Pilot's Handbook of Aeronautical Knowledge

2008

U.S. Department of Transportation
FEDERAL AVIATION ADMINISTRATION
Flight Standards Service

Preface

The Pilot's Handbook of Aeronautical Knowledge provides basic knowledge that is essential for pilots. This handbook introduces pilots to the broad spectrum of knowledge that will be needed as they progress in their pilot training. Except for the Code of Federal Regulations pertinent to civil aviation, most of the knowledge areas applicable to pilot certification are presented. This handbook is useful to beginning pilots, as well as those pursuing more advanced pilot certificates.

Occasionally the word "must" or similar language is used where the desired action is deemed critical. The use of such language is not intended to add to, interpret, or relieve a duty imposed by Title 14 of the Code of Federal Regulations (14 CFR).

It is essential for persons using this handbook to become familiar with and apply the pertinent parts of 14 CFR and the Aeronautical Information Manual (AIM). The AIM is available online at www.faa.gov. The current Flight Standards Service airman training and testing material and learning statements for all airman certificates and ratings can be obtained from www.faa.gov.

This handbook supersedes FAA-H-8083-25, Pilot's Handbook of Aeronautical Knowledge, dated 2003.

This handbook is available for download, in PDF format, from www.faa.gov.

This handbook is published by the United States Department of Transportation, Federal Aviation Administration, Airman Testing Standards Branch, AFS-630, P.O. Box 25082, Oklahoma City, OK 73125.

Comments regarding this publication should be sent, in email form, to the following address:

AFS630comments@faa.gov

Acknowledgments

The Pilot's Handbook of Aeronautical Knowledge was produced by the Federal Aviation Administration (FAA) with the assistance of Safety Research Corporation of America. The FAA wishes to acknowledge the following contributors:

Mrs. Nancy A. Wright for providing imagery of a de Haviland DH-4 inaugural air mail flight (Chapter 1)

The Raab Collection, Philadelphia, Pennsylvania, for images of the first pilot license (Chapter 1)

Sandy Kenyon and Rod Magner (magicair.com) for photo of 1929 TravelAir 4000 (Chapter 1)

Adventure Seaplanes for photos of a ski and float training plane (Chapter 2)

Jack Davis, Stearman Restorers Asociation, for photo of a 1941 PT-17 Army Air Corps trainer (Chapter 2)

Michael J. Hoke, Abaris Training Resources, Inc., for images and information about composite aircraft (Chapter 2)

M. van Leeuwen (www.zap16.com) for image of Piaggio P-180 (Chapter 5)

Greg Richter, Blue Mountain Avionics, for autopilot information and imagery (Chapter 5)

Mountain High E&S Company for various images provided regarding oxygen systems (Chapter 6)

Jeff Callahan, Aerox, for image of MSK-AS Silicone Mask without Microphone (Chapter 6)

Nonin Medical, Inc. for image of Onyx pulse oximeter (Chapter 6)

Pilotfriend.com for photo of a TKS Weeping Wing (Chapter 6)

Chelton Flight Systems for image of FlightLogic (Chapter 7)

Avidyne Corporation for image of the Entegra (Chapter 7)

Teledyne Controls for image of an air data computer (Chapter 7)

Watson Industries, Inc. (www.watson-gyro.com) for image of Attitude and Heading Reference system (Chapter 7)

Dr. Pat Veillette for information used on decision-making (Chapter 17)

John Park for image of spinning plates (Chapter 17)

Cessna Aircraft Company, Columbia Aircraft Manufacturing Corporation, Eclipse Aviation Corporation, Garmin Ltd., The Boeing Company for images provided and used throughout the Handbook.

Additional appreciation is extended to the Aircraft Owners and Pilots Association (AOPA), the AOPA Air Safety Foundation, the General Aviation Manufacturers Association (GAMA), and the National Business Aviation Association (NBAA) for their technical support and input.

Table of Contents

Preface iii

Acknowledgments...v

Table of Contents vii

Chapter 1
Introduction To Flying...............................1-1
Introduction... 1-1
History of Flight... 1-2
History of the Federal Aviation Administration (FAA) 1-3
   Transcontinental Air Mail Route............................1-4
   Federal Certification of Pilots and Mechanics 1-4
   The Civil Aeronautics Act of 1938 1-5
   The Federal Aviation Act of 1958...........................1-6
   Department of Transportation (DOT) 1-6
   Air Traffic Control (ATC) Automation.....................1-6
   The Professional Air Traffic Controllers
   Organization (PATCO) Strike..............................1-7
   The Airline Deregulation Act of 1978 1-7
Role of the Federal Aviation Administration (FAA).....1-7
   The Code of Federal Regulations (CFR)...................1-7
   Primary Locations of the FAA 1-8
     Field Offices...1-8
   Aviation Safety Inspector (ASI) 1-9
   FAA Safety Team (FAASTeam)...............................1-9
   Obtaining Assistance from the FAA 1-9
   FAA Reference Material 1-9
     Aeronautical Information Manual (AIM)..............1-9
     Handbooks 1-10
     Advisory Circulars (ACs) 1-10
     Flight Publications 1-11
   Pilot and Aeronautical Information 1-11
     Notices to Airmen (NOTAMs) 1-11
     Safety Program Airmen Notification
     System (SPANS) 1-12
Aircraft Types and Categories 1-12
   Ultralight Vehicles 1-12
   Light Sport Aircraft (LSA) Category 1-12

Pilot Certifications 1-13
   Sport Pilot..1-14
   Recreational Pilot 1-14
   Private Pilot 1-14
   Commercial Pilot..1-14
   Airline Transport Pilot 1-15
Selecting a Flight School 1-15
   How To Find a Reputable Flight Program 1-15
   How To Choose a Certificated Flight Instructor
   (CFI) 1-16
The Student Pilot 1-16
   Basic Requirements..1-16
     Medical Certification Requirements 1-17
Becoming a Pilot..1-17
Knowledge and Skill Examinations...........................1-18
   Knowledge Examination 1-18
     When To Take the Examination 1-18
     Where To Take the Examination 1-18
   Practical Examination 1-18
     When To Take the Practical Exam 1-19
     Who Administers the Practical Examination?......1-20
   Role of the Certificated Flight Instructor 1-20
   Role of the Designated Pilot Examiner 1-20
   Chapter Summary...1-21

Chapter 2
Aircraft Structure...2-1
Introduction..2-1
Lift and Basic Aerodynamics.....................................2-2
Major Components..2-3
   Fuselage...2-3
   Wings 2-3
   Empennage...2-5
   Landing Gear..2-6
   The Powerplant 2-6
Subcomponents..2-7
Types of Aircraft Construction 2-7
   Truss Structure 2-7
   Semimonocoque 2-8

Composite Construction 2-8
   History 2-8
   Composite Materials in Aircraft 2-9
   Advantages of Composites 2-9
   Disadvantages of Composites...........................2-9
   Fluid Spills on Composites 2-10
   Lightning Strike Protection.............................2-10
   The Future of Composites 2-11
Instrumentation: Moving into the Future 2-11
   Control Instruments 2-12
   Navigation Instruments 2-12
Global Positioning System (GPS)..............................2-12

Chapter 3
Principles of Flight 3-1
Introduction...3-1
Structure of the Atmosphere 3-1
   Atmospheric Pressure.......................................3-2
   Pressure Altitude 3-2
   Density Altitude 3-3
    Effect of Pressure on Density 3-3
    Effect of Temperature on Density 3-3
    Effect of Humidity (Moisture) on Density 3-3
Theories in the Production of Lift..................................3-4
   Newton's Basic Laws of Motion.......................3-4
   Magnus Effect 3-4
    Flow of Air Against a Nonrotating Cylinder..........3-5
    A Rotating Cylinder in a Motionless Fluid...........3-5
    A Rotating Cylinder in a Moving Fluid.............3-5
   Bernoulli's Principle of Differential Pressure 3-7
Airfoil Design 3-7
   Low Pressure Above 3-8
   High Pressure Below 3-9
   Pressure Distribution 3-9
   Airfoil Behavior 3-10
A Third Dimension 3-10
Chapter Summary 3-10

Chapter 4
Aerodynamics of Flight.....................................4-1
Forces Acting on the Aircraft 4-1
   Thrust 4-2
   Drag...4-3
    Parasite Drag...4-4
    Induced Drag 4-5
    Lift/Drag Ratio..4-6
   Weight 4-7
   Lift...4-7
Wingtip Vortices..4-8
   Formation of Vortices 4-8

   Avoiding Wake Turbulence 4-8
Ground Effect...4-9
Axes of an Aircraft...4-11
Moment and Moment Arm 4-12
Aircraft Design Characteristics 4-12
   Stability 4-12
    Static Stability...4-13
    Dynamic Stability 4-13
    Longitudinal Stability (Pitching) 4-14
    Lateral Stability (Rolling)...........................4-16
    Vertical Stability (Yawing).........................4-17
   Free Directional Oscillations (Dutch Roll) 4-18
   Spiral Instability 4-18
Aerodynamic Forces in Flight Maneuvers...................4-19
   Forces in Turns...4-19
   Forces in Climbs...4-21
   Forces in Descents 4-21
Stalls 4-22
Basic Propeller Principles 4-23
   Torque and P-Factor 4-26
   Torque Reaction 4-26
   Corkscrew Effect...4-26
   Gyroscopic Action..4-27
   Asymmetric Loading (P-Factor) 4-27
Load Factors...4-28
   Load Factors in Aircraft Design.......................4-28
   Load Factors in Steep Turns.............................4-29
   Load Factors and Stalling Speeds 4-30
   Load Factors and Flight Maneuvers.......................4-31
   Vg Diagram 4-32
   Rate of Turn 4-33
   Radius of Turn...4-34
Weight and Balance 4-35
   Effect of Weight on Flight Performance 4-37
   Effect of Weight on Aircraft Structure...................4-37
   Effect of Weight on Stability and Controllability 4-38
   Effect of Load Distribution 4-38
High Speed Flight 4-39
   Subsonic Versus Supersonic Flow 4-39
   Speed Ranges 4-40
   Mach Number Versus Airspeed 4-41
   Boundary Layer...4-41
    Laminar Boundary Layer Flow 4-41
    Turbulent Boundary Layer Flow 4-41
    Boundary Layer Separation 4-41
   Shock Waves 4-42
   Sweepback...4-43
   Mach Buffet Boundaries 4-44
   High Speed Flight Controls.............................4-45
Chapter Summary 4-46

Chapter 5

Flight Controls 5-1

Introduction...5-1

Flight Control Systems 5-2

  Flight Controls...5-2

  Primary Flight Controls..5-2

    Elevator..5-5

    T-Tail..5-6

    Stabilator..5-6

    Canard...5-7

    Rudder...5-7

    V-Tail..5-8

  Secondary Flight Controls....................................5-8

    Flaps...5-8

    Leading Edge Devices 5-9

    Spoilers 5-10

    Trim Tabs...5-10

    Balance Tabs..5-11

    Antiservo Tabs...5-11

    Ground Adjustable Tabs 5-11

    Adjustable Stabilizer..5-12

Autopilot...5-12

Chapter Summary 5-12

Chapter 6

Aircraft Systems 6-1

Introduction...6-1

Powerplant 6-1

  Reciprocating Engines..6-2

  Propeller 6-4

    Fixed-Pitch Propeller 6-5

    Adjustable-Pitch Propeller.................................6-6

  Induction Systems 6-7

  Carburetor Systems 6-7

    Mixture Control 6-8

    Carburetor Icing...6-8

    Carburetor Heat 6-9

    Carburetor Air Temperature Gauge.................6-10

  Outside Air Temperature Gauge 6-10

  Fuel Injection Systems 6-10

Superchargers and Turbosuperchargers.................6-11

  Superchargers 6-12

  Turbosuperchargers...6-12

    System Operation...6-13

    High Altitude Performance...............................6-14

Ignition System 6-14

Oil Systems 6-15

Engine Cooling Systems...6-16

Exhaust Systems 6-17

Starting System 6-18

Combustion...6-18

Full Authority Digital Engine Control (FADEC)........6-19

Turbine Engines..6-20

  Types of Turbine Engines 6-20

    Turbojet..6-20

    Turboprop 6-20

    Turbofan 6-20

    Turboshaft...6-20

  Turbine Engine Instruments 6-22

    Engine Pressure Ratio (EPR) 6-22

    Exhaust Gas Temperature (EGT) 6-22

    Torquemeter..6-22

    N_1 Indicator...6-22

    N_2 Indicator...6-22

  Turbine Engine Operational Considerations 6-22

    Engine Temperature Limitations 6-22

    Thrust Variations 6-22

    Foreign Object Damage (FOD) 6-23

    Turbine Engine Hot/Hung Start.......................6-23

    Compressor Stalls 6-23

    Flameout 6-23

  Performance Comparison....................................6-24

Airframe Systems 6-25

Fuel Systems 6-25

  Gravity-Feed System 6-25

  Fuel-Pump System 6-25

  Fuel Primer...6-25

  Fuel Tanks 6-25

  Fuel Gauges..6-26

  Fuel Selectors 6-26

  Fuel Strainers, Sumps, and Drains 6-26

  Fuel Grades 6-26

  Fuel Contamination 6-27

Refueling Procedures..6-27

Electrical System 6-28

Hydraulic Systems 6-30

  Landing Gear..6-31

    Tricycle Landing Gear Airplanes 6-31

    Tailwheel Landing Gear Airplanes...................6-31

    Fixed and Retractable Landing Gear 6-31

  Brakes...6-32

Pressurized Aircraft 6-32

Oxygen Systems..6-34

  Oxygen Masks..6-35

  Cannula...6-35

  Pressure-Demand Oxygen Systems 6-36

  Continuous-Flow Oxygen System 6-36

  Electrical Pulse-Demand Oxygen System.........6-36

  Pulse Oximeters..6-37

Servicing of Oxygen Systems 6-37
Anti-Ice and Deice Systems...................................6-37
   Airfoil Anti-Ice and Deice 6-37
   Windscreen Anti-Ice 6-38
   Propeller Anti-Ice...6-38
   Other Anti-Ice and Deice Systems.......................6-39
Chapter Summary 6-39

Chapter 7
Flight Instruments 7-1
Introduction...7-1
Pitot-Static Flight Instruments 7-1
   Impact Pressure Chamber and Lines......................7-2
   Static Pressure Chamber and Lines.......................7-2
   Altimeter..7-3
      Principle of Operation......................................7-3
      Effect of Nonstandard Pressure and Temperature..7-4
      Setting the Altimeter..7-5
      Altimeter Operation 7-6
      Types of Altitude 7-6
      Instrument Check 7-7
   Vertical Speed Indicator (VSI)...............................7-7
      Principle of Operation......................................7-7
      Instrument Check 7-8
   Airspeed Indicator (ASI) 7-8
      Airspeed Indicator Markings 7-9
      Other Airspeed Limitations 7-10
      Instrument Check 7-10
   Blockage of the Pitot-Static System.....................7-10
      Blocked Pitot System.....................................7-10
      Blocked Static System 7-11
Electronic Flight Display (EFD)..............................7-12
   Airspeed Tape 7-12
   Attitude Indicator 7-12
   Altimeter..7-12
   Vertical Speed Indicator (VSI).............................7-12
   Heading Indicator 7-12
   Turn Indicator..7-12
   Tachometer...7-12
   Slip/Skid Indicator...7-13
   Turn Rate Indicator 7-13
   Air Data Computer (ADC)....................................7-14
   Trend Vectors...7-14
Gyroscopic Flight Instruments.................................7-15
   Gyroscopic Principles 7-15
      Rigidity in Space...7-15
      Precession 7-15
   Sources of Power..7-16
   Turn Indicators 7-16
      Turn-and-Slip Indicator 7-17
      Turn Coordinator 7-17

      Inclinometer 7-18
      Yaw String 7-18
      Instrument Check 7-18
   Attitude Indicator 7-18
   Heading Indicator 7-20
   Attitude and Heading Reference System (AHRS)...7-20
   The Flux Gate Compass System 7-20
   Remote Indicating Compass..................................7-21
      Instrument Check 7-22
Compass Systems 7-22
   Magnetic Compass 7-22
      Magnetic Compass Induced Errors.................7-23
   The Vertical Card Magnetic Compass 7-26
      Lags or Leads..7-26
      Eddy Current Damping....................................7-26
Outside Air Temperature (OAT) Gauge 7-26
Chapter Summary 7-26

Chapter 8
Flight Manuals and Other Documents...............8-1
Introduction...8-1
   Preliminary Pages...8-2
   General (Section 1)..8-2
   Limitations (Section 2)..8-2
      Airspeed 8-2
      Powerplant 8-3
      Weight and Loading Distribution 8-3
      Flight Limits 8-4
      Placards...8-4
   Emergency Procedures (Section 3) 8-4
   Normal Procedures (Section 4) 8-4
   Performance (Section 5)..8-4
   Weight and Balance/Equipment List (Section 6).......8-4
   Systems Description (Section 7) 8-4
   Handling, Service, and Maintenance (Section 8).......8-4
   Supplements (Section 9)..8-5
   Safety Tips (Section 10) 8-5
Aircraft Documents..8-6
   Certificate of Aircraft Registration.......................8-6
   Light Sport Aircraft (LSA) 8-7
   Airworthiness Certificate......................................8-7
   Aircraft Maintenance..8-8
Aircraft Inspections...8-8
   Annual Inspection 8-8
   100-Hour Inspection...8-9
   Other Inspection Programs....................................8-9
      Altimeter System Inspection 8-9
      Transponder Inspection 8-9
      Emergency Locator Transmitter 8-9
      Preflight Inspections 8-9
Minimum Equipment Lists (MEL) and Operations With

Inoperative Equipment 8-9
Preventive Maintenance...8-11
    Maintenance Entries 8-11
    Examples of Preventive Maintenance 8-11
    Repairs and Alterations 8-12
    Special Flight Permits 8-12
Airworthiness Directives (ADs) 8-12
Aircraft Owner/Operator Responsibilities 8-13
Chapter Summary 8-14

Chapter 9
Weight and Balance 9-1
Introduction..9-1
Weight Control..9-1
    Effects of Weight 9-1
    Weight Changes 9-2
Balance, Stability, and Center of Gravity 9-2
    Effects of Adverse Balance 9-3
        Stability..9-3
        Control 9-3
    Management of Weight and Balance Control 9-4
    Terms and Definitions 9-4
    Principles of Weight and Balance Computations.......9-6
    Weight and Balance Restrictions 9-7
Determining Loaded Weight and CG 9-7
    Computational Method...9-7
    Graph Method 9-7
    Table Method 9-9
    Computations With a Negative Arm.....................9-10
    Computations With Zero Fuel Weight 9-10
    Shifting, Adding, and Removing Weight................9-10
        Weight Shifting..9-10
        Weight Addition or Removal.........................9-11
Chapter Summary 9-11

Chapter 10
Aircraft Performance...10-1
Introduction..10-1
Importance of Performance Data 10-1
Structure of the Atmosphere 10-2
Atmospheric Pressure 10-2
Pressure Altitude...10-3
Density Altitude 10-3
    Effects of Pressure on Density 10-4
    Effects of Temperature on Density 10-5
    Effects of Humidity (Moisture) on Density 10-5
Performance 10-5
    Straight-and-Level Flight 10-5
    Climb Performance 10-6
    Range Performance 10-8
    Region of Reversed Command 10-10

Takeoff and Landing Performance........................10-11
Runway Surface and Gradient..............................10-11
Water on the Runway and Dynamic Hydroplaning10-13
Takeoff Performance..10-13
Landing Performance 10-15
Performance Speeds..10-17
Performance Charts...10-17
    Interpolation 10-18
    Density Altitude Charts.....................................10-18
    Takeoff Charts...10-19
    Climb and Cruise Charts 10-20
    Crosswind and Headwind Component Chart 10-24
    Landing Charts 10-25
    Stall Speed Performance Charts 10-26
Transport Category Airplane Performance.................10-26
    Major Differences in Transport Category Versus Non-
    Transport Category Performance Requirements 10-27
    Performance Requirements 10-27
        Takeoff...10-27
        Landing 10-27
        Takeoff Planning 10-27
    Runway Requirements 10-27
        Balanced Field Length 10-28
Climb Requirements 10-30
    First Segment...10-30
    Second Segment 10-31
    Third or Acceleration Segment 10-31
    Fourth or Final Segment....................................10-31
    Second Segment Climb Limitations.....................10-31
Air Carrier Obstacle Clearance Requirements...........10-31
    Summary of Takeoff Requirements 10-32
    Landing Performance 10-32
        Planning the Landing....................................10-32
        Landing Requirements..................................10-32
        Approach Climb Requirements 10-32
        Landing Runway Required 10-33
    Summary of Landing Requirements 10-33
Chapter Summary 10-34

Chapter 11
Weather Theory 11-1
Introduction..11-1
Atmosphere 11-2
    Composition of the Atmosphere 11-2
    Atmospheric Circulation 11-3
    Atmospheric Pressure...11-3
Coriolis Force...11-3
Measurement of Atmosphere Pressure 11-4
Altitude and Atmospheric Pressure 11-5
Altitude and Flight..11-6
Altitude and the Human Body 11-6

Wind and Currents 11-7
  Wind Patterns 11-7
  Convective Currents 11-7
  Effect of Obstructions on Wind 11-8
  Low-Level Wind Shear 11-11
  Wind and Pressure Representation on Surface
  Weather Maps 11-11
Atmospheric Stability 11-12
  Inversion 11-13
  Moisture and Temperature 11-13
  Relative Humidity 11-13
  Temperature/Dew Point Relationship 11-13
  Methods by Which Air Reaches the
  Saturation Point 11-14
  Dew and Frost 11-15
  Fog 11-15
  Clouds 11-15
  Ceiling 11-17
  Visibility 11-18
  Precipitation 11-18
Air Masses 11-18
Fronts 11-18
  Warm Front 11-19
    Flight Toward an Approaching Warm Front 11-20
  Cold Front 11-20
    Fast-Moving Cold Front 11-21
    Flight Toward an Approaching Cold Front 11-21
  Comparison of Cold and Warm Fronts 11-22
  Wind Shifts 11-22
  Stationary Front 11-22
  Occluded Front 11-22
  Thunderstorms 11-22
    Hazards 11-23
    Squall Line 11-23
    Tornadoes 11-23
    Turbulence 11-24
    Icing 11-24
    Hail 11-24
    Ceiling and Visibility 11-25
    Effect on Altimeters 11-25
    Lightning 11-25
    Engine Water Ingestion 11-25
Chapter Summary 11-25

Chapter 12
Aviation Weather Services 12-1
Introduction 12-1
Observations 12-2
  Surface Aviation Weather Observations 12-2
    Air Route Traffic Control Center (ARTCC) 12-2

Upper Air Observations 12-2
Radar Observations 12-2
Satellite 12-3
  Satellite Weather 12-3
  Satellite Weather Products 12-4
Service Outlets 12-4
  Automated Flight Service Station (AFSS) 12-4
  Transcribed Information Briefing Service (TIBS) ... 12-4
  Direct User Access Terminal Service (DUATS) 12-4
  En Route Flight Advisory Service (EFAS) 12-5
  Hazardous Inflight Weather Advisory (HIWAS) 12-5
  Transcribed Weather Broadcast (TWEB) 12-5
Weather Briefings 12-5
  Standard Briefing 12-5
  Abbreviated Briefing 12-6
  Outlook Briefing 12-6
Aviation Weather Reports 12-6
  Aviation Routine Weather Report (METAR) 12-6
  Pilot Weather Reports (PIREPs) 12-8
  Radar Weather Reports (RAREP) 12-9
Aviation Forecasts 12-10
  Terminal Aerodrome Forecasts (TAF) 12-10
  Area Forecasts (FA) 12-11
  Inflight Weather Advisories 12-12
    AIRMET 12-12
    SIGMET 12-13
    Convective Significant Meteorological
    Information (WST) 12-14
  Winds and Temperature Aloft Forecast (FD) 12-14
Weather Charts 12-15
  Surface Analysis Chart 12-15
  Weather Depiction Chart 12-16
  Radar Summary Chart 12-17
  Significant Weather Prognostic Charts 12-18
ATC Radar Weather Displays 12-19
  Weather Avoidance Assistance 12-21
Electronic Flight Displays (EFD) /Multi-Function
Display (MFD) Weather 12-21
  Weather Products Age and Expiration 12-22
  The Next Generation Weather Radar System
  (NEXRAD) 12-22
    Level II Data Products 12-22
    Level III Data Products 12-22
    NEXRAD Abnormalities 12-23
    NEXRAD Limitations 12-23
  AIRMET/SIGMET Display 12-24
  Graphical METARs 12-24
Chapter Summary 12-26

Chapter 13
Airport Operations................................13-1

Introduction..13-1
Types of Airports 13-1
   Towered Airport...13-2
   Nontowered Airport 13-2
Sources for Airport Data..13-2
   Aeronautical Charts..13-3
   Airport/Facility Directory (A/FD)........................13-3
   Notices to Airmen (NOTAMs) 13-3
Airport Markings and Signs......................................13-4
   Runway Markings 13-4
   Taxiway Markings...13-5
   Other Markings 13-5
   Airport Signs 13-6
Airport Lighting 13-6
   Airport Beacon 13-6
   Approach Light Systems 13-7
   Visual Glideslope Indicators 13-7
     Visual Approach Slope Indicator (VASI)............13-7
     Other Glidepath Systems 13-7
   Runway Lighting...13-8
     Runway End Identifier Lights (REIL) 13-8
     Runway Edge Lights..13-8
     In-Runway Lighting...13-9
   Control of Airport Lighting...................................13-9
   Taxiway Lights..13-9
   Obstruction Lights..13-9
Wind Direction Indicators......................................13-10
Traffic Patterns 13-10
   Key to Traffic Pattern
   Operations—Single Runway................................13-11
   Key to Traffic Pattern
   Operations—Parallel Runways 13-11
Radio Communications..13-11
   Radio License..13-11
   Radio Equipment..13-12
   Lost Communication Procedures 13-12
Air Traffic Control (ATC) Services.........................13-13
   Primary Radar 13-13
   ATC Radar Beacon System (ATCRBS) 13-14
   Transponder..13-14
   Radar Traffic Advisories 13-14
Wake Turbulence 13-15
   Vortex Generation 13-16
   Vortex Strength 13-16
   Vortex Behavior 13-16
   Vortex Avoidance Procedures.............................13-17
Collision Avoidance..13-17
   Clearing Procedures 13-18
   Runway Incursion Avoidance 13-18
Chapter Summary 13-18

Chapter 14
Airspace 14-1

Introduction..14-1
Controlled Airspace 14-2
   Class A Airspace 14-2
   Class B Airspace 14-2
   Class C Airspace 14-2
   Class D Airspace 14-2
   Class E Airspace...14-2
Uncontrolled Airspace 14-3
   Class G Airspace 14-3
Special Use Airspace 14-3
   Prohibited Areas...14-3
   Restricted Areas 14-3
   Warning Areas..14-4
   Military Operation Areas (MOAs).........................14-4
   Alert Areas 14-4
   Controlled Firing Areas (CFAs)............................14-4
Other Airspace Areas 14-4
   Local Airport Advisory (LAA) 14-4
   Military Training Routes (MTRs) 14-6
   Temporary Flight Restrictions (TFR) 14-6
   Published VFR Routes 14-6
   Terminal Radar Service Areas (TRSAs).................14-6
   National Security Areas (NSAs) 14-6
Air Traffic Control and the National Airspace System 14-7
   Coordinating the Use of Airspace 14-7
   Operating in the Various Types of Airspace............14-7
     Basic VFR Weather Minimums...........................14-7
     Operating Rules and Pilot/Equipment
     Requirements..14-7
     Ultralight Vehicles..14-10
     Unmanned Free Balloons 14-10
     Parachute Jumps 14-10
Chapter Summary 14-10

Chapter 15
Navigation 15-1

Introduction..15-1
Aeronautical Charts 15-2
   Sectional Charts..15-2
   VFR Terminal Area Charts 15-2
   World Aeronautical Charts....................................15-2
Lattitude and Longitude (Meridians and Parallels) 15-3
   Time Zones...15-3
   Measurement of Direction.....................................15-5
   Variation...15-6
   Deviation 15-8
Effect of Wind..15-9
Basic Calculations..15-11
   Converting Minutes to Equivalent Hours...............15-11

Time T = D/GS 15-11
Distance D = GS X T...........................15-11
GS GS = D/T 15-11
Converting Knots to Miles Per Hour.....................15-11
Fuel Consumption 15-12
Flight Computers.....................................15-12
Plotter 15-12
Pilotage 15-12
Dead Reckoning...15-12
The Wind Triangle or Vector Analysis 15-12
Flight Planning..15-16
Assembling Necessary Material.........................15-16
Weather Check 15-17
Use of Airport/Facility Directory (A/FD) 15-17
Airplane Flight Manual or Pilot's Operating
Handbook (AFM/POH) 15-17
Charting the Course 15-17
Steps in Charting the Course 15-19
Filing a VFR Flight Plan.................................15-20
Radio Navigation 15-21
Very High Frequency (VHF) Omnidirectional
Range (VOR)...15-22
Using the VOR 15-23
Course Deviation Indicator (CDI).......................15-23
Horizontal Situation Indicator 15-24
Radio Magnetic Indicator (RMI).......................15-24
Tracking With VOR 15-25
Tips on Using the VOR 15-26
Time and Distance Check From a Station.............15-26
Course Intercept 15-27
Rate of Intercept 15-27
Angle of Intercept 15-27
Distance Measuring Equipment (DME)................15-27
VOR/DME RNAV 15-27
Automatic Direction Finder (ADF)......................15-29
Loran-C Navigation....................................15-30
Global Positioning System 15-32
Selective Availability.................................15-32
VFR Use of GPS 15-32
RAIM Capability 15-33
Tips for Using GPS for VFR Operations 15-33
VFR Waypoints 15-34
Lost Procedures..15-34
Flight Diversion 15-34
Chapter Summary 15-35

Chapter 16
Aeromedical Factors 16-1
Introduction..16-1
Obtaining a Medical Certificate 16-2
Health and Physiological Factors Affecting Pilot
Performance 16-2
Hypoxia 16-2
Hypoxic Hypoxia......................................16-2
Hypemic Hypoxia 16-2
Stagnant Hypoxia......................................16-3
Histotoxic Hypoxia 16-3
Symptoms of Hypoxia.................................16-3
Hyperventilation.......................................16-3
Middle Ear and Sinus Problems 16-4
Spatial Disorientation and Illusions 16-5
Vestibular Illusions....................................16-6
Visual Illusions...16-7
Postural Considerations..................................16-7
Demonstration of Spatial Disorientation..................16-8
Climbing While Accelerating 16-8
Climbing While Turning.................................16-8
Diving While Turning...................................16-8
Tilting to Right or Left 16-8
Reversal of Motion 16-8
Diving or Rolling Beyond the Vertical Plane.......16-8
Coping with Spatial Disorientation 16-8
Optical Illusions 16-9
Runway Width Illusion...................................16-9
Runway and Terrain Slopes Illusion....................16-9
Featureless Terrain Illusion 16-9
Water Refraction..16-9
Haze 16-9
Fog 16-9
Ground Lighting Illusions...............................16-9
How To Prevent Landing Errors Due to
Optical Illusions 16-11
Motion Sickness 16-11
Carbon Monoxide (CO) Poisoning 16-11
Stress 16-11
Fatigue 16-12
Dehydration and Heatstroke 16-12
Alcohol 16-13
Drugs 16-14
Altitude-Induced Decompression Sickness (DCS) 16-16
DCS After Scuba Diving 16-16

Vision in Flight 16-17
   Empty-Field Myopia 16-18
   Night Vision 16-18
   Night Vision Illusions 16-19
     Autokinesis 16-19
     False Horizon...............................16-19
   Night Landing Illusions........................16-19
Chapter Summary 16-20

Chapter 17
Aeronautical Decision-Making 17-1
Introduction...17-1
History of ADM...17-2
Crew Resource Management (CRM) and Single-Pilot
Resource Management.................................17-4
Hazard and Risk 17-4
   Hazardous Attitudes and Antidotes..........17-4
   Risk..17-4
     Assessing Risk 17-5
     Likelihood of an Event 17-6
     Severity of an Event.......................17-6
     Mitigating Risk 17-6
   The PAVE Checklist 17-6
     P = Pilot in Command (PIC) 17-8
     A = Aircraft 17-8
     V = EnVironment 17-8
     E = External Pressures 17-9
Human Behavior 17-10
The Decision-Making Process 17-11
   SRM and the 5P Check 17-11
     The Plan 17-12
     The Plane 17-13
     The Pilot 17-13
     The Passengers 17-13
     The Programming 17-13
   Perceive, Process, Perform (3P)............17-14
     Perceive, Process, Perform with
     CARE and TEAM..........................17-14
     Forming Good Safety Habits 17-16
   The OODA Loop..............................17-16

The DECIDE Model.................................17-17
   Detect (the Problem)..........................17-19
   Estimate (the Need To React)................17-19
   Choose (a Course of Action) 17-19
   Identify (Solutions)............................17-19
   Do (the Necessary Actions)..................17-19
   Evaluate (the Effect of the Action) 17-19
Decision-Making in a Dynamic Environment 17-19
   Automatic Decision-Making 17-20
     Operational Pitfalls........................17-20
   Stress Management 17-20
   Use of Resources............................17-20
     Internal Resources 17-20
     External Resources 17-22
Situational Awareness................................17-23
   Obstacles to Maintaining Situational Awareness...17-23
     Workload Management 17-23
     Managing Risks 17-24
Automation 17-25
   Results of the Study..........................17-27
   Equipment Use 17-29
     Autopilot Systems.........................17-29
     Familiarity.................................17-29
     Respect for Onboard Systems.............17-29
     Reinforcement of Onboard Suites 17-29
     Getting Beyond Rote Workmanship.......17-29
     Understand the Platform 17-29
   Managing Aircraft Automation 17-30
     Information Management 17-30
   Enhanced Situational Awareness 17-31
   Automation Management....................17-31
Risk Management 17-32
Chapter Summary 17-32

Appendix A-1

Glossary G-1

Index I-1

Chapter 1

Introduction To Flying

Introduction

The Pilot's Handbook of Aeronautical Knowledge provides basic knowledge for the student pilot learning to fly, as well as pilots seeking advanced pilot certification. For detailed information on a variety of specialized flight topics, see specific Federal Aviation Administration (FAA) handbooks and Advisory Circulars (ACs).

This chapter offers a brief history of flight, introduces the history and role of the FAA in civil aviation, FAA regulations and standards, government references and publications, eligibility for pilot certificates, available routes to flight instruction, the role of the Certificated Flight Instructor (CFI) and Designated Pilot Examiner (DPE) in flight training, and Practical Test Standards (PTS).

History of Flight

From prehistoric times, humans have watched the flight of birds, longed to imitate them, but lacked the power to do so. Logic dictated that if the small muscles of birds can lift them into the air and sustain them, then the larger muscles of humans should be able to duplicate the feat. No one knew about the intricate mesh of muscles, sinew, heart, breathing system, and devices not unlike wing flaps, variable-camber and spoilers of the modern airplane that enabled a bird to fly. Still, thousands of years and countless lives were lost in attempts to fly like birds.

The identity of the first "bird-men" who fitted themselves with wings and leapt off a cliff in an effort to fly are lost in time, but each failure gave those who wished to fly questions that needed answering. Where had the wing flappers gone wrong? Philosophers, scientists, and inventors offered solutions, but no one could add wings to the human body and soar like a bird. During the 1500s, Leonardo da Vinci filled pages of his notebooks with sketches of proposed flying machines, but most of his ideas were flawed because he clung to the idea of birdlike wings. *[Figure 1-1]* By 1655, mathematician, physicist, and inventor Robert Hooke concluded the human body does not possess the strength to power artificial wings. He believed human flight would require some form of artificial propulsion.

Figure 1-1. *Leonardo da Vinci's ornithopter wings.*

The quest for human flight led some practitioners in another direction. In 1783, the first manned hot air balloon, crafted by Joseph and Etienne Montgolfier, flew for 23 minutes. Ten days later, Professor Jacques Charles flew the first gas balloon. A madness for balloon flight captivated the public's imagination and for a time flying enthusiasts turned their expertise to the promise of lighter-than-air flight. But for all its majesty in the air, the balloon was little more than a billowing heap of cloth capable of no more than a one-way, downwind journey.

Balloons solved the problem of lift, but that was only one of the problems of human flight. The ability to control speed and direction eluded balloonists. The solution to that problem lay in a child's toy familiar to the East for 2,000 years, but not introduced to the West until the 13th century. The kite, used by the Chinese manned for aerial observation and to test winds for sailing, and unmanned as a signaling device and as a toy, held many of the answers to lifting a heavier-than-air device into the air.

One of the men who believed the study of kites unlocked the secrets of winged flight was Sir George Cayley. Born in England 10 years before the Mongolfier balloon flight, Cayley spent his 84 years seeking to develop a heavier-than-air vehicle supported by kite-shaped wings. *[Figure 1-2]* The "Father of Aerial Navigation," Cayley discovered the basic principles on which the modern science of aeronautics is founded, built what is recognized as the first successful flying model, and tested the first full-size man-carrying airplane.

For the half-century after Cayley's death, countless scientists, flying enthusiasts, and inventors worked toward building

Figure 1-2. *Glider from 1852 by Sir George Cayley, British aviator (1773–1857).*

a powered flying machine. Men, such as William Samuel Henson, who designed a huge monoplane that was propelled by a steam engine housed inside the fuselage, and Otto Lilienthal, who proved human flight in aircraft heavier than air was practical, worked toward the dream of powered flight. A dream turned into reality by Wilbur and Orville Wright at Kitty Hawk, North Carolina, on December 17, 1903.

The bicycle-building Wright brothers of Dayton, Ohio, had experimented for 4 years with kites, their own homemade wind tunnel, and different engines to power their biplane. One of their great achievements was proving the value of the scientific, rather than build-it-and-see approach to flight. Their biplane, The Flyer, combined inspired design and engineering with superior craftsmanship. *[Figure 1-3]* By the afternoon of December 17th, the Wright brothers had flown a total of 98 seconds on four flights. The age of flight had arrived.

Figure 1-3. *First flight by the Wright brothers.*

History of the Federal Aviation Administration (FAA)

During the early years of manned flight, aviation was a free for all because no government body was in place to establish policies or regulate and enforce safety standards. Individuals were free to conduct flights and operate aircraft with no government oversight. Most of the early flights were conducted for sport. Aviation was expensive and became the playground of the wealthy. Since these early airplanes were small, many people doubted their commercial value. One group of individuals believed otherwise and they became the genesis for modern airline travel.

P. E. Fansler, a Florida businessman living in St. Petersburg approached Tom Benoist of the Benoist Aircraft Company in St. Louis, Missouri, about starting a flight route from St. Petersburg across the waterway to Tampa. Benoist suggested

using his "Safety First" airboat and the two men signed an agreement for what would become the first scheduled airline in the United States. The first aircraft was delivered to St. Petersburg and made the first test flight on December 31, 1913. *[Figure 1-4]*

Figure 1-4. *Benoist airboat.*

A public auction decided who would win the honor of becoming the first paying airline customer. The former mayor of St. Petersburg, A. C. Pheil made the winning bid of $400.00 which secured his place in history as the first paying airline passenger.

On January 1, 1914, the first scheduled airline flight was conducted. The flight length was 21 miles and lasted 23 minutes due to a headwind. The return trip took 20 minutes. The line, which was subsidized by Florida businessmen, continued for 4 months and offered regular passage for $5.00 per person or $5.00 per 100 pounds of cargo. Shortly after the opening of the line, Benoist added a new airboat that afforded more protection from spray during takeoff and landing. The routes were also extended to Manatee, Bradenton, and Sarasota giving further credence to the idea of a profitable commercial airline.

The St. Petersburg-Tampa Airboat Line continued throughout the winter months with flights finally being suspended when the winter tourist industry began to dry up. The airline operated only for 4 months, but 1,205 passengers were carried without injury. This experiment proved commercial passenger airline travel was viable.

The advent of World War I offered the airplane a chance to demonstrate its varied capabilities. It began the war as a reconnaissance platform, but by 1918, airplanes were being mass produced to serve as fighters, bombers, trainers, as well as reconnaissance platforms.

Aviation advocates continued to look for ways to use airplanes. Airmail service was a popular idea, but the war prevented the Postal Service from having access to airplanes. The War Department and Postal Service reached an agreement in 1918. The Army would use the mail service to train its pilots in cross-country flying. The first airmail flight was conducted on May 15, 1918, between New York and Washington, DC. The flight was not considered spectacular; the pilot became lost and landed at the wrong airfield. In August of 1918, the United States Postal Service took control of the airmail routes and brought the existing Army airmail pilots and their planes into the program as postal employees.

Transcontinental Air Mail Route

Airmail routes continued to expand until the Transcontinental Mail Route was inaugurated. *[Figure 1-5]* This route spanned from San Francisco to New York for a total distance of 2,612 miles with 13 intermediate stops along the way. *[Figure 1-6]*

Figure 1-5. *The de Haviland DH-4 on the New York to San Francisco inaugural route in 1921.*

On May 20, 1926, Congress passed the Air Commerce Act, which served as the cornerstone for aviation within the United States. This legislation was supported by leaders in the aviation industry who felt that the airplane could not reach its full potential without assistance from the Federal Government in improving safety.

The Air Commerce Act charged the Secretary of Commerce with fostering air commerce, issuing and enforcing air traffic rules, licensing pilots, certificating aircraft, establishing airways, and operating and maintaining aids to air navigation. The Department of Commerce created a new Aeronautics Branch whose primary mission was to provide oversight for the aviation industry. In addition, the Aeronautics Branch took over the construction and operation of the nation's system of lighted airways. The Postal Service, as part of the

Figure 1-6. *The transcontinental airmail route ran from New York to San Francisco. Intermediate stops were: 2) Bellefonte, 3) Cleveland, 4) Bryan, 5) Chicago, 6) Iowa City, 7) Omaha, 8) North Platte, 9) Cheyenne, 10) Rawlins, 11) Rock Springs, 12) Salt Lake City, 13) Elko, and 14) Reno.*

Transcontinental Air Mail Route system, had initiated this system. The Department of Commerce made great advances in aviation communications, as well as introducing radio beacons as an effective means of navigation.

Built at intervals of approximately 10 miles, the standard beacon tower was 51 feet high, topped with a powerful rotating light. Below the rotating light, two course lights pointed forward and back along the airway. The course lights flashed a code to identify the beacon's number. The tower usually stood in the center of a concrete arrow 70 feet long. A generator shed, where required, stood at the "feather" end of the arrow. *[Figure 1-7]*

Federal Certification of Pilots and Mechanics

The Aeronautics Branch of the Department of Commerce began pilot certification with the first license issued on April 6, 1927. The recipient was the chief of the Aeronautics Branch, William P. MacCracken, Jr. *[Figure 1-8]* (Orville Wright, who was no longer an active flier, had declined the honor.) MacCracken's license was the first issued to a pilot by a civilian agency of the Federal Government. Some 3 months later, the Aeronautics Branch issued the first Federal aircraft mechanic license.

Equally important for safety was the establishment of a system of certification for aircraft. On March 29, 1927, the Aeronautics Branch issued the first airworthiness type certificate to the Buhl Airster CA-3, a three-place open biplane.

In 1934, to recognize the tremendous strides made in aviation and to display the enhanced status within the department,

Figure 1-7. *A standard airway beacon tower.*

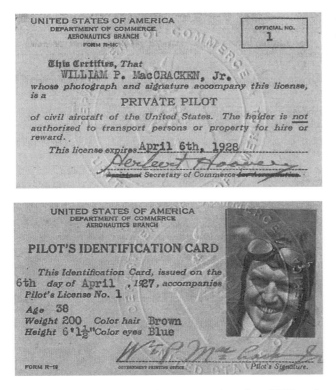

Figure 1-8. *The first pilot license was issued to William P. MacCracken, Jr.*

the Aeronautics Branch was renamed the Bureau of Air Commerce. *[Figure 1-9]* Within this time frame, the Bureau of Air Commerce brought together a group of airlines and encouraged them to form the first three Air Traffic Control (ATC) facilities along the established air routes. Then in 1936, the Bureau of Air Commerce took over the responsibilities of operating the centers and continued to advance the ATC facilities. ATC has come a long way from the early controllers using maps, chalkboards, and performing mental math calculations in order to separate aircraft along flight routes.

Figure 1-9. *The third head of the Aeronautics Branch, Eugene L. Vidal, is flanked by President Franklin D. Roosevelt (left) and Secretary of Agriculture Henry A. Wallace (right). The photograph was taken in 1933. During Vidal's tenure, the Aeronautics Branch was renamed the Bureau of Air Commerce on July 1, 1934. The new name more accurately reflected the status of the organization within the Department of Commerce.*

The Civil Aeronautics Act of 1938

In 1938, the Civil Aeronautics Act transferred the civil aviation responsibilities to a newly created, independent body, named the Civil Aeronautics Authority (CAA). This Act empowered the CAA to regulate airfares and establish new routes for the airlines to service.

President Franklin Roosevelt split the CAA into two agencies, the Civil Aeronautics Administration (CAA) and the Civil Aeronautics Board (CAB). Both agencies were still part of the Department of Commerce but the CAB functioned independently of the Secretary of Commerce. The role of the CAA was to facilitate ATC, certification of airmen and aircraft, rule enforcement, and the development of new airways. The CAB was charged with rule making to enhance safety, accident investigation, and the economic regulation of the airlines. Then in 1946, Congress gave the

CAA the responsibility of administering the Federal Aid Airport Program. This program was designed to promote the establishment of civil airports throughout the country.

The Federal Aviation Act of 1958

By mid-century, air traffic had increased and jet aircraft had been introduced into the civil aviation arena. A series of mid-air collisions underlined the need for more regulation of the aviation industry. Aircraft were not only increasing in numbers, but were now streaking across the skies at much higher speeds. The Federal Aviation Act of 1958 established a new independent body that assumed the roles of the CAA and transferred the rule making authority of the CAB to the newly created Federal Aviation Agency (FAA). In addition, the FAA was given complete control of the common civil-military system of air navigation and ATC. The man who was given the honor of being the first administrator of the FAA was former Air Force General Elwood Richard "Pete" Quesada. He served as the administrator from 1959–1961. *[Figure 1-10]*

Figure 1-10. *First Administrator of the FAA was General Elwood Richard "Pete" Quesada, 1959–1961.*

Department of Transportation (DOT)

On October 15, 1966, Congress established the Department of Transportation (DOT), which was given oversight of the transportation industry within the United States. The result was a combination of both air and surface transportation. Its mission was and is to serve the United States by ensuring a fast, safe, efficient, accessible, and convenient transportation system meeting vital national interests and enhancing the quality of life of the American people, then, now, and into the future. At this same time, the Federal Aviation Agency was renamed to the Federal Aviation Administration (FAA). The DOT began operation on April 1, 1967.

The role of the CAB was assumed by the newly created National Transportation Safety Board (NTSB), which was charged with the investigation of all transportation accidents within the United States.

As aviation continued to grow, the FAA took on additional duties and responsibilities. With the highjacking epidemic of the 1960s, the FAA was responsible for increasing the security duties of aviation both on the ground and in the air. After September 11, 2001, the duties were transferred to a newly created body called the Department of Homeland Security (DHS).

With numerous aircraft flying in and out of larger cities, the FAA began to concentrate on the environmental aspect of aviation by establishing and regulating the noise standards of aircraft. Additionally in the 1960s and 1970s, the FAA began to regulate high altitude (over 500 feet) kite and balloon flying. 1970 brought more duties to the FAA by adding the management of a new federal airport aid program and increased responsibility for airport safety.

Air Traffic Control (ATC) Automation

By the mid-1970s, the FAA had achieved a semi-automated ATC system based on a marriage of radar and computer technology. By automating certain routine tasks, the system allowed controllers to concentrate more efficiently on the vital task of providing aircraft separation. Data appearing directly on the controllers' scopes provided the identity, altitude, and groundspeed of aircraft carrying radar beacons. Despite its effectiveness, this system required enhancement to keep pace with the increased air traffic of the late 1970s. The increase was due in part to the competitive environment created by the Airline Deregulation Act of 1978. This law phased out CAB's economic regulation of the airlines, and CAB ceased to exist at the end of 1984.

To meet the challenge of traffic growth, the FAA unveiled the National Airspace System (NAS) Plan in January 1982. The new plan called for more advanced systems for en route and terminal ATC, modernized flight service stations, and improvements in ground-to-air surveillance and communication.

The Professional Air Traffic Controllers Organization (PATCO) Strike

While preparing the NAS Plan, the FAA faced a strike by key members of its workforce. An earlier period of discord between management and the Professional Air Traffic Controllers Organization (PATCO) culminated in a 1970 "sickout" by 3,000 controllers. Although controllers subsequently gained additional wage and retirement benefits, another period of tension led to an illegal strike in August 1981. The government dismissed over 11,000 strike participants and decertified PATCO. By the spring of 1984, the FAA ended the last of the special restrictions imposed to keep the airspace system operating safely during the strike.

The Airline Deregulation Act of 1978

Until 1978, the CAB regulated many areas of commercial aviation such as fares, routes, and schedules. The Airline Deregulation Act of 1978, however, removed many of these controls, thus changing the face of civil aviation in the United States. After deregulation, unfettered free competition ushered in a new era in passenger air travel.

The CAB had three main functions: to award routes to airlines, to limit the entry of air carriers into new markets, and to regulate fares for passengers. Much of the established practices of commercial passenger travel within the United States went back to the policies of Walter Folger Brown, the United States Postmaster General during the administration of President Herbert Hoover. Brown had changed the mail payments system to encourage the manufacture of passenger aircraft instead of mail-carrying aircraft. His influence was crucial in awarding contracts and helped create four major domestic airlines: United, American, Eastern, and Transcontinental and Western Air (TWA). Similarly, Brown had also helped give Pan American a monopoly on international routes.

The push to deregulate, or at least to reform the existing laws governing passenger carriers, was accelerated by President Jimmy Carter, who appointed economist and former professor Alfred Kahn, a vocal supporter of deregulation, to head the CAB. A second force to deregulate emerged from abroad. In 1977, Freddie Laker, a British entrepreneur who owned Laker Airways, created the Skytrain service, which offered extraordinarily cheap fares for transatlantic flights. Laker's offerings coincided with a boom in low-cost domestic flights as the CAB eased some limitations on charter flights, i.e., flights offered by companies that do not actually own planes but leased them from the major airlines. The big air carriers responded by proposing their own lower fares. For example, American Airlines, the country's second largest airline, obtained CAB approval for "SuperSaver" tickets.

All of these events proved to be favorable for large-scale deregulation. In November 1977, Congress formally deregulated air cargo. In late 1978, Congress passed the Airline Deregulation Act of 1978, legislation that had been principally authored by Senators Edward Kennedy and Howard Cannon. *[Figure 1-11]* There was stiff opposition to the bill—from the major airlines who feared free competition, from labor unions who feared nonunion employees, and from safety advocates who feared that safety would be sacrificed. Public support was, however, strong enough to pass the act. The act appeased the major airlines by offering generous subsidies and it pleased workers by offering high unemployment benefits if they lost their jobs as a result. The most important effect of the act, whose laws were slowly phased in, was on the passenger market. For the first time in 40 years, airlines could enter the market or (from 1981) expand their routes as they saw fit. Airlines (from 1982) also had full freedom to set their fares. In 1984, the CAB was finally abolished since its primary duty of regulating the airline industry was no longer necessary.

Figure 1-11. *President Jimmy Carter signs the Airline Deregulation Act in late 1978.*

The Role of the Federal Aviation Administration (FAA)

The Code of Federal Regulations (CFR)

The FAA is empowered by regulations to promote aviation safety and establish safety standards for civil aviation. The FAA achieves these objectives under the Code of Federal Regulations (CFR), which is the codification of the general and permanent rules published by the executive departments and agencies of the United States Government. The regulations are divided into 50 different codes, called Titles, that represent broad areas subject to Federal regulation. FAA regulations are listed under Title 14, Aeronautics and Space, which encompasses all aspects of civil aviation from how to earn a pilot's certificate to maintenance of an aircraft.

Title 14 CFR Chapter 1, Federal Aviation Administration, is broken down into subchapters A through N as illustrated in *Figure 1-12*.

Code of Federal Regulations	
Aeronautics and Space	
Subchapters	Chapter 1. Federal Aviation Administration
A	Definitions (definitions and abbreviations)
B	Procedural rules (rulemaking processes, claims, enforcement)
C	Aircraft (Aircraft certification procedures [21], Airworthiness standards [parts 25 through 33 depending on type of aircraft], airworthiness directives [39], maintenance [43], aircraft registration [47])
D	Airmen (certification of pilots and Instructors [61], (Medical standards [67])
E	Airspace (designation of airspace classification [71], special use airspace [73]
F	Air traffic and general rules (general operating and flight rules [91], special air traffic rules and airport traffic patterns [93])
G	Air carriers, air travel clubs. and operators for compensation or hire: certification and operations
H	Schools and other certified agencies
I	Airports
J	Navigational facilities
K	Administrative regulations
L–M	Reserved
N	War risk insurance

Figure 1-12. *Overview of 14 CFR, available online free from the FAA, and for purchase through commercial sources.*

For the pilot, certain parts of 14 CFR are more relevant than others. During flight training, it is helpful for the pilot to become familiar with the parts and subparts that relate to flight training and pilot certification. For instance, 14 CFR part 61 pertains to the certification of pilots, flight instructors, and ground instructors. It also defines the eligibility, aeronautical knowledge, flight proficiency, as well as training and testing requirements for each type of pilot certificate issued. 14 CFR part 91 provides guidance in the areas of general flight rules, visual flight rules (VFR), and instrument flight rules (IFR), while 14 CFR part 43 covers aircraft maintenance, preventive maintenance, rebuilding, and alterations.

Primary Locations of the FAA

The FAA headquarters are in Washington, D.C., and there are nine regional offices strategically located across the United States. The agency's two largest field facilities are the Mike Monroney Aeronautical Center (MMAC) in Oklahoma City, Oklahoma, and the William J. Hughes Technical Center (WJHTC) in Atlantic City, New Jersey. Home to FAA training and logistics services, the MMAC provides

a number of aviation safety-related and business support services. The WJHTC is the premier aviation research and development and test and evaluation facility in the country. The center's programs include testing and evaluation in ATC, communication, navigation, airports, aircraft safety, and security. Furthermore, the WJHTC is active in long-range development of innovative aviation systems and concepts, development of new ATC equipment and software, and modification of existing systems and procedures.

Field Offices
Flight Standards Service

Within the FAA, the Flight Standards Service promotes safe air transportation by setting the standards for certification and oversight of airmen, air operators, air agencies, and designees. It also promotes safety of flight of civil aircraft and air commerce by:

- Accomplishing certification, inspection, surveillance, investigation, and enforcement.

- Setting regulations and standards.

- Managing the system for registration of civil aircraft and all airmen records.

The focus of interaction between Flight Standards Service and the aviation community/general public is the Flight Standards District Office (FSDO).

Flight Standards District Office (FSDO)

The FAA has approximately 130 FSDOs. *[Figure 1-13]* These offices provide information and services for the aviation community. FSDO phone numbers are listed in the telephone directory under Government Offices, DOT, FAA. Another convenient method of finding a local office is to use the FSDO locator available at: www.faa.gov/about/office_org/headquarters_offices/avs/offices/afs/afs600.

Figure 1-13. *Atlanta Flight Standards District Office (FSDO).*

In addition to accident investigation and the enforcement of aviation regulations, the FSDO is also responsible for the certification and surveillance of air carriers, air operators, flight schools/training centers, and airmen including pilots and flight instructors. Each FSDO is staffed by Aviation Safety Inspectors (ASIs) who play a key role in making the nation's aviation system safe.

Aviation Safety Inspector (ASI)

The Aviation Safety Inspectors (ASIs) administer and enforce safety regulations and standards for the production, operation, maintenance, and/or modification of aircraft used in civil aviation. They also specialize in conducting inspections of various aspects of the aviation system, such as aircraft and parts manufacturing, aircraft operation, aircraft airworthiness, and cabin safety. ASIs must complete a training program at the FAA Academy in Oklahoma City, Oklahoma, which includes airman evaluation, and pilot testing techniques and procedures. ASIs also receive extensive on-the-job training and recurrent training on a regular basis. The FAA has approximately 3,700 inspectors located in its FSDO offices. All questions concerning pilot certification (and/or requests for other aviation information or services) should be directed to the local FSDO.

FAA Safety Team (FAASTeam)

The FAA is dedicated to improving the safety of United States civilian aviation by conveying safety principles and practices through training, outreach, and education. The FAA Safety Team (FAASTeam) exemplifies this commitment. The FAASTeam has replaced the Aviation Safety Program (ASP), whose education of airmen on all types of safety subjects successfully reduced accidents. Its success led to its demise because the easy-to-fix accident causes have been addressed. To take aviation safety one step further, Flight Standards Service created the FAASTeam, which is devoted to reducing aircraft accidents by using a coordinated effort to focus resources on elusive accident causes.

Each of the FAA's nine regions has a Regional FAASTeam Office dedicated to this new safety program and managed by the Regional FAASTeam Manager (RFM). The FAASTeam is "teaming" up with individuals and the aviation industry to create a unified effort against accidents and "tip" the safety culture in the right direction. To learn more about this effort to improve aviation safety, to take a course at their online learning center, or to join the FAASTeam, visit their web site at www.faasafety.gov/default.aspx.

Obtaining Assistance from the FAA

Information can be obtained from the FAA by phone, Internet/e-mail, or mail. To talk to the FAA toll-free 24 hours a day, call 1-866-TELL-FAA (1-866-835-5322). To visit the FAA's web site, go to www.faa.gov. Individuals can also e-mail an FAA representative at a local FSDO office by accessing the staff e-mail address available via the "Contact FAA" link at the bottom of the FAA home page. Letters can be sent to:

Federal Aviation Administration
800 Independence Ave, SW
Washington, DC 20591

FAA Reference Material

The FAA provides a variety of important reference material for the student, as well as the advanced civil aviation pilot. In addition to the regulations provided online by the FAA, several other publications are available to the user. Almost all reference material is available online at www.faa.gov in downloadable format. Commercial aviation publishers also provide published and online reference material to further aid the aviation pilot.

Aeronautical Information Manual (AIM)

The Aeronautical Information Manual (AIM) is the official guide to basic flight information and ATC procedures for the aviation community flying in the NAS of the United States. *[Figure 1-14]* An international version, containing parallel information, as well as specific information on international airports, is also available. The AIM also contains information of interest to pilots, such as health and medical facts, flight safety, a pilot/controller glossary of terms used in the system, and information on safety, accidents, and reporting of hazards.

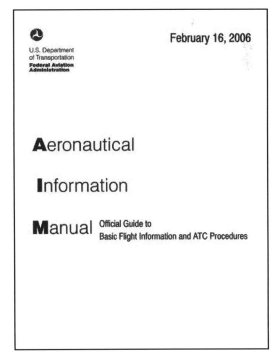

Figure 1-14. *Aeronautical Information Manual.*

This manual is offered for sale on a subscription basis or is available online at: http://bookstore.gpo.gov.

Order forms are provided at the beginning of the manual or online and should be sent to the Superintendent of Documents, United States Government Printing Office (GPO). The AIM is complemented by other operational publications, which are available via separate subscriptions or online.

Handbooks

Handbooks are developed to provide specific information about a particular topic that enhances training or understanding. The FAA publishes a variety of handbooks that generally fall into three categories: Aircraft, Aviation, and Examiners and Inspectors. *[Figure 1-15]* These handbooks can be purchased from the Superintendent of Documents or downloaded (www. faa.gov/regulations_policies). Aviation handbooks are also published by various commercial aviation companies. Aircraft flight manuals commonly called Pilot Operating Handbooks (POH) are documents developed by the airplane manufacturer, approved by the FAA, and are specific to a particular make and model aircraft by serial number. This subject is covered in greater detail in Chapter 8, Flight Manuals and Other Documents, of this handbook. *[Figure 1-16]*

Advisory Circulars (ACs)

Advisory circulars (ACs) provide a single, uniform, agency-wide system that the FAA uses to deliver advisory material to FAA customers, industry, the aviation community, and the public. An AC may be needed to:

- Provide an acceptable, clearly understood method for complying with a regulation.

- Standardize implementation of the regulation or harmonize implementation for the international aviation community.

- Resolve a general misunderstanding of a regulation.

- Respond to a request from some government entity, such as General Accounting Office, NTSB, or the Office of the Inspector General.

- Help the industry and FAA effectively implement a regulation.

- Explain requirements and limits of an FAA grant program.

- Expand on standards needed to promote aviation safety, including the safe operation of airports.

There are three parts to an AC number, as in 25-42C. The first part of the number identifies the subject matter area of the AC and corresponds to the appropriate 14 CFR part. For example, an AC on certification: Pilots and Flight and

---

Aeronautical Information Manual (AIM)

The Aeronautical Information Manual is designed to provide the aviation community with basic flight information and ATC procedures for use in the NAS of the United States. It also contains the fundamentals required in order to fly in the United States NAS, including items of interest to pilots concerning health/medical facts, factors affecting flight safety, etc.

Airplane Flying Handbook

The Airplane Flying Handbook is designed as a technical manual to introduce basic pilot skills and knowledge that are essential for piloting airplanes. It provides information on transition to other airplanes and the operation of various airplane systems.

Aviation Instructor's Handbook

The Aviation Instructor's Handbook provides the foundation for beginning instructors to understand and apply the fundamentals of instructing. This handbook also provides aviation instructors with up-to-date information on learning and teaching, and how to relate this information to the task of conveying aeronautical knowledge and skills to students. Experienced aviation instructors also find the new and updated information useful for improving their effectiveness in training activities.

Instrument Flying Handbook

The Instrument Flying Handbook is designed for use by instrument flight instructors and pilots preparing for instrument rating tests. Instructors find this handbook a valuable training aid as it includes basic reference material for knowledge testing and instrument flight training.

Instrument Procedures Handbook

The Instrument Procedures Handbook is designed as a technical reference for professional pilots who operate under IFR in the NAS and expands on information contained in the Instrument Flying Handbook.

Figure 1-15. *A few samples of the handbooks available to the public. Most are free of charge or can be downloaded from the FAA website.*

Figure 1-16. *Pilot Operating Handbooks from manufacturers.*

Ground Instructors is numbered as AC 61-65E. Since ACs are numbered sequentially within each subject area, the second part of the number beginning with the dash identifies this sequence. The third part of the number is a letter assigned by the originating office and shows the revision sequence if an AC is revised. The first version of an AC does not have a revision letter. In *Figure 1-17*, this is the fifth revision, as designated by the "E."

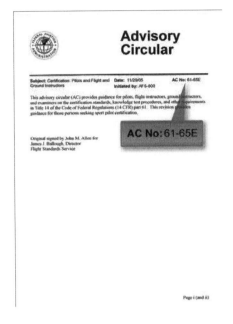

Figure 1-17. *Example of an Advisory Circular.*

Flight Publications

The FAA, in concert with other government agencies, orchestrates the publication and changes to publications that are key to safe flight. *Figure 1-18* illustrates some publications a pilot uses.

Pilot and Aeronautical Information
Notices to Airmen (NOTAMs)

Time-critical aeronautical information, which is of either a temporary nature or not sufficiently known in advance to permit publication on aeronautical charts or in other operational publications, receives immediate dissemination via the National Notice to Airmen (NOTAM) System. NOTAMs contain current notices to airmen, which are considered essential to the safety of flight, as well as supplemental data affecting other operational publications. NOTAM information is classified into two categories: NOTAM (D) or distant and Flight Data Center (FDC) NOTAMs.

NOTAM (D) information is disseminated for all navigational facilities that are part of the NAS, all public use airports, seaplane bases, and heliports listed in the Airport/Facility Directory (A/FD). NOTAM (D) information now includes such data as taxiway closures, personnel and equipment near or crossing runways, and airport lighting aids that do not affect instrument approach criteria, such as visual approach slope indicator (VASI).

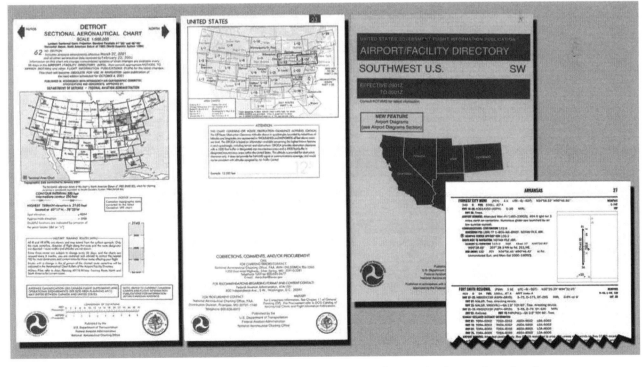

Figure 1-18. *From left to right, a sectional VFR chart, IFR chart, and A/FD with a sample of a page from that directory.*

FDC NOTAMs contain such things as amendments to published Instrument Approach Procedures (IAPs) and other current aeronautical charts. They are also used to advertise temporary flight restrictions caused by such things as natural disasters or large-scale public events that may generate a congestion of air traffic over a site.

NOTAMs are available in printed form through subscription from the Superintendent of Documents, from an FSS, or online at The Pilot Web Site (http://pilotweb.nas.faa.gov/distribution/atcscc.html), which provides access to current NOTAM information. *[Figure 1-19]*

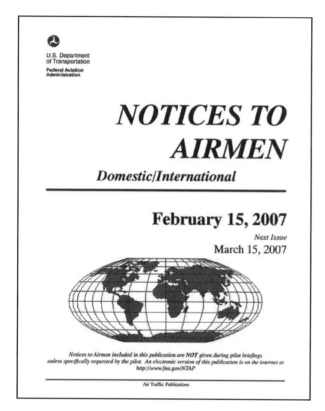

Figure 1-19. *A sample of NOTAM information available to the public. Most are free of charge or can be downloaded from the FAA website.*

Safety Program Airmen Notification System (SPANS)

The FAA recently launched the Safety Program Airmen Notification System (SPANS), an online event notification system that provides timely and easy-to-assess seminar and event information notification for airmen. The SPANS system is taking the place of the current paper based mail system. This transition will provide better service to airmen while reducing costs for the FAA. Anyone can search the SPANS system and register for events. To read more about SPANS, visit www.faasafety.gov/SPANS/default.aspx.

Aircraft Types and Categories

Ultralight Vehicles

An ultralight aircraft *[Figure 1-20]* is referred to as a vehicle because the FAA does not govern it if it:

- Is used or intended to be used by a single occupant.

- Is used for recreation or sport purposes.

- Does not have an airworthiness certificate.

- If unpowered, weighs less than 155 pounds.

- If powered, weighs less than 254 pounds empty weight, excluding floats and safety devices that are intended for deployment in a potentially catastrophic situation.

- Has a fuel capacity not exceeding 5 gallons.

- Is not capable of more than 55 knots calibrated airspeed at full power in level flight.

- Has a power-off stall speed, which does not exceed 24 knots calibrated airspeed.

Figure 1-20. *A typical ultralight vehicle, which weighs less than 254 pounds.*

Ultralight vehicles do not require any form of pilot license or certification if they are flown within 14 CFR 103 operating rules which generally limit the ultralight vehicle to uncontrolled airpsace and no flight over populated areas. Every person flying an ultralight should be familiar to the rules specified in 14 CFR 103.

Light Sport Aircraft (LSA) Category

In 2004, the FAA approved a new pilot certificate and aircraft category program to allow individuals to join the aviation community by reducing training requirements that affect the overall cost of learning to fly. The Sport Pilot Certificate was created for pilots flying light-weight, simple aircraft and offers limited privileges. The category of aircraft called the

Light Sport Aircraft (LSA) includes Airplane (Land/Sea), Gyroplane, Airship, Balloon, Weight-Shift Control (Land/Sea), Glider, and Powered Parachute. *[Figure 1-21]*

In order for an aircraft to fall in the Light Sport Category, it must meet the following criteria:

- The maximum gross takeoff weight may not exceed 1,320 pounds, or 1,430 pounds for seaplanes. Lighter-than-air maximum gross weight may not be more than 660 pounds.

- The maximum stall speed may not exceed 45 knots, and the inflight maximum speed in level flight with maximum continuous power is no greater than 120 knots.

- Seating is restricted to single or two-seat configuration only.

- The powerplant may be only a single, reciprocating engine (if powered), but may include rotary or diesel engines.

- The landing gear must be fixed, except gliders or those aircraft intended for operation on water.

- The aircraft can be manufactured and sold ready-to-fly under a new special LSA category, and certification must meet industry consensus standards. The aircraft may be used for sport, recreation, flight training, and aircraft rental.

- The aircraft will have an FAA registration N-number and may be operated at night if the aircraft is properly equipped and the pilot holds at least a private pilot certificate with a minimum of a third-class medical.

Pilot Certifications

The type of intended flying will influence what type of pilot's certificate is required. Eligibility, training, experience, and testing requirements differ depending on the type of certificates sought. *[Figure 1-22]*

Figure 1-21. *Some examples of LSA (from top to bottom: gyroplane, weight-shift control, and a powered parachute).*

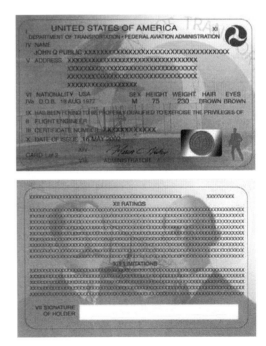

Figure 1-22. *Front side (top) and back side (bottom) of an airman certificate issued by the FAA.*

Sport Pilot

To become a sport pilot, the student pilot is required to have the following hours depending upon the aircraft:

- Airplane: 20 hours
- Powered Parachute: 12 hours
- Weight-Shift Control (Trikes): 20 hours
- Glider: 10 hours
- Rotorcraft (gyroplane only): 20 hours
- Lighter-Than-Air: 20 hours (airship) or 7 hours (balloon)

To earn a Sport Pilot Certificate, one must:

- Be at least 16 to become a student sport pilot (14 for glider).
- Be at least 17 to test for a sport pilot certificate (16 for gliders).
- Be able to read, write, and understand English.
- Hold a current and valid driver's license as evidence of medical eligibility.

Recreational Pilot

To become a recreational pilot, one must:

- Be at least 17 years old (16 to be a private glider pilot or be rated for free flight in a balloon.)
- Be able to read, write, speak and understand the English language
- Pass the required knowledge test
- Meet the aeronautical experience requirements
- A logbook endorsement from an instructor
- Pass the required practical test
- Third-class medical certificate issued under part 14 CFR part 67, except for gliders and balloons—medical eligibility not required

As a recreational pilot, cross-country flight is limited to a 50 NM range from departure airport but is permitted with additional training per 14 CFR section 61.101(c). Additional limitations include flight during the day, and no flying in airspace where communications with air traffic control are required.

The aeronautical experience requirements for a recreational pilot license

- 30 hours of flight time including at least:
- 15 hours of dual instruction
- 2 hours of enroute training

- 3 hours in preparation for the practical test
- 3 hours of solo flight

Private Pilot

A private pilot is one who flies for pleasure or personal business without accepting compensation for flying except in some very limited, specific circumstances. The Private Pilot Certificate is the certificate held by the majority of active pilots. It allows command of any aircraft (subject to appropriate ratings) for any noncommercial purpose, and gives almost unlimited authority to fly under VFR. Passengers may be carried, and flight in furtherance of a business is permitted; however, a private pilot may not be compensated in any way for services as a pilot, although passengers can pay a pro rata share of flight expenses, such as fuel or rental costs. If training under 14 CFR part 61, experience requirements include at least 40 hours of piloting time, including 20 hours of flight with an instructor and 10 hours of solo flight. *[Figure 1-23]*

Figure 1-23. *A typical aircraft a private pilot might fly.*

Commercial Pilot

A commercial pilot may be compensated for flying. Training for the certificate focuses on a better understanding of aircraft systems and a higher standard of airmanship. The Commercial Certificate itself does not allow a pilot to fly in instrument meteorological conditions (IMC), and commercial pilots without an instrument rating are restricted to daytime flight within 50 nautical miles (NM) when flying for hire.

A commercial airplane pilot must be able to operate a complex airplane, as a specific number of hours of complex (or turbine-powered) aircraft time are among the prerequisites, and at least a portion of the practical examination is performed in a complex aircraft. A complex aircraft must have retractable landing gear, movable flaps, and a controllable pitch propeller. See 14 CFR part 61, section 61.31(c) for additional information. *[Figure 1-24]*

Figure 1-24. *A complex aircraft.*

Airline Transport Pilot

The airline transport pilot (ATP) is tested to the highest level of piloting ability. The ATP Certificate is a prerequisite for acting as a pilot in command (PIC) of scheduled airline operations. The minimum pilot experience is 1,500 hours of flight time. In addition, the pilot must be at least 23 years of age, be able to read, write, speak, and understand the English language, and be "of good moral standing." *[Figure 1-25]*

Figure 1-25. *Type of aircraft flown by an airline transport pilot.*

Selecting a Flight School

Selection of a flight school is an important consideration in the flight training process. FAA-approved flight schools, noncertificated flying schools, and independent flight instructors conduct flight training in the United States. All flight training is conducted under the auspices of the FAA following the regulations outlined in either 14 CFR part 141 or 61. 14 CFR part 141 flight schools are certificated by the FAA. Application for certification is voluntary and the school must meet stringent requirements for personnel, equipment, maintenance, facilities, and teach an established curriculum, which includes a training course outline (TCO) approved by the FAA. The certificated schools may qualify for a ground school rating and a flight school rating. In addition, the school may be authorized to give its graduates practical (flight) tests and knowledge (computer administered written) tests. AC 140-2, as amended, FAA Certificated Pilot Schools Directory, lists certificated ground and flight schools and the pilot training courses each school offers. AC 140-2, as amended, can be found online at the FAA's Regulations and Guidance Library located on the FAA's web site at www.faa.gov.

Enrollment in a 14 CFR part 141 flight school ensures quality and continuity, and offers a structured approach to flight training because these facilities must document the training curriculum and have their flight courses approved by the FAA. These strictures allow 14 CFR part 141 schools to complete certificates and ratings in fewer flight hours, which can mean a savings on the cost of flight training for the student pilot. For example, the minimum requirement for a Private Pilot Certificate is 35 hours in a part 141-certificated school and 40 hours in part 61 schools. (This difference may be insignificant for a Private Pilot Certificate because the national average indicates most pilots require 60 to 75 hours of flight training.)

Many excellent flight schools find it impractical to qualify for the FAA part 141 certificates and are referred to as part 61 schools. 14 CFR part 61 outlines certificate and rating requirements for pilot certification through noncertificated schools and individual flight instructors. It also states what knowledge-based training must be covered and how much flight experience is required for each certificate and rating. Flight schools and flight instructors who train must adhere to the statutory requirements and train pilots to the standards found in 14 CFR part 61.

One advantage of flight training under 14 CFR part 61 is its flexibility. Flight lessons can be tailored to the individual student, because 14 CFR part 61 dictates the required minimum flight experience and knowledge-based training necessary to gain a specific pilot's license, but it does not stipulate how the training is to be organized. This flexibility can also be a disadvantage because a flight instructor who fails to organize the flight training can cost a student pilot time and expense through repetitious training. One way for a student pilot to avoid this problem is to insure the flight instructor has a well-documented training syllabus.

How To Find a Reputable Flight Program

To obtain information about pilot training, contact the local FSDO, which maintains a current file on all schools within its district. The choice of a flight school depends on what type of certificate is sought, whether an individual wishes to fly as a sport pilot or wishes to pursue a career as a professional pilot. Another consideration is the amount of time that can be devoted to training. Ground and flight training should be obtained as regularly and frequently as possible because this assures maximum retention of instruction and the achievement of requisite proficiency.

Do not make the determination based on financial concerns alone, because the quality of training is very important. Prior to making a final decision, visit the schools under consideration and talk with management, instructors, and students.

Be inquisitive and proactive when searching for a flight school, do some homework, and develop a checklist of questions by talking to pilots and reading articles in flight magazines. The checklist should include questions about aircraft reliability and maintenance practices, questions for current students such as whether or not there is a safe, clean aircraft available when they are scheduled to fly.

Questions for the training facility should be aimed at determining if the instruction fits available personal time. What are the school's operating hours? Does the facility have dedicated classrooms available for ground training required by the FAA? Is there an area available for preflight briefings, postflight debriefings, and critiques? Are these rooms private in nature in order to provide a nonthreatening environment in which the instructor can explain the content and outcome of the flight without making the student feel self-conscious?

Examine the facility before committing to any flight training. Evaluate the answers on the checklist, and then take time to think things over before making a decision. This proactive approach to choosing a flight school will ensure a student pilot contracts with a flight school or flight instructor best suited to individual needs.

How To Choose a Certificated Flight Instructor (CFI)

Whether an individual chooses to train under 14 CFR part 141 or part 61, the key to an effective flight program is the quality of the ground and flight training received from the CFI. The flight instructor assumes total responsibility for training an individual to meet the standards required for certification within an ever-changing operating environment.

A CFI should possess an understanding of the learning process, knowledge of the fundamentals of teaching, and the ability to communicate effectively with the student pilot. During the certification process, a flight instructor applicant is tested on the practical application of these skills in specific teaching situations. The flight instructor is crucial to the scenario-based training program endorsed by the FAA. He or she is trained to function in the learning environment as an advisor and guide for the learner. The duties, responsibilities, and authority of the CFI include the following:

- Orient the student to the scenario-based training system.

- Help the student become a confident planner and inflight manager of each flight and a critical evaluator of their own performance.

- Help the student understand the knowledge requirements present in real world applications.

- Diagnose learning difficulties and helping the student overcome them.

- Evaluate student progress and maintain appropriate records.

- Provide continuous review of student learning.

Should a student pilot find the selected CFI is not training in a manner conducive for learning, or the student and CFI do not have compatible schedules, the student pilot should find another CFI. Choosing the right CFI is important because the quality of instruction and the knowledge and skills acquired from this flight instructor affect a student pilot's entire flying career.

The Student Pilot

The first step in becoming a pilot is to select a type of aircraft. FAA rules for getting a pilot's certificate differ depending on the type of aircraft flown. Individuals can choose among airplanes, gyroplanes, weight-shift, helicopters, powered parachutes, gliders, balloons, or airships. A pilot does not need a certificate to fly ultralight vehicles.

Basic Requirements

A student pilot is one who is being trained by an instructor pilot for his or her first full certificate, and is permitted to fly alone (solo) under specific, limited circumstances. Upon request, an FAA-authorized aviation medical examiner (AME) will issue a combined medical certificate and Student Pilot Certificate after completion of a physical examination. Student Pilot Certificates may be issued by an FAA inspector or an FAA-designated pilot examiner. To be eligible for a Student Pilot's Certificate, an individual must be:

- Be 16 years old (14 years old to pilot a glider or balloon).

- Be able to read, write, speak, and understand English.

- Hold a current Third-Class Medical Certificate (or for glider or balloon, certify no medical defect exists that would prevent piloting a balloon or glider).

Medical Certification Requirements

The second step in becoming a pilot is to obtain a medical certificate and Student Pilot's Certificate if the choice of aircraft is an airplane, helicopter, gyroplane, or airship. *[Figure 1-26]* (The FAA suggests the individual get a medical certificate before beginning flight training to avoid the expense of flight training that cannot be continued due to a medical condition.) Balloon or glider pilots do not need a medical certificate, but do need to write a statement certifying that no medical defect exists that would prevent them from piloting a balloon or glider. The new sport pilot category does not require a medical examination; a driver's license can be used as proof of medical competence. Applicants who fail to meet certain requirements or who have physical disabilities which might limit, but not prevent, their acting as pilots, should contact the nearest FAA office.

Copy of FAA Form 8500-9 (Medical Certificate) or FAA Form 8420-2 (Medical Student Pilot Certificate) issued.

FF-

MEDICAL CERTIFICATE THIRD **CLASS AND STUDENT PILOT CERTIFICATE**

This certifies that *(Full name and address):*

JOHN DOE
123 ANYSTREET DR.
ANYTOWN, TN 37130

Date of Birth	Height	Weight	Hair	Eyes	Sex
12-17-73	70	182	BR	GR	M

has met the medical standards prescribed in 14 CFR part 67, for this class of Medical Certificate.

Limitations

MUST WEAR CORRECTIVE LENSES

Examiner

Date of Examination	Examiner's Designation No
10/17/89	1013-2

Signature *Joe Doctor*

Typed Name   JOE DOCTOR, D.O.

Airman's Signature

Figure 1-26. *A Third-Class Medical Certificate/Student Pilot Certificate.*

A medical certificate is obtained by passing a physical examination administered by a doctor who is an FAA-authorized AME. There are approximately 6,000 FAA-authorized AMEs in the nation. Medical certificates are designated as first class, second class, or third class. Generally, first class is designed for the airline transport pilot; second class for the commercial pilot; and third class for the student, recreational, and private pilot. A Student Pilot Certificate is issued by an AME at the time of the student's first medical examination. This certificate allows an individual who is being trained by a flight instructor to fly alone (solo) under specific, limited circumstances and must be carried with the student pilot while exercising solo flight privileges. The student pilot certificate is only required when exercising solo flight privileges. The student certificate is valid until the last day of the month, 24 months after it was issued.

Student Pilot Solo Requirements

Once a student has accrued sufficient training and experience, a CFI can endorse the student's certificate to authorize limited solo flight in a specific type (make and model) of aircraft. A student pilot may not carry passengers, fly in furtherance of a business, or operate an aircraft outside of the various endorsements provided by the flight instructor. There is no minimum aeronautical knowledge or experience requirement for the issuance of a student pilot certificate other than the medical requirements for the class of medical certificate the student certificate is based upon. There are, however, minimum aeronautical knowledge and experience requirements for student pilots to solo.

Becoming a Pilot

The course of instruction a student pilot follows depends on the type of certificate sought. It should include the ground and flight training necessary to acquire the knowledge and skills required to safely and efficiently function as a certificated pilot in the selected category and class of aircraft. The specific knowledge and skill areas for each category and class of aircraft are outlined in 14 CFR part 61. Eligibility, aeronautical knowledge, proficiency, and aeronautical requirements can be found in 14 CFR part 61, Certification: Pilots, Flight Instructors, and Ground Instructors.

- Recreational Pilot, see subpart D
- Private Pilot, see subpart E
- Sport Pilot, see subpart J

The knowledge-based portion of training is obtained through FAA handbooks such as this one, textbooks, and other sources of training and testing materials which are available in print form from the Superintendent of Documents, GPO, and online at the Regulatory Support Division: www.faa.gov/about/office_org/headquarters_offices/avs/offices/afs/afs600.

The CFI may also use commercial publications as a source of study materials, especially for aircraft categories where government materials are limited. A student pilot should follow the flight instructor's advice on what and when to study. Planning a definite study program and following it as closely as possible will help in scoring well on the knowledge test. Haphazard or disorganized study habits usually result in an unsatisfactory score.

In addition to learning aeronautical knowledge, such as the principles of flight, a student pilot is also required to gain skill in flight maneuvers. The selected category and class of aircraft determines the type of flight skills and number of flight hours to be obtained. There are four steps involved in learning a flight maneuver:

- The CFI introduces and demonstrates flight maneuver to the student.

- The CFI talks student pilot through the maneuver.

- The student pilot practices the maneuver under CFI supervision.

- The CFI authorizes the student pilot to practice the maneuver solo.

Once the student pilot has shown proficiency in the required knowledge areas, flight maneuvers, and accrued the required amount of flight hours, the CFI endorses the student pilot logbook, which allows the student pilot to take the written and practical exams for pilot certification.

Knowledge and Skill Examinations

Knowledge Examination

The knowledge test is the computer portion of the exams taken to obtain pilot certification. The test contains questions of the objective, multiple-choice type. This testing method conserves the applicant's time, eliminates any element of individual judgment in determining grades, and saves time in scoring.

If pursuing a recreational pilot or private pilot certificate, it is important to become familiar with 14 CFR part 61, section 61.23, Medical Certificates: Requirements and Duration; 14 CFR section 61.35, Knowledge Test: Prerequisites and Passing Grades; and 14 CFR section 61.83, Eligibility Requirements for Student Pilot, for detailed information pertaining to prerequisites and eligibility.

If pursuing a recreational pilot certificate, it is important to review 14 CFR section 61.96, Applicability and Eligibility Requirements: General, for additional detailed information pertaining to eligibility; and if pursuing a private pilot certificate, 14 CFR section 61.103, Eligibility Requirements: General, contains additional detailed information pertaining to eligibility. Sample test questions can be downloaded from Airmen Knowledge Test Questions: www.faa.gov/education_research/testing/airmen/test_questions/.

Each applicant must register to take the test, and provide proper identification and authorization proving eligibility to take a particular FAA test. The option to take an untimed sample test will be offered. The actual test is time limited, but most applicants have sufficient time to complete and review the test. Upon completion of the knowledge test, the applicant receives an Airman Knowledge Test Report that reflects the score and is embossed with the testing center's seal. To pass, a minimum score of 70 must be attained.

When To Take the Examination

The knowledge test is more meaningful to the applicant and more likely to result in a satisfactory grade if it is taken after beginning the flight portion of the training. Therefore, the FAA recommends the knowledge test be taken after the student pilot has completed a solo cross-country flight. The operational knowledge gained by this experience can be used to the student's advantage in the knowledge test. The student pilot's CFI is the best person to determine when the applicant is ready to take the knowledge exam.

Where To Take the Examination

The FAA has hundreds of designated computer testing centers worldwide that administer FAA knowledge tests. These testing centers offer the full range of airman knowledge tests. Applicants will be charged a fee for the administration of FAA knowledge tests. A complete list of test centers, their locations and phone numbers can be downloaded at "Airmen Certification Frequently Asked Questions" located at www.faa.gov/education_research/testing/airmen/test_questions/ or www.faa.gov/licenses_certificates/airmen_certification/airmen_FAQ/.

An applicant can also contact the local FSDO to obtain this information. If the student pilot chooses a 14 CFR part 141 flight school with test examining authority, the school will administer the knowledge test during the curriculum.

Practical Examination

The FAA has developed PTSs for FAA pilot certificates and associated ratings. *[Figure 1-27]* These practical tests are administered by FAA ASIs and DPEs. 14 CFR part 61 specifies the areas of operation in which knowledge and skill must be demonstrated by the applicant. Since the

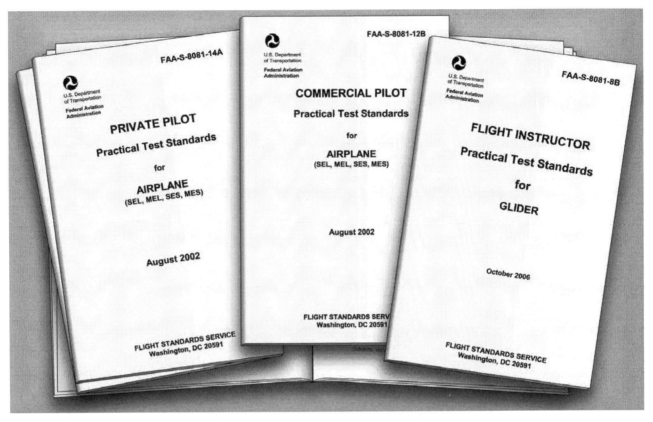

Figure 1-27. *Examples of Practical Test Standards.*

FAA requires all practical tests be conducted in accordance with the appropriate PTS, and the policies set forth in the Introduction section of the PTS book, the pilot applicant should become familiar with this book during training.

The PTS book is a testing document and not intended to be a training syllabus. An appropriately rated flight instructor is responsible for training the pilot applicant to acceptable standards in all subject matter areas, procedures, and maneuvers. Descriptions of tasks and information on how to perform maneuvers and procedures are contained in reference and teaching documents such as this handbook. A list of reference documents is contained in the Introduction section of each PTS book. Copies may obtained by:

- Downloading from the FAA website: www.faa.gov.

- Purchase of print copies from the GPO, Pittsburgh, Pennsylvania, or via their official online bookstore at www.access.gpo.gov.

The flight proficiency maneuvers listed in 14 CFR part 61 are the standard skill requirements for certification. They are outlined in the PTS as "areas of operation." These are phases of the practical test arranged in a logical sequence within the standard. They begin with preflight preparation and end with postflight procedures. Each area of operation

contains "tasks," which are comprised of knowledge areas, flight procedures, and/or flight maneuvers appropriate to the area of operation. The candidate is required to demonstrate knowledge and proficiency in all tasks for the original issuance of all pilot certificates.

When To Take the Practical Exam

14 CFR part 61 establishes the ground school and flight experience requirements for the type of certification and aircraft selected. However, the CFI best determines when an applicant is qualified for the practical test. A practice practical test is an important step in the flight training process.

The applicant will be asked to present the following documentation:

- FAA Form 8710-1 (8710.11 for sport pilot applicants), Application for an Airman Certificate and/or Rating, with the flight instructor's recommendation.

- An Airman Knowledge Test Report with a satisfactory grade.

- A medical certificate (not required for glider or balloon), and a student pilot certificate endorsed by a flight instructor for solo, solo cross-country (airplane and rotorcraft), and for the make and model aircraft to be used for the practical test (driver's license or medical certificate for sport pilot applicants).

- The pilot log book records.
- A graduation certificate from an FAA-approved school (if applicable).

The applicant must provide an airworthy aircraft with equipment relevant to the areas of operation required for the practical test. He or she will also be asked to produce and explain the:

- Aircraft's registration certificate
- Aircraft's airworthiness certificate
- Aircraft's operating limitations or FAA-approved aircraft flight manual (if required)
- Aircraft equipment list
- Required weight and balance data
- Maintenance records
- Applicable airworthiness directives (ADs)

For a detailed explanation of the required pilot maneuvers and performance standards, refer to the PTSs pertaining to the type of certification and aircraft selected. These standards may be downloaded free of charge from the FAA: www.faa.gov. They can also be purchased from the Superintendent of Documents or GPO bookstores. Most airport fixed-base operators and flight schools carry a variety of government publications and charts, as well as commercially published materials.

Who Administers the FAA Practical Examination?

Due to the varied responsibilities of the FSDOs, practical tests are usually given by DPEs. An applicant should schedule the practical test by appointment to avoid conflicts and wasted time. A list of examiner names can be obtained from the local FSDO. Since a DPE serves without pay from the government for conducting practical tests and processing the necessary reports, the examiner is allowed to charge a reasonable fee. There is no charge for the practical test when conducted by an FAA inspector.

Role of the Certificated Flight Instructor

To become a CFI, a pilot must meet the provisions of 14 CFR part 61. The FAA places full responsibility for student flight training on the shoulders of the CFI, who is the cornerstone of aviation safety. It is the job of the flight instructor to train the student pilot in all the knowledge areas and teach the skills necessary for the student pilot to operate safely and competently as a certificated pilot in the NAS. The training will include airmanship skills, pilot judgment and decision-making, and good operating practices.

A pilot training program depends on the quality of the ground and flight instruction the student pilot receives. The flight instructor must possess a thorough understanding of the learning process, knowledge of the fundamentals of teaching, and the ability to communicate effectively with the student pilot. He or she uses a syllabus and teaching style that embodies the "building block" method of instruction. In this method, the student progresses from the known to the unknown via a course of instruction laid out in such a way that each new maneuver embodies the principles involved in the performance of maneuvers previously learned. Thus, with the introduction of each new subject, the student not only learns a new principle or technique, but also broadens his or her application of those principles or techniques previously learned.

Insistence on correct techniques and procedures from the beginning of training by the flight instructor ensures that the student pilot develops proper flying habit patterns. Any deficiencies in the maneuvers or techniques must immediately be emphasized and corrected. A flight instructor serves as a role model for the student pilot who observes the flying habits of his or her flight instructor during flight instruction, as well as when the instructor conducts other pilot operations. Thus, the flight instructor becomes a model of flying proficiency for the student who, consciously or unconsciously, attempts to imitate the instructor. For this reason, a flight instructor should observe recognized safety practices, as well as regulations during all flight operations.

The student pilot who enrolls in a pilot training program commits considerable time, effort, and expense to achieve a pilot certificate. Students often judge the effectiveness of the flight instructor and the success of the pilot training program based on their ability to pass the requisite FAA practical test. A competent flight instructor stresses to the student that practical tests are a sampling of pilot ability compressed into a short period of time. The goal of a flight instructor is to train the "total" pilot.

Role of the Designated Pilot Examiner

The DPE plays an important role in the FAA's mission of promoting aviation safety by administering FAA practical tests for pilot and Flight Instructor Certificates and associated ratings. Although administering these tests is a responsibility of the ASI, the FAA's highest priority is making air travel safer by inspecting aircraft that fly in the United States. To satisfy the need for pilot testing and certification services, the FAA delegates certain of these responsibilities to private individuals who are not FAA employees.

Appointed in accordance with 14 CFR section 183.23, a DPE is an individual who meets the qualification requirements of the Pilot Examiner's Handbook, FAA Order 8710.3, and who:

- Is technically qualified.

- Holds all pertinent category, class, and type ratings for each aircraft related to their designation.

- Meets requirements of 14 CFR part 61, sections 61.56, 61.57, and 61.58, as appropriate.

- Is current and qualified to act as PIC of each aircraft for which he or she is authorized.

- Maintains at least a Third-Class Medical Certificate, if required.

- Maintains a current Flight Instructor Certificate, if required.

Designated to perform specific pilot certification tasks on behalf of the FAA, a DPE may charge a reasonable fee. Generally, a DPE's authority is limited to accepting applications and conducting practical tests leading to the issuance of specific pilot certificates and/or ratings. The majority of FAA practical tests at the private and commercial pilot levels are administered by DPEs.

DPE candidates must have good industry reputations for professionalism, integrity, a demonstrated willingness to serve the public, and adhere to FAA policies and procedures in certification matters. The FAA expects the DPE to administer practical tests with the same degree of professionalism, using the same methods, procedures, and standards as an FAA ASI.

Chapter Summary

The FAA has entered the second century of civil aviation as a robust government organization and is taking full advantage of technology, such as Global Positioning System (GPS) satellite technology to enhance the safety of civil aviation. The Internet has also become an important tool in promoting aviation safety and providing around-the-clock resources for the aviation community. Handbooks, regulations, standards, references, and online courses are now available at the FAA website.

In keeping with the FAA's belief that safety is a learned behavior, the FAA offers many courses and seminars to enhance air safety. The FAA puts the burden of instilling safe flying habits on the flight instructor, who should follow basic flight safety practices and procedures in every flight operation he or she undertakes with a student pilot. Operational safety practices include, but are not limited to, collision avoidance procedures consisting of proper scanning techniques, use of checklists, runway incursion avoidance, positive transfer of controls, and workload management. These safety practices will be discussed more fully within this handbook. Safe flight also depends on Scenario-Based Training (SBT) that teaches the student pilot how to respond in different flight situations. The FAA has incorporated these techniques along with decision-making methods, such as Aeronautical Decision-Making (ADM), risk management, and Crew Resource Management (CRM), which are covered more completely in Chapter 17, Aeronautical Decision-Making.

Chapter 2

Aircraft Structure

Introduction

An aircraft is a device that is used, or intended to be used, for flight, according to the current Title 14 of the Code of Federal Regulations (14 CFR) Part 1, Definitions and Abbreviations. Categories of aircraft for certification of airmen include airplane, rotorcraft, glider, lighter-than-air, powered-lift, powered parachute, and weight-shift control. 14 CFR part 1 also defines airplane as an engine-driven, fixed-wing aircraft that is supported in flight by the dynamic reaction of air against its wings. Another term, not yet codified in 14 CFR part 1, is advanced avionics aircraft, which refers to an aircraft that contains a global positioning system (GPS) navigation system with a moving map display, in conjunction with another system, such as an autopilot. This chapter provides a brief introduction to the structure of aircraft and uses an airplane for most illustrations. Light Sport Aircraft (LSA), such as weight-shift control, balloon, glider, powered parachute, and gyroplane have their own handbooks to include detailed information regarding aerodynamics and control.

Wing

Empennage

Powerplant

Fuselage

Landing gear

Lift and Basic Aerodynamics

In order to understand the operation of the major components and subcomponents of an aircraft, it is important to understand basic aerodynamic concepts. This chapter briefly introduces aerodynamics; a more detailed explanation can be found in Chapter 4, Aerodynamics of Flight.

Four forces act upon an aircraft in relation to straight-and-level, unaccelerated flight. These forces are thrust, lift, weight, and drag. *[Figure 2-1]*

Figure 2-1. *The four forces.*

Thrust is the forward force produced by the powerplant/propeller. It opposes or overcomes the force of drag. As a general rule, it is said to act parallel to the longitudinal axis. This is not always the case as explained later.

Drag is a rearward, retarding force, and is caused by disruption of airflow by the wing, fuselage, and other protruding objects. Drag opposes thrust, and acts rearward parallel to the relative wind.

Weight is the combined load of the airplane itself, the crew, the fuel, and the cargo or baggage. Weight pulls the airplane downward because of the force of gravity. It opposes lift, and acts vertically downward through the airplane's center of gravity (CG).

Lift opposes the downward force of weight, is produced by the dynamic effect of the air acting on the wing, and acts perpendicular to the flightpath through the wing's center of lift.

An aircraft moves in three dimensions and is controlled by moving it about one or more of its axes. The longitudinal or roll axis extends through the aircraft from nose to tail, with the line passing through the CG. The lateral or pitch axis extends across the aircraft on a line through the wing tips, again passing through the CG. The vertical, or yaw, axis passes through the aircraft vertically, intersecting the CG. All control movements cause the aircraft to move around one or more of these axes, and allows for the control of the airplane in flight. *[Figure 2-2]*

One of the most significant components of aircraft design is CG. It is the specific point where the mass or weight of an aircraft may be said to center; that is, a point around which, if the aircraft could be suspended or balanced, the aircraft would remain relatively level. The position of the CG of an aircraft determines the stability of the aircraft in flight. As the CG moves rearward (towards the tail) the aircraft becomes more and more dynamically unstable. In aircraft with fuel tanks situated in front of the CG, it is important that the CG is set with the fuel tank empty. Otherwise, as the fuel is used, the aircraft becomes unstable. *[Figure 2-3]* The CG is computed during initial design and construction, and is further affected by the installation of onboard equipment, aircraft loading, and other factors.

Figure 2-2. *Illustrates the pitch, roll, and yaw motion of the aircraft along the lateral, longitudinal, and vertical axes, respectively.*

Figure 2-3. *Center of gravity (CG).*

Major Components

Although airplanes are designed for a variety of purposes, most of them have the same major components. *[Figure 2-4]* The overall characteristics are largely determined by the original design objectives. Most airplane structures include a fuselage, wings, an empennage, landing gear, and a powerplant.

Fuselage

The fuselage is the central body of an airplane and is designed to accommodate the crew, passengers, and cargo. It also provides the structural connection for the wings and tail assembly. Older types of aircraft design utilized an open truss structure constructed of wood, steel, or aluminum tubing. *[Figure 2-5]* The most popular types of fuselage structures used in today's aircraft are the monocoque (French for "single shell") and semimonocoque. These structure types

Figure 2-4. *Airplane components.*

Figure 2-5. *Truss-type fuselage structure.*

are discussed in more detail under aircraft construction later in the chapter.

Wings

The wings are airfoils attached to each side of the fuselage and are the main lifting surfaces that support the airplane in flight. There are numerous wing designs, sizes, and shapes used by the various manufacturers. Each fulfills a certain need with respect to the expected performance for the particular airplane. How the wing produces lift is explained in Chapter 4, Aerodynamics of Flight.

Wings may be attached at the top, middle, or lower portion of the fuselage. These designs are referred to as high-, mid-, and low-wing, respectively. The number of wings can also vary. Airplanes with a single set of wings are referred to as

Figure 2-6. *Monoplane (left) and biplane (right).*

monoplanes, while those with two sets are called biplanes. *[Figure 2-6]*

Many high-wing airplanes have external braces, or wing struts, which transmit the flight and landing loads through the struts to the main fuselage structure. Since the wing struts are usually attached approximately halfway out on the wing, this type of wing structure is called semi-cantilever. A few high-wing and most low-wing airplanes have a full cantilever wing designed to carry the loads without external struts.

The principal structural parts of the wing are spars, ribs, and stringers. *[Figure 2-7]* These are reinforced by trusses, I-beams, tubing, or other devices, including the skin. The wing ribs determine the shape and thickness of the wing

(airfoil). In most modern airplanes, the fuel tanks either are an integral part of the wing's structure, or consist of flexible containers mounted inside of the wing.

Attached to the rear or trailing edges of the wings are two types of control surfaces referred to as ailerons and flaps. Ailerons extend from about the midpoint of each wing outward toward the tip, and move in opposite directions to create aerodynamic forces that cause the airplane to roll. Flaps extend outward from the fuselage to near the midpoint of each wing. The flaps are normally flush with the wing's surface during cruising flight. When extended, the flaps move simultaneously downward to increase the lifting force of the wing for takeoffs and landings. *[Figure 2-8]*

Figure 2-7. *Wing components.*

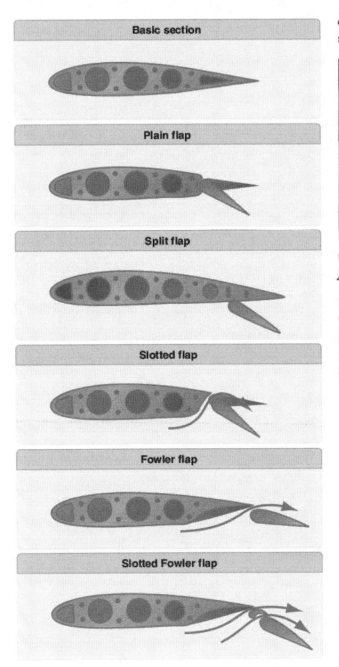

Figure 2-8. *Types of flaps.*

Alternate Types of Wings

With the Federal Aviation Administration's (FAA) recent addition of the LSA category, various methods are employed to control flight and to produce lift. These methods are discussed in Chapter 4, Aerodynamics of Flight, which provides information on the effect controls have on lifting surfaces from traditional wings to wings that use both flexing (due to billowing) and shifting (through the change of the aircraft's CG). Handbooks specific to each category of LSA are available for the interested pilot. LSA illustrate various lifting surfaces and control methods. For example, the wing

of the weight-shift control aircraft is highly swept, and the shifting of weight to provide controlled flight. *[Figure 2-9]*

Figure 2-9. *Weight-shift control aircraft use the shifting of weight for control.*

Empennage

The empennage includes the entire tail group and consists of fixed surfaces such as the vertical stabilizer and the horizontal stabilizer. The movable surfaces include the rudder, the elevator, and one or more trim tabs. *[Figure 2-10]*

Figure 2-10. *Empennage components.*

The rudder is attached to the back of the vertical stabilizer. During flight, it is used to move the airplane's nose left and right. The elevator, which is attached to the back of the horizontal stabilizer, is used to move the nose of the airplane up and down during flight. Trim tabs are small, movable portions of the trailing edge of the control surface. These movable trim tabs, which are controlled from the flight deck, reduce control pressures. Trim tabs may be installed on the ailerons, the rudder, and/or the elevator.

A second type of empennage design does not require an elevator. Instead, it incorporates a one-piece horizontal stabilizer that pivots from a central hinge point. This type of design is called a stabilator, and is moved using the control wheel, just as the elevator is moved. For example, when a pilot pulls back on the control wheel, the stabilator pivots so the trailing edge moves up. This increases the aerodynamic tail load and causes the nose of the airplane to move up. Stabilators have an antiservo tab extending across their trailing edge. [Figure 2-11]

Figure 2-11. *Stabilator components.*

The antiservo tab moves in the same direction as the trailing edge of the stabilator and helps make the stabilator less sensitive. The antiservo tab also functions as a trim tab to relieve control pressures and helps maintain the stabilator in the desired position.

Landing Gear

The landing gear is the principal support of the airplane when parked, taxiing, taking off, or landing. The most common type of landing gear consists of wheels, but airplanes can also be equipped with floats for water operations, or skis for landing on snow. [Figure 2-12]

The landing gear consists of three wheels—two main wheels and a third wheel positioned either at the front or rear of the airplane. Landing gear with a rear mounted wheel is called conventional landing gear.

Airplanes with conventional landing gear are sometimes referred to as tailwheel airplanes. When the third wheel is located on the nose, it is called a nosewheel, and the design is referred to as a tricycle gear. A steerable nosewheel or tailwheel permits the airplane to be controlled throughout all operations while on the ground. Most aircraft are steered by moving the rudder pedals, whether nosewheel or tailwheel. Additionally, some aircraft are steered by differential braking.

Figure 2-12. *Types of landing gear: floats (top), skis (middle), and wheels (bottom).*

The Powerplant

The powerplant usually includes both the engine and the propeller. The primary function of the engine is to provide the power to turn the propeller. It also generates electrical power, provides a vacuum source for some flight instruments, and in most single-engine airplanes, provides a source of heat for the pilot and passengers. [Figure 2-13] The engine is covered by a cowling, or a nacelle, which are both types of covered housings. The purpose of the cowling or nacelle

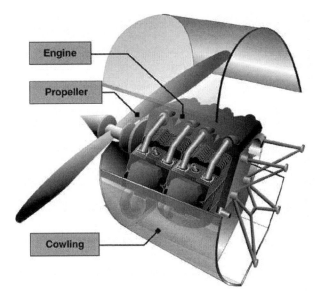

Figure 2-13. *Engine compartment.*

is to streamline the flow of air around the engine and to help cool the engine by ducting air around the cylinders.

The propeller, mounted on the front of the engine, translates the rotating force of the engine into thrust, a forward acting force that helps move the airplane through the air. The propeller may also be mounted on the rear of the engine as in a pusher-type aircraft. A propeller is a rotating airfoil that produces thrust through aerodynamic action. A low pressure area is formed at the back of the propeller's airfoil, and high pressure is produced at the face of the propeller, similar to the way lift is generated by an airfoil used as a lifting surface or wing. This pressure differential pulls air through the propeller, which in turn pulls the airplane forward.

There are two significant factors involved in the design of a propeller which impact its effectiveness. The angle of a propeller blade, as measured against the hub of the propeller, keeps the angle of attack relatively constant along the span of the propeller blade, reducing or eliminating the possibility of a stall. The pitch is defined as the distance a propeller would travel in one revolution if it were turning in a solid. These two factors combine to allow a measurement of the propeller's efficiency. Propellers are usually matched to a specific aircraft/powerplant combination to achieve the best efficiency at a particular power setting, and they pull or push depending on how the engine is mounted.

Subcomponents

The subcomponents of an airplane include the airframe, electrical system, flight controls, and brakes.

The airframe is the basic structure of an aircraft and is designed to withstand all aerodynamic forces, as well as the stresses imposed by the weight of the fuel, crew, and payload.

The primary function of an aircraft electrical system is to generate, regulate, and distribute electrical power throughout the aircraft. There are several different power sources on aircraft to power the aircraft electrical systems. These power sources include: engine-driven alternating current (AC) generators, auxiliary power units (APUs), and external power. The aircraft's electrical power system is used to operate the flight instruments, essential systems such as anti-icing, etc., and passenger services, such as cabin lighting.

The flight controls are the devices and systems which govern the attitude of an aircraft and, as a result, the flightpath followed by the aircraft. In the case of many conventional airplanes, the primary flight controls utilize hinged, trailing-edge surfaces called elevators for pitch, ailerons for roll, and the rudder for yaw. These surfaces are operated by the pilot in the flight deck or by an automatic pilot.

Airplane brakes consist of multiple pads (called caliper pads) that are hydraulically squeezed toward each other with a rotating disk (called a rotor) between them. The pads place pressure on the rotor which is turning with the wheels. As a result of the increased friction on the rotor, the wheels inherently slow down and stop turning. The disks and brake pads are made either from steel, like those in a car, or from a carbon material that weighs less and can absorb more energy. Because airplane brakes are used principally during landings and must absorb enormous amounts of energy, their life is measured in landings rather than miles.

Types of Aircraft Construction

The construction of aircraft fuselages evolved from the early wood truss structural arrangements to monocoque shell structures to the current semimonocoque shell structures.

Truss Structure

The main drawback of truss structure is its lack of a streamlined shape. In this construction method, lengths of tubing, called longerons, are welded in place to form a well-braced framework. Vertical and horizontal struts are welded to the longerons and give the structure a square or rectangular shape when viewed from the end. Additional struts are needed to resist stress that can come from any direction. Stringers and bulkheads, or formers, are added to shape the fuselage and support the covering.

As technology progressed, aircraft designers began to enclose the truss members to streamline the airplane and improve performance. This was originally accomplished with cloth fabric, which eventually gave way to lightweight metals such as aluminum. In some cases, the outside skin can support all or a major portion of the flight loads. Most modern aircraft use a form of this stressed skin structure known as monocoque or semimonocoque construction. [Figure 2-14]

Figure 2-14. *Semimonocoque and monocoque fuselage design.*

Monocoque

Monocoque construction uses stressed skin to support almost all loads much like an aluminum beverage can. Although very strong, monocoque construction is not highly tolerant to deformation of the surface. For example, an aluminum beverage can supports considerable forces at the ends of the can, but if the side of the can is deformed slightly while supporting a load, it collapses easily.

Because most twisting and bending stresses are carried by the external skin rather than by an open framework, the need for internal bracing was eliminated or reduced, saving weight and maximizing space. One of the notable and innovative methods for using monocoque construction was employed by Jack Northrop. In 1918, he devised a new way to construct a monocoque fuselage used for the Lockheed S-1 Racer. The technique utilized two molded plywood half-shells that were glued together around wooden hoops or stringers. To construct the half shells, rather than gluing many strips of plywood over a form, three large sets of spruce strips were soaked with glue and laid in a semi-circular concrete mold that looked like a bathtub. Then, under a tightly clamped lid, a rubber balloon was inflated in the cavity to press the plywood against the mold. Twenty-four hours later, the smooth half-shell was ready to be joined to another to create the fuselage. The two halves were each less than a quarter inch thick. Although employed in the early aviation period, monocoque construction would not reemerge for several decades due to the complexities involved. Every day examples of monocoque construction can be found in automobile manufacturing where the unibody is considered standard in manufacturing.

Semimonocoque

Semimonocoque construction, partial or one-half, uses a substructure to which the airplane's skin is attached. The substructure, which consists of bulkheads and/or formers of various sizes and stringers, reinforces the stressed skin by taking some of the bending stress from the fuselage. The main section of the fuselage also includes wing attachment points and a firewall. On single-engine airplanes, the engine is usually attached to the front of the fuselage. There is a fireproof partition between the rear of the engine and the flight deck or cabin to protect the pilot and passengers from accidental engine fires. This partition is called a firewall and is usually made of heat-resistant material such as stainless steel. However, a new emerging process of construction is the integration of composites or aircraft made entirely of composites.

Composite Construction
History

The use of composites in aircraft construction can be dated to World War II aircraft when soft fiberglass insulation was used in B-29 fuselages. By the late 1950s, European high performance sailplane manufacturers were using fiberglass as primary structures. In 1965, the FAA type certified the first all-fiberglass aircraft in the normal category, a Swiss sailplane called a Diamant HBV. Four years later, the FAA certified a four-seat single-engine Windecker Eagle in the normal category. By 2005, over 35 percent of new aircraft were constructed of composite materials.

Composite is a broad term and can mean materials such as fiberglass, carbon fiber cloth, Kevlar© cloth, and mixtures of all of the above. Composite construction offers two advantages: extremely smooth skins and the ability to easily form complex curved or streamlined structures. [Figure 2-15]

Figure 2-15. *Composite aircraft.*

Composite Materials in Aircraft

Composite materials are fiber-reinforced matrix systems. The matrix is the "glue" used to hold the fibers together and, when cured, gives the part its shape, but the fibers carry most of the load. There are many different types of fibers and matrix systems.

In aircraft, the most common matrix is epoxy resin, which is a type of thermosetting plastic. Compared to other choices such as polyester resin, epoxy is stronger and has good high-temperature properties. There are many different types of epoxies available, with a wide range of structural properties, cure times and temperatures, and costs.

The most common reinforcing fibers used in aircraft construction are fiberglass and carbon fiber. Fiberglass has good tensile and compressive strength, good impact resistance, is easy to work with, and is relatively inexpensive and readily available. Its main disadvantage is that it is relatively heavy, and it is difficult to make a fiberglass load-carrying structure lighter than a well designed equivalent aluminum structure.

Carbon fiber is generally stronger in tensile and compressive strength than fiberglass, and has much higher bending stiffness. It is also considerably lighter than fiberglass. However, it is relatively poor in impact resistance; the fibers are brittle and tend to shatter under sharp impact. This can be greatly improved with a "toughened" epoxy resin system, as used in the Boeing 787 horizontal and vertical stabilizers. Carbon fiber is more expensive than fiberglass, but the price has dropped due to innovations driven by the B-2 program in the 1980s, and Boeing 777 work in the 1990s. Very well-designed carbon fiber structures can be significantly lighter than an equivalent aluminum structure, sometimes by 30 percent or so.

Advantages of Composites

Composite construction offers several advantages over metal, wood, or fabric, with its lighter weight being the most frequently cited. Lighter weight is not always automatic. It must be remembered that building an aircraft structure out of composites does not guarantee it will be lighter, it depends on the structure, as well as the type of composite being used.

A more important advantage is that a very smooth, compound curved, aerodynamic structure made from composites reduces drag. This is the main reason sailplane designers switched from metal and wood to composites in the 1960s. In aircraft, the use of composites reduces drag for the Cirrus and Columbia line of production aircraft, leading to their high performance despite their fixed landing gear. Composites also help mask the radar signature of "stealth" aircraft designs, such as the B-2 and the F-22. Today, composites can be found in aircraft as varied as gliders to most new helicopters.

Lack of corrosion is a third advantage of composites. Boeing is designing the 787, with its all-composite fuselage, to have both a higher pressure differential and higher humidity in the cabin than previous airliners. Engineers are no longer as concerned about corrosion from moisture condensation on the hidden areas of the fuselage skins, such as behind insulation blankets. This should lead to lower long-term maintenance costs for the airlines.

Another advantage of composites is their good performance in a flexing environment, such as in helicopter rotor blades. Composites do not suffer from metal fatigue and crack growth as do metals. While it takes careful engineering, composite rotor blades can have considerably higher design lives than metal blades, and most new large helicopter designs have all composite blades, and in many cases, composite rotor hubs.

Disadvantages of Composites

Composite construction comes with its own set of disadvantages, the most important of which is the lack of visual proof of damage. Composites respond differently from other structural materials to impact, and there is often no obvious sign of damage. For example, if a car backs into an aluminum fuselage, it might dent the fuselage. If the fuselage is not dented, there is no damage. If the fuselage is dented, the damage is visible and repairs are made.

In a composite structure, a low energy impact, such as a bump or a tool drop, may not leave any visible sign of the impact on the surface. Underneath the impact site there may be extensive delaminations, spreading in a cone-shaped area from the impact location. The damage on the backside of the structure can be significant and extensive, but it may be hidden from view. Anytime one has reason to think there may have been an impact, even a minor one, it is best to get an inspector familiar with composites to examine the structure to determine underlying damage. The appearance of "whitish" areas in a fiberglass structure is a good tip-off that delaminations of fiber fracture has occurred.

A medium energy impact (perhaps the car backing into the structure) results in local crushing of the surface, which should be visible to the eye. The damaged area is larger than the visible crushed area, and will need to be repaired. A high energy impact, such as a bird strike or hail while in flight, results in a puncture and a severely damaged structure. In medium and high energy impacts, the damage is visible to the eye, but low energy impact is difficult to detect. *[Figure 2-16]*

Figure 2-16. *Impact energy affects the visibility, as well as the severity, of damage in composite structures. High and medium energy impacts, while severe, are easy to detect. Low energy impacts can easily cause hidden damage.*

If an impact results in delaminations, crushing of the surface, or a puncture, then a repair is mandatory. While waiting for the repair, the damaged area should be covered and protected from rain. Many composite parts are composed of thin skins over a honeycomb core, creating a "sandwich" structure. While excellent for structural stiffness reasons, such a structure is an easy target for water ingress (entering), leading to further problems later. A piece of "speed tape" over the puncture is a good way to protect it from water, but is not a structural repair. The use of a paste filler to cover up the damage, while acceptable for cosmetic purposes, is not a structural repair, either.

The potential for heat damage to the resin is another disadvantage of using composites. While "too hot" depends on the particular resin system chosen, many epoxies begin to weaken over 150° F. White paint on composites is often used to minimize this issue. For example, the bottom of a wing that is painted black facing a black asphalt ramp on a hot, sunny day, can get as hot as 220 °F. The same structure, painted white, rarely exceeds 140 °F. As a result, composite airplanes often have specific recommendations on allowable paint colors. If the airplane is repainted, these recommendations must be followed. Heat damage can also occur due to a fire. Even a quickly extinguished small brake fire can damage bottom wing skins, composite landing gear legs, or wheel pants.

Also, chemical paint strippers are very harmful to composites, and must not be used on them. If paint needs to be removed from composites, only mechanical methods are allowed, such as gentle grit blasting or sanding. Many expensive composite parts have been ruined by the use of paint stripper, and such damage is generally not repairable.

Fluid Spills on Composites

Some owners are concerned about fuel, oil, or hydraulic fluid spills on composite surfaces. These are generally not a problem with modern composites using epoxy resin. Usually, if the spill doesn't attack the paint, it won't hurt the underlying composite. Some aircraft use fiberglass fuel tanks, for example, in which the fuel rides directly against the composite surface with no sealant being used. If the fiberglass structure is made with some of the more inexpensive types of polyester resin, there can be a problem when using auto gas with ethanol blended into the mixture. The more expensive types of polyester resin, as well as epoxy resin, can be used with auto gas, as well as 100 octane aviation gas (avgas) and jet fuel.

Lightning Strike Protection

Lightning strike protection is an important consideration in aircraft design. When an aircraft is hit by lightning, a very large amount of energy is delivered to the structure. Whether flying a light general aviation (GA) airplane or a large airliner, the basic principle of lightning strike protection is the same. For any size aircraft, the energy from the strike must be spread over a large surface area to lower the "amps per square inch" to a harmless level.

If lightning strikes an aluminum airplane, the electrical energy naturally conducts easily through the aluminum structure. The challenge is to keep the energy out of avionics, fuel systems, etc., until it can be safely conducted overboard. The outer skin of the aircraft is the path of least resistance.

In a composite aircraft, fiberglass is an excellent electrical insulator, while carbon fiber conducts electricity, but not as easily as aluminum. Therefore, additional electrical conductivity needs to be added to the outside layer of composite skin. This is done typically with fine metal meshes bonded to the skin surfaces. Aluminum and copper mesh are the two most common types, with aluminum used on fiberglass and copper on carbon fiber. Any structural repairs on lightning-strike protected areas must also include the mesh as well as the underlying structure.

For composite aircraft with internal radio antennas, there must be "windows" in the lightning strike mesh in the area of the antenna. Internal radio antennas may be found in fiberglass composites because fiberglass is transparent to radio frequencies, where as carbon fiber is not.

The Future of Composites

In the decades since World War II, composites have earned an important role in aircraft structure design. Their design flexibility and corrosion resistance, as well as the high strength-to-weight ratios possible, will undoubtedly continue to lead to more innovative aircraft designs in the future. From the Cirrus SR-20 to the Boeing 787, it is obvious that composites have found a home in aircraft construction and are here to stay. *[Figure 2-17]*

Instrumentation: Moving into the Future

Until recently, most GA aircraft were equipped with individual instruments utilized collectively to safely operate and maneuver the aircraft. With the release of the electronic flight display (EFD) system, conventional instruments have been replaced by multiple liquid crystal display (LCD) screens. The first screen is installed in front of the left seat pilot position and is referred to as the primary flight display (PFD). The second screen, positioned approximately in the center of the instrument panel, is referred to as the multi-function display (MFD). These two screens de-clutter instrument panels while increasing safety. This has been accomplished through the utilization of solid state

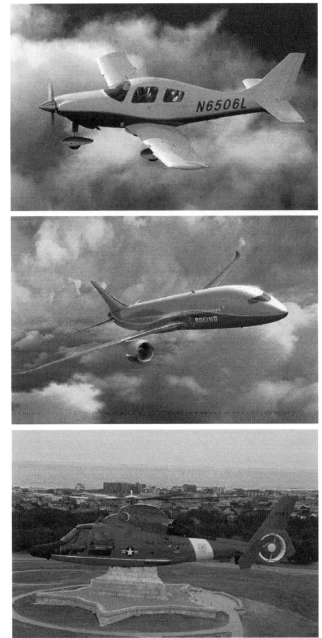

Figure 2-17. *Composite materials in aircraft, such as Columbia 350 (top), Boeing 787 (middle), and a Coast Guard HH-65 (bottom).*

instruments which have a failure rate far less than those of conventional analog instrumentation. *[Figure 2-18]*

With today's improvements in avionics and the introduction of EFDs, pilots at any level of experience need an astute knowledge of the onboard flight control systems as well as an understanding of how automation melds with Aeronautical Decision-Making (ADM). These subjects are covered in detail in Chapter 17, Aeronautical Decision-Making.

Figure 2-18. *Analog display (top) and digital display (bottom) from a Cessna 172.*

Whether an aircraft has analog or digital ("glass") instruments, the instrumentation falls into three different categories: performance, control, and navigation.

Performance Instruments

The performance instruments indicate the aircraft's actual performance. Performance is determined by reference to the altimeter, airspeed or vertical speed indicator (VSI), heading indicator, and turn-and-slip indicator. The performance instruments directly reflect the performance the aircraft is achieving. The speed of the aircraft can be referenced on the airspeed indicator. The altitude can be referenced on the altimeter. The aircraft's climb performance can be determined by referencing the VSI. Other performance instruments available are the heading indicator, angle of attack indicator, and the slip-skid indicator. *[Figure 2-19]*

Control Instruments

The control instruments *[Figure 2-20]* display immediate attitude and power changes, and are calibrated to permit adjustments in precise increments. The instrument for attitude display is the attitude indicator. The control instruments do not indicate aircraft speed or altitude. In order to determine

these variable and others, a pilot must reference the performance instruments.

Navigation Instruments

The navigation instruments indicate the position of the aircraft in relation to a selected navigation facility or fix. This group of instruments includes various types of course indicators, range indicators, glideslope indicators, and bearing pointers. Newer aircraft with more technologically advanced instrumentation provide blended information, giving the pilot more accurate positional information.

Navigation instruments are comprised of indicators that display GPS, very high frequency (VHF) omni-directional radio range (VOR), nondirectional beacon (NDB), and instrument landing system (ILS) information. The instruments indicate the position of the aircraft relative to a selected navigation facility or fix. They also provide pilotage information so the aircraft can be maneuvered to keep it on a predetermined path. The pilotage information can be in either two or three dimensions relative to the ground-based or space-based navigation information. *[Figures 2-21 and 2-22]*

Global Positioning System (GPS)

GPS is a satellite-based navigation system composed of a network of satellites placed into orbit by the United States Department of Defense (DOD). GPS was originally intended for military applications, but in the 1980s the government made the system available for civilian use. GPS works in all weather conditions, anywhere in the world, 24 hours a day. A GPS receiver must be locked onto the signal of at least three satellites to calculate a two-dimensional position (latitude and longitude) and track movement. With four or more satellites in view, the receiver can determine the user's three-dimensional position (latitude, longitude, and altitude). Other satellites must also be in view to offset signal loss and signal ambiguity. The use of the GPS is discussed in more detail in Chapter 15, Navigation. Additionally, GPS is discussed in the Aeronautical Information Manual (AIM).

Chapter Summary

This chapter provides an overview of aircraft structures. A more in-depth understanding of aircraft structures and controls can be gained through the use of flight simulation software or interactive programs available online through aviation organizations such as the Aircraft Owners and Pilots Association (AOPA). Pilots are also encouraged to subscribe to or review the various aviation periodicals which contain valuable flying information. As discussed in Chapter 1, the National Air and Space Administration (NASA) and the FAA also offer free information for pilots.

Figure 2-19. *Performance instruments.*

Figure 2-20. *Control instruments.*

2

The aircraft illustrated is heading 020°, but the course is to the left.

020°

HDG   CRS

1

Present position, inbound on 160° radial.

340°

HDG   CRS

View is from the pilots perspective, and the movable card is reset after each turn

A

2

1

160°

Figure 2-21. *A comparison of navigation information as depicted on both analog and digital displays.*

Fly down	Fly up
Glideslope needle indicates "fly down" to intercept glideslope	Glideslope needle indicates "fly up" to intercept glideslope

Glideslope

Figure 2-22. *Analog and digital indications for glideslope interception.*

Low angle of attack

Angle of attack

Normal angle of attack

Angle of attack

High angle of attack

Angle of attack

Standard Sea Level Pressure **29.92 Hg**	Inches of Mercury		Millibars	Standard Sea Level Pressure **1013 mb**
	30		1016	
	25		847	
	20		677	
	15		508	
	10		339	
	5		170	

Atmospheric Pressure

Chapter 3

Principles of Flight

Introduction

This chapter examines the fundamental physical laws governing the forces acting on an aircraft in flight, and what effect these natural laws and forces have on the performance characteristics of aircraft. To control an aircraft, be it an airplane, helicopter, glider, or balloon, the pilot must understand the principles involved and learn to use or counteract these natural forces.

Structure of the Atmosphere

The atmosphere is an envelope of air that surrounds the Earth and rests upon its surface. It is as much a part of the Earth as the seas or the land, but air differs from land and water as it is a mixture of gases. It has mass, weight, and indefinite shape.

The atmosphere is composed of 78 percent nitrogen, 21 percent oxygen, and 1 percent other gases, such as argon or helium. Some of these elements are heavier than others. The heavier elements, such as oxygen, settle to the surface of the Earth, while the lighter elements are lifted up to the region of higher altitude. Most of the atmosphere's oxygen is contained below 35,000 feet altitude.

Air, like fluid, is able to flow and change shape when subjected to even minute pressures because it lacks strong molecular cohesion. For example, gas completely fills any container into which it is placed, expanding or contracting to adjust its shape to the limits of the container.

Atmospheric Pressure

Although there are various kinds of pressure, pilots are mainly concerned with atmospheric pressure. It is one of the basic factors in weather changes, helps to lift an aircraft, and actuates some of the important flight instruments. These instruments are the altimeter, airspeed indicator, vertical speed indicator, and manifold pressure gauge.

Air is very light, but it has mass and is affected by the attraction of gravity. Therefore, like any other substance, it has weight, and because of its weight, it has force. Since it is a fluid substance, this force is exerted equally in all directions, and its effect on bodies within the air is called pressure. Under standard conditions at sea level, the average pressure exerted by the weight of the atmosphere is approximately 14.70 pounds per square inch (psi) of surface, or 1,013.2 millibars (mb). Its thickness is limited; therefore, the higher the altitude, the less air there is above. For this reason, the weight of the atmosphere at 18,000 feet is one-half what it is at sea level.

The pressure of the atmosphere varies with time and location. Due to the changing atmospheric pressure, a standard reference was developed. The standard atmosphere at sea level is a surface temperature of 59 °F or 15 °C and a surface pressure of 29.92 inches of mercury ("Hg), or 1,013.2 mb. *[Figure 3-1]*

Figure 3-1. *Standard sea level pressure.*

A standard temperature lapse rate is one in which the temperature decreases at the rate of approximately 3.5 °F or 2 °C per thousand feet up to 36,000 feet which is approximately -65 °F or -55 °C. Above this point, the temperature is considered constant up to 80,000 feet. A standard pressure lapse rate is one in which pressure decreases at a rate of approximately 1 "Hg per 1,000 feet of altitude gain to 10,000 feet. *[Figure 3-2]* The International Civil Aviation Organization (ICAO) has established this as a worldwide standard, and it is often referred to as International Standard Atmosphere (ISA) or ICAO Standard Atmosphere. Any temperature or pressure that differs from the standard lapse rates is considered nonstandard temperature and pressure.

Standard Atmosphere			
Altitude (ft)	Pressure (Hg)	Temperature	
		(°C)	(°F)
0	29.92	15.0	59.0
1,000	28.86	13.0	55.4
2,000	27.82	11.0	51.9
3,000	26.82	9.1	48.3
4,000	25.84	7.1	44.7
5,000	24.89	5.1	41.2
6,000	23.98	3.1	37.6
7,000	23.09	1.1	34.0
8,000	22.22	-0.9	30.5
9,000	21.38	-2.8	26.9
10,000	20.57	-4.8	23.3
11,000	19.79	-6.8	19.8
12,000	19.02	-8.8	16.2
13,000	18.29	-10.8	12.6
14,000	17.57	-12.7	9.1
15,000	16.88	-14.7	5.5
16,000	16.21	-16.7	1.9
17,000	15.56	-18.7	-1.6
18,000	14.94	-20.7	-5.2
19,000	14.33	-22.6	-8.8
20,000	13.74	-24.6	-12.3

Figure 3-2. *Properties of standard atmosphere.*

Since aircraft performance is compared and evaluated with respect to the standard atmosphere, all aircraft instruments are calibrated for the standard atmosphere. In order to account properly for the nonstandard atmosphere, certain related terms must be defined.

Pressure Altitude

Pressure altitude is the height above a standard datum plane (SDP), which is a theoretical level where the weight of the atmosphere is 29.92 "Hg (1,013.2 mb) as measured by a barometer. An altimeter is essentially a sensitive barometer calibrated to indicate altitude in the standard atmosphere. If the altimeter is set for 29.92 "Hg SDP, the altitude indicated is the pressure altitude. As atmospheric pressure changes, the SDP may be below, at, or above sea level. Pressure altitude is important as a basis for determining airplane performance, as well as for assigning flight levels to airplanes operating at or above 18,000 feet.

The pressure altitude can be determined by either of two methods:

1. Setting the barometric scale of the altimeter to 29.92 and reading the indicated altitude.

2. Applying a correction factor to the indicated altitude according to the reported altimeter setting.

Density Altitude

SDP is a theoretical pressure altitude, but aircraft operate in a nonstandard atmosphere and the term density altitude is used for correlating aerodynamic performance in the nonstandard atmosphere. Density altitude is the vertical distance above sea level in the standard atmosphere at which a given density is to be found. The density of air has significant effects on the aircraft's performance because as air becomes less dense, it reduces:

• Power because the engine takes in less air.

• Thrust because a propeller is less efficient in thin air.

• Lift because the thin air exerts less force on the airfoils.

Density altitude is pressure altitude corrected for nonstandard temperature. As the density of the air increases (lower density altitude), aircraft performance increases and conversely as air density decreases (higher density altitude), aircraft performance decreases. *A decrease in air density means a high density altitude; an increase in air density means a lower density altitude.* Density altitude is used in calculating aircraft performance, because under standard atmospheric conditions, air at each level in the atmosphere not only has a specific density, its pressure altitude and density altitude identify the same level.

The computation of density altitude involves consideration of pressure (pressure altitude) and temperature. Since aircraft performance data at any level is based upon air density under standard day conditions, such performance data apply to air density levels that may not be identical with altimeter indications. Under conditions higher or lower than standard, these levels cannot be determined directly from the altimeter.

Density altitude is determined by first finding pressure altitude, and then correcting this altitude for nonstandard temperature variations. Since density varies directly with pressure, and inversely with temperature, a given pressure altitude may exist for a wide range of temperature by allowing the density to vary. However, a known density occurs for any one temperature and pressure altitude. The density of the air has a pronounced effect on aircraft and engine performance.

Regardless of the actual altitude at which the aircraft is operating, it will perform as though it were operating at an altitude equal to the existing density altitude.

Air density is affected by changes in altitude, temperature, and humidity. High density altitude refers to thin air while low density altitude refers to dense air. The conditions that result in a high density altitude are high elevations, low atmospheric pressures, high temperatures, high humidity, or some combination of these factors. Lower elevations, high atmospheric pressure, low temperatures, and low humidity are more indicative of low density altitude.

Effect of Pressure on Density

Since air is a gas, it can be compressed or expanded. When air is compressed, a greater amount of air can occupy a given volume. Conversely, when pressure on a given volume of air is decreased, the air expands and occupies a greater space. At a lower pressure, the original column of air contains a smaller mass of air. The density is decreased because density is directly proportional to pressure. If the pressure is doubled, the density is doubled; if the pressure is lowered, the density is lowered. This statement is true only at a constant temperature.

Effect of Temperature on Density

Increasing the temperature of a substance decreases its density. Conversely, decreasing the temperature increases the density. Thus, the density of air varies inversely with temperature. This statement is true only at a constant pressure.

In the atmosphere, both temperature and pressure decrease with altitude, and have conflicting effects upon density. However, the fairly rapid drop in pressure as altitude is increased usually has the dominating effect. Hence, pilots can expect the density to decrease with altitude.

Effect of Humidity (Moisture) on Density

The preceding paragraphs refer to air that is perfectly dry. In reality, it is never completely dry. The small amount of water vapor suspended in the atmosphere may be almost negligible under certain conditions, but in other conditions humidity may become an important factor in the performance of an aircraft. Water vapor is lighter than air; consequently, moist air is lighter than dry air. Therefore, as the water content of the air increases, the air becomes less dense, increasing density altitude and decreasing performance. It is lightest or least dense when, in a given set of conditions, it contains the maximum amount of water vapor.

Humidity, also called relative humidity, refers to the amount of water vapor contained in the atmosphere, and is expressed as a percentage of the maximum amount of water vapor the air can hold. This amount varies with temperature. Warm air holds more water vapor, while colder air holds less. Perfectly dry air that contains no water vapor has a relative humidity of zero percent, while saturated air, which cannot hold any more water vapor, has a relative humidity of 100 percent. Humidity alone is usually not considered an important factor in calculating density altitude and aircraft performance, but it does contribute.

As temperature increases, the air can hold greater amounts of water vapor. When comparing two separate air masses, the first warm and moist (both qualities tending to lighten the air) and the second cold and dry (both qualities making it heavier), the first must be less dense than the second. Pressure, temperature, and humidity have a great influence on aircraft performance because of their effect upon density. There are no rules of thumb that can be easily conveyed but the affect of humidity can be determined using online formulas. In the first case, the pressure is needed at the altitude for which density altitude is being sought. Using *Figure 3-2,* select the barometric pressure closest to the associated altitude. As an example, the pressure at 8,000 feet is 22.22 "Hg. Using the National Oceanic and Atmospheric Administration (NOAA) website (http://www.srh.noaa.gov/elp/wxcalc/densityaltitude.html) for density altitude, enter the 22.22 for 8,000 feet in the station pressure window. Entering a temperature of 80° and a dew point of 75°. The result is a density altitude of 11,564 feet. With no humidity, the density altitude would be almost 500 feet lower.

Another site (http://wahiduddin.net/calc/density_altitude.htm) provides a more straight forward method of determining the effects of humidity on density altitude without using additional interpretive charts. In any case, the effects of humidity on density altitude include a decrease in overall performance in high humidity conditions.

Theories in the Production of Lift
Newton's Basic Laws of Motion
The formulation of lift has historically been the adaptation over the past few centuries of basic physical laws. These laws, although seemingly applicable to all aspects of lift, do not answer how lift is formulated. In fact, one must consider the many airfoils that are symmetrical, yet produce significant lift.

The fundamental physical laws governing the forces acting upon an aircraft in flight were adopted from postulated theories developed before any human successfully flew an aircraft. The use of these physical laws grew out of the Scientific Revolution, which began in Europe in the 1600s. Driven by the belief the universe operated in a predictable

manner open to human understanding, many philosophers, mathematicians, natural scientists, and inventors spent their lives unlocking the secrets of the universe. One of the best known was Sir Isaac Newton, who not only formulated the law of universal gravitation, but also described the three basic laws of motion.

Newton's First Law: "Every object persists in its state of rest or uniform motion in a straight line unless it is compelled to change that state by forces impressed on it."

This means that nothing starts or stops moving until some outside force causes it to do so. An aircraft at rest on the ramp remains at rest unless a force strong enough to overcome its inertia is applied. Once it is moving, its inertia keeps it moving, subject to the various other forces acting on it. These forces may add to its motion, slow it down, or change its direction.

Newton's Second Law: "Force is equal to the change in momentum per change in time. For a constant mass, force equals mass times acceleration."

When a body is acted upon by a constant force, its resulting acceleration is inversely proportional to the mass of the body and is directly proportional to the applied force. This takes into account the factors involved in overcoming Newton's First Law. It covers both changes in direction and speed, including starting up from rest (positive acceleration) and coming to a stop (negative acceleration or deceleration).

Newton's Third Law: "For every action, there is an equal and opposite reaction."

In an airplane, the propeller moves and pushes back the air; consequently, the air pushes the propeller (and thus the airplane) in the opposite direction—forward. In a jet airplane, the engine pushes a blast of hot gases backward; the force of equal and opposite reaction pushes against the engine and forces the airplane forward.

Magnus Effect
In 1852, the German physicist and chemist, Heinrich Gustav Magnus (1802–1870), made experimental studies of the aerodynamic forces on spinning spheres and cylinders. (The effect had already been mentioned by Newton in 1672, apparently in regard to spheres or tennis balls). These experiments led to the discovery of the Magnus Effect, which helps explain the theory of lift.

Flow of Air Against a Nonrotating Cylinder

If air flows against a cylinder that is not rotating, the flow of air above and below the cylinder is identical and the forces are the same. *[Figure 3-3A]*

A Rotating Cylinder in a Motionless Fluid

In *Figure 3-3B,* the cylinder is rotated clockwise and observed from the side while immersed in a fluid. The rotation of the cylinder affects the fluid surrounding the cylinder. The flow around the rotating cylinder differs from the flow around a stationary cylinder due to resistance caused by two factors: viscosity and friction.

Viscosity

Viscosity is the property of a fluid or semifluid that causes it to resist flowing. This resistance to flow is measurable due to the molecular tendency of fluids to adhere to each other to some extent. High-viscosity fluids resist flow; low-viscosity fluids flow easily.

Similar amounts of oil and water poured down two identical ramps demonstrate the difference in viscosity. The water seems to flow freely while the oil flows much more slowly. (An excellent website to demonstrate types of viscosity is found at the Cornell University website on viscosity, located at http://atlas.geo.cornell.edu/education/student/viscosity.html.)

Since molecular resistance to motion underlies viscosity, grease is very viscous because its molecules resist flow. Hot lava is another example of a viscous fluid. All fluids are viscous and have a resistance to flow whether this resistance is observed or not. Air is an example of a fluid whose viscosity can not be observed.

Since air has viscosity properties, it will resist flow to some extent. In the case of the rotating cylinder within an immersed fluid (oil, water, or air), the fluid (no matter what it is) resists flowing over the cylinder's surface.

Friction

Friction is the second factor at work when a fluid flows around a rotating cylinder. Friction is the resistance one surface or object encounters when moving over another and exists between a fluid and the surface over which it flows.

If identical fluids are poured down the ramp, they flow in the same manner and at the same speed. If one ramp's surface is coated with small pebbles, the flow down the two ramps differs significantly. The rough surface ramp impedes the flow of the fluid due to resistance from the surface (friction). It is important to remember that all surfaces, no matter how smooth they appear, are not smooth and impede the flow of a fluid. Both the surface of a wing and the rotating cylinder have a certain roughness, albeit at a microscopic level, causing resistance for a fluid to flow. This reduction in velocity of the airflow about a surface is caused by skin friction or drag.

When passing over a surface, molecules actually adhere (stick, cling) to the surface, illustrated by the rotating cylinder in a fluid that is not moving. Thus,

1. In the case of the rotating cylinder, air particles near the surface that resist motion have a relative velocity near zero. The roughness of the surface impedes their motion.

2. Due to the viscosity of the fluid, the molecules on the surface entrain, or pull, the surrounding flow above it in the direction of rotation due to the adhesion of the fluid to itself.

There is also a difference in flow around the rotating cylinder and in flow around a nonrotating cylinder. The molecules at the surface of the rotating cylinder are not in motion relative to the cylinder; they are moving clockwise with the cylinder. Due to viscosity, these molecules entrain others above them resulting in an increase in fluid flow in the clockwise direction. Substituting air for other fluids results in a higher velocity of air movement above the cylinder simply because more molecules are moving in a clockwise direction.

A Rotating Cylinder in a Moving Fluid

When the cylinder rotates in a fluid that is also moving, the result is a higher circulatory flow in the direction of the rotating cylinder. *[Figure 3-3C]* By adding fluid motion, the magnitude of the flow increases.

The highest differences of velocity are 90° from the relative motion between the cylinder and the airflow. Additionally, and as shown in *Figure 3-4,* at point "A," a stagnation point exists where the air stream impacts (impinges) on the front of the airfoil's surface and splits; some air goes over and some under. Another stagnation point exists at "B," where the two airstreams rejoin and resume at identical velocities. When viewed from the side, an upwash is created ahead of the airfoil and downwash at the rear.

In the case of *Figure 3-4,* the highest velocity is at the top of the airfoil with the lowest velocity at the bottom. Because these velocities are associated with an object (in this case, an airfoil) they are called local velocities as they do not exist outside the lift-producing system, in this case an airfoil. This concept can be readily applied to a wing or other lifting surface. Because there is a difference of velocity above and below the wing, the result is a a higher pressure at the bottom of the wing and a lower pressure on the top of the wing.

A. Flow of air against a nonrotating cylinder

B. Rotating cylinder in a fluid

C. Rotating cylinder in a moving fluid

D. Leading edge of wing

Leading edge

E. Leading edge of wing under 1,500x magnification

Figure 3-3. *A illustrates uniform circulation.* **B** *illustrates the increased airflow over the top of a rotating cylinder. The airflow speed is further increased when the rotating cylinder is in a moving stream of air (*C*). The air molecules near the surface of an object are slowed and almost stationary.* **D** *is an example of typical aircraft grade aluminum used in aircraft construction to include wings and leading edges of wings as shown in* **E** *(left). When magnified at 1,500x (*E*, right), polished aluminum is visibly rough. This demonstrates why airflow is affected by molecular irregularities of the surface.*

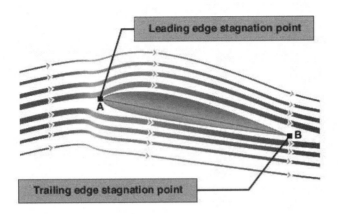

Figure 3-4. *Air circulation around an airfoil occurs when the front stagnation point is below the leading edge and the aft stagnation point is beyond the trailing edge.*

This low-pressure area produces an upward force known as the Magnus Effect, the physical phenomenon whereby an object's rotation affects its path through a fluid, to include air. Two early aerodynamicists, Martin Kutta and Nicolai Joukowski, eventually measured and calculated the forces for the lift equation on a rotating cylinder (the Kutta-Joukowski theorem).

To summarize the Magnus effect, an airfoil with a positive AOA develops air circulation about the upper surface of the wing. Its sharp trailing edge forces the rear stagnation point to be aft of the trailing edge, while the front stagnation point falls below the leading edge. *[Figure 3-4]*

Bernoulli's Principle of Differential Pressure

A half-century after Newton formulated his laws, Daniel Bernoulli, a Swiss mathematician, explained how the pressure of a moving fluid (liquid or gas) varies with its speed of motion. Bernoulli's Principle states that as the velocity of a moving fluid (liquid or gas) increases, the pressure within the fluid decreases. This principle explains what happens to air passing over the curved top of the airplane wing.

A practical application of Bernoulli's Principle is the venturi tube. The venturi tube has an air inlet that narrows to a throat (constricted point) and an outlet section that increases in diameter toward the rear. The diameter of the outlet is the same as that of the inlet. At the throat, the airflow speeds up and the pressure decreases; at the outlet, the airflow slows and the pressure increases. *[Figure 3-5]*

Since air is recognized as a body and it is accepted that it must follow the above laws, one can begin to see how and why an airplane wing develops lift. As the wing moves through the air, the flow of air across the curved top surface increases in velocity creating a low-pressure area.

Although Newton, Magnus, Bernoulli, and hundreds of other early scientists who studied the physical laws of the universe did not have the sophisticated laboratories available today, they provided great insight to the contemporary viewpoint of how lift is created.

Airfoil Design

An airfoil is a structure designed to obtain reaction upon its surface from the air through which it moves or that moves past such a structure. Air acts in various ways when submitted to different pressures and velocities; but this discussion is confined to the parts of an aircraft that a pilot is most concerned with in flight—namely, the airfoils designed to produce lift. By looking at a typical airfoil profile, such as the cross section of a wing, one can see several obvious characteristics of design. *[Figure 3-6]* Notice that there is a difference in the curvatures (called cambers) of the upper and lower surfaces of the airfoil. The camber of the upper surface is more pronounced than that of the lower surface, which is usually somewhat flat.

NOTE: The two extremities of the airfoil profile also differ in appearance. The end, which faces forward in flight, is called

Figure 3-5. *Air pressure decreases in a venturi tube.*

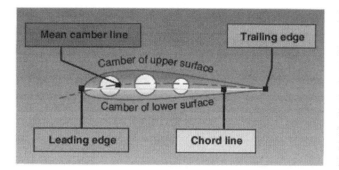

Figure 3-6. *Typical airfoil section.*

the leading edge, and is rounded; the other end, the trailing edge, is quite narrow and tapered.

A reference line often used in discussing the airfoil is the chord line, a straight line drawn through the profile connecting the extremities of the leading and trailing edges. The distance from this chord line to the upper and lower surfaces of the wing denotes the magnitude of the upper and lower camber at any point. Another reference line, drawn from the leading edge to the trailing edge, is the mean camber line. This mean line is equidistant at all points from the upper and lower surfaces.

An airfoil is constructed in such a way that its shape takes advantage of the air's response to certain physical laws. This develops two actions from the air mass: a positive pressure lifting action from the air mass below the wing, and a negative pressure lifting action from lowered pressure above the wing.

As the air stream strikes the relatively flat lower surface of a wing or rotor blade when inclined at a small angle to its direction of motion, the air is forced to rebound downward, causing an upward reaction in positive lift. At the same time, the air stream striking the upper curved section of the leading edge is deflected upward. An airfoil is shaped to cause an action on the air, and forces air downward, which provides an equal reaction from the air, forcing the airfoil upward. If a wing is constructed in such form that it causes a lift force greater than the weight of the aircraft, the aircraft will fly.

If all the lift required were obtained merely from the deflection of air by the lower surface of the wing, an aircraft would only need a flat wing like a kite. However, the balance of the lift needed to support the aircraft comes from the flow of air above the wing. Herein lies the key to flight.

It is neither accurate nor useful to assign specific values to the percentage of lift generated by the upper surface of an airfoil versus that generated by the lower surface. These are not constant values and vary, not only with flight conditions, but also with different wing designs.

Different airfoils have different flight characteristics. Many thousands of airfoils have been tested in wind tunnels and in actual flight, but no one airfoil has been found that satisfies every flight requirement. The weight, speed, and purpose of each aircraft dictate the shape of its airfoil. The most efficient airfoil for producing the greatest lift is one that has a concave, or "scooped out" lower surface. As a fixed design, this type of airfoil sacrifices too much speed while producing lift and is not suitable for high-speed flight. Advancements in engineering have made it possible for today's high-speed jets to take advantage of the concave airfoil's high lift characteristics. Leading edge (Kreuger) flaps and trailing edge (Fowler) flaps, when extended from the basic wing structure, literally change the airfoil shape into the classic concave form, thereby generating much greater lift during slow flight conditions.

On the other hand, an airfoil that is perfectly streamlined and offers little wind resistance sometimes does not have enough lifting power to take the airplane off the ground. Thus, modern airplanes have airfoils that strike a medium between extremes in design. The shape varies according to the needs of the airplane for which it is designed. *Figure 3-7* shows some of the more common airfoil sections.

Figure 3-7. *Airfoil designs.*

Low Pressure Above

In a wind tunnel or in flight, an airfoil is simply a streamlined object inserted into a moving stream of air. If the airfoil profile were in the shape of a teardrop, the speed and the pressure changes of the air passing over the top and bottom would be the same on both sides. But if the teardrop shaped airfoil were cut in half lengthwise, a form resembling the basic airfoil (wing) section would result. If the airfoil were then inclined so the airflow strikes it at an angle (angle of attack (AOA)), the air moving over the upper surface would be forced to move faster than the air moving along the bottom of the airfoil. This increased velocity reduces the pressure above the airfoil.

Applying Bernoulli's Principle of Pressure, the increase in the speed of the air across the top of an airfoil produces a drop in pressure. This lowered pressure is a component of total lift. The pressure difference between the upper and lower surface of a wing alone does not account for the total lift force produced.

The downward backward flow from the top surface of an airfoil creates a downwash. This downwash meets the flow from the bottom of the airfoil at the trailing edge. Applying Newton's third law, the reaction of this downward backward flow results in an upward forward force on the airfoil.

High Pressure Below

A certain amount of lift is generated by pressure conditions underneath the airfoil. Because of the manner in which air flows underneath the airfoil, a positive pressure results, particularly at higher angles of attack. But there is another aspect to this airflow that must be considered. At a point close to the leading edge, the airflow is virtually stopped (stagnation point) and then gradually increases speed. At some point near the trailing edge, it again reaches a velocity equal to that on the upper surface. In conformance with Bernoulli's principle, where the airflow was slowed beneath the airfoil, a positive upward pressure was created i.e., as the fluid speed decreases, the pressure must increase. Since the pressure differential between the upper and lower surface of the airfoil increases, total lift increases. Both Bernoulli's Principle and Newton's Laws are in operation whenever lift is being generated by an airfoil.

Pressure Distribution

From experiments conducted on wind tunnel models and on full size airplanes, it has been determined that as air flows along the surface of a wing at different angles of attack, there are regions along the surface where the pressure is negative, or less than atmospheric, and regions where the pressure is positive, or greater than atmospheric. This negative pressure on the upper surface creates a relatively larger force on the wing than is caused by the positive pressure resulting from the air striking the lower wing surface. *Figure 3-8* shows the pressure distribution along an airfoil at three different angles of attack. The average of the pressure variation for any given angle of attack is referred to as the center of pressure (CP). Aerodynamic force acts through this CP. At high angles of attack, the CP moves forward, while at low angles of attack the CP moves aft. In the design of wing structures, this CP

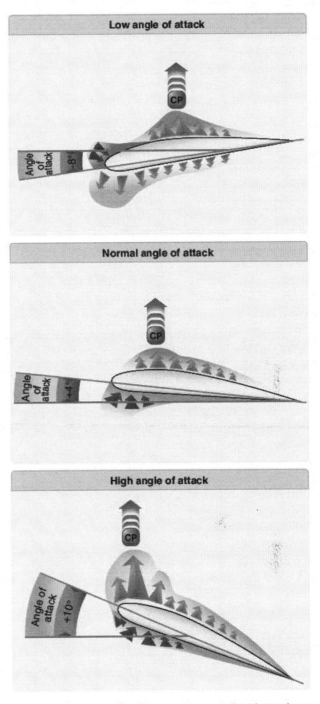

Figure 3-8. *Pressure distribution on an airfoil and CP changes with AOA.*

travel is very important, since it affects the position of the air loads imposed on the wing structure in both low and high AOA conditions. An airplane's aerodynamic balance and controllability are governed by changes in the CP.

Airfoil Behavior

Although specific examples can be cited in which each of the principles predict and contribute to the formation of lift, lift is a complex subject. The production of lift is much more complex than a simple differential pressure between upper and lower airfoil surfaces. In fact, many lifting airfoils do not have an upper surface longer than the bottom, as in the case of symmetrical airfoils. These are seen in high-speed aircraft having symmetrical wings, or on symmetrical rotor blades for many helicopters whose upper and lower surfaces are identical. In both examples, the relationship of the airfoil with the oncoming airstream (angle) is all that is different. A paper airplane, which is simply a flat plate, has a bottom and top exactly the same shape and length. Yet these airfoils do produce lift, and "flow turning" is partly (or fully) responsible for creating lift.

As an airfoil moves through air, the airfoil is inclined against the airflow, producing a different flow caused by the airfoil's relationship to the oncoming air. Think of a hand being placed outside the car window at a high speed. If the hand is inclined in one direction or another, the hand will move upward or downward. This is caused by deflection, which in turn causes the air to turn about the object within the air stream. As a result of this change, the velocity about the object changes in both magnitude and direction, in turn resulting in a measurable velocity force and direction.

A Third Dimension

To this point the discussion has centered on the flow across the upper and lower surfaces of an airfoil. While most of the lift is produced by these two dimensions, a third dimension, the tip of the airfoil also has an aerodynamic effect. The high-pressure area on the bottom of an airfoil pushes around the tip to the low-pressure area on the top. *[Figure 3-9]* This action creates a rotating flow called a tip vortex. The vortex flows behind the airfoil creating a downwash that extends back to the trailing edge of the airfoil. This downwash results in an overall reduction in lift for the affected portion of the airfoil.

Manufacturers have developed different methods to counteract this action. Winglets can be added to the tip of an airfoil to reduce this flow. The winglets act as a dam preventing the vortex from forming. Winglets can be on the top or bottom of the airfoil. Another method of countering the flow is to taper the airfoil tip, reducing the pressure differential and smoothing the airflow around the tip.

Chapter Summary

Modern general aviation aircraft have what may be considered high performance characteristics. Therefore, it is increasingly necessary that pilots appreciate and understand the principles upon which the art of flying is based. For additional information on the principles discussed in this chapter, visit the National Aeronautics and Space Administration (NASA) Beginner's Guide to Aerodynamics at http://www.grc.nasa.gov/WWW/K-12/airplane/index.html.

Figure 3-9. *Tip vortex.*

Chapter 4
Aerodynamics of Flight

Forces Acting on the Aircraft

Thrust, drag, lift, and weight are forces that act upon all aircraft in flight. Understanding how these forces work and knowing how to control them with the use of power and flight controls are essential to flight. This chapter discusses the aerodynamics of flight—how design, weight, load factors, and gravity affect an aircraft during flight maneuvers.

The four forces acting on an aircraft in straight-and-level, unaccelerated flight are thrust, drag, lift, and weight. They are defined as follows:

- Thrust—the forward force produced by the powerplant/propeller or rotor. It opposes or overcomes the force of drag. As a general rule, it acts parallel to the longitudinal axis. However, this is not always the case, as explained later.

- Drag—a rearward, retarding force caused by disruption of airflow by the wing, rotor, fuselage, and other protruding objects. Drag opposes thrust, and acts rearward parallel to the relative wind.

- Weight—the combined load of the aircraft itself, the crew, the fuel, and the cargo or baggage. Weight pulls the aircraft downward because of the force of gravity. It opposes lift, and acts vertically downward through the aircraft's center of gravity (CG).

- Lift—opposes the downward force of weight, is produced by the dynamic effect of the air acting on the airfoil, and acts perpendicular to the flightpath through the center of lift.

In steady flight, the sum of these opposing forces is always zero. There can be no unbalanced forces in steady, straight flight based upon Newton's Third Law, which states that for every action or force there is an equal, but opposite, reaction or force. This is true whether flying level or when climbing or descending.

It does not mean the four forces are equal. It means the opposing forces are equal to, and thereby cancel, the effects of each other. In *Figure 4-1* the force vectors of thrust, drag, lift, and weight appear to be equal in value. The usual explanation states (without stipulating that thrust and drag do not equal weight and lift) that thrust equals drag and lift equals weight. Although basically true, this statement can be misleading. It should be understood that in straight, level, unaccelerated flight, it is true that the opposing lift/weight forces are equal. They are also greater than the opposing forces of thrust/drag that are equal only to each other. Therefore, in steady flight:

- The sum of all upward forces (not just lift) equals the sum of all downward forces (not just weight).

- The sum of all forward forces (not just thrust) equals the sum of all backward forces (not just drag).

Figure 4-1. *Relationship of forces acting on an airplane.*

This refinement of the old "thrust equals drag; lift equals weight" formula explains that a portion of thrust is directed upward in climbs and acts as if it were lift while a portion of weight is directed backward and acts as if it were drag. *[Figure 4-2]*

Figure 4-2. *Force vectors during a stabilized climb.*

In glides, a portion of the weight vector is directed forward, and, therefore, acts as thrust. In other words, any time the flightpath of the aircraft is not horizontal, lift, weight, thrust, and drag vectors must each be broken down into two components.

Discussions of the preceding concepts are frequently omitted in aeronautical texts/handbooks/manuals. The reason is not that they are inconsequential, but because the main ideas with respect to the aerodynamic forces acting upon an airplane in flight can be presented in their most essential elements without being involved in the technicalities of the aerodynamicist. In point of fact, considering only level flight, and normal climbs and glides in a steady state, it is still true that lift provided by the wing or rotor is the primary upward force, and weight is the primary downward force.

By using the aerodynamic forces of thrust, drag, lift, and weight, pilots can fly a controlled, safe flight. A more detailed discussion of these forces follows.

Thrust

For an aircraft to move, thrust must be exerted and be greater than drag. The aircraft will continue to move and gain speed until thrust and drag are equal. In order to maintain a constant airspeed, thrust and drag must remain equal, just as lift and weight must be equal to maintain a constant altitude. If in level flight, the engine power is reduced, the thrust is lessened, and the aircraft slows down. As long as the thrust

Level high speed	Level cruise speed	Level low speed
Flightpath	Flightpath	Flightpath
Relative wind	Relative wind	Relative wind

Figure 4-3. *Angle of attack at various speeds.*

is less than the drag, the aircraft continues to decelerate until its airspeed is insufficient to support it in the air.

Likewise, if the engine power is increased, thrust becomes greater than drag and the airspeed increases. As long as the thrust continues to be greater than the drag, the aircraft continues to accelerate. When drag equals thrust, the aircraft flies at a constant airspeed.

Straight-and-level flight may be sustained at a wide range of speeds. The pilot coordinates angle of attack (AOA)—the acute angle between the chord line of the airfoil and the direction of the relative wind—and thrust in all speed regimes if the aircraft is to be held in level flight. Roughly, these regimes can be grouped in three categories: low-speed flight, cruising flight, and high-speed flight.

When the airspeed is low, the AOA must be relatively high if the balance between lift and weight is to be maintained. *[Figure 4-3]* If thrust decreases and airspeed decreases, lift becomes less than weight and the aircraft starts to descend. To maintain level flight, the pilot can increase the AOA an amount which will generate a lift force again equal to the weight of the aircraft. While the aircraft will be flying more slowly, it will still maintain level flight if the pilot has properly coordinated thrust and AOA.

Straight-and-level flight in the slow-speed regime provides some interesting conditions relative to the equilibrium of forces

because with the aircraft in a nose-high attitude, there is a vertical component of thrust that helps support it. For one thing, wing loading tends to be less than would be expected. Most pilots are aware that an airplane will stall, other conditions being equal, at a slower speed with the power on than with the power off. (Induced airflow over the wings from the propeller also contributes to this.) However, if analysis is restricted to the four forces as they are usually defined during slow-speed flight the thrust is equal to drag, and lift is equal to weight.

During straight-and-level flight when thrust is increased and the airspeed increases, the AOA must be decreased. That is, if changes have been coordinated, the aircraft will remain in level flight, but at a higher speed when the proper relationship between thrust and AOA is established.

If the AOA were not coordinated (decreased) with an increase of thrust, the aircraft would climb. But decreasing the AOA modifies the lift, keeping it equal to the weight, and the aircraft remains in level flight. Level flight at even slightly negative AOA is possible at very high speed. It is evident then, that level flight can be performed with any AOA between stalling angle and the relatively small negative angles found at high speed.

Some aircraft have the ability to change the direction of the thrust rather than changing the AOA. This is accomplished either by pivoting the engines or by vectoring the exhaust gases. *[Figure 4-4]*

Figure 4-4. *Some aircraft have the ability to change the direction of thrust.*

Drag

Drag is the force that resists movement of an aircraft through the air. There are two basic types: parasite drag and induced drag. The first is called parasite because it in no way functions to aid flight, while the second, induced drag, is a result of an airfoil developing lift.

Parasite Drag

Parasite drag is comprised of all the forces that work to slow an aircraft's movement. As the term parasite implies, it is the drag that is not associated with the production of lift. This includes the displacement of the air by the aircraft, turbulence generated in the airstream, or a hindrance of air moving over the surface of the aircraft and airfoil. There are three types of parasite drag: form drag, interference drag, and skin friction.

Form Drag

Form drag is the portion of parasite drag generated by the aircraft due to its shape and airflow around it. Examples include the engine cowlings, antennas, and the aerodynamic shape of other components. When the air has to separate to move around a moving aircraft and its components, it eventually rejoins after passing the body. How quickly and smoothly it rejoins is representative of the resistance that it creates which requires additional force to overcome. [Figure 4-5]

Figure 4-5. *Form drag.*

Notice how the flat plate in *Figure 4-5* causes the air to swirl around the edges until it eventually rejoins downstream. Form drag is the easiest to reduce when designing an aircraft. The solution is to streamline as many of the parts as possible.

Interference Drag

Interference drag comes from the intersection of airstreams that creates eddy currents, turbulence, or restricts smooth airflow. For example, the intersection of the wing and the fuselage at the wing root has significant interference drag. Air flowing around the fuselage collides with air flowing over the wing, merging into a current of air different from the two original currents. The most interference drag is observed when two surfaces meet at perpendicular angles. Fairings are used to reduce this tendency. If a jet fighter carries two identical wing tanks, the overall drag is greater than the sum of the individual tanks because both of these create and generate interference drag. Fairings and distance between lifting surfaces and external components (such as radar antennas hung from wings) reduce interference drag. [Figure 4-6]

Figure 4-6. *A wing root can cause interference drag.*

Skin Friction Drag

Skin friction drag is the aerodynamic resistance due to the contact of moving air with the surface of an aircraft. Every surface, no matter how apparently smooth, has a rough, ragged surface when viewed under a microscope. The air molecules, which come in direct contact with the surface of the wing, are virtually motionless. Each layer of molecules above the surface moves slightly faster until the molecules are moving at the velocity of the air moving around the aircraft. This speed is called the free-stream velocity. The area between the wing and the free-stream velocity level is about as wide as a playing card and is called the boundary layer. At the top of the boundary layer, the molecules increase velocity and move at the same speed as the molecules outside the boundary layer. The actual speed at which the molecules move depends upon the shape of the wing, the viscosity (stickiness) of the air through which the wing or airfoil is moving, and its compressibility (how much it can be compacted).

The airflow outside of the boundary layer reacts to the shape of the edge of the boundary layer just as it would to the physical surface of an object. The boundary layer gives any object an "effective" shape that is usually slightly different from the physical shape. The boundary layer may also separate from the body, thus creating an effective shape much different from the physical shape of the object. This change in the physical shape of the boundary layer causes a dramatic decrease in lift and an increase in drag. When this happens, the airfoil has stalled.

In order to reduce the effect of skin friction drag, aircraft designers utilize flush mount rivets and remove any irregularities which may protrude above the wing surface. In addition, a smooth and glossy finish aids in transition of air across the surface of the wing. Since dirt on an aircraft disrupts the free flow of air and increases drag, keep the surfaces of an aircraft clean and waxed.

Induced Drag

The second basic type of drag is induced drag. It is an established physical fact that no system that does work in the mechanical sense can be 100 percent efficient. This means that whatever the nature of the system, the required work is obtained at the expense of certain additional work that is dissipated or lost in the system. The more efficient the system, the smaller this loss.

In level flight the aerodynamic properties of a wing or rotor produce a required lift, but this can be obtained only at the expense of a certain penalty. The name given to this penalty is induced drag. Induced drag is inherent whenever an airfoil is producing lift and, in fact, this type of drag is inseparable from the production of lift. Consequently, it is always present if lift is produced.

An airfoil (wing or rotor blade) produces the lift force by making use of the energy of the free airstream. Whenever an airfoil is producing lift, the pressure on the lower surface of it is greater than that on the upper surface (Bernoulli's Principle). As a result, the air tends to flow from the high pressure area below the tip upward to the low pressure area on the upper surface. In the vicinity of the tips, there is a tendency for these pressures to equalize, resulting in a lateral flow outward from the underside to the upper surface. This lateral flow imparts a rotational velocity to the air at the tips, creating vortices, which trail behind the airfoil.

When the aircraft is viewed from the tail, these vortices circulate counterclockwise about the right tip and clockwise about the left tip. [Figure 4-7] Bearing in mind the direction of rotation of these vortices, it can be seen that they induce an upward flow of air beyond the tip, and a downwash flow behind the wing's trailing edge. This induced downwash has nothing in common with the downwash that is necessary to produce lift. It is, in fact, the source of induced drag. The greater the size and strength of the vortices and consequent downwash component on the net airflow over the airfoil, the greater the induced drag effect becomes. This downwash over the top of the airfoil at the tip has the same effect as bending the lift vector rearward; therefore, the lift is slightly aft of perpendicular to the relative wind, creating a rearward lift component. This is induced drag.

Figure 4-7. *Wingtip vortex from a crop duster.*

In order to create a greater negative pressure on the top of an airfoil, the airfoil can be inclined to a higher AOA. If the AOA of a symmetrical airfoil were zero, there would be no pressure differential, and consequently, no downwash component and no induced drag. In any case, as AOA increases, induced drag increases proportionally. To state this another way—the lower the airspeed the greater the AOA required to produce lift equal to the aircraft's weight and, therefore, the greater induced drag. The amount of induced drag varies inversely with the square of the airspeed.

Conversely, parasite drag increases as the square of the airspeed. Thus, as airspeed decreases to near the stalling speed, the total drag becomes greater, due mainly to the sharp rise in induced drag. Similarly, as the airspeed reaches the terminal velocity of the aircraft, the total drag again increases rapidly, due to the sharp increase of parasite drag. As seen in *Figure 4-8*, at some given airspeed, total drag is at its minimum amount. In figuring the maximum endurance and range of aircraft, the power required to overcome drag is at a minimum if drag is at a minimum.

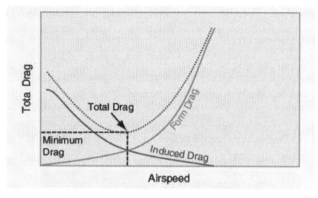

Figure 4-8. *Drag versus speed.*

Lift/Drag Ratio

Drag is the price paid to obtain lift. The lift to drag ratio (L/D) is the amount of lift generated by a wing or airfoil compared to its drag. A ratio of L/D indicates airfoil efficiency. Aircraft with higher L/D ratios are more efficient than those with lower L/D ratios. In unaccelerated flight with the lift and drag data steady, the proportions of the C_L and coefficient of drag (C_D) can be calculated for specific AOA. *[Figure 4-9]*

The L/D ratio is determined by dividing the C_L by the C_D, which is the same as dividing the lift equation by the drag equation. All terms except coefficients cancel out.
L = Lift in pounds
D = Drag

Where L is the lift force in pounds, C_L is the lift coefficient, ρ is density expressed in slugs per cubic feet, V is velocity in feet per second, q is dynamic pressure per square feet, and S is the wing area in square feet.

C_D= Ratio of drag pressure to dynamic pressure. Typically at low angles of attack, the drag coefficient is low and small changes in angle of attack create only slight changes in the drag coefficient. At high angles of attack, small changes in the angle of attack cause significant changes in drag.

$$ L = \frac{C_L \cdot \rho \cdot V^2 \cdot S}{2} $$

$$ D = \frac{C_D \cdot \rho \cdot V^2 \cdot S}{2} $$

The above formulas represent the coefficient of lift (C_L) and the coefficient of drag (C_D) respectively. The shape of an airfoil and other life producing devices (i.e., flaps) effect the production of lift and alter with changes in the AOA. The lift/drag ratio is used to express the relation between lift and drag and is determined by dividing the lift coefficient by the drag coefficient, C_L/C_D.

Notice in *Figure 4-9* that the lift curve (red) reaches its maximum for this particular wing section at 20° AOA, and then rapidly decreases. 15° AOA is therefore the stalling angle. The drag curve (yellow) increases very rapidly from 14° AOA and completely overcomes the lift curve at 21° AOA. The lift/drag ratio (green) reaches its maximum at 6° AOA, meaning that at this angle, the most lift is obtained for the least amount of drag.

Note that the maximum lift/drag ratio (L/D$_{MAX}$) occurs at one specific C_L and AOA. If the aircraft is operated in steady flight at L/D$_{MAX}$, the total drag is at a minimum. Any AOA lower or higher than that for L/D$_{MAX}$ reduces the L/D and

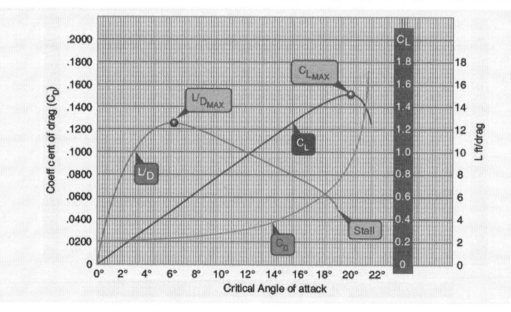

Figure 4-9. *Lift coefficients at various angles of attack.*

consequently increases the total drag for a given aircraft's lift. *Figure 4-8* depicts the L/D$_{MAX}$ by the lowest portion of the orange line labeled "total drag." The configuration of an aircraft has a great effect on the L/D.

Weight

Gravity is the pulling force that tends to draw all bodies to the center of the earth. The CG may be considered as a point at which all the weight of the aircraft is concentrated. If the aircraft were supported at its exact CG, it would balance in any attitude. It will be noted that CG is of major importance in an aircraft, for its position has a great bearing upon stability.

The location of the CG is determined by the general design of each particular aircraft. The designers determine how far the center of pressure (CP) will travel. They then fix the CG forward of the center of pressure for the corresponding flight speed in order to provide an adequate restoring moment to retain flight equilibrium.

Weight has a definite relationship to lift. This relationship is simple, but important in understanding the aerodynamics of flying. Lift is the upward force on the wing acting perpendicular to the relative wind. Lift is required to counteract the aircraft's weight (which is caused by the force of gravity acting on the mass of the aircraft). This weight (gravity) force acts downward through the airplane's CG. In stabilized level flight, when the lift force is equal to the weight force, the aircraft is in a state of equilibrium and neither gains nor loses altitude. If lift becomes less than weight, the aircraft loses altitude. When lift is greater than weight, the aircraft gains altitude.

Lift

The pilot can control the lift. Any time the control yoke or stick is moved fore or aft, the AOA is changed. As the AOA increases, lift increases (all other factors being equal). When the aircraft reaches the maximum AOA, lift begins to diminish rapidly. This is the stalling AOA, known as C$_{L-MAX}$ critical AOA. Examine *Figure 4-9*, noting how the C$_L$ increases until the critical AOA is reached, then decreases rapidly with any further increase in the AOA.

Before proceeding further with the topic of lift and how it can be controlled, velocity must be interjected. The shape of the wing or rotor cannot be effective unless it continually keeps "attacking" new air. If an aircraft is to keep flying, the lift-producing airfoil must keep moving. In a helicopter or gyro-plane this is accomplished by the rotation of the rotor blades. For other types of aircraft such as airplanes, weight-shift control, or gliders, air must be moving across the lifting surface. This is accomplished by the forward speed of the aircraft. Lift is proportional to the square of the aircraft's

velocity. For example, an airplane traveling at 200 knots has four times the lift as the same airplane traveling at 100 knots, if the AOA and other factors remain constant.

Actually, an aircraft could not continue to travel in level flight at a constant altitude and maintain the same AOA if the velocity is increased. The lift would increase and the aircraft would climb as a result of the increased lift force. Therefore, to maintain the lift and weight forces in balance, and to keep the aircraft straight and level (not accelerating upward) in a state of equilibrium, as velocity is increased, lift must be decreased. This is normally accomplished by reducing the AOA by lowering the nose. Conversely, as the aircraft is slowed, the decreasing velocity requires increasing the AOA to maintain lift sufficient to maintain flight. There is, of course, a limit to how far the AOA can be increased, if a stall is to be avoided.

All other factors being constant, for every AOA there is a corresponding airspeed required to maintain altitude in steady, unaccelerated flight (true only if maintaining "level flight"). Since an airfoil always stalls at the same AOA, if increasing weight, lift must also be increased. The only method of increasing lift is by increasing velocity if the AOA is held constant just short of the "critical," or stalling, AOA.

Lift and drag also vary directly with the density of the air. Density is affected by several factors: pressure, temperature, and humidity. At an altitude of 18,000 feet, the density of the air has one-half the density of air at sea level. In order to maintain its lift at a higher altitude, an aircraft must fly at a greater true airspeed for any given AOA.

Warm air is less dense than cool air, and moist air is less dense than dry air. Thus, on a hot humid day, an aircraft must be flown at a greater true airspeed for any given AOA than on a cool, dry day.

If the density factor is decreased and the total lift must equal the total weight to remain in flight, it follows that one of the other factors must be increased. The factor usually increased is the airspeed or the AOA, because these are controlled directly by the pilot.

Lift varies directly with the wing area, provided there is no change in the wing's planform. If the wings have the same proportion and airfoil sections, a wing with a planform area of 200 square feet lifts twice as much at the same AOA as a wing with an area of 100 square feet.

Two major aerodynamic factors from the pilot's viewpoint are lift and velocity because they can be controlled readily and accurately. Of course, the pilot can also control density by adjusting the altitude and can control wing area if the aircraft happens to have flaps of the type that enlarge wing area. However, for most situations, the pilot controls lift and velocity to maneuver an aircraft. For instance, in straight-and-level flight, cruising along at a constant altitude, altitude is maintained by adjusting lift to match the aircraft's velocity or cruise airspeed, while maintaining a state of equilibrium in which lift equals weight. In an approach to landing, when the pilot wishes to land as slowly as practical, it is necessary to increase lift to near maximum to maintain lift equal to the weight of the aircraft.

Wingtip Vortices

Formation of Vortices

The action of the airfoil that gives an aircraft lift also causes induced drag. When an airfoil is flown at a positive AOA, a pressure differential exists between the upper and lower surfaces of the airfoil. The pressure above the wing is less than atmospheric pressure and the pressure below the wing is equal to or greater than atmospheric pressure. Since air always moves from high pressure toward low pressure, and the path of least resistance is toward the airfoil's tips, there is a spanwise movement of air from the bottom of the airfoil outward from the fuselage around the tips. This flow of air results in "spillage" over the tips, thereby setting up a whirlpool of air called a "vortex." [Figure 4-10]

Figure 4-10. *Wingtip vortices.*

At the same time, the air on the upper surface has a tendency to flow in toward the fuselage and off the trailing edge. This air current forms a similar vortex at the inboard portion of the trailing edge of the airfoil, but because the fuselage limits the inward flow, the vortex is insignificant. Consequently, the deviation in flow direction is greatest at the outer tips where the unrestricted lateral flow is the strongest.

As the air curls upward around the tip, it combines with the wash to form a fast-spinning trailing vortex. These vortices increase drag because of energy spent in producing the turbulence. Whenever an airfoil is producing lift, induced drag occurs, and wingtip vortices are created.

Just as lift increases with an increase in AOA, induced drag also increases. This occurs because as the AOA is increased, there is a greater pressure difference between the top and bottom of the airfoil, and a greater lateral flow of air; consequently, this causes more violent vortices to be set up, resulting in more turbulence and more induced drag.

In *Figure 4-10*, it is easy to see the formation of wingtip vortices. The intensity or strength of the vortices is directly proportional to the weight of the aircraft and inversely proportional to the wingspan and speed of the aircraft. The heavier and slower the aircraft, the greater the AOA and the stronger the wingtip vortices. Thus, an aircraft will create wingtip vortices with maximum strength occurring during the takeoff, climb, and landing phases of flight. These vortices lead to a particularly dangerous hazard to flight, wake turbulence.

Avoiding Wake Turbulence

Wingtip vortices are greatest when the generating aircraft is "heavy, clean, and slow." This condition is most commonly encountered during approaches or departures because an aircraft's AOA is at the highest to produce the lift necessary to land or take off. To minimize the chances of flying through an aircraft's wake turbulence:

- Avoid flying through another aircraft's flightpath.

- Rotate prior to the point at which the preceding aircraft rotated, when taking off behind another aircraft.

- Avoid following another aircraft on a similar flightpath at an altitude within 1,000 feet. [Figure 4-11]

- Approach the runway above a preceding aircraft's path when landing behind another aircraft, and touch down after the point at which the other aircraft wheels contacted the runway. [Figure 4-12]

A hovering helicopter generates a down wash from its main rotor(s) similar to the vortices of an airplane. Pilots of small aircraft should avoid a hovering helicopter by at least three rotor disc diameters to avoid the effects of this down wash. In forward flight this energy is transformed into a pair of strong, high-speed trailing vortices similar to wing-tip vortices of larger fixed-wing aircraft. Helicopter vortices should be avoided because helicopter forward flight airspeeds are often very slow and can generate exceptionally strong wake turbulence.

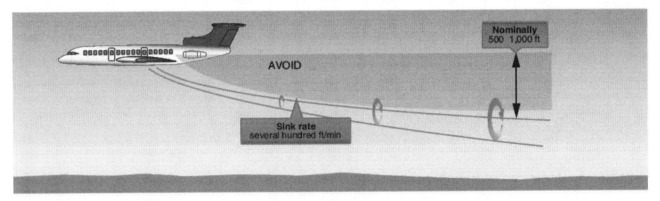

Figure 4-11. *Avoid following another aircraft at an altitude within 1,000 feet.*

Figure 4-12. *Avoid turbulence from another aircraft.*

Wind is an important factor in avoiding wake turbulence because wingtip vortices drift with the wind at the speed of the wind. For example, a wind speed of 10 knots causes the vortices to drift at about 1,000 feet in a minute in the wind direction. When following another aircraft, a pilot should consider wind speed and direction when selecting an intended takeoff or landing point. If a pilot is unsure of the other aircraft's takeoff or landing point, approximately 3 minutes provides a margin of safety that allows wake turbulence dissipation. For more information on wake turbulence, see Advisory Circular 90-23.

Ground Effect

It is possible to fly an aircraft just clear of the ground (or water) at a slightly slower airspeed than that required to sustain level flight at higher altitudes. This is the result of a phenomenon better known of than understood even by some experienced pilots.

When an aircraft in flight comes within several feet of the surface, ground or water, a change occurs in the three-dimensional flow pattern around the aircraft because the vertical component of the airflow around the wing is restricted by the surface. This alters the wing's upwash, downwash, and wingtip vortices. *[Figure 4-13]* Ground effect, then, is

Figure 4-13. *Ground effect changes airflow.*

due to the interference of the ground (or water) surface with the airflow patterns about the aircraft in flight.

While the aerodynamic characteristics of the tail surfaces and the fuselage are altered by ground effect, the principal effects due to proximity of the ground are the changes in the aerodynamic characteristics of the wing. As the wing encounters ground effect and is maintained at a constant lift coefficient, there is consequent reduction in the upwash, downwash, and wingtip vortices.

Induced drag is a result of the airfoil's work of sustaining the aircraft, and a wing or rotor lifts the aircraft simply by accelerating a mass of air downward. It is true that reduced pressure on top of an airfoil is essential to lift, but that is

4-9

only one of the things contributing to the overall effect of pushing an air mass downward. The more downwash there is, the harder the wing pushes the mass of air down. At high angles of attack, the amount of induced drag is high; since this corresponds to lower airspeeds in actual flight, it can be said that induced drag predominates at low speed.

However, the reduction of the wingtip vortices due to ground effect alters the spanwise lift distribution and reduces the induced AOA and induced drag. Therefore, the wing will require a lower AOA in ground effect to produce the same C_L. If a constant AOA is maintained, an increase in C_L results. [Figure 4-14]

Ground effect also alters the thrust required versus velocity. Since induced drag predominates at low speeds, the reduction of induced drag due to ground effect will cause the most significant reduction of thrust required (parasite plus induced drag) at low speeds.

The reduction in induced flow due to ground effect causes a significant reduction in induced drag but causes no direct effect on parasite drag. As a result of the reduction in induced drag, the thrust required at low speeds will be reduced. Due to the change in upwash, downwash, and wingtip vortices, there may be a change in position (installation) error of the airspeed system, associated with ground effect. In the majority of cases, ground effect will cause an increase in the local pressure at the static source and produce a lower indication of airspeed and altitude. Thus, an aircraft may be airborne at an indicated airspeed less than that normally required.

In order for ground effect to be of significant magnitude, the wing must be quite close to the ground. One of the direct results of ground effect is the variation of induced drag with wing height above the ground at a constant C_L. When the wing is at a height equal to its span, the reduction in induced drag is only 1.4 percent. However, when the wing is at a height equal to one-fourth its span, the reduction in induced

drag is 23.5 percent and, when the wing is at a height equal to one-tenth its span, the reduction in induced drag is 47.6 percent. Thus, a large reduction in induced drag will take place only when the wing is very close to the ground. Because of this variation, ground effect is most usually recognized during the liftoff for takeoff or just prior to touchdown when landing.

During the takeoff phase of flight, ground effect produces some important relationships. An aircraft leaving ground effect after takeoff encounters just the reverse of an aircraft entering ground effect during landing; i.e., the aircraft leaving ground effect will:

- Require an increase in AOA to maintain the same C_L.

- Experience an increase in induced drag and thrust required.

- Experience a decrease in stability and a nose-up change in moment.

- Experience a reduction in static source pressure and increase in indicated airspeed.

Ground effect must be considered during takeoffs and landings. For example, if a pilot fails to understand the relationship between the aircraft and ground effect during takeoff, a hazardous situation is possible because the recommended takeoff speed may not be achieved. Due to the reduced drag in ground effect, the aircraft may seem capable of takeoff well below the recommended speed. As the aircraft rises out of ground effect with a deficiency of speed, the greater induced drag may result in marginal initial climb performance. In extreme conditions, such as high gross weight, high density altitude, and high temperature, a deficiency of airspeed during takeoff may permit the aircraft to become airborne but be incapable of sustaining flight out of ground effect. In this case, the aircraft may become airborne initially with a deficiency of speed, and then settle back to the runway.

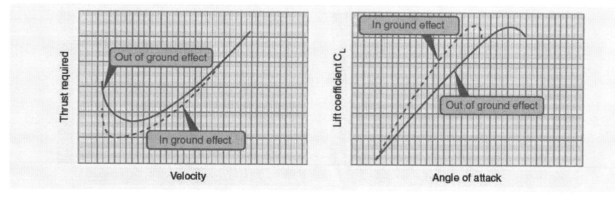

Figure 4-14. *Ground effect changes drag and lift.*

A pilot should not attempt to force an aircraft to become airborne with a deficiency of speed. The manufacturer's recommended takeoff speed is necessary to provide adequate initial climb performance. It is also important that a definite climb be established before a pilot retracts the landing gear or flaps. Never retract the landing gear or flaps prior to establishing a positive rate of climb, and only after achieving a safe altitude.

If, during the landing phase of flight, the aircraft is brought into ground effect with a constant AOA, the aircraft experiences an increase in C_L and a reduction in the thrust required, and a "floating" effect may occur. Because of the reduced drag and power-off deceleration in ground effect, any excess speed at the point of flare may incur a considerable "float" distance. As the aircraft nears the point of touchdown, ground effect is most realized at altitudes less than the wingspan. During the final phases of the approach as the aircraft nears the ground, a reduced power setting is necessary or the reduced thrust required would allow the aircraft to climb above the desired glidepath (GP).

Axes of an Aircraft

The axes of an aircraft are three imaginary lines that pass through an aircraft's CG. The axes can be considered as imaginary axles around which the aircraft turns. The three axes pass through the CG at 90° angles to each other. The axis from nose to tail is the longitudinal axis, the axis that passes from wingtip to wingtip is the lateral axis, and the axis that passes vertically through the CG is the vertical axis. Whenever an aircraft changes its flight attitude or position in flight, it rotates about one or more of the three axes. [Figure 4-15]

The aircraft's motion about its longitudinal axis resembles the roll of a ship from side to side. In fact, the names used to describe the motion about an aircraft's three axes were originally nautical terms. They have been adapted to aeronautical terminology due to the similarity of motion of aircraft and seagoing ships. The motion about the aircraft's longitudinal axis is "roll," the motion about its lateral axis is "pitch," and the motion about its vertical axis is "yaw." Yaw is the horizontal (left and right) movement of the aircraft's nose.

The three motions of the conventional airplane (roll, pitch, and yaw) are controlled by three control surfaces. Roll is controlled by the ailerons; pitch is controlled by the elevators; yaw is controlled by the rudder. The use of these controls is explained in Chapter 5, Flight Controls. Other types of aircraft may utilize different methods of controlling the movements about the various axes.

For example, weight-shift control aircraft control two axes, roll and pitch, using an "A" frame suspended from the flexible wing attached to a three-wheeled carriage. These aircraft are controlled by moving a horizontal bar (called a control bar) in roughly the same way hang glider pilots fly. [Figure 4-16] They are termed weight-shift control aircraft

Figure 4-16. *A weight-shift control aircraft.*

Figure 4-15. *Axes of an airplane.*

because the pilot controls the aircraft by shifting the CG. For more information on weight-shift control aircraft, see the Federal Aviation Administration (FAA) Weight-Shift Control Flying Handbook, FAA-H-8083-5. In the case of powered parachutes, aircraft control is accomplished by altering the airfoil via steering lines.

A powered parachute wing is a parachute that has a cambered upper surface and a flatter under surface. The two surfaces are separated by ribs that act as cells, which open to the airflow at the leading edge and have internal ports to allow lateral airflow. The principle at work holds that the cell pressure is greater than the outside pressure, thereby forming a wing that maintains its airfoil shape in flight. The pilot and passenger sit in tandem in front of the engine which is located at the rear of a vehicle. The airframe is attached to the parachute via two attachment points and lines. Control is accomplished by both power and the changing of the airfoil via the control lines. *[Figure 4-17]*

Figure 4-17. *A powered parachute.*

Moment and Moment Arm

A study of physics shows that a body that is free to rotate will always turn about its CG. In aerodynamic terms, the mathematical measure of an aircraft's tendency to rotate about its CG is called a "moment." A moment is said to be equal to the product of the force applied and the distance at which the force is applied. (A moment arm is the distance from a datum [reference point or line] to the applied force.) For aircraft weight and balance computations, "moments" are expressed in terms of the distance of the arm times the aircraft's weight, or simply, inch-pounds.

Aircraft designers locate the fore and aft position of the aircraft's CG as nearly as possible to the 20 percent point of the mean aerodynamic chord (MAC). If the thrust line is designed to pass horizontally through the CG, it will not cause the aircraft to pitch when power is changed, and there will be no difference in moment due to thrust for a power-on

or power-off condition of flight. Although designers have some control over the location of the drag forces, they are not always able to make the resultant drag forces pass through the CG of the aircraft. However, the one item over which they have the greatest control is the size and location of the tail. The objective is to make the moments (due to thrust, drag, and lift) as small as possible and, by proper location of the tail, to provide the means of balancing an aircraft longitudinally for any condition of flight.

The pilot has no direct control over the location of forces acting on the aircraft in flight, except for controlling the center of lift by changing the AOA. Such a change, however, immediately involves changes in other forces. Therefore, the pilot cannot independently change the location of one force without changing the effect of others. For example, a change in airspeed involves a change in lift, as well as a change in drag and a change in the up or down force on the tail. As forces such as turbulence and gusts act to displace the aircraft, the pilot reacts by providing opposing control forces to counteract this displacement.

Some aircraft are subject to changes in the location of the CG with variations of load. Trimming devices are used to counteract the forces set up by fuel burnoff, and loading or off-loading of passengers or cargo. Elevator trim tabs and adjustable horizontal stabilizers comprise the most common devices provided to the pilot for trimming for load variations. Over the wide ranges of balance during flight in large aircraft, the force which the pilot has to exert on the controls would become excessive and fatiguing if means of trimming were not provided.

Aircraft Design Characteristics

Each aircraft handles somewhat differently because each resists or responds to control pressures in its own way. For example, a training aircraft is quick to respond to control applications, while a transport aircraft feels heavy on the controls and responds to control pressures more slowly. These features can be designed into an aircraft to facilitate the particular purpose of the aircraft by considering certain stability and maneuvering requirements. The following discussion summarizes the more important aspects of an aircraft's stability, maneuverability and controllability qualities; how they are analyzed; and their relationship to various flight conditions.

Stability

Stability is the inherent quality of an aircraft to correct for conditions that may disturb its equilibrium, and to return to or to continue on the original flightpath. It is primarily an aircraft design characteristic. The flightpaths and attitudes an aircraft flies are limited by the aerodynamic characteristics of the aircraft, its propulsion system, and its structural strength. These limitations indicate the maximum performance and maneuverability of the aircraft. If the aircraft is to provide maximum utility, it must be safely controllable to the full extent of these limits without exceeding the pilot's strength or requiring exceptional flying ability. If an aircraft is to fly straight and steady along any arbitrary flightpath, the forces acting on it must be in static equilibrium. The reaction of any body when its equilibrium is disturbed is referred to as stability. The two types of stability are static and dynamic.

Static Stability

Static stability refers to the initial tendency, or direction of movement, back to equilibrium. In aviation, it refers to the aircraft's initial response when disturbed from a given AOA, slip, or bank.

- Positive static stability—the initial tendency of the aircraft to return to the original state of equilibrium after being disturbed [Figure 4-18]

- Neutral static stability—the initial tendency of the aircraft to remain in a new condition after its equilibrium has been disturbed [Figure 4-18]

- Negative static stability—the initial tendency of the aircraft to continue away from the original state of equilibrium after being disturbed [Figure 4-18]

Dynamic Stability

Static stability has been defined as the initial tendency to return to equilibrium that the aircraft displays after being disturbed from its trimmed condition. Occasionally, the initial tendency is different or opposite from the overall tendency, so a distinction must be made between the two.

Dynamic stability refers to the aircraft response over time when disturbed from a given AOA, slip, or bank. This type of stability also has three subtypes: [Figure 4-19]

- Positive dynamic stability—over time, the motion of the displaced object decreases in amplitude and, because it is positive, the object displaced returns toward the equilibrium state.

- Neutral dynamic stability—once displaced, the displaced object neither decreases nor increases in amplitude. A worn automobile shock absorber exhibits this tendency.

- Negative dynamic stability—over time, the motion of the displaced object increases and becomes more divergent.

Stability in an aircraft affects two areas significantly:

- Maneuverability—the quality of an aircraft that permits it to be maneuvered easily and to withstand the stresses imposed by maneuvers. It is governed by the aircraft's weight, inertia, size and location of flight controls, structural strength, and powerplant. It too is an aircraft design characteristic.

- Controllability—the capability of an aircraft to respond to the pilot's control, especially with regard to flightpath and attitude. It is the quality of the aircraft's response to the pilot's control application when maneuvering the aircraft, regardless of its stability characteristics.

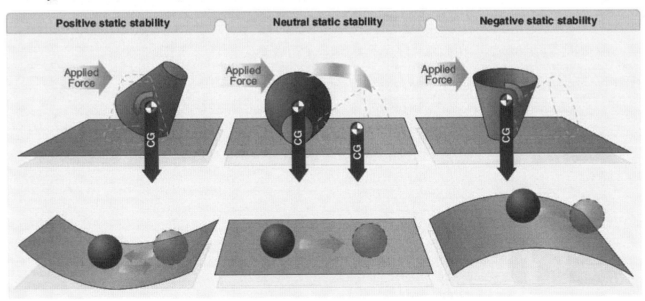

Figure 4-18. *Types of static stability.*

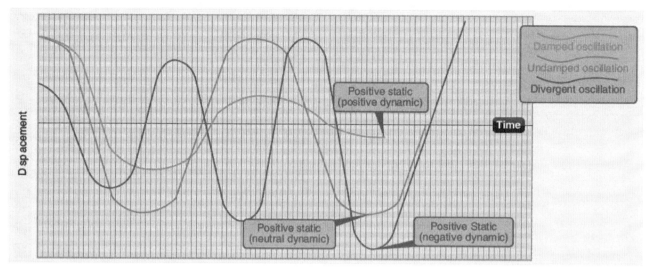

Figure 4-19. *Damped versus undamped stability.*

Longitudinal Stability (Pitching)

In designing an aircraft, a great deal of effort is spent in developing the desired degree of stability around all three axes. But longitudinal stability about the lateral axis is considered to be the most affected by certain variables in various flight conditions.

Longitudinal stability is the quality that makes an aircraft stable about its lateral axis. It involves the pitching motion as the aircraft's nose moves up and down in flight. A longitudinally unstable aircraft has a tendency to dive or climb progressively into a very steep dive or climb, or even a stall. Thus, an aircraft with longitudinal instability becomes difficult and sometimes dangerous to fly.

Static longitudinal stability or instability in an aircraft, is dependent upon three factors:

1. Location of the wing with respect to the CG

2. Location of the horizontal tail surfaces with respect to the CG

3. Area or size of the tail surfaces

In analyzing stability, it should be recalled that a body free to rotate always turns about its CG.

To obtain static longitudinal stability, the relation of the wing and tail moments must be such that, if the moments are initially balanced and the aircraft is suddenly nose up, the wing moments and tail moments change so that the sum of their forces provides an unbalanced but restoring moment which, in turn, brings the nose down again. Similarly, if the aircraft is nose down, the resulting change in moments brings the nose back up.

The CL in most asymmetrical airfoils has a tendency to change its fore and aft positions with a change in the AOA. The CL tends to move forward with an increase in AOA and to move aft with a decrease in AOA. This means that when the AOA of an airfoil is increased, the CL, by moving forward, tends to lift the leading edge of the wing still more. This tendency gives the wing an inherent quality of instability. (NOTE: CL is also known as the center of pressure (CP).)

Figure 4-20 shows an aircraft in straight-and-level flight. The line CG-CL-T represents the aircraft's longitudinal axis from the CG to a point T on the horizontal stabilizer.

Figure 4-20. *Longitudinal stability.*

Most aircraft are designed so that the wing's CL is to the rear of the CG. This makes the aircraft "nose heavy" and requires that there be a slight downward force on the horizontal stabilizer in order to balance the aircraft and keep the nose from continually pitching downward. Compensation for this nose heaviness is provided by setting the horizontal stabilizer at a slight negative AOA. The downward force thus produced holds the tail down, counterbalancing the "heavy" nose. It is as if the line CG-CL-T were a lever with an upward force at CL and two downward forces balancing each other, one a strong force at the CG point and the other, a much lesser force, at point T (downward air pressure on the stabilizer). To better visualize this physics principle: If an iron bar were suspended at point CL, with a heavy weight hanging on it at the CG, it would take downward pressure at point T to keep the "lever" in balance.

Even though the horizontal stabilizer may be level when the aircraft is in level flight, there is a downwash of air from the wings. This downwash strikes the top of the stabilizer and produces a downward pressure, which at a certain speed is just enough to balance the "lever." The faster the aircraft is flying, the greater this downwash and the greater the downward force on the horizontal stabilizer (except T-tails). *[Figure 4-21]* In aircraft with fixed-position horizontal stabilizers, the aircraft manufacturer sets the stabilizer at an angle that provides the best stability (or balance) during flight at the design cruising speed and power setting.

Figure 4-21. *Effect of speed on downwash.*

If the aircraft's speed decreases, the speed of the airflow over the wing is decreased. As a result of this decreased flow of air over the wing, the downwash is reduced, causing a lesser downward force on the horizontal stabilizer. In turn, the characteristic nose heaviness is accentuated, causing the aircraft's nose to pitch down more. *[Figure 4-22]* This places the aircraft in a nose-low attitude, lessening the wing's AOA and drag and allowing the airspeed to increase. As the aircraft continues in the nose-low attitude and its speed increases,

Figure 4-22. *Reduced power allows pitch down.*

the downward force on the horizontal stabilizer is once again increased. Consequently, the tail is again pushed downward and the nose rises into a climbing attitude.

As this climb continues, the airspeed again decreases, causing the downward force on the tail to decrease until the nose lowers once more. Because the aircraft is dynamically stable, the nose does not lower as far this time as it did before. The aircraft acquires enough speed in this more gradual dive to start it into another climb, but the climb is not as steep as the preceding one.

After several of these diminishing oscillations, in which the nose alternately rises and lowers, the aircraft finally settles down to a speed at which the downward force on the tail exactly counteracts the tendency of the aircraft to dive. When this condition is attained, the aircraft is once again in balanced flight and continues in stabilized flight as long as this attitude and airspeed are not changed.

A similar effect is noted upon closing the throttle. The downwash of the wings is reduced and the force at T in *Figure 4-20* is not enough to hold the horizontal stabilizer down. It seems as if the force at T on the lever were allowing the force of gravity to pull the nose down. This is a desirable characteristic because the aircraft is inherently trying to regain airspeed and reestablish the proper balance.

Power or thrust can also have a destabilizing effect in that an increase of power may tend to make the nose rise. The aircraft designer can offset this by establishing a "high thrust line" wherein the line of thrust passes above the CG. *[Figures 4-23 and 4-24]* In this case, as power or thrust is increased a moment is produced to counteract the down

Figure 4-23. *Thrust line affects longitudinal stability.*

Figure 4-24. *Power changes affect longitudinal stability.*

load on the tail. On the other hand, a very "low thrust line" would tend to add to the nose-up effect of the horizontal tail surface.

Conclusion: with CG forward of the CL and with an aerodynamic tail-down force, the aircraft usually tries to return to a safe flying attitude.

The following is a simple demonstration of longitudinal stability. Trim the aircraft for "hands off" control in level flight. Then, momentarily give the controls a slight push to nose the aircraft down. If, within a brief period, the nose rises to the original position and then stops, the aircraft is statically stable. Ordinarily, the nose passes the original position (that of level flight) and a series of slow pitching oscillations follows. If the oscillations gradually cease, the aircraft has positive stability; if they continue unevenly, the aircraft has neutral stability; if they increase, the aircraft is unstable.

Lateral Stability (Rolling)

Stability about the aircraft's longitudinal axis, which extends from the nose of the aircraft to its tail, is called lateral stability. This helps to stabilize the lateral or "rolling effect" when one wing gets lower than the wing on the opposite side of the aircraft. There are four main design factors that make an aircraft laterally stable: dihedral, sweepback, keel effect, and weight distribution.

Dihedral

The most common procedure for producing lateral stability is to build the wings with an angle of one to three degrees above perpendicular to the longitudinal axis. The wings on either side of the aircraft join the fuselage to form a slight V or angle called "dihedral." The amount of dihedral is measured by the angle made by each wing above a line parallel to the lateral axis.

Dihedral involves a balance of lift created by the wings' AOA on each side of the aircraft's longitudinal axis. If a momentary gust of wind forces one wing to rise and the other to lower, the aircraft banks. When the aircraft is banked without turning, the tendency to sideslip or slide downward toward the lowered wing occurs. *[Figure 4-25]* Since the wings have dihedral, the air strikes the lower wing at a much greater AOA than the higher wing. The increased AOA on the lower wing creates more lift than the higher wing. Increased lift causes the lower wing to begin to rise upward. As the wings approach the level position, the AOA on both wings once again are equal, causing the rolling tendency to subside. The effect of dihedral is to produce a rolling tendency to return the aircraft to a laterally balanced flight condition when a sideslip occurs.

The restoring force may move the low wing up too far, so that the opposite wing now goes down. If so, the process is repeated, decreasing with each lateral oscillation until a balance for wings-level flight is finally reached.

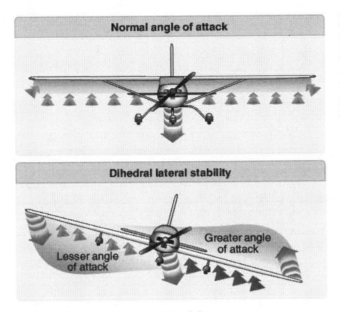

Figure 4-25. *Dihedral for lateral stability.*

Conversely, excessive dihedral has an adverse effect on lateral maneuvering qualities. The aircraft may be so stable laterally that it resists an intentional rolling motion. For this reason, aircraft that require fast roll or banking characteristics usually have less dihedral than those designed for less maneuverability.

Sweepback

Sweepback is an addition to the dihedral that increases the lift created when a wing drops from the level position. A sweptback wing is one in which the leading edge slopes backward. When a disturbance causes an aircraft with sweepback to slip or drop a wing, the low wing presents its leading edge at an angle that is perpendicular to the relative airflow. As a result, the low wing acquires more lift, rises, and the aircraft is restored to its original flight attitude.

Sweepback also contributes to directional stability. When turbulence or rudder application causes the aircraft to yaw to one side, the right wing presents a longer leading edge perpendicular to the relative airflow. The airspeed of the right wing increases and it acquires more drag than the left wing. The additional drag on the right wing pulls it back, turning the aircraft back to its original path.

Keel Effect and Weight Distribution

An aircraft always has the tendency to turn the longitudinal axis of the aircraft into the relative wind. This "weather vane" tendency is similar to the keel of a ship and exerts a steadying influence on the aircraft laterally about the longitudinal axis. When the aircraft is disturbed and one wing dips, the fuselage weight acts like a pendulum returning the airplane to its original attitude.

Laterally stable aircraft are constructed so that the greater portion of the keel area is above and behind the CG. *[Figure 4-26]* Thus, when the aircraft slips to one side, the combination of the aircraft's weight and the pressure of the airflow against the upper portion of the keel area (both acting about the CG) tends to roll the aircraft back to wings-level flight.

Figure 4-26. *Keel area for lateral stability.*

Vertical Stability (Yawing)

Stability about the aircraft's vertical axis (the sideways moment) is called yawing or directional stability. Yawing or directional stability is the most easily achieved stability in aircraft design. The area of the vertical fin and the sides of the fuselage aft of the CG are the prime contributors which make the aircraft act like the well known weather vane or arrow, pointing its nose into the relative wind.

In examining a weather vane, it can be seen that if exactly the same amount of surface were exposed to the wind in front of the pivot point as behind it, the forces fore and aft would be in balance and little or no directional movement would result. Consequently, it is necessary to have a greater surface aft of the pivot point than forward of it.

Similarly, the aircraft designer must ensure positive directional stability by making the side surface greater aft than ahead of the CG. *[Figure 4-27]* To provide additional positive stability to that provided by the fuselage, a vertical fin is added. The fin acts similar to the feather on an arrow in maintaining straight flight. Like the weather vane and the arrow, the farther aft this fin is placed and the larger its size, the greater the aircraft's directional stability.

If an aircraft is flying in a straight line, and a sideward gust of air gives the aircraft a slight rotation about its vertical axis (i.e., the right), the motion is retarded and stopped by the fin because while the aircraft is rotating to the right, the air is striking the left side of the fin at an angle. This causes pressure on the left side of the fin, which resists the turning motion and slows down the aircraft's yaw. In doing so, it

Figure 4-27. *Fuselage and fin for vertical stability.*

acts somewhat like the weather vane by turning the aircraft into the relative wind. The initial change in direction of the aircraft's flightpath is generally slightly behind its change of heading. Therefore, after a slight yawing of the aircraft to the right, there is a brief moment when the aircraft is still moving along its original path, but its longitudinal axis is pointed slightly to the right.

The aircraft is then momentarily skidding sideways, and during that moment (since it is assumed that although the yawing motion has stopped, the excess pressure on the left side of the fin still persists) there is necessarily a tendency for the aircraft to be turned partially back to the left. That is, there is a momentary restoring tendency caused by the fin.

This restoring tendency is relatively slow in developing and ceases when the aircraft stops skidding. When it ceases, the aircraft is flying in a direction slightly different from the original direction. In other words, it will not return of its own accord to the original heading; the pilot must reestablish the initial heading.

A minor improvement of directional stability may be obtained through sweepback. Sweepback is incorporated in the design of the wing primarily to delay the onset of compressibility during high-speed flight. In lighter and slower aircraft, sweepback aids in locating the center of pressure in the correct relationship with the CG. A longitudinally stable aircraft is built with the center of pressure aft of the CG.

Because of structural reasons, aircraft designers sometimes cannot attach the wings to the fuselage at the exact desired point. If they had to mount the wings too far forward, and at right angles to the fuselage, the center of pressure would not be far enough to the rear to result in the desired amount of longitudinal stability. By building sweepback into the wings, however, the designers can move the center of pressure toward the rear. The amount of sweepback and the position of the wings then place the center of pressure in the correct location.

The contribution of the wing to static directional stability is usually small. The swept wing provides a stable contribution depending on the amount of sweepback, but the contribution is relatively small when compared with other components.

Free Directional Oscillations (Dutch Roll)

Dutch roll is a coupled lateral/directional oscillation that is usually dynamically stable but is unsafe in an aircraft because of the oscillatory nature. The damping of the oscillatory mode may be weak or strong depending on the properties of the particular aircraft.

If the aircraft has a right wing pushed down, the positive sideslip angle corrects the wing laterally before the nose is realigned with the relative wind. As the wing corrects the position, a lateral directional oscillation can occur resulting in the nose of the aircraft making a figure eight on the horizon as a result of two oscillations (roll and yaw), which, although of about the same magnitude, are out of phase with each other.

In most modern aircraft, except high-speed swept wing designs, these free directional oscillations usually die out automatically in very few cycles unless the air continues to be gusty or turbulent. Those aircraft with continuing Dutch roll tendencies are usually equipped with gyro-stabilized yaw dampers. Manufacturers try to reach a midpoint between too much and too little directional stability. Because it is more desirable for the aircraft to have "spiral instability" than Dutch roll tendencies, most aircraft are designed with that characteristic.

Spiral Instability

Spiral instability exists when the static directional stability of the aircraft is very strong as compared to the effect of its dihedral in maintaining lateral equilibrium. When the lateral equilibrium of the aircraft is disturbed by a gust of air and a sideslip is introduced, the strong directional stability tends to yaw the nose into the resultant relative wind while the comparatively weak dihedral lags in restoring the lateral balance. Due to this yaw, the wing on the outside of the turning moment travels forward faster than the inside wing and, as a consequence, its lift becomes greater. This produces an overbanking tendency which, if not corrected by the pilot, results in the bank angle becoming steeper and steeper. At the same time, the strong directional stability that yaws the aircraft into the relative wind is actually forcing the nose to a lower pitch attitude. A slow downward spiral begins which, if not counteracted by the pilot, gradually increases into a steep spiral dive. Usually the rate of divergence in the spiral motion is so gradual the pilot can control the tendency without any difficulty.

All aircraft are affected to some degree by this characteristic, although they may be inherently stable in all other normal parameters. This tendency explains why an aircraft cannot be flown "hands off" indefinitely.

Much research has gone into the development of control devices (wing leveler) to correct or eliminate this instability. The pilot must be careful in application of recovery controls during advanced stages of this spiral condition or excessive loads may be imposed on the structure. Improper recovery from spiral instability leading to inflight structural failures has probably contributed to more fatalities in general aviation aircraft than any other factor. Since the airspeed in the spiral condition builds up rapidly, the application of back elevator force to reduce this speed and to pull the nose up only "tightens the turn," increasing the load factor. The results of the prolonged uncontrolled spiral are inflight structural failure or crashing into the ground, or both. The most common recorded causes for pilots who get into this situation are: loss of horizon reference, inability to control the aircraft by reference to instruments, or a combination of both.

Aerodynamic Forces in Flight Maneuvers

Forces in Turns

If an aircraft were viewed in straight-and-level flight from the front [Figure 4-28], and if the forces acting on the aircraft could be seen, lift and weight would be apparent: two forces. If the aircraft were in a bank it would be apparent that lift did not act directly opposite to the weight, rather it now acts in the direction of the bank. A basic truth about turns: when the aircraft banks, lift acts inward toward the center of the turn, as well as upward.

Newton's First Law of Motion, the Law of Inertia, states that an object at rest or moving in a straight line remains at rest or continues to move in a straight line until acted on by some other force. An aircraft, like any moving object, requires a sideward force to make it turn. In a normal turn, this force is supplied by banking the aircraft so that lift is exerted inward, as well as upward. The force of lift during a turn is separated into two components at right angles to each other. One component, which acts vertically and opposite to the weight (gravity), is called the "vertical component of lift." The other, which acts horizontally toward the center of the turn, is called the "horizontal component of lift," or centripetal force. The horizontal component of lift is the force that pulls the aircraft from a straight flightpath to make it turn. Centrifugal force is the "equal and opposite reaction" of the aircraft to the change in direction and acts equal and opposite to the horizontal component of lift. This explains why, in a correctly executed turn, the force that turns the aircraft is not supplied by the rudder. The rudder is used to correct any deviation between the straight track of the nose and tail of the aircraft. A good turn is one in which the nose and tail of the aircraft track along the same path. If no rudder is used in a turn, the nose of the aircraft yaws to the outside of the turn. The rudder is used to bring the nose back in line with the relative wind.

An aircraft is not steered like a boat or an automobile. In order for an aircraft to turn, it must be banked. If it is not banked, there is no force available to cause it to deviate from a straight flightpath. Conversely, when an aircraft is banked, it turns, provided it is not slipping to the inside of the turn.

Figure 4-28. *Forces during normal coordinated turn.*

Good directional control is based on the fact that the aircraft attempts to turn whenever it is banked. Pilots should keep this fact in mind when attempting to hold the aircraft in straight-and-level flight.

Merely banking the aircraft into a turn produces no change in the total amount of lift developed. Since the lift during the bank is divided into vertical and horizontal components, the amount of lift opposing gravity and supporting the aircraft's weight is reduced. Consequently, the aircraft loses altitude unless additional lift is created. This is done by increasing the AOA until the vertical component of lift is again equal to the weight. Since the vertical component of lift decreases as the bank angle increases, the AOA must be progressively increased to produce sufficient vertical lift to support the aircraft's weight. An important fact for pilots to remember when making constant altitude turns is that the vertical component of lift must be equal to the weight to maintain altitude.

At a given airspeed, the rate at which an aircraft turns depends upon the magnitude of the horizontal component of lift. It is found that the horizontal component of lift is proportional to the angle of bank—that is, it increases or decreases respectively as the angle of bank increases or decreases. As the angle of bank is increased, the horizontal component of lift increases, thereby increasing the ROT. Consequently, at any given airspeed, the ROT can be controlled by adjusting the angle of bank.

To provide a vertical component of lift sufficient to hold altitude in a level turn, an increase in the AOA is required. Since the drag of the airfoil is directly proportional to its AOA, induced drag increases as the lift is increased. This, in turn, causes a loss of airspeed in proportion to the angle of bank. A small angle of bank results in a small reduction in airspeed while a large angle of bank results in a large reduction in airspeed. Additional thrust (power) must be applied to prevent a reduction in airspeed in level turns. The required amount of additional thrust is proportional to the angle of bank.

To compensate for added lift, which would result if the airspeed were increased during a turn, the AOA must be decreased, or the angle of bank increased, if a constant altitude is to be maintained. If the angle of bank is held constant and the AOA decreased, the ROT decreases. In order to maintain a constant-ROT as the airspeed is increased, the AOA must remain constant and the angle of bank increased.

An increase in airspeed results in an increase of the turn radius, and centrifugal force is directly proportional to the radius of the turn. In a correctly executed turn, the horizontal component of lift must be exactly equal and opposite to the centrifugal force. As the airspeed is increased in a constant-rate level turn, the radius of the turn increases. This increase in the radius of turn causes an increase in the centrifugal force, which must be balanced by an increase in the horizontal component of lift, which can only be increased by increasing the angle of bank.

In a slipping turn, the aircraft is not turning at the rate appropriate to the bank being used, since the aircraft is yawed toward the outside of the turning flightpath. The aircraft is banked too much for the ROT, so the horizontal lift component is greater than the centrifugal force. *[Figure 4-29]* Equilibrium between the horizontal lift component and centrifugal force is reestablished by either decreasing the bank, increasing the ROT, or a combination of the two changes.

A skidding turn results from an excess of centrifugal force over the horizontal lift component, pulling the aircraft toward the outside of the turn. The ROT is too great for the angle of bank. Correction of a skidding turn thus involves a

Figure 4-29. *Normal, slipping, and skidding turns.*

reduction in the ROT, an increase in bank, or a combination of the two changes.

To maintain a given ROT, the angle of bank must be varied with the airspeed. This becomes particularly important in high-speed aircraft. For instance, at 400 miles per hour (mph), an aircraft must be banked approximately 44° to execute a standard-rate turn (3° per second). At this angle of bank, only about 79 percent of the lift of the aircraft comprises the vertical component of the lift. This causes a loss of altitude unless the AOA is increased sufficiently to compensate for the loss of vertical lift.

Forces in Climbs

For all practical purposes, the wing's lift in a steady state normal climb is the same as it is in a steady level flight at the same airspeed. Although the aircraft's flightpath changed when the climb was established, the AOA of the wing with respect to the inclined flightpath reverts to practically the same values, as does the lift. There is an initial momentary change as shown in *Figure 4-30*. During the transition from straight-and-level flight to a climb, a change in lift occurs when back elevator pressure is first applied. Raising the aircraft's nose increases the AOA and momentarily increases the lift. Lift at this moment is now greater than weight and starts the aircraft climbing. After the flightpath is stabilized on the upward incline, the AOA and lift again revert to about the level flight values.

Figure 4-30. *Changes in lift during climb entry.*

If the climb is entered with no change in power setting, the airspeed gradually diminishes because the thrust required to maintain a given airspeed in level flight is insufficient to maintain the same airspeed in a climb. When the flightpath is inclined upward, a component of the aircraft's weight acts in the same direction as, and parallel to, the total drag of the aircraft, thereby increasing the total effective drag. Consequently, the total drag is greater than the power, and the airspeed decreases. The reduction in airspeed gradually results in a corresponding decrease in drag until the total

drag (including the component of weight acting in the same direction) equals the thrust. *[Figure 4-31]* Due to momentum, the change in airspeed is gradual, varying considerably with differences in aircraft size, weight, total drag, and other factors. Consequently, the total drag is greater than the thrust, and the airspeed decreases.

Figure 4-31. *Changes in speed during climb entry.*

Generally, the forces of thrust and drag, and lift and weight, again become balanced when the airspeed stabilizes but at a value lower than in straight-and-level flight at the same power setting. Since the aircraft's weight is acting not only downward but rearward with drag while in a climb, additional power is required to maintain the same airspeed as in level flight. The amount of power depends on the angle of climb. When the climb is established steep enough that there is insufficient power available, a slower speed results.

The thrust required for a stabilized climb equals drag plus a percentage of weight dependent on the angle of climb. For example, a 10° climb would require thrust to equal drag plus 17 percent of weight. To climb straight up would require thrust to equal all of weight and drag. Therefore, the angle of climb for climb performance is dependent on the amount of excess power available to overcome a portion of weight. Note that aircraft are able to sustain a climb due to excess thrust. When the excess thrust is gone, the aircraft is no longer able to climb. At this point, the aircraft has reached its "absolute ceiling."

Forces in Descents

As in climbs, the forces which act on the aircraft go through definite changes when a descent is entered from straight-and-level flight. For the following example, the aircraft is descending at the same power as used in straight-and-level flight.

As forward pressure is applied to the control yoke to initiate the descent, the AOA is decreased momentarily. Initially, the momentum of the aircraft causes the aircraft to briefly continue along the same flightpath. For this instant, the AOA decreases causing the total lift to decrease. With weight now being greater than lift, the aircraft begins to descend. At the same time, the flightpath goes from level to a descending flightpath. Do not confuse a reduction in lift with the inability to generate sufficient lift to maintain level flight. The flightpath is being manipulated with available thrust in reserve and with the elevator.

To descend at the same airspeed as used in straight-and-level flight, the power must be reduced as the descent is entered. The component of weight acting forward along the flightpath increases as the angle of rate of descent increases and, conversely, decreases as the angle of rate of descent decreases. The component of weight acting forward along the flightpath increases as the angle of rate of descent increases and, conversely, decreases as the angle of rate of descent decreases.

Stalls

An aircraft stall results from a rapid decrease in lift caused by the separation of airflow from the wing's surface brought on by exceeding the critical AOA. A stall can occur at any pitch attitude or airspeed. Stalls are one of the most misunderstood areas of aerodynamics because pilots often believe an airfoil stops producing lift when it stalls. In a stall, the wing does not totally stop producing lift. Rather, it can not generate adequate lift to sustain level flight.

Since the C_L increases with an increase in AOA, at some point the C_L peaks and then begins to drop off. This peak is called the C_{L-MAX}. The amount of lift the wing produces drops dramatically after exceeding the C_{L-MAX} or critical AOA, but as stated above, it does not completely stop producing lift.

In most straight-wing aircraft, the wing is designed to stall the wing root first. The wing root reaches its critical AOA first making the stall progress outward toward the wingtip. By having the wing root stall first, aileron effectiveness is maintained at the wingtips, maintaining controllability of the aircraft. Various design methods are used to achieve the stalling of the wing root first. In one design, the wing is "twisted" to a higher AOA at the wing root. Installing stall strips on the first 20–25 percent of the wing's leading edge is another method to introduce a stall prematurely.

The wing never completely stops producing lift in a stalled condition. If it did, the aircraft would fall to the Earth. Most training aircraft are designed for the nose of the aircraft to drop during a stall, reducing the AOA and "unstalling" the wing. The "nose-down" tendency is due to the CL being aft of the CG. The CG range is very important when it comes to stall recovery characteristics. If an aircraft is allowed to

be operated outside of the CG, the pilot may have difficulty recovering from a stall. The most critical CG violation would occur when operating with a CG which exceeds the rear limit. In this situation, a pilot may not be able to generate sufficient force with the elevator to counteract the excess weight aft of the CG. Without the ability to decrease the AOA, the aircraft continues in a stalled condition until it contacts the ground.

The stalling speed of a particular aircraft is not a fixed value for all flight situations, but a given aircraft always stalls at the same AOA regardless of airspeed, weight, load factor, or density altitude. Each aircraft has a particular AOA where the airflow separates from the upper surface of the wing and the stall occurs. This critical AOA varies from 16° to 20° depending on the aircraft's design. But each aircraft has only one specific AOA where the stall occurs.

There are three flight situations in which the critical AOA can be exceeded: low speed, high speed, and turning.

The aircraft can be stalled in straight-and-level flight by flying too slowly. As the airspeed decreases, the AOA must be increased to retain the lift required for maintaining altitude. The lower the airspeed becomes, the more the AOA must be increased. Eventually, an AOA is reached which results in the wing not producing enough lift to support the aircraft which starts settling. If the airspeed is reduced further, the aircraft stalls, since the AOA has exceeded the critical angle and the airflow over the wing is disrupted.

Low speed is not necessary to produce a stall. The wing can be brought into an excessive AOA at any speed. For example, an aircraft is in a dive with an airspeed of 100 knots when the pilot pulls back sharply on the elevator control. *[Figure 4-32]* Gravity and centrifugal force prevent an immediate alteration

Figure 4-32. *Forces exerted when pulling out of a dive.*

of the flightpath, but the aircraft's AOA changes abruptly from quite low to very high. Since the flightpath of the aircraft in relation to the oncoming air determines the direction of the relative wind, the AOA is suddenly increased, and the aircraft would reach the stalling angle at a speed much greater than the normal stall speed.

The stalling speed of an aircraft is also higher in a level turn than in straight-and-level flight. *[Figure 4-33]* Centrifugal force is added to the aircraft's weight and the wing must produce sufficient additional lift to counterbalance the load imposed by the combination of centrifugal force and weight. In a turn, the necessary additional lift is acquired by applying back pressure to the elevator control. This increases the wing's AOA, and results in increased lift. The AOA must increase as the bank angle increases to counteract the increasing load caused by centrifugal force. If at any time during a turn the AOA becomes excessive, the aircraft stalls.

Figure 4-33. *Increase in stall speed and load factor.*

At this point, the action of the aircraft during a stall should be examined. To balance the aircraft aerodynamically, the CL is normally located aft of the CG. Although this makes the aircraft inherently nose-heavy, downwash on the horizontal stabilizer counteracts this condition. At the point of stall, when the upward force of the wing's lift and the downward tail force cease, an unbalanced condition exists. This allows the aircraft to pitch down abruptly, rotating about its CG. During this nose-down attitude, the AOA decreases and the airspeed again increases. The smooth flow of air over the wing begins again, lift returns, and the aircraft is again flying. Considerable altitude may be lost before this cycle is complete.

Airfoil shape and degradation of that shape must also be considered in a discussion of stalls. For example, if ice, snow, and frost are allowed to accumulate on the surface of an aircraft, the smooth airflow over the wing is disrupted. This causes the boundary layer to separate at an AOA lower than that of the critical angle. Lift is greatly reduced, altering

expected aircraft performance. If ice is allowed to accumulate on the aircraft during flight *[Figure 4-34]*, the weight of the aircraft is increased while the ability to generate lift is decreased. As little as 0.8 millimeter of ice on the upper wing surface increases drag and reduces aircraft lift by 25 percent.

Figure 4-34. *Inflight ice formation.*

Pilots can encounter icing in any season, anywhere in the country, at altitudes of up to 18,000 feet and sometimes higher. Small aircraft, including commuter planes, are most vulnerable because they fly at lower altitudes where ice is more prevalent. They also lack mechanisms common on jet aircraft that prevent ice buildup by heating the front edges of wings.

Icing can occur in clouds any time the temperature drops below freezing and super-cooled droplets build up on an aircraft and freeze. (Super-cooled droplets are still liquid even though the temperature is below 32 °Fahrenheit (F), or 0 °Celsius (C).

Basic Propeller Principles

The aircraft propeller consists of two or more blades and a central hub to which the blades are attached. Each blade of an aircraft propeller is essentially a rotating wing. As a result of their construction, the propeller blades are like airfoils and produce forces that create the thrust to pull, or push, the aircraft through the air. The engine furnishes the power needed to rotate the propeller blades through the air at high speeds, and the propeller transforms the rotary power of the engine into forward thrust.

A cross-section of a typical propeller blade is shown in *Figure 4-35*. This section or blade element is an airfoil comparable to a cross-section of an aircraft wing. One surface of the blade is cambered or curved, similar to the upper surface of an aircraft wing, while the other surface is flat like the bottom surface of a wing. The chord line is an imaginary line drawn through the blade from its leading edge to its trailing edge. As in a wing, the leading edge is the thick edge of the blade that meets the air as the propeller rotates.

Figure 4-35. *Airfoil sections of propeller blade.*

Blade angle, usually measured in degrees, is the angle between the chord of the blade and the plane of rotation and is measured at a specific point along the length of the blade. *[Figure 4-36]* Because most propellers have a flat blade "face," the chord line is often drawn along the face of the propeller blade. Pitch is not blade angle, but because pitch is largely determined by blade angle, the two terms are often used interchangeably. An increase or decrease in one is usually associated with an increase or decrease in the other.

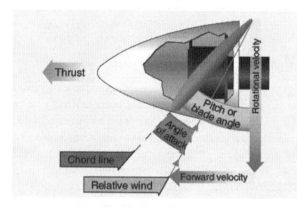

Figure 4-36. *Propeller blade angle.*

The pitch of a propeller may be designated in inches. A propeller designated as a "74-48" would be 74 inches in length and have an effective pitch of 48 inches. The pitch is the distance in inches, which the propeller would screw through the air in one revolution if there were no slippage.

When specifying a fixed-pitch propeller for a new type of aircraft, the manufacturer usually selects one with a pitch that operates efficiently at the expected cruising speed of the aircraft. Every fixed-pitch propeller must be a compromise because it can be efficient at only a given combination of airspeed and revolutions per minute (rpm). Pilots cannot change this combination in flight.

When the aircraft is at rest on the ground with the engine operating, or moving slowly at the beginning of takeoff, the propeller efficiency is very low because the propeller is restrained from advancing with sufficient speed to permit its fixed-pitch blades to reach their full efficiency. In this situation, each propeller blade is turning through the air at an AOA that produces relatively little thrust for the amount of power required to turn it.

To understand the action of a propeller, consider first its motion, which is both rotational and forward. As shown by the vectors of propeller forces in *Figure 4-36*, each section of a propeller blade moves downward and forward. The angle at which this air (relative wind) strikes the propeller blade is its AOA. The air deflection produced by this angle causes the dynamic pressure at the engine side of the propeller blade to be greater than atmospheric pressure, thus creating thrust.

The shape of the blade also creates thrust because it is cambered like the airfoil shape of a wing. As the air flows past the propeller, the pressure on one side is less than that on the other. As in a wing, a reaction force is produced in the direction of the lesser pressure. The airflow over the wing has less pressure, and the force (lift) is upward. In the case of the propeller, which is mounted in a vertical instead of a horizontal plane, the area of decreased pressure is in front of the propeller, and the force (thrust) is in a forward direction. Aerodynamically, thrust is the result of the propeller shape and the AOA of the blade.

Thrust can be considered also in terms of the mass of air handled by the propeller. In these terms, thrust equals mass of air handled multiplied by slipstream velocity minus velocity of the aircraft. The power expended in producing thrust depends on the rate of air mass movement. On average, thrust constitutes approximately 80 percent of the torque (total horsepower absorbed by the propeller). The other 20 percent is lost in friction and slippage. For any speed of rotation, the horsepower absorbed by the propeller balances the horsepower delivered by the engine. For any single revolution of the propeller, the amount of air handled depends on the blade angle, which determines how big a "bite" of air the propeller takes. Thus, the blade angle is an excellent means of adjusting the load on the propeller to control the engine rpm.

The blade angle is also an excellent method of adjusting the AOA of the propeller. On constant-speed propellers, the blade angle must be adjusted to provide the most efficient AOA at all engine and aircraft speeds. Lift versus drag curves, which are drawn for propellers, as well as wings, indicate that the most efficient AOA is small, varying from +2° to +4°. The actual blade angle necessary to maintain this small AOA varies with the forward speed of the aircraft.

Fixed-pitch and ground-adjustable propellers are designed for best efficiency at one rotation and forward speed. They are designed for a given aircraft and engine combination. A propeller may be used that provides the maximum efficiency for takeoff, climb, cruise, or high-speed flight. Any change in these conditions results in lowering the efficiency of both the propeller and the engine. Since the efficiency of any machine is the ratio of the useful power output to the actual power input, propeller efficiency is the ratio of thrust horsepower to brake horsepower. Propeller efficiency varies from 50 to 87 percent, depending on how much the propeller "slips."

Propeller slip is the difference between the geometric pitch of the propeller and its effective pitch. *[Figure 4-37]* Geometric pitch is the theoretical distance a propeller should advance in one revolution; effective pitch is the distance it actually advances. Thus, geometric or theoretical pitch is based on no slippage, but actual or effective pitch includes propeller slippage in the air.

Figure 4-38. *Propeller tips travel faster than the hub.*

A constant-speed propeller automatically keeps the blade angle adjusted for maximum efficiency for most conditions encountered in flight. During takeoff, when maximum power and thrust are required, the constant-speed propeller is at a low propeller blade angle or pitch. The low blade angle keeps the AOA small and efficient with respect to the relative wind. At the same time, it allows the propeller to handle a smaller mass of air per revolution. This light load allows the engine to turn at high rpm and to convert the maximum amount of fuel into heat energy in a given time. The high rpm also creates maximum thrust because, although the mass of air handled per revolution is small, the rpm and slipstream velocity are high, and with the low aircraft speed, there is maximum thrust.

Figure 4-37. *Propeller slippage.*

The reason a propeller is "twisted" is that the outer parts of the propeller blades, like all things that turn about a central point, travel faster than the portions near the hub. *[Figure 4-38]* If the blades had the same geometric pitch throughout their lengths, portions near the hub could have negative AOAs while the propeller tips would be stalled at cruise speed. Twisting or variations in the geometric pitch of the blades permits the propeller to operate with a relatively constant AOA along its length when in cruising flight. Propeller blades are twisted to change the blade angle in proportion to the differences in speed of rotation along the length of the propeller, keeping thrust more nearly equalized along this length.

Usually 1° to 4° provides the most efficient lift/drag ratio, but in flight the propeller AOA of a fixed-pitch propeller varies—normally from 0° to 15°. This variation is caused by changes in the relative airstream, which in turn results from changes in aircraft speed. Thus, propeller AOA is the product of two motions: propeller rotation about its axis and its forward motion.

After liftoff, as the speed of the aircraft increases, the constant-speed propeller automatically changes to a higher angle (or pitch). Again, the higher blade angle keeps the AOA small and efficient with respect to the relative wind. The higher blade angle increases the mass of air handled per revolution. This decreases the engine rpm, reducing fuel consumption and engine wear, and keeps thrust at a maximum.

After the takeoff climb is established in an aircraft having a controllable-pitch propeller, the pilot reduces the power output of the engine to climb power by first decreasing the manifold pressure and then increasing the blade angle to lower the rpm.

At cruising altitude, when the aircraft is in level flight and less power is required than is used in takeoff or climb, the pilot again reduces engine power by reducing the manifold pressure and then increasing the blade angle to decrease the rpm. Again, this provides a torque requirement to match the reduced engine power. Although the mass of air handled per revolution is greater, it is more than offset by a decrease in slipstream velocity and an increase in airspeed. The AOA is still small because the blade angle has been increased with an increase in airspeed.

Torque and P-Factor

To the pilot, "torque" (the left turning tendency of the airplane) is made up of four elements which cause or produce a twisting or rotating motion around at least one of the airplane's three axes. These four elements are:

1. Torque reaction from engine and propeller,

2. Corkscrewing effect of the slipstream,

3. Gyroscopic action of the propeller, and

4. Asymmetric loading of the propeller (P-factor).

Torque Reaction

Torque reaction involves Newton's Third Law of Physics— for every action, there is an equal and opposite reaction. As applied to the aircraft, this means that as the internal engine parts and propeller are revolving in one direction, an equal force is trying to rotate the aircraft in the opposite direction. *[Figure 4-39]*

Figure 4-39. *Torque reaction.*

When the aircraft is airborne, this force is acting around the longitudinal axis, tending to make the aircraft roll. To compensate for roll tendency, some of the older aircraft are rigged in a manner to create more lift on the wing that is being forced downward. The more modern aircraft are designed with the engine offset to counteract this effect of torque.

NOTE: Most United States built aircraft engines rotate the propeller clockwise, as viewed from the pilot's seat. The discussion here is with reference to those engines.

Generally, the compensating factors are permanently set so that they compensate for this force at cruising speed, since most of the aircraft's operating lift is at that speed. However, aileron trim tabs permit further adjustment for other speeds.

When the aircraft's wheels are on the ground during the takeoff roll, an additional turning moment around the vertical axis is induced by torque reaction. As the left side of the aircraft is being forced down by torque reaction, more weight is being placed on the left main landing gear. This results in more ground friction, or drag, on the left tire than on the right, causing a further turning moment to the left. The magnitude of this moment is dependent on many variables. Some of these variables are:

1. Size and horsepower of engine,

2. Size of propeller and the rpm,

3. Size of the aircraft, and

4. Condition of the ground surface.

This yawing moment on the takeoff roll is corrected by the pilot's proper use of the rudder or rudder trim.

Corkscrew Effect

The high-speed rotation of an aircraft propeller gives a corkscrew or spiraling rotation to the slipstream. At high propeller speeds and low forward speed (as in the takeoffs and approaches to power-on stalls), this spiraling rotation is very compact and exerts a strong sideward force on the aircraft's vertical tail surface. *[Figure 4-40]*

Figure 4-40. *Corkscrewing slipstream.*

When this spiraling slipstream strikes the vertical fin it causes a turning moment about the aircraft's vertical axis. The more compact the spiral, the more prominent this force is. As the forward speed increases, however, the spiral elongates and becomes less effective. The corkscrew flow of the slipstream also causes a rolling moment around the longitudinal axis.

Note that this rolling moment caused by the corkscrew flow of the slipstream is to the right, while the rolling moment caused by torque reaction is to the left—in effect one may be counteracting the other. However, these forces vary greatly and it is the pilot's responsibility to apply proper corrective action by use of the flight controls at all times. These forces must be counteracted regardless of which is the most prominent at the time.

Gyroscopic Action

Before the gyroscopic effects of the propeller can be understood, it is necessary to understand the basic principle of a gyroscope. All practical applications of the gyroscope are based upon two fundamental properties of gyroscopic action: rigidity in space and precession. The one of interest for this discussion is precession.

Precession is the resultant action, or deflection, of a spinning rotor when a deflecting force is applied to its rim. As can be seen in *Figure 4-41*, when a force is applied, the resulting force takes effect 90° ahead of and in the direction of rotation.

Figure 4-41. *Gyroscopic precession.*

The rotating propeller of an airplane makes a very good gyroscope and thus has similar properties. Any time a force is applied to deflect the propeller out of its plane of rotation, the resulting force is 90° ahead of and in the direction of rotation and in the direction of application, causing a pitching moment, a yawing moment, or a combination of the two depending upon the point at which the force was applied.

This element of torque effect has always been associated with and considered more prominent in tailwheel-type aircraft, and most often occurs when the tail is being raised during the takeoff roll. *[Figure 4-42]* This change in pitch attitude has the same effect as applying a force to the top of the propeller's plane of rotation. The resultant force acting 90° ahead causes a yawing moment to the left around the vertical axis. The magnitude of this moment depends on several variables, one of which is the abruptness with which the tail is raised (amount of force applied). However, precession, or gyroscopic action, occurs when a force is applied to any point on the rim of the propeller's plane of rotation; the

resultant force will still be 90° from the point of application in the direction of rotation. Depending on where the force is applied, the airplane is caused to yaw left or right, to pitch up or down, or a combination of pitching and yawing.

Figure 4-42. *Raising tail produces gyroscopic precession.*

It can be said that, as a result of gyroscopic action, any yawing around the vertical axis results in a pitching moment, and any pitching around the lateral axis results in a yawing moment. To correct for the effect of gyroscopic action, it is necessary for the pilot to properly use elevator and rudder to prevent undesired pitching and yawing.

Asymmetric Loading (P-Factor)

When an aircraft is flying with a high AOA, the "bite" of the downward moving blade is greater than the "bite" of the upward moving blade. This moves the center of thrust to the right of the prop disc area, causing a yawing moment toward the left around the vertical axis. To prove this explanation is complex because it would be necessary to work wind vector problems on each blade while considering both the AOA of the aircraft and the AOA of each blade.

This asymmetric loading is caused by the resultant velocity, which is generated by the combination of the velocity of the propeller blade in its plane of rotation and the velocity of the air passing horizontally through the propeller disc. With the aircraft being flown at positive AOAs, the right (viewed from the rear) or downswinging blade, is passing through an area of resultant velocity which is greater than that affecting the left or upswinging blade. Since the propeller blade is an airfoil, increased velocity means increased lift. The downswinging blade has more lift and tends to pull (yaw) the aircraft's nose to the left.

When the aircraft is flying at a high AOA, the downward moving blade has a higher resultant velocity, creating more lift than the upward moving blade. *[Figure 4-43]* This might be easier to visualize if the propeller shaft was mounted perpendicular to the ground (like a helicopter). If there were no air movement at all, except that generated by the

Figure 4-43. *Asymmetrical loading of propeller (P-factor).*

propeller itself, identical sections of each blade would have the same airspeed. With air moving horizontally across this vertically mounted propeller, the blade proceeding forward into the flow of air has a higher airspeed than the blade retreating with the airflow. Thus, the blade proceeding into the horizontal airflow is creating more lift, or thrust, moving the center of thrust toward that blade. Visualize rotating the vertically mounted propeller shaft to shallower angles relative to the moving air (as on an aircraft). This unbalanced thrust then becomes proportionately smaller and continues getting smaller until it reaches the value of zero when the propeller shaft is exactly horizontal in relation to the moving air.

The effects of each of these four elements of torque vary in value with changes in flight situations. In one phase of flight, one of these elements may be more prominent than another. In another phase of flight, another element may be more prominent. The relationship of these values to each other varies with different aircraft—depending on the airframe, engine, and propeller combinations, as well as other design features. To maintain positive control of the aircraft in all flight conditions, the pilot must apply the flight controls as necessary to compensate for these varying values.

Load Factors

In aerodynamics, load factor is the ratio of the maximum load an aircraft can sustain to the gross weight of the aircraft. The load factor is measured in Gs (acceleration of gravity), a unit of force equal to the force exerted by gravity on a body at rest and indicates the force to which a body is subjected when it is accelerated. Any force applied to an aircraft to deflect its flight from a straight line produces a stress on its structure, and the amount of this force is the load factor. While a course in aerodynamics is not a prerequisite for obtaining a pilot's license, the competent pilot should have a solid understanding of the forces that act on the aircraft, the advantageous use of these forces, and the operating limitations of the aircraft being flown.

For example, a load factor of 3 means the total load on an aircraft's structure is three times its gross weight. Since load factors are expressed in terms of Gs, a load factor of 3 may be spoken of as 3 Gs, or a load factor of 4 as 4 Gs.

If an aircraft is pulled up from a dive, subjecting the pilot to 3 Gs, he or she would be pressed down into the seat with a force equal to three times his or her weight. Since modern aircraft operate at significantly higher speeds than older aircraft, increasing the magnitude of the load factor, this effect has become a primary consideration in the design of the structure of all aircraft.

With the structural design of aircraft planned to withstand only a certain amount of overload, a knowledge of load factors has become essential for all pilots. Load factors are important for two reasons:

1. It is possible for a pilot to impose a dangerous overload on the aircraft structures.

2. An increased load factor increases the stalling speed and makes stalls possible at seemingly safe flight speeds.

Load Factors in Aircraft Design

The answer to the question "How strong should an aircraft be?" is determined largely by the use to which the aircraft is subjected. This is a difficult problem because the maximum possible loads are much too high for use in efficient design. It is true that any pilot can make a very hard landing or an extremely sharp pull up from a dive, which would result in abnormal loads. However, such extremely abnormal loads must be dismissed somewhat if aircraft are built that take off quickly, land slowly, and carry worthwhile payloads.

The problem of load factors in aircraft design becomes how to determine the highest load factors that can be expected in normal operation under various operational situations. These load factors are called "limit load factors." For reasons of safety, it is required that the aircraft be designed to withstand these load factors without any structural damage. Although the Code of Federal Regulations (CFR) requires the aircraft structure be capable of supporting one and one-half times these limit load factors without failure, it is accepted that parts of the aircraft may bend or twist under these loads and that some structural damage may occur.

This 1.5 load limit factor is called the "factor of safety" and provides, to some extent, for loads higher than those expected under normal and reasonable operation. This strength reserve is not something which pilots should willfully abuse; rather, it is there for protection when encountering unexpected conditions.

The above considerations apply to all loading conditions, whether they be due to gusts, maneuvers, or landings. The gust load factor requirements now in effect are substantially the same as those that have been in existence for years. Hundreds of thousands of operational hours have proven them adequate for safety. Since the pilot has little control over gust load factors (except to reduce the aircraft's speed when rough air is encountered), the gust loading requirements are substantially the same for most general aviation type aircraft regardless of their operational use. Generally, the gust load factors control the design of aircraft which are intended for strictly nonacrobatic usage.

An entirely different situation exists in aircraft design with maneuvering load factors. It is necessary to discuss this matter separately with respect to: (1) aircraft designed in accordance with the category system (i.e., normal, utility, acrobatic); and (2) older designs built according to requirements which did not provide for operational categories.

Aircraft designed under the category system are readily identified by a placard in the flight deck, which states the operational category (or categories) in which the aircraft is certificated. The maximum safe load factors (limit load factors) specified for aircraft in the various categories are:

CATEGORY	LIMIT LOAD FACTOR
Normal[1]	3.8 to −1.52
Utility (mild acrobatics, including spins)	4.4 to −1.76
Acrobatic	6.0 to −3.00

[1] For aircraft with gross weight of more than 4,000 pounds, the limit load factor is reduced. To the limit loads given above, a safety factor of 50 percent is added.

There is an upward graduation in load factor with the increasing severity of maneuvers. The category system provides for maximum utility of an aircraft. If normal operation alone is intended, the required load factor (and consequently the weight of the aircraft) is less than if the aircraft is to be employed in training or acrobatic maneuvers as they result in higher maneuvering loads.

Aircraft that do not have the category placard are designs that were constructed under earlier engineering requirements in which no operational restrictions were specifically given to the pilots. For aircraft of this type (up to weights of about 4,000 pounds), the required strength is comparable to present-day utility category aircraft, and the same types of operation are permissible. For aircraft of this type over 4,000 pounds, the load factors decrease with weight. These aircraft should be regarded as being comparable to the normal category

aircraft designed under the category system, and they should be operated accordingly.

Load Factors in Steep Turns

In a constant altitude, coordinated turn in any aircraft, the load factor is the result of two forces: centrifugal force and gravity. *[Figure 4-44]* For any given bank angle, the ROT varies with the airspeed—the higher the speed, the slower the ROT. This compensates for added centrifugal force, allowing the load factor to remain the same.

Figure 4-44. *Two forces cause load factor during turns.*

Figure 4-45 reveals an important fact about turns—the load factor increases at a terrific rate after a bank has reached 45° or 50°. The load factor for any aircraft in a 60° bank is 2 Gs. The load factor in an 80° bank is 5.76 Gs. The wing must produce lift equal to these load factors if altitude is to be maintained.

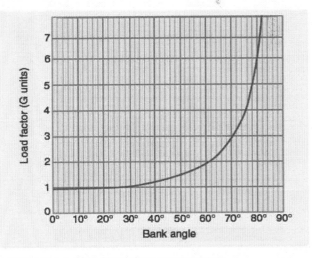

Figure 4-45. *Angle of bank changes load factor.*

It should be noted how rapidly the line denoting load factor rises as it approaches the 90° bank line, which it never quite reaches because a 90° banked, constant altitude turn is not mathematically possible. An aircraft may be banked to 90°, but not in a coordinated turn. An aircraft which can be held in a 90° banked slipping turn is capable of straight knife-edged flight. At slightly more than 80°, the load factor exceeds the limit of 6 Gs, the limit load factor of an acrobatic aircraft.

For a coordinated, constant altitude turn, the approximate maximum bank for the average general aviation aircraft is 60°. This bank and its resultant necessary power setting reach the limit of this type of aircraft. An additional 10° bank increases the load factor by approximately 1 G, bringing it close to the yield point established for these aircraft. [Figure 4-46]

Load Factors and Stalling Speeds

Any aircraft, within the limits of its structure, may be stalled at any airspeed. When a sufficiently high AOA is imposed, the smooth flow of air over an airfoil breaks up and separates, producing an abrupt change of flight characteristics and a sudden loss of lift, which results in a stall.

A study of this effect has revealed that the aircraft's stalling speed increases in proportion to the square root of the load factor. This means that an aircraft with a normal unaccelerated stalling speed of 50 knots can be stalled at 100 knots by inducing a load factor of 4 Gs. If it were possible for this aircraft to withstand a load factor of nine, it could be stalled at a speed of 150 knots. A pilot should be aware:

- Of the danger of inadvertently stalling the aircraft by increasing the load factor, as in a steep turn or spiral;

- When intentionally stalling an aircraft above its design maneuvering speed, a tremendous load factor is imposed.

Figures 4-45 and 4-46 show that banking an aircraft greater than 72° in a steep turn produces a load factor of 3, and the stalling speed is increased significantly. If this turn is made in an aircraft with a normal unaccelerated stalling speed of 45 knots, the airspeed must be kept greater than 75 knots to prevent inducing a stall. A similar effect is experienced in a quick pull up, or any maneuver producing load factors above 1 G. This sudden, unexpected loss of control, particularly in a steep turn or abrupt application of the back elevator control near the ground, has caused many accidents.

Since the load factor is squared as the stalling speed doubles, tremendous loads may be imposed on structures by stalling an aircraft at relatively high airspeeds.

The maximum speed at which an aircraft may be stalled safely is now determined for all new designs. This speed is called the "design maneuvering speed" (V_A) and must be entered in the FAA-approved Airplane Flight Manual/Pilot's Operating Handbook (AFM/POH) of all recently designed aircraft. For older general aviation aircraft, this speed is approximately 1.7 times the normal stalling speed. Thus, an older aircraft which normally stalls at 60 knots must never be stalled at above 102 knots (60 knots × 1.7 = 102 knots). An aircraft with a normal stalling speed of 60 knots stalled at 102 knots undergoes a load factor equal to the square of the increase in speed, or 2.89 Gs (1.7 × 1.7 = 2.89 Gs). (The above figures are approximations to be considered as a guide, and are not the exact answers to any set of problems. The design maneuvering speed should be determined from the particular aircraft's operating limitations provided by the manufacturer.)

Figure 4-46. *Load factor changes stall speed.*

Since the leverage in the control system varies with different aircraft (some types employ "balanced" control surfaces while others do not), the pressure exerted by the pilot on the controls cannot be accepted as an index of the load factors produced in different aircraft. In most cases, load factors can be judged by the experienced pilot from the feel of seat pressure. Load factors can also be measured by an instrument called an "accelerometer," but this instrument is not common in general aviation training aircraft. The development of the ability to judge load factors from the feel of their effect on the body is important. A knowledge of these principles is essential to the development of the ability to estimate load factors.

A thorough knowledge of load factors induced by varying degrees of bank and the V_A aids in the prevention of two of the most serious types of accidents:

1. Stalls from steep turns or excessive maneuvering near the ground

2. Structural failures during acrobatics or other violent maneuvers resulting from loss of control

Load Factors and Flight Maneuvers

Critical load factors apply to all flight maneuvers except unaccelerated straight flight where a load factor of 1 G is always present. Certain maneuvers considered in this section are known to involve relatively high load factors.

Turns

Increased load factors are a characteristic of all banked turns. As noted in the section on load factors in steep turns, load factors become significant to both flight performance and load on wing structure as the bank increases beyond approximately 45°.

The yield factor of the average light plane is reached at a bank of approximately 70° to 75°, and the stalling speed is increased by approximately one-half at a bank of approximately 63°.

Stalls

The normal stall entered from straight-and-level flight, or an unaccelerated straight climb, does not produce added load factors beyond the 1 G of straight-and-level flight. As the stall occurs, however, this load factor may be reduced toward zero, the factor at which nothing seems to have weight. The pilot experiences a sensation of "floating free in space." If recovery is effected by snapping the elevator control forward, negative load factors (or those that impose a down load on the wings and raise the pilot from the seat) may be produced.

During the pull up following stall recovery, significant load factors are sometimes induced. These may be further increased inadvertently during excessive diving (and consequently high airspeed) and abrupt pull ups to level flight. One usually leads to the other, thus increasing the load factor. Abrupt pull ups at high diving speeds may impose critical loads on aircraft structures and may produce recurrent or secondary stalls by increasing the AOA to that of stalling.

As a generalization, a recovery from a stall made by diving only to cruising or design maneuvering airspeed, with a gradual pull up as soon as the airspeed is safely above stalling, can be effected with a load factor not to exceed 2 or 2.5 Gs. A higher load factor should never be necessary unless recovery has been effected with the aircraft's nose near or beyond the vertical attitude, or at extremely low altitudes to avoid diving into the ground.

Spins

A stabilized spin is not different from a stall in any element other than rotation and the same load factor considerations apply to spin recovery as apply to stall recovery. Since spin recoveries are usually effected with the nose much lower than is common in stall recoveries, higher airspeeds and consequently higher load factors are to be expected. The load factor in a proper spin recovery usually is found to be about 2.5 Gs.

The load factor during a spin varies with the spin characteristics of each aircraft, but is usually found to be slightly above the 1 G of level flight. There are two reasons for this:

1. Airspeed in a spin is very low, usually within 2 knots of the unaccelerated stalling speeds.

2. Aircraft pivots, rather than turns, while it is in a spin.

High Speed Stalls

The average light plane is not built to withstand the repeated application of load factors common to high speed stalls. The load factor necessary for these maneuvers produces a stress on the wings and tail structure, which does not leave a reasonable margin of safety in most light aircraft.

The only way this stall can be induced at an airspeed above normal stalling involves the imposition of an added load factor, which may be accomplished by a severe pull on the elevator control. A speed of 1.7 times stalling speed (about 102 knots in a light aircraft with a stalling speed of 60 knots) produces a load factor of 3 Gs. Only a very narrow margin for error can be allowed for acrobatics in light aircraft. To illustrate how rapidly the load factor increases with airspeed, a high-speed stall at 112 knots in the same aircraft would produce a load factor of 4 Gs.

Chandelles and Lazy Eights

A chandelle is a maximum performance climbing turn beginning from approximately straight-and-level flight, and ending at the completion of a precise 180° of turn in a wings-level, nose-high attitude at the minimum controllable airspeed. In this flight maneuver, the aircraft is in a steep climbing turn and almost stalls to gain altitude while changing direction. A lazy eight derives its name from the manner in which the extended longitudinal axis of the aircraft is made to trace a flight pattern in the form of a figure "8" lying on its side. It would be difficult to make a definite statement concerning load factors in these maneuvers as both involve smooth, shallow dives and pull ups. The load factors incurred depend directly on the speed of the dives and the abruptness of the pull ups during these maneuvers.

Generally, the better the maneuver is performed, the less extreme the load factor induced. A chandelle or lazy eight in which the pull-up produces a load factor greater than 2 Gs will not result in as great a gain in altitude, and in low-powered aircraft it may result in a net loss of altitude.

The smoothest pull up possible, with a moderate load factor, delivers the greatest gain in altitude in a chandelle and results in a better overall performance in both chandelles and lazy eights. The recommended entry speed for these maneuvers is generally near the manufacturer's design maneuvering speed which allows maximum development of load factors without exceeding the load limits.

Rough Air

All standard certificated aircraft are designed to withstand loads imposed by gusts of considerable intensity. Gust load factors increase with increasing airspeed, and the strength used for design purposes usually corresponds to the highest level flight speed. In extremely rough air, as in thunderstorms or frontal conditions, it is wise to reduce the speed to the design maneuvering speed. Regardless of the speed held, there may be gusts that can produce loads which exceed the load limits.

Each specific aircraft is designed with a specific G loading that can be imposed on the aircraft without causing structural damage. There are two types of load factors factored into aircraft design, limit load and ultimate load. The limit load is a force applied to an aircraft that causes a bending of the aircraft structure that does not return to the original shape. The ultimate load is the load factor applied to the aircraft beyond the limit load and at which point the aircraft material experiences structural failure (breakage). Load factors lower than the limit load can be sustained without compromising the integrity of the aircraft structure.

Speeds up to but not exceeding the maneuvering speed allows an aircraft to stall prior to experiencing an increase in load factor that would exceed the limit load of the aircraft.

Most AFM/POH now include turbulent air penetration information, which help today's pilots safely fly aircraft capable of a wide range of speeds and altitudes. It is important for the pilot to remember that the maximum "never-exceed" placard dive speeds are determined for smooth air only. High speed dives or acrobatics involving speed above the known maneuvering speed should never be practiced in rough or turbulent air.

Vg Diagram

The flight operating strength of an aircraft is presented on a graph whose vertical scale is based on load factor. [Figure 4-47] The diagram is called a Vg diagram—velocity versus G loads or load factor. Each aircraft has its own Vg diagram which is valid at a certain weight and altitude.

The lines of maximum lift capability (curved lines) are the first items of importance on the Vg diagram. The aircraft in the Figure 4-47 is capable of developing no more than +1 G at 62 mph, the wing level stall speed of the aircraft. Since the maximum load factor varies with the square of the airspeed, the maximum positive lift capability of this aircraft is 2 G at 92 mph, 3 G at 112 mph, 4.4 G at 137 mph, and so forth. Any load factor above this line is unavailable aerodynamically (i.e., the aircraft cannot fly above the line of maximum lift capability because it stalls). The same situation exists for negative lift flight with the exception that the speed necessary to produce a given negative load factor is higher than that to produce the same positive load factor.

If the aircraft is flown at a positive load factor greater than the positive limit load factor of 4.4, structural damage is possible. When the aircraft is operated in this region, objectionable permanent deformation of the primary structure may take place and a high rate of fatigue damage is incurred. Operation above the limit load factor must be avoided in normal operation.

There are two other points of importance on the Vg diagram. One point is the intersection of the positive limit load factor and the line of maximum positive lift capability. The airspeed at this point is the minimum airspeed at which the limit load can be developed aerodynamically. Any airspeed greater than this provides a positive lift capability sufficient to damage the aircraft. Conversely, any airspeed less than this does not provide positive lift capability sufficient to cause damage from excessive flight loads. The usual term given to this speed is "maneuvering speed," since consideration of subsonic

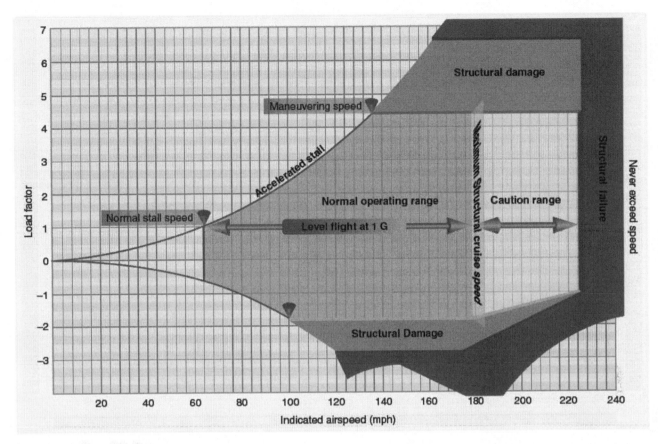

Figure 4-47. *Typical Vg diagram.*

aerodynamics would predict minimum usable turn radius or maneuverability to occur at this condition. The maneuver speed is a valuable reference point, since an aircraft operating below this point cannot produce a damaging positive flight load. Any combination of maneuver and gust cannot create damage due to excess airload when the aircraft is below the maneuver speed.

The other point of importance on the Vg diagram is the intersection of the negative limit load factor and line of maximum negative lift capability. Any airspeed greater than this provides a negative lift capability sufficient to damage the aircraft; any airspeed less than this does not provide negative lift capability sufficient to damage the aircraft from excessive flight loads.

The limit airspeed (or redline speed) is a design reference point for the aircraft—this aircraft is limited to 225 mph. If flight is attempted beyond the limit airspeed, structural damage or structural failure may result from a variety of phenomena.

The aircraft in flight is limited to a regime of airspeeds and Gs which do not exceed the limit (or redline) speed, do not exceed the limit load factor, and cannot exceed the maximum lift capability. The aircraft must be operated within this "envelope" to prevent structural damage and ensure the anticipated service lift of the aircraft is obtained. The pilot must appreciate the Vg diagram as describing the allowable combination of airspeeds and load factors for safe operation. Any maneuver, gust, or gust plus maneuver outside the structural envelope can cause structural damage and effectively shorten the service life of the aircraft.

Rate of Turn

The rate of turn (ROT) is the number of degrees (expressed in degrees per second) of heading change that an aircraft makes. The ROT can be determined by taking the constant of 1,091, multiplying it by the tangent of any bank angle and dividing that product by a given airspeed in knots as illustrated in *Figure 4-48*. If the airspeed is increased and the ROT desired is to be constant, the angle of bank must be increased, otherwise, the ROT decreases. Likewise, if the airspeed is held constant, an aircraft's ROT increases if the bank angle is increased. The formula in *Figures 4-48* through *4-50* depicts the relationship between bank angle and airspeed as they affect the ROT.

NOTE: All airspeed discussed in this section is true airspeed (TAS).

$$\text{ROT} = \frac{1{,}091 \times \text{tangent of the bank angle}}{\text{airspeed (in knots)}}$$

Example The rate of turn for an aircraft in a coordinated turn of 30° and traveling at 120 knots would have a ROT as follows.

$$\text{ROT} = \frac{1{,}091 \times \text{tangent of } 30°}{120 \text{ knots}}$$

$$\text{ROT} = \frac{1{,}091 \times 0.5773 \text{ (tangent of } 30°)}{120 \text{ knots}}$$

$$\text{ROT} = 5.25 \text{ degrees per second}$$

Figure 4-48. *Rate of turn for a given airspeed (knots, TAS) and bank angle.*

Example Suppose we were to increase the speed to 240 knots, what is the rate of turn? Using the same formula from above we see that:

$$\text{ROT} = \frac{1{,}091 \times \text{tangent of } 30°}{240 \text{ knots}}$$

$$\text{ROT} = 2.62 \text{ degrees per second}$$

An increase in speed causes a decrease in the rate of turn when using the same bank angle.

Figure 4-49 *Rate of turn when increasing speed*

Example Suppose we wanted to know what bank angle would give us a rate of turn of 5.25° per second at 240 knots. A slight rearrangement of the formula would indicate it will take a 49° angle of bank to achieve the same ROT used at the lower airspeed of 120 knots.

$$\text{ROT (5.25)} = \frac{1{,}091 \times \text{tangent of } X}{240 \text{ knots}}$$

$$240 \times 5.25 = 1{,}091 \times \text{tangent of } X$$

$$\frac{240 \times 5.25}{1{,}091} = \text{tangent of } X$$

$$1.1549 = \text{tangent of } X$$

$$49° = X$$

Figure 4-50. *To achieve the same rate of turn of an aircraft traveling at 120 knots, an increase of bank angle is required.*

Airspeed significantly effects an aircraft's ROT. If airspeed is increased, the ROT is reduced if using the same angle of bank used at the lower speed. Therefore, if airspeed is increased as illustrated in *Figure 4-49*, it can be inferred that the angle of bank must be increased in order to achieve the same ROT achieved in *Figure 4-50*.

What does this mean on a practicable side? If a given airspeed and bank angle produces a specific ROT, additional conclusions can be made. Knowing the ROT is a given number of degrees of change per second, the number of seconds it takes to travel 360° (a circle) can be determined by simple division. For example, if moving at 120 knots with a 30° bank angle, the ROT is 5.25° per second and it takes 68.6 seconds (360° divided by 5.25 = 68.6 seconds) to make a complete circle. Likewise, if flying at 240 knots TAS and using a 30° angle of bank, the ROT is only about 2.63° per second and it takes about 137 seconds to complete a 360° circle. Looking at the formula, any increase in airspeed is directly proportional to the time the aircraft takes to travel an arc.

So why is this important to understand? Once the ROT is understood, a pilot can determine the distance required to make that particular turn which is explained in radius of turn.

Radius of Turn

The radius of turn is directly linked to the ROT, which explained earlier is a function of both bank angle and airspeed. If the bank angle is held constant and the airspeed is increased, the radius of the turn changes (increases). A higher airspeed causes the aircraft to travel through a longer arc due to a greater speed. An aircraft traveling at 120 knots is able to turn a 360° circle in a tighter radius than an aircraft traveling at 240 knots. In order to compensate for the increase in airspeed, the bank angle would need to be increased.

The radius of turn (R) can be computed using a simple formula. The radius of turn is equal to the velocity squared (V^2) divided by 11.26 times the tangent of the bank angle.

$$R = \frac{V^2}{11.26 \times \text{tangent of bank angle}}$$

Using the examples provided in *Figures 4-48* through *4-50*, the turn radius for each of the two speeds can be computed. Note that if the speed is doubled, the radius is squared. *[Figures 4-51 and 4-52]*

120 knots

$$R = \frac{V^2}{11.26 \times \text{tangent of bank angle}}$$

$$R = \frac{120^2}{11.26 \times \text{tangent of } 30°}$$

$$R = \frac{14{,}400}{11.26 \times 0.5773}$$

$$R = 2{,}215 \text{ feet}$$

The radius of a turn required by an aircraft traveling at 120 knots and using a bank angle of 30° is 2,215 feet.

Figure 4-51. *Radius at 120 knots with bank angle of 30°.*

240 knots

$$R = \frac{V^2}{11.26 \times \text{tangent of bank angle}}$$

$$R = \frac{240^2}{11.26 \times \text{tangent of } 30°}$$

$$R = \frac{57,600}{11.26 \times 0.57735}$$

$$R = 8,861 \text{ feet}$$
(four times the radius at 120 knots)

The radius of a turn required by an aircraft traveling at 240 knots using the same bank angle in *Figure 4-51* is 8,861 feet. Speed is a major factor in a turn.

Figure 4-52. *Radius at 240 knots.*

Another way to determine the radius of turn is speed in using feet per second (fps), π (3.1415) and the ROT. Using the example on page 4-34 in the upper right column, it was determined that an aircraft with a ROT of 5.25 degrees per second required 68.6 seconds to make a complete circle. An aircraft's speed (in knots) can be converted to fps by multiplying it by a constant of 1.69. Therefore, an aircraft traveling at 120 knots (TAS) travels at 202.8 fps. Knowing the speed in fps (202.8) multiplied by the time an aircraft takes to complete a circle (68.6 seconds) can determine the size of the circle; 202.8 times 68.6 equals 13,912 feet. Dividing by π yields a diameter of 4,428 feet, which when divided by 2 equals a radius of 2,214 feet *[Figure 4-53]*, a foot within that determined through use of the formula in *Figure 4-51*.

$$r = \frac{\text{speed (fps)} \times \frac{360}{\text{ROT}}}{\frac{\text{Pi }(\pi)}{2}}$$

$$r = \frac{202.8 \times 68.6}{\frac{\pi}{2}}$$

$$r = \frac{13,912}{\frac{\pi}{2}}$$

$$r = \frac{4,428}{2} = 2,214 \text{ feet}$$

Figure 4-53. *Another formula that can be used for radius.*

In *Figure 4-54*, the pilot enters a canyon and decides to turn 180° to exit. The pilot uses a 30° bank angle in his turn.

Weight and Balance

The aircraft's weight and balance data is important information for a pilot that must be frequently reevaluated. Although the aircraft was weighed during the certification process, this data is not valid indefinitely. Equipment changes or modifications affect the weight and balance data. Too often pilots reduce the aircraft weight and balance into a "rule of thumb" such as: "If I have three passengers, I can load only 100 gallons of fuel; four passengers, 70 gallons."

Weight and balance computations should be part of every preflight briefing. Never assume three passengers are always of equal weight. Instead, do a full computation of all items to be loaded on the aircraft, including baggage, as well as the pilot and passenger. It is recommended that all bags be weighed to make a precise computation of how the aircraft CG is positioned.

The importance of the CG was stressed in the discussion of stability, controllability, and performance. Unequal load distribution causes accidents. A competent pilot understands and respects the effects of CG on an aircraft.

Weight and balance are critical components in the utilization of an aircraft to its fullest potential. The pilot must know how much fuel can be loaded onto the aircraft without violating CG limits, as well as weight limits to conduct long or short flights with or without a full complement of allowable passengers. For example, an aircraft has four seats and can carry 60 gallons of fuel. How many passengers can the aircraft safely carry? Can all those seats be occupied at all times with the varying fuel loads? Four people who each weigh 150 pounds leads to a different weight and balance computation than four people who each weigh 200 pounds. The second scenario loads an additional 200 pounds onto the aircraft and is equal to about 30 gallons of fuel.

The additional weight may or may not place the CG outside of the CG envelope, but the maximum gross weight could be exceeded. The excess weight can overstress the aircraft and degrade the performance.

Aircraft are certified for weight and balance for two principal reasons:

1. The effect of the weight on the aircraft's primary structure and its performance characteristics

2. The effect of the location of this weight on flight characteristics, particularly in stall and spin recovery and stability

Aircraft, such as balloons and weight-shift control, do not require weight and balance computations because the load is suspended below the lifting mechanism. The CG range in these types of aircraft is such that it is difficult to exceed loading limits. For example, the rear seat position and fuel of a weight-shift control aircraft are as close as possible to the hang point with the aircraft in a suspended attitude. Thus, load variations have little effect on the CG. This also holds true for the balloon basket or gondola. While it is difficult

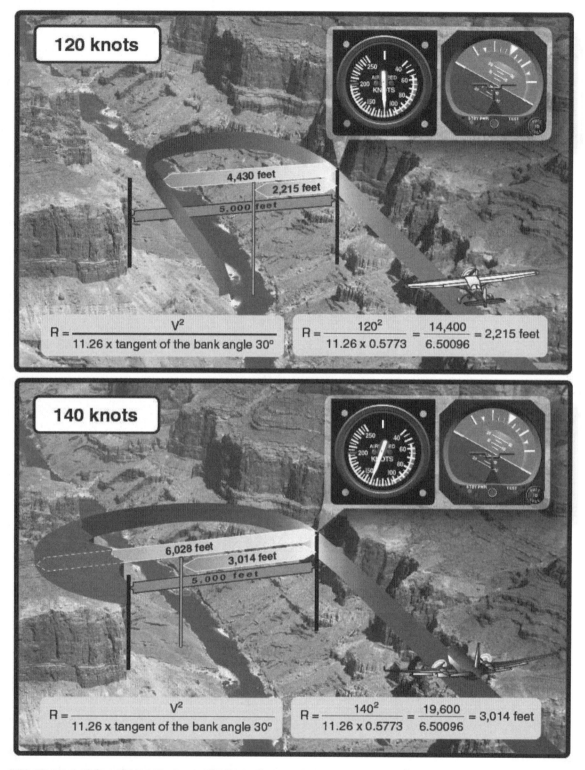

Figure 4-54. *Two aircraft have flown into a canyon by error. The canyon is 5,000 feet across and has sheer cliffs on both sides. The pilot in the top image is flying at 120 knots. After realizing the error, the pilot banks hard and uses a 30° bank angle to reverse course. This aircraft requires about 4,000 feet to turn 180°, and makes it out of the canyon safely. The pilot in the bottom image is flying at 140 knots and also uses a 30° angle of bank in an attempt to reverse course. The aircraft, although flying just 20 knots faster than the aircraft in the top image, requires over 6,000 feet to reverse course to safety. Unfortunately, the canyon is only 5,000 feet across and the aircraft will hit the canyon wall. The point is that airspeed is the most influential factor in determining how much distance is required to turn. Many pilots have made the error of increasing the steepness of their bank angle when a simple reduction of speed would have been more appropriate.*

to exceed CG limits in these aircraft, pilots should never overload an aircraft because overloading causes structural damage and failures. Weight and balance computations are not required, but pilots should calculate weight and remain within the manufacturer's established limit.

Effect of Weight on Flight Performance

The takeoff/climb and landing performance of an aircraft are determined on the basis of its maximum allowable takeoff and landing weights. A heavier gross weight results in a longer takeoff run and shallower climb, and a faster touchdown speed and longer landing roll. Even a minor overload may make it impossible for the aircraft to clear an obstacle that normally would not be a problem during takeoff under more favorable conditions.

The detrimental effects of overloading on performance are not limited to the immediate hazards involved with takeoffs and landings. Overloading has an adverse effect on all climb and cruise performance which leads to overheating during climbs, added wear on engine parts, increased fuel consumption, slower cruising speeds, and reduced range.

The manufacturers of modern aircraft furnish weight and balance data with each aircraft produced. Generally, this information may be found in the FAA-approved AFM/POH and easy-to-read charts for determining weight and balance data are now provided. Increased performance and load-carrying capability of these aircraft require strict adherence to the operating limitations prescribed by the manufacturer. Deviations from the recommendations can result in structural damage or complete failure of the aircraft's structure. Even if an aircraft is loaded well within the maximum weight limitations, it is imperative that weight distribution be within the limits of CG location. The preceding brief study of aerodynamics and load factors points out the reasons for this precaution. The following discussion is background information into some of the reasons why weight and balance conditions are important to the safe flight of an aircraft.

In some aircraft, it is not possible to fill all seats, baggage compartments, and fuel tanks, and still remain within approved weight or balance limits. For example, in several popular four-place aircraft, the fuel tanks may not be filled to capacity when four occupants and their baggage are carried. In a certain two-place aircraft, no baggage may be carried in the compartment aft of the seats when spins are to be practiced. It is important for a pilot to be aware of the weight and balance limitations of the aircraft being flown and the reasons for these limitations.

Effect of Weight on Aircraft Structure

The effect of additional weight on the wing structure of an aircraft is not readily apparent. Airworthiness requirements prescribe that the structure of an aircraft certificated in the normal category (in which acrobatics are prohibited) must be strong enough to withstand a load factor of 3.8 Gs to take care of dynamic loads caused by maneuvering and gusts. This means that the primary structure of the aircraft can withstand a load of 3.8 times the approved gross weight of the aircraft without structural failure occurring. If this is accepted as indicative of the load factors that may be imposed during operations for which the aircraft is intended, a 100-pound overload imposes a potential structural overload of 380 pounds. The same consideration is even more impressive in the case of utility and acrobatic category aircraft, which have load factor requirements of 4.4 and 6.0, respectively.

Structural failures which result from overloading may be dramatic and catastrophic, but more often they affect structural components progressively in a manner that is difficult to detect and expensive to repair. Habitual overloading tends to cause cumulative stress and damage that may not be detected during preflight inspections and result in structural failure later during completely normal operations. The additional stress placed on structural parts by overloading is believed to accelerate the occurrence of metallic fatigue failures.

A knowledge of load factors imposed by flight maneuvers and gusts emphasizes the consequences of an increase in the gross weight of an aircraft. The structure of an aircraft about to undergo a load factor of 3 Gs, as in recovery from a steep dive, must be prepared to withstand an added load of 300 pounds for each 100-pound increase in weight. It should be noted that this would be imposed by the addition of about 16 gallons of unneeded fuel in a particular aircraft. FAA-certificated civil aircraft have been analyzed structurally and tested for flight at the maximum gross weight authorized and within the speeds posted for the type of flights to be performed. Flights at weights in excess of this amount are quite possible and often are well within the performance capabilities of an aircraft. This fact should not mislead the pilot, as the pilot may not realize that loads for which the aircraft was not designed are being imposed on all or some part of the structure.

In loading an aircraft with either passengers or cargo, the structure must be considered. Seats, baggage compartments, and cabin floors are designed for a certain load or concentration of load and no more. For example, a light plane baggage compartment may be placarded for 20 pounds because of the limited strength of its supporting structure even though the aircraft may not be overloaded or out of CG limits with more weight at that location.

Effect of Weight on Stability and Controllability

Overloading also effects stability. An aircraft that is stable and controllable when loaded normally may have very different flight characteristics when overloaded. Although the distribution of weight has the most direct effect on this, an increase in the aircraft's gross weight may be expected to have an adverse effect on stability, regardless of location of the CG. The stability of many certificated aircraft is completely unsatisfactory if the gross weight is exceeded.

Effect of Load Distribution

The effect of the position of the CG on the load imposed on an aircraft's wing in flight is significant to climb and cruising performance. An aircraft with forward loading is "heavier" and consequently, slower than the same aircraft with the CG further aft.

Figure 4-55 illustrates why this is true. With forward loading, "nose-up" trim is required in most aircraft to maintain level cruising flight. Nose-up trim involves setting the tail surfaces to produce a greater down load on the aft portion of the fuselage, which adds to the wing loading and the total lift required from the wing if altitude is to be maintained. This requires a higher AOA of the wing, which results in more drag and, in turn, produces a higher stalling speed.

Figure 4-55. *Effect of load distribution on balance.*

With aft loading and "nose-down" trim, the tail surfaces exert less down load, relieving the wing of that much wing loading and lift required to maintain altitude. The required AOA of the wing is less, so the drag is less, allowing for a faster

cruise speed. Theoretically, a neutral load on the tail surfaces in cruising flight would produce the most efficient overall performance and fastest cruising speed, but it would also result in instability. Modern aircraft are designed to require a down load on the tail for stability and controllability.

A zero indication on the trim tab control is not necessarily the same as "neutral trim" because of the force exerted by downwash from the wings and the fuselage on the tail surfaces.

The effects of the distribution of the aircraft's useful load have a significant influence on its flight characteristics, even when the load is within the CG limits and the maximum permissible gross weight. Important among these effects are changes in controllability, stability, and the actual load imposed on the wing.

Generally, an aircraft becomes less controllable, especially at slow flight speeds, as the CG is moved further aft. An aircraft which cleanly recovers from a prolonged spin with the CG at one position may fail completely to respond to normal recovery attempts when the CG is moved aft by one or two inches.

It is common practice for aircraft designers to establish an aft CG limit that is within one inch of the maximum which allows normal recovery from a one-turn spin. When certificating an aircraft in the utility category to permit intentional spins, the aft CG limit is usually established at a point several inches forward of that permissible for certification in the normal category.

Another factor affecting controllability, which has become more important in current designs of large aircraft, is the effect of long moment arms to the positions of heavy equipment and cargo. The same aircraft may be loaded to maximum gross weight within its CG limits by concentrating fuel, passengers, and cargo near the design CG, or by dispersing fuel and cargo loads in wingtip tanks and cargo bins forward and aft of the cabin.

With the same total weight and CG, maneuvering the aircraft or maintaining level flight in turbulent air requires the application of greater control forces when the load is dispersed. The longer moment arms to the positions of the heavy fuel and cargo loads must be overcome by the action of the control surfaces. An aircraft with full outboard wing tanks or tip tanks tends to be sluggish in roll when control situations are marginal, while one with full nose and aft cargo bins tends to be less responsive to the elevator controls.

The rearward CG limit of an aircraft is determined largely by considerations of stability. The original airworthiness requirements for a type certificate specify that an aircraft in flight at a certain speed dampens out vertical displacement of the nose within a certain number of oscillations. An aircraft loaded too far rearward may not do this. Instead, when the nose is momentarily pulled up, it may alternately climb and dive becoming steeper with each oscillation. This instability is not only uncomfortable to occupants, but it could even become dangerous by making the aircraft unmanageable under certain conditions.

The recovery from a stall in any aircraft becomes progressively more difficult as its CG moves aft. This is particularly important in spin recovery, as there is a point in rearward loading of any aircraft at which a "flat" spin develops. A flat spin is one in which centrifugal force, acting through a CG located well to the rear, pulls the tail of the aircraft out away from the axis of the spin, making it impossible to get the nose down and recover.

An aircraft loaded to the rear limit of its permissible CG range handles differently in turns and stall maneuvers and has different landing characteristics than when it is loaded near the forward limit.

The forward CG limit is determined by a number of considerations. As a safety measure, it is required that the trimming device, whether tab or adjustable stabilizer, be capable of holding the aircraft in a normal glide with the power off. A conventional aircraft must be capable of a full stall, power-off landing in order to ensure minimum landing speed in emergencies. A tailwheel-type aircraft loaded excessively nose-heavy is difficult to taxi, particularly in high winds. It can be nosed over easily by use of the brakes, and it is difficult to land without bouncing since it tends to pitch down on the wheels as it is slowed down and flared for landing. Steering difficulties on the ground may occur in nosewheel-type aircraft, particularly during the landing roll and takeoff. To summarize the effects of load distribution:

- The CG position influences the lift and AOA of the wing, the amount and direction of force on the tail, and the degree of deflection of the stabilizer needed to supply the proper tail force for equilibrium. The latter is very important because of its relationship to elevator control force.

- The aircraft stalls at a higher speed with a forward CG location. This is because the stalling AOA is reached at a higher speed due to increased wing loading.

- Higher elevator control forces normally exist with a forward CG location due to the increased stabilizer deflection required to balance the aircraft.

- The aircraft cruises faster with an aft CG location because of reduced drag. The drag is reduced because a smaller AOA and less downward deflection of the stabilizer are required to support the aircraft and overcome the nose-down pitching tendency.

- The aircraft becomes less stable as the CG is moved rearward. This is because when the CG is moved rearward it causes an increase in the AOA. Therefore, the wing contribution to the aircraft's stability is now decreased, while the tail contribution is still stabilizing. When the point is reached that the wing and tail contributions balance, then neutral stability exists. Any CG movement further aft results in an unstable aircraft.

- A forward CG location increases the need for greater back elevator pressure. The elevator may no longer be able to oppose any increase in nose-down pitching. Adequate elevator control is needed to control the aircraft throughout the airspeed range down to the stall.

A detailed discussion and additional information relating to weight and balance can be found in Chapter 9, Weight and Balance.

High Speed Flight

Subsonic Versus Supersonic Flow

In subsonic aerodynamics, the theory of lift is based upon the forces generated on a body and a moving gas (air) in which it is immersed. At speeds of approximately 260 knots, air can be considered incompressible in that, at a fixed altitude, its density remains nearly constant while its pressure varies. Under this assumption, air acts the same as water and is classified as a fluid. Subsonic aerodynamic theory also assumes the effects of viscosity (the property of a fluid that tends to prevent motion of one part of the fluid with respect to another) are negligible, and classifies air as an ideal fluid, conforming to the principles of ideal-fluid aerodynamics such as continuity, Bernoulli's principle, and circulation.

In reality, air is compressible and viscous. While the effects of these properties are negligible at low speeds, compressibility effects in particular become increasingly important as speed increases. Compressibility (and to a lesser extent viscosity) is of paramount importance at speeds approaching the speed of sound. In these speed ranges, compressibility causes a change in the density of the air around an aircraft.

During flight, a wing produces lift by accelerating the airflow over the upper surface. This accelerated air can, and does, reach sonic speeds even though the aircraft itself may be flying subsonic. At some extreme AOAs, in some aircraft, the speed of the air over the top surface of the wing may be double the aircraft's speed. It is therefore entirely possible to have both supersonic and subsonic airflow on an aircraft at the same time. When flow velocities reach sonic speeds at some location on an aircraft (such as the area of maximum camber on the wing), further acceleration results in the onset of compressibility effects such as shock wave formation, drag increase, buffeting, stability, and control difficulties. Subsonic flow principles are invalid at all speeds above this point. [Figure 4-56]

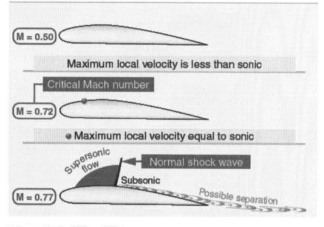

Figure 4-56. *Wing airflow.*

Speed Ranges

The speed of sound varies with temperature. Under standard temperature conditions of 15 °C, the speed of sound at sea level is 661 knots. At 40,000 feet, where the temperature is –55 °C, the speed of sound decreases to 574 knots. In high-speed flight and/or high-altitude flight, the measurement of speed is expressed in terms of a "Mach number"—the ratio of the true airspeed of the aircraft to the speed of sound in the same atmospheric conditions. An aircraft traveling at the speed of sound is traveling at Mach 1.0. Aircraft speed regimes are defined approximately as follows:

Subsonic—Mach numbers below 0.75

Transonic—Mach numbers from 0.75 to 1.20

Supersonic—Mach numbers from 1.20 to 5.00

Hypersonic—Mach numbers above 5.00

While flights in the transonic and supersonic ranges are common occurrences for military aircraft, civilian jet aircraft normally operate in a cruise speed range of Mach 0.7 to Mach 0.90.

The speed of an aircraft in which airflow over any part of the aircraft or structure under consideration first reaches (but does not exceed) Mach 1.0 is termed "critical Mach number" or "Mach Crit." Thus, critical Mach number is

the boundary between subsonic and transonic flight and is largely dependent on the wing and airfoil design. Critical Mach number is an important point in transonic flight. When shock waves form on the aircraft, airflow separation followed by buffet and aircraft control difficulties can occur. Shock waves, buffet, and airflow separation take place above critical Mach number. A jet aircraft typically is most efficient when cruising at or near its critical Mach number. At speeds 5–10 percent above the critical Mach number, compressibility effects begin. Drag begins to rise sharply. Associated with the "drag rise" are buffet, trim and stability changes, and a decrease in control surface effectiveness. This is the point of "drag divergence." [Figure 4-57]

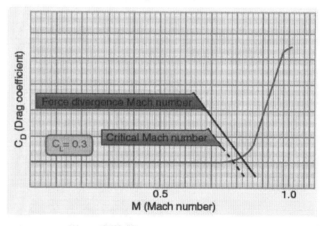

Figure 4-57. *Critical Mach.*

V_{MO}/M_{MO} is defined as the maximum operating limit speed. V_{MO} is expressed in knots calibrated airspeed (KCAS), while M_{MO} is expressed in Mach number. The V_{MO} limit is usually associated with operations at lower altitudes and deals with structural loads and flutter. The M_{MO} limit is associated with operations at higher altitudes and is usually more concerned with compressibility effects and flutter. At lower altitudes, structural loads and flutter are of concern; at higher altitudes, compressibility effects and flutter are of concern.

Adherence to these speeds prevents structural problems due to dynamic pressure or flutter, degradation in aircraft control response due to compressibility effects (e.g., Mach Tuck, aileron reversal, or buzz), and separated airflow due to shock waves resulting in loss of lift or vibration and buffet. Any of these phenomena could prevent the pilot from being able to adequately control the aircraft.

For example, an early civilian jet aircraft had a V_{MO} limit of 306 KCAS up to approximately FL 310 (on a standard day). At this altitude (FL 310), an M_{MO} of 0.82 was approximately equal to 306 KCAS. Above this altitude, an M_{MO} of 0.82 always equaled a KCAS less than 306 KCAS and, thus, became the operating limit as you could not reach the V_{MO} limit without first reaching the M_{MO} limit. For example, at FL 380, an M_{MO} of 0.82 is equal to 261 KCAS.

Mach Number Versus Airspeed

It is important to understand how airspeed varies with Mach number. As an example, consider how the stall speed of a jet transport aircraft varies with an increase in altitude. The increase in altitude results in a corresponding drop in air density and outside temperature. Suppose this jet transport is in the clean configuration (gear and flaps up) and weighs 550,000 pounds. The aircraft might stall at approximately 152 KCAS at sea level. This is equal to (on a standard day) a true velocity of 152 KTAS and a Mach number of 0.23. At FL 380, the aircraft will still stall at approximately 152 KCAS but the true velocity is about 287 KTAS with a Mach number of 0.50.

Although the stalling speed has remained the same for our purposes, both the Mach number and TAS have increased. With increasing altitude, the air density has decreased; this requires a faster true airspeed in order to have the same pressure sensed by the pitot tube for the same KCAS or KIAS (for our purposes, KCAS and KIAS are relatively close to each other). The dynamic pressure the wing experiences at FL 380 at 287 KTAS is the same as at sea level at 152 KTAS. However, it is flying at higher Mach number.

Another factor to consider is the speed of sound. A decrease in temperature in a gas results in a decrease in the speed of sound. Thus, as the aircraft climbs in altitude with outside temperature dropping, the speed of sound is dropping. At sea level, the speed of sound is approximately 661 KCAS, while at FL 380 it is 574 KCAS. Thus, for our jet transport aircraft, the stall speed (in KTAS) has gone from 152 at sea level to 287 at FL 380. Simultaneously, the speed of sound (in KCAS) has decreased from 661 to 574 and the Mach number has increased from 0.23 (152 KTAS divided by 661 KTAS) to 0.50 (287 KTAS divided by 574 KTAS). All the while the KCAS for stall has remained constant at 152. This describes what happens when the aircraft is at a constant KCAS with increasing altitude, but what happens when the pilot keeps Mach constant during the climb? In normal jet flight operations, the climb is at 250 KIAS (or higher (e.g. heavy)) to 10,000 feet and then at a specified en route climb airspeed (such as about 330 if a DC10) until reaching an altitude in the "mid-twenties" where the pilot then climbs at a constant Mach number to cruise altitude.

Assuming for illustration purposes that the pilot climbs at a M_{MO} of 0.82 from sea level up to FL 380. KCAS goes from 543 to 261. The KIAS at each altitude would follow the same behavior and just differ by a few knots. Recall from the earlier discussion that the speed of sound is decreasing with the drop in temperature as the aircraft climbs. The Mach number is simply the ratio of the true airspeed to the speed of sound at flight conditions. The significance of this is that at a constant Mach number climb, the KCAS (and KTAS or KIAS as well) is falling off.

If the aircraft climbed high enough at this constant M_{MO} with decreasing KIAS, KCAS, and KTAS, it would begin to approach its stall speed. At some point the stall speed of the aircraft in Mach number could equal the M_{MO} of the aircraft, and the pilot could neither slow up (without stalling) nor speed up (without exceeding the max operating speed of the aircraft). This has been dubbed the "coffin corner."

Boundary Layer

The viscous nature of airflow reduces the local velocities on a surface and is responsible for skin friction. As discussed earlier in the chapter, the layer of air over the wing's surface that is slowed down or stopped by viscosity, is the boundary layer. There are two different types of boundary layer flow: laminar and turbulent.

Laminar Boundary Layer Flow

The laminar boundary layer is a very smooth flow, while the turbulent boundary layer contains swirls or "eddies." The laminar flow creates less skin friction drag than the turbulent flow, but is less stable. Boundary layer flow over a wing surface begins as a smooth laminar flow. As the flow continues back from the leading edge, the laminar boundary layer increases in thickness.

Turbulent Boundary Layer Flow

At some distance back from the leading edge, the smooth laminar flow breaks down and transitions to a turbulent flow. From a drag standpoint, it is advisable to have the transition from laminar to turbulent flow as far aft on the wing as possible, or have a large amount of the wing surface within the laminar portion of the boundary layer. The low energy laminar flow, however, tends to break down more suddenly than the turbulent layer.

Boundary Layer Separation

Another phenomenon associated with viscous flow is separation. Separation occurs when the airflow breaks away from an airfoil. The natural progression is from laminar boundary layer to turbulent boundary layer and then to airflow separation. Airflow separation produces high drag and ultimately destroys lift. The boundary layer separation point moves forward on the wing as the AOA is increased. *[Figure 4-58]*

Figure 4-58. *Boundary layer.*

Vortex generators are used to delay or prevent shock wave induced boundary layer separation encountered in transonic flight. They are small low aspect ratio airfoils placed at a 12° to 15° AOA to the airstream. Usually spaced a few inches apart along the wing ahead of the ailerons or other control surfaces, vortex generators create a vortex which mixes the boundary airflow with the high energy airflow just above the surface. This produces higher surface velocities and increases the energy of the boundary layer. Thus, a stronger shock wave is necessary to produce airflow separation.

Shock Waves

When an airplane flies at subsonic speeds, the air ahead is "warned" of the airplane's coming by a pressure change transmitted ahead of the airplane at the speed of sound. Because of this warning, the air begins to move aside before the airplane arrives and is prepared to let it pass easily. When the airplane's speed reaches the speed of sound, the pressure change can no longer warn the air ahead because the airplane is keeping up with its own pressure waves. Rather, the air particles pile up in front of the airplane causing a sharp decrease in the flow velocity directly in front of the airplane with a corresponding increase in air pressure and density.

As the airplane's speed increases beyond the speed of sound, the pressure and density of the compressed air ahead of it increase, the area of compression extending some distance ahead of the airplane. At some point in the airstream, the air particles are completely undisturbed, having had no advanced warning of the airplane's approach, and in the next instant the same air particles are forced to undergo sudden and drastic changes in temperature, pressure, density, and velocity. The boundary between the undisturbed air and the region of compressed air is called a shock or "compression" wave. This same type of wave is formed whenever a supersonic airstream is slowed to subsonic without a change in direction, such as when the airstream is accelerated to sonic speed over the cambered portion of a wing, and then decelerated to subsonic speed as the area of maximum camber is passed. A shock wave forms as a boundary between the supersonic and subsonic ranges.

Whenever a shock wave forms perpendicular to the airflow, it is termed a "normal" shock wave, and the flow immediately behind the wave is subsonic. A supersonic airstream passing through a normal shock wave experiences these changes:

- The airstream is slowed to subsonic.

- The airflow immediately behind the shock wave does not change direction.

- The static pressure and density of the airstream behind the wave is greatly increased.

- The energy of the airstream (indicated by total pressure—dynamic plus static) is greatly reduced.

Shock wave formation causes an increase in drag. One of the principal effects of a shock wave is the formation of a dense high pressure region immediately behind the wave. The instability of the high pressure region, and the fact that part of the velocity energy of the airstream is converted to heat as it flows through the wave is a contributing factor in the drag increase, but the drag resulting from airflow separation is much greater. If the shock wave is strong, the boundary layer may not have sufficient kinetic energy to withstand airflow separation. The drag incurred in the transonic region due to shock wave formation and airflow separation is known as "wave drag." When speed exceeds the critical Mach number by about 10 percent, wave drag increases sharply. A considerable increase in thrust (power) is required to increase flight speed beyond this point into the supersonic range where, depending on the airfoil shape and the angle of attack, the boundary layer may reattach.

Normal shock waves form on the wing's upper surface and form an additional area of supersonic flow and a normal shock wave on the lower surface. As flight speed approaches the speed of sound, the areas of supersonic flow enlarge and the shock waves move nearer the trailing edge. *[Figure 4-59]*

Associated with "drag rise" are buffet (known as Mach buffet), trim and stability changes, and a decrease in control

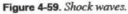

Figure 4-59. *Shock waves.*

force effectiveness. The loss of lift due to airflow separation results in a loss of downwash, and a change in the position of the center pressure on the wing. Airflow separation produces a turbulent wake behind the wing, which causes the tail surfaces to buffet (vibrate). The nose-up and nose-down pitch control provided by the horizontal tail is dependent on the downwash behind the wing. Thus, an increase in downwash decreases the horizontal tail's pitch control effectiveness since it effectively increases the angle of attack that the tail surface is seeing. Movement of the wing CP affects the wing pitching moment. If the CP moves aft, a diving moment referred to as "Mach tuck" or "tuck under" is produced, and if it moves forward, a nose-up moment is produced. This is the primary reason for the development of the T-tail configuration on many turbine-powered aircraft, which places the horizontal stabilizer as far as practical from the turbulence of the wings.

Sweepback

Most of the difficulties of transonic flight are associated with shock wave induced flow separation. Therefore, any means of delaying or alleviating the shock induced separation improves aerodynamic performance. One method is wing sweepback. Sweepback theory is based upon the concept that it is only the component of the airflow perpendicular to the leading edge of the wing that affects pressure distribution and formation of shock waves. *[Figure 4-60]*

On a straight wing aircraft, the airflow strikes the wing leading edge at 90°, and its full impact produces pressure and lift. A wing with sweepback is struck by the same airflow at an angle smaller than 90°. This airflow on the swept wing has

Figure 4-60. *Sweepback effect.*

the effect of persuading the wing into believing that it is flying slower than it really is; thus the formation of shock waves is delayed. Advantages of wing sweep include an increase in critical Mach number, force divergence Mach number, and the Mach number at which drag rises peaks. In other words, sweep delays the onset of compressibility effects.

The Mach number, which produces a sharp change in drag coefficient, is termed the "force divergence" Mach number and, for most airfoils, usually exceeds the critical Mach number by 5 to 10 percent. At this speed, the airflow separation induced by shock wave formation can create significant variations in the drag, lift, or pitching moment coefficients. In addition to the delay of the onset of compressibility effects, sweepback reduces the magnitude in the changes of drag, lift or moment coefficients. In other words, the use of sweepback "softens" the force divergence.

A disadvantage of swept wings is that they tend to stall at the wingtips rather than at the wing roots. *[Figure 4-61]* This is because the boundary layer tends to flow spanwise toward the tips and to separate near the leading edges. Because the tips of a swept wing are on the aft part of the wing (behind the CL), a wingtip stall causes the CL to move forward on the wing, forcing the nose to rise further. The tendency for tip stall is greatest when wing sweep and taper are combined.

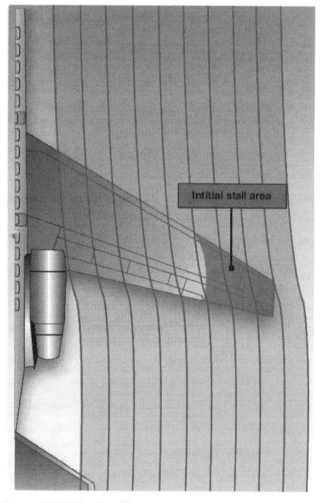

Figure 4-61. *Wingtip stall.*

The stall situation can be aggravated by a T-tail configuration, which affords little or no pre-stall warning in the form of tail control surface buffet. *[Figure 4-62]* The T-tail, being above the wing wake remains effective even after the wing has begun to stall, allowing the pilot to inadvertently drive the wing into a deeper stall at a much greater AOA. If the horizontal tail surfaces then become buried in the wing's wake, the elevator may lose all effectiveness, making it impossible to reduce pitch attitude and break the stall. In the pre-stall and immediate post-stall regimes, the lift/drag qualities of a swept wing aircraft (specifically the enormous increase in drag at low speeds) can cause an increasingly

descending flightpath with no change in pitch attitude, further increasing the AOA. In this situation, without reliable AOA information, a nose-down pitch attitude with an increasing airspeed is no guarantee that recovery has been effected, and up-elevator movement at this stage may merely keep the aircraft stalled.

Figure 4-62. *T-tail stall.*

It is a characteristic of T-tail aircraft to pitch up viciously when stalled in extreme nose-high attitudes, making recovery difficult or violent. The stick pusher inhibits this type of stall. At approximately one knot above stall speed, pre-programmed stick forces automatically move the stick forward, preventing the stall from developing. A G-limiter may also be incorporated into the system to prevent the pitch down generated by the stick pusher from imposing excessive loads on the aircraft. A "stick shaker," on the other hand provides stall warning when the airspeed is five to seven percent above stall speed.

Mach Buffet Boundaries

Mach buffet is a function of the speed of the airflow over the wing—not necessarily the speed of the aircraft. Any time that too great a lift demand is made on the wing, whether from too fast an airspeed or from too high an AOA near the MMO, the "high-speed" buffet occurs. There are also occasions when the buffet can be experienced at much lower speeds known as the "low-speed Mach buffet."

An aircraft flown at a speed too slow for its weight and altitude necessitating a high AOA is the most likely situation to cause a low-speed Mach buffet. This very high AOA has the effect of increasing airflow velocity over the upper surface of the wing until the same effects of the shock waves and buffet occur as in the high-speed buffet situation. The AOA of the wing has the greatest effect on inducing the Mach buffet at either the high-speed or low-speed boundaries for the aircraft. The conditions that increase the AOA, the speed of the airflow over the wing, and chances of Mach buffet are:

- High altitudes—the higher an aircraft flies, the thinner the air and the greater the AOA required to produce the lift needed to maintain level flight.

- Heavy weights—the heavier the aircraft, the greater the lift required of the wing, and all other things being equal, the greater the AOA.

- G loading—an increase in the G loading on the aircraft has the same effect as increasing the weight of the aircraft. Whether the increase in G forces is caused by turns, rough control usage, or turbulence, the effect of increasing the wing's AOA is the same.

High Speed Flight Controls

On high-speed aircraft, flight controls are divided into primary flight controls and secondary or auxiliary flight controls. The primary flight controls maneuver the aircraft about the pitch, roll, and yaw axes. They include the ailerons, elevator, and rudder. Secondary or auxiliary flight controls include tabs, leading edge flaps, trailing edge flaps, spoilers, and slats.

Spoilers are used on the upper surface of the wing to spoil or reduce lift. High speed aircraft, due to their clean low drag design use spoilers as speed brakes to slow them down. Spoilers are extended immediately after touchdown to dump lift and thus transfer the weight of the aircraft from the wings onto the wheels for better braking performance. [Figure 4-63]

Jet transport aircraft have small ailerons. The space for ailerons is limited because as much of the wing trailing edge as possible is needed for flaps. Also, a conventional size aileron would cause wing twist at high speed. For that reason, spoilers are used in unison with ailerons to provide additional roll control.

Some jet transports have two sets of ailerons, a pair of outboard low-speed ailerons and a pair of high-speed inboard ailerons. When the flaps are fully retracted after takeoff, the outboard ailerons are automatically locked out in the faired position.

When used for roll control, the spoiler on the side of the up-going aileron extends and reduces the lift on that side, causing the wing to drop. If the spoilers are extended as

speed brakes, they can still be used for roll control. If they are the differential type, they extend further on one side and retract on the other side. If they are the non-differential type, they extend further on one side but do not retract on the other side. When fully extended as speed brakes, the non-differential spoilers remain extended and do not supplement the ailerons.

To obtain a smooth stall and a higher AOA without airflow separation, the wing's leading edge should have a well-rounded almost blunt shape that the airflow can adhere to at the higher AOA. With this shape, the airflow separation starts at the trailing edge and progresses forward gradually as AOA is increased.

The pointed leading edge necessary for high-speed flight results in an abrupt stall and restricts the use of trailing edge flaps because the airflow cannot follow the sharp curve around the wing leading edge. The airflow tends to tear loose rather suddenly from the upper surface at a moderate AOA. To utilize trailing edge flaps, and thus increase the C_{L-MAX}, the wing must go to a higher AOA without airflow separation. Therefore, leading edge slots, slats, and flaps are used to improve the low-speed characteristics during takeoff, climb, and landing. Although these devices are not as powerful as trailing edge flaps, they are effective when used full span in combination with high-lift trailing edge flaps. With the aid of these sophisticated high-lift devices, airflow separation is delayed and the C_{L-MAX} is increased considerably. In fact, a 50 knot reduction in stall speed is not uncommon.

The operational requirements of a large jet transport aircraft necessitate large pitch trim changes. Some requirements are:

- A large CG range

- A large speed range

- The ability to perform large trim changes due to wing leading edge and trailing edge high-lift devices without limiting the amount of elevator remaining

- Maintaining trim drag to a minimum

These requirements are met by the use of a variable incidence horizontal stabilizer. Large trim changes on a fixed-tail aircraft require large elevator deflections. At these large deflections, little further elevator movement remains in the same direction. A variable incidence horizontal stabilizer is designed to take out the trim changes. The stabilizer is larger than the elevator, and consequently does not need to be moved through as large an angle. This leaves the elevator streamlining the tail plane with a full range of movement up and down. The variable incidence horizontal stabilizer can

Figure 4-63. *Control surfaces.*

be set to handle the bulk of the pitch control demand, with the elevator handling the rest. On aircraft equipped with a variable incidence horizontal stabilizer, the elevator is smaller and less effective in isolation than it is on a fixed-tail aircraft. In comparison to other flight controls, the variable incidence horizontal stabilizer is enormously powerful in its effect.

Because of the size and high speeds of jet transport aircraft, the forces required to move the control surfaces can be beyond the strength of the pilot. Consequently, the control surfaces are actuated by hydraulic or electrical power units. Moving the controls in the flight deck signals the control angle required, and the power unit positions the actual control surface. In the event of complete power unit failure, movement of the control surface can be effected by manually controlling the control tabs. Moving the control tab upsets the aerodynamic balance which causes the control surface to move.

Chapter Summary

In order to sustain an aircraft in flight, a pilot must understand how thrust, drag, lift, and weight act on the aircraft. By understanding the aerodynamics of flight, how design, weight, load factors, and gravity affect an aircraft during flight maneuvers from stalls to high speed flight, the pilot learns how to control the balance between these forces. For information on stall speeds, load factors, and other important aircraft data, always consult the AFM/POH for specific information pertaining to the aircraft being flown.

Chapter 5
Flight Controls

Introduction

This chapter focuses on the flight control systems a pilot uses to control the forces of flight, and the aircraft's direction and attitude. It should be noted that flight control systems and characteristics can vary greatly depending on the type of aircraft flown. The most basic flight control system designs are mechanical and date back to early aircraft. They operate with a collection of mechanical parts such as rods, cables, pulleys, and sometimes chains to transmit the forces of the flight deck controls to the control surfaces. Mechanical flight control systems are still used today in small general and sport category aircraft where the aerodynamic forces are not excessive. *[Figure 5-1]*

Nose-down trim

Elevator

Trim tab

Tab up—Elevator down

Nose-up trim

Elevator

Trim tab

Tab down—Elevator up

Figure 5-1. *Mechanical flight control system.*

As aviation matured and aircraft designers learned more about aerodynamics, the industry produced larger and faster aircraft. Therefore, the aerodynamic forces acting upon the control surfaces increased exponentially. To make the control force required by pilots manageable, aircraft engineers designed more complex systems. At first, hydromechanical designs, consisting of a mechanical circuit and a hydraulic circuit, were used to reduce the complexity, weight, and limitations of mechanical flight controls systems. *[Figure 5-2]*

Figure 5-2. *Hydromechanical flight control system.*

As aircraft became more sophisticated, the control surfaces were actuated by electric motors, digital computers, or fiber optic cables. Called "fly-by-wire," this flight control system replaces the physical connection between pilot controls and the flight control surfaces with an electrical interface. In addition, in some large and fast aircraft, controls are boosted by hydraulically or electrically actuated systems. In both the fly-by-wire and boosted controls, the feel of the control reaction is fed back to the pilot by simulated means.

Current research at the National Aeronautics and Space Administration (NASA) Dryden Flight Research Center involves Intelligent Flight Control Systems (IFCS). The goal

of this project is to develop an adaptive neural network-based flight control system. Applied directly to flight control system feedback errors, IFCS provides adjustments to improve aircraft performance in normal flight as well as with system failures. With IFCS, a pilot is able to maintain control and safely land an aircraft that has suffered a failure to a control surface or damage to the airframe. It also improves mission capability, increases the reliability and safety of flight, and eases the pilot workload.

Today's aircraft employ a variety of flight control systems. For example, some aircraft in the sport pilot category rely on weight-shift control to fly while balloons use a standard burn technique. Helicopters utilize a cyclic to tilt the rotor in the desired direction along with a collective to manipulate rotor pitch and anti-torque pedals to control yaw. *[Figure 5-3]*

Figure 5-3. *Helicopter flight control system.*

For additional information on flight control systems, refer to the appropriate handbook for information related to the flight control systems and characteristics of specific types of aircraft.

Flight Control Systems
Flight Controls
Aircraft flight control systems consist of primary and secondary systems. The ailerons, elevator (or stabilator), and rudder constitute the primary control system and are required to control an aircraft safely during flight. Wing flaps, leading edge devices, spoilers, and trim systems constitute the secondary control system and improve the performance characteristics of the airplane or relieve the pilot of excessive control forces.

Primary Flight Controls
Aircraft control systems are carefully designed to provide adequate responsiveness to control inputs while allowing a

natural feel. At low airspeeds, the controls usually feel soft and sluggish, and the aircraft responds slowly to control applications. At higher airspeeds, the controls become increasingly firm and aircraft response is more rapid.

Movement of any of the three primary flight control surfaces (ailerons, elevator or stabilator, or rudder), changes the airflow and pressure distribution over and around the airfoil. These changes affect the lift and drag produced by the airfoil/control surface combination, and allow a pilot to control the aircraft about its three axes of rotation.

Design features limit the amount of deflection of flight control surfaces. For example, control-stop mechanisms may be incorporated into the flight control linkages, or movement of the control column and/or rudder pedals may be limited. The purpose of these design limits is to prevent the pilot from inadvertently overcontrolling and overstressing the aircraft during normal maneuvers.

A properly designed airplane is stable and easily controlled during normal maneuvering. Control surface inputs cause movement about the three axes of rotation. The types of stability an airplane exhibits also relate to the three axes of rotation. *[Figure 5-4]*

Ailerons

Ailerons control roll about the longitudinal axis. The ailerons are attached to the outboard trailing edge of each wing and move in the opposite direction from each other. Ailerons are connected by cables, bellcranks, pulleys and/or push-pull tubes to a control wheel or control stick.

Moving the control wheel or control stick to the right causes the right aileron to deflect upward and the left aileron to deflect downward. The upward deflection of the right aileron decreases the camber resulting in decreased lift on the right wing. The corresponding downward deflection of the left aileron increases the camber resulting in increased lift on the left wing. Thus, the increased lift on the left wing and the decreased lift on the right wing causes the airplane to roll to the right.

Adverse Yaw

Since the downward deflected aileron produces more lift as evidenced by the wing raising, it also produces more drag. This added drag causes the wing to slow down slightly. This results in the aircraft yawing toward the wing which had experienced an increase in lift (and drag). From the pilot's perspective, the yaw is opposite the direction of the bank. The adverse yaw is a result of differential drag and the slight difference in the velocity of the left and right wings. *[Figure 5-5]*

Figure 5-5. *Adverse yaw is caused by higher drag on the outside wing, which is producing more lift.*

Adverse yaw becomes more pronounced at low airspeeds. At these slower airspeeds aerodynamic pressure on control surfaces are low and larger control inputs are required to effectively maneuver the airplane. As a result, the increase in aileron deflection causes an increase in adverse yaw. The yaw is especially evident in aircraft with long wing spans.

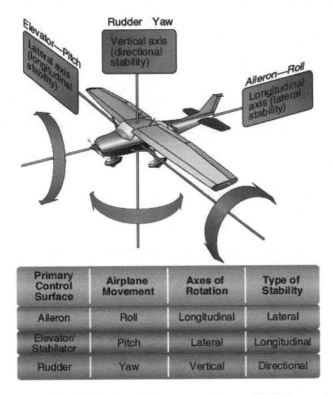

Primary Control Surface	Airplane Movement	Axes of Rotation	Type of Stability
Aileron	Roll	Longitudinal	Lateral
Elevator/Stabilator	Pitch	Lateral	Longitudinal
Rudder	Yaw	Vertical	Directional

Figure 5-4. *Airplane controls, movement, axes of rotation, and type of stability.*

Application of rudder is used to counteract adverse yaw. The amount of rudder control required is greatest at low airspeeds, high angles of attack, and with large aileron deflections. Like all control surfaces at lower airspeeds, the vertical stabilizer/rudder becomes less effective, and magnifies the control problems associated with adverse yaw.

All turns are coordinated by use of ailerons, rudder, and elevator. Applying aileron pressure is necessary to place the aircraft in the desired angle of bank, while simultaneous application of rudder pressure is necessary to counteract the resultant adverse yaw. Additionally, because more lift is required during a turn than when in straight-and-level flight, the angle of attack (AOA) must be increased by applying elevator back pressure. The steeper the turn, the more elevator back pressure is needed.

As the desired angle of bank is established, aileron and rudder pressures should be relaxed. This stops the angle of bank from increasing, because the aileron and rudder control surfaces are in a neutral and streamlined position. Elevator back pressure should be held constant to maintain altitude. The roll-out from a turn is similar to the roll-in, except the flight controls are applied in the opposite direction. Aileron and rudder are applied in the direction of the roll-out or toward the high wing. As the angle of bank decreases, the elevator back pressure should be relaxed as necessary to maintain altitude.

In an attempt to reduce the effects of adverse yaw, manufacturers have engineered four systems: differential ailerons, frise-type ailerons, coupled ailerons and rudder, and flaperons.

Differential Ailerons

With differential ailerons, one aileron is raised a greater distance than the other aileron is lowered for a given movement of the control wheel or control stick. This produces an increase in drag on the descending wing. The greater drag results from deflecting the up aileron on the descending wing to a greater angle than the down aileron on the rising wing. While adverse yaw is reduced, it is not eliminated completely. [Figure 5-6]

Frise-Type Ailerons

With a frise-type aileron, when pressure is applied to the control wheel or control stick, the aileron that is being raised pivots on an offset hinge. This projects the leading edge of the aileron into the airflow and creates drag. It helps equalize the drag created by the lowered aileron on the opposite wing and reduces adverse yaw. [Figure 5-7]

The frise-type aileron also forms a slot so air flows smoothly over the lowered aileron, making it more effective at high

Figure 5-6. *Differential ailerons.*

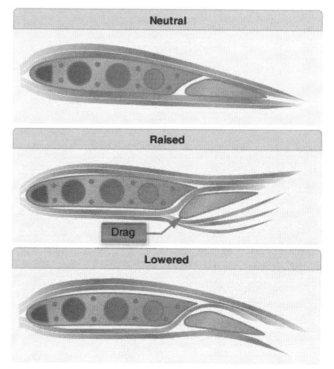

Figure 5-7. *Frise-type ailerons.*

angles of attack. Frise-type ailerons may also be designed to function differentially. Like the differential aileron, the frise-type aileron does not eliminate adverse yaw entirely. Coordinated rudder application is still needed wherever ailerons are applied.

Coupled Ailerons and Rudder

Coupled ailerons and rudder are linked controls. This is accomplished with rudder-aileron interconnect springs, which help correct for aileron drag by automatically deflecting the rudder at the same time the ailerons are deflected. For example, when the control wheel or control stick is moved to produce a left roll, the interconnect cable and spring pulls forward on the left rudder pedal just enough to prevent the nose of the aircraft from yawing to the right. The force applied

Rudder deflects with ailerons

Rudder/Aileron interconnecting springs

Figure 5-8. *Coupled ailerons and rudder.*

to the rudder by the springs can be overridden if it becomes necessary to slip the aircraft. *[Figure 5-8]*

Flaperons

Flaperons combine both aspects of flaps and ailerons. In addition to controlling the bank angle of an aircraft like conventional ailerons, flaperons can be lowered together to function much the same as a dedicated set of flaps. The pilot retains separate controls for ailerons and flaps. A mixer is used to combine the separate pilot inputs into this single set of control surfaces called flaperons. Many designs that incorporate flaperons mount the control surfaces away from the wing to provide undisturbed airflow at high angles of attack and/or low airspeeds. *[Figure 5-9]*

Elevator

The elevator controls pitch about the lateral axis. Like the ailerons on small aircraft, the elevator is connected to the control column in the flight deck by a series of mechanical linkages. Aft movement of the control column deflects the trailing edge of the elevator surface up. This is usually referred to as up "elevator." *[Figure 5-10]*

Figure 5-9. *Flaperons on a Skystar Kitfox MK 7.*

The up-elevator position decreases the camber of the elevator and creates a downward aerodynamic force, which is greater than the normal tail-down force that exists in straight-and-level flight. The overall effect causes the tail of the aircraft to move down and the nose to pitch up. The pitching moment occurs about the center of gravity (CG). The strength of the pitching moment is determined by the distance between the CG and the horizontal tail surface, as well as by the aerodynamic effectiveness of the horizontal tail surface. Moving the control column forward has the opposite effect. In this case, elevator camber increases, creating more lift (less tail-down force) on the horizontal stabilizer/elevator. This moves the tail upward and pitches the nose down. Again, the pitching moment occurs about the CG.

As mentioned earlier in the coverage on stability, power, thrustline, and the position of the horizontal tail surfaces on the empennage are factors in elevator effectiveness controlling pitch. For example, the horizontal tail surfaces may be attached near the lower part of the vertical stabilizer, at the midpoint, or at the high point, as in the T-tail design.

Control column Aft

Nose up

Up elevator

Tail down

Downward aerodynamic force

Figure 5-10. *The elevator is the primary control for changing the pitch attitude of an airplane.*

T-Tail

In a T-tail configuration, the elevator is above most of the effects of downwash from the propeller as well as airflow around the fuselage and/or wings during normal flight conditions. Operation of the elevators in this undisturbed air allows control movements that are consistent throughout most flight regimes. T-tail designs have become popular on many light and large aircraft, especially those with aft fuselage-mounted engines because the T-tail configuration removes the tail from the exhaust blast of the engines. Seaplanes and amphibians often have T-tails in order to keep the horizontal surfaces as far from the water as possible. An additional benefit is reduced vibration and noise inside the aircraft.

At slow speeds, the elevator on a T-tail aircraft must be moved through a larger number of degrees of travel to raise the nose a given amount than on a conventional-tail aircraft. This is because the conventional-tail aircraft has the downwash from the propeller pushing down on the tail to assist in raising the nose.

Since controls on aircraft are rigged so that increasing control forces are required for increased control travel, the forces required to raise the nose of a T-tail aircraft are greater than those for a conventional-tail aircraft. Longitudinal stability of a trimmed aircraft is the same for both types of configuration, but the pilot must be aware that the required control forces are greater at slow speeds during takeoffs, landings, or stalls than for similar size aircraft equipped with conventional tails.

T-tail airplanes also require additional design considerations to counter the problem of flutter. Since the weight of the horizontal surfaces is at the top of the vertical stabilizer, the moment arm created causes high loads on the vertical stabilizer which can result in flutter. Engineers must compensate for this by increasing the design stiffness of the vertical stabilizer, usually resulting in a weight penalty over conventional tail designs.

When flying at a very high AOA with a low airspeed and an aft CG, the T-tail aircraft may be susceptible to a deep stall. In a deep stall, the airflow over the horizontal tail is blanketed by the disturbed airflow from the wings and fuselage. In these circumstances, elevator or stabilator control could be diminished, making it difficult to recover from the stall. It should be noted that an aft CG is often a contributing factor in these incidents, since similar recovery problems are also found with conventional tail aircraft with an aft CG. [Figure 5-11]

Since flight at a high AOA with a low airspeed and an aft CG position can be dangerous, many aircraft have systems to compensate for this situation. The systems range from

Figure 5-11. *Airplane with a T-tail design at a high AOA and an aft CG.*

control stops to elevator down springs. An elevator down spring assists in lowering the nose of the aircraft to prevent a stall caused by the aft CG position. The stall occurs because the properly trimmed airplane is flying with the elevator in a trailing edge down position, forcing the tail up and the nose down. In this unstable condition, if the aircraft encounters turbulence and slows down further, the trim tab no longer positions the elevator in the nose-down position. The elevator then streamlines, and the nose of the aircraft pitches upward, possibly resulting in a stall.

The elevator down spring produces a mechanical load on the elevator, causing it to move toward the nose-down position if not otherwise balanced. The elevator trim tab balances the elevator down spring to position the elevator in a trimmed position. When the trim tab becomes ineffective, the down spring drives the elevator to a nose-down position. The nose of the aircraft lowers, speed builds up, and a stall is prevented. [Figure 5-12]

The elevator must also have sufficient authority to hold the nose of the aircraft up during the roundout for a landing. In this case, a forward CG may cause a problem. During the landing flare, power is usually reduced, which decreases the airflow over the empennage. This, coupled with the reduced landing speed, makes the elevator less effective.

As this discussion demonstrates, pilots must understand and follow proper loading procedures, particularly with regard to the CG position. More information on aircraft loading, as well as weight and balance, is included in Chapter 9, Weight and Balance.

Stabilator

As mentioned in Chapter 2, Aircraft Structure, a stabilator is essentially a one-piece horizontal stabilizer that pivots

Figure 5-12. *When the aerodynamic efficiency of the horizontal tail surface is inadequate due to an aft CG condition, an elevator down spring may be used to supply a mechanical load to lower the nose.*

from a central hinge point. When the control column is pulled back, it raises the stabilator's trailing edge, pulling the airplane's nose up. Pushing the control column forward lowers the trailing edge of the stabilator and pitches the nose of the airplane down.

Because stabilators pivot around a central hinge point, they are extremely sensitive to control inputs and aerodynamic loads. Antiservo tabs are incorporated on the trailing edge to decrease sensitivity. They deflect in the same direction as the stabilator. This results in an increase in the force required to move the stabilator, thus making it less prone to pilot-induced overcontrolling. In addition, a balance weight is usually incorporated in front of the main spar. The balance weight may project into the empennage or may be incorporated on the forward portion of the stabilator tips. *[Figure 5-13]*

Canard

The canard design utilizes the concept of two lifting surfaces, the canard functioning as a horizontal stabilizer located in front of the main wings. In effect, the canard is an airfoil similar to the horizontal surface on a conventional aft-tail design. The difference is that the canard actually creates lift and holds the nose up, as opposed to the aft-tail design which exerts downward force on the tail to prevent the nose from rotating downward. *[Figure 5-14]*

The canard design dates back to the pioneer days of aviation, most notably used on the Wright Flyer. Recently, the canard configuration has regained popularity and is appearing on newer aircraft. Canard designs include two types—one with a horizontal surface of about the same size as a normal aft-tail

Figure 5-13. *The stabilator is a one-piece horizontal tail surface that pivots up and down about a central hinge point.*

design, and the other with a surface of the same approximate size and airfoil of the aft-mounted wing known as a tandem wing configuration. Theoretically, the canard is considered more efficient because using the horizontal surface to help lift the weight of the aircraft should result in less drag for a given amount of lift.

Rudder

The rudder controls movement of the aircraft about its vertical axis. This motion is called yaw. Like the other primary control surfaces, the rudder is a movable surface hinged to a fixed surface, in this case to the vertical stabilizer, or fin. Moving the left or right rudder pedal controls the rudder.

When the rudder is deflected into the airflow, a horizontal force is exerted in the opposite direction. *[Figure 5-15]* By pushing the left pedal, the rudder moves left. This alters the airflow around the vertical stabilizer/rudder, and creates a

Figure 5-14. *The Piaggio P180 includes a variable-sweep canard design, which provides longitudinal stability about the lateral axis.*

sideward lift that moves the tail to the right and yaws the nose of the airplane to the left. Rudder effectiveness increases with speed; therefore, large deflections at low speeds and small deflections at high speeds may be required to provide the desired reaction. In propeller-driven aircraft, any slipstream flowing over the rudder increases its effectiveness.

Figure 5-15. *The effect of left rudder pressure.*

V-Tail

The V-tail design utilizes two slanted tail surfaces to perform the same functions as the surfaces of a conventional elevator and rudder configuration. The fixed surfaces act as both horizontal and vertical stabilizers. *[Figure 5-16]*

Figure 5-16. *Beechcraft Bonanza V35.*

The movable surfaces, which are usually called ruddervators, are connected through a special linkage that allows the control wheel to move both surfaces simultaneously. On the other hand, displacement of the rudder pedals moves the surfaces differentially, thereby providing directional control.

When both rudder and elevator controls are moved by the pilot, a control mixing mechanism moves each surface the appropriate amount. The control system for the V-tail is more complex than that required for a conventional tail. In addition, the V-tail design is more susceptible to Dutch roll tendencies than a conventional tail, and total reduction in drag is minimal.

Secondary Flight Controls

Secondary flight control systems may consist of wing flaps, leading edge devices, spoilers, and trim systems.

Flaps

Flaps are the most common high-lift devices used on aircraft. These surfaces, which are attached to the trailing edge of the wing, increase both lift and induced drag for any given AOA. Flaps allow a compromise between high cruising speed and low landing speed, because they may be extended when needed, and retracted into the wing's structure when not needed. There are four common types of flaps: plain, split, slotted, and Fowler flaps. *[Figure 5-17]*

The plain flap is the simplest of the four types. It increases the airfoil camber, resulting in a significant increase in the coefficient of lift (C_L) at a given AOA. At the same time, it greatly increases drag and moves the center of pressure (CP) aft on the airfoil, resulting in a nose-down pitching moment.

The split flap is deflected from the lower surface of the airfoil and produces a slightly greater increase in lift than the plain flap. More drag is created because of the turbulent air pattern produced behind the airfoil. When fully extended, both plain and split flaps produce high drag with little additional lift.

The most popular flap on aircraft today is the slotted flap. Variations of this design are used for small aircraft, as well as for large ones. Slotted flaps increase the lift coefficient significantly more than plain or split flaps. On small aircraft, the hinge is located below the lower surface of the flap, and when the flap is lowered, a duct forms between the flap well in the wing and the leading edge of the flap. When the slotted flap is lowered, high energy air from the lower surface is ducted to the flap's upper surface. The high energy air from the slot accelerates the upper surface boundary layer and delays airflow separation, providing a higher C_L. Thus, the slotted flap produces much greater increases in maximum coefficient of lift (C_{L-MAX}) than the plain or split flap. While there are many types of slotted flaps, large aircraft often have double- and even triple-slotted flaps. These allow the maximum increase in drag without the airflow over the flaps separating and destroying the lift they produce.

Figure 5-17. *Five common types of flaps.*

Fowler flaps are a type of slotted flap. This flap design not only changes the camber of the wing, it also increases the wing area. Instead of rotating down on a hinge, it slides backwards on tracks. In the first portion of its extension, it increases the drag very little, but increases the lift a great deal as it increases both the area and camber. As the extension continues, the flap deflects downward. During the last portion of its travel, the flap increases the drag with little additional increase in lift.

Leading Edge Devices

High-lift devices also can be applied to the leading edge of the airfoil. The most common types are fixed slots, movable slats, leading edge flaps, and cuffs. *[Figure 5-18]*

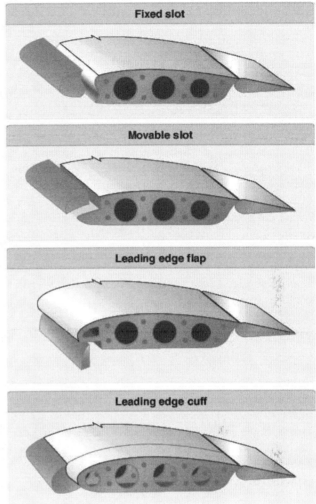

Figure 5-18. *Leading edge high lift devices.*

Fixed slots direct airflow to the upper wing surface and delay airflow separation at higher angles of attack. The slot does not increase the wing camber, but allows a higher maximum C_L because the stall is delayed until the wing reaches a greater AOA.

Movable slats consist of leading edge segments, which move on tracks. At low angles of attack, each slat is held flush against the wing's leading edge by the high pressure that forms at the wing's leading edge. As the AOA increases, the high-pressure area moves aft below the lower surface of the wing, allowing the slats to move forward. Some slats, however, are pilot operated and can be deployed at any AOA. Opening a slat allows the air below the wing to flow over the wing's upper surface, delaying airflow separation.

Leading edge flaps, like trailing edge flaps, are used to increase both C_{L-MAX} and the camber of the wings. This type of leading edge device is frequently used in conjunction with trailing edge flaps and can reduce the nose-down pitching movement produced by the latter. As is true with trailing edge flaps, a small increment of leading edge flaps increases lift to a much greater extent than drag. As greater amounts of flaps are extended, drag increases at a greater rate than lift.

Leading edge cuffs, like leading edge flaps and trailing edge flaps are used to increase both C_{L-MAX} and the camber of the wings. Unlike leading edge flaps and trailing edge flaps, leading edge cuffs are fixed aerodynamic devices. In most cases leading edge cuffs extend the leading edge down and forward. This causes the airflow to attach better to the upper surface of the wing at higher angles of attack, thus lowering an aircraft's stall speed. The fixed nature of leading edge cuffs extracts a penalty in maximum cruise airspeed, but recent advances in design and technology have reduced this penalty.

Spoilers

Found on many gliders and some aircraft, high drag devices called spoilers are deployed from the wings to spoil the smooth airflow, reducing lift and increasing drag. On gliders, spoilers are most often used to control rate of descent for accurate landings. On other aircraft, spoilers are often used for roll control, an advantage of which is the elimination of adverse yaw. To turn right, for example, the spoiler on the right wing is raised, destroying some of the lift and creating more drag on the right. The right wing drops, and the aircraft banks and yaws to the right. Deploying spoilers on both wings at the same time allows the aircraft to descend without gaining speed. Spoilers are also deployed to help reduce ground roll after landing. By destroying lift, they transfer weight to the wheels, improving braking effectiveness. [Figure 5-19]

Trim Systems

Although an aircraft can be operated throughout a wide range of attitudes, airspeeds, and power settings, it can be designed to fly hands-off within only a very limited combination of these variables. Trim systems are used to relieve the pilot of the need to maintain constant pressure on the flight controls, and usually consist of flight deck controls and small hinged devices attached to the trailing edge of one or more of the primary flight control surfaces. Designed to help minimize a pilot's workload, trim systems aerodynamically assist movement and position of the flight control surface to which they are attached. Common types of trim systems include trim

Figure 5-19. *Spoilers reduce lift and increase drag during descent and landing.*

tabs, balance tabs, antiservo tabs, ground adjustable tabs, and an adjustable stabilizer.

Trim Tabs

The most common installation on small aircraft is a single trim tab attached to the trailing edge of the elevator. Most trim tabs are manually operated by a small, vertically mounted control wheel. However, a trim crank may be found in some aircraft. The flight deck control includes a trim tab position indicator. Placing the trim control in the full nose-down position moves the trim tab to its full up position. With the trim tab up and into the airstream, the airflow over the horizontal tail surface tends to force the trailing edge of the elevator down. This causes the tail of the airplane to move up, and the nose to move down. [Figure 5-20]

If the trim tab is set to the full nose-up position, the tab moves to its full down position. In this case, the air flowing under the horizontal tail surface hits the tab and forces the trailing edge of the elevator up, reducing the elevator's AOA. This causes the tail of the airplane to move down, and the nose to move up.

In spite of the opposing directional movement of the trim tab and the elevator, control of trim is natural to a pilot. If the pilot needs to exert constant back pressure on a control column, the need for nose-up trim is indicated. The normal trim procedure is to continue trimming until the aircraft is balanced and the nose-heavy condition is no longer apparent. Pilots normally establish the desired power, pitch attitude, and configuration first, and then trim the aircraft to relieve control pressures that may exist for that flight condition. Any time power, pitch attitude, or configuration is changed, expect that retrimming will be necessary to relieve the control pressures for the new flight condition.

Figure 5-20. *The movement of the elevator is opposite to the direction of movement of the elevator trim tab.*

stabilator moves up, the linkage forces the trailing edge of the tab up. When the stabilator moves down, the tab also moves down. Conversely, trim tabs on elevators move opposite of the control surface. *[Figure 5-21]*

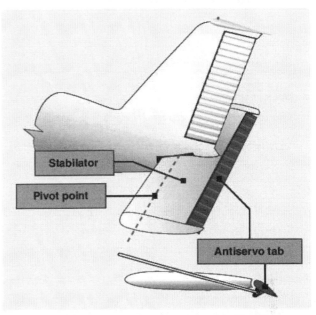

Figure 5-21. *An antiservo tab attempts to streamline the control surface and is used to make the stabilator less sensitive by opposing the force exerted by the pilot.*

Balance Tabs

The control forces may be excessively high in some aircraft, and, in order to decrease them, the manufacturer may use balance tabs. They look like trim tabs and are hinged in approximately the same places as trim tabs. The essential difference between the two is that the balancing tab is coupled to the control surface rod so that when the primary control surface is moved in any direction, the tab automatically moves in the opposite direction. The airflow striking the tab counterbalances some of the air pressure against the primary control surface, and enables the pilot to move more easily and hold the control surface in position.

If the linkage between the balance tab and the fixed surface is adjustable from the flight deck, the tab acts as a combination trim and balance tab that can be adjusted to any desired deflection.

Antiservo Tabs

Antiservo tabs work in the same manner as balance tabs except, instead of moving in the opposite direction, they move in the same direction as the trailing edge of the stabilator. In addition to decreasing the sensitivity of the stabilator, an antiservo tab also functions as a trim device to relieve control pressure and maintain the stabilator in the desired position. The fixed end of the linkage is on the opposite side of the surface from the horn on the tab; when the trailing edge of the

Ground Adjustable Tabs

Many small aircraft have a nonmovable metal trim tab on the rudder. This tab is bent in one direction or the other while on the ground to apply a trim force to the rudder. The correct displacement is determined by trial and error. Usually, small adjustments are necessary until the aircraft no longer skids left or right during normal cruising flight. *[Figure 5-22]*

Figure 5-22. *A ground adjustable tab is used on the rudder of many small airplanes to correct for a tendency to fly with the fuselage slightly misaligned with the relative wind.*

Adjustable Stabilizer

Rather than using a movable tab on the trailing edge of the elevator, some aircraft have an adjustable stabilizer. With this arrangement, linkages pivot the horizontal stabilizer about its rear spar. This is accomplished by use of a jackscrew mounted on the leading edge of the stabilator. *[Figure 5-23]*

Figure 5-23. *Some airplanes, including most jet transports, use an adjustable stabilizer to provide the required pitch trim forces.*

On small aircraft, the jackscrew is cable operated with a trim wheel or crank. On larger aircraft, it is motor driven. The trimming effect and flight deck indications for an adjustable stabilizer are similar to those of a trim tab.

Autopilot

Autopilot is an automatic flight control system that keeps an aircraft in level flight or on a set course. It can be directed by the pilot, or it may be coupled to a radio navigation signal. Autopilot reduces the physical and mental demands on a pilot and increases safety. The common features available on an autopilot are altitude and heading hold.

The simplest systems use gyroscopic attitude indicators and magnetic compasses to control servos connected to the flight control system. *[Figure 5-24]* The number and location of these servos depends on the complexity of the system. For example, a single-axis autopilot controls the aircraft about the longitudinal axis and a servo actuates the ailerons. A three-axis autopilot controls the aircraft about the longitudinal, lateral, and vertical axes. Three different servos actuate ailerons, elevator, and rudder. More advanced systems often include a vertical speed and/or indicated airspeed hold mode. Advanced autopilot systems are coupled to navigational aids through a flight director.

Figure 5-24. *Basic autopilot system integrated into the flight control system.*

The autopilot system also incorporates a disconnect safety feature to disengage the system automatically or manually. These autopilots work with inertial navigation systems, global positioning systems (GPS), and flight computers to control the aircraft. In fly-by-wire systems, the autopilot is an integrated component.

Additionally, autopilots can be manually overridden. Because autopilot systems differ widely in their operation, refer to the autopilot operating instructions in the Airplane Flight Manual (AFM) or the Pilot's Operating Handbook (POH).

Chapter Summary

Because flight control systems and aerodynamic characteristics vary greatly between aircraft, it is essential that a pilot become familiar with the primary and secondary flight control systems of the aircraft being flown. The primary source of this information is the AFM or the POH. Various manufacturer and owner group websites can also be a valuable source of additional information.

Chapter 6

Aircraft Systems

Introduction

This chapter covers the primary systems found on most aircraft. These include the engine, propeller, induction, ignition, as well as the fuel, lubrication, cooling, electrical, landing gear, and environmental control systems.

Powerplant

An aircraft engine, or powerplant, produces thrust to propel an aircraft. Reciprocating engines and turboprop engines work in combination with a propeller to produce thrust. Turbojet and turbofan engines produce thrust by increasing the velocity of air flowing through the engine. All of these powerplants also drive the various systems that support the operation of an aircraft.

Two-stroke compression ignition

Forced air   Exhaust valve   Fuel injector

Piston

Reciprocating Engines

Most small aircraft are designed with reciprocating engines. The name is derived from the back-and-forth, or reciprocating, movement of the pistons which produces the mechanical energy necessary to accomplish work.

Driven by a revitalization of the general aviation (GA) industry and advances in both material and engine design, reciprocating engine technology has improved dramatically over the past two decades. The integration of computerized engine management systems has improved fuel efficiency, decreased emissions, and reduced pilot workload.

Reciprocating engines operate on the basic principle of converting chemical energy (fuel) into mechanical energy. This conversion occurs within the cylinders of the engine through the process of combustion. The two primary reciprocating engine designs are the spark ignition and the compression ignition. The spark ignition reciprocating engine has served as the powerplant of choice for many years. In an effort to reduce operating costs, simplify design, and improve reliability, several engine manufacturers are turning to compression ignition as a viable alternative. Often referred to as jet fuel piston engines, compression ignition engines have the added advantage of utilizing readily available and lower cost diesel or jet fuel.

The main mechanical components of the spark ignition and the compression ignition engine are essentially the same. Both use cylindrical combustion chambers and pistons that travel the length of the cylinders to convert linear motion into the rotary motion of the crankshaft. The main difference between spark ignition and compression ignition is the process of igniting the fuel. Spark ignition engines use a spark plug to ignite a pre-mixed fuel/air mixture. (Fuel/air mixture is the ratio of the "weight" of fuel to the "weight" of air in the mixture to be burned.) A compression ignition engine first compresses the air in the cylinder, raising its temperature to a degree necessary for automatic ignition when fuel is injected into the cylinder.

These two engine designs can be further classified as:

1. Cylinder arrangement with respect to the crankshaft—radial, in-line, v-type, or opposed.

2. Operating cycle—two or four.

3. Method of cooling—liquid or air.

Radial engines were widely used during World War II and many are still in service today. With these engines, a row or rows of cylinders are arranged in a circular pattern around the crankcase. The main advantage of a radial engine is the favorable power-to-weight ratio. *[Figure 6-1]*

Figure 6-1. *Radial engine.*

In-line engines have a comparatively small frontal area, but their power-to-weight ratios are relatively low. In addition, the rearmost cylinders of an air-cooled, in-line engine receive very little cooling air, so these engines are normally limited to four or six cylinders. V-type engines provide more horsepower than in-line engines and still retain a small frontal area.

Continued improvements in engine design led to the development of the horizontally-opposed engine which remains the most popular reciprocating engines used on smaller aircraft. These engines always have an even number of cylinders, since a cylinder on one side of the crankcase "opposes" a cylinder on the other side. *[Figure 6-2]* The majority of these engines are air cooled and usually are mounted in a horizontal position when installed on fixed-wing airplanes. Opposed-type engines have high power-to-weight ratios because they have a comparatively small, lightweight crankcase. In addition, the compact cylinder arrangement reduces the engine's frontal area and allows a streamlined installation that minimizes aerodynamic drag.

Figure 6-2. *Horizontally opposed engine.*

Depending on the engine manufacturer, all of these arrangements can be designed to utilize spark or compression ignition, and operate on either a two- or four-stroke cycle.

In a two-stroke engine, the conversion of chemical energy into mechanical energy occurs over a two-stroke operating cycle. The intake, compression, power, and exhaust processes occur in only two strokes of the piston rather than the more common four strokes. Because a two-stroke engine has a power stroke each revolution of the crankshaft, it typically has higher power-to-weight ratio than a comparable four-stroke engine. Due to the inherent inefficiency and disproportionate emissions of the earliest designs, use of the two-stroke engine has been limited in aviation.

Recent advances in material and engine design have reduced many of the negative characteristics associated with two-stroke engines. Modern two-stroke engines often use conventional oil sumps, oil pumps and full pressure fed lubrication systems. The use of direct fuel injection and pressurized air, characteristic of advanced compression ignition engines, make two-stroke compression ignition engines a viable alternative to the more common four-stroke spark ignition designs. *[Figure 6-3]*

Figure 6-3. *Two-stroke compression ignition.*

Spark ignition four-stroke engines remain the most common design used in general aviation today. *[Figure 6-4]* The main parts of a spark ignition reciprocating engine include the cylinders, crankcase, and accessory housing. The intake/exhaust valves, spark plugs, and pistons are located in the cylinders. The crankshaft and connecting rods are located in the crankcase. The magnetos are normally located on the engine accessory housing.

Figure 6-4. *Main components of a spark ignition reciprocating engine.*

In a four-stroke engine the conversion of chemical energy into mechanical energy occurs over a four stroke operating cycle. The intake, compression, power, and exhaust processes occur in four separate strokes of the piston.

1. The intake stroke begins as the piston starts its downward travel. When this happens, the intake valve opens and the fuel/air mixture is drawn into the cylinder.

2. The compression stroke begins when the intake valve closes and the piston starts moving back to the top of the cylinder. This phase of the cycle is used to obtain a much greater power output from the fuel/air mixture once it is ignited.

3. The power stroke begins when the fuel/air mixture is ignited. This causes a tremendous pressure increase in the cylinder, and forces the piston downward away from the cylinder head, creating the power that turns the crankshaft.

4. The exhaust stroke is used to purge the cylinder of burned gases. It begins when the exhaust valve opens and the piston starts to move toward the cylinder head once again.

Even when the engine is operated at a fairly low speed, the four-stroke cycle takes place several hundred times each minute. *[Figure 6-5]* In a four-cylinder engine, each cylinder operates on a different stroke. Continuous rotation of a crankshaft is maintained by the precise timing of the power strokes in each cylinder. Continuous operation of the engine depends on the simultaneous function of auxiliary systems, including the induction, ignition, fuel, oil, cooling, and exhaust systems.

Figure 6-5. *The arrows in this illustration indicate the direction of motion of the crankshaft and piston during the four-stroke cycle.*

The latest advance in aircraft reciprocating engines was pioneered in the mid-1960s by Frank Thielert, who looked to the automotive industry for answers on how to integrate diesel technology into an aircraft engine. The advantage of a diesel-fueled reciprocating engine lies in the physical similarity of diesel and kerosene. Aircraft equipped with a diesel piston engine runs on standard aviation fuel kerosene which provides more independence, higher reliability, lower consumption, and operational cost saving.

In 1999, Thielert formed Thielert Aircraft Engines (TAE) to design, develop, certify, and manufacture a brand-new Jet-A-burning diesel cycle engine (also known as jet-fueled piston engine) for the GA industry. By March 2001, the first prototype engine became the first certified diesel engine since World War II. TAE continues to design and develop diesel cycle engines and other engine manufacturers such as Société de Motorisations Aéronautiques (SMA) now offer jet-fueled piston engines as well. TAE engines can be found on the Diamond DA40 single and the DA42 Twin Star, the first diesel engine to be part of the type certificate of a new original equipment manufacturer (OEM) aircraft.

These engines have also gained a toehold in the retrofit market with a supplemental type certificate (STC) to re-engine the Cessna 172 models and the Piper PA-28 family. The jet-fueled piston engines technology has continued to progress and a full authority digital engine control (FADEC, discussed more fully later in the chapter) is standard on such equipped aircraft which minimizes complication of engine control. By 2007, various jet-fueled piston aircraft had logged well over 600,000 hours of service.

Propeller

The propeller is a rotating airfoil, subject to induced drag, stalls, and other aerodynamic principles that apply to any airfoil. It provides the necessary thrust to pull, or in some cases push, the aircraft through the air. The engine power is used to rotate the propeller, which in turn generates thrust very similar to the manner in which a wing produces lift. The amount of thrust produced depends on the shape of the airfoil, the angle of attack of the propeller blade, and the revolutions per minute (rpm) of the engine. The propeller itself is twisted so the blade angle changes from hub to tip. The greatest angle of incidence, or the highest pitch, is at the hub while the smallest angle of incidence or smallest pitch is at the tip. *[Figure 6-6]*

The reason for the twist is to produce uniform lift from the hub to the tip. As the blade rotates, there is a difference in the actual speed of the various portions of the blade. The tip of the blade travels faster than the part near the hub, because the tip travels a greater distance than the hub in the same length of time. *[Figure 6-7]* Changing the angle of incidence (pitch) from the hub to the tip to correspond with the speed produces uniform lift throughout the length of the blade. A

Figure 6-6. *Changes in propeller blade angle from hub to tip.*

propeller blade designed with the same angle of incidence throughout its entire length would be inefficient because as airspeed increases in flight, the portion near the hub would have a negative angle of attack while the blade tip would be stalled.

Figure 6-7. *Relationship of travel distance and speed of various portions of propeller blade.*

Small aircraft are equipped with either one of two types of propellers. One is the fixed pitch, and the other is the adjustable pitch.

Fixed-Pitch Propeller

A propeller with fixed blade angles is a fixed-pitch propeller. The pitch of this propeller is set by the manufacturer and cannot be changed. Since a fixed-pitch propeller achieves the best efficiency only at a given combination of airspeed and rpm, the pitch setting is ideal for neither cruise nor climb. Thus, the aircraft suffers a bit in each performance category. The fixed-pitch propeller is used when low weight, simplicity, and low cost are needed.

There are two types of fixed-pitch propellers: climb and cruise. Whether the airplane has a climb or cruise propeller installed depends upon its intended use. The climb propeller has a lower pitch, therefore less drag. Less drag results in higher rpm and more horsepower capability, which increases performance during takeoffs and climbs, but decreases performance during cruising flight.

The cruise propeller has a higher pitch, therefore more drag. More drag results in lower rpm and less horsepower capability, which decreases performance during takeoffs and climbs, but increases efficiency during cruising flight.

The propeller is usually mounted on a shaft, which may be an extension of the engine crankshaft. In this case, the rpm of the propeller would be the same as the crankshaft rpm. On some engines, the propeller is mounted on a shaft geared to the engine crankshaft. In this type, the rpm of the propeller is different than that of the engine.

In a fixed-pitch propeller, the tachometer is the indicator of engine power. *[Figure 6-8]* A tachometer is calibrated in hundreds of rpm and gives a direct indication of the engine and propeller rpm. The instrument is color coded, with a green arc denoting the maximum continuous operating rpm. Some tachometers have additional markings to reflect engine and/or propeller limitations. The manufacturer's recommendations should be used as a reference to clarify any misunderstanding of tachometer markings.

Figure 6-8. *Engine rpm is indicated on the tachometer.*

The rpm is regulated by the throttle, which controls the fuel/air flow to the engine. At a given altitude, the higher the tachometer reading, the higher the power output of the engine.

When operating altitude increases, the tachometer may not show correct power output of the engine. For example, 2,300 rpm at 5,000 feet produces less horsepower than 2,300 rpm at sea level because power output depends on air density. Air density decreases as altitude increases and a decrease in air density (higher density altitude) decreases the power output of the engine. As altitude changes, the position of the throttle must be changed to maintain the same rpm. As altitude is increased, the throttle must be opened further to indicate the same rpm as at a lower altitude.

Adjustable-Pitch Propeller

The adjustable-pitch propeller was the forerunner of the constant-speed propeller. It is a propeller with blades whose pitch can be adjusted on the ground with the engine not running, but which cannot be adjusted in flight. It is also referred to as a ground adjustable propeller. By the 1930s, pioneer aviation inventors were laying the ground work for automatic pitch-change mechanisms, which is why the term sometimes refers to modern constant-speed propellers that are adjustable in flight.

The first adjustable-pitch propeller systems provided only two pitch settings: low and high. Today, most adjustable-pitch propeller systems are capable of a range of pitch settings.

A constant-speed propeller is a controllable-pitch propeller whose pitch is automatically varied in flight by a governor maintaining constant rpm despite varying air loads. It is the most common type of adjustable-pitch propeller. The main advantage of a constant-speed propeller is that it converts a high percentage of brake horsepower (BHP) into thrust horsepower (THP) over a wide range of rpm and airspeed combinations. A constant-speed propeller is more efficient than other propellers because it allows selection of the most efficient engine rpm for the given conditions.

An aircraft with a constant-speed propeller has two controls: the throttle and the propeller control. The throttle controls power output and the propeller control regulates engine rpm. This in turn regulates propeller rpm which is registered on the tachometer.

Once a specific rpm is selected, a governor automatically adjusts the propeller blade angle as necessary to maintain the selected rpm. For example, after setting the desired rpm during cruising flight, an increase in airspeed or decrease in propeller load will cause the propeller blade angle to increase as necessary to maintain the selected rpm. A reduction in airspeed or increase in propeller load will cause the propeller blade angle to decrease.

The propeller's constant-speed range, defined by the high and low pitch stops, is the range of possible blade angles for a constant-speed propeller. As long as the propeller blade angle is within the constant-speed range and not against either pitch stop, a constant engine rpm will be maintained. If the propeller blades contact a pitch stop, the engine rpm will increase or decrease as appropriate, with changes in airspeed and propeller load. For example, once a specific rpm has been selected, if aircraft speed decreases enough to rotate the propeller blades until they contact the low pitch stop, any further decrease in airspeed will cause engine rpm to decrease the same way as if a fixed-pitch propeller were installed. The same holds true when an aircraft equipped with a constant-speed propeller accelerates to a faster airspeed. As the aircraft accelerates, the propeller blade angle increases to maintain the selected rpm until the high pitch stop is reached. Once this occurs, the blade angle cannot increase any further and engine rpm increases.

On aircraft equipped with a constant-speed propeller, power output is controlled by the throttle and indicated by a manifold pressure gauge. The gauge measures the absolute pressure of the fuel/air mixture inside the intake manifold and is more correctly a measure of manifold absolute pressure (MAP). At a constant rpm and altitude, the amount of power produced is directly related to the fuel/air flow being delivered to the combustion chamber. As the throttle setting is increased, more fuel and air flows to the engine and MAP increases. When the engine is not running, the manifold pressure gauge indicates ambient air pressure (i.e., 29.92 inches mercury (29.92 "Hg)). When the engine is started, the manifold pressure indication will decrease to a value less than ambient pressure (i.e., idle at 12 "Hg). Engine failure or power loss is indicated on the manifold gauge as an increase in manifold pressure to a value corresponding to the ambient air pressure at the altitude where the failure occurred. [Figure 6-9]

Figure 6-9. *Engine power output is indicated on the manifold pressure gauge.*

The manifold pressure gauge is color coded to indicate the engine's operating range. The face of the manifold pressure gauge contains a green arc to show the normal operating range, and a red radial line to indicate the upper limit of manifold pressure.

For any given rpm, there is a manifold pressure that should not be exceeded. If manifold pressure is excessive for a given rpm, the pressure within the cylinders could be exceeded, placing undue stress on the cylinders. If repeated too frequently, this stress can weaken the cylinder components and eventually cause engine failure. As a general rule, manifold pressure (inches) should be less than the rpm.

A pilot can avoid conditions that overstress the cylinders by being constantly aware of the rpm, especially when increasing the manifold pressure. Conform to the manufacturer's recommendations for power settings of a particular engine to maintain the proper relationship between manifold pressure and rpm.

When both manifold pressure and rpm need to be changed, avoid engine overstress by making power adjustments in the proper order:

- When power settings are being decreased, reduce manifold pressure before reducing rpm. If rpm is reduced before manifold pressure, manifold pressure will automatically increase, possibly exceeding the manufacturer's tolerances.

- When power settings are being increased, reverse the order—increase rpm first, then manifold pressure.

- To prevent damage to radial engines, minimize operating time at maximum rpm and manifold pressure, and avoid operation at maximum rpm and low manifold pressure.

The engine and/or airframe manufacturer's recommendations should be followed to prevent severe wear, fatigue, and damage to high-performance reciprocating engines.

Induction Systems
The induction system brings in air from the outside, mixes it with fuel, and delivers the fuel/air mixture to the cylinder where combustion occurs. Outside air enters the induction system through an intake port on the front of the engine cowling. This port normally contains an air filter that inhibits the entry of dust and other foreign objects. Since the filter may occasionally become clogged, an alternate source of air must be available. Usually, the alternate air comes from inside the engine cowling, where it bypasses a clogged air filter. Some alternate air sources function automatically, while others operate manually.

Two types of induction systems are commonly used in small aircraft engines:

1. The carburetor system, which mixes the fuel and air in the carburetor before this mixture enters the intake manifold

2. The fuel injection system, which mixes the fuel and air immediately before entry into each cylinder or injects fuel directly into each cylinder

Carburetor Systems
Carburetors are classified as either float type or pressure type. The float type of carburetor, complete with idling, accelerating, mixture control, idle cutoff, and power enrichment systems is probably the most common of all carburetor types. Pressure carburetors are usually not found on small aircraft. The basic difference between a float-type and a pressure-type carburetor is the delivery of fuel. The pressure-type carburetor delivers fuel under pressure by a fuel pump.

In the operation of the float-type carburetor system, the outside air first flows through an air filter, usually located at an air intake in the front part of the engine cowling. This filtered air flows into the carburetor and through a venturi, a narrow throat in the carburetor. When the air flows through the venturi, a low-pressure area is created, which forces the fuel to flow through a main fuel jet located at the throat. The fuel then flows into the airstream where it is mixed with the flowing air. *[Figure 6-10]*

The fuel/air mixture is then drawn through the intake manifold and into the combustion chambers where it is ignited. The float-type carburetor acquires its name from a float, which rests on fuel within the float chamber. A needle attached to the float opens and closes an opening at the bottom of the carburetor bowl. This meters the correct amount of fuel into the carburetor, depending upon the position of the float, which is controlled by the level of fuel in the float chamber. When the level of the fuel forces the float to rise, the needle valve closes the fuel opening and shuts off the fuel flow to the carburetor. The needle valve opens again when the engine requires additional fuel. The flow of the fuel/air mixture to the combustion chambers is regulated by the throttle valve, which is controlled by the throttle in the flight deck.

The float-type carburetor has several distinct disadvantages. In the first place, imagine the effect that abrupt maneuvers have on the float action. In the second place, the fact that its fuel must be discharged at low pressure leads to incomplete vaporization and difficulty in discharging fuel into some types of supercharged systems. The chief disadvantage of the float carburetor, however, is its icing tendency. Since the float carburetor must discharge fuel at a point of low

FUEL/AIR MIXTURE
The blend of fuel and air is routed to the combustion chambers to be burned.

THROTTLE VALVE
The flow of the fuel/air mixture is controlled by the throttle valve. The throttle valve is adjusted from the flight deck by the throttle.

VENTURI
The shape of the venturi creates an area of low pressure.

DISCHARGE NOZZLE
Fuel is forced through the discharge nozzle into the venturi by greater atmospheric pressure in the float chamber.

FLOAT CHAMBER
Fuel level is maintained by a float-type device.

FUEL INLET
Fuel is received into the carburetor through the fuel inlet.

FUEL

MIXTURE NEEDLE
The mixture needle controls fuel to the discharge nozzle. Mixture needle position can be adjusted using the mixture control.

AIR INLET
Air enters the carburetor through the air inlet.

AIR BLEED
The air bleed allows air to be mixed with fuel being drawn out of the discharge nozzle to decrease fuel density and promote fuel vaporization.

Figure 6-10. *Float-type carburetor.*

pressure, the discharge nozzle must be located at the venturi throat, and the throttle valve must be on the engine side of the discharge nozzle. This means the drop in temperature due to fuel vaporization takes place within the venturi. As a result, ice readily forms in the venturi and on the throttle valve.

A pressure-type carburetor discharges fuel into the airstream at a pressure well above atmospheric. This results in better vaporization and permits the discharge of fuel into the airstream on the engine side of the throttle valve. With the discharge nozzle located at this point, the drop in temperature due to fuel vaporization takes place after the air has passed the throttle valve and at a point where engine heat tends to offset it. Thus, the danger of fuel vaporization icing is practically eliminated. The effects of rapid maneuvers and rough air on the pressure-type carburetors are negligible since their fuel chambers remain filled under all operating conditions

Mixture Control

Carburetors are normally calibrated at sea-level pressure, where the correct fuel-to-air mixture ratio is established with the mixture control set in the FULL RICH position. However, as altitude increases, the density of air entering the carburetor decreases, while the density of the fuel remains the same. This creates a progressively richer mixture, which can result in engine roughness and an appreciable loss of power. The roughness normally is due to spark plug fouling

from excessive carbon buildup on the plugs. Carbon buildup occurs because the rich mixture lowers the temperature inside the cylinder, inhibiting complete combustion of the fuel. This condition may occur during the pretakeoff runup at high-elevation airports and during climbs or cruise flight at high altitudes. To maintain the correct fuel/air mixture, the mixture must be leaned using the mixture control. Leaning the mixture decreases fuel flow, which compensates for the decreased air density at high altitude.

During a descent from high altitude, the mixture must be enriched, or it may become too lean. An overly lean mixture causes detonation, which may result in rough engine operation, overheating, and a loss of power. The best way to maintain the proper mixture is to monitor the engine temperature and enrich the mixture as needed. Proper mixture control and better fuel economy for fuel-injected engines can be achieved by use of an exhaust gas temperature (EGT) gauge. Since the process of adjusting the mixture can vary from one aircraft to another, it is important to refer to the airplane flight manual (AFM) or the pilot's operating handbook (POH) to determine the specific procedures for a given aircraft.

Carburetor Icing

As mentioned earlier, one disadvantage of the float-type carburetor is its icing tendency. Carburetor ice occurs due to the effect of fuel vaporization and the decrease in air pressure in the venturi, which causes a sharp temperature drop in the carburetor. If water vapor in the air condenses when the carburetor temperature is at or below freezing, ice may form on internal surfaces of the carburetor, including the throttle valve. *[Figure 6-11]*

Figure 6-11. *The formation of carburetor ice may reduce or block fuel/air flow to the engine.*

The reduced air pressure, as well as the vaporization of fuel, contributes to the temperature decrease in the carburetor. Ice generally forms in the vicinity of the throttle valve and in the venturi throat. This restricts the flow of the fuel/air mixture and reduces power. If enough ice builds up, the engine may cease to operate. Carburetor ice is most likely to occur when temperatures are below 70 degrees Fahrenheit (°F) or 21 degrees Celsius (°C) and the relative humidity is above 80 percent. Due to the sudden cooling that takes place in the carburetor, icing can occur even with temperatures as high as 100 °F (38 °C) and humidity as low as 50 percent. This temperature drop can be as much as 60 to 70 °F (15 to 21 °C). Therefore, at an outside air temperature of 100 °F (37 °C), a temperature drop of 70 °F (21 °C) results in an air temperature in the carburetor of 30 °F (-1 °C). *[Figure 6-12]*

The first indication of carburetor icing in an aircraft with a fixed-pitch propeller is a decrease in engine rpm, which may be followed by engine roughness. In an aircraft with a constant-speed propeller, carburetor icing is usually indicated

Figure 6-12. *Although carburetor ice is most likely to form when the temperature and humidity are in ranges indicated by this chart, carburetor ice is possible under conditions not depicted.*

by a decrease in manifold pressure, but no reduction in rpm. Propeller pitch is automatically adjusted to compensate for loss of power. Thus, a constant rpm is maintained. Although carburetor ice can occur during any phase of flight, it is particularly dangerous when using reduced power during a descent. Under certain conditions, carburetor ice could build unnoticed until power is added. To combat the effects of carburetor ice, engines with float-type carburetors employ a carburetor heat system.

Carburetor Heat

Carburetor heat is an anti-icing system that preheats the air before it reaches the carburetor, and is intended to keep the fuel/air mixture above the freezing temperature to prevent the formation of carburetor ice. Carburetor heat can be used to melt ice that has already formed in the carburetor if the accumulation is not too great, but using carburetor heat as a preventative measure is the better option. Additionally, the use of carburetor heat as an alternate air source can be used if the intake filter clogs such as in sudden or unexpected airframe icing conditions. The carburetor heat should be checked during the engine runup. When using carburetor heat, follow the manufacturer's recommendations.

When conditions are conducive to carburetor icing during flight, periodic checks should be made to detect its presence. If detected, full carburetor heat should be applied immediately, and it should be left in the ON position until the pilot is certain all the ice has been removed. If ice is present, applying partial heat or leaving heat on for an insufficient time might aggravate the situation. In extreme cases of carburetor icing, even after the ice has been removed, full carburetor heat should be used to prevent further ice formation. If installed, a carburetor temperature gauge is useful in determining when to use carburetor heat.

Whenever the throttle is closed during flight, the engine cools rapidly and vaporization of the fuel is less complete than if the engine is warm. Also, in this condition, the engine is more susceptible to carburetor icing. If carburetor icing conditions are suspected and closed-throttle operation anticipated, adjust the carburetor heat to the full ON position before closing the throttle and leave it on during the closed-throttle operation. The heat will aid in vaporizing the fuel and help prevent the formation of carburetor ice. Periodically, open the throttle smoothly for a few seconds to keep the engine warm; otherwise, the carburetor heater may not provide enough heat to prevent icing.

The use of carburetor heat causes a decrease in engine power, sometimes up to 15 percent, because the heated air is less dense than the outside air that had been entering the engine. This enriches the mixture. When ice is present in an aircraft with a fixed-pitch propeller and carburetor heat is being used, there is a decrease in rpm, followed by a gradual increase in rpm as the ice melts. The engine also should run more smoothly after the ice has been removed. If ice is not present, the rpm will decrease and then remain constant. When carburetor heat is used on an aircraft with a constant-speed propeller and ice is present, a decrease in the manifold pressure will be noticed, followed by a gradual increase. If carburetor icing is not present, the gradual increase in manifold pressure will not be apparent until the carburetor heat is turned off.

It is imperative for a pilot to recognize carburetor ice when it forms during flight because a loss of power, altitude, and/or airspeed will occur. These symptoms may sometimes be accompanied by vibration or engine roughness. Once a power loss is noticed, immediate action should be taken to eliminate ice already formed in the carburetor, and to prevent further ice formation. This is accomplished by applying full carburetor heat, which will cause a further reduction in power, and possibly engine roughness as melted ice goes through the engine. These symptoms may last from 30 seconds to several minutes, depending on the severity of the icing. During this period, the pilot must resist the temptation to decrease the carburetor heat usage. Carburetor heat must remain in the full-hot position until normal power returns.

Since the use of carburetor heat tends to reduce the output of the engine and to increase the operating temperature, carburetor heat should not be used when full power is required (as during takeoff) or during normal engine operation, except to check for the presence or to remove carburetor ice.

Carburetor Air Temperature Gauge

Some aircraft are equipped with a carburetor air temperature gauge, which is useful in detecting potential icing conditions.

Usually, the face of the gauge is calibrated in degrees Celsius, with a yellow arc indicating the carburetor air temperatures where icing may occur. This yellow arc typically ranges between -15 °C and +5 °C (5 °F and 41 °F). If the air temperature and moisture content of the air are such that carburetor icing is improbable, the engine can be operated with the indicator in the yellow range with no adverse effects. If the atmospheric conditions are conducive to carburetor icing, the indicator must be kept outside the yellow arc by application of carburetor heat.

Certain carburetor air temperature gauges have a red radial, which indicates the maximum permissible carburetor inlet air temperature recommended by the engine manufacturer. If present, a green arc indicates the normal operating range.

Outside Air Temperature Gauge

Most aircraft are also equipped with an outside air temperature (OAT) gauge calibrated in both degrees Celsius and Fahrenheit. It provides the outside or ambient air temperature for calculating true airspeed, and also is useful in detecting potential icing conditions.

Fuel Injection Systems

In a fuel injection system, the fuel is injected directly into the cylinders, or just ahead of the intake valve. The air intake for the fuel injection system is similar to that used in a carburetor system, with an alternate air source located within the engine cowling. This source is used if the external air source is obstructed. The alternate air source is usually operated automatically, with a backup manual system that can be used if the automatic feature malfunctions.

A fuel injection system usually incorporates six basic components: an engine-driven fuel pump, a fuel/air control unit, fuel manifold (fuel distributor), discharge nozzles, an auxiliary fuel pump, and fuel pressure/flow indicators. [Figure 6-13]

The auxiliary fuel pump provides fuel under pressure to the fuel/air control unit for engine starting and/or emergency use. After starting, the engine-driven fuel pump provides fuel under pressure from the fuel tank to the fuel/air control unit.

This control unit, which essentially replaces the carburetor, meters fuel based on the mixture control setting, and sends it to the fuel manifold valve at a rate controlled by the throttle. After reaching the fuel manifold valve, the fuel is distributed to the individual fuel discharge nozzles. The discharge nozzles, which are located in each cylinder head, inject the fuel/air mixture directly into each cylinder intake port.

Figure 6-13. *Fuel injection system.*

A fuel injection system is considered to be less susceptible to icing than the carburetor system, but impact icing on the air intake is a possibility in either system. Impact icing occurs when ice forms on the exterior of the aircraft, and blocks openings such as the air intake for the injection system.

Advantages of fuel injection:

- Reduction in evaporative icing
- Better fuel flow
- Faster throttle response
- Precise control of mixture
- Better fuel distribution
- Easier cold weather starts

Disadvantages:

- Difficulty in starting a hot engine
- Vapor locks during ground operations on hot days
- Problems associated with restarting an engine that quits because of fuel starvation

Superchargers and Turbosuperchargers

To increase an engine's horsepower, manufacturers have developed forced induction systems called supercharger and turbosupercharger systems. They both compress the intake air to increase its density. The key difference lies in the power supply. A supercharger relies on an engine-driven air pump or compressor, while a turbocharger gets its power from the exhaust stream that runs through a turbine, which in turn spins the compressor. Aircraft with these systems have a manifold pressure gauge, which displays MAP within the engine's intake manifold.

On a standard day at sea level with the engine shut down, the manifold pressure gauge will indicate the ambient absolute air pressure of 29.92 "Hg. Because atmospheric pressure decreases approximately 1 "Hg per 1,000 feet of altitude increase, the manifold pressure gauge will indicate approximately 24.92 "Hg at an airport that is 5,000 feet above sea level with standard day conditions.

As a normally aspirated aircraft climbs, it eventually reaches an altitude where the MAP is insufficient for a normal climb. That altitude limit is the aircraft's service ceiling, and it is directly affected by the engine's ability to produce power. If the induction air entering the engine is pressurized, or boosted, by either a supercharger or a turbosupercharger, the aircraft's service ceiling can be increased. With these systems, an aircraft can fly at higher altitudes with the advantage of higher true airspeeds and the increased ability to circumnavigate adverse weather.

Superchargers

A supercharger is an engine-driven air pump or compressor that provides compressed air to the engine to provide additional pressure to the induction air so the engine can produce additional power. It increases manifold pressure and forces the fuel/air mixture into the cylinders. The higher the manifold pressure, the more dense the fuel/air mixture, and the more power an engine can produce. With a normally aspirated engine, it is not possible to have manifold pressure higher than the existing atmospheric pressure. A supercharger is capable of boosting manifold pressure above 30 "Hg.

For example, at 8,000 feet a typical engine may be able to produce 75 percent of the power it could produce at mean sea level (MSL) because the air is less dense at the higher altitude. The supercharger compresses the air to a higher density allowing a supercharged engine to produce the same manifold pressure at higher altitudes as it could produce at sea level. Thus, an engine at 8,000 feet MSL could still produce 25 "Hg of manifold pressure whereas without a supercharger it could produce only 22 "Hg. Superchargers are especially valuable at high altitudes (such as 18,000 feet) where the air density is 50 percent that of sea level. The use of a supercharger in many cases will supply air to the engine at the same density it did at sea level. With a normally aspirated engine, it is not possible to have manifold pressure higher than the existing atmospheric pressure. A supercharger is capable of boosting manifold pressure above 30 "Hg.

The components in a supercharged induction system are similar to those in a normally aspirated system, with the addition of a supercharger between the fuel metering device and intake manifold. A supercharger is driven by the engine through a gear train at one speed, two speeds, or variable speeds. In addition, superchargers can have one or more stages. Each stage also provides an increase in pressure and superchargers may be classified as single stage, two stage, or multistage, depending on the number of times compression occurs.

An early version of a single-stage, single-speed supercharger may be referred to as a sea-level supercharger. An engine equipped with this type of supercharger is called a sea-level engine. With this type of supercharger, a single gear-driven impeller is used to increase the power produced by an engine at all altitudes. The drawback with this type of supercharger is a decrease in engine power output with an increase in altitude.

Single-stage, single-speed superchargers are found on many high-powered radial engines and use an air intake that faces forward so the induction system can take full advantage of the ram air. Intake air passes through ducts to a carburetor, where fuel is metered in proportion to the airflow. The fuel/air charge is then ducted to the supercharger, or blower impeller, which

accelerates the fuel/air mixture outward. Once accelerated, the fuel/air mixture passes through a diffuser, where air velocity is traded for pressure energy. After compression, the resulting high pressure fuel/air mixture is directed to the cylinders.

Some of the large radial engines developed during World War II have a single-stage, two-speed supercharger. With this type of supercharger, a single impeller may be operated at two speeds. The low impeller speed is often referred to as the low blower setting, while the high impeller speed is called the high blower setting. On engines equipped with a two-speed supercharger, a lever or switch in the flight deck activates an oil-operated clutch that switches from one speed to the other.

Under normal operations, takeoff is made with the supercharger in the low blower position. In this mode, the engine performs as a ground-boosted engine, and the power output decreases as the aircraft gains altitude. However, once the aircraft reaches a specified altitude, a power reduction is made, and the supercharger control is switched to the high blower position. The throttle is then reset to the desired manifold pressure. An engine equipped with this type of supercharger is called an altitude engine. *[Figure 6-14]*

Figure 6-14. *Power output of normally aspirated engine compared to a single-stage, two-speed supercharged engine.*

Turbosuperchargers

The most efficient method of increasing horsepower in an engine is by use of a turbosupercharger or turbocharger. Installed on an engine, this booster uses the engine's exhaust gases to drive an air compressor to increase the pressure of the air going into the engine through the carburetor or fuel injection system to boost power at higher altitude.

The major disadvantage of the gear-driven supercharger—use of a large amount of the engine's power output for the amount of power increase produced—is avoided with a turbocharger, because turbochargers are powered by an engine's exhaust gases. This means a turbocharger recovers energy from hot exhaust gases that would otherwise be lost.

A second advantage of turbochargers over superchargers is the ability to maintain control over an engine's rated sea-level horsepower from sea level up to the engine's critical altitude. Critical altitude is the maximum altitude at which a turbocharged engine can produce its rated horsepower. Above the critical altitude, power output begins to decrease like it does for a normally aspirated engine.

Turbochargers increase the pressure of the engine's induction air, which allows the engine to develop sea level or greater horsepower at higher altitudes. A turbocharger is comprised of two main elements: a compressor and turbine. The compressor section houses an impeller that turns at a high rate of speed. As induction air is drawn across the impeller blades, the impeller accelerates the air, allowing a large volume of air to be drawn into the compressor housing. The impeller's action subsequently produces high-pressure, high-density air, which is delivered to the engine. To turn the impeller, the engine's exhaust gases are used to drive a turbine wheel that is mounted on the opposite end of the impeller's drive

shaft. By directing different amounts of exhaust gases to flow over the turbine, more energy can be extracted, causing the impeller to deliver more compressed air to the engine. The waste gate, essentially an adjustable butterfly valve installed in the exhaust system, is used to vary the mass of exhaust gas flowing into the turbine. When closed, most of the exhaust gases from the engine are forced to flow through the turbine. When open, the exhaust gases are allowed to bypass the turbine by flowing directly out through the engine's exhaust pipe. [Figure 6-15]

Since the temperature of a gas rises when it is compressed, turbocharging causes the temperature of the induction air to increase. To reduce this temperature and lower the risk of detonation, many turbocharged engines use an intercooler. This small heat exchanger uses outside air to cool the hot compressed air before it enters the fuel metering device.

System Operation

On most modern turbocharged engines, the position of the waste gate is governed by a pressure-sensing control mechanism coupled to an actuator. Engine oil directed into or away from this actuator moves the waste gate position. On these systems, the actuator is automatically positioned to produce the desired MAP simply by changing the position of the throttle control.

TURBOCHARGER
The turbocharger incorporates a turbine, which is driven by exhaust gases, and a compressor that pressurizes the incoming air.

THROTTLE BODY
This regulates airflow to the engine.

INTAKE MANIFOLD
Pressurized air from the turbocharger is supplied to the cylinders.

EXHAUST GAS DISCHARGE

WASTE GATE
This controls the amount of exhaust through the turbine. Waste gate position is actuated by engine oil pressure.

AIR INTAKE
Intake air is ducted to the turbocharger where it is compressed.

EXHAUST MANIFOLD
Exhaust gas is ducted through the exhaust manifold and is used to turn the turbine which drives the compressor.

Figure 6-15. *Turbocharger components.*

Other turbocharging system designs use a separate manual control to position the waste gate. With manual control, the manifold pressure gauge must be closely monitored to determine when the desired MAP has been achieved. Manual systems are often found on aircraft that have been modified with aftermarket turbocharging systems. These systems require special operating considerations. For example, if the waste gate is left closed after descending from a high altitude, it is possible to produce a manifold pressure that exceeds the engine's limitations. This condition, called an overboost, may produce severe detonation because of the leaning effect resulting from increased air density during descent.

Although an automatic waste gate system is less likely to experience an overboost condition, it can still occur. If takeoff power is applied while the engine oil temperature is below its normal operating range, the cold oil may not flow out of the waste gate actuator quickly enough to prevent an overboost. To help prevent overboosting, advance the throttle cautiously to prevent exceeding the maximum manifold pressure limits.

A pilot flying an aircraft with a turbocharger should be aware of system limitations. For example, a turbocharger turbine and impeller can operate at rotational speeds in excess of 80,000 rpm while at extremely high temperatures. To achieve high rotational speed, the bearings within the system must be constantly supplied with engine oil to reduce the frictional forces and high temperature. To obtain adequate lubrication, the oil temperature should be in the normal operating range before high throttle settings are applied. In addition, allow the turbocharger to cool and the turbine to slow down before shutting the engine down. Otherwise, the oil remaining in the bearing housing will boil, causing hard carbon deposits to form on the bearings and shaft. These deposits rapidly deteriorate the turbocharger's efficiency and service life. For further limitations, refer to the AFM/POH.

High Altitude Performance

As an aircraft equipped with a turbocharging system climbs, the waste gate is gradually closed to maintain the maximum allowable manifold pressure. At some point, the waste gate will be fully closed and further increases in altitude will cause the manifold pressure to decrease. This is the critical altitude, which is established by the aircraft or engine manufacturer. When evaluating the performance of the turbocharging system, be aware that if the manifold pressure begins decreasing before the specified critical altitude, the engine and turbocharging system should be inspected by a qualified aviation maintenance technician to verify the system's proper operation.

Ignition System

In a spark ignition engine the ignition system provides a spark that ignites the fuel/air mixture in the cylinders and is made up of magnetos, spark plugs, high-tension leads, and the ignition switch. *[Figure 6-16]*

A magneto uses a permanent magnet to generate an electrical current completely independent of the aircraft's electrical system. The magneto generates sufficiently high voltage to jump a spark across the spark plug gap in each cylinder. The system begins to fire when the starter is engaged and the crankshaft begins to turn. It continues to operate whenever the crankshaft is rotating.

Most standard certificated aircraft incorporate a dual ignition system with two individual magnetos, separate sets of wires, and spark plugs to increase reliability of the ignition system. Each magneto operates independently to fire one of the two spark plugs in each cylinder. The firing of two spark plugs improves combustion of the fuel/air mixture and results in a slightly higher power output. If one of the magnetos fails, the other is unaffected. The engine will continue to operate normally, although a slight decrease in engine power can be expected. The same is true if one of the two spark plugs in a cylinder fails.

The operation of the magneto is controlled in the flight deck by the ignition switch. The switch has five positions:

1. OFF
2. R (right)
3. L (left)
4. BOTH
5. START

With RIGHT or LEFT selected, only the associated magneto is activated. The system operates on both magnetos with BOTH selected.

A malfunctioning ignition system can be identified during the pretakeoff check by observing the decrease in rpm that occurs when the ignition switch is first moved from BOTH to RIGHT, and then from BOTH to LEFT. A small decrease in engine rpm is normal during this check. The permissible decrease is listed in the AFM or POH. If the engine stops running when switched to one magneto or if the rpm drop exceeds the allowable limit, do not fly the aircraft until the problem is corrected. The cause could be fouled plugs, broken or shorted wires between the magneto and the plugs, or improperly timed firing of the plugs. It should be noted

Upper magneto wires
Lower magneto wires

Upper spark plugs

Lower spark plugs

Left magneto

Right magneto

Figure 6-16. *Ignition system components.*

that "no drop" in rpm is not normal, and in that instance, the aircraft should not be flown.

Following engine shutdown, turn the ignition switch to the OFF position. Even with the battery and master switches OFF, the engine can fire and turn over if the ignition switch is left ON and the propeller is moved because the magneto requires no outside source of electrical power. Be aware of the potential for serious injury in this situation.

Even with the ignition switch in the OFF position, if the ground wire between the magneto and the ignition switch becomes disconnected or broken, the engine could accidentally start if the propeller is moved with residual fuel in the cylinder. If this occurs, the only way to stop the engine is to move the mixture lever to the idle cutoff position, then have the system checked by a qualified aviation maintenance technician.

Oil Systems

The engine oil system performs several important functions:

- Lubrication of the engine's moving parts
- Cooling of the engine by reducing friction
- Removing heat from the cylinders
- Providing a seal between the cylinder walls and pistons
- Carrying away contaminants

Reciprocating engines use either a wet-sump or a dry-sump oil system. In a wet-sump system, the oil is located in a sump, which is an integral part of the engine. In a dry-sump system, the oil is contained in a separate tank, and circulated through the engine by pumps. *[Figure 6-17]*

The main component of a wet-sump system is the oil pump, which draws oil from the sump and routes it to the engine. After the oil passes through the engine, it returns to the sump. In some engines, additional lubrication is supplied by the rotating crankshaft, which splashes oil onto portions of the engine.

An oil pump also supplies oil pressure in a dry-sump system, but the source of the oil is located external to the engine in a separate oil tank. After oil is routed through the engine, it is pumped from the various locations in the engine back to the oil tank by scavenge pumps. Dry-sump systems allow for a greater volume of oil to be supplied to the engine, which makes them more suitable for very large reciprocating engines.

The oil pressure gauge provides a direct indication of the oil system operation. It ensures the pressure in pounds per square inch (psi) of the oil supplied to the engine. Green indicates the normal operating range, while red indicates the minimum and maximum pressures. There should be an indication of oil pressure during engine start. Refer to the AFM/POH for manufacturer limitations.

Figure 6-17. *Wet-sump oil system.*

The oil temperature gauge measures the temperature of oil. A green area shows the normal operating range and the red line indicates the maximum allowable temperature. Unlike oil pressure, changes in oil temperature occur more slowly. This is particularly noticeable after starting a cold engine, when it may take several minutes or longer for the gauge to show any increase in oil temperature.

Check oil temperature periodically during flight especially when operating in high or low ambient air temperature. High oil temperature indications may signal a plugged oil line, a low oil quantity, a blocked oil cooler, or a defective temperature gauge. Low oil temperature indications may signal improper oil viscosity during cold weather operations.

The oil filler cap and dipstick (for measuring the oil quantity) are usually accessible through a panel in the engine cowling. If the quantity does not meet the manufacturer's recommended operating levels, oil should be added. The AFM/POH or placards near the access panel provide information about the correct oil type and weight, as well as the minimum and maximum oil quantity. *[Figure 6-18]*

Engine Cooling Systems

The burning fuel within the cylinders produces intense heat, most of which is expelled through the exhaust system. Much of the remaining heat, however, must be removed, or at least dissipated, to prevent the engine from overheating. Otherwise, the extremely high engine temperatures can lead

Figure 6-18. *Always check the engine oil level during the preflight inspection.*

to loss of power, excessive oil consumption, detonation, and serious engine damage.

While the oil system is vital to the internal cooling of the engine, an additional method of cooling is necessary for the engine's external surface. Most small aircraft are air cooled, although some are liquid cooled.

Air cooling is accomplished by air flowing into the engine compartment through openings in front of the engine cowling. Baffles route this air over fins attached to the engine cylinders, and other parts of the engine, where the air absorbs the engine heat. Expulsion of the hot air takes place through one or more openings in the lower, aft portion of the engine cowling. *[Figure 6-19]*

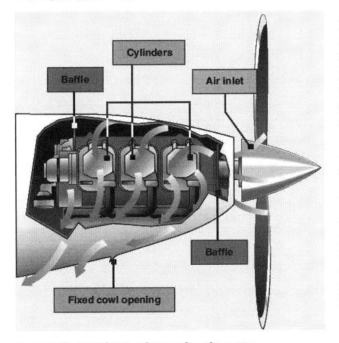

Figure 6-19. *Outside air aids in cooling the engine.*

The outside air enters the engine compartment through an inlet behind the propeller hub. Baffles direct it to the hottest parts of the engine, primarily the cylinders, which have fins that increase the area exposed to the airflow.

The air cooling system is less effective during ground operations, takeoffs, go-arounds, and other periods of high-power, low-airspeed operation. Conversely, high-speed descents provide excess air and can shock cool the engine, subjecting it to abrupt temperature fluctuations.

Operating the engine at higher than its designed temperature can cause loss of power, excessive oil consumption, and detonation. It will also lead to serious permanent damage, such as scoring the cylinder walls, damaging the pistons and rings, and burning and warping the valves. Monitoring the flight deck engine temperature instruments will aid in avoiding high operating temperature.

Under normal operating conditions in aircraft not equipped with cowl flaps, the engine temperature can be controlled by changing the airspeed or the power output of the engine. High engine temperatures can be decreased by increasing the airspeed and/or reducing the power.

The oil temperature gauge gives an indirect and delayed indication of rising engine temperature, but can be used for determining engine temperature if this is the only means available.

Most aircraft are equipped with a cylinder-head temperature gauge which indicates a direct and immediate cylinder temperature change. This instrument is calibrated in degrees Celsius or Fahrenheit, and is usually color coded with a green arc to indicate the normal operating range. A red line on the instrument indicates maximum allowable cylinder head temperature.

To avoid excessive cylinder head temperatures, increase airspeed, enrich the mixture, and/or reduce power. Any of these procedures help to reduce the engine temperature. On aircraft equipped with cowl flaps, use the cowl flap positions to control the temperature. Cowl flaps are hinged covers that fit over the opening through which the hot air is expelled. If the engine temperature is low, the cowl flaps can be closed, thereby restricting the flow of expelled hot air and increasing engine temperature. If the engine temperature is high, the cowl flaps can be opened to permit a greater flow of air through the system, thereby decreasing the engine temperature.

Exhaust Systems

Engine exhaust systems vent the burned combustion gases overboard, provide heat for the cabin, and defrost the windscreen. An exhaust system has exhaust piping attached to the cylinders, as well as a muffler and a muffler shroud. The exhaust gases are pushed out of the cylinder through the exhaust valve and then through the exhaust pipe system to the atmosphere.

For cabin heat, outside air is drawn into the air inlet and is ducted through a shroud around the muffler. The muffler is heated by the exiting exhaust gases and, in turn, heats the air around the muffler. This heated air is then ducted to the cabin for heat and defrost applications. The heat and defrost are controlled in the flight deck, and can be adjusted to the desired level.

Exhaust gases contain large amounts of carbon monoxide, which is odorless and colorless. Carbon monoxide is deadly, and its presence is virtually impossible to detect. The exhaust system must be in good condition and free of cracks.

Some exhaust systems have an EGT probe. This probe transmits the EGT to an instrument in the flight deck. The EGT gauge measures the temperature of the gases at the exhaust manifold. This temperature varies with the ratio of fuel to air entering the cylinders and can be used as a basis for regulating the fuel/air mixture. The EGT gauge is highly accurate in indicating the correct mixture setting. When using the EGT to aid in leaning the fuel/air mixture, fuel consumption can be reduced. For specific procedures, refer to the manufacturer's recommendations for leaning the mixture.

Starting System

Most small aircraft use a direct-cranking electric starter system. This system consists of a source of electricity, wiring, switches, and solenoids to operate the starter and a starter motor. Most aircraft have starters that automatically engage and disengage when operated, but some older aircraft have starters that are mechanically engaged by a lever actuated by the pilot. The starter engages the aircraft flywheel, rotating the engine at a speed that allows the engine to start and maintain operation.

Electrical power for starting is usually supplied by an onboard battery, but can also be supplied by external power through an external power receptacle. When the battery switch is turned on, electricity is supplied to the main power bus bar through the battery solenoid. Both the starter and the starter switch draw current from the main bus bar, but the starter will not operate until the starting solenoid is energized by the starter switch being turned to the "start" position. When the starter switch is released from the "start" position, the solenoid removes power from the starter motor. The starter motor is protected from being driven by the engine through a clutch in the starter drive that allows the engine to run faster than the starter motor. *[Figure 6-20]*

When starting an engine, the rules of safety and courtesy should be strictly observed. One of the most important is to make sure there is no one near the propeller. In addition, the wheels should be chocked and the brakes set, to avoid hazards caused by unintentional movement. To avoid damage to the propeller and property, the aircraft should be in an area where the propeller will not stir up gravel or dust.

Combustion

During normal combustion, the fuel/air mixture burns in a very controlled and predictable manner. In a spark ignition engine the process occurs in a fraction of a second. The mixture actually begins to burn at the point where it is ignited by the spark plugs, then burns away from the plugs until it is all consumed. This type of combustion causes a smooth build-up of temperature and pressure and ensures that the expanding gases deliver the maximum force to the piston at exactly the right time in the power stroke. *[Figure 6-21]*

Figure 6-20. *Typical starting circuit.*

Figure 6-21. *Normal combustion and explosive combustion.*

Detonation is an uncontrolled, explosive ignition of the fuel/air mixture within the cylinder's combustion chamber. It causes excessive temperatures and pressures which, if not corrected, can quickly lead to failure of the piston, cylinder, or valves. In less severe cases, detonation causes engine overheating, roughness, or loss of power.

Detonation is characterized by high cylinder head temperatures and is most likely to occur when operating at high power settings. Common operational causes of detonation are:

- Use of a lower fuel grade than that specified by the aircraft manufacturer.

- Operation of the engine with extremely high manifold pressures in conjunction with low rpm.

- Operation of the engine at high power settings with an excessively lean mixture.

- Maintaining extended ground operations or steep climbs in which cylinder cooling is reduced.

Detonation may be avoided by following these basic guidelines during the various phases of ground and flight operations:

- Make sure the proper grade of fuel is used.

- Keep the cowl flaps (if available) in the full-open position while on the ground to provide the maximum airflow through the cowling.

- Use an enriched fuel mixture, as well as a shallower climb angle to increase cylinder cooling during takeoff and initial climb.

- Avoid extended, high power, steep climbs.

- Develop the habit of monitoring the engine instruments to verify proper operation according to procedures established by the manufacturer.

Preignition occurs when the fuel/air mixture ignites prior to the engine's normal ignition event. Premature burning is usually caused by a residual hot spot in the combustion chamber, often created by a small carbon deposit on a spark plug, a cracked spark plug insulator, or other damage in the cylinder that causes a part to heat sufficiently to ignite the fuel/air charge. Preignition causes the engine to lose power, and produces high operating temperature. As with detonation, preignition may also cause severe engine damage, because the expanding gases exert excessive pressure on the piston while still on its compression stroke.

Detonation and preignition often occur simultaneously and one may cause the other. Since either condition causes high engine temperature accompanied by a decrease in engine performance, it is often difficult to distinguish between the two. Using the recommended grade of fuel and operating the engine within its proper temperature, pressure, and rpm ranges reduce the chance of detonation or preignition.

Full Authority Digital Engine Control (FADEC)

FADEC is a system consisting of a digital computer and ancillary components that control an aircraft's engine and propeller. First used in turbine-powered aircraft, and referred to as full authority digital electronic control, these sophisticated control systems are increasingly being used in piston powered aircraft.

In a spark ignition reciprocating engine the FADEC uses speed, temperature, and pressure sensors to monitor the status of each cylinder. A digital computer calculates the ideal pulse for each injector and adjusts ignition timing as necessary to achieve optimal performance. In a compression ignition engine the FADEC operates similarly and performs all of the same functions, excluding those specifically related to the spark ignition process.

FADEC systems eliminate the need for magnetos, carburetor heat, mixture controls, and engine priming. A single throttle lever is characteristic of an aircraft equipped with a FADEC system. The pilot simply positions the throttle lever to a desired detent such as start, idle, cruise power, or max power, and the FADEC system adjusts the engine and propeller automatically for the mode selected. There is no need for the pilot to monitor or control the air/fuel mixture.

During aircraft starting, the FADEC primes the cylinders, adjusts the mixture, and positions the throttle based on engine temperature and ambient pressure. During cruise flight, the FADEC constantly monitors the engine and adjusts fuel flow, and ignition timing individually in each cylinder. This precise control of the combustion process often results in decreased fuel consumption and increased horsepower.

FADEC systems are considered an essential part of the engine and propeller control, and may be powered by the aircraft's main electrical system. In many aircraft FADEC uses power from a separate generator connected to the engine. In either case, there must be a backup electrical source available because failure of a FADEC system could result in a complete loss of engine thrust. To prevent loss of thrust, two separate and identical digital channels are incorporated for redundancy, each channel capable of providing all engine and propeller functions without limitations.

Turbine Engines

An aircraft turbine engine consists of an air inlet, compressor, combustion chambers, a turbine section, and exhaust. Thrust is produced by increasing the velocity of the air flowing through the engine. Turbine engines are highly desirable aircraft powerplants. They are characterized by smooth operation and a high power-to-weight ratio, and they use readily available jet fuel. Prior to recent advances in material, engine design, and manufacturing processes, the use of turbine engines in small/light production aircraft was cost prohibitive. Today, several aviation manufacturers are producing or plan to produce small/light turbine-powered aircraft. These smaller turbine-powered aircraft typically seat between three and seven passengers and are referred to as very light jets (VLJs) or microjets. [Figure 6-22]

Figure 6-22. *Eclipse 500 VLJ.*

Types of Turbine Engines

Turbine engines are classified according to the type of compressors they use. There are three types of compressors—centrifugal flow, axial flow, and centrifugal-axial flow. Compression of inlet air is achieved in a centrifugal flow engine by accelerating air outward perpendicular to the longitudinal axis of the machine. The axial-flow engine compresses air by a series of rotating and stationary airfoils moving the air parallel to the longitudinal axis. The centrifugal-axial flow design uses both kinds of compressors to achieve the desired compression.

The path the air takes through the engine and how power is produced determines the type of engine. There are four types of aircraft turbine engines—turbojet, turboprop, turbofan, and turboshaft.

Turbojet

The turbojet engine consists of four sections: compressor, combustion chamber, turbine section, and exhaust. The compressor section passes inlet air at a high rate of speed to the combustion chamber. The combustion chamber contains the fuel inlet and igniter for combustion. The expanding air drives a turbine, which is connected by a shaft to the compressor, sustaining engine operation. The accelerated exhaust gases from the engine provide thrust. This is a basic application of compressing air, igniting the fuel-air mixture, producing power to self-sustain the engine operation, and exhaust for propulsion. [Figure 6-23]

Turbojet engines are limited in range and endurance. They are also slow to respond to throttle applications at slow compressor speeds.

Turboprop

A turboprop engine is a turbine engine that drives a propeller through a reduction gear. The exhaust gases drive a power turbine connected by a shaft that drives the reduction gear assembly. Reduction gearing is necessary in turboprop engines because optimum propeller performance is achieved at much slower speeds than the engine's operating rpm. Turboprop engines are a compromise between turbojet engines and reciprocating powerplants. Turboprop engines are most efficient at speeds between 250 and 400 mph and altitudes between 18,000 and 30,000 feet. They also perform well at the slow airspeeds required for takeoff and landing, and are fuel efficient. The minimum specific fuel consumption of the turboprop engine is normally available in the altitude range of 25,000 feet to the tropopause. [Figure 6-24]

Turbofan

Turbofans were developed to combine some of the best features of the turbojet and the turboprop. Turbofan engines are designed to create additional thrust by diverting a secondary airflow around the combustion chamber. The turbofan bypass air generates increased thrust, cools the engine, and aids in exhaust noise suppression. This provides turbojet-type cruise speed and lower fuel consumption.

The inlet air that passes through a turbofan engine is usually divided into two separate streams of air. One stream passes through the engine core, while a second stream bypasses the engine core. It is this bypass stream of air that is responsible for the term "bypass engine." A turbofan's bypass ratio refers to the ratio of the mass airflow that passes through the fan divided by the mass airflow that passes through the engine core. [Figure 6-25]

Turboshaft

The fourth common type of jet engine is the turboshaft. [Figure 6-26] It delivers power to a shaft that drives something other than a propeller. The biggest difference between a turbojet and turboshaft engine is that on a

Figure 6-23. *Turbojet engine.*

Figure 6-24. *Turboprop engine.*

Figure 6-25. *Turbofan engine.*

Figure 6-26. *Turboshaft engine.*

turboshaft engine, most of the energy produced by the expanding gases is used to drive a turbine rather than produce thrust. Many helicopters use a turboshaft gas turbine engine. In addition, turboshaft engines are widely used as auxiliary power units on large aircraft.

Turbine Engine Instruments

Engine instruments that indicate oil pressure, oil temperature, engine speed, exhaust gas temperature, and fuel flow are common to both turbine and reciprocating engines. However, there are some instruments that are unique to turbine engines. These instruments provide indications of engine pressure ratio, turbine discharge pressure, and torque. In addition, most gas turbine engines have multiple temperature-sensing instruments, called thermocouples, which provide pilots with temperature readings in and around the turbine section.

Engine Pressure Ratio (EPR)

An engine pressure ratio (EPR) gauge is used to indicate the power output of a turbojet/turbofan engine. EPR is the ratio of turbine discharge to compressor inlet pressure. Pressure measurements are recorded by probes installed in the engine inlet and at the exhaust. Once collected, the data is sent to a differential pressure transducer, which is indicated on a flight deck EPR gauge.

EPR system design automatically compensates for the effects of airspeed and altitude. Changes in ambient temperature require a correction be applied to EPR indications to provide accurate engine power settings.

Exhaust Gas Temperature (EGT)

A limiting factor in a gas turbine engine is the temperature of the turbine section. The temperature of a turbine section must be monitored closely to prevent overheating the turbine blades and other exhaust section components. One common way of monitoring the temperature of a turbine section is with an EGT gauge. EGT is an engine operating limit used to monitor overall engine operating conditions.

Variations of EGT systems bear different names based on the location of the temperature sensors. Common turbine temperature sensing gauges include the turbine inlet temperature (TIT) gauge, turbine outlet temperature (TOT) gauge, interstage turbine temperature (ITT) gauge, and turbine gas temperature (TGT) gauge.

Torquemeter

Turboprop/turboshaft engine power output is measured by the torquemeter. Torque is a twisting force applied to a shaft. The torquemeter measures power applied to the shaft. Turboprop and turboshaft engines are designed to produce torque for driving a propeller. Torquemeters are calibrated in percentage units, foot-pounds, or psi.

N_1 Indicator

N_1 represents the rotational speed of the low pressure compressor and is presented on the indicator as a percentage of design rpm. After start the speed of the low pressure compressor is governed by the N_1 turbine wheel. The N_1 turbine wheel is connected to the low pressure compressor through a concentric shaft.

N_2 Indicator

N_2 represents the rotational speed of the high pressure compressor and is presented on the indicator as a percentage of design rpm. The high pressure compressor is governed by the N_2 turbine wheel. The N_2 turbine wheel is connected to the high pressure compressor through a concentric shaft. [Figure 6-27]

Figure 6-27. *Dual-spool axial-flow compressor.*

Turbine Engine Operational Considerations

The great variety of turbine engines makes it impractical to cover specific operational procedures, but there are certain operational considerations common to all turbine engines. They are engine temperature limits, foreign object damage, hot start, compressor stall, and flameout.

Engine Temperature Limitations

The highest temperature in any turbine engine occurs at the turbine inlet. Turbine inlet temperature is therefore usually the limiting factor in turbine engine operation.

Thrust Variations

Turbine engine thrust varies directly with air density. As air density decreases, so does thrust. Additionally, because air density decreases with an increase in temperature, increased temperatures will also result in decreased thrust. While both turbine and reciprocating powered engines are affected to some degree by high relative humidity, turbine engines will experience a negligible loss of thrust, while reciprocating engines a significant loss of brake horsepower.

Foreign Object Damage (FOD)

Due to the design and function of a turbine engine's air inlet, the possibility of ingestion of debris always exists. This causes significant damage, particularly to the compressor and turbine sections. When ingestion of debris occurs, it is called foreign object damage (FOD). Typical FOD consists of small nicks and dents caused by ingestion of small objects from the ramp, taxiway, or runway, but FOD damage caused by bird strikes or ice ingestion also occur. Sometimes FOD results in total destruction of an engine.

Prevention of FOD is a high priority. Some engine inlets have a tendency to form a vortex between the ground and the inlet during ground operations. A vortex dissipater may be installed on these engines. Other devices, such as screens and/or deflectors, may also be utilized. Preflight procedures include a visual inspection for any sign of FOD.

Turbine Engine Hot/Hung Start

When the EGT exceeds the safe limit of an aircraft, it experiences a "hot start." It is caused by too much fuel entering the combustion chamber, or insufficient turbine rpm. Any time an engine has a hot start, refer to the AFM/POH or an appropriate maintenance manual for inspection requirements.

If the engine fails to accelerate to the proper speed after ignition or does not accelerate to idle rpm, a hung or false start has occurred. A hung start may be caused by an insufficient starting power source or fuel control malfunction.

Compressor Stalls

Compressor blades are small airfoils and are subject to the same aerodynamic principles that apply to any airfoil. A compressor blade has an angle of attack which is a result of inlet air velocity and the compressor's rotational velocity. These two forces combine to form a vector, which defines the airfoil's actual angle of attack to the approaching inlet air.

A compressor stall is an imbalance between the two vector quantities, inlet velocity and compressor rotational speed. Compressor stalls occur when the compressor blades' angle of attack exceeds the critical angle of attack. At this point, smooth airflow is interrupted and turbulence is created with pressure fluctuations. Compressor stalls cause air flowing

in the compressor to slow down and stagnate, sometimes reversing direction. *[Figure 6-28]*

Figure 6-28. *Comparison of normal and distorted airflow into the compressor section.*

Compressor stalls can be transient and intermittent or steady and severe. Indications of a transient/intermittent stall are usually an intermittent "bang" as backfire and flow reversal take place. If the stall develops and becomes steady, strong vibration and a loud roar may develop from the continuous flow reversal. Often, the flight deck gauges do not show a mild or transient stall, but they do indicate a developed stall. Typical instrument indications include fluctuations in rpm and an increase in exhaust gas temperature. Most transient stalls are not harmful to the engine and often correct themselves after one or two pulsations. The possibility of severe engine damage from a steady state stall is immediate. Recovery must be accomplished by quickly reducing power, decreasing the aircraft's angle of attack, and increasing airspeed.

Although all gas turbine engines are subject to compressor stalls, most models have systems that inhibit them. One system uses a variable inlet guide vane (VIGV) and variable stator vanes, which direct the incoming air into the rotor blades at an appropriate angle. To prevent air pressure stalls, operate the aircraft within the parameters established by the manufacturer. If a compressor stall does develop, follow the procedures recommended in the AFM/POH.

Flameout

A flameout occurs in the operation of a gas turbine engine in which the fire in the engine unintentionally goes out. If the rich limit of the fuel/air ratio is exceeded in the combustion chamber, the flame will blow out. This condition is often referred to as a rich flameout. It generally results from very fast engine acceleration, in which an overly rich mixture causes the fuel temperature to drop below the combustion temperature. It may also be caused by insufficient airflow to support combustion.

A more common flameout occurrence is due to low fuel pressure and low engine speeds, which typically are associated with high-altitude flight. This situation may also occur with the engine throttled back during a descent, which can set up the lean-condition flameout. A weak mixture can easily cause the flame to die out, even with a normal airflow through the engine.

Any interruption of the fuel supply can result in a flameout. This may be due to prolonged unusual attitudes, a malfunctioning fuel control system, turbulence, icing or running out of fuel.

Symptoms of a flameout normally are the same as those following an engine failure. If the flameout is due to a transitory condition, such as an imbalance between fuel flow and engine speed, an airstart may be attempted once the condition is corrected. In any case, pilots must follow the applicable emergency procedures outlined in the AFM/POH. Generally these procedures contain recommendations concerning altitude and airspeed where the airstart is most likely to be successful.

Performance Comparison

It is possible to compare the performance of a reciprocating powerplant and different types of turbine engines. For the comparison to be accurate, thrust horsepower (usable horsepower) for the reciprocating powerplant must be used rather than brake horsepower, and net thrust must be used for the turbine-powered engines. In addition, aircraft design configuration and size must be approximately the same. When comparing performance, the following definitions are useful:

Brake horsepower (BHP)—the horsepower actually delivered to the output shaft. Brake horsepower is the actual usable horsepower.

Net thrust—the thrust produced by a turbojet or turbofan engine.

Thrust horsepower (THP)—the horsepower equivalent of the thrust produced by a turbojet or turbofan engine.

Equivalent shaft horsepower (ESHP)—with respect to turboprop engines, the sum of the shaft horsepower (SHP) delivered to the propeller and THP produced by the exhaust gases.

Figure 6-29 shows how four types of engines compare in net thrust as airspeed is increased. This figure is for explanatory purposes only and is not for specific models of engines. The following are the four types of engines:

- Reciprocating powerplant
- Turbine, propeller combination (turboprop)
- Turbine engine incorporating a fan (turbofan)
- Turbojet (pure jet)

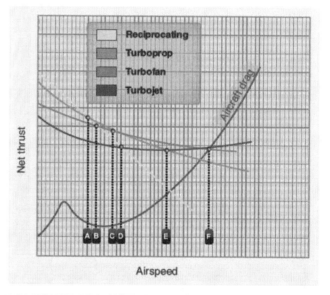

Figure 6-29. *Engine net thrust versus aircraft speed and drag. Points* **A** *through* **F** *are explained in the text below.*

By plotting the performance curve for each engine, a comparison can be made of maximum aircraft speed variation with the type of engine used. Since the graph is only a means of comparison, numerical values for net thrust, aircraft speed, and drag are not included.

Comparison of the four powerplants on the basis of net thrust makes certain performance capabilities evident. In the speed range shown to the left of line A, the reciprocating powerplant outperforms the other three types. The turboprop outperforms the turbofan in the range to the left of line C. The turbofan engine outperforms the turbojet in the range to the left of line F. The turbofan engine outperforms the reciprocating powerplant to the right of line B and the turboprop to the right of line C. The turbojet outperforms the reciprocating powerplant to the right of line D, the turboprop to the right of line E, and the turbofan to the right of line F.

The points where the aircraft drag curve intersects the net thrust curves are the maximum aircraft speeds. The vertical lines from each of the points to the baseline of the graph indicate that the turbojet aircraft can attain a higher maximum speed than aircraft equipped with the other types of engines. Aircraft equipped with the turbofan engine will attain a higher maximum speed than aircraft equipped with a turboprop or reciprocating powerplant.

Airframe Systems

Fuel, electrical, hydraulic, and oxygen systems make up the airframe systems.

Fuel Systems

The fuel system is designed to provide an uninterrupted flow of clean fuel from the fuel tanks to the engine. The fuel must be available to the engine under all conditions of engine power, altitude, attitude, and during all approved flight maneuvers. Two common classifications apply to fuel systems in small aircraft: gravity-feed and fuel-pump systems.

Gravity-Feed System

The gravity-feed system utilizes the force of gravity to transfer the fuel from the tanks to the engine. For example, on high-wing airplanes, the fuel tanks are installed in the wings. This places the fuel tanks above the carburetor, and the fuel is gravity fed through the system and into the carburetor. If the design of the aircraft is such that gravity cannot be used to transfer fuel, fuel pumps are installed. For example, on low-wing airplanes, the fuel tanks in the wings are located below the carburetor. *[Figure 6-30]*

Fuel-Pump System

Aircraft with fuel-pump systems have two fuel pumps. The main pump system is engine driven with an electrically driven auxiliary pump provided for use in engine starting and in the event the engine pump fails. The auxiliary pump, also known as a boost pump, provides added reliability to the fuel system. The electrically driven auxiliary pump is controlled by a switch in the flight deck.

Fuel Primer

Both gravity-feed and fuel-pump systems may incorporate a fuel primer into the system. The fuel primer is used to draw fuel from the tanks to vaporize fuel directly into the cylinders prior to starting the engine. During cold weather, when engines are difficult to start, the fuel primer helps because there is not enough heat available to vaporize the fuel in the carburetor. It is important to lock the primer in place when it is not in use. If the knob is free to move, it may vibrate out during flight and can cause an excessively rich mixture. To avoid overpriming, read the priming instructions for the aircraft.

Figure 6-30. *Gravity-feed and fuel-pump systems.*

Fuel Tanks

The fuel tanks, normally located inside the wings of an airplane, have a filler opening on top of the wing through which they can be filled. A filler cap covers this opening. The tanks are vented to the outside to maintain atmospheric pressure inside the tank. They may be vented through the filler cap or through a tube extending through the surface of the wing. Fuel tanks also include an overflow drain that may stand alone or be collocated with the fuel tank vent. This allows fuel to expand with increases in temperature without damage to the tank itself. If the tanks have been filled on a hot day, it is not unusual to see fuel coming from the overflow drain.

Fuel Gauges

The fuel quantity gauges indicate the amount of fuel measured by a sensing unit in each fuel tank and is displayed in gallons or pounds. Aircraft certification rules require accuracy in fuel gauges only when they read "empty." Any reading other than "empty" should be verified. Do not depend solely on the accuracy of the fuel quantity gauges. Always visually check the fuel level in each tank during the preflight inspection, and then compare it with the corresponding fuel quantity indication.

If a fuel pump is installed in the fuel system, a fuel pressure gauge is also included. This gauge indicates the pressure in the fuel lines. The normal operating pressure can be found in the AFM/POH or on the gauge by color coding.

Fuel Selectors

The fuel selector valve allows selection of fuel from various tanks. A common type of selector valve contains four positions: LEFT, RIGHT, BOTH, and OFF. Selecting the LEFT or RIGHT position allows fuel to feed only from that tank, while selecting the BOTH position feeds fuel from both tanks. The LEFT or RIGHT position may be used to balance the amount of fuel remaining in each wing tank. *[Figure 6-31]*

Figure 6-31. *Fuel selector valve.*

Fuel placards will show any limitations on fuel tank usage, such as "level flight only" and/or "both" for landings and takeoffs.

Regardless of the type of fuel selector in use, fuel consumption should be monitored closely to ensure that a tank does not run completely out of fuel. Running a fuel tank dry will not only cause the engine to stop, but running for prolonged periods on one tank causes an unbalanced fuel load between tanks. Running a tank completely dry may allow air to enter the fuel system and cause vapor lock, which makes it difficult to restart the engine. On fuel-injected engines, the fuel becomes so hot it vaporizes in the fuel line, not allowing fuel to reach the cylinders.

Fuel Strainers, Sumps, and Drains

After leaving the fuel tank and before it enters the carburetor, the fuel passes through a strainer which removes any moisture and other sediments in the system. Since these contaminants are heavier than aviation fuel, they settle in a sump at the bottom of the strainer assembly. A sump is a low point in a fuel system and/or fuel tank. The fuel system may contain sump, fuel strainer, and fuel tank drains, which may be collocated.

The fuel strainer should be drained before each flight. Fuel samples should be drained and checked visually for water and contaminants.

Water in the sump is hazardous because in cold weather the water can freeze and block fuel lines. In warm weather, it can flow into the carburetor and stop the engine. If water is present in the sump, more water in the fuel tanks is probable and they should be drained until there is no evidence of water. Never take off until all water and contaminants have been removed from the engine fuel system.

Because of the variation in fuel systems, become thoroughly familiar with the systems that apply to the aircraft being flown. Consult the AFM/POH for specific operating procedures.

Fuel Grades

Aviation gasoline (AVGAS) is identified by an octane or performance number (grade), which designates the antiknock value or knock resistance of the fuel mixture in the engine cylinder. The higher the grade of gasoline, the more pressure the fuel can withstand without detonating. Lower grades of fuel are used in lower-compression engines because these fuels ignite at a lower temperature. Higher grades are used in higher-compression engines, because they ignite at higher temperatures, but not prematurely. If the proper grade of fuel is not available, use the next higher grade as a substitute. Never use a grade lower than recommended. This can cause the cylinder head temperature and engine oil temperature to exceed their normal operating ranges, which may result in detonation.

Several grades of AVGAS are available. Care must be exercised to ensure that the correct aviation grade is being used for the specific type of engine. The proper fuel grade is stated in the AFM/POH, on placards in the flight deck, and next to the filler caps. Auto gas should NEVER be used in aircraft engines unless the aircraft has been modified with a Supplemental Type Certificate (STC) issued by the Federal Aviation Administration (FAA).

The current method identifies AVGAS for aircraft with reciprocating engines by the octane and performance number, along with the abbreviation AVGAS. These aircraft use AVGAS 80, 100, and 100LL. Although AVGAS 100LL performs the same as grade 100, the "LL" indicates it has a low lead content. Fuel for aircraft with turbine engines is classified as JET A, JET A-1, and JET B. Jet fuel is basically kerosene and has a distinctive kerosene smell. Since use of the correct fuel is critical, dyes are added to help identify the type and grade of fuel. *[Figure 6-32]*

Figure 6-32. *Aviation fuel color-coding system.*

In addition to the color of the fuel itself, the color-coding system extends to decals and various airport fuel handling equipment. For example, all AVGAS is identified by name, using white letters on a red background. In contrast, turbine fuels are identified by white letters on a black background.

Fuel Contamination

Accidents attributed to powerplant failure from fuel contamination have often been traced to:

- Inadequate preflight inspection by the pilot.

- Servicing aircraft with improperly filtered fuel from small tanks or drums.

- Storing aircraft with partially filled fuel tanks.

- Lack of proper maintenance.

Fuel should be drained from the fuel strainer quick drain and from each fuel tank sump into a transparent container, and then checked for dirt and water. When the fuel strainer is being drained, water in the tank may not appear until all the fuel has been drained from the lines leading to the tank. This indicates that water remains in the tank, and is not forcing the fuel out of the fuel lines leading to the fuel strainer. Therefore, drain enough fuel from the fuel strainer to be certain that fuel is being drained from the tank. The amount will depend on the length of fuel line from the tank to the drain. If water or other contaminants are found in the first sample, drain further samples until no trace appears.

Water may also remain in the fuel tanks after the drainage from the fuel strainer has ceased to show any trace of water.

This residual water can be removed only by draining the fuel tank sump drains.

Water is the principal fuel contaminant. Suspended water droplets in the fuel can be identified by a cloudy appearance of the fuel, or by the clear separation of water from the colored fuel, which occurs after the water has settled to the bottom of the tank. As a safety measure, the fuel sumps should be drained before every flight during the preflight inspection.

Fuel tanks should be filled after each flight or after the last flight of the day to prevent moisture condensation within the tank. To prevent fuel contamination, avoid refueling from cans and drums.

In remote areas or in emergency situations, there may be no alternative to refueling from sources with inadequate anti-contamination systems. While a chamois skin and funnel may be the only possible means of filtering fuel, using them is hazardous. Remember, the use of a chamois will not always ensure decontaminated fuel. Worn-out chamois will not filter water; neither will a new, clean chamois that is already water-wet or damp. Most imitation chamois skins will not filter water.

Refueling Procedures

Static electricity is formed by the friction of air passing over the surfaces of an aircraft in flight and by the flow of fuel through the hose and nozzle during refueling. Nylon, Dacron, or wool clothing is especially prone to accumulate and discharge static electricity from the person to the funnel or nozzle. To guard against the possibility of static electricity igniting fuel fumes, a ground wire should be attached to the aircraft before the fuel cap is removed from the tank. Because both the aircraft and refueler have different static charges, bonding both components to each other is critical. By bonding both components to each other, the static differential charge is equalized. The refueling nozzle should be bonded to the aircraft before refueling begins and should remain bonded throughout the refueling process. When a fuel truck is used, it should be grounded prior to the fuel nozzle contacting the aircraft.

If fueling from drums or cans is necessary, proper bonding and grounding connections are important. Drums should be placed near grounding posts and the following sequence of connections observed:

1. Drum to ground

2. Ground to aircraft

3. Bond drum to aircraft or nozzle to aircraft before the fuel cap is removed

When disconnecting, reverse the order.

The passage of fuel through a chamois increases the charge of static electricity and the danger of sparks. The aircraft must be properly grounded and the nozzle, chamois filter, and funnel bonded to the aircraft. If a can is used, it should be connected to either the grounding post or the funnel. Under no circumstances should a plastic bucket or similar nonconductive container be used in this operation.

Electrical System

Most aircraft are equipped with either a 14- or a 28-volt direct current electrical system. A basic aircraft electrical system consists of the following components:

- Alternator/generator
- Battery
- Master/battery switch
- Alternator/generator switch
- Bus bar, fuses, and circuit breakers
- Voltage regulator
- Ammeter/loadmeter
- Associated electrical wiring

Engine-driven alternators or generators supply electric current to the electrical system. They also maintain a sufficient electrical charge in the battery. Electrical energy stored in a battery provides a source of electrical power for starting the engine and a limited supply of electrical power for use in the event the alternator or generator fails.

Most direct-current generators will not produce a sufficient amount of electrical current at low engine rpm to operate the entire electrical system. During operations at low engine rpm, the electrical needs must be drawn from the battery, which can quickly be depleted.

Alternators have several advantages over generators. Alternators produce sufficient current to operate the entire electrical system, even at slower engine speeds, by producing alternating current, which is converted to direct current. The electrical output of an alternator is more constant throughout a wide range of engine speeds.

Some aircraft have receptacles to which an external ground power unit (GPU) may be connected to provide electrical energy for starting. These are very useful, especially during cold weather starting. Follow the manufacturer's recommendations for engine starting using a GPU.

The electrical system is turned on or off with a master switch. Turning the master switch to the ON position provides electrical energy to all the electrical equipment circuits except the ignition system. Equipment that commonly uses the electrical system for its source of energy includes:

- Position lights
- Anticollision lights
- Landing lights
- Taxi lights
- Interior cabin lights
- Instrument lights
- Radio equipment
- Turn indicator
- Fuel gauges
- Electric fuel pump
- Stall warning system
- Pitot heat
- Starting motor

Many aircraft are equipped with a battery switch that controls the electrical power to the aircraft in a manner similar to the master switch. In addition, an alternator switch is installed which permits the pilot to exclude the alternator from the electrical system in the event of alternator failure. [Figure 6-33]

Figure 6-33. *On this master switch, the left half is for the alternator and the right half is for the battery.*

With the alternator half of the switch in the OFF position, the entire electrical load is placed on the battery. All nonessential electrical equipment should be turned off to conserve battery power.

A bus bar is used as a terminal in the aircraft electrical system to connect the main electrical system to the equipment using electricity as a source of power. This simplifies the wiring system and provides a common point from which voltage can be distributed throughout the system. [Figure 6-34]

Fuses or circuit breakers are used in the electrical system to protect the circuits and equipment from electrical overload.

Spare fuses of the proper amperage limit should be carried in the aircraft to replace defective or blown fuses. Circuit breakers have the same function as a fuse but can be manually reset, rather than replaced, if an overload condition occurs in the electrical system. Placards at the fuse or circuit breaker panel identify the circuit by name and show the amperage limit.

Figure 6-34. *Electrical system schematic.*

An ammeter is used to monitor the performance of the aircraft electrical system. The ammeter shows if the alternator/generator is producing an adequate supply of electrical power. It also indicates whether or not the battery is receiving an electrical charge.

Ammeters are designed with the zero point in the center of the face and a negative or positive indication on either side. *[Figure 6-35]* When the pointer of the ammeter is on the plus side, it shows the charging rate of the battery. A minus indication means more current is being drawn from the battery than is being replaced. A full-scale minus deflection indicates a malfunction of the alternator/generator. A full-scale positive deflection indicates a malfunction of the regulator. In either case, consult the AFM or POH for appropriate action to be taken.

Figure 6-35. *Ammeter and loadmeter.*

Not all aircraft are equipped with an ammeter. Some have a warning light that, when lighted, indicates a discharge in the system as a generator/alternator malfunction. Refer to the AFM or POH for appropriate action to be taken.

Another electrical monitoring indicator is a loadmeter. This type of gauge has a scale beginning with zero and shows the load being placed on the alternator/generator. *[Figure 6-35]* The loadmeter reflects the total percentage of the load placed on the generating capacity of the electrical system by the electrical accessories and battery. When all electrical components are turned off, it reflects only the amount of charging current demanded by the battery.

A voltage regulator controls the rate of charge to the battery by stabilizing the generator or alternator electrical output. The generator/alternator voltage output should be higher than the battery voltage. For example, a 12-volt battery would be fed by a generator/alternator system of approximately 14 volts. The difference in voltage keeps the battery charged.

Hydraulic Systems

There are multiple applications for hydraulic use in aircraft, depending on the complexity of the aircraft. For example,

hydraulics is often used on small airplanes to operate wheel brakes, retractable landing gear, and some constant-speed propellers. On large airplanes, hydraulics is used for flight control surfaces, wing flaps, spoilers, and other systems.

A basic hydraulic system consists of a reservoir, pump (either hand, electric, or engine driven), a filter to keep the fluid clean, selector valve to control the direction of flow, relief valve to relieve excess pressure, and an actuator. *[Figure 6-36]*

Figure 6-36. *Basic hydraulic system.*

The hydraulic fluid is pumped through the system to an actuator or servo. A servo is a cylinder with a piston inside that turns fluid power into work and creates the power needed to move an aircraft system or flight control. Servos can be either single-acting or double-acting, based on the needs of the system. This means that the fluid can be applied to one or both sides of the servo, depending on the servo type. A single-acting servo provides power in one direction. The selector valve allows the fluid direction to be controlled. This is necessary for operations such as the extension and retraction of landing gear during which the fluid must work in two different directions. The relief valve provides an outlet for the system in the event of excessive fluid pressure in the system. Each system incorporates different components to meet the individual needs of different aircraft.

A mineral-based hydraulic fluid is the most widely used type for small aircraft. This type of hydraulic fluid, a kerosene-like petroleum product, has good lubricating properties, as well as additives to inhibit foaming and prevent the formation of corrosion. It is chemically stable, has very little viscosity change with temperature, and is dyed for identification. Since several types of hydraulic fluids are commonly used, an aircraft must be serviced with the type specified by the manufacturer. Refer to the AFM/POH or the Maintenance Manual.

Landing Gear

The landing gear forms the principal support of an aircraft on the surface. The most common type of landing gear consists of wheels, but aircraft can also be equipped with floats for water operations or skis for landing on snow. *[Figure 6-37]*

Figure 6-37. *The landing gear supports the airplane during the takeoff run, landing, taxiing, and when parked.*

The landing gear on small aircraft consists of three wheels: two main wheels (one located on each side of the fuselage) and a third wheel positioned either at the front or rear of the airplane. Landing gear employing a rear-mounted wheel is called conventional landing gear. Airplanes with conventional landing gear are often referred to as tailwheel airplanes. When the third wheel is located on the nose, it is called a nosewheel, and the design is referred to as a tricycle gear. A steerable nosewheel or tailwheel permits the airplane to be controlled throughout all operations while on the ground.

Tricycle Landing Gear Airplanes

A tricycle gear airplane has three advantages:

1. It allows more forceful application of the brakes during landings at high speeds without causing the aircraft to nose over.

2. It permits better forward visibility for the pilot during takeoff, landing, and taxiing.

3. It tends to prevent ground looping (swerving) by providing more directional stability during ground operation since the aircraft's center of gravity (CG) is forward of the main wheels. The forward CG keeps the airplane moving forward in a straight line rather than ground looping.

Nosewheels are either steerable or castering. Steerable nosewheels are linked to the rudders by cables or rods, while castering nosewheels are free to swivel. In both cases, the aircraft is steered using the rudder pedals. Aircraft with a castering nosewheel may require the pilot to combine the use of the rudder pedals with independent use of the brakes.

Tailwheel Landing Gear Airplanes

Tailwheel landing gear aircraft have two main wheels attached to the airframe ahead of its CG that support most of the weight of the structure. A tailwheel at the very back of the fuselage provides a third point of support. This arrangement allows adequate ground clearance for a larger propeller and is more desirable for operations on unimproved fields. *[Figure 6-38]*

Figure 6-38. *Tailwheel landing gear.*

With the CG located behind the main gear, directional control of this type aircraft becomes more difficult while on the ground. This is the main disadvantage of the tailwheel landing gear. For example, if the pilot allows the aircraft to swerve while rolling on the ground at a low speed, he or she may not have sufficient rudder control and the CG will attempt to get ahead of the main gear which may cause the airplane to ground loop.

Lack of good forward visibility when the tailwheel is on or near the ground is a second disadvantage of tailwheel landing gear aircraft. These inherent problems mean specific training is required in tailwheel aircraft.

Fixed and Retractable Landing Gear

Landing gear can also be classified as either fixed or retractable. A fixed gear always remains extended and has the advantage of simplicity combined with low maintenance. A retractable gear is designed to streamline the airplane by allowing the landing gear to be stowed inside the structure during cruising flight. *[Figure 6-39]*

Figure 6-39. *Fixed (left) and retractable (right) gear airplanes.*

Brakes

Airplane brakes are located on the main wheels and are applied by either a hand control or by foot pedals (toe or heel). Foot pedals operate independently and allow for differential braking. During ground operations, differential braking can supplement nosewheel/tailwheel steering.

Pressurized Aircraft

Aircraft are flown at high altitudes for two reasons. First, an aircraft flown at high altitude consumes less fuel for a given airspeed than it does for the same speed at a lower altitude because the aircraft is more efficient at a high altitude. Second, bad weather and turbulence may be avoided by flying in relatively smooth air above the storms. Many modern aircraft are being designed to operate at high altitudes, taking advantage of that environment. In order to fly at higher altitudes, the aircraft must be pressurized. It is important for pilots who fly these aircraft to be familiar with the basic operating principles.

In a typical pressurization system, the cabin, flight compartment, and baggage compartments are incorporated into a sealed unit capable of containing air under a pressure higher than outside atmospheric pressure. On aircraft powered by turbine engines, bleed air from the engine compressor section is used to pressurize the cabin. Superchargers may be used on older model turbine-powered aircraft to pump air into the sealed fuselage. Piston-powered aircraft may use air supplied from each engine turbocharger through a sonic venturi (flow limiter). Air is released from the fuselage by a device called an outflow valve. By regulating the air exit, the outflow valve allows for a constant inflow of air to the pressurized area. *[Figure 6-40]*

A cabin pressurization system typically maintains a cabin pressure altitude of approximately 8,000 feet at the maximum designed cruising altitude of an aircraft. This prevents rapid changes of cabin altitude that may be uncomfortable or cause

Figure 6-40. *High performance airplane pressurization system.*

injury to passengers and crew. In addition, the pressurization system permits a reasonably fast exchange of air from the inside to the outside of the cabin. This is necessary to eliminate odors and to remove stale air. *[Figure 6-41]*

Pressurization of the aircraft cabin is an accepted method of protecting occupants against the effects of hypoxia. Within a pressurized cabin, occupants can be transported comfortably

Atmosphere pressure	
Altitude (ft)	Pressure (psi)
Sea level	14.7
2,000	13.7
4,000	12.7
6,000	11.8
8,000	10.9
10,000	10.1
12,000	9.4
14,000	8.6
16,000	8.0
18,000	7.3
20,000	6.8
22,000	6.2
24,000	5.7
26,000	5.2
28,000	4.8
30,000	4.4

The altitude at which the standard air pressure is equal to 10.9 psi can be found at 8,000 feet.

At an altitude of 28,000 feet, standard atmospheric pressure is 4.8 psi. By adding this pressure to the cabin pressure differential of 6.1 psi difference (psid), a total air pressure of 10.9 psi is obtained.

Figure 6-41. *Standard atmospheric pressure chart.*

and safely for long periods of time, particularly if the cabin altitude is maintained at 8,000 feet or below, where the use of oxygen equipment is not required. The flight crew in this type of aircraft must be aware of the danger of accidental loss of cabin pressure and be prepared to deal with such an emergency whenever it occurs.

The following terms will aid in understanding the operating principles of pressurization and air conditioning systems:

- Aircraft altitude—the actual height above sea level at which the aircraft is flying

- Ambient temperature—the temperature in the area immediately surrounding the aircraft

- Ambient pressure—the pressure in the area immediately surrounding the aircraft

- Cabin altitude—cabin pressure in terms of equivalent altitude above sea level

- Differential pressure—the difference in pressure between the pressure acting on one side of a wall and the pressure acting on the other side of the wall. In aircraft air-conditioning and pressurizing systems, it is the difference between cabin pressure and atmospheric pressure.

The cabin pressure control system provides cabin pressure regulation, pressure relief, vacuum relief, and the means for selecting the desired cabin altitude in the isobaric and differential range. In addition, dumping of the cabin pressure is a function of the pressure control system. A cabin pressure regulator, an outflow valve, and a safety valve are used to accomplish these functions.

The cabin pressure regulator controls cabin pressure to a selected value in the isobaric range and limits cabin pressure to a preset differential value in the differential range. When an aircraft reaches the altitude at which the difference between the pressure inside and outside the cabin is equal to the highest differential pressure for which the fuselage structure is designed, a further increase in aircraft altitude will result in a corresponding increase in cabin altitude. Differential control is used to prevent the maximum differential pressure, for which the fuselage was designed, from being exceeded. This differential pressure is determined by the structural strength of the cabin and often by the relationship of the cabin size to the probable areas of rupture, such as window areas and doors.

The cabin air pressure safety valve is a combination pressure relief, vacuum relief, and dump valve. The pressure relief valve prevents cabin pressure from exceeding a predetermined differential pressure above ambient pressure. The vacuum relief prevents ambient pressure from exceeding cabin pressure by allowing external air to enter the cabin when ambient pressure exceeds cabin pressure. The flight deck control switch actuates the dump valve. When this switch is positioned to ram, a solenoid valve opens, causing the valve to dump cabin air to atmosphere.

The degree of pressurization and the operating altitude of the aircraft are limited by several critical design factors. Primarily, the fuselage is designed to withstand a particular maximum cabin differential pressure.

Several instruments are used in conjunction with the pressurization controller. The cabin differential pressure gauge indicates the difference between inside and outside pressure. This gauge should be monitored to assure that the cabin does not exceed the maximum allowable differential pressure. A cabin altimeter is also provided as a check on the performance of the system. In some cases, these two instruments are combined into one. A third instrument indicates the cabin rate of climb or descent. A cabin rate-of-climb instrument and a cabin altimeter are illustrated in *Figure 6-42*.

Decompression is defined as the inability of the aircraft's pressurization system to maintain its designed pressure differential. This can be caused by a malfunction in the pressurization system or structural damage to the aircraft.

Physiologically, decompressions fall into two categories:

- Explosive decompression—a change in cabin pressure faster than the lungs can decompress, possibly causing lung damage. Normally, the time required to release air from the lungs without restrictions, such as masks, is 0.2 seconds. Most authorities consider any

Cabin rate-of-climb indicator

Cabin/differential pressure indicator

Cabin differential pressure indicator (pounds per square inch differential)

Cabin pressure altitude indicator (thousands of feet)

Maximum cabin differential pressure limit

Figure 6-42. *Cabin pressurization instruments.*

decompression that occurs in less than 0.5 seconds to be explosive and potentially dangerous.

• Rapid decompression—a change in cabin pressure in which the lungs decompress faster than the cabin, resulting in no likelihood of lung damage.

During an explosive decompression, there may be noise, and one may feel dazed for a moment. The cabin air fills with fog, dust, or flying debris. Fog occurs due to the rapid drop in temperature and the change of relative humidity. Normally, the ears clear automatically. Air rushes from the mouth and nose due to the escape of air from the lungs, and may be noticed by some individuals.

Rapid decompression decreases the period of useful consciousness because oxygen in the lungs is exhaled rapidly, reducing pressure on the body. This decreases the partial pressure of oxygen in the blood and reduces the pilot's effective performance time by one-third to one-fourth its normal time. For this reason, an oxygen mask should be worn when flying at very high altitudes (35,000 feet or higher). It is recommended that the crewmembers select the 100 percent oxygen setting on the oxygen regulator at high altitude if the aircraft is equipped with a demand or pressure demand oxygen system.

The primary danger of decompression is hypoxia. Quick, proper utilization of oxygen equipment is necessary to avoid unconsciousness. Another potential danger that pilots, crew, and passengers face during high altitude decompressions is evolved gas decompression sickness. This occurs when the pressure on the body drops sufficiently, nitrogen comes out of solution, and forms bubbles that can have adverse effects on some body tissues.

Decompression caused by structural damage to the aircraft presents another type of danger to pilots, crew, and passengers—being tossed or blown out of the aircraft if they are located near openings. Individuals near openings should wear safety harnesses or seatbelts at all times when the aircraft is pressurized and they are seated. Structural damage also has the potential to expose them to wind blasts and extremely cold temperatures.

Rapid descent from altitude is necessary if these problems are to be minimized. Automatic visual and aural warning systems are included in the equipment of all pressurized aircraft.

Oxygen Systems

Most high altitude aircraft come equipped with some type of fixed oxygen installation. If the aircraft does not have a fixed installation, portable oxygen equipment must be readily accessible during flight. The portable equipment usually consists of a container, regulator, mask outlet, and pressure gauge. Aircraft oxygen is usually stored in high pressure system containers of 1,800–2,200 psi. When the ambient temperature surrounding an oxygen cylinder decreases, pressure within that cylinder decreases because pressure varies directly with temperature if the volume of a gas remains constant. If a drop in indicated pressure on a supplemental oxygen cylinder is noted, there is no reason to suspect depletion of the oxygen supply, which has simply been compacted due to storage of the containers in an unheated area of the aircraft. High pressure oxygen containers should be marked with the psi tolerance (i.e., 1,800 psi) before filling the container to that pressure. The containers should be supplied with aviation oxygen only, which is 100 percent pure oxygen. Industrial oxygen is not intended for breathing and may contain impurities, and medical oxygen contains water vapor that can freeze in the regulator when exposed to cold temperatures. To assure safety, periodic inspection and servicing of the oxygen system should be done.

An oxygen system consists of a mask or cannula and a regulator that supplies a flow of oxygen dependent upon cabin altitude. Cannulas are not approved for flights above 18,000 feet. Regulators approved for use up to 40,000 feet are designed to provide zero percent cylinder oxygen and 100 percent cabin air at cabin altitudes of 8,000 feet or less, with the ratio changing to 100 percent oxygen and zero percent cabin air at approximately 34,000 feet cabin altitude. [Figure 6-43] Regulators approved up to 45,000 feet are designed to provide 40 percent cylinder oxygen and 60 percent cabin air at lower altitudes, with the ratio changing to 100 percent at the higher altitude. Pilots should avoid flying above 10,000 feet without oxygen during the day and above 8,000 feet at night.

Figure 6-43. *Oxygen system regulator.*

Pilots should be aware of the danger of fire when using oxygen. Materials that are nearly fireproof in ordinary air may be susceptible to combustion in oxygen. Oils and greases may ignite if exposed to oxygen, and cannot be used for sealing the valves and fittings of oxygen equipment. Smoking during any kind of oxygen equipment use is prohibited. Before each flight, the pilot should thoroughly inspect and test all oxygen equipment. The inspection should include a thorough examination of the aircraft oxygen equipment, including available supply, an operational check of the system, and assurance that the supplemental oxygen is readily accessible. The inspection should be accomplished with clean hands and should include a visual inspection of the mask and tubing for tears, cracks, or deterioration; the regulator for valve and lever condition and positions; oxygen quantity; and the location and functioning of oxygen pressure gauges, flow indicators and connections. The mask should be donned and the system should be tested. After any oxygen use, verify that all components and valves are shut off.

Oxygen Masks

There are numerous types and designs of oxygen masks in use. The most important factor in oxygen mask use is to insure the masks and oxygen system are compatible. Crew masks are fitted to the user's face with a minimum of leakage and usually contain a microphone. Most masks are the oronasal type, which covers only the mouth and nose.

A passenger mask may be a simple, cup-shaped rubber molding sufficiently flexible to obviate individual fitting. It may have a simple elastic head strap or the passenger may hold it to his or her face.

All oxygen masks should be kept clean to reduce the danger of infection and prolong the life of the mask. To clean the mask, wash it with a mild soap and water solution and rinse it with clear water. If a microphone is installed, use a clean swab, instead of running water, to wipe off the soapy solution. The mask should also be disinfected. A gauze pad that has been soaked in a water solution of Merthiolate can be used to swab out the mask. This solution used should contain one-fifth teaspoon of Merthiolate per quart of water. Wipe the mask with a clean cloth and air dry.

Cannula

A cannula is an ergonomic piece of plastic tubing which runs under the nose and is often used to administer oxygen in non-pressurized aircraft. [Figure 6-44] Cannulas are typically more comfortable then masks and can be used up to 18,000 feet. Altitudes greater than 18,000 feet require the

Figure 6-44. *Cannula with green flow detector.*

use of an oxygen mask. Many cannulas have a flow meter in the line. If equipped, a periodic check of the green flow detector should be part of a pilot's regular scan.

Diluter-Demand Oxygen Systems

Diluter-demand oxygen systems supply oxygen only when the user inhales through the mask. An automix lever allows the regulators to automatically mix cabin air and oxygen or supply 100 percent oxygen, depending on the altitude. The demand mask provides a tight seal over the face to prevent dilution with outside air and can be used safely up to 40,000 feet. A pilot who has a beard or mustache should be sure it is trimmed in a manner that will not interfere with the sealing of the oxygen mask. The fit of the mask around the beard or mustache should be checked on the ground for proper sealing.

Pressure-Demand Oxygen Systems

Pressure-demand oxygen systems are similar to diluter demand oxygen equipment, except that oxygen is supplied to the mask under pressure at cabin altitudes above 34,000 feet. Pressure-demand regulators create airtight and oxygen-tight seals, but they also provide a positive pressure application of oxygen to the mask face piece that allows the user's lungs to be pressurized with oxygen. This feature makes pressure demand regulators safe at altitudes above 40,000 feet. Some systems may have a pressure demand mask with the regulator attached directly to the mask, rather than mounted on the instrument panel or other area within the flight deck. The mask-mounted regulator eliminates the problem of a long hose that must be purged of air before 100 percent oxygen begins flowing into the mask.

Continuous-Flow Oxygen System

Continuous-flow oxygen systems are usually provided for passengers. The passenger mask typically has a reservoir bag, which collects oxygen from the continuous-flow oxygen system during the time when the mask user is exhaling. The oxygen collected in the reservoir bag allows a higher aspiratory flow rate during the inhalation cycle, which reduces the amount of air dilution. Ambient air is added to the supplied oxygen during inhalation after the reservoir bag oxygen supply is depleted. The exhaled air is released to the cabin. [Figure 6-45]

Electrical Pulse-Demand Oxygen System

Portable electrical pulse-demand oxygen systems deliver oxygen by detecting an individual's inhalation effort and provide oxygen flow during the initial portion of inhalation. Pulse demand systems do not waste oxygen during the breathing cycle because oxygen is only delivered during inhalation. Compared to continuous-flow systems, the pulse-demand method of oxygen delivery can reduce the amount

Figure 6-45. *Continuous flow mask and rebreather bag.*

of oxygen needed by 50–85 percent. Most pulse-demand oxygen systems also incorporate an internal barometer that automatically compensates for changes in altitude by increasing the amount of oxygen delivered for each pulse as altitude is increased. [Figure 6-46]

Figure 6-46. *EDS-011 portable pulse-demand oxygen system.*

6-36

Pulse Oximeters

A pulse oximeter is a device that measures the amount of oxygen in an individual's blood, in addition to heart rate. This non-invasive device measures the color changes that red blood cells undergo when they become saturated with oxygen. By transmitting a special light beam through a fingertip to evaluate the color of the red cells, a pulse oximeter can calculate the degree of oxygen saturation within one percent of directly measured blood oxygen. Because of their portability and speed, pulse oximeters are very useful for pilots operating in nonpressurized aircraft above 12,500 feet where supplemental oxygen is required. A pulse oximeter permits crewmembers and passengers of an aircraft to evaluate their actual need for supplemental oxygen. *[Figure 6-47]*

Figure 6-47. *Onyx pulse oximeter.*

Servicing of Oxygen Systems

Before servicing any aircraft with oxygen, consult the specific aircraft service manual to determine the type of equipment required and procedures to be used. Certain precautions should be observed whenever aircraft oxygen systems are to be serviced. Oxygen system servicing should be accomplished only when the aircraft is located outside of the hangars. Personal cleanliness and good housekeeping are imperative when working with oxygen. Oxygen under pressure and petroleum products create spontaneous results when they are brought in contact with each other. Service people should be certain to wash dirt, oil, and grease (including lip salves and hair oil) from their hands before working around oxygen equipment. It is also essential that clothing and tools are free of oil, grease, and dirt. Aircraft with permanently installed oxygen tanks usually require two persons to accomplish servicing of the system. One should be stationed at the service equipment control valves, and the other stationed where he or she can observe the aircraft system pressure gauges. Oxygen system servicing is not recommended during aircraft fueling operations or while other work is performed that could provide a source of ignition. Oxygen system servicing while passengers are on board the aircraft is not recommended.

Anti-Ice and Deice Systems

Anti-icing equipment is designed to prevent the formation of ice, while deicing equipment is designed to remove ice once it has formed. These systems protect the leading edge of wing and tail surfaces, pitot and static port openings, fuel tank vents, stall warning devices, windshields, and propeller blades. Ice detection lighting may also be installed on some aircraft to determine the extent of structural icing during night flights.

Most light aircraft have only a heated pitot tube and are not certified for flight in icing. These light aircraft have limited cross-country capability in the cooler climates during late fall, winter, and early spring. Noncertificated aircraft must exit icing conditions immediately. Refer to the AFM/POH for details.

Airfoil Anti-Ice and Deice

Inflatable deicing boots consist of a rubber sheet bonded to the leading edge of the airfoil. When ice builds up on the leading edge, an engine-driven pneumatic pump inflates the rubber boots. Many turboprop aircraft divert engine bleed air to the wing to inflate the rubber boots. Upon inflation, the ice is cracked and should fall off the leading edge of the wing. Deicing boots are controlled from the flight deck by a switch and can be operated in a single cycle or allowed to cycle at automatic, timed intervals. *[Figure 6-48]*

Figure 6-48. *Deicing boots on the leading edge of the wing.*

In the past it was believed that if the boots were cycled too soon after encountering ice, the ice layer would expand instead of breaking off, resulting in a condition referred to as ice "bridging." Consequently, subsequent deice boot cycles would be ineffective at removing the ice buildup. Although some residual ice may remain after a boot cycle, "bridging" does not occur with any modern boots. Pilots can cycle the boots as soon as an ice accumulation is observed. Consult the AFM/POH for information on the operation of deice boots on an aircraft.

Many deicing boot systems use the instrument system suction gauge and a pneumatic pressure gauge to indicate proper boot operation. These gauges have range markings that indicate the operating limits for boot operation. Some systems may also incorporate an annunciator light to indicate proper boot operation.

Proper maintenance and care of deicing boots are important for continued operation of this system. They need to be carefully inspected during preflight.

Another type of leading edge protection is the thermal anti-ice system. Heat provides one of the most effective methods for preventing ice accumulation on an airfoil. High performance turbine aircraft often direct hot air from the compressor section of the engine to the leading edge surfaces. The hot air heats the leading edge surfaces sufficiently to prevent the formation of ice. A newer type of thermal anti-ice system referred to as thermawing uses electrically heated graphite foil laminate applied to the leading edge of the wing and horizontal stabilizer. Thermawing systems typically have two zones of heat application. One zone on the leading edge receives continuous heat; the second zone further aft receives heat in cycles to dislodge the ice allowing aerodynamic forces to remove it. Thermal anti-ice systems should be activated prior to entering icing conditions.

An alternate type of leading edge protection that is not as common as thermal anti-ice and deicing boots is known as a weeping wing. The weeping-wing design uses small holes located in the leading edge of the wing to prevent the formation and build-up of ice. An antifreeze solution is pumped to the leading edge and weeps out through the holes. Additionally, the weeping wing is capable of deicing an aircraft. When ice has accumulated on the leading edges, application of the antifreeze solution chemically breaks down the bond between the ice and airframe, allowing aerodynamic forces to remove the ice. [Figure 6-48]

Windscreen Anti-Ice

There are two main types of windscreen anti-ice systems. The first system directs a flow of alcohol to the windscreen.

Figure 6-48. *TKS weeping wing anti-ice/deicing system.*

If used early enough, the alcohol will prevent ice from building up on the windscreen. The rate of alcohol flow can be controlled by a dial in the flight deck according to procedures recommended by the aircraft manufacturer.

Another effective method of anti-icing equipment is the electric heating method. Small wires or other conductive material is imbedded in the windscreen. The heater can be turned on by a switch in the flight deck, causing an electrical current to be passed across the shield through the wires to provide sufficient heat to prevent the formation of ice on the windscreen. The heated windscreen should only be used during flight. Do not leave it on during ground operations, as it can overheat and cause damage to the windscreen. Warning: the electrical current can cause compass deviation errors by as much as 40°.

Propeller Anti-Ice

Propellers are protected from icing by the use of alcohol or electrically heated elements. Some propellers are equipped with a discharge nozzle that is pointed toward the root of the blade. Alcohol is discharged from the nozzles, and centrifugal force drives the alcohol down the leading edge of the blade. The boots are also grooved to help direct the flow of alcohol. This prevents ice from forming on the leading edge of the propeller. Propellers can also be fitted with propeller anti-ice boots. The propeller boot is divided into two sections—the inboard and the outboard sections. The boots are imbedded with electrical wires that carry current for heating the propeller. The prop anti-ice system can be monitored for proper operation by monitoring the prop anti-ice ammeter. During the preflight inspection, check the propeller boots for proper operation. If a boot fails to heat one blade, an unequal blade loading can result, and may cause severe propeller vibration. [Figure 6-49]

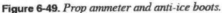

Figure 6-49. *Prop ammeter and anti-ice boots.*

Other Anti-Ice and Deice Systems

Pitot and static ports, fuel vents, stall-warning sensors, and other optional equipment may be heated by electrical elements. Operational checks of the electrically heated systems are to be checked in accordance with the AFM /POH.

Operation of aircraft anti-icing and deicing systems should be checked prior to encountering icing conditions. Encounters with structural ice require immediate action. Anti-icing and deicing equipment are not intended to sustain long-term flight in icing conditions.

Chapter Summary

All aircraft have a requirement for essential systems such as the engine, propeller, induction, ignition systems as well as the fuel, lubrication, cooling, electrical, landing gear, and environmental control systems to support flight. Understanding the aircraft systems of the aircraft being flown is critical to its safe operation and proper maintenance. Consult the AFM/POH for specific information pertaining to the aircraft being flown. Various manufacturer and owners group websites can also be a valuable source of additional information.

Chapter 7

Flight Instruments

Introduction

In order to safely fly any aircraft, a pilot must understand how to interpret and operate the flight instruments. The pilot also needs to be able to recognize associated errors and malfunctions of these instruments. This chapter addresses the pitot-static system and associated instruments, the vacuum system and related instruments, gyroscopic instruments, and the magnetic compass. When a pilot understands how each instrument works and recognizes when an instrument is malfunctioning, he or she can safely utilize the instruments to their fullest potential.

Pitot-Static Flight Instruments

The pitot-static system is a combined system that utilizes the static air pressure, and the dynamic pressure due to the motion of the aircraft through the air. These combined pressures are utilized for the operation of the airspeed indicator (ASI), altimeter, and vertical speed indicator (VSI). *[Figure 7-1]*

Climbing left bank

Level left bank

Descending left bank

Figure 7-1. *Pitot-static system and instruments.*

Impact Pressure Chamber and Lines

The pitot tube is utilized to measure the total combined pressures that are present when an aircraft moves through the air. Static pressure, also known as ambient pressure, is always present whether an aircraft is moving or at rest. It is simply the barometric pressure in the local area. Dynamic pressure is present only when an aircraft is in motion; therefore, it can be thought of as a pressure due to motion. Wind also generates dynamic pressure. It does not matter if the aircraft is moving through still air at 70 knots or if the aircraft is facing a wind with a speed of 70 knots, the same dynamic pressure is generated.

When the wind blows from an angle less than 90° off the nose of the aircraft, dynamic pressure can be depicted on the ASI. The wind moving across the airfoil at 20 knots is the same as the aircraft moving through calm air at 20 knots. The pitot tube captures the dynamic pressure, as well as the static pressure that is always present.

The pitot tube has a small opening at the front which allows the total pressure to enter the pressure chamber. The total pressure is made up of dynamic pressure plus static pressure. In addition to the larger hole in the front of the pitot tube, there is a small hole in the back of the chamber which allows moisture to drain from the system should the aircraft enter precipitation. Both openings in the pitot tube need to

be checked prior to flight to insure that neither is blocked. Many aircraft have pitot tube covers installed when they sit for extended periods of time. This helps to keep bugs and other objects from becoming lodged in the opening of the pitot tube.

The one instrument that utilizes the pitot tube is the ASI. The total pressure is transmitted to the ASI from the pitot tube's pressure chamber via a small tube. The static pressure is also delivered to the opposite side of the ASI which serves to cancel out the two static pressures, thereby leaving the dynamic pressure to be indicated on the instrument. When the dynamic pressure changes, the ASI shows either increase or decrease, corresponding to the direction of change. The two remaining instruments (altimeter and VSI) utilize only the static pressure which is derived from the static port.

Static Pressure Chamber and Lines

The static chamber is vented through small holes to the free undisturbed air on the side(s) of the aircraft. As the atmospheric pressure changes, the pressure is able to move freely in and out of the instruments through the small lines which connect the instruments into the static system. An alternate static source is provided in some aircraft to provide static pressure should the primary static source become blocked. The alternate static source is normally found inside of the flight deck. Due to the venturi effect of the air flowing around the fuselage, the air pressure inside the flight deck is lower than the exterior pressure.

When the alternate static source pressure is used, the following instrument indications are observed:

1. The altimeter indicates a slightly higher altitude than actual.

2. The ASI indicates an airspeed greater than the actual airspeed.

3. The VSI shows a momentary climb and then stabilizes if the altitude is held constant.

Each pilot is responsible for consulting the Aircraft Flight Manual (AFM) or the Pilot's Operating Handbook (POH) to determine the amount of error that is introduced into the system when utilizing the alternate static source. In an aircraft not equipped with an alternate static source, an alternate method of introducing static pressure into the system should a blockage occur is to break the glass face of the VSI. This most likely renders the VSI inoperative. The reason for choosing the VSI as the instrument to break is that it is the least important static source instrument for flight.

Altimeter

The altimeter is an instrument that measures the height of an aircraft above a given pressure level. Pressure levels are discussed later in detail. Since the altimeter is the only instrument that is capable of indicating altitude, this is one of the most vital instruments installed in the aircraft. To use the altimeter effectively, the pilot must understand the operation of the instrument, as well as the errors associated with the altimeter and how each effect the indication.

A stack of sealed aneroid wafers comprise the main component of the altimeter. An aneroid wafer is a sealed wafer that is evacuated to an internal pressure of 29.92 inches of mercury (29.92 "Hg). These wafers are free to expand and contract with changes to the static pressure. A higher static pressure presses down on the wafers and causes them to collapse. A lower static pressure (less than 29.92 "Hg) allows the wafers to expand. A mechanical linkage connects the wafer movement to the needles on the indicator face, which translates compression of the wafers into a decrease in altitude and translates an expansion of the wafers into an increase in altitude. [Figure 7-2]

Notice how the static pressure is introduced into the rear of the sealed altimeter case. The altimeter's outer chamber is sealed, which allows the static pressure to surround the aneroid wafers. If the static pressure is higher than the pressure in the aneroid wafers (29.92 "Hg), then the wafers are compressed until the pressure inside the wafers is equal to the surrounding

Figure 7-2. *Altimeter.*

static pressure. Conversely, if the static pressure is less than the pressure inside of the wafers, the wafers are able to expand which increases the volume. The expansion and contraction of the wafers moves the mechanical linkage, which drives the needles on the face of the ASI.

Principle of Operation

The pressure altimeter is an aneroid barometer that measures the pressure of the atmosphere at the level where the altimeter is located, and presents an altitude indication in feet. The altimeter uses static pressure as its source of operation. Air is denser at sea level than aloft—as altitude increases, atmospheric pressure decreases. This difference in pressure at various levels causes the altimeter to indicate changes in altitude.

The presentation of altitude varies considerably between different types of altimeters. Some have one pointer while others have two or more. Only the multipointer type is discussed in this handbook. The dial of a typical altimeter is graduated with numerals arranged clockwise from zero to nine. Movement of the aneroid element is transmitted through gears to the three hands that indicate altitude. The shortest hand indicates altitude in tens of thousands of feet, the intermediate hand in thousands of feet, and the longest hand in hundreds of feet.

This indicated altitude is correct, however, only when the sea level barometric pressure is standard (29.92 "Hg), the sea level free air temperature is standard (+15 degrees Celsius (°C) or 59 degrees Fahrenheit (°F)), and the pressure and temperature decrease at a standard rate with an increase in altitude. Adjustments for nonstandard pressures are accomplished by setting the corrected pressure into a barometric scale located on the face of the altimeter. The barometric pressure window is sometimes referred to as the Kollsman window; only after the altimeter is set does it indicate the correct altitude. The word "correct" will need to be better explained when referring to types of altitudes, but is commonly used in this case to denote the approximate altitude above sea level. In other words, the indicated altitude refers to the altitude read off of the altitude which is uncorrected, after the barometric pressure setting is dialed into the Kollsman window. The additional types of altitudes are further explained later.

Effect of Nonstandard Pressure and Temperature

It is easy to maintain a consistent height above ground if the barometric pressure and temperature remain constant, but this is rarely the case. The pressure temperature can change between takeoff and landing even on a local flight. If these changes are not taken into consideration, flight becomes dangerous.

If altimeters could not be adjusted for nonstandard pressure, a hazardous situation could occur. For example, if an aircraft is flown from a high pressure area to a low pressure area without adjusting the altimeter, a constant altitude will be displayed, but the actual height of the aircraft above the ground would be lower then the indicated altitude. There is an old aviation axiom: "GOING FROM A HIGH TO A LOW, LOOK OUT BELOW." Conversely, if an aircraft is flown from a low pressure area to a high pressure area without an adjustment of the altimeter, the actual altitude of the aircraft is higher than the indicated altitude. Once in flight, it is important to frequently obtain current altimeter settings en route to ensure terrain and obstruction clearance.

Many altimeters do not have an accurate means of being adjusted for barometric pressures in excess of 31.00 inches of mercury ("Hg). When the altimeter cannot be set to the higher pressure setting, the aircraft actual altitude will be higher than the altimeter indicates. When low barometric pressure conditions occur (below 28.00), flight operations by aircraft unable to set the actual altimeter setting are not recommended.

Adjustments to compensate for nonstandard pressure do not compensate for nonstandard temperature. Since cold air is denser than warm air, when operating in temperatures that are colder than standard, the altitude is lower than the altimeter indication. [Figure 7-3] It is the magnitude of this "difference" that determines the magnitude of the error. It is the difference due to colder temperatures that concerns the pilot. When flying into a cooler air mass while maintaining a constant indicated altitude, true altitude is lower. If terrain or obstacle clearance is a factor in selecting a cruising altitude, particularly in mountainous terrain, remember to anticipate that a colder-than-standard temperature places the aircraft lower than the altimeter indicates. Therefore, a higher indicated altitude may be required to provide adequate terrain clearance. A variation of the memory aid used for pressure can be employed: "FROM HOT TO COLD, LOOK OUT BELOW." When the air is warmer than standard, the aircraft is higher than the

Figure 7-3. *Effects of nonstandard temperature on an altimeter.*

altimeter indicates. Altitude corrections for temperature can be computed on the navigation computer.

Extremely cold temperatures will also affect altimeter indications. *Figure 7-4*, which was derived from ICAO formulas, indicates how much error can exist when the temperature is extremely cold.

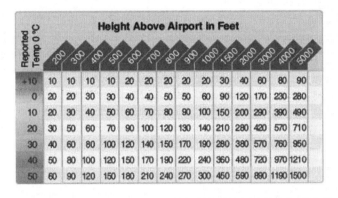

Reported Temp 0 °C	Height Above Airport in Feet													
	200	300	400	500	600	700	800	900	1000	1500	2000	3000	4000	5000
+10	10	10	10	10	20	20	20	20	20	30	40	60	80	90
0	20	20	30	30	40	40	50	50	60	90	120	170	230	280
10	20	30	40	50	60	70	80	90	100	150	200	290	390	490
20	30	50	60	70	90	100	120	130	140	210	280	420	570	710
30	40	60	80	100	120	140	150	170	190	280	380	570	760	950
40	50	80	100	120	150	170	190	220	240	360	480	720	970	1210
50	60	90	120	150	180	210	240	270	300	450	590	890	1190	1500

Figure 7-4. *Look at the chart using a temperature of –10 °C and the aircraft altitude is 1,000 feet above the airport elevation. The chart shows that the reported current altimeter setting may place the aircraft as much as 100 feet below the altitude indicated by the altimeter.*

Setting the Altimeter

Most altimeters are equipped with a barometric pressure setting window (or Kollsman window) providing a means to adjust the altimeter. A knob is located at the bottom of the instrument for this adjustment.

To adjust the altimeter for variation in atmospheric pressure, the pressure scale in the altimeter setting window, calibrated in inches of mercury ("Hg) and/or millibars (mb), is adjusted to match the given altimeter setting. Altimeter setting is defined as station pressure reduced to sea level, but, an altimeter setting is accurate only in the vicinity of the reporting station. Therefore, the altimeter must be adjusted as the flight progresses from one station to the next. Air traffic control (ATC) will advise when updated altimeter settings are available. If a pilot is not utilizing ATC assistance, local altimeter settings can be obtained by monitoring local automated weather observing system/automated surface observation system (AWOS/ASOS) or automatic terminal information service (ATIS) broadcasts.

Many pilots confidently expect the current altimeter setting will compensate for irregularities in atmospheric pressure at all altitudes, but this is not always true. The altimeter setting broadcast by ground stations is the station pressure corrected to mean sea level. It does not account for the irregularities at higher levels, particularly the effect of nonstandard temperature.

If each pilot in a given area is using the same altimeter setting, each altimeter should be equally affected by temperature and pressure variation errors, making it possible to maintain the desired vertical separation between aircraft. This does not guarantee vertical separation though. It is still imperative to maintain a regimented visual scan for intruding air traffic.

When flying over high, mountainous terrain, certain atmospheric conditions cause the altimeter to indicate an altitude of 1,000 feet or more higher than the actual altitude. For this reason, a generous margin of altitude should be allowed—not only for possible altimeter error, but also for possible downdrafts that might be associated with high winds.

To illustrate the use of the altimeter setting system, follow a flight from Dallas Love Field, Texas, to Abilene Municipal Airport, Texas, via Mineral Wells. Before taking off from Love Field, the pilot receives a current altimeter setting of 29.85 "Hg from the control tower or ATIS, and sets this value in the altimeter setting window. The altimeter indication should then be compared with the known airport elevation of 487 feet. Since most altimeters are not perfectly calibrated, an error may exist.

When over Mineral Wells, assume the pilot receives a current altimeter setting of 29.94 "Hg and sets this in the altimeter window. Before entering the traffic pattern at Abilene Municipal Airport, a new altimeter setting of 29.69 "Hg is received from the Abilene Control Tower, and set in the altimeter setting window. If the pilot desires to fly the traffic pattern at approximately 800 feet above the terrain, and the field elevation of Abilene is 1,791 feet, an indicated altitude of 2,600 feet should be maintained (1,791 feet + 800 feet = 2,591 feet, rounded to 2,600 feet).

The importance of properly setting the altimeter cannot be overemphasized. Assume the pilot did not adjust the altimeter at Abilene to the current setting and continued using the Mineral Wells setting of 29.94 "Hg. When entering the Abilene traffic pattern at an indicated altitude of 2,600 feet, the aircraft would be approximately 250 feet below the proper traffic pattern altitude. Upon landing, the altimeter would indicate approximately 250 feet higher than the field elevation.

Mineral Wells altimeter setting	29.94
Abilene altimeter setting	29.69
Difference	0.25

(Since 1 inch of pressure is equal to approximately 1,000 feet of altitude, 0.25 × 1,000 feet = 250 feet.)

When determining whether to add or subtract the amount of altimeter error, remember that, when the actual pressure is lower than what is set in the altimeter window, the actual altitude of the aircraft is lower than what is indicated on the altimeter.

The following is another method of computing the altitude deviation. Start by subtracting the current altimeter setting from 29.94 "Hg. Always remember to place the original setting as the top number. Then subtract the current altimeter setting.

Mineral Wells altimeter setting	29.94
Abilene altimeter setting	29.69
29.94 – 29.69 = Difference	0.25

(Since 1 inch of pressure is equal to approximately 1,000 feet of altitude, 0.25 x 1,000 feet = 250 feet.) Always subtract the number from the indicated altitude.

$$2,600 – 250 = 2,350$$

Now, try a lower pressure setting. Adjust from altimeter setting 29.94 to 30.56 "Hg.

Mineral Wells altimeter setting	29.94
Altimeter setting	30.56
29.94 – 30.56 = Difference	–0.62

(Since 1 inch of pressure is equal to approximately 1,000 feet of altitude, 0.62 x 1,000 feet = 620 feet.) Always subtract the number from the indicated altitude.

$$2,600 – (–620) = 3,220$$

The pilot will be 620 feet high.

Notice the difference is a negative number. Starting with the current indicated altitude of 2,600 feet, subtracting a negative number is the same as adding the two numbers. By utilizing this method, a pilot should be able to better understand what is happening with the aircraft's altitude. This method always yields the correct result and tells a pilot what the altitude is and the direction. (The implications of not understanding where the errors lie and in what direction are important to a safe flight.) If the altitude was lower than actually indicated, an aircraft could be in danger of colliding with an obstacle.

Altimeter Operation

There are two means by which the altimeter pointers can be moved. The first is a change in air pressure, while the other is an adjustment to the barometric scale. When the aircraft climbs or descends, changing pressure within the altimeter case expands or contracts the aneroid barometer.

This movement is transmitted through mechanical linkage to rotate the pointers.

A decrease in pressure causes the altimeter to indicate an increase in altitude, and an increase in pressure causes the altimeter to indicate a decrease in altitude. Accordingly, if the aircraft is sitting on the ground with a pressure level of 29.98 "Hg and the pressure level changes to 29.68 "Hg, the altimeter would show an increase of approximately 300 feet in altitude. This pressure change is most noticeable when the aircraft is left parked over night. As the pressure falls, the altimeter interprets this as a climb. The altimeter indicates an altitude above the actual field elevation. If the barometric pressure setting is reset to the current altimeter setting of 29.68 "Hg, then the field elevation is again indicated on the altimeter.

This pressure change is not as easily noticed in flight since aircraft fly specific altitudes. The aircraft steadily decreases true altitude while the altimeter is held constant through pilot action as discussed in the previous section.

Knowing the aircraft's altitude is vitally important to a pilot. The pilot must be sure that the aircraft is flying high enough to clear the highest terrain or obstruction along the intended route. It is especially important to have accurate altitude information when visibility is restricted. To clear obstructions, the pilot must constantly be aware of the altitude of the aircraft and the elevation of the surrounding terrain. To reduce the possibility of a midair collision, it is essential to maintain altitude in accordance with air traffic rules.

Types of Altitude

Altitude in itself is a relevant term only when it is specifically stated to which type of altitude a pilot is referring to. Normally when the term altitude is used, it is referring to altitude above sea level since this is the altitude which is used to depict obstacles and airspace, as well as to separate air traffic.

Altitude is vertical distance above some point or level used as a reference. There are as many kinds of altitude as there are reference levels from which altitude is measured, and each may be used for specific reasons. Pilots are mainly concerned with five types of altitudes:

1. Indicated altitude—read directly from the altimeter (uncorrected) when it is set to the current altimeter setting.

2. True altitude—the vertical distance of the aircraft above sea level—the actual altitude. It is often expressed as feet above mean sea level (MSL). Airport, terrain,

and obstacle elevations on aeronautical charts are true altitudes.

3. Absolute altitude—the vertical distance of an aircraft above the terrain, or above ground level (AGL).

4. Pressure altitude—the altitude indicated when the altimeter setting window (barometric scale) is adjusted to 29.92 "Hg. This is the altitude above the standard datum plane, which is a theoretical plane where air pressure (corrected to 15 °C) equals 29.92" Hg. Pressure altitude is used to compute density altitude, true altitude, true airspeed (TAS), and other performance data.

5. Density altitude—pressure altitude corrected for variations from standard temperature. When conditions are standard, pressure altitude and density altitude are the same. If the temperature is above standard, the density altitude is higher than pressure altitude. If the temperature is below standard, the density altitude is lower than pressure altitude. This is an important altitude because it is directly related to the aircraft's performance.

A pilot must understand how the performance of the aircraft is directly related to the density of the air. The density of the air affects how much power a naturally aspirated engine produces, as well as how efficient the airfoils are. If there are fewer air molecules (lower pressure) to accelerate through the propeller, the acceleration to rotation speed is longer and thus produces a longer takeoff roll, which translates to a decrease in performance.

As an example, consider an airport with a field elevation of 5,048 feet MSL where the standard temperature is 5 °C. Under these conditions, pressure altitude and density altitude are the same—5,048 feet. If the temperature changes to 30 °C, the density altitude increases to 7,855 feet. This means an aircraft would perform on takeoff as though the field elevation were 7,855 feet at standard temperature. Conversely, a temperature of –25 °C would result in a density altitude of 1,232 feet. An aircraft would perform much better under these conditions.

Instrument Check

Prior to each flight, a pilot should examine the altimeter for proper indications in order to verify its validity. To determine the condition of an altimeter, set the barometric scale to the current reported altimeter setting transmitted by the local automated flight service station (AFSS) or any other reliable source, such as ATIS, AWOS, or ASOS. The altimeter pointers should indicate the surveyed field elevation of the airport. If the indication is off more than 75 feet from the surveyed field elevation, the instrument should be referred to a certificated instrument repair station for recalibration.

Vertical Speed Indicator (VSI)

The VSI, which is sometimes called a vertical velocity indicator (VVI), indicates whether the aircraft is climbing, descending, or in level flight. The rate of climb or descent is indicated in feet per minute (fpm). If properly calibrated, the VSI indicates zero in level flight. *[Figure 7-5]*

Figure 7-5. *Vertical speed indicator (VSI).*

Principle of Operation

Although the VSI operates solely from static pressure, it is a differential pressure instrument. It contains a diaphragm with connecting linkage and gearing to the indicator pointer inside an airtight case. The inside of the diaphragm is connected directly to the static line of the pitot-static system. The area outside the diaphragm, which is inside the instrument case, is also connected to the static line, but through a restricted orifice (calibrated leak).

Both the diaphragm and the case receive air from the static line at existing atmospheric pressure. The diaphragm receives unrestricted air while the case receives the static pressure via the metered leak. When the aircraft is on the ground or in level flight, the pressures inside the diaphragm and the instrument case are equal and the pointer is at the zero indication. When the aircraft climbs or descends, the pressure inside the diaphragm changes immediately, but due to the metering action of the restricted passage, the case pressure remains higher or lower for a short time, causing the diaphragm to contract or expand. This causes a pressure differential that is indicated on the instrument needle as a climb or descent.

Figure 7-6. *An IVSI incorporates accelerometers to help the instrument immediately indicate changes in vertical speed.*

When the pressure differential stabilizes at a definite ratio, the needle indicates the rate of altitude change.

The VSI displays two different types of information:

- Trend information shows an immediate indication of an increase or decrease in the aircraft's rate of climb or descent.

- Rate information shows a stabilized rate of change in altitude.

The trend information is the direction of movement of the VSI needle. For example, if an aircraft is maintaining level flight and the pilot pulls back on the control yoke causing the nose of the aircraft to pitch up, the VSI needle moves upward to indicate a climb. If the pitch attitude is held constant, the needle stabilizes after a short period (6–9 seconds) and indicates the rate of climb in hundreds of fpm. The time period from the initial change in the rate of climb, until the VSI displays an accurate indication of the new rate, is called the lag. Rough control technique and turbulence can extend the lag period and cause erratic and unstable rate indications. Some aircraft are equipped with an instantaneous vertical speed indicator (IVSI), which incorporates accelerometers to compensate for the lag in the typical VSI. *[Figure 7-6]*

Instrument Check

As part of a preflight check, proper operation of the VSI must be established. Make sure the VSI indicates near zero prior to leaving the ramp area and again just before takeoff. If the VSI indicates anything other than zero, that indication can be referenced as the zero mark. Normally, if the needle is not exactly zero, it is only slightly above or below the zero line. After takeoff, the VSI should trend upward to indicate

a positive rate of climb and then, once a stabilized climb is established, a rate of climb can be referenced.

Airspeed Indicator (ASI)

The ASI is a sensitive, differential pressure gauge which measures and promptly indicates the difference between pitot (impact/dynamic pressure) and static pressure. These two pressures are equal when the aircraft is parked on the ground in calm air. When the aircraft moves through the air, the pressure on the pitot line becomes greater than the pressure in the static lines. This difference in pressure is registered by the airspeed pointer on the face of the instrument, which is calibrated in miles per hour, knots (nautical miles per hour), or both. *[Figure 7-7]*

Figure 7-7. *Airspeed indicator (ASI).*

The ASI is the one instrument that utilizes both the pitot, as well as the static system. The ASI introduces the static pressure into the airspeed case while the pitot pressure (dynamic) is introduced into the diaphragm. The dynamic pressure expands or contracts one side of the diaphragm, which is attached to an indicating system. The system drives the mechanical linkage and the airspeed needle.

Just as in altitudes, there are multiple types of airspeeds. Pilots need to be very familiar with each type.

- Indicated airspeed (IAS)—the direct instrument reading obtained from the ASI, uncorrected for variations in atmospheric density, installation error, or instrument error. Manufacturers use this airspeed as the basis for determining aircraft performance. Takeoff, landing, and stall speeds listed in the AFM/POH are IAS and do not normally vary with altitude or temperature.

- Calibrated airspeed (CAS)—IAS corrected for installation error and instrument error. Although manufacturers attempt to keep airspeed errors to a minimum, it is not possible to eliminate all errors throughout the airspeed operating range. At certain airspeeds and with certain flap settings, the installation and instrument errors may total several knots. This error is generally greatest at low airspeeds. In the cruising and higher airspeed ranges, IAS and CAS are approximately the same. Refer to the airspeed calibration chart to correct for possible airspeed errors.

- True airspeed (TAS)—CAS corrected for altitude and nonstandard temperature. Because air density decreases with an increase in altitude, an aircraft has to be flown faster at higher altitudes to cause the same pressure difference between pitot impact pressure and static pressure. Therefore, for a given CAS, TAS increases as altitude increases; or for a given TAS, CAS decreases as altitude increases. A pilot can find TAS by two methods. The most accurate method is to use a flight computer. With this method, the CAS is corrected for temperature and pressure variation by using the airspeed correction scale on the computer. Extremely accurate electronic flight computers are also available. Just enter the CAS, pressure altitude, and temperature, and the computer calculates the TAS. A second method, which is a rule of thumb, provides the approximate TAS. Simply add 2 percent to the CAS for each 1,000 feet of altitude. The TAS is the speed which is used for flight planning and is used when filing a flight plan.

- Groundspeed (GS)—the actual speed of the airplane over the ground. It is TAS adjusted for wind. GS decreases with a headwind, and increases with a tailwind.

Airspeed Indicator Markings

Aircraft weighing 12,500 pounds or less, manufactured after 1945, and certificated by the FAA, are required to have ASIs marked in accordance with a standard color-coded marking system. This system of color-coded markings enables a pilot to determine at a glance certain airspeed limitations that are important to the safe operation of the aircraft. For example, if during the execution of a maneuver, it is noted that the airspeed needle is in the yellow arc and rapidly approaching the red line, the immediate reaction should be to reduce airspeed.

As shown in *Figure 7-8*, ASIs on single-engine small aircraft include the following standard color-coded markings:

- White arc—commonly referred to as the flap operating range since its lower limit represents the full flap stall speed and its upper limit provides the maximum flap speed. Approaches and landings are usually flown at speeds within the white arc.

- Lower limit of white arc (V_{S0})—the stalling speed or the minimum steady flight speed in the landing configuration. In small aircraft, this is the power-off stall speed at the maximum landing weight in the landing configuration (gear and flaps down).

- Upper limit of the white arc (V_{FE})—the maximum speed with the flaps extended.

- Green arc—the normal operating range of the aircraft. Most flying occurs within this range.

- Lower limit of green arc (V_{S1})—the stalling speed or the minimum steady flight speed obtained in a specified configuration. For most aircraft, this is the power-off stall speed at the maximum takeoff weight in the clean configuration (gear up, if retractable, and flaps up).

- Upper limit of green arc (V_{NO})—the maximum structural cruising speed. Do not exceed this speed except in smooth air.

- Yellow arc—caution range. Fly within this range only in smooth air, and then, only with caution.

Figure 7-8. *Airspeed indicator (ASI).*

- Red line (V_{NE})—never exceed speed. Operating above this speed is prohibited since it may result in damage or structural failure.

Other Airspeed Limitations

Some important airspeed limitations are not marked on the face of the ASI, but are found on placards and in the AFM/POH. These airspeeds include:

- Design maneuvering speed (V_A)—the maximum speed at which the structural design's limit load can be imposed (either by gusts or full deflection of the control surfaces) without causing structural damage. It is important to consider weight when referencing this speed. For example, VA may be 100 knots when an airplane is heavily loaded, but only 90 knots when the load is light.

- Landing gear operating speed (V_{LO})—the maximum speed for extending or retracting the landing gear if flying an aircraft with retractable landing gear.

- Landing gear extended speed (V_{LE})—the maximum speed at which an aircraft can be safely flown with the landing gear extended.

- Best angle-of-climb speed (V_X)—the airspeed at which an aircraft gains the greatest amount of altitude in a given distance. It is used during a short-field takeoff to clear an obstacle.

- Best rate-of-climb speed (V_Y)—the airspeed that provides the most altitude gain in a given period of time.

- Single-engine best rate-of-climb (V_{YSE})—the best rate-of-climb or minimum rate-of-sink in a light twin-engine aircraft with one engine inoperative. It is marked on the ASI with a blue line. V_{YSE} is commonly referred to as "Blue Line."

- Minimum control speed (V_{MC})—the minimum flight speed at which a light, twin-engine aircraft can be satisfactorily controlled when an engine suddenly becomes inoperative and the remaining engine is at takeoff power.

Instrument Check

Prior to takeoff, the ASI should read zero. However, if there is a strong wind blowing directly into the pitot tube, the ASI may read higher than zero. When beginning the takeoff, make sure the airspeed is increasing at an appropriate rate.

Blockage of the Pitot-Static System

Errors almost always indicate blockage of the pitot tube, the static port(s), or both. Blockage may be caused by moisture (including ice), dirt, or even insects. During preflight, make sure the pitot tube cover is removed. Then, check the pitot and static port openings. A blocked pitot tube affects the accuracy of the ASI, but, a blockage of the static port not only affects the ASI, but also causes errors in the altimeter and VSI.

Blocked Pitot System

The pitot system can become blocked completely or only partially if the pitot tube drain hole remains open. If the pitot tube becomes blocked and its associated drain hole remains clear, ram air no longer is able to enter the pitot system. Air already in the system vents through the drain hole, and the remaining pressure drops to ambient (outside) air pressure. Under these circumstances, the ASI reading decreases to zero, because the ASI senses no difference between ram and static air pressure. The ASI no longer operates since dynamic pressure can not enter the pitot tube opening. Static pressure is able to equalize on both sides since the pitot drain hole is still open. The apparent loss of airspeed is not usually instantaneous but happens very quickly. *[Figure 7-9]*

Figure 7-9. *A blocked pitot tube, but clear drain hole.*

If both the pitot tube opening and the drain hole should become clogged simultaneously, then the pressure in the pitot tube is trapped. No change is noted on the airspeed indication should the airspeed increase or decrease. If the static port is unblocked and the aircraft should change altitude, then a change is noted on the ASI. The change is not related to a change in airspeed but a change in static pressure. The total pressure in the pitot tube does not change due to the blockage; however, the static pressure will change.

Because airspeed indications rely upon both static and dynamic pressure together, the blockage of either of these systems affects the ASI reading. Remember that the ASI has a diaphragm in which dynamic air pressure is entered. Behind this diaphragm is a reference pressure called static pressure that comes from the static ports. The diaphragm pressurizes against this static pressure and as a result changes the airspeed indication via levers and indicators. *[Figure 7-10]*

Figure 7-10. *Blocked pitot system with clear static system.*

For example, take an aircraft and slow it down to zero knots at given altitude. If the static port (providing static pressure) and the pitot tube (providing dynamic pressure) are both unobstructed, the following claims can be made:

1. The ASI would be zero.

2. There must be a relationship between both dynamic and static pressure. At zero speed, dynamic pressure and static pressure are the same: static air pressure.

3. Because both dynamic and static air pressure are equal at zero speed with increased speed, dynamic pressure must include two components: static pressure and dynamic pressure.

It can be inferred that airspeed indication must be based upon a relationship between these two pressures, and indeed it is. An ASI uses the static pressure as a reference pressure and as a result, the ASI's case is kept at this pressure behind the diaphragm. On the other hand, the dynamic pressure through the pitot tube is connected to a highly sensitive diaphragm within the ASI case. Because an aircraft in zero motion (regardless of altitude) results in a zero airspeed, the pitot tube always provides static pressure in addition to dynamic pressure.

Therefore, the airspeed indication is the result of two pressures: the pitot tube static and dynamic pressure within the diaphragm as measured against the static pressure in case. What does this mean if the pitot tube is obstructed?

If the aircraft were to descend, the pressure in the pitot system including the diaphragm would remain constant. It is clogged and the diaphragm is at a single pressure. But as the descent is made, the static pressure would increase against the diaphragm causing it to compress thereby resulting in an indication of decreased airspeed. Conversely, if the aircraft were to climb, the static pressure would decrease allowing the diaphragm to expand, thereby showing an indication of greater airspeed. *[Figure 7-10]*

The pitot tube may become blocked during flight due to visible moisture. Some aircraft may be equipped with pitot heat for flight in visible moisture. Consult the AFM/POH for specific procedures regarding the use of pitot heat.

Blocked Static System

If the static system becomes blocked but the pitot tube remains clear, the ASI continues to operate; however, it is inaccurate. The airspeed indicates lower than the actual airspeed when the aircraft is operated above the altitude where the static ports became blocked, because the trapped static pressure is higher than normal for that altitude. When operating at a lower altitude, a faster than actual airspeed is displayed due to the relatively low static pressure trapped in the system.

Revisiting the ratios that were used to explain a blocked pitot tube, the same principle applies for a blocked static port. If the aircraft descends, the static pressure increases on the pitot side showing an increase on the ASI. This assumes that the aircraft does not actually increase its speed. The increase in static pressure on the pitot side is equivalent to an increase in dynamic pressure since the pressure can not change on the static side.

If an aircraft begins to climb after a static port becomes blocked, the airspeed begins to show a decrease as the aircraft continues to climb. This is due to the decrease in static pressure on the pitot side, while the pressure on the static side is held constant.

A blockage of the static system also affects the altimeter and VSI. Trapped static pressure causes the altimeter to freeze at the altitude where the blockage occurred. In the case of the VSI, a blocked static system produces a continuous zero indication. *[Figure 7-11]*

Figure 7-11. *Blocked static system.*

Some aircraft are equipped with an alternate static source in the flight deck. In the case of a blocked static source, opening the alternate static source introduces static pressure from the flight deck back into the system. Flight deck static pressure is lower than outside static pressure. Check the aircraft AOM/POH for airspeed corrections when utilizing alternate static pressure.

Electronic Flight Display (EFD)

Advances in digital displays and solid state electronic components have been introduced into the flight decks of general aviation (GA) aircraft. In addition to the improvement in system reliability, which increases overall safety, electronic flight displays (EFD) have decreased the overall cost of equipping aircraft with state-of-the-art instrumentation. Primary electronic instrumentation packages are less prone to failure than their analogue counterparts. No longer is it necessary for aircraft designers to create cluttered panel layouts in order to accommodate all necessary flight instruments. Instead, multi-panel digital flight displays combine all flight instruments onto a single screen which is called a primary flight display (PFD). The traditional "six pack" of instruments is now displayed on one liquid crystal display (LCD) screen.

Airspeed Tape

Configured similarly to traditional panel layouts, the ASI is located on the left side of the screen and is displayed as a vertical speed tape. As the aircraft increases in speed, the larger numbers descend from the top of the tape. The TAS is displayed at the bottom of the tape through the input to the air data computer (ADC) from the outside air temperature probe. Airspeed markings for V_X, V_Y, and rotation speed (V_R) are

displayed for pilot reference. An additional pilot-controlled airspeed bug is available to set at any desired reference speed. As on traditional analogue ASIs, the electronic airspeed tape displays the color-coded ranges for the flap operating range, normal range, and caution range. *[Figure 7-12]* The number value changes color to red when the airspeed exceeds V_{NE} to warn the pilot of exceeding the maximum speed limitation.

Attitude Indicator

One improvement over analogue instrumentation is the larger attitude indicator on EFD. The artificial horizon spans the entire width of the PFD. *[Figure 7-12]* This expanded instrumentation offers better reference through all phases of flight and all flight maneuvers. The attitude indicator receives its information from the Attitude Heading and Reference System (AHRS).

Altimeter

The altimeter is located on the right side of the PFD. *[Figure 7-12]* As the altitude increases, the larger numbers descend from the top of the display tape, with the current altitude being displayed in the black box in the center of the display tape. The altitude is displayed in increments of 20 feet.

Vertical Speed Indicator (VSI)

The VSI is displayed to the right of the altimeter tape and can take the form of an arced indicator or a vertical speed tape. *[Figure 7-12]* Both are equipped with a vertical speed bug.

Heading Indicator

The heading indicator is located below the artificial horizon and is normally modeled after a Horizontal Situation Indicator (HSI). *[Figure 7-12]* As in the case of the attitude indicator, the heading indicator receives its information from the magnetometer which feeds information to the AHRS unit and then out to the PFD.

Turn Indicator

The turn indicator takes a slightly different form than the traditional instrumentation. A sliding bar moves left and right below the triangle to indicate deflection from coordinated flight. *[Figure 7-12]* Reference for coordinated flight comes from accelerometers contained in the AHRS unit.

Tachometer

The sixth instrument normally associated with the "six pack" package is the tachometer. This is the only instrument that is not located on the PFD. The tachometer is normally located on the multi-function display (MFD). In the event of a display screen failure, it is displayed on the remaining screen with the PFD flight instrumentation. *[Figure 7-13]*

Slip/Skid Indicator

The slip/skid indicator *[Figure 7-12]* is the horizontal line below the roll pointer. Like a ball in a turn-and-slip indicator, a bar width off center is equal to one ball width displacement.

Turn Rate Indicator

The turn rate indicator, illustrated in *Figure 7-12*, is typically found directly above the rotating compass card. Tick marks to the left and right of the luber line denote the turn (standard-rate versus half standard-rate). Typically denoted by a trend line, if the trend vector is extended to the second tick mark the aircraft is in a standard-rate turn.

Figure 7-12. *Primary flight display. Note that the actual location of indications vary depending on manufacturers.*

Figure 7-13. *Multi-function display.*

Individual panel displays are able to be configured for a variety of aircraft simply by installing different software packages. *[Figure 7-14]* Manufacturers are also able to upgrade existing instrument displays in a similar manner, eliminating the need to replace individual gauges in order to upgrade.

Figure 7-14. *Chelton's FlightLogic (top) and Avidyne's Entegra (bottom) are examples of panel displays that are configurable.*

Air Data Computer (ADC)

Electronic flight displays utilize the same type of instrument inputs as traditional analogue gauges; however, the processing system is different. The pitot static inputs are received by an ADC. The ADC computes the difference between the total pressure and the static pressure, and generates the information necessary to display the airspeed on the PFD. Outside air temperatures are also monitored and introduced into various components within the system, as well as being displayed on the PFD screen. *[Figure 7-15]*

The ADC is a separate solid state device which, in addition to providing data to the PFD, is capable of providing data to the

Figure 7-15. *Teledyne's 90004 TAS/Plus Air Data Computer (ADC) computes air data information from the pitot-static pneumatic system, aircraft temperature probe, and barometric correction device to help create a clear picture of flight characteristics.*

autopilot control system. In the event of system malfunction, the ADC can quickly be removed and replaced in order to decrease down time and maintenance turn-around times.

Altitude information is derived from the static pressure port just as an analogue system does; however, the static pressure does not enter a diaphragm. The ADC computes the received barometric pressure and sends a digital signal to the PFD to display the proper altitude readout. Electronic flight displays also show trend vectors which show the pilot how the altitude and airspeed are progressing.

Trend Vectors

Trend vectors are magenta lines which move up and down both the ASI and the altimeter. *[Figures 7-16 and 7-17]* The

Figure 7-16. *Airspeed trend vector.*

Figure 7-17. *Altimeter trend vector.*

ADC computes the rate of change and displays the 6-second projection of where the aircraft will be. Pilots can utilize the trend vectors to better control the aircraft's attitude. By including the trend vectors in the instrument scan, pilots are able to precisely control airspeed and altitude. Additional information can be obtained by referencing the Instrument Flying Handbook or specific avionics manufacturer's training material.

Gyroscopic Flight Instruments

Several flight instruments utilize the properties of a gyroscope for their operation. The most common instruments containing gyroscopes are the turn coordinator, heading indicator, and the attitude indicator. To understand how these instruments operate requires knowledge of the instrument power systems, gyroscopic principles, and the operating principles of each instrument.

Gyroscopic Principles

Any spinning object exhibits gyroscopic properties. A wheel or rotor designed and mounted to utilize these properties is called a gyroscope. Two important design characteristics of an instrument gyro are great weight for its size, or high density, and rotation at high speed with low friction bearings.

There are two general types of mountings; the type used depends upon which property of the gyro is utilized. A freely or universally mounted gyroscope is free to rotate in any direction about its center of gravity. Such a wheel is said to have three planes of freedom. The wheel or rotor is free to rotate in any plane in relation to the base and is balanced so that, with the gyro wheel at rest, it remains in the position in which it is placed. Restricted or semi-rigidly mounted gyroscopes are those mounted so that one of the planes of freedom is held fixed in relation to the base.

There are two fundamental properties of gyroscopic action: rigidity in space and precession.

Rigidity in Space

Rigidity in space refers to the principle that a gyroscope remains in a fixed position in the plane in which it is spinning. An example of rigidity in space is that of a bicycle wheel. As the bicycle wheels increase speed, they become more and more stable in their plane of rotation. This is why a bicycle is very unstable and very maneuverable at low speeds and very stable and less maneuverable at higher speeds.

By mounting this wheel, or gyroscope, on a set of gimbal rings, the gyro is able to rotate freely in any direction. Thus, if the gimbal rings are tilted, twisted, or otherwise moved, the gyro remains in the plane in which it was originally spinning. [*Figure 7-18*]

Figure 7-18. *Regardless of the position of its base, a gyro tends to remain rigid in space, with its axis of rotation pointed in a constant direction.*

Precession

Precession is the tilting or turning of a gyro in response to a deflective force. The reaction to this force does not occur at the point at which it was applied; rather, it occurs at a point that is 90° later in the direction of rotation. This principle allows the gyro to determine a rate of turn by sensing the amount of pressure created by a change in direction. The rate at which the gyro precesses is inversely proportional to the speed of the rotor and proportional to the deflective force.

Using the example of the bicycle, precession acts on the wheels in order to allow the bicycle to turn. While riding at normal speed, it is not necessary to turn the handle bars in the direction of the desired turn. A rider simply leans in the direction that he or she wishes to go. Since the wheels are rotating in a clockwise direction when viewed from the right side of the bicycle, if a rider leans to the left, a force is applied to the top of the wheel to the left. The force actually acts 90° in the direction of rotation, which has the effect of applying a force to the front of the tire, causing the bicycle to move to the left. There is a need to turn the handlebars at low speeds because of the instability of the slowly turning gyros, and also to increase the rate of turn.

Precession can also create some minor errors in some instruments. [Figure 7-19] Precession can cause a freely spinning gyro to become displaced from its intended plane of rotation through bearing friction, etc. Certain instruments may require corrective realignment during flight, such as the heading indicator.

Figure 7-19. *Precession of a gyroscope resulting from an applied deflective force.*

Sources of Power

In some aircraft, all the gyros are vacuum, pressure, or electrically operated. In other aircraft, vacuum or pressure systems provide the power for the heading and attitude indicators, while the electrical system provides the power for the turn coordinator. Most aircraft have at least two sources of power to ensure at least one source of bank information is available if one power source fails. The vacuum or pressure system spins the gyro by drawing a stream of air against the rotor vanes to spin the rotor at high speed, much like the operation of a waterwheel or turbine. The amount of vacuum

or pressure required for instrument operation varies, but is usually between 4.5 "Hg and 5.5 "Hg.

One source of vacuum for the gyros is a vane-type engine-driven pump that is mounted on the accessory case of the engine. Pump capacity varies in different airplanes, depending on the number of gyros.

A typical vacuum system consists of an engine-driven vacuum pump, relief valve, air filter, gauge, and tubing necessary to complete the connections. The gauge is mounted in the aircraft's instrument panel and indicates the amount of pressure in the system (vacuum is measured in inches of mercury less than ambient pressure).

As shown in *Figure 7-20,* air is drawn into the vacuum system by the engine-driven vacuum pump. It first goes through a filter, which prevents foreign matter from entering the vacuum or pressure system. The air then moves through the attitude and heading indicators, where it causes the gyros to spin. A relief valve prevents the vacuum pressure, or suction, from exceeding prescribed limits. After that, the air is expelled overboard or used in other systems, such as for inflating pneumatic deicing boots.

It is important to monitor vacuum pressure during flight, because the attitude and heading indicators may not provide reliable information when suction pressure is low. The vacuum, or suction, gauge is generally marked to indicate the normal range. Some aircraft are equipped with a warning light that illuminates when the vacuum pressure drops below the acceptable level.

When the vacuum pressure drops below the normal operating range, the gyroscopic instruments may become unstable and inaccurate. Cross checking the instruments routinely is a good habit to develop.

Turn Indicators

Aircraft use two types of turn indicators: turn-and-slip indicator and turn coordinator. Because of the way the gyro is mounted, the turn-and-slip indicator shows only the rate of turn in degrees per second. The turn coordinator is mounted at an angle, or canted, so it can initially show roll rate. When the roll stabilizes, it indicates rate of turn. Both instruments indicate turn direction and quality (coordination), and also serve as a backup source of bank information in the event an attitude indicator fails. Coordination is achieved by referring to the inclinometer, which consists of a liquid-filled curved tube with a ball inside. [Figure 7-21]

Figure 7-20. *Typical vacuum system.*

Turn-and-Slip Indicator

The gyro in the turn-and-slip indicator rotates in the vertical plane, corresponding to the aircraft's longitudinal axis. A single gimbal limits the planes in which the gyro can tilt, and a spring tries to return it to center. Because of precession, a yawing force causes the gyro to tilt left or right, as viewed from the pilot seat. The turn-and-slip indicator uses a pointer, called the turn needle, to show the direction and rate of turn. The turn-and-slip indicator is incapable of "tumbling" off its rotational axis because of the restraining springs. When extreme forces are applied to a gyro, the gyro is displaced from its normal plane of rotation, rendering its indications invalid. Certain instruments have specific pitch and bank limits that induce a tumble of the gyro.

Turn Coordinator

The gimbal in the turn coordinator is canted; therefore, its gyro can sense both rate of roll and rate of turn. Since turn coordinators are more prevalent in training aircraft, this discussion concentrates on that instrument. When rolling into or out of a turn, the miniature aircraft banks in the direction the aircraft is rolled. A rapid roll rate causes the miniature aircraft to bank more steeply than a slow roll rate.

Figure 7-21. *Turn indicators rely on controlled precession for their operation.*

The turn coordinator can be used to establish and maintain a standard-rate turn by aligning the wing of the miniature aircraft with the turn index. *Figure 7-22* shows a picture of a turn coordinator. There are two marks on each side (left and right) of the face of the instrument. The first mark is used to reference a wings level zero rate of turn. The second mark on the left and right side of the instrument serve to indicate a standard rate of turn. A standard-rate turn is defined as a turn rate of 3° per second. The turn coordinator indicates only the rate and direction of turn; it does not display a specific angle of bank.

Slipping turn

Skidding turn

Coordinated turn

Figure 7-22. *If inadequate right rudder is applied in a right turn, a slip results. Too much right rudder causes the aircraft to skid through the turn. Centering the ball results in a coordinated turn.*

Inclinometer

The inclinometer is used to depict aircraft yaw, which is the side-to-side movement of the aircraft's nose. During coordinated, straight-and-level flight, the force of gravity causes the ball to rest in the lowest part of the tube, centered between the reference lines. Coordinated flight is maintained by keeping the ball centered. If the ball is not centered, it can be centered by using the rudder.

To center the ball, apply rudder pressure on the side to which the ball is deflected. Use the simple rule, "step on the ball," to remember which rudder pedal to press. If aileron and rudder are coordinated during a turn, the ball remains centered in the tube. If aerodynamic forces are unbalanced, the ball moves away from the center of the tube. As shown in *Figure 7-22*, in a slip, the rate of turn is too slow for the angle of bank, and the ball moves to the inside of the turn. In a skid, the rate of

turn is too great for the angle of bank, and the ball moves to the outside of the turn. To correct for these conditions, and improve the quality of the turn, remember to "step on the ball." Varying the angle of bank can also help restore coordinated flight from a slip or skid. To correct for a slip, decrease bank and/or increase the rate of turn. To correct for a skid, increase the bank and/or decrease the rate of turn.

Yaw String

One additional tool which can be added to the aircraft is a yaw string. A yaw string is simply a string or piece of yarn attached to the center of the wind screen. When in coordinated flight, the string trails straight back over the top of the wind screen. When the aircraft is either slipping or skidding, the yaw string moves to the right or left depending on the direction of slip or skid.

Instrument Check

During the preflight, check to see that the inclinometer is full of fluid and has no air bubbles. The ball should also be resting at its lowest point. When taxiing, the turn coordinator should indicate a turn in the correct direction while the ball moves opposite the direction of the turn.

Attitude Indicator

The attitude indicator, with its miniature aircraft and horizon bar, displays a picture of the attitude of the aircraft. The relationship of the miniature aircraft to the horizon bar is the same as the relationship of the real aircraft to the actual horizon. The instrument gives an instantaneous indication of even the smallest changes in attitude.

The gyro in the attitude indicator is mounted in a horizontal plane and depends upon rigidity in space for its operation. The horizon bar represents the true horizon. This bar is fixed to the gyro and remains in a horizontal plane as the aircraft is pitched or banked about its lateral or longitudinal axis, indicating the attitude of the aircraft relative to the true horizon. *[Figure 7-23]*

The gyro spins in the horizontal plane and resists deflection of the rotational path. Since the gyro relies on rigidity in space, the aircraft actually rotates around the spinning gyro.

An adjustment knob is provided with which the pilot may move the miniature aircraft up or down to align the miniature aircraft with the horizon bar to suit the pilot's line of vision. Normally, the miniature aircraft is adjusted so that the wings overlap the horizon bar when the aircraft is in straight-and-level cruising flight.

Figure 7-23. *Attitude indicator.*

The pitch and bank limits depend upon the make and model of the instrument. Limits in the banking plane are usually from 100° to 110°, and the pitch limits are usually from 60° to 70°. If either limit is exceeded, the instrument will tumble or spill and will give incorrect indications until realigned. A number of modern attitude indicators do not tumble.

Every pilot should be able to interpret the banking scale illustrated in *Figure 7-24.* Most banking scale indicators on the top of the instrument move in the same direction from that in which the aircraft is actually banked. Some other models move in the opposite direction from that in which the aircraft is actually banked. This may confuse the pilot if the indicator is used to determine the direction of bank. This scale should be used only to control the degree of desired bank. The relationship of the miniature aircraft to the horizon bar should be used for an indication of the direction of bank.

Figure 7-24. *Attitude representation by the attitude indicator corresponds to the relation of the aircraft to the real horizon.*

The attitude indicator is reliable and the most realistic flight instrument on the instrument panel. Its indications are very close approximations of the actual attitude of the aircraft.

Heading Indicator

The heading indicator is fundamentally a mechanical instrument designed to facilitate the use of the magnetic compass. Errors in the magnetic compass are numerous, making straight flight and precision turns to headings difficult to accomplish, particularly in turbulent air. A heading indicator, however, is not affected by the forces that make the magnetic compass difficult to interpret. *[Figure 7-25]*

Figure 7-25. *A heading indicator displays headings based on a 360° azimuth, with the final zero omitted. For example, "6" represents 060°, while "21" indicates 210°. The adjustment knob is used to align the heading indicator with the magnetic compass.*

The operation of the heading indicator depends upon the principle of rigidity in space. The rotor turns in a vertical plane and fixed to the rotor is a compass card. Since the rotor remains rigid in space, the points on the card hold the same position in space relative to the vertical plane of the gyro. The aircraft actually rotates around the rotating gyro, not the other way around. As the instrument case and the aircraft revolve around the vertical axis of the gyro, the card provides clear and accurate heading information.

Because of precession caused by friction, the heading indicator creeps or drifts from a heading to which it is set. Among other factors, the amount of drift depends largely upon the condition of the instrument. If the bearings are worn, dirty, or improperly lubricated, the drift may be excessive. Another error in the heading indicator is caused by the fact that the gyro is oriented in space, and the Earth rotates in space at a rate of 15° in 1 hour. Thus, discounting precession

caused by friction, the heading indicator may indicate as much as 15° error per every hour of operation.

Some heading indicators referred to as horizontal situation indicators (HSI) receive a magnetic north reference from a magnetic slaving transmitter, and generally need no adjustment. The magnetic slaving transmitter is called a magnetometer.

Attitude and Heading Reference System (AHRS)

Electronic flight displays have replaced free-spinning gyros with solid-state laser systems that are capable of flight at any attitude without tumbling. This capability is the result of the development of the Attitude and Heading Reference System (AHRS).

The AHRS sends attitude information to the PFD in order to generate the pitch and bank information of the attitude indicator. The heading information is derived from a magnetometer which senses the earth's lines of magnetic flux. This information is then processed and sent out to the PFD to generate the heading display. *[Figure 7-26]*

Figure 7-26. *Attitude and heading reference system (AHRS).*

The Flux Gate Compass System

As mentioned earlier, the lines of flux in the Earth's magnetic field have two basic characteristics: a magnet aligns with them, and an electrical current is induced, or generated, in any wire crossed by them.

The flux gate compass that drives slaved gyros uses the characteristic of current induction. The flux valve is a small, segmented ring, like the one in *Figure 7-27*, made of soft iron that readily accepts lines of magnetic flux. An electrical coil is wound around each of the three legs to accept the current

Figure 7-27. *The soft iron frame of the flux valve accepts the flux from the Earth's magnetic field each time the current in the center coil reverses. This flux causes current to flow in the three pickup coils.*

induced in this ring by the Earth's magnetic field. A coil wound around the iron spacer in the center of the frame has 400 Hz alternating current (AC) flowing through it. During the times when this current reaches its peak, twice during each cycle, there is so much magnetism produced by this coil that the frame cannot accept the lines of flux from the Earth's field.

As the current reverses between the peaks, it demagnetizes the frame so it can accept the flux from the Earth's field. As this flux cuts across the windings in the three coils, it causes current to flow in them. These three coils are connected in such a way that the current flowing in them changes as the heading of the aircraft changes. *[Figure 7-28]*

The three coils are connected to three similar but smaller coils in a synchro inside the instrument case. The synchro rotates the dial of a radio magnetic indicator (RMI) or a HSI.

Remote Indicating Compass

Remote indicating compasses were developed to compensate for the errors and limitations of the older type of heading indicators. The two panel-mounted components of a typical system are the pictorial navigation indicator and the slaving control and compensator unit. *[Figure 7-29]* The pictorial navigation indicator is commonly referred to as an HSI.

Figure 7-28. *The current in each of the three pickup coils changes with the heading of the aircraft..*

The slaving control and compensator unit has a push button that provides a means of selecting either the "slaved gyro" or "free gyro" mode. This unit also has a slaving meter and two manual heading-drive buttons. The slaving meter indicates the difference between the displayed heading and the magnetic heading. A right deflection indicates a clockwise error of the compass card; a left deflection indicates a counterclockwise error. Whenever the aircraft is in a turn and the card rotates, the slaving meter shows a full deflection to one side or the other. When the system is in "free gyro" mode, the compass card may be adjusted by depressing the appropriate heading-drive button.

A separate unit, the magnetic slaving transmitter is mounted remotely, usually in a wingtip to eliminate the possibility of

Figure 7-29. *Pictorial navigation indicator (HSI, top), slaving meter (lower right), and slaving control compensator unit (lower left).*

magnetic interference. It contains the flux valve, which is the direction-sensing device of the system. A concentration of lines of magnetic force, after being amplified, becomes a signal relayed to the heading indicator unit, which is also remotely mounted. This signal operates a torque motor in the heading indicator unit that processes the gyro unit until it is aligned with the transmitter signal. The magnetic slaving transmitter is connected electrically to the HSI.

There are a number of designs of the remote indicating compass; therefore, only the basic features of the system are covered here. Instrument pilots must become familiar with the characteristics of the equipment in their aircraft.

As instrument panels become more crowded and the pilot's available scan time is reduced by a heavier flight deck workload, instrument manufacturers have worked toward combining instruments. One good example of this is the RMI in *Figure 7-30.* The compass card is driven by signals from the flux valve, and the two pointers are driven by an automatic direction finder (ADF) and a very high frequency (VHF) omni-directional radio range (VOR).

Figure 7-30. *Driven by signals from a flux valve, the compass card in this RMI indicates the heading of the aircraft opposite the upper center index mark. The green pointer is driven by the ADF.*

Heading indicators that do not have this automatic northseeking capability are called "free" gyros, and require periodic adjustment. It is important to check the indications frequently (approximately every 15 minutes) and reset the heading indicator to align it with the magnetic compass when required. Adjust the heading indicator to the magnetic compass heading when the aircraft is straight and level at a constant speed to avoid compass errors.

The bank and pitch limits of the heading indicator vary with the particular design and make of instrument. On some heading indicators found in light aircraft, the limits are approximately 55° of pitch and 55° of bank. When either of these attitude limits is exceeded, the instrument "tumbles" or "spills" and no longer gives the correct indication until reset. After spilling, it may be reset with the caging knob. Many of the modern instruments used are designed in such a manner that they do not tumble.

An additional precession error may occur due to a gyro not spinning fast enough to maintain its alignment. When the vacuum system stops producing adequate suction to maintain the gyro speed, the heading indicator and the attitude indicator gyros begin to slow down. As they slow, they become more susceptible to deflection from the plane of rotation. Some aircraft have warning lights to indicate that a low vacuum situation has occurred. Other aircraft may have only a vacuum gauge that indicates the suction.

Instrument Check

As the gyro spools up, make sure there are no abnormal sounds. While taxiing, the instrument should indicate turns in the correct direction, and precession should not be abnormal. At idle power settings, the gyroscopic instruments using the vacuum system might not be up to operating speeds and precession might occur more rapidly than during flight.

Compass Systems

The Earth is a huge magnet, spinning in space, surrounded by a magnetic field made up of invisible lines of flux. These lines leave the surface at the magnetic north pole and reenter at the magnetic South Pole.

Lines of magnetic flux have two important characteristics: any magnet that is free to rotate will align with them, and an electrical current is induced into any conductor that cuts across them. Most direction indicators installed in aircraft make use of one of these two characteristics.

Magnetic Compass

One of the oldest and simplest instruments for indicating direction is the magnetic compass. It is also one of the basic instruments required by Title 14 of the Code of Federal Regulations (14 CFR) part 91 for both VFR and IFR flight.

A magnet is a piece of material, usually a metal containing iron, which attracts and holds lines of magnetic flux. Regardless of size, every magnet has two poles: north and south. When one magnet is placed in the field of another, the unlike poles attract each other, and like poles repel.

An aircraft magnetic compass, such as the one in *Figure 7-30*, has two small magnets attached to a metal float sealed inside a bowl of clear compass fluid similar to kerosene. A graduated scale, called a card, is wrapped around the float and viewed through a glass window with a lubber line across it. The card is marked with letters representing the cardinal directions, north, east, south, and west, and a number for each 30° between these letters. The final "0" is omitted from these directions. For example, 3 = 30°, 6 = 60°, and 33 = 330°. There are long and short graduation marks between the letters and numbers, each long mark representing 10° and each short mark representing 5°.

Figure 7-31. *A magnetic compass. The vertical line is called the lubber line.*

The float and card assembly has a hardened steel pivot in its center that rides inside a special, spring-loaded, hard glass jewel cup. The buoyancy of the float takes most of the weight off the pivot, and the fluid damps the oscillation of the float and card. This jewel-and-pivot type mounting allows the float freedom to rotate and tilt up to approximately 18° angle of bank. At steeper bank angles, the compass indications are erratic and unpredictable.

The compass housing is entirely full of compass fluid. To prevent damage or leakage when the fluid expands and contracts with temperature changes, the rear of the compass case is sealed with a flexible diaphragm, or with a metal bellows in some compasses.

The magnets align with the Earth's magnetic field and the pilot reads the direction on the scale opposite the lubber line. Note that in *Figure 7-31*, the pilot sees the compass card from its backside. When the pilot is flying north as the compass shows, east is to the pilot's right. On the card, "33", which represents 330° (west of north), is to the right of north. The reason for this apparent backward graduation is that the card remains stationary, and the compass housing and the pilot turn around it, always viewing the card from its backside.

A compensator assembly mounted on the top or bottom of the compass allows an aviation maintenance technician (AMT) to create a magnetic field inside the compass housing that cancels the influence of local outside magnetic fields. This is done to correct for deviation error. The compensator assembly has two shafts whose ends have screwdriver slots accessible from the front of the compass. Each shaft rotates one or two small compensating magnets. The end of one shaft is marked E-W, and its magnets affect the compass when the aircraft is pointed east or west. The other shaft is marked N-S and its magnets affect the compass when the aircraft is pointed north or south.

Magnetic Compass Induced Errors

The magnetic compass is the simplest instrument in the panel, but it is subject to a number of errors that must be considered.

Variation

The Earth rotates about its geographic axis; maps and charts are drawn using meridians of longitude that pass through the geographic poles. Directions measured from the geographic poles are called true directions. The magnetic North Pole to which the magnetic compass points is not collocated with the geographic North Pole, but is some 1,300 miles away; directions measured from the magnetic poles are called magnetic directions. In aerial navigation, the difference between true and magnetic directions is called variation. This same angular difference in surveying and land navigation is called declination.

Figure 7-32 shows the isogonic lines that identify the number of degrees of variation in their area. The line that passes near Chicago is called the agonic line. Anywhere along this line the two poles are aligned, and there is no variation. East of this line, the magnetic North Pole is to the west of the geographic North Pole and a correction must be applied to a compass indication to get a true direction.

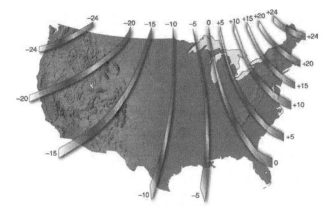

Figure 7-32. *Isogonic lines are lines of equal variation.*

Flying in the Washington, D.C., area, for example, the variation is 10° west. If a pilot wants to fly a true course of south (180°), the variation must be added to this, resulting in a magnetic course of 190° to fly. Flying in the Los Angeles, California, area, the variation is 14° east. To fly a true course of 180° there, the pilot would have to subtract the variation and fly a magnetic course of 166°. The variation error does not change with the heading of the aircraft; it is the same anywhere along the isogonic line.

Deviation

The magnets in a compass align with any magnetic field. Local magnetic fields in an aircraft caused by electrical current flowing in the structure, in nearby wiring or any magnetized part of the structure, conflict with the Earth's magnetic field and cause a compass error called deviation.

Deviation, unlike variation, is different on each heading, but it is not affected by the geographic location. Variation error cannot be reduced or changed, but deviation error can be minimized when an AMT performs the maintenance task known as "swinging the compass."

Most airports have a compass rose, which is a series of lines marked out on a ramp or maintenance runup area where there is no magnetic interference. Lines, oriented to magnetic north, are painted every 30°, as shown in *Figure 7-33.*

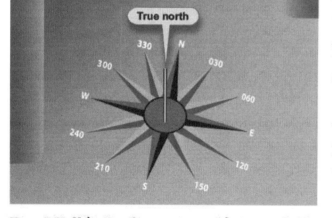

Figure 7-33. *Utilization of a compass rose aids compensation for deviation errors.*

The AMT aligns the aircraft on each magnetic heading and adjusts the compensating magnets to minimize the difference between the compass indication and the actual magnetic heading of the aircraft. Any error that cannot be removed is recorded on a compass correction card, like the one in *Figure 7-34*, and placed in a cardholder near the compass. The pilot can taxi the aircraft to the compass rose and maneuver the aircraft to the headings prescribed by the AMT, and if authorized to do so, the AMT can also taxi and maneuver the aircraft; however, only the AMT can adjust the compass or

FOR STEER	000	030	060	090	120	150
RDO. ON	001	032	062	095	123	155
RDO. OFF	002	031	064	094	125	157

FOR STEER	180	210	240	270	300	330
RDO. ON	176	210	243	271	296	325
RDO. OFF	174	210	240	273	298	327

Figure 7-34. *A compass correction card shows the deviation correction for any heading.*

complete the compass coreection card. If the pilot wants to fly a magnetic heading of 120° and the aircraft is operating with the radios on, the pilot should fly a compass heading of 123°.

The corrections for variation and deviation must be applied in the correct sequence and is shown below, starting from the true course desired.

Step 1: Determine the Magnetic Course
True Course (180°) ± Variation (+10°) = Magnetic Course (190°)

The magnetic course (190°) is steered if there is no deviation error to be applied. The compass card must now be considered for the compass course of 190°.

Step 2: Determine the Compass Course
Magnetic Course (190°, from step 1) ± Deviation (–2°, from correction card) = Compass Course (188°)

NOTE: Intermediate magnetic courses between those listed on the compass card need to be interpreted. Therefore, to steer a true course of 180°, the pilot would follow a compass course of 188°.

To find the true course that is being flown when the compass course is known:
Compass Course ± Deviation = Magnetic Course ± Variation= True Course

Dip Errors

The lines of magnetic flux are considered to leave the Earth at the magnetic North Pole and enter at the magnetic South Pole. At both locations the lines are perpendicular to the Earth's surface. At the magnetic equator, which is halfway between the poles, the lines are parallel with the surface. The magnets in a compass align with this field, and near the poles they dip, or tilt, the float and card. The float is balanced with a small dip-compensating weight, to dampen the effects of dip when operating in the middle latitudes of the northern hemisphere. This dip (and weight) causes two very noticeable errors: northerly turning error and acceleration error.

The pull of the vertical component of the Earth's magnetic field causes northerly turning error, which is apparent on a heading of north or south. When an aircraft flying on a heading of north makes a turn toward east, the aircraft banks to the right, and the compass card tilts to the right. The vertical component of the Earth's magnetic field pulls the northseeking end of the magnet to the right, and the float rotates, causing the card to rotate toward west, the direction opposite the direction the turn is being made. [Figure 7-35]

If the turn is made from north to west, the aircraft banks to the left and the compass card tilts down on the left side. The magnetic field pulls on the end of the magnet that causes the card to rotate toward east. This indication is again opposite to the direction the turn is being made. The rule for this error is: when starting a turn from a northerly heading, the compass indication lags behind the turn.

When an aircraft is flying on a heading of south and begins a turn toward east, the Earth's magnetic field pulls on the end of the magnet that rotates the card toward east, the same direction the turn is being made. If the turn is made from south toward west, the magnetic pull starts the card rotating toward west—again, in the same direction the turn is being made. The rule for this error is: when starting a turn from a southerly heading, the compass indication leads the turn.

In acceleration error, the dip-correction weight causes the end of the float and card marked N (the south-seeking end) to be heavier than the opposite end. When the aircraft is flying at a constant speed on a heading of east or west, the float and card is level. The effects of magnetic dip and the weight are approximately equal. If the aircraft accelerates on a heading of east [Figure 7-36], the inertia of the weight holds its end of the float back and the card rotates toward north. As soon as the

Figure 7-35. *Northerly turning error.*

Figure 7-36. *Effects of acceleration error.*

speed of the aircraft stabilizes, the card swings back to its east indication. If, while flying on this easterly heading, the aircraft decelerates, the inertia causes the weight to move ahead and the card rotates toward south until the speed again stabilizes.

When flying on a heading of west, the same things happen. Inertia from acceleration causes the weight to lag, and the card rotates toward north. When the aircraft decelerates on a heading of west, inertia causes the weight to move ahead and the card rotates toward south.

A mnemonic, or memory jogger, for the effect of acceleration error is the word "ANDS" (acceleration—north, deceleration—south). Acceleration causes an indication toward north; deceleration causes an indication toward south.

Oscillation Error

Oscillation is a combination of all of the other errors, and it results in the compass card swinging back and forth around the heading being flown. When setting the gyroscopic heading indicator to agree with the magnetic compass, use the average indication between the swings.

The Vertical Card Magnetic Compass

The floating magnet type of compass not only has all the errors just described, but also lends itself to confused reading. It is easy to begin a turn in the wrong direction because its card appears backward. East is on what the pilot would expect to be the west side. The vertical card magnetic compass eliminates some of the errors and confusion. The dial of this compass is graduated with letters representing the cardinal directions, numbers every 30°, and tick marks every 5°. The dial is rotated by a set of gears from the shaft-mounted magnet, and the nose of the symbolic aircraft on the instrument glass represents the lubber line for reading the heading of the aircraft from the dial. Eddy currents induced into an aluminum-damping cup damp, or decrease, oscillation of the magnet. [Figure 7-37]

Figure 7-37. *Vertical card compass.*

Lags or Leads

When starting a turn from a northerly heading, the compass lags behind the turn. When starting a turn from a southerly heading, the compass leads the turn.

Eddy Current Damping

The decreased amplitude of oscillations by the interaction of magnetic fields. In the case of a vertical card magnetic compass, flux from the oscillating permanent magnet produces eddy currents in a damping disk or cup. The magnetic flux produced by the eddy currents opposes the flux from the permanent magnet and decreases the oscillations.

Outside Air Temperature (OAT) Gauge

The outside air temperature (OAT) gauge is a simple and effective device mounted so that the sensing element is exposed to the outside air. The sensing element consists of a bimetallic-type thermometer in which two dissimilar materials are welded together in a single strip and twisted into a helix. One end is anchored into protective tube and the other end is affixed to the pointer, which reads against the calibration on a circular face. OAT gauges are calibrated in degrees °C, °F, or both. An accurate air temperature provides the pilot with useful information about temperature lapse rate with altitude change. [Figure 7-38]

Figure 7-38. *Outside air temperature (OAT) gauge.*

Chapter Summary

Flight instruments enable an aircraft to be operated with maximum performance and enhanced safety, especially when flying long distances. Manufacturers provide the necessary flight instruments, but to use them effectively, pilots need to understand how they operate. As a pilot, it is important to become very familiar with the operational aspects of the pitot-static system and associated instruments, the vacuum system and associated instruments, the gyroscopic instruments, and the magnetic compass.

Chapter 8

Flight Manuals and Other Documents

Introduction

Each aircraft comes with documentation and a set of manuals with which a pilot must be familiar in order to fly that aircraft. This chapter covers airplane flight manuals (AFM), the pilot's operating handbook (POH), and aircraft documents pertaining to ownership, airworthiness, maintenance, and operations with inoperative equipment. Knowledge of these required documents and manuals is essential for a pilot to conduct a safe flight.

Airplane Flight Manuals (AFM)

Flight manuals and operating handbooks are concise reference books that provide specific information about a particular aircraft or subject. They contain basic facts, information, and/or instructions for the pilot about the operation of an aircraft, flying techniques, etc., and are intended to be kept at hand for ready reference.

The aircraft owner/information manual is a document developed by the manufacturer and contains general information about the make and model of aircraft. The manual is not pproved by the Federal Aviation Administration (FAA) and is not specific to an individual aircraft. The manual provides general information about the operation of an aircraft, is not kept current, and cannot be substituted for the AFM/POH.

An AFM is a document developed by the manufacturer and approved by the FAA. This book contains the information and instructions required to operate an aircraft safely. A pilot must comply with this information which is specific to a particular make and model aircraft, usually by serial number. An AFM contains the operating procedures and limitations of that aircraft. Title 14 of the Code of Federal Regulations (14 CFR) part 91 requires that pilots comply with the operating limitations specified in the approved flight manuals, markings, and placards.

Originally, flight manuals followed whatever format and content the manufacturer felt was appropriate, but this changed with the acceptance of Specification No. 1 prepared by the General Aviation Manufacturers Association (GAMA). Specification No. 1 established a standardized format for all general aviation airplane and helicopter flight manuals.

The POH is a document developed by the aircraft manufacturer and contains FAA approved AFM information. If "POH" is used in the main title, a statement must be included on the title page indicating that sections of the document are FAA approved as the AFM.

The POH for most light aircraft built after 1975 is also designated as the FAA-approved flight manual. The typical AFM/POH contains the following nine sections: General; Limitations; Emergency Procedures; Normal Procedures; Performance; Weight and Balance/Equipment List; Systems Description; Handling, Service, and Maintenance; and Supplements. Manufacturers also have the option of including additional sections, such as one on Safety and Operational Tips or an alphabetical index at the end of the POH.

Preliminary Pages

While the AFM/POH may appear similar for the same make and model of aircraft, each manual is unique and contains specific information about a particular aircraft, such as the equipment installed and weight and balance information. Manufacturers are required to include the serial number and registration on the title page to identify the aircraft to which the manual belongs. If a manual does not indicate a specific aircraft registration and serial number, it is limited to general study purposes only.

Most manufacturers include a table of contents, which identifies the order of the entire manual by section number and title. Usually, each section also contains a table of contents for that section. Page numbers reflect the section and page within that section (1-1, 1-2, 2-1, 3-1, etc.). If the manual is published in loose-leaf form, each section is usually marked with a divider tab indicating the section number or title, or both. The Emergency Procedures section may have a red tab for quick identification and reference.

General (Section 1)

The General section provides the basic descriptive information on the airframe and powerplant(s). Some manuals include a three-dimensional drawing of the aircraft that provides dimensions of various components. Included are such items as wingspan, maximum height, overall length, wheelbase length, main landing gear track width, diameter of the rotor system, maximum propeller diameter, propeller ground clearance, minimum turning radius, and wing area. This section serves as a quick reference and helps a pilot become familiar with the aircraft.

The last segment of the General section contains definitions, abbreviations, explanations of symbology, and some of the terminology used in the POH. At the option of the manufacturer, metric and other conversion tables may also be included.

Limitations (Section 2)

The Limitations section contains only those limitations required by regulation or that are necessary for the safe operation of the aircraft, powerplant, systems, and equipment. It includes operating limitations, instrument markings, color-coding, and basic placards. Some of the limitation areas are: airspeed, powerplant, weight and loading distribution, and flight.

Airspeed

Airspeed limitations are shown on the airspeed indicator (ASI) by color coding and on placards or graphs in the aircraft. [Figure 8-1] A red line on the ASI shows the airspeed limit beyond which structural damage could occur. This is called the never-exceed speed (V_{NE}). A yellow arc indicates the speed range between maximum structural cruising speed (V_{NO}) and V_{NE}. Operation of an airplane in the yellow airspeed arc is for smooth air only, and then only with caution. A green arc depicts the normal operating speed range, with the upper end at V_{NO}, and the lower end at stalling speed at maximum weight with the landing gear and flaps retracted (V_{S1}). For airplanes the flap operating range is depicted by the white arc, with the upper end at the maximum flap extended speed (V_{FE}), and the lower end at the stalling speed with the landing gear and flaps in the landing configuration (V_{SO}).

Figure 8-1. *Single-engine airspeed indicator.*

In addition to the markings listed above, small multi-engine airplanes will have a red radial line to indicate single-engine minimum controllable airspeed (VMC). A blue radial line is used to indicate single-engine best rate of climb speed at maximum weight at sea level (V_{YSE}). *[Figure 8-2]*

Figure 8-2. *Multi-engine airspeed indicator.*

Powerplant

The Powerplant Limitations portion describes operating limitations on an aircraft's reciprocating or turbine engine(s). These include limitations for takeoff power, maximum continuous power, and maximum normal operating power, which is the maximum power the engine can produce without any restrictions and is depicted by a green arc. Other items that can be included in this area are the minimum and maximum oil and fuel pressures, oil and fuel grades, and propeller operating limits. *[Figure 8-3]*

All reciprocating-engine powered aircraft must have a revolutions per minute (rpm) indicator for each engine. Aircraft equipped with a constant-speed propeller or rotor system use a manifold pressure gauge to monitor power output and a tachometer to monitor propeller or rotor speed. Both instruments depict the maximum operating limit with

Figure 8-3. *Minimum, maximum, and normal operating range markings on oil gauge.*

a red radial line and the normal operating range with a green arc. *[Figure 8-4]* Some instruments may have a yellow arc to indicate a caution area.

Weight and Loading Distribution

Weight and Loading Distribution contains the maximum certificated weights, as well as the center of gravity (CG) range. The location of the reference datum used in balance computations is included in this section. Weight and balance computations are not provided in this area, but rather in the weight and balance section of the AFM/POH.

Figure 8-4. *Manifold pressure gauge (top) and tachometer (bottom).*

Flight Limits

Flight Limits list authorized maneuvers with appropriate entry speeds, flight load factor limits, and kinds of operation limits. It also indicates those maneuvers that are prohibited, such as spins or acrobatic flight, as well as operational limitations such as flight into known icing conditions.

Placards

Most aircraft display one or more placards that contain information having a direct bearing on the safe operation of the aircraft. These placards are located in conspicuous places and are reproduced in the Limitations section or as directed by an Airworthiness Directive (AD). *[Figure 8-5]*

Figure 8-5. *Placards are used to depict aircraft limitations.*

Emergency Procedures (Section 3)

Checklists describing the recommended procedures and airspeeds for coping with various types of emergencies or critical situations are located in the Emergency Procedures section. Some of the emergencies covered include: engine failure, fire, and system failure. The procedures for inflight engine restarting and ditching may also be included. Manufacturers may first show an emergency checklist in an abbreviated form, with the order of items reflecting the sequence of action. Amplified checklists that provide additional information on the procedures follow the abbreviated checklist. To be prepared for emergency situations, memorize the immediate action items and, after completion, refer to the appropriate checklist.

Manufacturers may include an optional subsection titled "Abnormal Procedures." This subsection describes recommended procedures for handling malfunctions that are not considered emergencies.

Normal Procedures (Section 4)

This section begins with a list of the airspeeds for normal operations. The next area consists of several checklists that may include preflight inspection, before starting procedures, starting engine, before taxiing, taxiing, before takeoff, climb, cruise, descent, before landing, balked landing, after landing, and post flight procedures. An Amplified Procedures area follows the checklists to provide more detailed information about the various previously mentioned procedures.

To avoid missing important steps, always use the appropriate checklists when available. Consistent adherence to approved checklists is a sign of a disciplined and competent pilot.

Performance (Section 5)

The Performance section contains all the information required by the aircraft certification regulations, and any additional performance information the manufacturer deems important to pilot ability to safely operate the aircraft. Performance charts, tables, and graphs vary in style, but all contain the same basic information. Examples of the performance information found in most flight manuals include a graph or table for converting calibrated airspeed to true airspeed; stall speeds in various configurations; and data for determining takeoff and climb performance, cruise performance, and landing performance. *Figure 8-6* is an example of a typical performance graph. For more information on use of the charts, graphs, and tables, refer to Chapter 10, Aircraft Performance.

Weight and Balance/Equipment List (Section 6)

The Weight and Balance/Equipment List section contains all the information required by the FAA to calculate the weight and balance of an aircraft. Manufacturers include sample weight and balance problems. Weight and balance is discussed in greater detail in Chapter 9, Weight and Balance.

Systems Description (Section 7)

This section describes the aircraft systems in a manner appropriate to the pilot most likely to operate the aircraft. For example, a manufacturer might assume an experienced pilot will be reading the information for an advanced aircraft. For more information on aircraft systems, refer to Chapter 6, Aircraft Systems.

Handling, Service, and Maintenance (Section 8)

The Handling, Service, and Maintenance section describes the maintenance and inspections recommended by the manufacturer (and the regulations). Additional maintenance or inspections may be required by the issuance of AD applicable to the airframe, engine, propeller, or components.

EXAMPLE

Gross weight: 2,170 pounds
Angle of bank: 20°
Flap position: 40°
Stall speed, indicated: 44 knots

Calibrated stall speed
Indicated stall speed

Maximum weight - 2,440 (pounds)

Stall speed (knots)

0° Flaps

0° Flaps   40° Flaps

40° Flaps

2,400   2,200   2,000   1,800   1,600   0°   20°   40°   60°

Gross weight (pounds)   Angle of bank (degrees)

70
60
50
40
30

Figure 8-6. *Stall speed chart.*

This section also describes preventive maintenance that may be accomplished by certificated pilots, as well as the manufacturer's recommended ground handling procedures. It includes considerations for hangaring, tie-down, and general storage procedures for the aircraft.

Supplements (Section 9)

The Supplements section contains information necessary to safely and efficiently operate the aircraft when equipped with optional systems and equipment (not provided with the standard aircraft). Some of this information may be supplied by the aircraft manufacturer or by the manufacturer of the optional equipment. The appropriate information is inserted into the flight manual at the time the equipment is installed. Autopilots, navigation systems, and air-conditioning systems are examples of equipment described in this section. *[Figure 8-7]*

Safety Tips (Section 10)

The Safety Tips section is an optional section containing a review of information that enhances the safe operation of the aircraft. For example, physiological factors, general weather information, fuel conservation procedures, high altitude operations, or cold weather operations might be discussed.

Figure 8-7. *Supplements provide information on optional equipment.*

Aircraft Documents

Certificate of Aircraft Registration

Before an aircraft can be flown legally, it must be registered with the FAA Aircraft Registry. The Certificate of Aircraft Registration, which is issued to the owner as evidence of the registration, must be carried in the aircraft at all times. [Figure 8-8]

The Certificate of Aircraft Registration cannot be used for operations when:

- The aircraft is registered under the laws of a foreign country.

- The aircraft's registration is canceled upon written request of the certificate holder.

- The aircraft is totally destroyed or scrapped.

- The ownership of the aircraft is transferred.

- The certificate holder loses United States citizenship.

For additional information, see 14 CFR section 47.41. When one of the events listed in 14 CFR section 47.41 occurs, the previous owner must notify the FAA by filling in the back of the Certificate of Aircraft Registration, and mailing it to:

FAA Aircraft Registration Branch, AFS-750
P.O. Box 25504
Oklahoma City, OK 73125-0504

A dealer's aircraft registration certificate is another form of registration certificate, but is valid only for required flight tests by the manufacturer or in flights that are necessary for the sale of the aircraft by the manufacturer or a dealer. The dealer must remove the certificate when the aircraft is sold.

Upon complying with 14 CFR section 47.31, the pink copy of the application for an Aircraft Registration Application, Aeronautical Center (AC) Form 8050-1, provides authorization to operate an unregistered aircraft for a period not to exceed 90 days. Since the aircraft is

Figure 8-8. AC Form 8050-3, Certificate of Aircraft Registration.

unregistered, it cannot be operated outside of the United States until a permanent Certificate of Aircraft Registration is received and placed in the aircraft.

The FAA does not issue any certificate of ownership or endorse any information with respect to ownership on a Certificate of Aircraft Registration.

NOTE: For additional information concerning the Aircraft Registration Application or the Aircraft Bill of Sale, contact the nearest FAA Flight Standards District Office (FSDO).

Light Sport Aircraft (LSA)

The FAA recently added a new category called Light Sport Aircraft (LSA). Requirements for registration of these aircraft differ from those of other aircraft. The following guidelines are provided for LSA registration, but a more detailed explanation can be found on the FAA website at http//www.faa.gov.

An existing LSA that has not been issued a United States or foreign airworthiness certificate, and does not meet the provisions of 14 CFR section 103.1, must meet specific criteria in order to be certificated as an experimental LSA under 14 CFR section 21.191 (i)(l) before January 31, 2008. The following items must be provided: evidence of ownership of the parts or the manufacturer's kit, Aircraft Registration Application (AC Form 8050-1), and a $5.00 registration fee.

If evidence of ownership can not be supplied, an affidavit stating why it is not available must be submitted on the AC Form 8050-88A.

If an owner wants to register a newly manufactured LSA that will be certificated as an experimental light sport aircraft under 14 CFR section 21.191(i)(2), the following items must be provided: AC Form 8050-88A or its equivalent (completed by the LSA manufacturer, unless previously submitted to the Registry by the manufacturer), evidence from the manufacturer of ownership of an aircraft (kit-built or fly-away), AC Form 8050-1, and a $5.00 registration fee.

Airworthiness Certificate

An Airworthiness Certificate is issued by a representative of the FAA after the aircraft has been inspected, is found to meet the requirements of 14 CFR part 21, and is in condition for safe operation. The Airworthiness Certificate must be displayed in the aircraft so it is legible to the passengers and crew whenever it is operated. The Airworthiness Certificate is transferred with the aircraft except when it is sold to a foreign purchaser.

A Standard Airworthiness Certificate is issued for aircraft type certificated in the normal, utility, acrobatic, commuter, transport categories, and manned free balloons. *Figure 8-9* illustrates a Standard Airworthiness Certificate, and an explanation of each item in the certificate follows.

Figure 8-9. *FAA Form 8100-2, Standard Airworthiness Certificate.*

1. Nationality and Registration Marks. The "N" indicates the aircraft is registered in the United States. Registration marks consist of a series of up to five numbers or numbers and letters. In this case, N2631A is the registration number assigned to this airplane.

2. Manufacturer and Model. Indicates the manufacturer, make, and model of the aircraft.

3. Aircraft Serial Number. Indicates the manufacturer's serial number assigned to the aircraft, as noted on the aircraft data plate.

4. Category. Indicates the category in which the aircraft must be operated. In this case, it must be operated in accordance with the limitations specified for the "NORMAL" category.

5. Authority and Basis for Issuance. Indicates the aircraft conforms to its type certificate and is considered in condition for safe operation at the time of inspection and issuance of the certificate. Any exemptions from the applicable airworthiness standards are briefly noted here and the exemption number given. The word "NONE" is entered if no exemption exists.

6. Terms and Conditions. Indicates the Airworthiness Certificate is in effect indefinitely if the aircraft is maintained in accordance with 14 CFR parts 21, 43, and 91, and the aircraft is registered in the United States.

Also included are the date the certificate was issued and the signature and office identification of the FAA representative.

A Standard Airworthiness Certificate remains in effect if the aircraft receives the required maintenance and is properly registered in the United States. Flight safety relies in part on the condition of the aircraft, which is determined by inspections performed by mechanics, approved repair stations, or manufacturers that meet specific requirements of 14 CFR part 43.

A Special Airworthiness Certificate is issued for all aircraft certificated in other than the Standard classifications, such as Experimental, Restricted, Limited, Provisional, and LSA. LSA receive a pink special airworthiness certificate. There are exceptions. For example, the Piper Cub is in the new LSA category, but it was certificated as a normal aircraft during its manufacture. When purchasing an aircraft classified as other than Standard, it is recommended that the local FSDO be contacted for an explanation of the pertinent airworthiness requirements and the limitations of such a certificate.

Aircraft Maintenance

Maintenance is defined as the preservation, inspection, overhaul, and repair of an aircraft, including the replacement of parts. Regular and proper maintenance ensures that an aircraft meets an acceptable standard of airworthiness throughout its operational life.

Although maintenance requirements vary for different types of aircraft, experience shows that aircraft need some type of preventive maintenance every 25 hours of flying time or less, and minor maintenance at least every 100 hours. This is influenced by the kind of operation, climatic conditions, storage facilities, age, and construction of the aircraft. Manufacturers supply maintenance manuals, parts catalogs, and other service information that should be used in maintaining the aircraft.

Aircraft Inspections

14 CFR part 91 places primary responsibility on the owner or operator for maintaining an aircraft in an airworthy condition. Certain inspections must be performed on the aircraft, and the owner must maintain the airworthiness of the aircraft during the time between required inspections by having any defects corrected.

14 CFR part 91, subpart E, requires the inspection of all civil aircraft at specific intervals to determine the overall condition. The interval depends upon the type of operations in which the aircraft is engaged. All aircraft need to be inspected at least once each 12 calendar months, while inspection is required for others after each 100 hours of operation. Some aircraft are inspected in accordance with an inspection system set up to provide for total inspection of the aircraft on the basis of calendar time, time in service, number of system operations, or any combination of these.

All inspections should follow the current manufacturer's maintenance manual, including the Instructions for Continued Airworthiness concerning inspections intervals, parts replacement, and life-limited items as applicable to the aircraft.

Annual Inspection

Any reciprocating engine or single-engine turbojet/turbopropeller-powered small aircraft (12,500 pounds and under) flown for business or pleasure and not flown for compensation or hire is required to be inspected at least annually. The inspection shall be performed by a certificated airframe and powerplant (A&P) mechanic who holds an inspection authorization (IA) by the manufacturer of the aircraft or by a certificated and appropriately rated repair station. The aircraft may not be operated unless the annual inspection has been performed within the preceding 12 calendar months. A period of 12 calendar months extends from any day of a month to the last day of the same month the following year. An aircraft overdue for an annual inspection may be operated under a Special Flight Permit issued by the FAA for the purpose of flying the aircraft to a location where the annual inspection can be performed. However, all applicable ADs that are due must be complied with before the flight.

100-Hour Inspection

All aircraft under 12,500 pounds (except turbojet/turbopropeller-powered multi-engine airplanes and turbine powered rotorcraft), used to carry passengers for hire, must have received a 100-hour inspection within the preceding 100 hours of time in service and have been approved for return to service. Additionally, an aircraft used for flight instruction for hire, when provided by the person giving the flight instruction, must also have received a 100-hour inspection. This inspection must be performed by an FAA-certificated A&P mechanic, an appropriately rated FAA-certificated repair station, or by the aircraft manufacturer. An annual inspection, or an inspection for the issuance of an Airworthiness Certificate may be substituted for a required 100-hour inspection. The 100-hour limitation may be exceeded by not more than 10 hours while en route to reach a place where the inspection can be done. The excess time used to reach a place where the inspection can be done must be included in computing the next 100 hours of time in service.

Other Inspection Programs

The annual and 100-hour inspection requirements do not apply to large (over 12,500 pounds) airplanes, turbojets, or turbopropeller-powered multi-engine airplanes or to aircraft for which the owner complies with a progressive inspection program. Details of these requirements may be determined by reference to 14 CFR section 43.11 and 14 CFR part 91, subpart E, and by inquiring at a local FSDO.

Altimeter System Inspection

14 CFR section 91.411 requires that the altimeter, encoding altimeter, and related system be tested and inspected in the preceding 24 months before operated in controlled airspace under instrument flight rules (IFR).

Transponder Inspection

14 CFR section 91.413 requires that before a transponder can be used under 14 CFR section 91.215(a), it shall be tested and inspected within the preceding 24 months.

Emergency Locator Transmitter

An emergency locator transmitter (ELT) is required by 14 CFR section 91.207 and must be inspected within 12 calendar months after the last inspection for the following:

- Proper installation
- Battery corrosion
- Operation of the controls and crash sensor
- The presence of a sufficient signal radiated from its antenna

The ELT must be attached to the airplane in such a manner that the probablity of damage to the transmitter in the event of crash impact is minimized. Fixed and deployable automatic type transmitters must be attached to the airplane as far aft as practicable. Batteries used in the ELTs must be replaced (or recharged, if the batteries are rechargeable):

- When the transmitter has been in use for more than 1 cumulative hour.
- When 50 percent of the battery useful life (or, for rechargeable batteries, 50 percent of useful life of the charge) has expired.

An expiration date for replacing (or recharging) the battery must be legibly marked on the outside of the transmitter and entered in the aircraft maintenance record. This does not apply to batteries that are essentially unaffected during storage intervals, such as water-activated batteries.

Preflight Inspections

The preflight inspection is a thorough and systematic means by which a pilot determines if the aircraft is airworthy and in condition for safe operation. POHs and owner/information manuals contain a section devoted to a systematic method of performing a preflight inspection.

Minimum Equipment Lists (MEL) and Operations With Inoperative Equipment

14 CFR requires that all aircraft instruments and installed equipment be operative prior to each departure. When the FAA adopted the minimum equipment list (MEL) concept for 14 CFR part 91 operations, this allowed operations with inoperative equipment determined to be nonessential for safe flight. At the same time, it allowed part 91 operators, without an MEL, to defer repairs on nonessential equipment within the guidelines of part 91.

The FAA has two acceptable methods of deferring maintenance on small rotorcraft, non-turbine powered airplanes, gliders, or lighter-than-air aircraft operated under part 91. They are the deferral provision of 14 CFR section 91.213(d) and an FAA-approved MEL.

The deferral provision of 14 CFR section 91.213(d) is widely used by most pilot/operators. Its popularity is due to simplicity and minimal paperwork. When inoperative equipment is found during preflight or prior to departure, the decision should be to cancel the flight, obtain maintenance prior to flight, or to defer the item or equipment.

Maintenance deferrals are not used for inflight discrepancies. The manufacturer's AFM/POH procedures are to be used in those situations. The discussion that follows assumes that the pilot wishes to defer maintenance that would ordinarily be required prior to flight.

Using the deferral provision of 14 CFR section 91.213(d), the pilot determines whether the inoperative equipment is required by type design, 14 CFR, or ADs. If the inoperative item is not required, and the aircraft can be safely operated without it, the deferral may be made. The inoperative item shall be deactivated or removed and an INOPERATIVE placard placed near the appropriate switch, control, or indicator. If deactivation or removal involves maintenance (removal always will), it must be accomplished by certificated maintenance personnel and recorded in accordance with 14 CFR part 43.

For example, if the position lights (installed equipment) were discovered to be inoperative prior to a daytime flight, the pilot would follow the requirements of 14 CFR section 91.213(d).

The deactivation may be a process as simple as the pilot positioning a circuit breaker to the OFF position, or as complex as rendering instruments or equipment totally inoperable. Complex maintenance tasks require a certificated and appropriately rated maintenance person to perform the deactivation. In all cases, the item or equipment must be placarded INOPERATIVE.

All small rotorcraft, non-turbine powered airplanes, gliders, or lighter-than-air aircraft operated under 14 CFR part 91 are eligible to use the maintenance deferral provisions of 14 CFR section 91.213(d). However, once an operator requests an MEL, and a Letter of Authorization (LOA) is issued by the FAA, then the use of the MEL becomes mandatory for that aircraft. All maintenance deferrals must be accomplished in accordance with the terms and conditions of the MEL and the operator-generated procedures document.

The use of an MEL for an aircraft operated under 14 CFR part 91 also allows for the deferral of inoperative items or equipment. The primary guidance becomes the FAA-approved MEL issued to that specific operator and N-numbered aircraft.

The FAA has developed master minimum equipment lists (MMELs) for aircraft in current use. Upon written request by an operator, the local FSDO may issue the appropriate make and model MMEL, along with an LOA, and the preamble. The operator then develops operations and maintenance (O&M) procedures from the MMEL. This MMEL with O&M procedures now becomes the operator's MEL. The MEL, LOA, preamble, and procedures document developed by the operator must be on board the aircraft when it is operated. The FAA considers an approved MEL to be a supplemental type certificate (STC) issued to an aircraft by serial number and registration number. It, therefore, becomes the authority to operate that aircraft in a condition other than originally type certificated.

With an approved MEL, if the position lights were discovered inoperative prior to a daytime flight, the pilot would make an entry in the maintenance record or discrepancy record provided for that purpose. The item is then either repaired or deferred in accordance with the MEL. Upon confirming that daytime flight with inoperative position lights is acceptable in accordance with the provisions of the MEL, the pilot would leave the position lights switch OFF, open the circuit breaker (or whatever action is called for in the procedures document), and placard the position light switch as INOPERATIVE.

There are exceptions to the use of the MEL for deferral. For example, should a component fail that is not listed in the MEL as deferrable (the tachometer, flaps, or stall warning device, for example), then repairs are required to be performed prior to departure. If maintenance or parts are not readily available at that location, a special flight permit can be obtained from the nearest FSDO. This permit allows the aircraft to be flown to another location for maintenance. This allows an aircraft that may not currently meet applicable airworthiness requirements, but is capable of safe flight, to be operated under the restrictive special terms and conditions attached to the special flight permit.

Deferral of maintenance is not to be taken lightly, and due consideration should be given to the effect an inoperative component may have on the operation of an aircraft, particularly if other items are inoperative. Further information regarding MELs and operations with inoperative equipment can be found in AC 91-67, Minimum Equipment Requirements for General Aviation Operations Under CFR Part 91.

Preventive Maintenance

Preventive maintenance is considered to be simple or minor preservation operations and the replacement of small standard parts, not involving complex assembly operations. Allowed items of preventative maintenance are listed and limited to the items of 14 CFR part 43, appendix A(c).

Maintenance Entries

All pilots who maintain or perform preventive maintenance must make an entry in the maintenance record of the aircraft. The entry must include:

1. A description of the work, such as "changed oil (Shell Aero-50) at 2,345 hours."

2. The date of completion of the work performed.

3. The entry of the pilot's name, signature, certificate number, and type of certificate held.

Examples of Preventive Maintenance

The following examples of preventive maintenance are taken from 14 CFR Part 43, Maintenance, Preventive Maintenance, Rebuilding, and Alternation, which should be consulted for a more in-depth look at preventive maintenance a pilot can perform on an aircraft. Remember, preventive maintenance is limited to work that does not involve complex assembly operations and includes:

- Removal, installation, and repair of landing gear tires and shock cords; servicing landing gear shock struts by adding oil, air, or both; servicing gear wheel bearings; replacing defective safety wiring or cotter keys; lubrication not requiring disassembly other than removal of nonstructural items such as cover plates, cowlings, and fairings; making simple fabric patches not requiring rib stitching or the removal of structural parts or control surfaces. In the case of balloons, the making of small fabric repairs to envelopes (as defined in, and in accordance with, the balloon manufacturer's instructions) not requiring load tape repair or replacement.

- Replenishing hydraulic fluid in the hydraulic reservoir; refinishing decorative coating of fuselage, balloon baskets, wings, tail group surfaces (excluding balanced control surfaces), fairings, cowlings, landing gear, cabin, or flight deck interior when removal or disassembly of any primary structure or operating system is not required; applying preservative or protective material to components where no disassembly of any primary structure or operating system is involved and where such coating is not prohibited or is not contrary to good practices; repairing upholstery and decorative furnishings of the cabin, flight deck, or balloon basket interior when the repair does not require disassembly of any primary structure or operating system or interfere with an operating system or affect the primary structure of the aircraft; making small, simple repairs to fairings, nonstructural cover plates, cowlings, and small patches and reinforcements not changing the contour to interfere with proper air flow; replacing side windows where that work does not interfere with the structure or any operating system such as controls, electrical equipment, etc.

- Replacing safety belts, seats or seat parts with replacement parts approved for the aircraft, not involving disassembly of any primary structure or operating system, bulbs, reflectors, and lenses of position and landing lights.

- Replacing wheels and skis where no weight-and-balance computation is involved; replacing any cowling not requiring removal of the propeller or disconnection of flight controls; replacing or cleaning spark plugs and setting of spark plug gap clearance; replacing any hose connection, except hydraulic connections; however, prefabricated fuel lines may be replaced.

- Cleaning or replacing fuel and oil strainers or filter elements; servicing batteries, cleaning of balloon burner pilot and main nozzles in accordance with the balloon manufacturer's instructions.

- The interchange of balloon baskets and burners on envelopes when the basket or burner is designated as interchangeable in the balloon type certificate data and the baskets and burners are specifically designed for quick removal and installation; adjustment of nonstructural standard fasteners incidental to operations.

- The installations of anti-misfueling devices to reduce the diameter of fuel tank filler openings only if the specific device has been made a part of the aircraft type certificate data by the aircraft manufacturer, the aircraft manufacturer has provided FAA-approved instructions for installation of the specific device, and installation does not involve the disassembly of the existing tank filler opening; troubleshooting and repairing broken circuits in landing light wiring circuits.

- Removing and replacing self-contained, front instrument panel-mounted navigation and communication devices employing tray-mounted connectors that connect the unit when the unit is installed into the instrument panel; excluding automatic flight control systems, transponders, and microwave frequency distance measuring equipment (DME). The approved unit must be designed to be readily and repeatedly removed and replaced, and pertinent instructions must be provided.

Prior to the unit's intended use, an operational check must be performed in accordance with the applicable sections of 14 CFR part 91 on checking, removing, and replacing magnetic chip detectors.

- Inspection and maintenance tasks prescribed and specifically identified as preventive maintenance in a primary category aircraft type certificate or supplemental type certificate holder's approved special inspection and preventive maintenance program when accomplished on a primary category aircraft.

- Updating self-contained, front instrument panel-mounted air traffic control (ATC) navigational software databases (excluding those of automatic flight control systems, transponders, and microwave frequency DME) only if no disassembly of the unit is required and pertinent instructions are provided; prior to the unit's intended use, an operational check must be performed in accordance with applicable sections of 14 CFR part 91.

Certificated pilots, excluding student pilots, sport pilots, and recreational pilots, may perform preventive maintenance on any aircraft that is owned or operated by them provided that aircraft is not used in air carrier service or 14 CFR part 121, 129, or 135. A pilot holding a sport pilot certificate may perform preventive maintenance on an aircraft owned or operated by that pilot if that aircraft is issued a special airworthiness certificate in the LSA category. (Sport pilots operating LSA should refer to 14 CFR part 65 for maintenance privileges.) 14 CFR part 43, appendix A, contains a list of the operations that are considered to be preventive maintenance.

Repairs and Alterations

Repairs and alterations are classified as either major or minor. 14 CFR part 43, appendix A, describes the alterations and repairs considered major. Major repairs or alterations shall be approved for return to service on FAA Form 337, Major Repair and Alteration, by an appropriately rated certificated repair station, an FAA-certificated A&P mechanic holding an IA, or a representative of the Administrator. Minor repairs and minor alterations may be approved for return to service with a proper entry in the maintenance records by an FAA-certificated A&P mechanic or an appropriately certificated repair station.

For modifications of experimental aircraft, refer to the operating limitations issued to that aircraft. Modifications in accordance with FAA Order 8130.2, Airworthiness Certification of Aircraft and Related Products, may require the notification of the issuing authority.

Special Flight Permits

A special flight permit is a Special Airworthiness Certificate authorizing operation of an aircraft that does not currently meet applicable airworthiness requirements but is safe for a specific flight. Before the permit is issued, an FAA inspector may personally inspect the aircraft, or require it to be inspected by an FAA-certificated A&P mechanic or an appropriately certificated repair station to determine its safety for the intended flight. The inspection shall be recorded in the aircraft records.

The special flight permit is issued to allow the aircraft to be flown to a base where repairs, alterations, or maintenance can be performed; for delivering or exporting the aircraft; or for evacuating an aircraft from an area of impending danger. A special flight permit may be issued to allow the operation of an overweight aircraft for flight beyond its normal range over water or land areas where adequate landing facilities or fuel is not available.

If a special flight permit is needed, assistance and the necessary forms may be obtained from the local FSDO or Designated Airworthiness Representative (DAR). [Figure 8-10]

Airworthiness Directives (ADs)

A primary safety function of the FAA is to require correction of unsafe conditions found in an aircraft, aircraft engine, propeller, or appliance when such conditions exist and are likely to exist or develop in other products of the same design. The unsafe condition may exist because of a design defect, maintenance, or other causes. 14 CFR part 39 and Airworthiness Directives (ADs) define the authority and responsibility of the Administrator for requiring the necessary corrective action. ADs are used to notify aircraft owners and other interested persons of unsafe conditions and to specify the conditions under which the product may continue to be operated. ADs are divided into two categories:

1. Those of an emergency nature requiring immediate compliance prior to further flight

2. Those of a less urgent nature requiring compliance within a specified period of time

ADs are regulatory and shall be complied with unless a specific exemption is granted. It is the responsibility of the aircraft owner or operator to ensure compliance with all pertinent ADs, including those ADs that require recurrent or continuing action. For example, an AD may require a repetitive inspection each 50 hours of operation, meaning the particular inspection shall be accomplished and recorded

Figure 8-10. *FAA Form 8130-7, Special Airworthiness Certificate.*

every 50 hours of time in service. Owners/operators are reminded there is no provision to overfly the maximum hour requirement of an AD unless it is specifically written into the AD. To help determine if an AD applies to an amateur-built aircraft, contact the local FSDO.

14 CFR section 91.417 requires a record to be maintained that shows the current status of applicable ADs, including the method of compliance; the AD number and revision date, if recurring; next due date and time; the signature; kind of certificate; and certificate number of the repair station or mechanic who performed the work. For ready reference, many aircraft owners have a chronological listing of the pertinent ADs in the back of their aircraft, engine, and propeller maintenance records.

All ADs and the AD Biweekly are free on the Internet at http://rgl.faa.gov. In July of 2007, the FAA made ADs available through e-mail. Individuals can enroll for the e-mail service at the link above. Mailing paper copies of ADs will be discontinued when the e-mail system is proven to be effective.

Paper copies of the Summary of Airworthiness Directives and the AD Biweekly may be purchased from the Superintendent of Documents. The Summary contains all the valid ADs previously published and is divided into two areas. The small aircraft and helicopter books contain all ADs applicable to small aircraft (12,500 pounds or less maximum certificated takeoff weight) and ADs applicable to all helicopters. The large aircraft books contain all ADs applicable to large aircraft.

For current information on how to order paper copies of AD books and the AD Biweekly visit the FAA online regulatory and guidance library at: http://rgl.faa.gov.

Aircraft Owner/Operator Responsibilities

The registered owner/operator of an aircraft is responsible for:

- Having a current Airworthiness Certificate and a Certificate of Aircraft Registration in the aircraft.

- Maintaining the aircraft in an airworthy condition, including compliance with all applicable ADs, and assuring that maintenance is properly recorded.

- Keeping abreast of current regulations concerning the operation and maintenance of the aircraft.

- Notifying the FAA Aircraft Registry immediately of any change of permanent mailing address, or of the sale or export of the aircraft, or of the loss of the eligibility to register an aircraft. (Refer to 14 CFR section 47.41.)

- Having a current Federal Communications Commission (FCC) radio station license if equipped with radios, including emergency locator transmitter (ELT), if operated outside of the United States.

Chapter Summary

Knowledge of an aircraft's AFM/POH and documents such as ADs help a pilot to have ready access to pertinent information needed to safely fly a particular aircraft. By understanding the operations, limitations, and performance characteristics of the aircraft, the pilot can make good flight decisions. By learning what preventive maintenance is allowed on the aircraft, a pilot can maintain his or her aircraft in an airworthy condition. The goal of every pilot is a safe flight; flight manuals and aircraft documentation are essential tools used to reach that goal.

Chapter 9
Weight and Balance

Introduction

Compliance with the weight and balance limits of any aircraft is critical to flight safety. Operating above the maximum weight limitation compromises the structural integrity of an aircraft and adversely affects its performance. Operation with the center of gravity (CG) outside the approved limits results in control difficulty.

Weight Control

As discussed in Chapter 4, Aerodynamics of Flight, weight is the force with which gravity attracts a body toward the center of the Earth. It is a product of the mass of a body and the acceleration acting on the body. Weight is a major factor in aircraft construction and operation, and demands respect from all pilots.

The force of gravity continuously attempts to pull an aircraft down toward Earth. The force of lift is the only force that counteracts weight and sustains an aircraft in flight. The amount of lift produced by an airfoil is limited by the airfoil design, angle of attack (AOA), airspeed, and air density. To assure that the lift generated is sufficient to counteract weight, loading an aircraft beyond the manufacturer's recommended weight must be avoided. If the weight is greater than the lift generated, the aircraft may be incapable of flight.

Effects of Weight

Any item aboard the aircraft that increases the total weight is undesirable for performance. Manufacturers attempt to make an aircraft as light as possible without sacrificing strength or safety.

The pilot should always be aware of the consequences of overloading. An overloaded aircraft may not be able to leave the ground, or if it does become airborne, it may exhibit unexpected and unusually poor flight characteristics. If not properly loaded, the initial indication of poor performance usually takes place during takeoff.

Excessive weight reduces the flight performance in almost every respect. For example, the most important performance deficiencies of an overloaded aircraft are:

- Higher takeoff speed
- Longer takeoff run
- Reduced rate and angle of climb
- Lower maximum altitude
- Shorter range
- Reduced cruising speed
- Reduced maneuverability
- Higher stalling speed
- Higher approach and landing speed
- Longer landing roll
- Excessive weight on the nose wheel or tail wheel

The pilot must be knowledgeable about the effect of weight on the performance of the particular aircraft being flown. Preflight planning should include a check of performance charts to determine if the aircraft's weight may contribute to hazardous flight operations. Excessive weight in itself reduces the safety margins available to the pilot, and becomes even more hazardous when other performance-reducing factors are combined with excess weight. The pilot must also consider the consequences of an overweight aircraft if an emergency condition arises. If an engine fails on takeoff or airframe ice forms at low altitude, it is usually too late to reduce an aircraft's weight to keep it in the air.

Weight Changes

The operating weight of an aircraft can be changed by simply altering the fuel load. Gasoline has considerable weight—6 pounds per gallon. Thirty gallons of fuel may weigh more than one passenger. If a pilot lowers airplane weight by reducing fuel, the resulting decrease in the range of the airplane must be taken into consideration during flight planning. During flight, fuel burn is normally the only weight change that takes place. As fuel is used, an aircraft becomes lighter and performance is improved.

Changes of fixed equipment have a major effect upon the weight of an aircraft. The installation of extra radios or instruments, as well as repairs or modifications may also affect the weight of an aircraft.

Balance, Stability, and Center of Gravity

Balance refers to the location of the CG of an aircraft, and is important to stability and safety in flight. The CG is a point at which the aircraft would balance if it were suspended at that point.

The primary concern in balancing an aircraft is the fore and aft location of the CG along the longitudinal axis. The CG is not necessarily a fixed point; its location depends on the distribution of weight in the aircraft. As variable load items are shifted or expended, there is a resultant shift in CG location. The distance between the forward and back limits for the position of the center for gravity or CG range is certified for an aircraft by the manufacturer. The pilot should realize that if the CG is displaced too far forward on the longitudinal axis, a nose-heavy condition will result. Conversely, if the CG is displaced too far aft on the longitudinal axis, a tail heavy condition results. It is possible that the pilot could not control the aircraft if the CG location produced an unstable condition. *[Figure 9-1]*

Location of the CG with reference to the lateral axis is also important. For each item of weight existing to the left of the fuselage centerline, there is an equal weight existing at a corresponding location on the right. This may be upset by unbalanced lateral loading. The position of the lateral CG is not computed in all aircraft, but the pilot must be aware that adverse effects arise as a result of a laterally unbalanced condition. In an airplane, lateral unbalance occurs if the fuel load is mismanaged by supplying the engine(s) unevenly from tanks on one side of the airplane. The pilot can compensate for the resulting wing-heavy condition by adjusting the

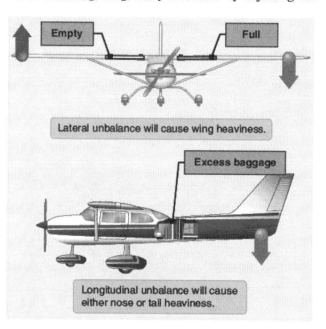

Figure 9-1. *Lateral and longitudinal unbalance.*

trim or by holding a constant control pressure. This action places the aircraft controls in an out-of-streamline condition, increases drag, and results in decreased operating efficiency. Since lateral balance is addressed when needed in the aircraft flight manual (AFM) and longitudinal balance is more critical, further reference to balance in this handbook means longitudinal location of the CG. A single pilot operating a small rotorcraft, may require additional weight to keep the aircraft laterally balanced.

Flying an aircraft that is out of balance can produce increased pilot fatigue with obvious effects on the safety and efficiency of flight. The pilot's natural correction for longitudinal unbalance is a change of trim to remove the excessive control pressure. Excessive trim, however, has the effect of reducing not only aerodynamic efficiency but also primary control travel distance in the direction the trim is applied.

Effects of Adverse Balance

Adverse balance conditions affect flight characteristics in much the same manner as those mentioned for an excess weight condition. It is vital to comply with weight and balance limits established for all aircraft, especially rotorcraft. Operating above the maximum weight limitation compromises the structural integrity of the rotorcraft and adversely affects performance. Balance is also critical because on some fully loaded rotorcraft, CG deviations as small as three inches can dramatically change handling characteristics. Stability and control are also affected by improper balance.

Stability

Loading in a nose-heavy condition causes problems in controlling and raising the nose, especially during takeoff and landing. Loading in a tail heavy condition has a serious effect upon longitudinal stability, and reduces the capability to recover from stalls and spins. Tail heavy loading also produces very light control forces, another undesirable characteristic. This makes it easy for the pilot to inadvertently overstress an aircraft.

It is important to reevaluate the balance in a rotorcraft whenever loading changes. In most aircraft, off-loading a passenger is unlikely to adversely affect the CG, but off-loading a passenger from a rotorcraft can create an unsafe flight condition. An out-of-balance loading condition also decreases maneuverability since cyclic control is less effective in the direction opposite to the CG location.

Limits for the location of the CG are established by the manufacturer. These are the fore and aft limits beyond which the CG should not be located for flight. These limits are published for each aircraft in the Type Certificate Data Sheet (TCDS), or aircraft specification and the AFM or pilot's operating handbook (POH). If the CG is not within the allowable limits after loading, it will be necessary to relocate some items before flight is attempted.

The forward CG limit is often established at a location that is determined by the landing characteristics of an aircraft. During landing, one of the most critical phases of flight, exceeding the forward CG limit may result in excessive loads on the nosewheel, a tendency to nose over on tailwheel type airplanes, decreased performance, higher stalling speeds, and higher control forces.

Control

In extreme cases, a CG location that is beyond the forward limit may result in nose heaviness, making it difficult or impossible to flare for landing. Manufacturers purposely place the forward CG limit as far rearward as possible to aid pilots in avoiding damage when landing. In addition to decreased static and dynamic longitudinal stability, other undesirable effects caused by a CG location aft of the allowable range may include extreme control difficulty, violent stall characteristics, and very light control forces which make it easy to overstress an aircraft inadvertently.

A restricted forward CG limit is also specified to assure that sufficient elevator/control deflection is available at minimum airspeed. When structural limitations do not limit the forward CG position, it is located at the position where full-up elevator/control deflection is required to obtain a high AOA for landing.

The aft CG limit is the most rearward position at which the CG can be located for the most critical maneuver or operation. As the CG moves aft, a less stable condition occurs, which decreases the ability of the aircraft to right itself after maneuvering or turbulence.

For some aircraft, both fore and aft CG limits may be specified to vary as gross weight changes. They may also be changed for certain operations, such as acrobatic flight, retraction of the landing gear, or the installation of special loads and devices that change the flight characteristics.

The actual location of the CG can be altered by many variable factors and is usually controlled by the pilot. Placement of baggage and cargo items determines the CG location. The assignment of seats to passengers can also be used as a means of obtaining a favorable balance. If an aircraft is tail heavy, it is only logical to place heavy passengers in forward seats.

Fuel burn can also affect the CG based on the location of the fuel tanks. For example, most small aircraft carry fuel in the wings very near the CG and burning off fuel has little effect on the loaded CG. On rotorcraft, the fuel tanks are often located behind the CG and fuel consumption from a tank aft of the rotor mast causes the loaded CG to move forward. A rotorcraft in this condition has a nose-low attitude when coming to a hover following a vertical takeoff. Excessive rearward displacement of the cyclic control is needed to maintain a hover in a no-wind condition. Flight should not be continued since rearward cyclic control fades as fuel is consumed. Deceleration to a stop may also be impossible. In the event of engine failure and autorotation, there may not be enough cyclic control to flare properly for a landing.

Management of Weight and Balance Control

Title 14 of the Code of Federal Regulations (14 CFR) section 23.23 requires establishment of the ranges of weights and CGs within which an aircraft may be operated safely. The manufacturer provides this information, which is included in the approved AFM, TCDS, or aircraft specifications.

While there are no specified requirements for a pilot operating under 14 CFR part 91 to conduct weight and balance calculations prior to each flight, 14 CFR section 91.9 requires the pilot in command (PIC) to comply with the operating limits in the approved AFM. These limits include the weight and balance of the aircraft. To enable pilots to make weight and balance computations, charts and graphs are provided in the approved AFM.

Weight and balance control should be a matter of concern to all pilots. The pilot controls loading and fuel management (the two variable factors that can change both total weight and CG location) of a particular aircraft. The aircraft owner or operator should make certain that up-to-date information is available for pilot use, and should ensure that appropriate entries are made in the records when repairs or modifications have been accomplished. The removal or addition of equipment results in changes to the CG.

Weight changes must be accounted for and the proper notations made in weight and balance records. The equipment list must be updated, if appropriate. Without such information, the pilot has no foundation upon which to base the necessary calculations and decisions.

Standard parts with negligible weight or the addition of minor items of equipment such as nuts, bolts, washers, rivets, and similar standard parts of negligible weight on fixed-wing aircraft do not require a weight and balance check. Rotorcraft are, in general, more critical with respect to control with changes in the CG position. The following

criteria for negligible weight change is outlined in Advisory Circular (AC) 43.13-1 (as revised), Methods Techniques and Practices—Aircraft Inspection and Repair:

- One pound or less for an aircraft whose weight empty is less than 5,000 pounds;
- Two pounds or less for aircraft with an empty weight of more than 5,000 pounds to 50,000 pounds;
- Five pounds or less for aircraft with an empty weight of more than 50,000 pounds.

Negligible CG change is any change of less than 0.05 percent Mean Aerodynamic Chord (MAC) for fixed-wing aircraft, 0.2 percent of the maximum allowable CG range for rotorcraft. Exceeding these limits would require a weight and balance check.

Before any flight, the pilot should determine the weight and balance condition of the aircraft. Simple and orderly procedures based on sound principles have been devised by the manufacturer for the determination of loading conditions. The pilot uses these procedures and exercises good judgment when determining weight and balance. In many modern aircraft, it is not possible to fill all seats, baggage compartments, and fuel tanks, and still remain within the approved weight and balance limits. If the maximum passenger load is carried, the pilot must often reduce the fuel load or reduce the amount of baggage.

14 CFR part 125 requires aircraft with 20 or more seats or weighing 6,000 pounds or more to be weighed every 36 calendar months. Multi-engine aircraft operated under a 14 CFR part 135 are also required to be weighed every 36 months. Aircraft operated under 14 CFR part 135 are exempt from the 36 month requirement if operated under a weight and balance system approved in the operations specifications of the certificate holder. AC 43.13-1, Acceptable Methods, Techniques and Practices—Aircraft Inspection and Repair also requires that the aircraft mechanic must ensure the weight and balance data in the aircraft records is current and accurate after a 100-hour or annual inspection.

Terms and Definitions

The pilot should be familiar with terms used in working problems related to weight and balance. The following list of terms and their definitions is standardized, and knowledge of these terms aids the pilot to better understand weight and balance calculations of any aircraft. Terms defined by the General Aviation Manufacturers Association (GAMA) as industry standard are marked in the titles with GAMA.

- Arm (moment arm)—the horizontal distance in inches from the reference datum line to the CG of an item. The algebraic sign is plus (+) if measured aft of the datum, and minus (–) if measured forward of the datum.

- Basic empty weight (GAMA)—the standard empty weight plus the weight of optional and special equipment that have been installed.

- Center of gravity (CG)—the point about which an aircraft would balance if it were possible to suspend it at that point. It is the mass center of the aircraft, or the theoretical point at which the entire weight of the aircraft is assumed to be concentrated. It may be expressed in inches from the reference datum, or in percent of MAC. The CG is a three-dimensional point with longitudinal, lateral, and vertical positioning in the aircraft.

- CG limits—the specified forward and aft points within which the CG must be located during flight. These limits are indicated on pertinent aircraft specifications.

- CG range—the distance between the forward and aft CG limits indicated on pertinent aircraft specifications.

- Datum (reference datum)—an imaginary vertical plane or line from which all measurements of arm are taken. The datum is established by the manufacturer. Once the datum has been selected, all moment arms and the location of CG range are measured from this point.

- Delta—a Greek letter expressed by the symbol $\triangle$ to indicate a change of values. As an example, $\triangle$CG indicates a change (or movement) of the CG.

- Floor load limit—the maximum weight the floor can sustain per square inch/foot as provided by the manufacturer.

- Fuel load—the expendable part of the load of the aircraft. It includes only usable fuel, not fuel required to fill the lines or that which remains trapped in the tank sumps.

- Licensed empty weight—the empty weight that consists of the airframe, engine(s), unusable fuel, and undrainable oil plus standard and optional equipment as specified in the equipment list. Some manufacturers used this term prior to GAMA standardization.

- Maximum landing weight—the greatest weight that an aircraft normally is allowed to have at landing.

- Maximum ramp weight—the total weight of a loaded aircraft, and includes all fuel. It is greater than the takeoff weight due to the fuel that will be burned during the taxi and runup operations. Ramp weight may also be referred to as taxi weight.

- Maximum takeoff weight—the maximum allowable weight for takeoff.

- Maximum weight—the maximum authorized weight of the aircraft and all of its equipment as specified in the TCDS for the aircraft.

- Maximum zero fuel weight (GAMA)—the maximum weight, exclusive of usable fuel.

- Mean aerodynamic chord (MAC)—the average distance from the leading edge to the trailing edge of the wing.

- Moment—the product of the weight of an item multiplied by its arm. Moments are expressed in pound-inches (in-lb). Total moment is the weight of the airplane multiplied by the distance between the datum and the CG.

- Moment index (or index)—a moment divided by a constant such as 100, 1,000, or 10,000. The purpose of using a moment index is to simplify weight and balance computations of aircraft where heavy items and long arms result in large, unmanageable numbers.

- Payload (GAMA)—the weight of occupants, cargo, and baggage.

- Standard empty weight (GAMA)—aircraft weight that consists of the airframe, engines, and all items of operating equipment that have fixed locations and are permanently installed in the aircraft, including fixed ballast, hydraulic fluid, unusable fuel, and full engine oil.

- Standard weights—established weights for numerous items involved in weight and balance computations. These weights should not be used if actual weights are available. Some of the standard weights are:

  Gasoline .... 6 lb/US gal

  Jet A, Jet A-1 .... 6.8 lb/US gal

  Jet B .... 6.5 lb/US gal

  Oil .... 7.5 lb/US gal

  Water .... 8.35 lb/US gal

- Station—a location in the aircraft that is identified by a number designating its distance in inches from the datum. The datum is, therefore, identified as station zero. An item located at station +50 would have an arm of 50 inches.

- Useful load—the weight of the pilot, copilot, passengers, baggage, usable fuel, and drainable oil. It is the basic empty weight subtracted from the maximum allowable gross weight. This term applies to general aviation (GA) aircraft only.

Principles of Weight and Balance Computations

It might be advantageous at this point to review and discuss some of the basic principles of weight and balance determination. The following method of computation can be applied to any object or vehicle for which weight and balance information is essential.

By determining the weight of the empty aircraft and adding the weight of everything loaded on the aircraft, a total weight can be determined—a simple concept. A greater problem, particularly if the basic principles of weight and balance are not understood, is distributing this weight in such a manner that the entire mass of the loaded aircraft is balanced around a point (CG) that must be located within specified limits.

The point at which an aircraft balances can be determined by locating the CG, which is, as stated in the definitions of terms, the imaginary point at which all the weight is concentrated. To provide the necessary balance between longitudinal stability and elevator control, the CG is usually located slightly forward of the center of lift. This loading condition causes a nose-down tendency in flight, which is desirable during flight at a high AOA and slow speeds.

As mentioned earlier, a safe zone within which the balance point (CG) must fall is called the CG range. The extremities of the range are called the forward CG limits and aft CG limits. These limits are usually specified in inches, along the longitudinal axis of the airplane, measured from a reference point called a datum reference. The datum is an arbitrary point, established by aircraft designers, which may vary in location between different aircraft. [Figure 9-2]

The distance from the datum to any component part or any object loaded on the aircraft, is called the arm. When the object or component is located aft of the datum, it is measured in positive inches; if located forward of the datum, it is measured as negative inches, or minus inches. The location

of the object or part is often referred to as the station. If the weight of any object or component is multiplied by the distance from the datum (arm), the product is the moment. The moment is the measurement of the gravitational force that causes a tendency of the weight to rotate about a point or axis and is expressed in inch-pounds (in-lb).

To illustrate, assume a weight of 50 pounds is placed on the board at a station or point 100 inches from the datum. The downward force of the weight can be determined by multiplying 50 pounds by 100 inches, which produces a moment of 5,000 in-lb. [Figure 9-3]

Figure 9-3. *Determining moment.*

To establish a balance, a total of 5,000 in-lb must be applied to the other end of the board. Any combination of weight and distance which, when multiplied, produces a 5,000 in-lb moment will balance the board. For example (illustrated in *Figure 9-4*), if a 100-pound weight is placed at a point (station) 25 inches from the datum, and another 50-pound weight is placed at a point (station) 50 inches from the datum, the sum of the product of the two weights and their distances will total a moment of 5,000 in-lb, which will balance the board.

Figure 9-2. *Weight and balance.*

Figure 9-4. *Establishing a balance.*

Weight and Balance Restrictions

An aircraft's weight and balance restrictions should be closely followed. The loading conditions and empty weight of a particular aircraft may differ from that found in the AFM/POH because modifications or equipment changes may have been made. Sample loading problems in the AFM/POH are intended for guidance only; therefore, each aircraft must be treated separately. Although an aircraft is certified for a specified maximum gross takeoff weight, it will not safely take off with this load under all conditions. Conditions that affect takeoff and climb performance, such as high elevations, high temperatures, and high humidity (high density altitudes) may require a reduction in weight before flight is attempted. Other factors to consider prior to takeoff are runway length, runway surface, runway slope, surface wind, and the presence of obstacles. These factors may require a reduction in weight prior to flight.

Some aircraft are designed so that it is difficult to load them in a manner that will place the CG out of limits. These are usually small aircraft with the seats, fuel, and baggage areas located near the CG limit. Pilots must be aware that while within CG limits these aircraft can be overloaded in weight. Other aircraft can be loaded in such a manner that they will be out of CG limits even though the useful load has not been exceeded. Because of the effects of an out-of-balance or overweight condition, a pilot should always be sure that an aircraft is properly loaded.

Determining Loaded Weight and CG

There are various methods for determining the loaded weight and CG of an aircraft. There is the computational method, as well as methods that utilize graphs and tables provided by the aircraft manufacturer.

Computational Method

The following is an example of the computational method involving the application of basic math functions.

Aircraft Allowances:

Maximum gross weight....................... 3,400 pounds

CG range.. 78–86 inches

Given:

Weight of front seat occupants............. 340 pounds

Weight of rear seat occupants.............. 350 pounds

Fuel.. 75 gallons

Weight of baggage in area 1.................... 80 pounds

1. List the weight of the aircraft, occupants, fuel, and baggage. Remember that aviation gas (AVGAS) weighs 6 pounds per gallon and is used in this example.

2. Enter the moment for each item listed. Remember "weight X arm = moment."

3. Find the total weight and total moment.

4. To determine the CG, divide the total moment by the total weight.

NOTE: The weight and balance records for a particular aircraft will provide the empty weight and moment, as well as the information on the arm distance. *[Figure 9-5]*

Item	Weight	Arm	Moment
Aircraft Empty Weight	2,100	78.3	164,430
Front Seat Occupants	340	85.0	28,900
Rear Seat Occupants	350	121.0	42,350
Fuel	450	75.0	33,750
Baggage Area 1	80	150.0	12,000
Total	3,320		281,430
			281,430 ÷ 3,320 = 84.8

Figure 9-5. *Example of weight and balance computations.*

The total loaded weight of 3,320 pounds does not exceed the maximum gross weight of 3,400 pounds, and the CG of 84.8 is within the 78–86 inch range; therefore, the aircraft is loaded within limits.

Graph Method

Another method for determining the loaded weight and CG is the use of graphs provided by the manufacturers. To simplify calculations, the moment may sometimes be divided by 100, 1,000, or 10,000. *[Figures 9-6, 9-7, and 9-8]*

Front seat occupants...................................340 pounds

Rear seat occupants ....300 pounds

Fuel..40 gallons

Baggage area 1 ....20 pounds

Sample Loading Problem	Weight (lb)	Moment (in-lb/1,000)
1. Basic Empty Weight (Use data pertaining to aircraft as it is presently equipped.) Includes unusable fuel and full oil	1,467	57.3
2. Usable Fuel (At 6 lb/gal) ▪ Standard Tanks (40 gal maximum) ▪ Long Range Tanks (50 gal maximum) ▪ Integral Tanks (62 gal maximum) ▪ Integral Reduced Fuel (42 gal)	240	11.5
3. Pilot and Front Passenger (Station 34 to 46)	340	12.7
4. Rear Passengers	300	21.8
5. Baggage Area 1 or Passenger on Child's Seat (Station 82 to 108, 120 lb maximum)	20	1.9
6. Baggage Area 2 (Station 108 to 142, 50 lb maximum)		
7. Weight and Moment	2,367	105.2

Figure 9-6. *Weight and balance data.*

Figure 9-7. *Loading graph.*

Figure 9-8. *CG moment envelope.*

The same steps should be followed as in the computational method except the graphs provided will calculate the moments and allow the pilot to determine if the aircraft is loaded within limits. To determine the moment using the loading graph, find the weight and draw a line straight across until it intercepts the item for which the moment is to be calculated. Then draw a line straight down to determine the moment. (The red line on the loading graph represents the moment for the pilot and front passenger. All other moments were determined in the same way.) Once this has been done for each item, total the weight and moments and draw a line for both weight and moment on the CG envelope graph. If the lines intersect within the envelope, the aircraft is loaded within limits. In this sample loading problem, the aircraft is loaded within limits.

Table Method

The table method applies the same principles as the computational and graph methods. The information and limitations are contained in tables provided by the manufacturer. *Figure 9-9* is an example of a table and a weight and balance calculation based on that table. In this problem, the total weight of 2,799 pounds and moment of 2,278/100 are within the limits of the table.

Usable Fuel

Main Wing Tanks Arm 75

Gallons	Weight	Moment 100
5	30	22
10	60	45
15	90	68
20	120	90
25	150	112
30	180	135
35	210	158
40	240	180
44	264	198

Occupants

Front Seat Arm 85		Rear Seats Arm 121	
Weight	Moment 100	Weight	Moment 100
120	102	120	145
130	110	130	157
140	119	140	169
150	128	150	182
160	136	160	194
170	144	170	206
180	153	180	218
190	162	190	230
200	170	200	242

Weight	Minimum Moment 100	Maximum Moment 100
2,400	1,848	2,057
2,410	1,856	2,065
2,420	1,863	2,074
2,430	1,871	2,083
2,440	1,879	2,091
2,450	1,887	2,100
2,460	1,894	2,108
2,470	1,092	2,117
2,480	1,911	2,125
2,490	1,921	2,134
2,500	1,932	2,143
2,510	1,942	2,151
2,520	1,953	2,160
2,530	1,963	2,168
2,540	1,974	2,176
2,550	1,984	2,184
2,560	1,995	2,192
2,570	2,005	2,200
2,580	2,016	2,208
2,590	2,026	2,216
2,600	2,037	2,224
2,610	2,048	2,232
2,620	2,058	2,239
2,630	2,069	2,247
2,640	2,080	2,255
2,650	2,090	2,263
2,660	2,101	2,271
2,670	2,112	2,279
2,680	2,123	2,287
2,690	2,133	2,295
2,700	2,144	2,303
2,710	2,155	2,311
2,720	2,166	2,319
2,730	2,177	2,326
2,740	2,188	2,334
2,750	2,199	2,342
2,760	2,210	2,350
2,770	2,221	2,358
2,780	2,232	2,366
2,790	2,243	2,374
2,800	2,254	2,381
2,810	2,265	2,389
2,820	2,276	2,397
2,830	2,287	2,405
2,840	2,298	2,413
2,850	2,309	2,421
2,860	2,320	2,426
2,870	2,332	2,436
2,880	2,343	2,444
2,890	2,354	2,452
2,900	2,365	3,460
2,910	2,377	2,468
2,920	2,388	2,475
2,930	2,399	2,483
2,940	2,411	2,491
2,950	2,422	2,499

*Oil

Quarts	Weight	Moment 100
10	19	5

*Included in basic empty weight

Empty Weight – 2,015
MOM/100 – 1,554

Baggage or 5th Seat Occupant Arm 140

Weight	Moment 100
10	14
20	28
30	42
40	56
50	70
60	84
70	98
80	112
90	126
100	140
110	154
	168

Weight	Minimum Moment 100	Maximum Moment 100
2,100	1,617	1,800
2,110	1,625	1,808
2,120	1,632	1,817
2,130	1,640	1,825
2,140	1,648	1,834
2,150	1,656	1,843
2,160	1,663	1,851
2,170	1,671	1,860
2,180	1,679	1,868
2,190	1,686	1,877
2,200	1,694	1,885
2,210	1,702	1,894
2,220	1,709	1,903
2,230	1,717	1,911
2,240	1,725	1,920
2,250	1,733	1,928
2,260	1,740	1,937
2,270	1,748	1,945
2,280	1,756	1,954
2,290	1,763	1,963
2,300	1,771	1,971
2,310	1,779	1,980
2,320	1,786	1,988
2,330	1,794	1,997
2,340	1,802	2,005
2,350	1,810	2,014
2,360	1,817	2,023
2,370	1,825	2,031
2,380	1,833	2,040
2,390	1,840	2,048

Moment Limits vs Weight

Moment limits are based on the following weight and center of gravity limit data (landing gear down).

Weight Condition	Forward CG Limit	AFT CG Limit
2,950 lb (takeoff or landing)	82.1	84.7
2,525 lb	77.5	85.7
2,475 lb or less	77.0	85.7

Sample Loading Problem

	Weight	Moment
Basic empty weight	2,015	1,554
Fuel main tanks (44 gal)	264	198
*Front seat passengers	300	254
*Rear seat passengers	190	230
Baggage	30	42
Total	2,799	2,278/100

* Interpolate or, as in this case, add appropriate numbers.

Figure 9-9. *Loading schedule placard.*

Computations With a Negative Arm

Figure 9-10 is a sample of weight and balance computation using an airplane with a negative arm. It is important to remember that a positive times a negative equals a negative, and a negative would be subtracted from the total moments.

Item	Weight	Arm	Moment
Licensed Empty Weight	1,011.9	68.6	69,393.0
Oil (6 quarts)	11.0	31.0	341.0
Fuel (18 gallons)	108.0	84.0	9,072.0
Fuel, Auxiliary (18 gallons)	108.0	84.0	9,072.0
Pilot	170.0	81.0	13,770.0
Passenger	170.0	81.0	13,770.0
Baggage	70.0	105.0	7,350.0
Total	1,648.9		122,086.0
CG		74.0	

Figure 9-10. *Sample weight and balance using a negative.*

Computations With Zero Fuel Weight

Figure 9-11 is a sample of weight and balance computation using an aircraft with a zero fuel weight. In this example, the total weight of the aircraft less fuel is 4,240 pounds, which is under the zero fuel weight of 4,400 pounds. If the total weight of the aircraft without fuel had exceeded 4,400 pounds, passengers or cargo would have needed to be reduced to bring the weight at or below the max zero fuel weight.

Item	Weight	Arm	Moment
Basic Empty Weight	3,230	CG 90.5	292,315.0
Front Seat Occupants	335	89.0	29,815.0
3rd & 4th Seat Occupants Forward Facing	350	126.0	44,100.0
5th & 6th Seat Occupants	200	157.0	31,400.0
Nose Baggage	100	10.0	1,000.0
Aft Baggage	25	183.0	4,575.0
Zero Fuel Weight Max 4,400 pounds Subtotal	4,240	CG 95.1	403,205.0
Fuel	822	113.0	92,886.0
Ramp Weight Max 5,224 pounds Subtotal Ramp Weight	5,062	CG 98.0	496,091.0
* Less Fuel for Start, Taxi, and Takeoff	24	113.0	2,712.0
Subtotal Takeoff Weight	5,038	CG 97.9	493,379.0
Less Fuel to Destination	450	113.0	50,850.0
Max Landing Weight 4,940 pounds Actual Landing Weight	4,588	CG 96.5	442,529.0
*Fuel for start, taxi, and takeoff is normally 24 pounds.			

Figure 9-11. *Sample weight and balance using an aircraft with a published zero fuel weight.*

Shifting, Adding, and Removing Weight

A pilot must be able to solve any problems accurately that involve the shift, addition, or removal of weight. For example, the pilot may load the aircraft within the allowable takeoff weight limit, then find a CG limit has been exceeded. The most satisfactory solution to this problem is to shift baggage, passengers, or both. The pilot should be able to determine the minimum load shift needed to make the aircraft safe for flight. Pilots should be able to determine if shifting a load to a new location will correct an out-of-limit condition. There are some standardized calculations that can help make these determinations.

Weight Shifting

When weight is shifted from one location to another, the total weight of the aircraft is unchanged. The total moments, however, do change in relation and proportion to the direction and distance the weight is moved. When weight is moved forward, the total moments decrease; when weight is moved aft, total moments increase. The moment change is proportional to the amount of weight moved. Since many aircraft have forward and aft baggage compartments, weight may be shifted from one to the other to change the CG. If starting with a known aircraft weight, CG, and total moments, calculate the new CG (after the weight shift) by dividing the new total moments by the total aircraft weight.

To determine the new total moments, find out how many moments are gained or lost when the weight is shifted. Assume that 100 pounds has been shifted from station 30 to station 150. This movement increases the total moments of the aircraft by 12,000 in-lb.

Moment when
at station 150 $= 100 \text{ lb} \times 150 \text{ in} = 15,000 \text{ in-lb}$

Moment when
at station 30 $= 100 \text{ lb} \times 30 \text{ in} = 3,000 \text{ in-lb}$

Moment change $= [15,000 - 3,000] = 12,000 \text{ in-lb}$

By adding the moment change to the original moment (or subtracting if the weight has been moved forward instead of aft), the new total moments are obtained. Then determine the new CG by dividing the new moments by the total weight:

$$\text{Total moments} =$$
$$616,000 \text{ in-lb} + 12,000 \text{ in-lb} = 628,000 \text{ in-lb}$$

$$CG = \frac{628,000 \text{ in-lb}}{8,000 \text{ lb}} = 78.5 \text{ in}$$

The shift has caused the CG to shift to station 78.5.

A simpler solution may be obtained by using a computer or calculator and a proportional formula. This can be done because the CG will shift a distance that is proportional to the distance the weight is shifted.

Example

$$\frac{\text{Weight shifted}}{\text{Total weight}} = \frac{\Delta CG \text{ (change of CG)}}{\text{Distance weight is shifted}}$$

$$\frac{100}{8,000} = \frac{\Delta CG}{120}$$

$$\Delta CG = 1.5 \text{ in}$$

The change of CG is added to (or subtracted from when appropriate) the original CG to determine the new CG:
77 + 1.5 = 78.5 inches aft of datum

The shifting weight proportion formula can also be used to determine how much weight must be shifted to achieve a particular shift of the CG. The following problem illustrates a solution of this type.

Example

Given:
Aircraft total weight . . . . 7,800 lb
CG station. . . . . 81.5 in
Aft CG limit . . . . 80.5 in

Determine how much cargo must be shifted from the aft cargo compartment at station 150 to the forward cargo compartment at station 30 to move the CG to exactly the aft limit.

Solution:

$$\frac{\text{Weight to be shifted}}{\text{Total weight}} = \frac{\Delta CG}{\text{Distance weight is shifted}}$$

$$\frac{\text{Weight to be shifted}}{7,800 \text{ lb}} = \frac{1.0 \text{ in}}{120 \text{ in}}$$

$$\text{Weight to be shifted} = 65 \text{ lb}$$

Weight Addition or Removal

In many instances, the weight and balance of the aircraft will be changed by the addition or removal of weight. When this happens, a new CG must be calculated and checked against the limitations to see if the location is acceptable. This type of weight and balance problem is commonly encountered

Example

Given:
Aircraft total weight . . . . 6,860 lb
CG station. . . . . 80.0 in

Determine the location of the CG if 140 pounds of baggage is added to station 150.

Solution:

$$\frac{\text{Added weight}}{\text{New total weight}} = \frac{\Delta CG}{\text{Distance between weight and old CG}}$$

$$\frac{140 \text{ lb}}{6,860 \text{ lb} + 140 \text{ lb}} = \frac{\Delta CG}{150 \text{ in} - 80 \text{ in}}$$

$$\frac{140 \text{ lb}}{7,000 \text{ lb}} = \frac{\Delta CG}{70 \text{ in}}$$

$$CG = 1.4 \text{ in aft}$$

Add ΔCG to old CG
New CG = 80 in + 1.4 in = 81.4 in

Example

Given:
Aircraft total weight . . . . 6,100 lb
CG station. . . . . 80.0 in

Determine the location of the CG if 100 pounds is removed from station 150.

Solution:

$$\frac{\text{Weight removed}}{\text{New total weight}} = \frac{\Delta CG}{\text{Distance between weight and old CG}}$$

$$\frac{100 \text{ lb}}{6,100 \text{ lb} - 100 \text{ lb}} = \frac{\Delta CG}{150 \text{ in} - 80 \text{ in}}$$

$$\frac{100 \text{ lb}}{6,000 \text{ lb}} = \frac{\Delta CG}{70 \text{ in}}$$

$$CG = 1.2 \text{ in forward}$$

Subtract ΔCG from old CG
New CG = 80 in - 1.2 in = 78.8 in

when the aircraft burns fuel in flight, thereby reducing the weight located at the fuel tanks. Most small aircraft are designed with the fuel tanks positioned close to the CG; therefore, the consumption of fuel does not affect the CG to any great extent.

The addition or removal of cargo presents a CG change problem that must be calculated before flight. The problem may always be solved by calculations involving total moments. A typical problem may involve the calculation of a new CG for an aircraft which, when loaded and ready for flight, receives some additional cargo or passengers just before departure time.

In the previous examples, the $\triangle CG$ is either added or subtracted from the old CG. Deciding which to accomplish is best handled by mentally calculating which way the CG will shift for the particular weight change. If the CG is shifting aft, the $\triangle CG$ is added to the old CG; if the CG is shifting forward, the $\triangle CG$ is subtracted from the old CG.

Chapter Summary

Operating an aircraft within the weight and balance limits is critical to flight safety. Pilots must ensure that the CG is and remains within approved limits for all phases of a flight. Additional information on weight, balance, CG, and aircraft stability can be found in FAA-H-8083-1, Aircraft Weight and Balance Handbook. Those pilots flying helicopters or gyroplanes should consult the Rotorcraft Flying Handbook, FAA-H-8083-21, for specific information relating to aircraft type.

Chapter 10
Aircraft Performance

Introduction

This chapter discusses the factors that affect aircraft performance, which include the aircraft weight, atmospheric conditions, runway environment, and the fundamental physical laws governing the forces acting on an aircraft.

Importance of Performance Data

The performance or operational information section of the Aircraft Flight Manual/Pilot's Operating Handbook (AFM/POH) contains the operating data for the aircraft; that is, the data pertaining to takeoff, climb, range, endurance, descent, and landing. The use of this data in flying operations is mandatory for safe and efficient operation. Considerable knowledge and familiarity of the aircraft can be gained through study of this material.

It must be emphasized that the manufacturers' information and data furnished in the AFM/POH is not standardized. Some provide the data in tabular form, while others use graphs. In addition, the performance data may be presented on the basis of standard atmospheric conditions, pressure altitude, or density altitude. The performance information in the AFM/POH has little or no value unless the user recognizes those variations and makes the necessary adjustments.

To be able to make practical use of the aircraft's capabilities and limitations, it is essential to understand the significance of the operational data. The pilot must be cognizant of the basis for the performance data, as well as the meanings of the various terms used in expressing performance capabilities and limitations.

Since the characteristics of the atmosphere have a major effect on performance, it is necessary to review two dominant factors—pressure and temperature.

Structure of the Atmosphere

The atmosphere is an envelope of air that surrounds the Earth and rests upon its surface. It is as much a part of the Earth as its land and water. However, air differs from land and water inasmuch as it is a mixture of gases. It has mass, weight, and indefinite shape.

Air, like any other fluid, is able to flow and change its shape when subjected to even minute pressures because of the lack of strong molecular cohesion. For example, gas will completely fill any container into which it is placed, expanding or contracting to adjust its shape to the limits of the container.

The atmosphere is composed of 78 percent nitrogen, 21 percent oxygen, and 1 percent other gases, such as argon or helium. Most of the oxygen is contained below 35,000 feet altitude.

Atmospheric Pressure

Though there are various kinds of pressure, pilots are mainly concerned with atmospheric pressure. It is one of the basic factors in weather changes, helps to lift the aircraft, and actuates some of the most important flight instruments in the aircraft. These instruments often include the altimeter, the airspeed indicator (ASI), the vertical speed indicator, and the manifold pressure gauge.

Though air is very light, it has mass and is affected by the attraction of gravity. Therefore, like any other substance, it has weight; because it has weight, it has force. Since it is a fluid substance, this force is exerted equally in all directions, and its effect on bodies within the air is called pressure. Under standard conditions at sea level, the average pressure exerted by the weight of the atmosphere is approximately 14.7

pounds per square inch (psi). The density of air has significant effects on the aircraft's performance. As air becomes less dense, it reduces:

- Power, because the engine takes in less air.

- Thrust, because the propeller is less efficient in thin air.

- Lift, because the thin air exerts less force on the airfoils.

The pressure of the atmosphere varies with time and altitude. Due to the changing atmospheric pressure, a standard reference was developed. The standard atmosphere at sea level is a surface temperature of 59 degrees Fahrenheit (°F) or 15 degrees Celsius (°C) and a surface pressure of 29.92 inches of mercury ("Hg) or 1013.2 millibars (mb). [Figure 10-1]

Figure 10-1. *Standard sea level pressure.*

A standard temperature lapse rate is one in which the temperature decreases at the rate of approximately 3.5 °F or 2 °C per thousand feet up to 36,000 feet. Above this point, the temperature is considered constant up to 80,000 feet. A standard pressure lapse rate is one in which pressure decreases at a rate of approximately 1 "Hg per 1,000 feet of altitude gain to 10,000 feet. [Figure 10-2] The International Civil Aviation Organization (ICAO) has established this as a worldwide standard, and it is often referred to as International Standard Atmosphere (ISA) or ICAO Standard Atmosphere. Any temperature or pressure that differs from the standard lapse rates is considered nonstandard temperature and pressure. Adjustments for nonstandard temperatures and pressures are provided on the manufacturer's performance charts.

Altitude (ft)	Pressure ("Hg)	Temperature	
		(°C)	(°F)
0	29.92	15.0	59.0
1,000	28.86	13.0	55.4
2,000	27.82	11.0	51.9
3,000	26.82	9.1	48.3
4,000	25.84	7.1	44.7
5,000	24.89	5.1	41.2
6,000	23.98	3.1	37.6
7,000	23.09	1.1	34.0
8,000	22.22	−0.9	30.5
9,000	21.38	−2.8	26.9
10,000	20.57	−4.8	23.3
11,000	19.79	−6.8	19.8
12,000	19.02	−8.8	16.2
13,000	18.29	−10.8	12.6
14,000	17.57	−12.7	9.1
15,000	16.88	−14.7	5.5
16,000	16.21	−16.7	1.9
17,000	15.56	−18.7	−1.6
18,000	14.94	−20.7	−5.2
19,000	14.33	−22.6	−8.8
20,000	13.74	−24.6	−12.3

Figure 10-2. *Properties of standard atmosphere.*

Since all aircraft performance is compared and evaluated with respect to the standard atmosphere, all aircraft instruments are calibrated for the standard atmosphere. Thus, certain corrections must apply to the instrumentation, as well as the aircraft performance, if the actual operating conditions do not fit the standard atmosphere. In order to account properly for the nonstandard atmosphere, certain related terms must be defined.

Pressure Altitude

Pressure altitude is the height above the standard datum plane (SDP). The aircraft altimeter is essentially a sensitive barometer calibrated to indicate altitude in the standard atmosphere. If the altimeter is set for 29.92 "Hg SDP, the altitude indicated is the pressure altitude—the altitude in the standard atmosphere corresponding to the sensed pressure.

The SDP is a theoretical level where the pressure of the atmosphere is 29.92 "Hg and the weight of air is 14.7 psi. As atmospheric pressure changes, the SDP may be below, at, or above sea level. Pressure altitude is important as a basis for determining aircraft performance, as well as for assigning flight levels to aircraft operating at above 18,000 feet.

The pressure altitude can be determined by either of two methods:

1. By setting the barometric scale of the altimeter to 29.92 "Hg and reading the indicated altitude, or

2. By applying a correction factor to the indicated altitude according to the reported "altimeter setting."

Density Altitude

The more appropriate term for correlating aerodynamic performance in the nonstandard atmosphere is density altitude—the altitude in the standard atmosphere corresponding to a particular value of air density.

Density altitude is pressure altitude corrected for nonstandard temperature. As the density of the air increases (lower density altitude), aircraft performance increases. Conversely, as air density decreases (higher density altitude), aircraft performance decreases. A decrease in air density means a high density altitude; an increase in air density means a lower density altitude. Density altitude is used in calculating aircraft performance. Under standard atmospheric condition, air at each level in the atmosphere has a specific density; under standard conditions, pressure altitude and density altitude identify the same level. Density altitude, then, is the vertical distance above sea level in the standard atmosphere at which a given density is to be found.

The computation of density altitude must involve consideration of pressure (pressure altitude) and temperature. Since aircraft performance data at any level is based upon air density under standard day conditions, such performance data apply to air density levels that may not be identical to altimeter indications. Under conditions higher or lower than standard, these levels cannot be determined directly from the altimeter.

Density altitude is determined by first finding pressure altitude, and then correcting this altitude for nonstandard temperature variations. Since density varies directly with pressure, and inversely with temperature, a given pressure altitude may exist for a wide range of temperature by allowing the density to vary. However, a known density occurs for any one temperature and pressure altitude. The density of the air, of course, has a pronounced effect on aircraft and engine performance. Regardless of the actual altitude at which the aircraft is operating, it will perform as though it were operating at an altitude equal to the existing density altitude.

For example, when set at 29.92 "Hg, the altimeter may indicate a pressure altitude of 5,000 feet. According to the AFM/POH, the ground run on takeoff may require a distance of 790 feet under standard temperature conditions.

However, if the temperature is 20 °C above standard, the expansion of air raises the density level. Using temperature correction data from tables or graphs, or by deriving the density altitude with a computer, it may be found that the density level is above 7,000 feet, and the ground run may be closer to 1,000 feet.

Air density is affected by changes in altitude, temperature, and humidity. High density altitude refers to thin air while low density altitude refers to dense air. The conditions that result in a high density altitude are high elevations, low atmospheric pressures, high temperatures, high humidity, or some combination of these factors. Lower elevations, high atmospheric pressure, low temperatures, and low humidity are more indicative of low density altitude.

Using a flight computer, density altitude can be computed by inputting the pressure altitude and outside air temperature at flight level. Density altitude can also be determined by referring to the table and chart in *Figures 10-3 and 10-4.*

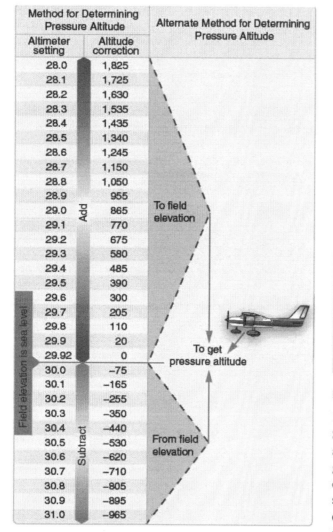

Method for Determining Pressure Altitude		Alternate Method for Determining Pressure Altitude
Altimeter setting	Altitude correction	
28.0	1,825	
28.1	1,725	
28.2	1,630	
28.3	1,535	
28.4	1,435	
28.5	1,340	
28.6	1,245	
28.7	1,150	
28.8	1,050	
28.9	955	
29.0	865	To field elevation
29.1	770	
29.2	675	
29.3	580	
29.4	485	
29.5	390	
29.6	300	
29.7	205	
29.8	110	
29.9	20	
29.92	0	To get pressure altitude
30.0	−75	
30.1	−165	
30.2	−255	
30.3	−350	
30.4	−440	
30.5	−530	From field elevation
30.6	−620	
30.7	−710	
30.8	−805	
30.9	−895	
31.0	−965	

Figure 10-3. *Field elevation versus pressure. The aircraft is located on a field which happens to be at sea level. Set the altimeter to the current altimeter setting (29.7). The difference of 205 feet is added to the elevation or a PA of 205 feet.*

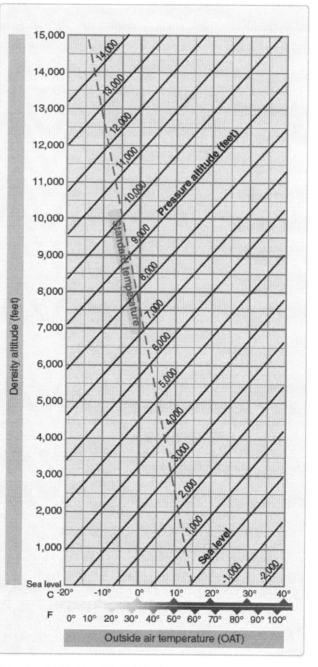

Figure 10-4. *Density altitude chart.*

Effects of Pressure on Density

Since air is a gas, it can be compressed or expanded. When air is compressed, a greater amount of air can occupy a given volume. Conversely, when pressure on a given volume of air is decreased, the air expands and occupies a greater space. That is, the original column of air at a lower pressure contains a smaller mass of air. In other words, the density is decreased. In fact, density is directly proportional to pressure. If the pressure is doubled, the density is doubled, and if the pressure is lowered, so is the density. This statement is true only at a constant temperature.

Effects of Temperature on Density

Increasing the temperature of a substance decreases its density. Conversely, decreasing the temperature increases the density. Thus, the density of air varies inversely with temperature. This statement is true only at a constant pressure.

In the atmosphere, both temperature and pressure decrease with altitude, and have conflicting effects upon density. However, the fairly rapid drop in pressure as altitude is increased usually has the dominant effect. Hence, pilots can expect the density to decrease with altitude.

Effects of Humidity (Moisture) on Density

The preceding paragraphs are based on the presupposition of perfectly dry air. In reality, it is never completely dry. The small amount of water vapor suspended in the atmosphere may be negligible under certain conditions, but in other conditions humidity may become an important factor in the performance of an aircraft. Water vapor is lighter than air; consequently, moist air is lighter than dry air. Therefore, as the water content of the air increases, the air becomes less dense, increasing density altitude and decreasing performance. It is lightest or least dense when, in a given set of conditions, it contains the maximum amount of water vapor.

Humidity, also called relative humidity, refers to the amount of water vapor contained in the atmosphere, and is expressed as a percentage of the maximum amount of water vapor the air can hold. This amount varies with the temperature; warm air can hold more water vapor, while colder air can hold less. Perfectly dry air that contains no water vapor has a relative humidity of zero percent, while saturated air that cannot hold any more water vapor has a relative humidity of 100 percent. Humidity alone is usually not considered an essential factor in calculating density altitude and aircraft performance; however, it does contribute.

The higher the temperature, the greater amount of water vapor that the air can hold. When comparing two separate air masses, the first warm and moist (both qualities making air lighter) and the second cold and dry (both qualities making it heavier), the first must be less dense than the second. Pressure, temperature, and humidity have a great influence on aircraft performance because of their effect upon density. There is no rule-of-thumb or chart used to compute the effects of humidity on density altitude, but it must be taken into consideration. Expect a decrease in overall performance in high humidity conditions.

Performance

Performance is a term used to describe the ability of an aircraft to accomplish certain things that make it useful for certain purposes. For example, the ability of an aircraft to land and take off in a very short distance is an important factor to the pilot who operates in and out of short, unimproved airfields. The ability to carry heavy loads, fly at high altitudes at fast speeds, or travel long distances is essential performance for operators of airline and executive type aircraft.

The primary factors most affected by performance are the takeoff and landing distance, rate of climb, ceiling, payload, range, speed, maneuverability, stability, and fuel economy. Some of these factors are often directly opposed: for example, high speed versus short landing distance, long range versus great payload, and high rate of climb versus fuel economy. It is the preeminence of one or more of these factors that dictates differences between aircraft and explains the high degree of specialization found in modern aircraft.

The various items of aircraft performance result from the combination of aircraft and powerplant characteristics. The aerodynamic characteristics of the aircraft generally define the power and thrust requirements at various conditions of flight, while powerplant characteristics generally define the power and thrust available at various conditions of flight. The matching of the aerodynamic configuration with the powerplant is accomplished by the manufacturer to provide maximum performance at the specific design condition (e.g., range, endurance, and climb).

Straight-and-Level Flight

All of the principal components of flight performance involve steady-state flight conditions and equilibrium of the aircraft. For the aircraft to remain in steady, level flight, equilibrium must be obtained by a lift equal to the aircraft weight and a powerplant thrust equal to the aircraft drag. Thus, the aircraft drag defines the thrust required to maintain steady, level flight. As presented in Chapter 4, Aerodynamics of Flight, all parts of an aircraft contribute to the drag, either induced (from lifting surfaces) or parasite drag.

While the parasite drag predominates at high speed, induced drag predominates at low speed. *[Figure 10-5]* For example,

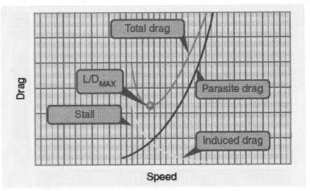

Figure 10-5. *Drag versus speed.*

if an aircraft in a steady flight condition at 100 knots is then accelerated to 200 knots, the parasite drag becomes four times as great, but the power required to overcome that drag is eight times the original value. Conversely, when the aircraft is operated in steady, level flight at twice as great a speed, the induced drag is one-fourth the original value, and the power required to overcome that drag is only one-half the original value.

When an aircraft is in steady, level flight, the condition of equilibrium must prevail. The unaccelerated condition of flight is achieved with the aircraft trimmed for lift equal to weight and the powerplant set for a thrust to equal the aircraft drag.

The maximum level flight speed for the aircraft will be obtained when the power or thrust required equals the maximum power or thrust available from the powerplant. *[Figure 10-6]* The minimum level flight airspeed is not usually defined by thrust or power requirement since conditions of stall or stability and control problems generally predominate.

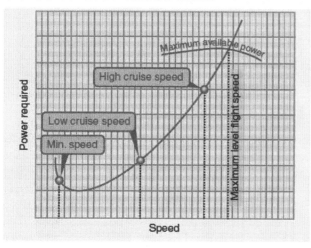

Figure 10-6. *Power versus speed.*

Climb Performance

Climb performance is a result of using the aircrafts potential energy provided by one, or a combination of two factors. The first is the use of excess power above that required for level flight. An aircraft equipped with an engine capable of 200 horsepower (at a given altitude) but using 130 horsepower to sustain level flight (at a given airspeed) has 70 excess horsepower available for climbing. A second factor is that the aircraft can tradeoff its kinetic energy and increase its potential energy by reducing its airspeed. The reduction in airspeed will increase the aircraft's potential energy thereby also making the aircraft climb. Both terms, power and thrust are often used in aircraft performance however, they should not be confused.

Although the terms "power" and "thrust" are sometimes used interchangeably, erroneously implying that they are synonymous, it is important to distinguish between the two when discussing climb performance. Work is the product of a force moving through a distance and is usually independent of time. Work is measured by several standards; the most common unit is called a foot-pound. If a one pound mass is raised one foot, a work unit of one foot-pound has been performed. The common unit of mechanical power is horsepower; one horsepower is work equivalent to lifting 33,000 pounds a vertical distance of one foot in one minute. The term power implies work rate or units of work per unit of time, and as such is a function of the speed at which the force is developed. Thrust, also a function of work, means the force that imparts a change in the velocity of a mass. This force is measured in pounds but has no element of time or rate. It can be said then, that during a steady climb, the rate of climb is a function of excess thrust.

This relationship means that, for a given weight of an aircraft, the angle of climb depends on the difference between thrust and drag, or the excess power. *[Figure 10-7]* Of course, when the excess thrust is zero, the inclination of the flightpath is zero, and the aircraft will be in steady, level flight. When the thrust is greater than the drag, the excess thrust will allow a climb angle depending on the value of excess thrust. On the other hand, when the thrust is less than the drag, the deficiency of thrust will allow an angle of descent.

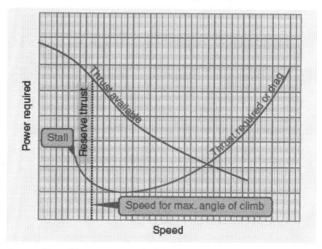

Figure 10-7. *Thrust versus climb angle.*

The most immediate interest in the climb angle performance involves obstacle clearance. The most obvious purpose for which it might be used is to clear obstacles when climbing out of short or confined airports.

The maximum angle of climb would occur where there exists the greatest difference between thrust available and thrust required; i.e., for the propeller-powered airplane, the maximum excess thrust and angle of climb will occur at some speed just above the stall speed. Thus, if it is necessary to clear an obstacle after takeoff, the propeller-powered airplane will attain maximum angle of climb at an airspeed close to—if not at—the takeoff speed.

Of greater interest in climb performance are the factors that affect the rate of climb. The vertical velocity of an aircraft depends on the flight speed and the inclination of the flightpath. In fact, the rate of climb is the vertical component of the flightpath velocity.

For rate of climb, the maximum rate would occur where there exists the greatest difference between power available and power required. *[Figure 10-8]* The above relationship means that, for a given weight of an aircraft, the rate of climb depends on the difference between the power available and the power required, or the excess power. Of course, when the excess power is zero, the rate of climb is zero and the aircraft is in steady, level flight. When power available is greater than the power required, the excess power will allow a rate of climb specific to the magnitude of excess power.

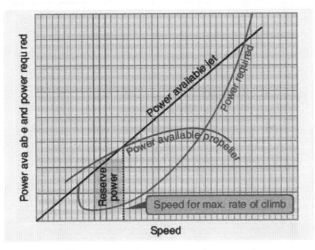

Figure 10-8. *Power versus climb rate.*

During a steady climb, the rate of climb will depend on excess power while the angle of climb is a function of excess thrust.

The climb performance of an aircraft is affected by certain variables. The conditions of the aircraft's maximum climb angle or maximum climb rate occur at specific speeds, and variations in speed will produce variations in climb performance. There is sufficient latitude in most aircraft that small variations in speed from the optimum do not produce large changes in climb performance, and certain operational considerations may require speeds slightly different from

the optimum. Of course, climb performance would be most critical with high gross weight, at high altitude, in obstructed takeoff areas, or during malfunction of a powerplant. Then, optimum climb speeds are necessary.

Weight has a very pronounced effect on aircraft performance. If weight is added to an aircraft, it must fly at a higher angle of attack (AOA) to maintain a given altitude and speed. This increases the induced drag of the wings, as well as the parasite drag of the aircraft. Increased drag means that additional thrust is needed to overcome it, which in turn means that less reserve thrust is available for climbing. Aircraft designers go to great effort to minimize the weight since it has such a marked effect on the factors pertaining to performance.

A change in an aircraft's weight produces a twofold effect on climb performance. First, a change in weight will change the drag and the power required. This alters the reserve power available, which in turn, affects both the climb angle and the climb rate. Secondly, an increase in weight will reduce the maximum rate of climb, but the aircraft must be operated at a higher climb speed to achieve the smaller peak climb rate.

An increase in altitude also will increase the power required and decrease the power available. Therefore, the climb performance of an aircraft diminishes with altitude. The speeds for maximum rate of climb, maximum angle of climb, and maximum and minimum level flight airspeeds vary with altitude. As altitude is increased, these various speeds finally converge at the absolute ceiling of the aircraft. At the absolute ceiling, there is no excess of power and only one speed will allow steady, level flight. Consequently, the absolute ceiling of an aircraft produces zero rate of climb. The service ceiling is the altitude at which the aircraft is unable to climb at a rate greater than 100 feet per minute (fpm). Usually, these specific performance reference points are provided for the aircraft at a specific design configuration. *[Figure 10-9]*

In discussing performance, it frequently is convenient to use the terms power loading, wing loading, blade loading, and disk loading. Power loading is expressed in pounds per horsepower and is obtained by dividing the total weight of the aircraft by the rated horsepower of the engine. It is a significant factor in an aircraft's takeoff and climb capabilities. Wing loading is expressed in pounds per square foot and is obtained by dividing the total weight of an airplane in pounds by the wing area (including ailerons) in square feet. It is the airplane's wing loading that determines the landing speed. Blade loading is expressed in pounds per square foot and is obtained by dividing the total weight of a helicopter by the area of the rotor blades. Blade loading is not to be confused with disk loading, which is the total weight of a helicopter divided by the area of the disk swept by the rotor blades.

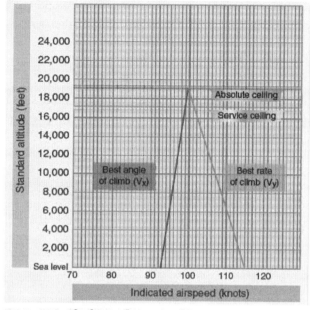

Figure 10-9. *Absolute and service ceiling.*

Range Performance

The ability of an aircraft to convert fuel energy into flying distance is one of the most important items of aircraft performance. In flying operations, the problem of efficient range operation of an aircraft appears in two general forms:

1. To extract the maximum flying distance from a given fuel load

2. To fly a specified distance with a minimum expenditure of fuel

A common element for each of these operating problems is the specific range; that is, nautical miles (NM) of flying distance versus the amount of fuel consumed. Range must be clearly distinguished from the item of endurance. Range involves consideration of flying distance, while endurance involves consideration of flying time. Thus, it is appropriate to define a separate term, specific endurance.

$$\text{specific endurance} = \frac{\text{flight hours}}{\text{pounds of fuel}}$$

or

$$\text{specific endurance} = \frac{\text{flight hours/hour}}{\text{pounds of fuel/hour}}$$

or

$$\text{specific endurance} = \frac{1}{\text{fuel flow}}$$

Fuel flow can be defined in either pounds or gallons. If maximum endurance is desired, the flight condition must provide a minimum fuel flow. In *Figure 10-10* at point A the airspeed is low and fuel flow is high. This would occur during ground operations or when taking off and climbing. As airspeed is increased, power requirements decrease due to aerodynamic factors and fuel flow decreases to point B. This is the point of maximum endurance. Beyond this point increases in airspeed come at a cost. Airspeed increases require additional power and fuel flow increases with additional power.

Cruise flight operations for maximum range should be conducted so that the aircraft obtains maximum specific range throughout the flight. The specific range can be defined by the following relationship.

$$\text{specific range} = \frac{\text{NM}}{\text{pounds of fuel}}$$

or

$$\text{specific range} = \frac{\text{NM/hour}}{\text{pounds of fuel/hour}}$$

or

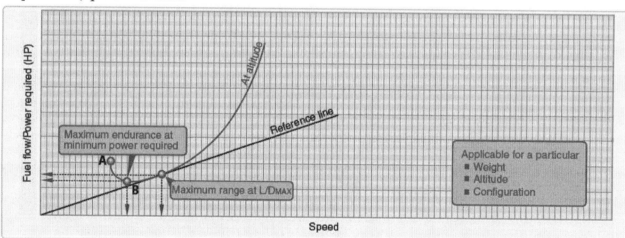

Figure 10-10. *Airspeed for maximum endurance.*

$$\text{specific range} = \frac{\text{knots}}{\text{fuel flow}}$$

If maximum specific range is desired, the flight condition must provide a maximum of speed per fuel flow. While the peak value of specific range would provide maximum range operation, long-range cruise operation is generally recommended at some slightly higher airspeed. Most long-range cruise operations are conducted at the flight condition that provides 99 percent of the absolute maximum specific range. The advantage of such operation is that one percent of range is traded for three to five percent higher cruise speed. Since the higher cruise speed has a great number of advantages, the small sacrifice of range is a fair bargain. The values of specific range versus speed are affected by three principal variables:

1. Aircraft gross weight

2. Altitude

3. The external aerodynamic configuration of the aircraft.

These are the source of range and endurance operating data included in the performance section of the AFM/POH.

Cruise control of an aircraft implies that the aircraft is operated to maintain the recommended long-range cruise condition throughout the flight. Since fuel is consumed during cruise, the gross weight of the aircraft will vary and optimum airspeed, altitude, and power setting can also vary. Cruise control means the control of the optimum airspeed, altitude, and power setting to maintain the 99 percent maximum specific range condition. At the beginning of cruise flight, the relatively high initial weight of the aircraft will require specific values of airspeed, altitude, and power setting to produce the recommended cruise condition. As fuel is consumed and the aircraft's gross weight decreases, the optimum airspeed and power setting may decrease, or, the optimum altitude may increase. In addition, the optimum specific range will increase. Therefore, the pilot must provide the proper cruise control procedure to ensure that optimum conditions are maintained.

Total range is dependent on both fuel available and specific range. When range and economy of operation are the principal goals, the pilot must ensure that the aircraft is operated at the recommended long-range cruise condition. By this procedure, the aircraft will be capable of its maximum design-operating radius, or can achieve flight distances less than the maximum with a maximum of fuel reserve at the destination.

A propeller-driven aircraft combines the propeller with the reciprocating engine for propulsive power. Fuel flow is determined mainly by the shaft power put into the propeller rather than thrust. Thus, the fuel flow can be related directly to the power required to maintain the aircraft in steady, level

flight and on performance charts power can be substituted for fuel flow. This fact allows for the determination of range through analysis of power required versus speed.

The maximum endurance condition would be obtained at the point of minimum power required since this would require the lowest fuel flow to keep the airplane in steady, level flight. Maximum range condition would occur where the ratio of speed to power required is greatest. *[Figure 10-10]*

The maximum range condition is obtained at maximum lift/drag ratio (L/D_{MAX}), and it is important to note that for a given aircraft configuration, the L/D_{MAX} occurs at a particular AOA and lift coefficient, and is unaffected by weight or altitude. A variation in weight will alter the values of airspeed and power required to obtain the L/D_{MAX}. *[Figure 10-11]*

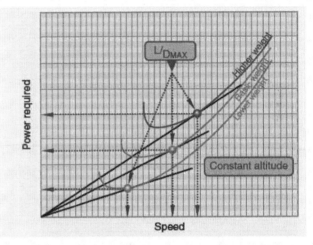

Figure 10-11. *Effect of weight.*

The variations of speed and power required must be monitored by the pilot as part of the cruise control procedure to maintain the L/D_{MAX}. When the aircraft's fuel weight is a small part of the gross weight and the aircraft's range is small, the cruise control procedure can be simplified to essentially maintaining a constant speed and power setting throughout the time of cruise flight. However, a long-range aircraft has a fuel weight that is a considerable part of the gross weight, and cruise control procedures must employ scheduled airspeed and power changes to maintain optimum range conditions.

The variations of speed and power required must be monitored by the pilot as part of the cruise control procedure to maintain the L/D_{MAX}. When the aircraft's fuel weight is a small part of the gross weight and the aircraft's range is small, the cruise control procedure can be simplified to essentially maintaining a constant speed and power setting throughout the time of cruise flight. However, a long-range aircraft has a fuel weight that is a considerable part of the gross weight, and cruise control procedures must employ scheduled airspeed and power changes to maintain optimum range conditions.

The effect of altitude on the range of a propeller-driven aircraft is illustrated in *Figure 10-12*. A flight conducted at high altitude has a greater true airspeed (TAS), and the power required is proportionately greater than when conducted at sea level. The drag of the aircraft at altitude is the same as the drag at sea level, but the higher TAS causes a proportionately greater power required. NOTE: The straight line that is tangent to the sea level power curve is also tangent to the altitude power curve.

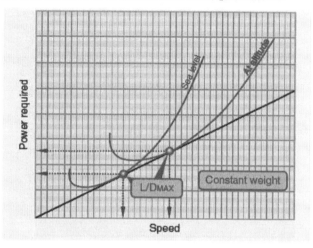

Figure 10-12. *Effect of altitude on range.*

The effect of altitude on specific range also can be appreciated from the previous relationships. If a change in altitude causes identical changes in speed and power required, the proportion of speed to power required would be unchanged. The fact implies that the specific range of a propeller-driven aircraft would be unaffected by altitude. Actually, this is true to the extent that specific fuel consumption and propeller efficiency are the principal factors that could cause a variation of specific range with altitude. If compressibility effects are negligible, any variation of specific range with altitude is strictly a function of engine/propeller performance.

An aircraft equipped with a reciprocating engine will experience very little, if any, variation of specific range up to its absolute altitude. There is negligible variation of brake specific fuel consumption for values of brake horsepower below the maximum cruise power rating of the engine that is the lean range of engine operation. Thus, an increase in altitude will produce a decrease in specific range only when the increased power requirement exceeds the maximum cruise power rating of the engine. One advantage of supercharging is that the cruise power may be maintained at high altitude, and the aircraft may achieve the range at high altitude with the corresponding increase in TAS. The principal differences in the high altitude cruise and low altitude cruise are the TAS and climb fuel requirements.

Region of Reversed Command

The aerodynamic properties of an aircraft generally determine the power requirements at various conditions of flight, while the powerplant capabilities generally determine the power available at various conditions of flight. When an aircraft is in steady, level flight, a condition of equilibrium must prevail. An unaccelerated condition of flight is achieved when lift equals weight, and the powerplant is set for thrust equal to drag. The power required to achieve equilibrium in constant-altitude flight at various airspeeds is depicted on a power required curve. The power required curve illustrates the fact that at low airspeeds near the stall or minimum controllable airspeed, the power setting required for steady, level flight is quite high.

Flight in the region of normal command means that while holding a constant altitude, a higher airspeed requires a higher power setting and a lower airspeed requires a lower power setting. The majority of aircraft flying (climb, cruise, and maneuvers) is conducted in the region of normal command.

Flight in the region of reversed command means flight in which a higher airspeed requires a lower power setting and a lower airspeed requires a higher power setting to hold altitude. It does not imply that a decrease in power will produce lower airspeed. The region of reversed command is encountered in the low speed phases of flight. Flight speeds below the speed for maximum endurance (lowest point on the power curve) require higher power settings with a decrease in airspeed. Since the need to increase the required power setting with decreased speed is contrary to the normal command of flight, the regime of flight speeds between the speed for minimum required power setting and the stall speed (or minimum control speed) is termed the region of reversed command. In the region of reversed command, a decrease in airspeed must be accompanied by an increased power setting in order to maintain steady flight.

Figure 10-13 shows the maximum power available as a curved line. Lower power settings, such as cruise power, would also appear in a similar curve. The lowest point on the power required curve represents the speed at which the lowest brake horsepower will sustain level flight. This is termed the best endurance airspeed.

An airplane performing a low airspeed, high pitch attitude power approach for a short-field landing is an example of operating in the region of reversed command. If an unacceptably high sink rate should develop, it may be possible for the pilot to reduce or stop the descent by applying power. But without further use of power, the airplane would probably stall or be incapable of flaring for the landing.

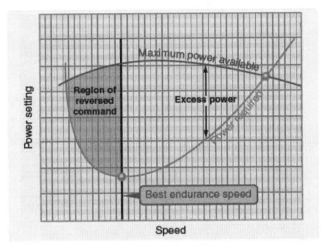

Figure 10-13. *Power required curve.*

Merely lowering the nose of the airplane to regain flying speed in this situation, without the use of power, would result in a rapid sink rate and corresponding loss of altitude.

If during a soft-field takeoff and climb, for example, the pilot attempts to climb out of ground effect without first attaining normal climb pitch attitude and airspeed, the airplane may inadvertently enter the region of reversed command at a dangerously low altitude. Even with full power, the airplane may be incapable of climbing or even maintaining altitude. The pilot's only recourse in this situation is to lower the pitch attitude in order to increase airspeed, which will inevitably result in a loss of altitude.

Airplane pilots must give particular attention to precise control of airspeed when operating in the low flight speeds of the region of reversed command.

Takeoff and Landing Performance

The majority of pilot-caused aircraft accidents occur during the takeoff and landing phase of flight. Because of this fact, the pilot must be familiar with all the variables that influence the takeoff and landing performance of an aircraft and must strive for exacting, professional procedures of operation during these phases of flight.

Takeoff and landing performance is a condition of accelerated and decelerated motion. For instance, during takeoff, an aircraft starts at zero speed and accelerates to the takeoff speed to become airborne. During landing, the aircraft touches down at the landing speed and decelerates to zero speed. The important factors of takeoff or landing performance are:

- The takeoff or landing speed is generally a function of the stall speed or minimum flying speed.

- The rate of acceleration/deceleration during the takeoff or landing roll. The speed (acceleration and deceleration) experienced by any object varies directly with the imbalance of force and inversely with the mass of the object. An airplane on the runway moving at 75 knots has four times the energy it has traveling at 37 knots. Thus, an airplane requires four times as much distance to stop as required at half the speed.

- The takeoff or landing roll distance is a function of both acceleration/deceleration and speed.

Runway Surface and Gradient

Runway conditions affect takeoff and landing performance. Typically, performance chart information assumes paved, level, smooth, and dry runway surfaces. Since no two runways are alike, the runway surface differs from one runway to another, as does the runway gradient or slope. *[Figure 10-14]*

TAKEOFF DISTANCE
MAXIMUM WEIGHT 3800 LBS

SHORT FIELD

CONDITIONS:
Flaps 10°
2850 RPM, Full Throttle and Mixture Set at Placard Fuel Flow Prior to Brake Release
Cowl Flaps Open
Paved, Level, Dry Runway
Zero Wind

MIXTURE SETTING	
PRESS ALT	PPH
S.L.	144
2000	138
4000	132
6000	126
8000	120

NOTES:
1. Short field technique as specified in Section 4.
2. Landing gear extended until takeoff obstacle is cleared.
3. Where distance value has been deleted, climb performance after lift-off is less than 150 fpm. Rate of climb is based on landing gear extended and flaps 10° at takeoff speed.
4. Decrease distances 10% for each 10 knots headwind. For operation with tailwinds up to 10 knots, increase distances by 10% for each 2.5 knots.
5. For operation on a dry, grass runway, increase distances by 15% of the "ground roll" figure.

WEIGHT LBS	TAKEOFF SPEED KIAS		PRESS ALT FT	0°C		10°C		20°C		30°C		40°C	
	LIFT	AT		GRND	TOTAL TO CLEAR	GRND	TOTAL TO CLEAR	GRND	TOTAL TO CLEAR	GRND	TOTAL TO CLEAR	GRND	TOTAL TO CLEAR

Figure 10-14. *Takeoff distance chart.*

Figure 10-15. *An aircraft's performance depends greatly on the runway surface.*

Runway surfaces vary widely from one airport to another. The runway surface encountered may be concrete, asphalt, gravel, dirt, or grass. The runway surface for a specific airport is noted in the Airport/Facility Directory (A/FD). Any surface that is not hard and smooth will increase the ground roll during takeoff. This is due to the inability of the tires to roll smoothly along the runway. Tires can sink into soft, grassy, or muddy runways. Potholes or other ruts in the pavement can be the cause of poor tire movement along the runway. Obstructions such as mud, snow, or standing water reduce the airplane's acceleration down the runway. Although muddy and wet surface conditions can reduce friction between the runway and the tires, they can also act as obstructions and reduce the landing distance. *[Figure 10-15]* Braking effectiveness is another consideration when dealing with various runway types. The condition of the surface affects the braking ability of the airplane.

The amount of power that is applied to the brakes without skidding the tires is referred to as braking effectiveness.

Ensure that runways are adequate in length for takeoff acceleration and landing deceleration when less than ideal surface conditions are being reported.

The gradient or slope of the runway is the amount of change in runway height over the length of the runway. The gradient is expressed as a percentage such as a 3 percent gradient. This means that for every 100 feet of runway length, the runway height changes by 3 feet. A positive gradient indicates the runway height increases, and a negative gradient indicates the runway decreases in height. An upsloping runway impedes acceleration and results in a longer ground run during takeoff. However, landing on an upsloping runway typically reduces the landing roll. A downsloping runway aids in acceleration on takeoff resulting in shorter takeoff distances. The opposite is true when landing, as landing on a downsloping runway increases landing distances. Runway slope information is contained in the A/FD. *[Figure 10-16]*

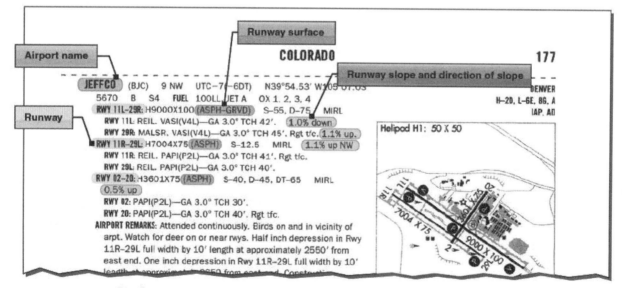

Figure 10-16. *Airport/facility directory (A/FD) information.*

Water on the Runway and Dynamic Hydroplaning

Water on the runways reduces the friction between the tires and the ground, and can reduce braking effectiveness. The ability to brake can be completely lost when the tires are hydroplaning because a layer of water separates the tires from the runway surface. This is also true of braking effectiveness when runways are covered in ice.

When the runway is wet, the pilot may be confronted with dynamic hydroplaning. Dynamic hydroplaning is a condition in which the aircraft tires ride on a thin sheet of water rather than on the runway's surface. Because hydroplaning wheels are not touching the runway, braking and directional control are almost nil. To help minimize dynamic hydroplaning, some runways are grooved to help drain off water; most runways are not.

Tire pressure is a factor in dynamic hydroplaning. Using the simple formula in *Figure 10-17*, a pilot can calculate the minimum speed, in knots, at which hydroplaning will begin. In plain language, the minimum hydroplaning speed is determined by multiplying the square root of the main gear tire pressure in psi by nine. For example, if the main gear tire pressure is at 36 psi, the aircraft would begin hydroplaning at 54 knots.

Minimum dynamic hydroplaning speed (rounded off) =

$$9 \times \sqrt{\text{Tire pressure (in psi)}}$$

$$\sqrt{36} \quad 6$$
$$9 \times 6 \quad 54 \text{ knots}$$

Figure 10-17. *Tire pressure.*

Landing at higher than recommended touchdown speeds will expose the aircraft to a greater potential for hydroplaning. And once hydroplaning starts, it can continue well below the minimum initial hydroplaning speed.

On wet runways, directional control can be maximized by landing into the wind. Abrupt control inputs should be avoided. When the runway is wet, anticipate braking problems well before landing and be prepared for hydroplaning. Opt for a suitable runway most aligned with the wind. Mechanical braking may be ineffective, so aerodynamic braking should be used to its fullest advantage.

Takeoff Performance

The minimum takeoff distance is of primary interest in the operation of any aircraft because it defines the runway requirements. The minimum takeoff distance is obtained by taking off at some minimum safe speed that allows sufficient margin above stall and provides satisfactory control and initial rate of climb. Generally, the lift-off speed is some fixed percentage of the stall speed or minimum control speed for the aircraft in the takeoff configuration. As such, the lift-off will be accomplished at some particular value of lift coefficient and AOA. Depending on the aircraft characteristics, the lift-off speed will be anywhere from 1.05 to 1.25 times the stall speed or minimum control speed.

To obtain minimum takeoff distance at the specific lift-off speed, the forces that act on the aircraft must provide the maximum acceleration during the takeoff roll. The various forces acting on the aircraft may or may not be under the control of the pilot, and various procedures may be necessary in certain aircraft to maintain takeoff acceleration at the highest value.

The powerplant thrust is the principal force to provide the acceleration and, for minimum takeoff distance, the output thrust should be at a maximum. Lift and drag are produced as soon as the aircraft has speed, and the values of lift and drag depend on the AOA and dynamic pressure.

In addition to the important factors of proper procedures, many other variables affect the takeoff performance of an aircraft. Any item that alters the takeoff speed or acceleration rate during the takeoff roll will affect the takeoff distance.

For example, the effect of gross weight on takeoff distance is significant and proper consideration of this item must be made in predicting the aircraft's takeoff distance. Increased gross weight can be considered to produce a threefold effect on takeoff performance:

1. Higher lift-off speed

2. Greater mass to accelerate

3. Increased retarding force (drag and ground friction)

If the gross weight increases, a greater speed is necessary to produce the greater lift necessary to get the aircraft airborne at the takeoff lift coefficient. As an example of the effect of a change in gross weight, a 21 percent increase in takeoff weight will require a 10 percent increase in lift-off speed to support the greater weight.

A change in gross weight will change the net accelerating force and change the mass that is being accelerated. If the aircraft has a relatively high thrust-to-weight ratio, the change in the net accelerating force is slight and the principal effect on acceleration is due to the change in mass.

For example, a 10 percent increase in takeoff gross weight would cause:

- A 5 percent increase in takeoff velocity.
- At least a 9 percent decrease in rate of acceleration.
- At least a 21 percent increase in takeoff distance.

With ISA conditions, increasing the takeoff weight of the average Cessna 182 from 2,400 pounds to 2,700 pounds (11 percent increase) results in an increased takeoff distance from 440 feet to 575 feet (23 percent increase).

For the aircraft with a high thrust-to-weight ratio, the increase in takeoff distance might be approximately 21 to 22 percent, but for the aircraft with a relatively low thrust-to-weight ratio, the increase in takeoff distance would be approximately 25 to 30 percent. Such a powerful effect requires proper consideration of gross weight in predicting takeoff distance.

The effect of wind on takeoff distance is large, and proper consideration also must be provided when predicting takeoff distance. The effect of a headwind is to allow the aircraft to reach the lift-off speed at a lower groundspeed while the effect of a tailwind is to require the aircraft to achieve a greater groundspeed to attain the lift-off speed.

A headwind that is 10 percent of the takeoff airspeed will reduce the takeoff distance approximately 19 percent. However, a tailwind that is 10 percent of the takeoff airspeed will increase the takeoff distance approximately 21 percent. In the case where the headwind speed is 50 percent of the takeoff speed, the takeoff distance would be approximately 25 percent of the zero wind takeoff distance (75 percent reduction).

The effect of wind on landing distance is identical to its effect on takeoff distance. *Figure 10-18* illustrates the general effect of wind by the percent change in takeoff or landing distance as a function of the ratio of wind velocity to takeoff or landing speed.

The effect of proper takeoff speed is especially important when runway lengths and takeoff distances are critical. The takeoff speeds specified in the AFM/POH are generally the minimum safe speeds at which the aircraft can become airborne. Any attempt to take off below the recommended speed means that the aircraft could stall, be difficult to

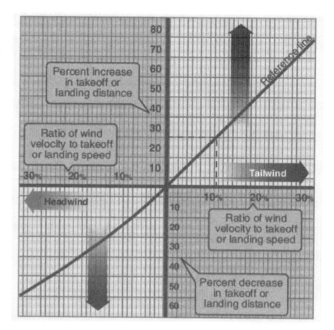

Figure 10-18. *Effect of wind on takeoff and landing.*

control, or have a very low initial rate of climb. In some cases, an excessive AOA may not allow the aircraft to climb out of ground effect. On the other hand, an excessive airspeed at takeoff may improve the initial rate of climb and "feel" of the aircraft, but will produce an undesirable increase in takeoff distance. Assuming that the acceleration is essentially unaffected, the takeoff distance varies with the square of the takeoff velocity.

Thus, ten percent excess airspeed would increase the takeoff distance 21 percent. In most critical takeoff conditions, such an increase in takeoff distance would be prohibitive, and the pilot must adhere to the recommended takeoff speeds.

The effect of pressure altitude and ambient temperature is to define the density altitude and its effect on takeoff performance. While subsequent corrections are appropriate for the effect of temperature on certain items of powerplant performance, density altitude defines specific effects on takeoff performance. An increase in density altitude can produce a twofold effect on takeoff performance:

1. Greater takeoff speed

2. Decreased thrust and reduced net accelerating force

If an aircraft of given weight and configuration is operated at greater heights above standard sea level, the aircraft requires the same dynamic pressure to become airborne at the takeoff lift coefficient. Thus, the aircraft at altitude will take off at the same indicated airspeed (IAS) as at sea level, but because of the reduced air density, the TAS will be greater.

The effect of density altitude on powerplant thrust depends much on the type of powerplant. An increase in altitude above standard sea level will bring an immediate decrease in power output for the unsupercharged reciprocating engine. However, an increase in altitude above standard sea level will not cause a decrease in power output for the supercharged reciprocating engine until the altitude exceeds the critical operating altitude. For those powerplants that experience a decay in thrust with an increase in altitude, the effect on the net accelerating force and acceleration rate can be approximated by assuming a direct variation with density. Actually, this assumed variation would closely approximate the effect on aircraft with high thrust-to-weight ratios.

Proper accounting of pressure altitude and temperature is mandatory for accurate prediction of takeoff roll distance. The most critical conditions of takeoff performance are the result of some combination of high gross weight, altitude, temperature, and unfavorable wind. In all cases, the pilot must make an accurate prediction of takeoff distance from the performance data of the AFM/POH, regardless of the runway available, and strive for a polished, professional takeoff procedure.

In the prediction of takeoff distance from the AFM/POH data, the following primary considerations must be given:

- Pressure altitude and temperature—to define the effect of density altitude on distance

- Gross weight—a large effect on distance

- Wind—a large effect due to the wind or wind component along the runway

- Runway slope and condition—the effect of an incline and retarding effect of factors such as snow or ice

Landing Performance

In many cases, the landing distance of an aircraft will define the runway requirements for flight operations. The minimum landing distance is obtained by landing at some minimum safe speed, which allows sufficient margin above stall and provides satisfactory control and capability for a go-around. Generally, the landing speed is some fixed percentage of the stall speed or minimum control speed for the aircraft in the landing configuration. As such, the landing will be accomplished at some particular value of lift coefficient and AOA. The exact values will depend on the aircraft characteristics but, once defined, the values are independent of weight, altitude, and wind.

To obtain minimum landing distance at the specified landing speed, the forces that act on the aircraft must provide maximum deceleration during the landing roll. The forces acting on the aircraft during the landing roll may require various procedures to maintain landing deceleration at the peak value.

A distinction should be made between the procedures for minimum landing distance and an ordinary landing roll with considerable excess runway available. Minimum landing distance will be obtained by creating a continuous peak deceleration of the aircraft; that is, extensive use of the brakes for maximum deceleration. On the other hand, an ordinary landing roll with considerable excess runway may allow extensive use of aerodynamic drag to minimize wear and tear on the tires and brakes. If aerodynamic drag is sufficient to cause deceleration, it can be used in deference to the brakes in the early stages of the landing roll; i.e., brakes and tires suffer from continuous hard use, but aircraft aerodynamic drag is free and does not wear out with use. The use of aerodynamic drag is applicable only for deceleration to 60 or 70 percent of the touchdown speed. At speeds less than 60 to 70 percent of the touchdown speed, aerodynamic drag is so slight as to be of little use, and braking must be utilized to produce continued deceleration. Since the objective during the landing roll is to decelerate, the powerplant thrust should be the smallest possible positive value (or largest possible negative value in the case of thrust reversers).

In addition to the important factors of proper procedures, many other variables affect the landing performance. Any item that alters the landing speed or deceleration rate during the landing roll will affect the landing distance.

The effect of gross weight on landing distance is one of the principal items determining the landing distance. One effect of an increased gross weight is that a greater speed will be required to support the aircraft at the landing AOA and lift coefficient. For an example of the effect of a change in gross weight, a 21 percent increase in landing weight will require a ten percent increase in landing speed to support the greater weight.

When minimum landing distances are considered, braking friction forces predominate during the landing roll and, for the majority of aircraft configurations, braking friction is the main source of deceleration.

The minimum landing distance will vary in direct proportion to the gross weight. For example, a ten percent increase in gross weight at landing would cause a:

- Five percent increase in landing velocity

- Ten percent increase in landing distance

A contingency of this is the relationship between weight and braking friction force.

The effect of wind on landing distance is large and deserves proper consideration when predicting landing distance. Since the aircraft will land at a particular airspeed independent of the wind, the principal effect of wind on landing distance is the change in the groundspeed at which the aircraft touches down. The effect of wind on deceleration during the landing is identical to the effect on acceleration during the takeoff.

The effect of pressure altitude and ambient temperature is to define density altitude and its effect on landing performance. An increase in density altitude increases the landing speed but does not alter the net retarding force. Thus, the aircraft at altitude lands at the same IAS as at sea level but, because of the reduced density, the TAS is greater. Since the aircraft lands at altitude with the same weight and dynamic pressure, the drag and braking friction throughout the landing roll have the same values as at sea level. As long as the condition is within the capability of the brakes, the net retarding force is unchanged, and the deceleration is the same as with the landing at sea level. Since an increase in altitude does not alter deceleration, the effect of density altitude on landing distance is due to the greater TAS.

The minimum landing distance at 5,000 feet is 16 percent greater than the minimum landing distance at sea level. The approximate increase in landing distance with altitude is approximately three and one-half percent for each 1,000 feet of altitude. Proper accounting of density altitude is necessary to accurately predict landing distance.

The effect of proper landing speed is important when runway lengths and landing distances are critical. The landing speeds specified in the AFM/POH are generally the minimum safe speeds at which the aircraft can be landed. Any attempt to land at below the specified speed may mean that the aircraft may stall, be difficult to control, or develop high rates of descent. On the other hand, an excessive speed at landing may improve the controllability slightly (especially in crosswinds), but causes an undesirable increase in landing distance.

A ten percent excess landing speed causes at least a 21 percent increase in landing distance. The excess speed places a greater working load on the brakes because of the additional kinetic energy to be dissipated. Also, the additional speed causes increased drag and lift in the normal ground attitude, and the increased lift reduces the normal force on the braking surfaces. The deceleration during this range of speed immediately after touchdown may suffer, and it is more probable for a tire to be blown out from braking at this point.

The most critical conditions of landing performance are combinations of high gross weight, high density altitude, and unfavorable wind. These conditions produce the greatest required landing distances and critical levels of energy dissipation required of the brakes. In all cases, it is necessary to make an accurate prediction of minimum landing distance to compare with the available runway. A polished, professional landing procedure is necessary because the landing phase of flight accounts for more pilot-caused aircraft accidents than any other single phase of flight.

In the prediction of minimum landing distance from the AFM/POH data, the following considerations must be given:

- Pressure altitude and temperature—to define the effect of density altitude

- Gross weight—which defines the CAS for landing.

- Wind—a large effect due to wind or wind component along the runway

- Runway slope and condition—relatively small correction for ordinary values of runway slope, but a significant effect of snow, ice, or soft ground

A tail wind of ten knots increases the landing distance by about 21 percent. An increase of landing speed by ten percent increases the landing distance by 20 percent. Hydroplaning makes braking ineffective until a decrease of speed to that determined using *Figure 10-17*.

For instance, a pilot is downwind for runway 18, and the tower asks if runway 27 could be accepted. There is a light rain and the winds are out of the east at ten knots. The pilot accepts because he or she is approaching the extended centerline of runway 27. The turn is tight and the pilot must descend (dive) to get to runway 27. After becoming aligned with the runway and at 50 feet AGL, the pilot is already 1,000 feet down the 3,500 feet runway. The airspeed is still high by about ten percent (should be at 70 knots and is at about 80 knots). The wind of ten knots is blowing from behind.

First, the airspeed being high by about ten percent (80 knots versus 70 knots), as presented in the performance chapter, results in a 20 percent increase in the landing distance. In performance planning, the pilot determined that at 70 knots the distance would be 1,600 feet. However, now it is increased by 20 percent and the required distance is now 1,920 feet.

The newly revised landing distance of 1,920 feet is also affected by the wind. In looking at *Figure 10-18*, the affect of the wind is an additional 20 percent for every ten miles per hour (mph) in wind. This is computed not on the original estimate but on the estimate based upon the increased airspeed. Now the landing distance is increased by another

320 feet for a total requirement of 2,240 feet to land the airplane after reaching 50 feet AGL.

That is the original estimate of 1,600 under planned conditions plus the additional 640 feet for excess speed and the tailwind. Given the pilot overshot the threshhold by 1,000 feet, the total length required is 3, 240 on a 3,500 foot runway; 260 feet to spare. But this is in a perfect environment. Most pilots become fearful as the end of the runway is facing them just ahead. A typical pilot reaction is to brake—and brake hard. Because the aircraft does not have antilock braking features like a car, the brakes lock, and the aircraft hydroplanes on the wet surface of the runway until decreasing to a speed of about 54 knots (the square root of the tire pressure ($\sqrt{36}$) x 9). Braking is ineffective when hydroplaning.

The 260 feet that a pilot might feel is left over has long since evaporated as the aircraft hydroplaned the first 300–500 feet when the brakes locked. This is an example of a true story, but one which only changes from year to year because of new participants and aircraft with different N-numbers.

In this example, the pilot actually made many bad decisions. Bad decisions, when combined, have a synergy greater than the individual errors. Therefore, the corrective actions become larger and larger until correction is almost impossible. Aeronautical decision-making will be discussed more fully in Chapter 17, Aeronautical Decision-Making (ADM).

Performance Speeds

True Airspeed (TAS)—the speed of the aircraft in relation to the air mass in which it is flying.

Indicated Airspeed (IAS)—the speed of the aircraft as observed on the ASI. It is the airspeed without correction for indicator, position (or installation), or compressibility errors.

Calibrated Airspeed (CAS)—the ASI reading corrected for position (or installation), and instrument errors. (CAS is equal to TAS at sea level in standard atmosphere.) The color coding for various design speeds marked on ASIs may be IAS or CAS.

Equivalent Airspeed (EAS)—the ASI reading corrected for position (or installation), or instrument error, and for adiabatic compressible flow for the particular altitude. (EAS is equal to CAS at sea level in standard atmosphere.)

V_{S0}—the calibrated power-off stalling speed or the minimum steady flight speed at which the aircraft is controllable in the landing configuration.

V_{S1}—the calibrated power-off stalling speed or the minimum steady flight speed at which the aircraft is controllable in a specified configuration.

V_Y—the speed at which the aircraft will obtain the maximum increase in altitude per unit of time. This best rate-of-climb speed normally decreases slightly with altitude.

V_X—the speed at which the aircraft will obtain the highest altitude in a given horizontal distance. This best angle-of-climb speed normally increases slightly with altitude.

V_{LE}—the maximum speed at which the aircraft can be safely flown with the landing gear extended. This is a problem involving stability and controllability.

V_{LO}—the maximum speed at which the landing gear can be safely extended or retracted. This is a problem involving the air loads imposed on the operating mechanism during extension or retraction of the gear.

V_{FE}—the highest speed permissible with the wing flaps in a prescribed extended position. This is because of the air loads imposed on the structure of the flaps.

V_A—the calibrated design maneuvering airspeed. This is the maximum speed at which the limit load can be imposed (either by gusts or full deflection of the control surfaces) without causing structural damage. Operating at or below manuevering speed does not provide structural protection against multiple full control inputs in one axis or full control inputs in more than one axis at the same time.

V_{NO}—the maximum speed for normal operation or the maximum structural cruising speed. This is the speed at which exceeding the limit load factor may cause permanent deformation of the aircraft structure.

V_{NE}—the speed which should *never* be exceeded. If flight is attempted above this speed, structural damage or structural failure may result.

Performance Charts

Performance charts allow a pilot to predict the takeoff, climb, cruise, and landing performance of an aircraft. These charts, provided by the manufacturer, are included in the AFM/POH. Information the manufacturer provides on these charts has been gathered from test flights conducted in a new aircraft, under normal operating conditions while using average piloting skills, and with the aircraft and engine in good working order. Engineers record the flight data and create performance charts based on the behavior of the aircraft during the test flights. By using these performance charts, a pilot can determine the runway length needed to take off and land, the amount of fuel to be used during flight, and the time required to arrive at the destination. It is important to remember that the data from the charts will not be accurate if the aircraft is not in good working order or when operating under adverse conditions. Always consider the necessity to compensate for the performance numbers if the aircraft is not in good working order or piloting skills are below average. Each aircraft performs differently and, therefore, has different performance numbers. Compute the performance of the aircraft prior to every flight, as every flight is different. (See appendix for examples of performance charts for a Cessna Model 172R and Challenger 605.)

Every chart is based on certain conditions and contains notes on how to adapt the information for flight conditions. It is important to read every chart and understand how to use it. Read the instructions provided by the manufacturer. For an explanation on how to use the charts, refer to the example provided by the manufacturer for that specific chart. *[Figure 10-19]*

The information manufacturers furnish is not standardized. Information may be contained in a table format, and other information may be contained in a graph format. Sometimes combined graphs incorporate two or more graphs into one chart to compensate for multiple conditions of flight. Combined graphs allow the pilot to predict aircraft performance for variations in density altitude, weight, and winds all on one chart. Because of the vast amount of information that can be extracted from this type of chart, it is important to be very accurate in reading the chart. A small error in the beginning can lead to a large error at the end.

The remainder of this section covers performance information for aircraft in general and discusses what information the charts contain and how to extract information from the charts by direct reading and interpolation methods. Every chart contains a wealth of information that should be used when flight planning. Examples of the table, graph, and combined graph formats for all aspects of flight will be discussed.

Interpolation

Not all of the information on the charts is easily extracted. Some charts require interpolation to find the information for specific flight conditions. Interpolating information means that by taking the known information, a pilot can compute intermediate information. However, pilots sometimes round off values from charts to a more conservative figure.

Using values that reflect slightly more adverse conditions provides a reasonable estimate of performance information and gives a slight margin of safety. The following illustration is an example of interpolating information from a takeoff distance chart. *[Figure 10-20]*

Density Altitude Charts

Use a density altitude chart to figure the density altitude at the departing airport. Using *Figure 10-21*, determine the density altitude based on the given information.

Sample Problem 1

Airport Elevation..5,883 feet

OAT..70 °F

Altimeter...30.10" Hg

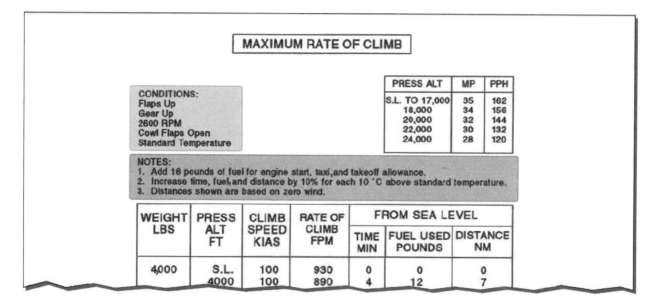

Figure 10-19. *Conditions notes chart.*

Conditions														

Conditions: Flaps 10° / Full throttle prior to brake release / Paved level runway / Zero wind

TAKEOFF DISTANCE — MAXIMUM WEIGHT 2,400 LB

Weight (lb)	Takeoff speed KIAS Lift off	Takeoff speed KIAS AT 50 ft	Press ALT (feet)	0 °C Grnd Roll (feet)	0 °C Total feet to clear 50 ft OBS	10 °C Grnd Roll (feet)	10 °C Total feet to clear 50 ft OBS	20 °C Grnd Roll (feet)	20 °C Total feet to clear 50 ft OBS	30 °C Grnd Roll (feet)	30 °C Total feet to clear 50 ft OBS	40 °C Grnd Roll (feet)	40 °C Total feet to clear 50 ft OBS
2,400	51	56	S.L.	795	1,460	860	1,570	925	1,685	995	1,810	1,065	1,945
			1,000	875	1,605	940	1,725	1,015	1,860	1,090	2,000	1,170	2,155
			2,000	960	1,770	1,035	1,910	1,115	2,060	1,200	2,220	1,290	2,395
			3,000	1,055	1,960	1,140	2,120	1,230	2,295	1,325	2,480	1,425	2,685
			4,000	1,165	2,185	1,260	2,365	1,355	2,570	1,465	2,790	1,575	3,030
			5,000	1,285	2,445	1,390	2,660	1,500	2,895	1,620	3,160	1,745	3,455
			6,000	1,425	2,755	1,540	3,015	1,665	3,300	1,800	3,620	1,940	3,990
			7,000	1,580	3,140	1,710	3,450	1,850	3,805	2,000	4,220	---	---
			8,000	1,755	3,615	1,905	4,015	2,060	4,480	---	---	---	---

To find the takeoff distance for a pressure altitude of 2,500 feet at 20 °C, average the ground roll for 2,000 feet and 3,000 feet.

$$\frac{1,115 + 1,230}{2} = 1,173 \text{ feet}$$

Figure 10-20. *Interpolating charts.*

First, compute the pressure altitude conversion. Find 30.10 under the altimeter heading. Read across to the second column. It reads "–165." Therefore, it is necessary to subtract 165 from the airport elevation giving a pressure altitude of 5,718 feet. Next, locate the outside air temperature on the scale along the bottom of the graph. From 70°, draw a line up to the 5,718 feet pressure altitude line, which is about two-thirds of the way up between the 5,000 and 6,000 foot lines. Draw a line straight across to the far left side of the graph and read the approximate density altitude. The approximate density altitude in thousands of feet is 7,700 feet.

Takeoff Charts

Takeoff charts are typically provided in several forms and allow a pilot to compute the takeoff distance of the aircraft with no flaps or with a specific flap configuration. A pilot can also compute distances for a no flap takeoff over a 50 foot obstacle scenario, as well as with flaps over a 50 foot obstacle. The takeoff distance chart provides for various aircraft weights, altitudes, temperatures, winds, and obstacle heights.

Sample Problem 2

Pressure Altitude...2,000 feet

OAT...22 °C

Takeoff Weight..2,600 pounds

Headwind...6 knots

Obstacle Height...50 foot obstacle

Refer to *Figure 10-22.* This chart is an example of a combined takeoff distance graph. It takes into consideration pressure altitude, temperature, weight, wind, and obstacles all on one chart. First, find the correct temperature on the bottom left-

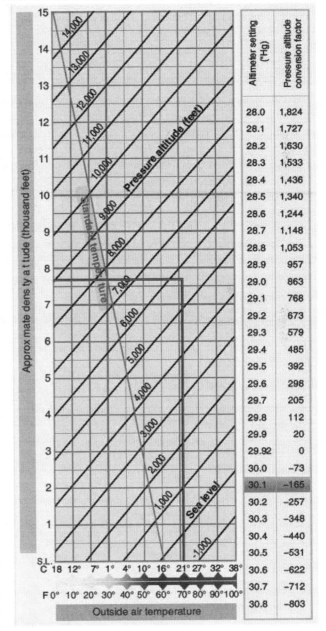

Altimeter setting ("Hg)	Pressure altitude conversion factor
28.0	1,824
28.1	1,727
28.2	1,630
28.3	1,533
28.4	1,436
28.5	1,340
28.6	1,244
28.7	1,148
28.8	1,053
28.9	957
29.0	863
29.1	768
29.2	673
29.3	579
29.4	485
29.5	392
29.6	298
29.7	205
29.8	112
29.9	20
29.92	0
30.0	–73
30.1	–165
30.2	–257
30.3	–348
30.4	–440
30.5	–531
30.6	–622
30.7	–712
30.8	–803

Figure 10-21. *Density altitude chart.*

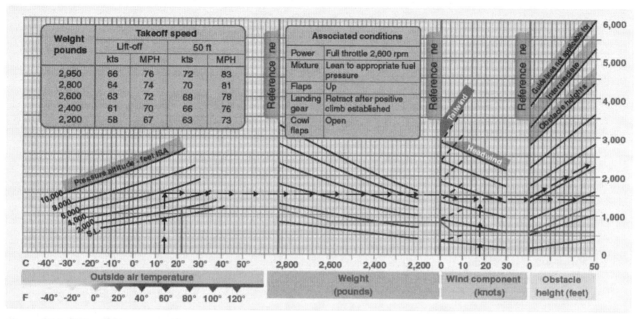

Figure 10-22. *Takeoff distance graph.*

hand side of the graph. Follow the line from 22° C straight up until it intersects the 2,000 foot altitude line. From that point, draw a line straight across to the first dark reference line. Continue to draw the line from the reference point in a diagonal direction following the surrounding lines until it intersects the corresponding weight line. From the intersection of 2,600 pounds, draw a line straight across until it reaches the second reference line. Once again, follow the lines in a diagonal manner until it reaches the six knot headwind mark. Follow straight across to the third reference line and from here, draw a line in two directions. First, draw a line straight across to figure the ground roll distance. Next, follow the diagonal lines again until it reaches the corresponding obstacle height. In this case, it is a 50 foot obstacle. Therefore, draw the diagonal line to the far edge of the chart. This results in a 600 foot ground roll distance and a total distance of 1,200 feet over a 50 foot obstacle. To find the corresponding takeoff speeds at lift-off and over the 50 foot obstacle, refer to the table on the top of the chart. In this case, the lift-off speed at 2,600 pounds would be 63 knots and over the 50 foot obstacle would be 68 knots.

Sample Problem 3

Pressure Altitude	3,000 feet
OAT	30 °C
Takeoff Weight	2,400 pounds
Headwind	18 knots

Refer to *Figure 10-23.* This chart is an example of a takeoff distance table for short-field takeoffs. For this table, first find the takeoff weight. Once at 2,400 pounds, begin reading from

left to right across the table. The takeoff speed is in the second column and, in the third column under pressure altitude, find the pressure altitude of 3,000 feet. Carefully follow that line to the right until it is under the correct temperature column of 30 °C. The ground roll total reads 1,325 feet and the total required to clear a 50 foot obstacle is 2,480 feet. At this point, there is an 18 knot headwind. According to the notes section under point number two, decrease the distances by ten percent for each 9 knots of headwind. With an 18 knot headwind, it is necessary to decrease the distance by 20 percent. Multiply 1,325 feet by 20 percent (1,325 x .20 = 265), subtract the product from the total distance (1,325 – 265 = 1,060). Repeat this process for the total distance over a 50 foot obstacle. The ground roll distance is 1,060 feet and the total distance over a 50 foot obstacle is 1,984 feet.

Climb and Cruise Charts

Climb and cruise chart information is based on actual flight tests conducted in an aircraft of the same type. This information is extremely useful when planning a cross-country to predict the performance and fuel consumption of the aircraft. Manufacturers produce several different charts for climb and cruise performance. These charts include everything from fuel, time, and distance to climb, to best power setting during cruise, to cruise range performance.

The first chart to check for climb performance is a fuel, time, and distance-to-climb chart. This chart will give the fuel amount used during the climb, the time it will take to accomplish the climb, and the ground distance that will be covered during the climb. To use this chart, obtain the

Conditions
Flaps 10°
Full throttle prior to brake release
Paved level runway
Zero wind

TAKEOFF DISTANCE
MAXIMUM WEIGHT 2,400 LB

SHORT FIELD

Notes
1. Prior to takeoff from fields above 3,000 feet elevation, the mixture should be leaned to give maximum rpm in a full throttle, static runup.
2. Decrease distances 10% for each 9 knots headwind. For operation with tailwind up to 10 knots, increase distances by 10% for each 2 knots.
3. For operation on a dry, grass runway, increase distances by 15% of the "ground roll" figure.

Weight (lb)	Takeoff speed KIAS		Press ALT (FT)	0 °C		10 °C		20 °C		30 °C		40 °C	
	Lift off	AT 50 ft		Grnd Roll (FT)	Total feet to clear 50 ft OBS	Grnd Roll (FT)	Total feet to clear 50 ft OBS	Grnd Roll (FT)	Total feet to clear 50 ft OBS	Grnd Roll (FT)	Total feet to clear 50 ft OBS	Grnd Roll (FT)	Total feet to clear 50 ft OBS
2,400	51	56	S.L.	795	1,460	860	1,570	925	1,685	995	1,810	1,065	1,945
			1,000	875	1,605	940	1,725	1,015	1,860	1,090	2,000	1,170	2,155
			2,000	960	1,770	1,035	1,910	1,115	2,060	1,200	2,220	1,290	2,395
			3,000	1,055	1,960	1,140	2,120	1,230	2,295	1,325	2,480	1,425	2,685
			4,000	1,165	2,185	1,260	2,365	1,355	2,570	1,465	2,790	1,575	3,030
			5,000	1,285	2,445	1,390	2,660	1,500	2,895	1,620	3,160	1,745	3,455
			6,000	1,425	2,755	1,540	3,015	1,665	3,300	1,800	3,620	1,940	3,990
			7,000	1,580	3,140	1,710	3,450	1,850	3,805	2,000	4,220	---	---
			8,000	1,755	3,615	1,905	4,015	2,060	4,480	---	---	---	---
2,200	49	54	S.L.	650	1,195	700	1,280	750	1,375	805	1,470	865	1,575
			1,000	710	1,310	765	1,405	825	1,510	885	1,615	950	1,735
			2,000	780	1,440	840	1,545	905	1,660	975	1,785	1,045	1,915
			3,000	855	1,585	925	1,705	995	1,835	1,070	1,975	1,150	2,130
			4,000	945	1,750	1,020	1,890	1,100	2,040	1,180	2,200	1,270	2,375
			5,000	1,040	1,945	1,125	2,105	1,210	2,275	1,305	2,465	1,405	2,665
			6,000	1,150	2,170	1,240	2,355	1,340	2,555	1,445	2,775	1,555	3,020
			7,000	1,270	2,440	1,375	2,655	1,485	2,890	1,605	3,155	1,730	3,450
			8,000	1,410	2,760	1,525	3,015	1,650	3,305	1,785	3,630	1,925	4,005
2,000	46	51	S.L.	525	970	565	1,035	605	1,110	650	1,185	695	1,265
			1,000	570	1,060	615	1,135	665	1,215	710	1,295	765	1,385
			2,000	625	1,160	675	1,240	725	1,330	780	1,425	840	1,525
			3,000	690	1,270	740	1,365	800	1,465	860	1,570	920	1,685
			4,000	755	1,400	815	1,500	880	1,615	945	1,735	1,015	1,865
			5,000	830	1,545	900	1,660	970	1,790	2,145	1,925	1,120	2,070
			6,000	920	1,710	990	1,845	1,070	1,990	2,405	2,145	1,235	2,315
			7,000	1,015	1,900	1,095	2,055	1,180	2,225	2,715	2,405	1,370	2,605
			8,000	1,125	2,125	1,215	2,305	1,310	2,500	1,410	2,715	1,520	2,950

Figure 10-23. *Takeoff distance short field charts.*

information for the departing airport and for the cruise altitude. Using *Figure 10-24,* calculate the fuel, time, and distance to climb based on the information provided.

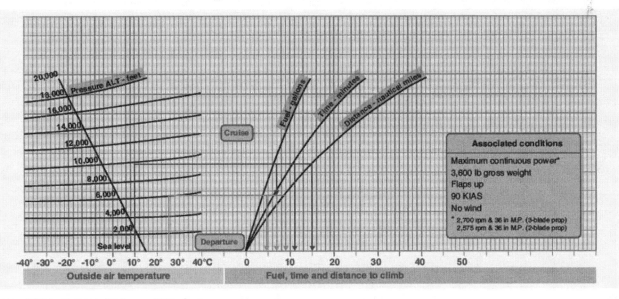

Figure 10-24. *Fuel time distance climb chart.*

Sample Problem 4

Departing Airport Pressure Altitude.................6,000 feet

Departing Airport OAT...25 °C

Cruise Pressure Altitude...................................10,000 feet

Cruise OAT...10 °C

First, find the information for the departing airport. Find the OAT for the departing airport along the bottom, left-hand side of the graph. Follow the line from 25 °C straight up until it intersects the line corresponding to the pressure altitude of 6,000 feet. Continue this line straight across until it intersects all three lines for fuel, time, and distance. Draw a line straight down from the intersection of altitude and fuel, altitude and time, and a third line at altitude and distance. It should read three and one-half gallons of fuel, 6.5 minutes of time, and nine NM. Next, repeat the steps to find the information for the cruise altitude. It should read six and one-half gallons of fuel, 11.5 minutes of time, and 15 NM. Take each set of numbers for fuel, time, and distance and subtract them from one another (6.5 – 3.5 = 3 gallons of fuel). It will take three gallons of fuel and 5 minutes of time to climb to 10,000 feet. During that climb, the distance covered is six NM. Remember, according to the notes at the top of the chart, these numbers do not take into account wind, and it is assumed maximum continuous power is being used.

The next example is a fuel, time, and distance-to-climb table. For this table, use the same basic criteria as for the previous chart. However, it is necessary to figure the information in a different manner. Refer to *Figure 10-25* to work the following sample problem.

Sample Problem 5

Departing Airport Pressure Altitude...................Sea level

Departing Airport OAT...22 °C

Cruise Pressure Altitude.....................................8,000 feet

Takeoff Weight...3,400 pounds

To begin, find the given weight of 3,400 in the first column of the chart. Move across to the pressure altitude column to find the sea level altitude numbers. At sea level, the numbers read zero. Next, read the line that corresponds with the cruising altitude of 8,000 feet. Normally, a pilot would subtract these two sets of number from one another, but given the fact that the numbers read zero at sea level, it is known that the time to climb from sea level to 8,000 feet is 10 minutes. It is also known that 21 pounds of fuel will be used and 20 NM will be covered during the climb. However, the temperature is 22 °C, which is 7° above the standard temperature of 15 °C. The notes section of this chart indicate that the findings must be increased

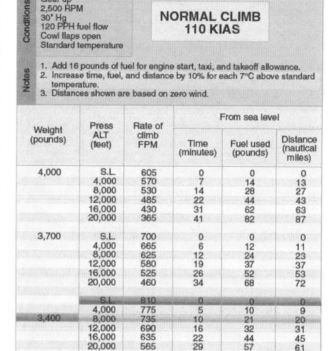

Figure 10-25. *Fuel time distance climb.*

Weight (pounds)	Press ALT (feet)	Rate of climb FPM	From sea level		
			Time (minutes)	Fuel used (pounds)	Distance (nautical miles)
4,000	S.L.	605	0	0	0
	4,000	570	7	14	13
	8,000	530	14	28	27
	12,000	485	22	44	43
	16,000	430	31	62	63
	20,000	365	41	82	87
3,700	S.L.	700	0	0	0
	4,000	665	6	12	11
	8,000	625	12	24	23
	12,000	580	19	37	37
	16,000	525	26	52	53
	20,000	460	34	68	72
3,400	S.L.	810	0	0	0
	4,000	775	5	10	9
	8,000	735	10	21	20
	12,000	690	16	32	31
	16,000	635	22	44	45
	20,000	565	29	57	61

by ten percent for each 7° above standard. Multiply the findings by ten percent or .10 (10 × .10 = 1, 1 + 10 = 11 minutes). After accounting for the additional ten percent, the findings should read 11 minutes, 23.1 pounds of fuel, and 22 NM. Notice that the fuel is reported in pounds of fuel, not gallons. Aviation fuel weighs six pounds per gallon, so 23.1 pounds of fuel is equal to 3.85 gallons of fuel (23.1 ÷ 6 = 3.85).

The next example is a cruise and range performance chart. This type of table is designed to give TAS, fuel consumption, endurance in hours, and range in miles at specific cruise configurations. Use *Figure 10-26* to determine the cruise and range performance under the given conditions.

Sample Problem 6

Pressure Altitude...5,000 feet

RPM...2,400 rpm

Fuel Carrying Capacity..................38 gallons, no reserve

Find 5,000 feet pressure altitude in the first column on the left-hand side of the table. Next, find the correct rpm of 2,400 in the second column. Follow that line straight across and read the TAS of 116 mph, and a fuel burn rate of 6.9 gallons per hour. As per the example, the aircraft is equipped with a fuel carrying capacity of 38 gallons. Under this column,

The conditions block in the figure reads:
Flaps up / Gear up / 2,500 RPM / 30" Hg / 120 PPH fuel flow / Cowl flaps open / Standard temperature

NORMAL CLIMB
110 KIAS

Notes:
1. Add 16 pounds of fuel for engine start, taxi, and takeoff allowance.
2. Increase time, fuel, and distance by 10% for each 7°C above standard temperature.
3. Distances shown are based on zero wind.

						38 gal (no reserve)		48 gal (no reserve)	
ALT	RPM	% BHP	TAS MPH	GAL/ Hour		Endr. hours	Range miles	Endr. hours	Range miles
2,500	2,700	86	134	9.7		3.9	525	4.9	660
	2,600	79	129	8.6		4.4	570	5.6	720
	2,500	72	123	7.8		4.9	600	6.2	760
	2,400	65	117	7.2		5.3	620	6.7	780
	2,300	58	111	6.7		5.7	630	7.2	795
	2,200	52	103	6.3		6.1	625	7.7	790
5,000	2,700	82	134	9.0		4.2	565	5.3	710
	2,600	75	128	8.1		4.7	600	5.9	760
	2,500	68	122	7.4		5.1	625	6.4	790
	2,400	61	116	6.9		5.5	635	6.9	805
	2,300	55	108	6.5		5.9	635	7.4	805
	2,200	49	100	6.0		6.3	630	7.9	795
7,500	2,700	78	133	8.4		4.5	600	5.7	755
	2,600	71	127	7.7		4.9	625	6.2	790
	2,500	64	121	7.1		5.3	645	6.7	810
	2,400	58	113	6.7		5.7	645	7.2	820
	2,300	52	105	6.2		6.1	640	7.7	810
10,000	2,650	70	129	7.6		5.0	640	6.3	810
	2,600	67	124	7.3		5.2	650	6.5	820
	2,500	61	118	6.9		5.5	655	7.0	830
	2,400	55	110	6.4		5.9	650	7.5	825
	2,300	49	100	6.0		6.3	635	8.0	800

Conditions:
Gross weight 2,300 lb.
Standard conditions
Zero wind
Lean mixture

Notes: Maximum cruise is normally limited to 75% power.

Figure 10-26. *Cruise and range performance.*

read that the endurance in hours is 5.5 hours and the range in miles is 635 miles.

Cruise power setting tables are useful when planning cross-country flights. The table gives the correct cruise power settings, as well as the fuel flow and airspeed performance numbers at that altitude and airspeed.

Sample Problem 7

Pressure Altitude at Cruise..................................6,000 feet

OAT...36 °F above standard

Refer to *Figure 10-27* for this sample problem. First, locate the pressure altitude of 6,000 feet on the far left side of the table. Follow that line across to the far right side of the table under the 20 °C (or 36 °F) column. At 6,000 feet, the rpm setting of 2,450 will maintain 65 percent continuous power at 21.0 "Hg with a fuel flow rate of 11.5 gallons per hour and airspeed of 161 knots.

Another type of cruise chart is a best power mixture range graph. This graph gives the best range based on power setting and altitude. Using *Figure 10-28,* find the range at 65 percent power with and without a reserve based on the provided conditions.

Sample Problem 8

OAT...Standard

Pressure Altitude...5,000 feet

First, move up the left side of the graph to 5,000 feet and standard temperature. Follow the line straight across the graph until it intersects the 65 percent line under both the reserve and no reserve categories. Draw a line straight down from both intersections to the bottom of the graph. At 65 percent power with a reserve, the range is approximately 522 miles. At 65 percent power with no reserve, the range should be 581 miles.

The last cruise chart referenced is a cruise performance graph. This graph is designed to tell the TAS performance of the airplane depending on the altitude, temperature, and power

CRUISE POWER SETTING
65% MAXIMUM CONTINUOUS POWER (OR FULL THROTTLE)
2,800 POUNDS

Press ALT	ISA -20° (-36 °F)								Standard day (ISA)								ISA +20° (+36 °F)							
	IOAT		Engine speed	Man. press	Fuel flow per engine		TAS		IOAT		Engine speed	Man. press	Fuel flow per engine		TAS		IOAT		Engine speed	Man. press	Fuel flow per engine		TAS	
	°F	°C	RPM	"HG	PSI	GPH	kts	MPH	°F	°C	RPM	"HG	PSI	GPH	kts	MPH	°F	°C	RPM	"HG	PSI	GPH	kts	MPH
S.L.	27	-3	2,450	20.7	6.6	11.5	147	169	63	17	2,450	21.2	6.6	11.5	150	173	99	37	2,450	21.8	6.6	11.5	153	176
2,000	19	-7	2,450	20.4	6.6	11.5	149	171	55	13	2,450	21.0	6.6	11.5	153	176	91	33	2,450	21.5	6.6	11.5	156	180
4,000	12	-11	2,450	20.1	6.6	11.5	152	175	48	9	2,450	20.7	6.6	11.5	156	180	84	29	2,450	21.3	6.6	11.5	159	183
6,000	5	-15	2,450	19.8	6.6	11.5	155	178	41	5	2,450	20.4	6.6	11.5	158	182	79	26	2,450	21.0	6.6	11.5	161	185
8,000	-2	-19	2,450	19.5	6.6	11.5	157	181	36	2	2,450	20.2	6.6	11.5	161	185	72	22	2,450	20.8	6.6	11.5	164	189
10,000	-8	-22	2,450	19.2	6.6	11.5	160	184	28	-2	2,450	19.9	6.6	11.5	163	188	64	18	2,450	20.3	6.5	11.4	166	191
12,000	-15	-26	2,450	18.8	6.4	11.3	162	186	21	-6	2,450	18.8	6.1	10.9	163	188	57	14	2,450	18.8	5.9	10.6	163	188
14,000	-22	-30	2,450	17.4	5.8	10.5	159	183	14	-10	2,450	17.4	5.6	10.1	160	184	50	10	2,450	17.4	5.4	9.8	160	184
16,000	-29	-34	2,450	16.1	5.3	9.7	156	180	7	-14	2,450	16.1	5.1	9.4	156	180	43	6	2,450	16.1	4.9	9.1	155	178

Notes:
1. Full throttle manifold pressure settings are approximate.
2. Shaded area represents operation with full throttle.

Figure 10-27. *Cruise power setting.*

Figure 10-28. *Best power mixture range.*

setting. Using *Figure 10-29*, find the TAS performance based on the given information.

Sample Problem 9

OAT	16 °C
Pressure Altitude	6,000 feet
Power Setting	65 percent, best power
Wheel Fairings	Not installed

Begin by finding the correct OAT on the bottom, left side of the graph. Move up that line until it intersects the pressure altitude of 6,000 feet. Draw a line straight across to the 65 percent, best power line. This is the solid line, which represents best economy. Draw a line straight down from this intersection to the bottom of the graph. The TAS at 65 percent best power is 140 knots. However, it is necessary to subtract 8 knots from the speed since there are no wheel fairings. This note is listed under the title and conditions. The TAS will be 132 knots.

Crosswind and Headwind Component Chart

Every aircraft is tested according to Federal Aviation Administration (FAA) regulations prior to certification. The aircraft is tested by a pilot with average piloting skills in 90° crosswinds with a velocity up to 0.2 V_{SO} or two-tenths of the aircraft's stalling speed with power off, gear down, and flaps down. This means that if the stalling speed of the aircraft is 45 knots, it must be capable of landing in a 9-knot, 90° crosswind. The maximum demonstrated crosswind component is published in the AFM/POH. The crosswind and headwind component chart allows for figuring the headwind and crosswind component for any given wind direction and velocity.

Sample Problem 10

Runway	17
Wind	140° at 25 knots

Refer to *Figure 10-30* to solve this problem. First, determine how many degrees difference there is between the runway and the wind direction. It is known that runway 17 means a direction of 170°; from that subtract the wind direction of 140°. This gives a 30° angular difference, or wind angle. Next, locate the 30° mark and draw a line from there until it intersects

Figure 10-29. *Cruise performance graph.*

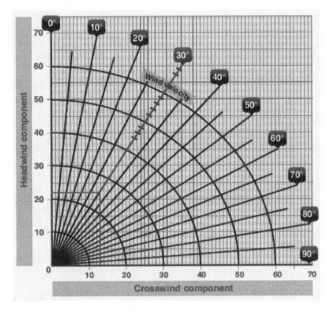

Figure 10-30. *Crosswind component chart.*

the correct wind velocity of 25 knots. From there, draw a line straight down and a line straight across. The headwind component is 22 knots and the crosswind component is 13 knots. This information is important when taking off and landing so that, first of all, the appropriate runway can be picked if more than one exists at a particular airport, but also so that the aircraft is not pushed beyond its tested limits.

Landing Charts

Landing performance is affected by variables similar to those affecting takeoff performance. It is necessary to compensate for differences in density altitude, weight of the airplane, and headwinds. Like takeoff performance charts, landing distance information is available as normal landing information, as well as landing distance over a 50 foot obstacle. As usual, read the associated conditions and notes in order to ascertain the basis of the chart information. Remember, when calculating landing distance that the landing weight will not be the same as the takeoff weight. The weight must be recalculated to compensate for the fuel that was used during the flight.

Sample Problem 11

Pressure Altitude	1,250 feet
Temperature	Standard

Refer to *Figure 10-31*. This example makes use of a landing distance table. Notice that the altitude of 1,250 feet is not on this table. It is, therefore, necessary to interpolate to find the correct landing distance. The pressure altitude of 1,250 is halfway between sea level and 2,500 feet. First, find the column for sea level and the column for 2,500 feet. Take the total distance of 1,075 for sea level and the total distance of 1,135 for 2,500 and add them together. Divide the total by two to obtain the distance for 1,250 feet. The distance is 1,105 feet total landing distance to clear a 50 foot obstacle. Repeat this process to obtain the ground roll distance for the pressure altitude. The ground roll should be 457.5 feet.

Sample Problem 12

OAT	57 °F
Pressure Altitude	4,000 feet
Landing Weight	2,400 pounds
Headwind	6 knots
Obstacle Height	50 feet

Using the given conditions and *Figure 10-32*, determine the landing distance for the aircraft. This graph is an example of a combined landing distance graph and allows compensation for temperature, weight, headwinds, tailwinds, and varying obstacle height. Begin by finding the correct OAT on the scale on the left side of the chart. Move up in a straight line to the correct pressure altitude of 4,000 feet. From this intersection, move straight across to the first dark reference line. Follow the lines in the same diagonal fashion until the correct landing weight is reached. At 2,400 pounds, continue in a straight line across to the second dark reference line. Once again, draw a line in a diagonal manner to the correct wind component and then straight across to the third dark

		LANDING DISTANCE							
Conditions Flaps lowered to 40° Power off Hard surface runway Zero wind									
Gross weight lb	Approach speed IAS, MPH	At sea level & 59 °F		At 2,500 ft & 59 °F		At 5,000 ft & 41 °F		At 7,500 ft & 32 °F	
		Ground roll	Total to clear 50 ft OBS	Ground roll	Total to clear 50 ft OBS	Ground roll	Total to clear 50 ft OBS	Ground roll	Total to clear 50 ft OBS
1,600	60	445	1,075	470	1,135	495	1,195	520	1,255
Note 1. Decrease the distances shown by 10% for each 4 knots of headwind. 2. Increase the distance by 10% for each 60 °F temperature increase above standard. 3. For operation on a dry, grass runway, increase distances (both "ground roll" and "total to clear 50 ft obstacle") by 20% of the "total to clear 50 ft obstacle" figure.									

Figure 10-31. *Landing distance table.*

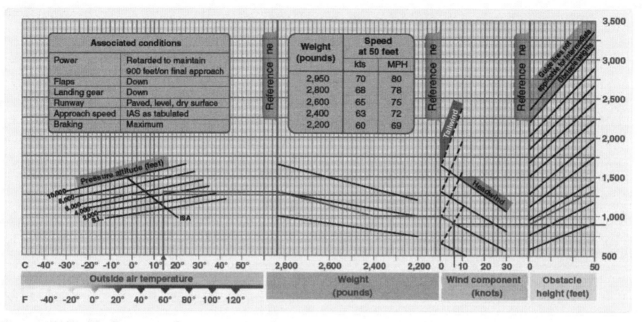

Figure 10-32. *Landing distance graph.*

reference line. From this point, draw a line in two separate directions: one straight across to figure the ground roll and one in a diagonal manner to the correct obstacle height. This should be 900 feet for the total ground roll and 1,300 feet for the total distance over a 50 foot obstacle.

Stall Speed Performance Charts

Stall speed performance charts are designed to give an understanding of the speed at which the aircraft will stall in a given configuration. This type of chart will typically take into account the angle of bank, the position of the gear and flaps, and the throttle position. Use *Figure 10-33* and the accompanying conditions to find the speed at which the airplane will stall.

Sample Problem 13

Power... OFF

Flaps.. Down

Gear... Down

Angle of Bank.. 45°

First, locate the correct flap and gear configuration. The bottom half of the chart should be used since the gear and flaps are down. Next, choose the row corresponding to a power-off situation. Now, find the correct angle of bank column, which is 45°. The stall speed is 78 mph, and the stall speed in knots would be 68 knots.

Gross weight 2,750 lb			Angle of bank			
			Level	30°	45°	60°
			Gear and flaps up			
Power	On	MPH	62	67	74	88
		knots	54	58	64	76
	Off	MPH	75	81	89	106
		knots	65	70	77	92
			Gear and flaps down			
Power	On	MPH	54	58	64	76
		knots	47	50	56	66
	Off	MPH	66	71	78	93
		knots	57	62	68	81

Figure 10-33. *Stall speed table.*

Performance charts provide valuable information to the pilot. Take advantage of these charts. A pilot can predict the performance of the aircraft under most flying conditions, and this enables a better plan for every flight. The Code of Federal Regulations (CFR) requires that a pilot be familiar with all information available prior to any flight. Pilots should use the information to their advantage as it can only contribute to safety in flight.

Transport Category Airplane Performance

Transport category aircraft are certificated under Title 14 of the CFR (14 CFR) parts 25 and 29. The airworthiness certification standards of part 25 and 29 require proven levels of performance and guarantee safety margins for these aircraft, regardless of the specific operating regulations under which they are employed.

Major Differences in Transport Category Versus Non-Transport Category Performance Requirements

- Full temperature accountability—all of the performance charts for the transport category aircraft require that takeoff and climb performance be computed with the full effects of temperature considered.

- Climb performance expressed as percent gradient of climb—the transport category aircraft's climb performance is expressed as a percent gradient of climb rather than a figure calculated in fpm of climb. This percent gradient of climb is a much more practical expression of performance since it is the aircraft's angle of climb that is critical in an obstacle clearance situation.

- Change in lift-off technique—lift-off technique in transport category aircraft allows the reaching of V_2 (takeoff safety speed) after the aircraft is airborne. This is possible because of the excellent acceleration and reliability characteristics of the engines on these aircraft and due to the larger surplus of power.

- Performance requirements applicable to all segments of aviation—all aircraft certificated by the FAA in the transport category, whatever the size, must be operated in accordance with the same performance criteria. This applies to both commercial and non-commercial operations.

Performance Requirements

The performance requirements that the transport category aircraft must meet are:

Takeoff

- Takeoff speeds
- Takeoff runway required
- Takeoff climb required
- Obstacle clearance requirements

Landing

- Landing speeds
- Landing runway required
- Landing climb required

Takeoff Planning

Listed below are the speeds that affect the transport category aircraft's takeoff performance. The flight crew must be thoroughly familiar with each of these speeds and how they are used in takeoff planning.

- V_S—stalling speed or the minimum steady flight speed at which the aircraft is controllable.

- V_{MCG}—minimum control speed on the ground, with one engine inoperative, (critical engine on two-engine airplanes) takeoff power on other engine(s), using aerodynamic controls only for directional control (must be less than V_1).

- V_{MCA}—minimum control speed in the air, with one engine inoperative, (critical engine on two-engine aircraft) operating engine(s) at takeoff power, maximum of 5° bank into the good engine(s).

- V_1—critical engine failure speed or decision speed. Engine failure below this speed shall result in an aborted takeoff; above this speed the takeoff run should be continued.

- V_R—speed at which the rotation of the aircraft is initiated to takeoff attitude. The speed cannot be less than V_1 or less than 1.05 times V_{MC}. With an engine failure, it must also allow for the acceleration to V_2 at the 35-foot height at the end of the runway.

- V_{LOF}—lift-off speed. The speed at which the aircraft first becomes airborne.

- V_2—the takeoff safety speed which must be attained at the 35-foot height at the end of the required runway distance. This is essentially the best one-engine operative angle of climb speed for the aircraft and should be held until clearing obstacles after takeoff, or until at least 400 feet above the ground.

- V_{FS}—final segment climb speed, which is based upon one-engine inooerative climb, clean configuration, and mximum continuos power setting.

All of the V speeds should be considered during every takeoff. The V_1, V_R, V_2, and V_{FS} speeds should be visibly posted in the flightdeck for reference during the takeoff.

Takeoff speeds vary with aircraft weight. Before takeoff speeds can be computed, the pilot must first determine the maximum allowable takeoff weight. The three items that can limit takeoff weight are runway requirements, takeoff climb requirements, and obstacle clearance requirements.

Runway Requirements

The runway requirements for takeoff are affected by:

- Pressure altitude
- Temperature
- Headwind component
- Runway gradient or slope
- Aircraft weight

The runway required for takeoff must be based upon the possible loss of an engine at the most critical point, which is at V₁ (decision speed). By regulation, the aircraft's takeoff weight has to accommodate the longest of three distances:

1. Accelerate-go distance—the distance required to accelerate to V_1 with all engines at takeoff power, experience an engine failure at V_1 and continue the takeoff on the remaining engine(s). The runway required includes the distance required to climb to 35 feet by which time V_2 speed must be attained.

2. Accelerate-stop distance—the distance required to accelerate to V_1 with all engines at takeoff power, experience an engine failure at V_1, and abort the takeoff and bring the aircraft to a stop using braking action only (use of thrust reversing is not considered).

3. Takeoff distance—the distance required to complete an all-engines operative takeoff to the 35-foot height. It must be at least 15 percent less than the distance required for a one-engine inoperative engine takeoff. This distance is not normally a limiting factor as it is usually less than the one-engine inoperative takeoff distance.

These three required takeoff runway considerations are shown in *Figure 10-34.*

Balanced Field Length

In most cases, the pilot will be working with a performance chart for takeoff runway required, which will give "balanced field length" information. This means that the distance

Figure 10-34. *Minimum required takeoff.*

shown for the takeoff will include both the accelerate-go and accelerate-stop distances. One effective means of presenting the normal takeoff data is shown in the tabulated chart in *Figure 10-35*.

The chart in *Figure 10-35* shows the runway distance required under normal conditions and is useful as a quick reference chart for the standard takeoff. The V speeds for the various weights and conditions are also shown.

For other than normal takeoff conditions, such as with engine anti-ice, anti-skid brakes inoperative, or extremes in temperature or runway slope, the pilot should consult the appropriate takeoff performance charts in the performance section of the AFM.

There are other occasions of very high weight and temperature where the runway requirement may be dictated by the maximum brake kinetic energy limits that affect

Conditions: Cabin pressurization On / Zero slope runway / No flaps—Anti-ice RAM air inlets Off / Anti-skid On / Distances—100 feet (V₁ – KIAS)

TAKEOFF RUNWAY REQUIREMENTS
Standard ISA conditions

Notes: Shaded area indicates conditions that do not meet second segment climb requirements. Refer to F.M. for takeoff limitations.

Takeoff gross weight at brake release	°F	°C	Sea level (V₁)	1,000 (V₁)	2,000 (V₁)	3,000 (V₁)	4,000 (V₁)	5,000 (V₁)	6,000 (V₁)	Headwind (knots)
19,612 V_R = 126 V_2 = 134	30	-1.1	47 (121)	48 (121)	50 (120)	53 (121)	57 (122)	62 (123)	70 (123)	0
	50	10	48 (121)	51 (121)	55 (121)	60 (122)	63 (123)	69 (124)	77 (125)	
	70	21	53 (122)	56 (122)	60 (123)	65 (124)	70 (125)	77 (125)	85 (126)	
	90	32	58 (123)	62 (124)	68 (124)	73 (125)	78 (126)	85 (127)	95 (129)	
	30	-1.1	43 (121)	43 (121)	45 (120)	48 (121)	52 (122)	56 (123)	64 (123)	20
	50	10	43 (121)	46 (121)	50 (122)	55 (122)	57 (123)	63 (124)	70 (125)	
	70	21	48 (122)	51 (122)	55 (123)	59 (124)	63 (125)	70 (125)	77 (126)	
	90	32	53 (123)	57 (124)	62 (124)	66 (125)	71 (126)	77 (127)	85 (129)	
19,000 V_R = 124 V_2 = 131	30	-1.1	45 (118)	45 (118)	47 (117)	50 (118)	54 (119)	59 (120)	66 (120)	0
	50	10	46 (118)	48 (118)	51 (118)	56 (119)	59 (120)	65 (121)	73 (121)	
	70	21	50 (118)	53 (119)	57 (120)	66 (121)	66 (121)	72 (122)	80 (123)	
	90	32	55 (120)	59 (121)	64 (121)	73 (122)	73 (123)	80 (124)	90 (124)	
	30	-1.1	40 (118)	41 (118)	43 (118)	45 (118)	49 (119)	54 (120)	60 (120)	20
	50	10	42 (118)	44 (118)	46 (118)	51 (119)	54 (120)	59 (121)	66 (121)	
	70	21	45 (118)	48 (119)	52 (120)	56 (121)	60 (121)	65 (122)	72 (123)	
	90	32	50 (120)	54 (121)	58 (121)	63 (122)	66 (123)	73 (124)	81 (124)	
18,000 V_R = 119 V_2 = 127	30	-1.1	40 (114)	41 (114)	42 (113)	45 (113)	49 (114)	53 (115)	60 (115)	0
	50	10	41 (115)	43 (114)	46 (115)	50 (115)	53 (115)	59 (116)	66 (117)	
	70	21	45 (114)	48 (115)	51 (115)	56 (116)	59 (116)	65 (116)	72 (117)	
	90	32	50 (115)	53 (116)	58 (116)	62 (117)	66 (118)	73 (118)	80 (119)	
	30	-1.1	36 (114)	37 (114)	38 (113)	41 (113)	45 (114)	48 (115)	54 (115)	20
	50	10	37 (115)	39 (114)	42 (114)	46 (115)	48 (115)	54 (116)	60 (117)	
	70	21	41 (114)	44 (115)	46 (115)	51 (116)	56 (116)	59 (116)	65 (117)	
	90	32	46 (115)	48 (116)	53 (116)	56 (117)	60 (118)	66 (118)	73 (119)	
17,000 V_R = 115 V_2 = 124	30	-1.1	36 (108)	37 (108)	38 (107)	40 (108)	44 (109)	48 (110)	53 (111)	0
	50	10	37 (110)	39 (108)	41 (109)	45 (110)	48 (110)	53 (111)	59 (112)	
	70	21	40 (108)	43 (110)	46 (111)	50 (111)	53 (112)	58 (111)	65 (113)	
	90	32	45 (111)	46 (112)	52 (112)	56 (113)	59 (114)	65 (114)	72 (114)	
	30	-1.1	32 (108)	33 (108)	34 (107)	36 (108)	40 (109)	44 (110)	48 (111)	20
	50	10	34 (110)	35 (108)	37 (109)	41 (110)	44 (110)	48 (111)	54 (112)	
	70	21	36 (108)	39 (110)	42 (111)	45 (111)	48 (112)	53 (111)	59 (113)	
	90	32	41 (111)	44 (112)	47 (112)	51 (113)	54 (114)	59 (114)	65 (114)	
16,000 V_R = 111 V_2 = 120	30	-1.1	32 (104)	33 (103)	34 (103)	36 (103)	39 (105)	43 (106)	48 (106)	0
	50	10	34 (105)	35 (103)	37 (104)	41 (105)	43 (106)	47 (107)	53 (107)	
	70	21	36 (104)	38 (105)	41 (105)	45 (106)	48 (107)	52 (107)	58 (108)	
	90	32	41 (106)	43 (107)	46 (107)	50 (108)	53 (108)	58 (109)	64 (110)	
	30	-1.1	29 (104)	30 (103)	31 (103)	32 (103)	35 (105)	39 (106)	44 (106)	20
	50	10	31 (105)	32 (103)	33 (104)	37 (105)	39 (106)	43 (107)	48 (107)	
	70	21	32 (104)	34 (105)	37 (105)	41 (106)	44 (107)	47 (107)	53 (108)	
	90	32	37 (106)	39 (107)	42 (107)	45 (108)	48 (108)	53 (109)	58 (110)	
15,000 V_R = 106 V_2 = 116	30	-1.1	28 (98)	30 (98)	30 (98)	32 (98)	35 (99)	38 (101)	42 (101)	0
	50	10	30 (100)	31 (98)	33 (99)	36 (100)	38 (101)	42 (102)	46 (102)	
	70	21	32 (99)	34 (100)	37 (101)	40 (102)	42 (102)	46 (102)	51 (103)	
	90	32	36 (101)	38 (102)	41 (102)	44 (103)	47 (104)	51 (104)	56 (105)	
	30	-1.1	25 (98)	27 (98)	27 (98)	29 (98)	32 (99)	34 (101)	38 (101)	20
	50	10	27 (100)	29 (98)	30 (99)	32 (100)	34 (101)	38 (102)	42 (102)	
	70	21	29 (99)	31 (100)	33 (101)	36 (102)	38 (102)	42 (102)	46 (103)	
	90	32	32 (101)	34 (102)	37 (102)	40 (103)	43 (104)	46 (104)	51 (105)	

Figure 10-35. *Normal takeoff runway required.*

the aircraft's ability to stop. Under these conditions, the accelerate-stop distance may be greater than the accelerate-go. The procedure to bring performance back to a balanced field takeoff condition is to limit the V_1 speed so that it does not exceed the maximum brake kinetic energy speed (sometimes called VBE). This procedure also results in a reduction in allowable takeoff weight.

Climb Requirements

After the aircraft has reached the 35 foot height with one engine inoperative, there is a requirement that it be able to climb at a specified climb gradient. This is known as the takeoff flightpath requirement. The aircraft's performance must be considered based upon a one-engine inoperative climb up to 1,500 feet above the ground. The takeoff flightpath profile with required gradients of climb for the various segments and configurations is shown in Figure 10-36.

NOTE: Climb gradient can best be described as being a specific gain of vertical height for a given distance covered horizontally. For instance, a 2.4 percent gradient means that 24 feet of altitude would be gained for each 1,000 feet of distance covered horizontally across the ground.

The following brief explanation of the one-engine inoperative climb profile may be helpful in understanding the chart in Figure 10-36.

First Segment

This segment is included in the takeoff runway required charts, and is measured from the point at which the aircraft becomes airborne until it reaches the 35-foot height at the end of the runway distance required. Speed initially is V_{LO} and must be V_2 at the 35 foot height.

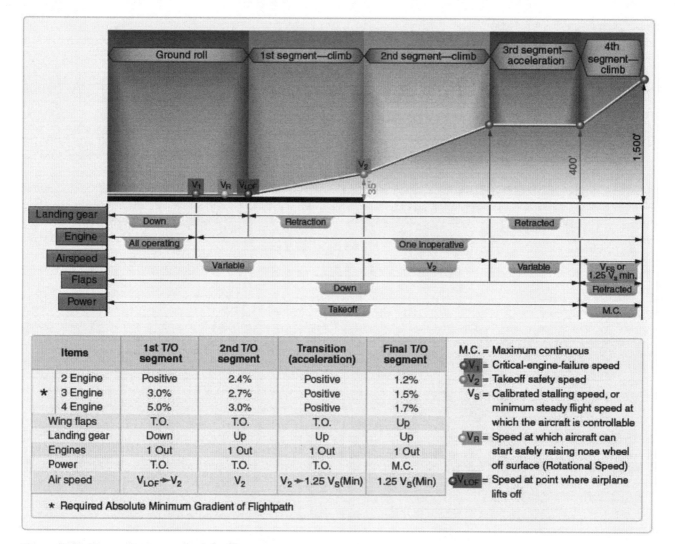

Items		1st T/O segment	2nd T/O segment	Transition (acceleration)	Final T/O segment
	2 Engine	Positive	2.4%	Positive	1.2%
★	3 Engine	3.0%	2.7%	Positive	1.5%
	4 Engine	5.0%	3.0%	Positive	1.7%
	Wing flaps	T.O.	T.O.	T.O.	Up
	Landing gear	Down	Up	Up	Up
	Engines	1 Out	1 Out	1 Out	1 Out
	Power	T.O.	T.O.	T.O.	M.C.
	Air speed	$V_{LOF} \rightarrow V_2$	V_2	$V_2 \rightarrow 1.25\,V_S$(Min)	$1.25\,V_S$(Min)

★ Required Absolute Minimum Gradient of Flightpath

M.C. = Maximum continuous
V_1 = Critical-engine-failure speed
V_2 = Takeoff safety speed
V_S = Calibrated stalling speed, or minimum steady flight speed at which the aircraft is controllable
V_R = Speed at which aircraft can start safely raising nose wheel off surface (Rotational Speed)
V_{LOF} = Speed at point where airplane lifts off

Figure 10-36. One engine inoperative takeoff.

Second Segment

This is the most critical segment of the profile. The second segment is the climb from the 35 foot height to 400 feet above the ground. The climb is done at full takeoff power on the operating engine(s), at V_2 speed, and with the flaps in the takeoff configuration. The required climb gradient in this segment is 2.4 percent for two-engine aircraft, 2.7 percent for three-engine aircraft, and 3.0 percent for four-engine aircraft.

Third or Acceleration Segment

During this segment, the airplane is considered to be maintaining the 400 feet above the ground and accelerating from the V_2 speed to the V_{FS} speed before the climb profile is continued. The flaps are raised at the beginning of the acceleration segment and power is maintained at the takeoff setting as long as possible (5 minutes maximum).

Fourth or Final Segment

This segment is from the 400 to 1,500 foot AGL altitude with power set at maximum continuous. The required climb in this segment is a gradient of 1.2 percent for two-engine airplanes, 1.55 for three-engine airplanes, and 1.7 percent for four-engine airplanes.

Second Segment Climb Limitations

The second segment climb requirements, from 35 to 400 feet, are the most restrictive (or hardest to meet) of the climb segments. The pilot must determine that the second segment climb is met for each takeoff. In order to achieve this performance at the higher density altitude conditions, it may be necessary to limit the takeoff weight of the aircraft.

It must be realized that, regardless of the actual available length of the takeoff runway, takeoff weight must be adjusted so that the second segment climb requirements can be met. The aircraft may well be capable of lifting off with one engine inoperative, but it must then be able to climb and clear obstacles. Although second segment climb may not present much of a problem at the lower altitudes, at the higher altitude airports and higher temperatures, the second segment climb chart should be consulted to determine the effects on maximum takeoff weights before figuring takeoff runway distance required.

Air Carrier Obstacle Clearance Requirements

Regulations require that large transport category turbine powered aircraft certificated after September 30, 1958, be taken off at a weight that allows a net takeoff flightpath (one engine inoperative) that clears all obstacles either by a height of at least 35 feet vertically, or by at least 200 feet horizontally within the airport boundaries and by at least 300 feet horizontally after passing the boundaries. The takeoff flightpath is considered to begin 35 feet above the takeoff surface at the end of the takeoff distance, and extends to a point in the takeoff at which the aircraft is 1,500 feet above the takeoff surface, or at which the transition from the takeoff to the en route configuration is completed. The net takeoff flightpath is the actual takeoff flightpath reduced at each point by 0.8 percent for two engine aircraft, 0.9 percent for three-engine aircraft, and 1.0 percent for four-engine aircraft.

Air carrier pilots therefore are responsible not only for determining that there is enough runway available for an engine inoperative takeoff (balanced field length), and the ability to meet required climb gradients; but they must also assure that the aircraft will safely be able to clear any obstacles that may be in the takeoff flightpath. The net takeoff flightpath and obstacle clearance required are shown in *Figure 10-37*.

Figure 10-37. *Takeoff obstacle clearance.*

The usual method of computing net takeoff flightpath performance is to add up the total ground distances required for each of the climb segments and/or use obstacle clearance performance charts in the AFM. Although this obstacle clearance requirement is seldom a limitation at the normally used airports, it is quite often an important consideration under critical conditions such as high takeoff weight and/or high density altitude. Consider that at a 2.4 percent climb gradient (2.4 feet up for every 100 feet forward) a 1,500 foot altitude gain would take a horizontal distance of 10.4 NM to achieve.

Summary of Takeoff Requirements

In order to establish the allowable takeoff weight for a transport category aircraft, at any airfield, the following must be considered:

- Airfield pressure altitude
- Temperature
- Headwind component
- Runway length
- Runway gradient or slope
- Obstacles in the flightpath

Once the above details are known and applied to the appropriate performance charts, it is possible to determine the maximum allowable takeoff weight. This weight would be the lower of the maximum weights as allowed by:

- Balanced field length required
- Engine inoperative climb ability (second segment limited)
- Obstacle clearance requirement

In practice, restrictions to takeoff weight at low altitude airports are usually due to runway length limitations; engine inoperative climb limitations are most common at the higher altitude airports. All limitations to weight must be observed. Since the combined weight of fuel and payload in the aircraft may amount to nearly half the maximum takeoff weight, it is usually possible to reduce fuel weight to meet takeoff limitations. If this is done, however, flight planning must be recalculated in light of reduced fuel and range.

Landing Performance

As in the takeoff planning, certain speeds must be considered during landing. These speeds are shown below.

- V_{SO}—stalling speed or the minimum steady flight speed in the landing configuration.

- V_{REF}—1.3 times the stalling speed in the landing configuration. This is the required speed at the 50-foot height above the threshold end of the runway.

- Approach climb—the speed which gives the best climb performance in the approach confguration, with one engine inoperative, and with maximum takeoff power on the operating engine(s). The required gradient of climb in this configuration is 2.1 percent for two-engine aircraft, 2.4 percent for three-emgine aircraft, and 2.7 percent for four-engine aircraft.

- Landing climb—the speed giving the best performance in the full landing configuration with maximum takeoff power on all engines. The gradient of climb required in this configuration is 3.2 percent.

Planning the Landing

As in the takeoff, the landing speeds shown above should be precomputed and visible to both pilots prior to the landing. The V_{REF} speed, or threshold speed, is used as a reference speed throughout the traffic pattern or instrument approach as in the following example:

V_{REF} plus 30K	Downwind or procedure turn
V_{REF} plus 20K	Base leg or final course inbound to final fix
V_{REF} plus 10K	Final or final course inbound from fix (ILS final)
V_{REF}	Speed at the 50 foot height above the threshold

Landing Requirements

The maximum landing weight of an aircraft can be restricted by either the approach climb requirements or by the landing runway available.

Approach Climb Requirements

The approach climb is usually more limiting (or more difficult to meet) than the landing climb, primarily because it is based upon the ability to execute a missed approach with one engine inoperative. The required climb gradient can be affected by pressure altitude and temperature and, as in the second segment climb in the takeoff, aircraft weight must be limited as needed in order to comply with this climb requirement.

Landing Runway Required

The runway distance needed for landing can be affected by the following:

- Pressure altitude
- Temperature
- Headwind component
- Runway gradient or slope
- Aircraft weight

In computing the landing distance required, some manufacturers do not include all of the above items in their charts, since the regulations state that only pressure altitude, wind, and aircraft weight must be considered. Charts are provided for anti-skid on and anti-skid off conditions, but the use of reverse thrust is not used in computing required landing distances.

The landing distance, as required by the regulations, is that distance needed to land and come to a complete stop from a point 50 feet above the threshold end of the runway. It includes the air distance required to travel from the 50 foot height to touchdown (which can consume 1,000 feet of runway distance), plus the stopping distance, with no margin left over. This is all that is required for 14 CFR part 91 operators (non-air carrier), and all that is shown on some landing distance required charts.

For air carriers and other commercial operators subject to 14 CFR part 121, a different set of rules applies stating that the required landing distance from the 50 foot height cannot exceed 60 percent of the actual runway length available. In all cases, the minimum airspeed allowed at the 50 foot height must be no less than 1.3 times the aircraft's stalling speed in the landing configuration. This speed is commonly called the aircraft's V_{REF} speed and varies with landing weight. *Figure 10-38* is a diagram of these landing runway requirements.

Summary of Landing Requirements

In order to establish the allowable landing weight for a transport category aircraft, the following details must be considered:

- Airfield pressure altitude
- Temperature
- Headwind component
- Runway length
- Runway gradient or slope
- Runway surface condition

With these details, it is possible to establish the maximum allowable landing weight, which will be the lower of the weights as dictated by:

- Landing runway requirements
- Approach climb requirements

In practice, the approach climb limitations (ability to climb in approach configuration with one engine inoperative) are seldom encountered because the landing weights upon arrival at the destination airport are usually low. However, as in the second segment climb requirement for takeoff, this approach climb gradient must be met and landing weights must be restricted if necessary. The most likely conditions that would make the approach climb critical would be the landings at high weights and high pressure altitudes and temperatures, which might be encountered if a landing were required shortly after takeoff.

Landing field requirements can more frequently limit an aircraft's allowable landing weight than the approach climb limitations. Again, however, unless the runway is particularly short, this is seldom problematical as the average landing weight at the destination rarely approaches the maximum design landing weight due to fuel burn off.

Figure 10-38. *Landing runway requirements.*

Chapter Summary

Performance characteristics and capabilities vary greatly among aircraft. Moreover, aircraft weight, atmospheric conditions, and external environmental factors can significantly affect aircraft performance. It is essential that a pilot become intimately familiar with the performance characteristics and capabilities of the aircraft being flown. The primary source of this information is the AFM/POH.

Chapter II

Weather Theory

Introduction

Weather is an important factor that influences aircraft performance and flying safety. It is the state of the atmosphere at a given time and place, with respect to variables such as temperature (heat or cold), moisture (wetness or dryness), wind velocity (calm or storm), visibility (clearness or cloudiness), and barometric pressure (high or low). The term weather can also apply to adverse or destructive atmospheric conditions, such as high winds.

This chapter explains basic weather theory and offers pilots background knowledge of weather principles. It is designed to help them gain a good understanding of how weather affects daily flying activities. Understanding the theories behind weather helps a pilot make sound weather decisions based on the reports and forecasts obtained from a Flight Service Station (FSS) weather specialist and other aviation weather services.

Be it a local flight or a long cross-country flight, decisions based on weather can dramatically affect the safety of the flight.

Atmosphere

The atmosphere is a blanket of air made up of a mixture of gases that surrounds the Earth and reaches almost 350 miles from the surface of the Earth. This mixture is in constant motion. If the atmosphere were visible, it might look like an ocean with swirls and eddies, rising and falling air, and waves that travel for great distances.

Life on Earth is supported by the atmosphere, solar energy, and the planet's magnetic fields. The atmosphere absorbs energy from the Sun, recycles water and other chemicals, and works with the electrical and magnetic forces to provide a moderate climate. The atmosphere also protects life on Earth from high energy radiation and the frigid vacuum of space.

Composition of the Atmosphere

In any given volume of air, nitrogen accounts for 78 percent of the gases that comprise the atmosphere, while oxygen makes up 21 percent. Argon, carbon dioxide, and traces of other gases make up the remaining one percent. This cubic foot also contains some water vapor, varying from zero to about five percent by volume. This small amount of water vapor is responsible for major changes in the weather. *[Figure 11-1]*

The envelope of gases surrounding the Earth changes from the ground up. Four distinct layers or spheres of the atmosphere have been identified using thermal characteristics

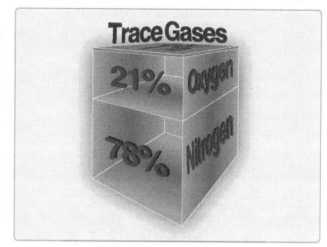

Figure 11-1. *Composition of the atmosphere.*

(temperature changes), chemical composition, movement, and density. *[Figure 11-2]*

The first layer, known as the troposphere, extends from sea level up to 20,000 feet (8 kilometers (km)) over the northern and southern poles and up to 48,000 feet (14.5 km) over the equatorial regions. The vast majority of weather, clouds, storms, and temperature variances occur within this first layer of the atmosphere. Inside the troposphere, the temperature decreases at a rate of about 2 °Celsius (C) every 1,000 feet of altitude gain, and the pressure decreases at a rate of about one inch per 1,000 feet of altitude gain.

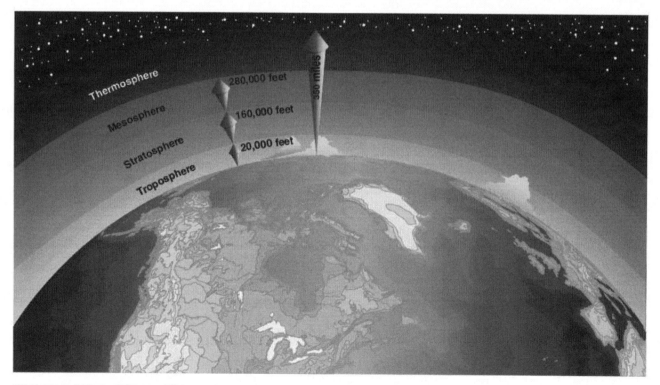

Figure 11-2. *Layers of the atmosphere.*

At the top of the troposphere is a boundary known as the tropopause, which traps moisture and the associated weather in the troposphere. The altitude of the tropopause varies with latitude and with the season of the year; therefore, it takes on an elliptical shape, as opposed to round. Location of the tropopause is important because it is commonly associated with the location of the jet stream and possible clear air turbulence.

Above the tropopause are three more atmospheric levels. The first is the stratosphere, which extends from the tropopause to a height of about 160,000 feet (50 km). Little weather exists in this layer and the air remains stable although certain types of clouds occasionally extend in it. Above the stratosphere are the mesosphere and thermosphere which have little influence over weather.

Atmospheric Circulation

As noted earlier, the atmosphere is in constant motion. Certain factors combine to set the atmosphere in motion, but a major factor is the uneven heating of the Earth's surface. This heating upsets the equilibrium of the atmosphere, creating changes in air movement and atmospheric pressure. The movement of air around the surface of the Earth is called atmospheric circulation.

Heating of the Earth's surface is accomplished by several processes, but in the simple convection-only model used for this discussion, the Earth is warmed by energy radiating from the sun. The process causes a circular motion that results when warm air rises and is replaced by cooler air.

Warm air rises because heat causes air molecules to spread apart. As the air expands, it becomes less dense and lighter than the surrounding air. As air cools, the molecules pack together more closely, becoming denser and heavier than warm air. As a result, cool, heavy air tends to sink and replace warmer, rising air.

Because the Earth has a curved surface that rotates on a tilted axis while orbiting the sun, the equatorial regions of the Earth receive a greater amount of heat from the sun than the polar regions. The amount of sun that heats the Earth depends on the time of year and the latitude of the specific region. All of these factors affect the length of time and the angle at which sunlight strikes the surface.

Solar heating causes higher temperatures in equatorial areas which causes the air to be less dense and rise. As the warm air flows toward the poles, it cools, becoming denser, and sinks back toward the surface. *[Figure 11-3]*

Figure 11-3. *Circulation pattern in a static environment.*

Atmospheric Pressure

The unequal heating of the Earth's surface not only modifies air density and creates circulation patterns; it also causes changes in air pressure or the force exerted by the weight of air molecules. Although air molecules are invisible, they still have weight and take up space.

Imagine a sealed column of air that has a footprint of one square inch and is 350 miles high. It would take 14.7 pounds of effort to lift that column. This represents the air's weight; if the column is shortened, the pressure exerted at the bottom (and its weight) would be less.

The weight of the shortened column of air at 18,000 feet is approximately 7.4 pounds; almost 50 percent that at sea level. For instance, if a bathroom scale (calibrated for sea level) were raised to 18,000 feet, the column of air weighing 14.7 pounds at sea level would be 18,000 feet shorter, and would weigh approximately 7.3 pounds (50 percent) less than at sea level. *[Figure 11-4]*

The actual pressure at a given place and time differs with altitude, temperature, and density of the air. These conditions also affect aircraft performance, especially with regard to takeoff, rate of climb, and landings.

Coriolis Force

In general atmospheric circulation theory, areas of low pressure exist over the equatorial regions and areas of high pressure exist over the polar regions due to a difference in temperature. The resulting low pressure allows the high-pressure air at the poles to flow along the planet's surface

Figure 11-4. *Atmosphere weights.*

Figure 11-5. *Three-cell circulation pattern due to the rotation of the Earth.*

toward the equator. While this pattern of air circulation is correct in theory, the circulation of air is modified by several forces, the most important of which is the rotation of the Earth.

The force created by the rotation of the Earth is known as the Coriolis force. This force is not perceptible to humans as they walk around because humans move slowly and travel relatively short distances compared to the size and rotation rate of the Earth. However, the Coriolis force significantly affects bodies that move over great distances, such as an air mass or body of water.

The Coriolis force deflects air to the right in the Northern Hemisphere, causing it to follow a curved path instead of a straight line. The amount of deflection differs depending on the latitude. It is greatest at the poles, and diminishes to zero at the equator. The magnitude of Coriolis force also differs with the speed of the moving body—the greater the speed, the greater the deviation. In the Northern Hemisphere, the rotation of the Earth deflects moving air to the right and changes the general circulation pattern of the air.

The speed of the Earth's rotation causes the general flow to break up into three distinct cells in each hemisphere. *[Figure 11-5]* In the Northern Hemisphere, the warm air at the equator rises upward from the surface, travels northward, and is deflected eastward by the rotation of the Earth. By the time it has traveled one-third of the distance from the equator to the North Pole, it is no longer moving northward, but eastward. This air cools and sinks in a belt-like area at

about 30° latitude, creating an area of high pressure as it sinks toward the surface. Then, it flows southward along the surface back toward the equator. Coriolis force bends the flow to the right, thus creating the northeasterly trade winds that prevail from 30° latitude to the equator. Similar forces create circulation cells that encircle the Earth between 30° and 60° latitude, and between 60° and the poles. This circulation pattern results in the prevailing westerly winds in the conterminous United States.

Circulation patterns are further complicated by seasonal changes, differences between the surfaces of continents and oceans, and other factors such as frictional forces caused by the topography of the Earth's surface which modify the movement of the air in the atmosphere. For example, within 2,000 feet of the ground, the friction between the surface and the atmosphere slows the moving air. The wind is diverted from its path because the frictional force reduces the Coriolis force. Thus, the wind direction at the surface varies somewhat from the wind direction just a few thousand feet above the Earth.

Measurement of Atmosphere Pressure

Atmospheric pressure is typically measured in inches of mercury ("Hg) by a mercurial barometer. *[Figure 11-6]* The barometer measures the height of a column of mercury inside a glass tube. A section of the mercury is exposed to the pressure of the atmosphere, which exerts a force on the mercury. An increase in pressure forces the mercury to rise inside the tube. When the pressure drops, mercury drains out of the tube, decreasing the height of the column. This type of barometer is typically used in a laboratory or weather observation station, is not easily transported, and difficult to read.

At sea level in a standard atmosphere, the weight of the atmosphere (14.7 lb/in²) supports a column of mercury 29.92 inches high.

Height of mercury 29.92" (760 mm)

Atmospheric pressure

Sea level

29.92 "Hg = 1,013.2 mb (hPa) = 14.7 lb/in²

Figure 11-6. *Mercurial barometer.*

An aneroid barometer is an alternative to a mercurial barometer; it is easier to read and transport. *[Figure 11-7]* The aneroid barometer contains a closed vessel, called an aneroid cell that contracts or expands with changes in pressure. The aneroid cell attaches to a pressure indicator with a mechanical linkage to provide pressure readings. The pressure sensing part of an aircraft altimeter is essentially an aneroid barometer. It is important to note that due to the linkage mechanism of an aneroid barometer, it is not as accurate as a mercurial barometer.

Atmospheric pressure

Higher

Lower

Sealed aneroid cell
Sealed aneroid cell
Sealed aneroid cell

Figure 11-7. *Aneroid barometer.*

To provide a common reference, the International Standard Atmosphere (ISA) has been established. These standard conditions are the basis for certain flight instruments and most aircraft performance data. Standard sea level pressure is defined as 29.92 "Hg and a standard temperature of 59 °F (15 °C). Atmospheric pressure is also reported in millibars (mb), with 1 "Hg equal to approximately 34 mb. Standard sea level pressure is 1,013.2 mb. Typical mb pressure readings range from 950.0 to 1,040.0 mb. Constant pressure charts and hurricane pressure reports are written using mb.

Since weather stations are located around the globe, all local barometric pressure readings are converted to a sea level pressure to provide a standard for records and reports. To achieve this, each station converts its barometric pressure by adding approximately 1 "Hg for every 1,000 feet of elevation. For example, a station at 5,000 feet above sea level, with a reading of 24.92 "Hg, reports a sea level pressure reading of 29.92 "Hg. *[Figure 11-8]* Using common sea level pressure readings helps ensure aircraft altimeters are set correctly, based on the current pressure readings.

By tracking barometric pressure trends across a large area, weather forecasters can more accurately predict movement of pressure systems and the associated weather. For example, tracking a pattern of rising pressure at a single weather station generally indicates the approach of fair weather. Conversely, decreasing or rapidly falling pressure usually indicates approaching bad weather and, possibly, severe storms.

Altitude and Atmospheric Pressure

As altitude increases, atmospheric pressure decreases. On average, with every 1,000 feet of increase in altitude, the atmospheric pressure decreases 1 "Hg. As pressure decreases, the air becomes less dense or "thinner." This is the equivalent of being at a higher altitude and is referred to as density altitude (DA). As pressure decreases, DA increases and has a pronounced effect on aircraft performance.

Differences in air density caused by changes in temperature result in a change in pressure. This, in turn, creates motion in the atmosphere, both vertically and horizontally, in the form of currents and wind. The atmosphere is almost constantly in motion as it strives to reach equilibrium. These never-ending air movements set up chain reactions which cause a continuing variety in the weather.

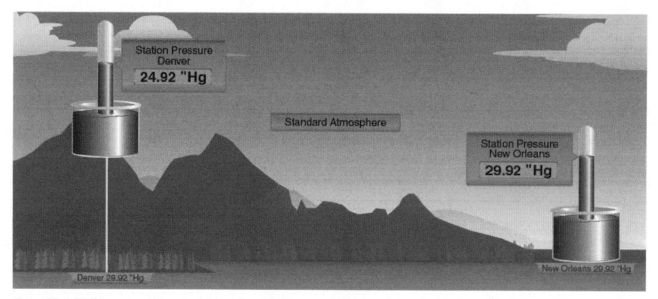

Figure 11-8. *Station pressure is converted to and reported in sea level pressure.*

Altitude and Flight

Altitude affects every aspect of flight from aircraft performance to human performance. At higher altitudes, with a decreased atmospheric pressure, takeoff and landing distances are increased, as are climb rates.

When an aircraft takes off, lift must be developed by the flow of air around the wings. If the air is thin, more speed is required to obtain enough lift for takeoff; therefore, the ground run is longer. An aircraft that requires 745 feet of ground run at sea level requires more than double that at a pressure altitude of 8,000 feet. *[Figure 11-9]*. It is also true that at higher altitudes, due to the decreased density of the air, aircraft engines and propellers are less efficient. This leads to reduced rates of climb and a greater ground run for obstacle clearance.

Altitude and the Human Body

As discussed earlier, nitrogen and other trace gases make up 79 percent of the atmosphere, while the remaining 21

TAKEOFF DISTANCE
MAXIMUM WEIGHT 2,400 LB

Pressure altitude (feet)	0 °C	
	Ground roll (feet)	Total feet to clear 50 foot obstacle
S.L.	745	1,320
1,000	815	1,445
2,000	895	1,585
3,000	980	1,740
4,000	1,075	1,920
5,000	1,185	2,125
6,000	1,305	2,360
7,000	1,440	2,635
8,000	1,590	2,960

Figure 11-9. *Takeoff distances increase with increased altitude.*

11-6

percent is life sustaining, atmospheric oxygen. At sea level, atmospheric pressure is great enough to support normal growth, activity, and life. By 18,000 feet, the partial pressure of oxygen is reduced and adversely affects the normal activities and functions of the human body.

The reactions of the average person become impaired at an altitude of about 10,000 feet, but for some people impairment can occur at an altitude as low as 5,000 feet. The physiological reactions to hypoxia or oxygen deprivation are insidious and affect people in different ways. These symptoms range from mild disorientation to total incapacitation, depending on body tolerance and altitude. Supplemental oxygen or cabin pressurization systems help pilots fly at higher altitudes and overcome the effects of oxygen deprivation.

Wind and Currents

Air flows from areas of high pressure into areas of low pressure because air always seeks out lower pressure. Air pressure, temperature changes, and the Coriolis force work in combination to create two kinds of motion in the atmosphere—vertical movement of ascending and descending currents, and horizontal movement in the form of wind. Currents and winds are important as they affect takeoff, landing, and cruise flight operations. Most importantly, currents and winds or atmospheric circulation cause weather changes.

Wind Patterns

In the Northern Hemisphere, the flow of air from areas of high to low pressure is deflected to the right and produces a clockwise circulation around an area of high pressure. This is known as anticyclonic circulation. The opposite is true of low-pressure areas; the air flows toward a low and is deflected to create a counterclockwise or cyclonic circulation. *[Figure 11-10]*

High pressure systems are generally areas of dry, stable, descending air. Good weather is typically associated with high pressure systems for this reason. Conversely, air flows into a low pressure area to replace rising air. This air tends to be unstable, and usually brings increasing cloudiness and precipitation. Thus, bad weather is commonly associated with areas of low pressure.

A good understanding of high and low pressure wind patterns can be of great help when planning a flight, because a pilot can take advantage of beneficial tailwinds. *[Figure 11-11]* When planning a flight from west to east, favorable winds would be encountered along the northern side of a high pressure system or the southern side of a low pressure system. On the return flight, the most favorable winds would be along the southern side of the same high pressure system or the northern side of a low pressure system. An added advantage

Figure 11-10. *Circulation pattern about areas of high and low pressure.*

is a better understanding of what type of weather to expect in a given area along a route of flight based on the prevailing areas of highs and lows.

While the theory of circulation and wind patterns is accurate for large scale atmospheric circulation, it does not take into account changes to the circulation on a local scale. Local conditions, geological features, and other anomalies can change the wind direction and speed close to the Earth's surface.

Convective Currents

Different surfaces radiate heat in varying amounts. Plowed ground, rocks, sand, and barren land give off a large amount of heat; water, trees, and other areas of vegetation tend to absorb and retain heat. The resulting uneven heating of the air creates small areas of local circulation called convective currents.

Convective currents cause the bumpy, turbulent air sometimes experienced when flying at lower altitudes during warmer weather. On a low altitude flight over varying surfaces, updrafts are likely to occur over pavement or barren places, and downdrafts often occur over water or expansive areas of vegetation like a group of trees. Typically, these turbulent conditions can be avoided by flying at higher altitudes, even above cumulus cloud layers. *[Figure 11-12]*

Convective currents are particularly noticeable in areas with a land mass directly adjacent to a large body of water, such as an ocean, large lake, or other appreciable area of water. During the day, land heats faster than water, so the air over the land becomes warmer and less dense. It rises and is replaced

Figure 11-11. *Favorable winds near a high pressure system.*

Figure 11-12. *Convective turbulence avoidance.*

by cooler, denser air flowing in from over the water. This causes an onshore wind, called a sea breeze. Conversely, at night land cools faster than water, as does the corresponding air. In this case, the warmer air over the water rises and is replaced by the cooler, denser air from the land, creating an offshore wind called a land breeze. This reverses the local wind circulation pattern. Convective currents can occur anywhere there is an uneven heating of the Earth's surface. *[Figure 11-13]*

Convective currents close to the ground can affect a pilot's ability to control the aircraft. For example, on final approach, the rising air from terrain devoid of vegetation sometimes produces a ballooning effect that can cause a pilot to overshoot the intended landing spot. On the other hand, an approach over a large body of water or an area of thick vegetation tends to create a sinking effect that can cause an unwary pilot to land short of the intended landing spot. *[Figure 11-14]*

Effect of Obstructions on Wind

Another atmospheric hazard exists that can create problems for pilots. Obstructions on the ground affect the flow of wind and can be an unseen danger. Ground topography and large buildings can break up the flow of the wind and create wind gusts that change rapidly in direction and speed. These obstructions range from manmade structures like hangars to large natural obstructions, such as mountains, bluffs, or canyons. It is especially important to be vigilant when flying in or out of airports that have large buildings or natural obstructions located near the runway. *[Figure 11-15]*

The intensity of the turbulence associated with ground obstructions depends on the size of the obstacle and the primary velocity of the wind. This can affect the takeoff and landing performance of any aircraft and can present a very serious hazard. During the landing phase of flight, an aircraft

Figure 11-13. *Sea breeze and land breeze wind circulation patterns.*

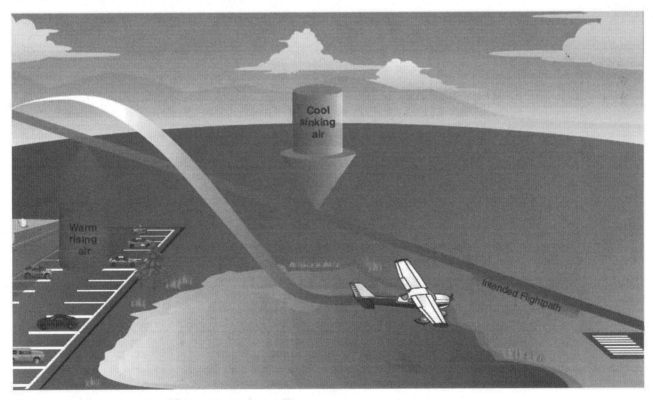

Figure 11-14. *Currents generated by varying surface conditions.*

Figure 11-15. *Turbulence caused by manmade obstructions.*

may "drop in" due to the turbulent air and be too low to clear obstacles during the approach.

This same condition is even more noticeable when flying in mountainous regions. *[Figure 11-16]* While the wind flows smoothly up the windward side of the mountain and the upward currents help to carry an aircraft over the peak of the mountain, the wind on the leeward side does not act in a similar manner. As the air flows down the leeward side of the mountain, the air follows the contour of the terrain and is increasingly turbulent. This tends to push an aircraft into the side of a mountain. The stronger the wind, the greater the downward pressure and turbulence become.

Due to the effect terrain has on the wind in valleys or canyons, downdrafts can be severe. Before conducting a flight in or near mountainous terrain, it is helpful for a pilot unfamiliar with a mountainous area to get a checkout with a mountain qualified flight instructor.

Figure 11-16. *Turbulence in mountainous regions.*

Low-Level Wind Shear

Wind shear is a sudden, drastic change in wind speed and/or direction over a very small area. Wind shear can subject an aircraft to violent updrafts and downdrafts, as well as abrupt changes to the horizontal movement of the aircraft. While wind shear can occur at any altitude, low-level wind shear is especially hazardous due to the proximity of an aircraft to the ground. Directional wind changes of 180° and speed changes of 50 knots or more are associated with low-level wind shear. Low-level wind shear is commonly associated with passing frontal systems, thunderstorms, and temperature inversions with strong upper level winds (greater than 25 knots).

Wind shear is dangerous to an aircraft for several reasons. The rapid changes in wind direction and velocity change the wind's relation to the aircraft disrupting the normal flight attitude and performance of the aircraft. During a wind shear situation, the effects can be subtle or very dramatic depending on wind speed and direction of change. For example, a tailwind that quickly changes to a headwind causes an increase in airspeed and performance. Conversely, when a headwind changes to a tailwind, the airspeed rapidly decreases and there is a corresponding decrease in performance. In either case, a pilot must be prepared to react immediately to the changes to maintain control of the aircraft.

In general, the most severe type of low-level wind shear is associated with convective precipitation or rain from thunderstorms. One critical type of shear associated with convective precipitation is known as a microburst. A typical microburst occurs in a space of less than one mile horizontally and within 1,000 feet vertically. The lifespan of a microburst is about 15 minutes during which it can produce downdrafts of up to 6,000 feet per minute (fpm). It can also produce a hazardous wind direction change of 45 degrees or more, in a matter of seconds.

When encountered close to the ground, these excessive downdrafts and rapid changes in wind direction can produce a situation in which it is difficult to control the aircraft. *[Figure 11-17]* During an inadvertent takeoff into a microburst, the plane first experiences a performance-increasing headwind (1), followed by performance-decreasing downdrafts (2). Then, the wind rapidly shears to a tailwind (3), and can result in terrain impact or flight dangerously close to the ground (4).

Microbursts are often difficult to detect because they occur in relatively confined areas. In an effort to warn pilots of low-level wind shear, alert systems have been installed at several airports around the country. A series of anemometers, placed around the airport, form a net to detect changes in wind speeds. When wind speeds differ by more than 15 knots, a warning for wind shear is given to pilots. This system is known as the low-level wind shear alert system (LLWAS).

It is important to remember that wind shear can affect any flight and any pilot at any altitude. While wind shear may be reported, it often remains undetected and is a silent danger to aviation. Always be alert to the possibility of wind shear, especially when flying in and around thunderstorms and frontal systems.

Wind and Pressure Representation on Surface Weather Maps

Surface weather maps provide information about fronts, areas of high and low pressure, and surface winds and pressures for each station. This type of weather map allows pilots to

Figure 11-17. *Effects of a microburst wind.*

see the locations of fronts and pressure systems, but more importantly, it depicts the wind and pressure at the surface for each location. For more information on surface analysis and weather depiction charts, see Chapter 12, Weather Aviation Services.

Wind conditions are reported by an arrow attached to the station location circle. *[Figure 11-18]* The station circle represents the head of the arrow, with the arrow pointing in the direction from which the wind is blowing. Winds are described by the direction from which they blow, thus a northwest wind means that the wind is blowing from the northwest toward the southeast. The speed of the wind is depicted by barbs or pennants placed on the wind line. Each barb represents a speed of ten knots, while half a barb is equal to five knots, and a pennant is equal to 50 knots.

Figure 11-18. *Depiction of winds on a surface weather chart.*

The pressure for each station is recorded on the weather chart and is shown in mb. Isobars are lines drawn on the chart to depict areas of equal pressure. These lines result in a pattern that reveals the pressure gradient or change in pressure over distance. *[Figure 11-19]* Isobars are similar to contour lines on a topographic map that indicate terrain altitudes and slope steepness. For example, isobars that are closely spaced indicate a steep wind gradient and strong winds prevail. Shallow gradients, on the other hand, are represented by isobars that are spaced far apart, and are indicative of light winds. Isobars help identify low and high pressure systems as well as the location of ridges, troughs, and cut-off lows (cols). A high is an area of high pressure surrounded by lower pressure; a low is an area of low pressure surrounded by higher pressure. A ridge is an elongated area of high pressure, and a trough is an elongated area of low pressure. A col is the intersection between a ridge and a trough, or an area of neutrality between two highs or two lows.

Isobars furnish valuable information about winds in the first few thousand feet above the surface. Close to the ground, wind direction is modified by the surface and wind speed decreases due to friction with the surface. At levels 2,000 to

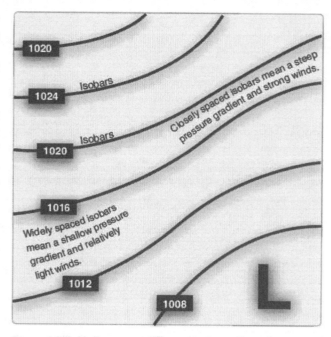

Figure 11-19. *Isobars reveal the pressure gradient of an area of high- or low-pressure areas.*

3,000 feet above the surface, however, the speed is greater and the direction becomes more parallel to the isobars. Therefore, the surface winds are shown on the weather map, as well as the winds at a slightly higher altitude.

Generally, the wind 2,000 feet above ground level (AGL) is 20° to 40° to the right of surface winds, and the wind speed is greater. The change of wind direction is greatest over rough terrain and least over flat surfaces, such as open water. In the absence of winds aloft information, this rule of thumb allows for a rough estimate of the wind conditions a few thousand feet above the surface.

Atmospheric Stability

The stability of the atmosphere depends on its ability to resist vertical motion. A stable atmosphere makes vertical movement difficult, and small vertical disturbances dampen out and disappear. In an unstable atmosphere, small vertical air movements tend to become larger, resulting in turbulent airflow and convective activity. Instability can lead to significant turbulence, extensive vertical clouds, and severe weather.

Rising air expands and cools due to the decrease in air pressure as altitude increases. The opposite is true of descending air; as atmospheric pressure increases, the temperature of descending air increases as it is compressed. Adiabatic heating and adiabatic cooling are terms used to describe this temperature change.

The adiabatic process takes place in all upward and downward moving air. When air rises into an area of lower pressure, it expands to a larger volume. As the molecules of air expand, the temperature of the air lowers. As a result, when a parcel of air rises, pressure decreases, volume increases, and temperature decreases. When air descends, the opposite is true. The rate at which temperature decreases with an increase in altitude is referred to as its lapse rate. As air ascends through the atmosphere, the average rate of temperature change is 2 °C (3.5 °F) per 1,000 feet.

Since water vapor is lighter than air, moisture decreases air density, causing it to rise. Conversely, as moisture decreases, air becomes denser and tends to sink. Since moist air cools at a slower rate, it is generally less stable than dry air since the moist air must rise higher before its temperature cools to that of the surrounding air. The dry adiabatic lapse rate (unsaturated air) is 3 °C (5.4 °F) per 1,000 feet. The moist adiabatic lapse rate varies from 1.1 °C to 2.8 °C (2 °F to 5 °F) per 1,000 feet.

The combination of moisture and temperature determine the stability of the air and the resulting weather. Cool, dry air is very stable and resists vertical movement, which leads to good and generally clear weather. The greatest instability occurs when the air is moist and warm, as it is in the tropical regions in the summer. Typically, thunderstorms appear on a daily basis in these regions due to the instability of the surrounding air.

Inversion

As air rises and expands in the atmosphere, the temperature decreases. There is an atmospheric anomaly that can occur; however, that changes this typical pattern of atmospheric behavior. When the temperature of the air rises with altitude, a temperature inversion exists. Inversion layers are commonly shallow layers of smooth, stable air close to the ground. The temperature of the air increases with altitude to a certain point, which is the top of the inversion. The air at the top of the layer acts as a lid, keeping weather and pollutants trapped below. If the relative humidity of the air is high, it can contribute to the formation of clouds, fog, haze, or smoke, resulting in diminished visibility in the inversion layer.

Surface based temperature inversions occur on clear, cool nights when the air close to the ground is cooled by the lowering temperature of the ground. The air within a few hundred feet of the surface becomes cooler than the air above it. Frontal inversions occur when warm air spreads over a layer of cooler air, or cooler air is forced under a layer of warmer air.

Moisture and Temperature

The atmosphere, by nature, contains moisture in the form of water vapor. The amount of moisture present in the atmosphere is dependent upon the temperature of the air. Every 20 °F increase in temperature doubles the amount of moisture the air can hold. Conversely, a decrease of 20 °F cuts the capacity in half.

Water is present in the atmosphere in three states: liquid, solid, and gaseous. All three forms can readily change to another, and all are present within the temperature ranges of the atmosphere. As water changes from one state to another, an exchange of heat takes place. These changes occur through the processes of evaporation, sublimation, condensation, deposition, melting, or freezing. However, water vapor is added into the atmosphere only by the processes of evaporation and sublimation.

Evaporation is the changing of liquid water to water vapor. As water vapor forms, it absorbs heat from the nearest available source. This heat exchange is known as the latent heat of evaporation. A good example is the evaporation of human perspiration. The net effect is a cooling sensation as heat is extracted from the body. Similarly, sublimation is the changing of ice directly to water vapor, completely bypassing the liquid stage. Though dry ice is not made of water, but rather carbon dioxide, it demonstrates the principle of sublimation, when a solid turns directly into vapor.

Relative Humidity

Humidity refers to the amount of water vapor present in the atmosphere at a given time. Relative humidity is the actual amount of moisture in the air compared to the total amount of moisture the air could hold at that temperature. For example, if the current relative humidity is 65 percent, the air is holding 65 percent of the total amount of moisture that it is capable of holding at that temperature and pressure. While much of the western United States rarely sees days of high humidity, relative humidity readings of 75 to 90 percent are not uncommon in the southern United States during warmer months. *[Figure 11-20]*

Temperature/Dew Point Relationship

The relationship between dew point and temperature defines the concept of relative humidity. The dew point, given in degrees, is the temperature at which the air can hold no more moisture. When the temperature of the air is reduced to the dew point, the air is completely saturated and moisture begins to condense out of the air in the form of fog, dew, frost, clouds, rain, hail, or snow.

At sea level pressure, air can hold

9 g H₂O/cubic foot of air at 10 °C
17 g H₂O/cubic foot of air at 20 °C
30 g H₂O/cubic foot of air at 30 °C

If the temperature is lowered to 10 °C, the air can hold only 9 g of water vapor, and 8 g of water will condense as water droplets. The relative humidity will still be at 100%.

A cubic foot of air with 17 grams (g) of water vapor at 20 °C is at saturation, or 100% relative humidity. Any further cooling will cause condensation (fog, clouds, dew) to form. Thus, 20 °C is the dewpoint for this situation.

If the same cubic foot of air warms to 30 °C, the 17 g of water vapor will produce a relative humidity of 56%. (17 g is 56% of the 30 g the air could hold at this temperature.)

Figure 11-20. *Relationship between relative humidity, temperature, and dewpoint.*

As moist, unstable air rises, clouds often form at the altitude where temperature and dew point reach the same value. When lifted, unsaturated air cools at a rate of 5.4 °F per 1,000 feet and the dew point temperature decreases at a rate of 1 °F per 1,000 feet. This results in a convergence of temperature and dew point at a rate of 4.4 °F. Apply the convergence rate to the reported temperature and dew point to determine the height of the cloud base.

Given:

Temperature (T) = 85 °F

Dew point (DP) = 71 °F

Convergence Rate (CR) = 4.4°

T – DP = Temperature Dew Point Spread (TDS)

TDS ÷ CR = X

X × 1,000 feet = height of cloud base AGL

Example:

85 °F–71 °F = 14 °F

14 °F ÷ 4.4 °F = 3.18

3.18 × 1,000 = 3,180 feet AGL

The height of the cloud base is 3,180 feet AGL.

Explanation:

With an outside air temperature (OAT) of 85 °F at the surface, and dew point at the surface of 71 °F, the spread is 14°. Divide the temperature dew point spread by the convergence rate of 4.4 °F, and multiply by 1,000 to determine the approximate height of the cloud base.

Methods by Which Air Reaches the Saturation Point

If air reaches the saturation point while temperature and dew point are close together, it is highly likely that fog, low clouds, and precipitation will form. There are four methods by which air can reach the complete saturation point. First, when warm air moves over a cold surface, the air temperature drops and reaches the saturation point. Second, the saturation point may be reached when cold air and warm air mix. Third, when air cools at night through contact with the cooler ground, air reaches its saturation point. The fourth method occurs when air is lifted or is forced upward in the atmosphere.

As air rises, it uses heat energy to expand. As a result, the rising air loses heat rapidly. Unsaturated air loses heat at a rate of 3.0 °C (5.4 °F) for every 1,000 feet of altitude gain. No matter what causes the air to reach its saturation point, saturated air brings clouds, rain, and other critical weather situations.

Dew and Frost

On cool, calm nights, the temperature of the ground and objects on the surface can cause temperatures of the surrounding air to drop below the dew point. When this occurs, the moisture in the air condenses and deposits itself on the ground, buildings, and other objects like cars and aircraft. This moisture is known as dew and sometimes can be seen on grass in the morning. If the temperature is below freezing, the moisture is deposited in the form of frost. While dew poses no threat to an aircraft, frost poses a definite flight safety hazard. Frost disrupts the flow of air over the wing and can drastically reduce the production of lift. It also increases drag, which, when combined with lowered lift production, can adversely affect the ability to take off. An aircraft must be thoroughly cleaned and free of frost prior to beginning a flight.

Fog

Fog is a cloud that begins within 50 feet of the surface. It typically occurs when the temperature of air near the ground is cooled to the air's dew point. At this point, water vapor in the air condenses and becomes visible in the form of fog. Fog is classified according to the manner in which it forms and is dependent upon the current temperature and the amount of water vapor in the air.

On clear nights, with relatively little to no wind present, radiation fog may develop. *[Figure 11-21]* Usually, it forms in low-lying areas like mountain valleys. This type of fog occurs when the ground cools rapidly due to terrestrial radiation, and the surrounding air temperature reaches its dew point. As the sun rises and the temperature increases, radiation fog lifts and eventually burns off. Any increase in wind also speeds the dissipation of radiation fog. If radiation fog is less than 20 feet thick, it is known as ground fog.

When a layer of warm, moist air moves over a cold surface, advection fog is likely to occur. Unlike radiation fog, wind is required to form advection fog. Winds of up to 15 knots allow the fog to form and intensify; above a speed of 15 knots, the fog usually lifts and forms low stratus clouds. Advection fog is common in coastal areas where sea breezes can blow the air over cooler landmasses.

Upslope fog occurs when moist, stable air is forced up sloping land features like a mountain range. This type of fog also requires wind for formation and continued existence. Upslope and advection fog, unlike radiation fog, may not burn off with the morning sun, but instead can persist for days. They can also extend to greater heights than radiation fog.

Steam fog, or sea smoke, forms when cold, dry air moves over warm water. As the water evaporates, it rises and resembles smoke. This type of fog is common over bodies of water during the coldest times of the year. Low-level turbulence and icing are commonly associated with steam fog.

Ice fog occurs in cold weather when the temperature is much below freezing and water vapor forms directly into ice crystals. Conditions favorable for its formation are the same as for radiation fog except for cold temperature, usually –25 °F or colder. It occurs mostly in the arctic regions, but is not unknown in middle latitudes during the cold season.

Clouds

Clouds are visible indicators and are often indicative of future weather. For clouds to form, there must be adequate water vapor and condensation nuclei, as well as a method by which the air can be cooled. When the air cools and reaches its saturation point, the invisible water vapor changes into a visible state. Through the processes of deposition (also referred to as sublimation) and condensation, moisture condenses or sublimates onto miniscule particles of matter like dust, salt, and smoke known as condensation nuclei. The nuclei are important because they provide a means for the moisture to change from one state to another.

Cloud type is determined by its height, shape, and behavior. They are classified according to the height of their bases as low, middle, or high clouds, as well as clouds with vertical development. *[Figure 11-22]*

Low clouds are those that form near the Earth's surface and extend up to 6,500 feet AGL. They are made primarily of water droplets, but can include supercooled water droplets that induce hazardous aircraft icing. Typical low clouds are stratus, stratocumulus, and nimbostratus. Fog is also classified as a type of low cloud formation. Clouds in this family create low ceilings, hamper visibility, and can change rapidly. Because of this, they influence flight planning and can make visual flight rules (VFR) flight impossible.

Figure 11-21. *Radiation fog.*

Figure 11-22. *Basic cloud types.*

Middle clouds form around 6,500 feet AGL and extend up to 20,000 feet AGL. They are composed of water, ice crystals, and supercooled water droplets. Typical middle-level clouds include altostratus and altocumulus. These types of clouds may be encountered on cross-country flights at higher altitudes. Altostratus clouds can produce turbulence and may contain moderate icing. Altocumulus clouds, which usually form when altostratus clouds are breaking apart, also may contain light turbulence and icing.

High clouds form above 20,000 feet AGL and usually form only in stable air. They are made up of ice crystals and pose no real threat of turbulence or aircraft icing. Typical high level clouds are cirrus, cirrostratus, and cirrocumulus.

Clouds with extensive vertical development are cumulus clouds that build vertically into towering cumulus or cumulonimbus clouds. The bases of these clouds form in the low to middle cloud base region but can extend into high altitude cloud levels. Towering cumulus clouds indicate areas of instability in the atmosphere, and the air around and inside them is turbulent. These types of clouds often develop into cumulonimbus clouds or thunderstorms. Cumulonimbus clouds contain large amounts of moisture and unstable air, and usually produce hazardous weather phenomena, such as lightning, hail, tornadoes, gusty winds, and wind shear. These extensive vertical clouds can be obscured by other cloud formations and are not always visible from the ground or while in flight. When this happens, these clouds are said to be embedded, hence the term, embedded thunderstorms.

To pilots, the cumulonimbus cloud is perhaps the most dangerous cloud type. It appears individually or in groups and is known as either an air mass or orographic thunderstorm. Heating of the air near the Earth's surface creates an air mass thunderstorm; the upslope motion of air in the mountainous regions causes orographic thunderstorms. Cumulonimbus clouds that form in a continuous line are nonfrontal bands of thunderstorms or squall lines.

Since rising air currents cause cumulonimbus clouds, they are extremely turbulent and pose a significant hazard to flight safety. For example, if an aircraft enters a thunderstorm, the aircraft could experience updrafts and downdrafts that exceed 3,000 fpm. In addition, thunderstorms can produce large hailstones, damaging lightning, tornadoes, and large quantities of water, all of which are potentially hazardous to aircraft.

A thunderstorm makes its way through three distinct stages before dissipating. It begins with the cumulus stage, in which lifting action of the air begins. If sufficient moisture and instability are present, the clouds continue to increase in vertical height. Continuous, strong updrafts prohibit moisture from falling. The updraft region grows larger than the individual thermals feeding the storm. Within approximately 15 minutes, the thunderstorm reaches the mature stage, which is the most violent time period of the thunderstorm's life cycle. At this point, drops of moisture, whether rain or ice, are too heavy for the cloud to support and begin falling in the form of rain or hail. This creates a downward motion of the air. Warm, rising air; cool, precipitation-induced descending air; and violent turbulence all exist within and near the cloud. Below the cloud, the down-rushing air increases surface winds and decreases the temperature. Once the vertical motion near the top of the cloud slows down, the top of the cloud spreads out and takes on an anvil-like shape. At this point, the storm enters the dissipating stage. This is when the downdrafts spread out and replace the updrafts needed to sustain the storm. *[Figure 11-23]*

It is impossible to fly over thunderstorms in light aircraft. Severe thunderstorms can punch through the tropopause and reach staggering heights of 50,000 to 60,000 feet depending on latitude. Flying under thunderstorms can subject aircraft to rain, hail, damaging lightning, and violent turbulence. A good rule of thumb is to circumnavigate thunderstorms identified as severe or giving an intense radar echo by at least 20 nautical miles (NM) since hail may fall for miles

outside of the clouds. If flying around a thunderstorm is not an option, stay on the ground until it passes.

Cloud classification can be further broken down into specific cloud types according to the outward appearance and cloud composition. Knowing these terms can help a pilot identify visible clouds.

The following is a list of cloud classifications:

- Cumulus—heaped or piled clouds
- Stratus—formed in layers
- Cirrus—ringlets, fibrous clouds, also high level clouds above 20,000 feet
- Castellanus—common base with separate vertical development, castle-like
- Lenticularus—lens shaped, formed over mountains in strong winds
- Nimbus—rain-bearing clouds
- Fracto—ragged or broken
- Alto—meaning high, also middle level clouds existing at 5,000 to 20,000 feet

Ceiling
For aviation purposes, a ceiling is the lowest layer of clouds reported as being broken or overcast, or the vertical visibility into an obscuration like fog or haze. Clouds are reported

Figure 11-23. *Life cycle of a thunderstorm.*

as broken when five-eighths to seven-eighths of the sky is covered with clouds. Overcast means the entire sky is covered with clouds. Current ceiling information is reported by the aviation routine weather report (METAR) and automated weather stations of various types.

Visibility

Closely related to cloud cover and reported ceilings is visibility information. Visibility refers to the greatest horizontal distance at which prominent objects can be viewed with the naked eye. Current visibility is also reported in METAR and other aviation weather reports, as well as by automated weather systems. Visibility information, as predicted by meteorologists, is available for a pilot during a preflight weather briefing.

Precipitation

Precipitation refers to any type of water particles that form in the atmosphere and fall to the ground. It has a profound impact on flight safety. Depending on the form of precipitation, it can reduce visibility, create icing situations, and affect landing and takeoff performance of an aircraft.

Precipitation occurs because water or ice particles in clouds grow in size until the atmosphere can no longer support them. It can occur in several forms as it falls toward the Earth, including drizzle, rain, ice pellets, hail, snow, and ice.

Drizzle is classified as very small water droplets, smaller than 0.02 inches in diameter. Drizzle usually accompanies fog or low stratus clouds. Water droplets of larger size are referred to as rain. Rain that falls through the atmosphere but evaporates prior to striking the ground is known as virga. Freezing rain and freezing drizzle occur when the temperature of the surface is below freezing; the rain freezes on contact with the cooler surface.

If rain falls through a temperature inversion, it may freeze as it passes through the underlying cold air and fall to the ground in the form of ice pellets. Ice pellets are an indication of a temperature inversion and that freezing rain exists at a higher altitude. In the case of hail, freezing water droplets are carried up and down by drafts inside clouds, growing larger in size as they come in contact with more moisture. Once the updrafts can no longer hold the freezing water, it falls to the Earth in the form of hail. Hail can be pea sized, or it can grow as large as five inches in diameter, larger than a softball.

Snow is precipitation in the form of ice crystals that falls at a steady rate or in snow showers that begin, change in intensity, and end rapidly. Falling snow also varies in size, being very small grains or large flakes. Snow grains are the equivalent of drizzle in size.

Precipitation in any form poses a threat to safety of flight. Often, precipitation is accompanied by low ceilings and reduced visibility. Aircraft that have ice, snow, or frost on their surfaces must be carefully cleaned prior to beginning a flight because of the possible airflow disruption and loss of lift. Rain can contribute to water in the fuel tanks. Precipitation can create hazards on the runway surface itself, making takeoffs and landings difficult, if not impossible, due to snow, ice, or pooling water and very slick surfaces.

Air Masses

Air masses are classified according to the regions where they originate. They are large bodies of air that take on the characteristics of the surrounding area, or source region. A source region is typically an area in which the air remains relatively stagnant for a period of days or longer. During this time of stagnation, the air mass takes on the temperature and moisture characteristics of the source region. Areas of stagnation can be found in polar regions, tropical oceans, and dry deserts. Air masses are generally identified as polar or tropical based on temperature characteristics and maritime or continental based on moisture content.

A continental polar air mass forms over a polar region and brings cool, dry air with it. Maritime tropical air masses form over warm tropical waters like the Caribbean Sea and bring warm, moist air. As the air mass moves from its source region and passes over land or water, the air mass is subjected to the varying conditions of the land or water, and these modify the nature of the air mass. *[Figure 11-24]*

An air mass passing over a warmer surface is warmed from below, and convective currents form, causing the air to rise. This creates an unstable air mass with good surface visibility. Moist, unstable air causes cumulus clouds, showers, and turbulence to form.

Conversely, an air mass passing over a colder surface does not form convective currents, but instead creates a stable air mass with poor surface visibility. The poor surface visibility is due to the fact that smoke, dust, and other particles cannot rise out of the air mass and are instead trapped near the surface. A stable air mass can produce low stratus clouds and fog.

Fronts

As an air mass moves across bodies of water and land, it eventually comes in contact with another air mass with different characteristics. The boundary layer between two types of air masses is known as a front. An approaching front of any type always means changes to the weather are imminent.

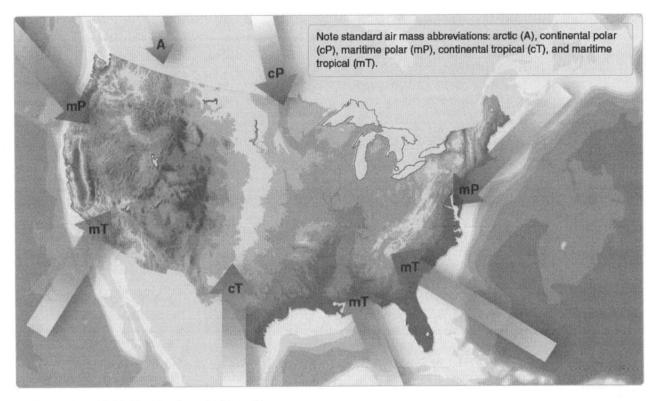

Figure 11-24. *North American air mass source regions.*

There are four types of fronts, which are named according to the temperature of the advancing air relative to the temperature of the air it is replacing: *[Figure 11-25]*

- Warm
- Cold
- Stationary
- Occluded

Any discussion of frontal systems must be tempered with the knowledge that no two fronts are the same. However, generalized weather conditions are associated with a specific type of front that helps identify the front.

Symbols for surface fronts and other significant lines shown on the surface analysis chart

Warm front (red)*

Cold front (blue)*

Stationary front (red/blue)*

Occluded front (purple)*

* Note: Fronts may be black and white or color, depending on their source. Also, fronts shown in color code will not necessarily show frontal symbols.

Figure 11-25. *Common chart symbology to depict weather front location.*

Warm Front

A warm front occurs when a warm mass of air advances and replaces a body of colder air. Warm fronts move slowly, typically 10 to 25 miles per hour (mph). The slope of the advancing front slides over the top of the cooler air and gradually pushes it out of the area. Warm fronts contain warm air that often have very high humidity. As the warm air is lifted, the temperature drops and condensation occurs.

Generally, prior to the passage of a warm front, cirriform or stratiform clouds, along with fog, can be expected to form along the frontal boundary. In the summer months, cumulonimbus clouds (thunderstorms) are likely to develop. Light to moderate precipitation is probable, usually in the form of rain, sleet, snow, or drizzle, accentuated by poor visibility. The wind blows from the south-southeast, and the outside temperature is cool or cold, with an increasing dew point. Finally, as the warm front approaches, the barometric pressure continues to fall until the front passes completely.

During the passage of a warm front, stratiform clouds are visible and drizzle may be falling. The visibility is generally poor, but improves with variable winds. The temperature rises steadily from the inflow of relatively warmer air. For the most part, the dew point remains steady and the pressure levels off.

After the passage of a warm front, stratocumulus clouds predominate and rain showers are possible. The visibility eventually improves, but hazy conditions may exist for a short period after passage. The wind blows from the south-southwest. With warming temperatures, the dew point rises and then levels off. There is generally a slight rise in barometric pressure, followed by a decrease of barometric pressure.

Flight Toward an Approaching Warm Front

By studying a typical warm front, much can be learned about the general patterns and atmospheric conditions that exist when a warm front is encountered in flight. *Figure 11-26* depicts a warm front advancing eastward from St. Louis, Missouri, toward Pittsburgh, Pennsylvania.

At the time of departure from Pittsburgh, the weather is good VFR with a scattered layer of cirrus clouds at 15,000 feet. As the flight progresses westward to Columbus and closer to the oncoming warm front, the clouds deepen and become increasingly stratiform in appearance with a ceiling of 6,000 feet. The visibility decreases to six miles in haze with a falling barometric pressure. Approaching Indianapolis, the weather deteriorates to broken clouds at 2,000 feet with three miles visibility and rain. With the temperature and dew

point the same, fog is likely. At St. Louis, the sky is overcast with low clouds and drizzle and the visibility is one mile. Beyond Indianapolis, the ceiling and visibility would be too low to continue VFR. Therefore, it would be wise to remain in Indianapolis until the warm front had passed, which might require a day or two.

Cold Front

A cold front occurs when a mass of cold, dense, and stable air advances and replaces a body of warmer air.

Cold fronts move more rapidly than warm fronts, progressing at a rate of 25 to 30 mph. However, extreme cold fronts have been recorded moving at speeds of up to 60 mph. A typical cold front moves in a manner opposite that of a warm front. It is so dense, it stays close to the ground and acts like a snowplow, sliding under the warmer air and forcing the less dense air aloft. The rapidly ascending air causes the temperature to decrease suddenly, forcing the creation of clouds. The type of clouds that form depends on the stability of the warmer air mass. A cold front in the Northern Hemisphere is normally oriented in a northeast to southwest manner and can be several hundred miles long, encompassing a large area of land.

Figure 11-26. *Warm front cross-section with surface weather chart depiction and associated METAR.*

Prior to the passage of a typical cold front, cirriform or towering cumulus clouds are present, and cumulonimbus clouds are possible. Rain showers and haze are possible due to the rapid development of clouds. The wind from the south-southwest helps to replace the warm temperatures with the relative colder air. A high dew point and falling barometric pressure are indicative of imminent cold front passage.

As the cold front passes, towering cumulus or cumulonimbus clouds continue to dominate the sky. Depending on the intensity of the cold front, heavy rain showers form and might be accompanied by lightning, thunder, and/or hail. More severe cold fronts can also produce tornadoes. During cold front passage, the visibility is poor, with winds variable and gusty, and the temperature and dew point drop rapidly. A quickly falling barometric pressure bottoms out during frontal passage, then begins a gradual increase.

After frontal passage, the towering cumulus and cumulonimbus clouds begin to dissipate to cumulus clouds with a corresponding decrease in the precipitation. Good visibility eventually prevails with the winds from the west-northwest. Temperatures remain cooler and the barometric pressure continues to rise.

Fast-Moving Cold Front

Fast-moving cold fronts are pushed by intense pressure systems far behind the actual front. The friction between the ground and the cold front retards the movement of the front and creates a steeper frontal surface. This results in a very narrow band of weather, concentrated along the leading edge of the front. If the warm air being overtaken by the cold front is relatively stable, overcast skies and rain may occur for some distance ahead of the front. If the warm air is unstable, scattered thunderstorms and rain showers may form. A continuous line of thunderstorms, or squall line, may form along or ahead of the front. Squall lines present a serious hazard to pilots as squall type thunderstorms are intense and move quickly. Behind a fast-moving cold front, the skies usually clear rapidly and the front leaves behind gusty, turbulent winds and colder temperatures.

Flight Toward an Approaching Cold Front

Like warm fronts, not all cold fronts are the same. Examining a flight toward an approaching cold front, pilots can get a better understanding of the type of conditions that can be encountered in flight. *Figure 11-27* shows a flight from Pittsburgh, Pennsylvania, toward St. Louis, Missouri.

Figure 11-27. *Cold front cross-section with surface weather chart depiction and associated METAR.*

At the time of departure from Pittsburgh, the weather is VFR with three miles visibility in smoke and a scattered layer of clouds at 3,500 feet. As the flight progresses westward to Columbus and closer to the oncoming cold front, the clouds show signs of vertical development with a broken layer at 2,500 feet. The visibility is six miles in haze with a falling barometric pressure. Approaching Indianapolis, the weather has deteriorated to overcast clouds at 1,000 feet, and three miles visibility with thunderstorms and heavy rain showers. At St. Louis, the weather gets better with scattered clouds at 1,000 feet and a ten mile visibility.

A pilot using sound judgment based on the knowledge of frontal conditions would most likely remain in Indianapolis until the front had passed. Trying to fly below a line of thunderstorms or a squall line is hazardous, and flight over the top of or around the storm is not an option. Thunderstorms can extend up to well over the capability of small airplanes and can extend in a line for 300 to 500 miles.

Comparison of Cold and Warm Fronts

Warm fronts and cold fronts are very different in nature as are the hazards associated with each front. They vary in speed, composition, weather phenomenon, and prediction. Cold fronts, which move at 20 to 35 mph, move very quickly in comparison to warm fronts, which move at only 10 to 25 mph. Cold fronts also possess a steeper frontal slope. Violent weather activity is associated with cold fronts, and the weather usually occurs along the frontal boundary, not in advance. However, squall lines can form during the summer months as far as 200 miles in advance of a severe cold front. Whereas warm fronts bring low ceilings, poor visibility, and rain, cold fronts bring sudden storms, gusty winds, turbulence, and sometimes hail or tornadoes.

Cold fronts are fast approaching with little or no warning, and they make a complete weather change in just a few hours. The weather clears rapidly after passage and drier air with unlimited visibilities prevail. Warm fronts, on the other hand, provide advance warning of their approach and can take days to pass through a region.

Wind Shifts

Wind around a high pressure system rotates in a clockwise fashion, while low pressure winds rotate in a counter-clockwise manner. When two pressure systems are adjacent, the winds are almost in direct opposition to each other at the point of contact. Fronts are the boundaries between two areas of pressure, and therefore, wind shifts are continually occurring within a front. Shifting wind direction is most pronounced in conjunction with cold fronts.

Stationary Front

When the forces of two air masses are relatively equal, the boundary or front that separates them remains stationary and influences the local weather for days. This front is called a stationary front. The weather associated with a stationary front is typically a mixture that can be found in both warm and cold fronts.

Occluded Front

An occluded front occurs when a fast-moving cold front catches up with a slow-moving warm front. As the occluded front approaches, warm front weather prevails, but is immediately followed by cold front weather. There are two types of occluded fronts that can occur, and the temperatures of the colliding frontal systems play a large part in defining the type of front and the resulting weather. A cold front occlusion occurs when a fast moving cold front is colder than the air ahead of the slow moving warm front. When this occurs, the cold air replaces the cool air and forces the warm front aloft into the atmosphere. Typically, the cold front occlusion creates a mixture of weather found in both warm and cold fronts, providing the air is relatively stable. A warm front occlusion occurs when the air ahead of the warm front is colder than the air of the cold front. When this is the case, the cold front rides up and over the warm front. If the air forced aloft by the warm front occlusion is unstable, the weather is more severe than the weather found in a cold front occlusion. Embedded thunderstorms, rain, and fog are likely to occur.

Figure 11-28 depicts a cross-section of a typical cold front occlusion. The warm front slopes over the prevailing cooler air and produces the warm front type weather. Prior to the passage of the typical occluded front, cirriform and stratiform clouds prevail, light to heavy precipitation is falling, visibility is poor, dew point is steady, and barometric pressure is falling. During the passage of the front, nimbostratus and cumulonimbus clouds predominate, and towering cumulus may also be possible. Light to heavy precipitation is falling, visibility is poor, winds are variable, and the barometric pressure is leveling off. After the passage of the front, nimbostratus and altostratus clouds are visible, precipitation is decreasing and clearing, and visibility is improving.

Thunderstorms

For a thunderstorm to form, the air must have sufficient water vapor, an unstable lapse rate, and an initial lifting action to start the storm process. Some storms occur at random in unstable air, last for only an hour or two, and produce only moderate wind gusts and rainfall. These are known as air

Figure 11-28. *Occluded front cross-section with a weather chart depiction and associated METAR.*

mass thunderstorms and are generally a result of surface heating. Steady-state thunderstorms are associated with weather systems. Fronts, converging winds, and troughs aloft force upward motion spawning these storms which often form into squall lines. In the mature stage, updrafts become stronger and last much longer than in air mass storms, hence the name steady state. *[Figure 11-29]*

Knowledge of thunderstorms and the hazards associated with them is critical to the safety of flight.

Hazards

Weather can pose serious hazards to flight and a thunderstorm packs just about every weather hazard known to aviation into one vicious bundle. These hazards occur individually or in combinations and most can be found in a squall line.

Squall Line

A squall line is a narrow band of active thunderstorms. Often it develops on or ahead of a cold front in moist, unstable air, but it may develop in unstable air far removed from any front. The line may be too long to detour easily and too wide and severe to penetrate. It often contains steady-state thunderstorms and presents the single most intense weather hazard to aircraft. It usually forms rapidly, generally reaching

maximum intensity during the late afternoon and the first few hours of darkness.

Tornadoes

The most violent thunderstorms draw air into their cloud bases with great vigor. If the incoming air has any initial rotating motion, it often forms an extremely concentrated vortex from the surface well into the cloud. Meteorologists have estimated that wind in such a vortex can exceed 200 knots with pressure inside the vortex quite low. The strong winds gather dust and debris and the low pressure generates a funnel-shaped cloud extending downward from the cumulonimbus base. If the cloud does not reach the surface, it is a funnel cloud; if it touches a land surface, it is a tornado.

Tornadoes occur with both isolated and squall line thunderstorms. Reports for forecasts of tornadoes indicate that atmospheric conditions are favorable for violent turbulence. An aircraft entering a tornado vortex is almost certain to suffer structural damage. Since the vortex extends well into the cloud, any pilot inadvertently caught on instruments in a severe thunderstorm could encounter a hidden vortex.

Families of tornadoes have been observed as appendages of the main cloud extending several miles outward from the area

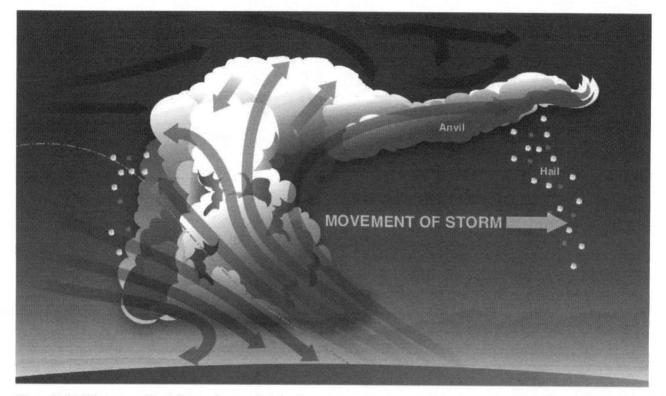

Figure 11-29. *Movement and turbulence of a maturing thunderstorm.*

of lightning and precipitation. Thus, any cloud connected to a severe thunderstorm carries a threat of violence.

Turbulence

Potentially hazardous turbulence is present in all thunderstorms, and a severe thunderstorm can destroy an aircraft. Strongest turbulence within the cloud occurs with shear between updrafts and downdrafts. Outside the cloud, shear turbulence has been encountered several thousand feet above and 20 miles laterally from a severe storm. A low-level turbulent area is the shear zone associated with the gust front. Often, a "roll cloud" on the leading edge of a storm marks the top of the eddies in this shear and it signifies an extremely turbulent zone. Gust fronts often move far ahead (up to 15 miles) of associated precipitation. The gust front causes a rapid and sometimes drastic change in surface wind ahead of an approaching storm. Advisory Circular (AC) 00-50A, Low Level Wind Shear, explains in detail the hazards associated with gust fronts. Figure 1 in the AC shows a schematic truss section of a thunderstorm with areas outside the cloud where turbulence may be encountered.

Icing

Updrafts in a thunderstorm support abundant liquid water with relatively large droplet sizes. When carried above the freezing level, the water becomes supercooled. When temperature in the upward current cools to about –15 °C, much of the remaining water vapor sublimates as ice crystals. Above this level, at lower temperatures, the amount of supercooled water decreases.

Supercooled water freezes on impact with an aircraft. Clear icing can occur at any altitude above the freezing level, but at high levels, icing from smaller droplets may be rime or mixed rime and clear ice. The abundance of large, supercooled water droplets makes clear icing very rapid between 0 °C and –15 °C and encounters can be frequent in a cluster of cells. Thunderstorm icing can be extremely hazardous.

Thunderstorms are not the only area where pilots could encounter icing conditions. Pilots should be alert for icing anytime the temperature approaches 0 °C and visible moisture is present.

Hail

Hail competes with turbulence as the greatest thunderstorm hazard to aircraft. Supercooled drops above the freezing level begin to freeze. Once a drop has frozen, other drops latch on and freeze to it, so the hailstone grows—sometimes into a huge ice ball. Large hail occurs with severe thunderstorms with strong updrafts that have built to great heights. Eventually, the hailstones fall, possibly some distance from the storm core. Hail may be encountered in clear air several miles from thunderstorm clouds.

As hailstones fall through air whose temperature is above 0 °C, they begin to melt and precipitation may reach the ground as either hail or rain. Rain at the surface does not mean the absence of hail aloft. Possible hail should be anticipated with any thunderstorm, especially beneath the anvil of a large cumulonimbus. Hailstones larger than one-half inch in diameter can significantly damage an aircraft in a few seconds.

Ceiling and Visibility

Generally, visibility is near zero within a thunderstorm cloud. Ceiling and visibility also may be restricted in precipitation and dust between the cloud base and the ground. The restrictions create the same problem as all ceiling and visibility restrictions; but the hazards are multiplied when associated with the other thunderstorm hazards of turbulence, hail, and lightning.

Effect on Altimeters

Pressure usually falls rapidly with the approach of a thunderstorm, rises sharply with the onset of the first gust and arrival of the cold downdraft and heavy rain showers, and then falls back to normal as the storm moves on. This cycle of pressure change may occur in 15 minutes. If the pilot does not receive a corrected altimeter setting, the altimeter may be more than 100 feet in error.

Lightning

A lightning strike can puncture the skin of an aircraft and damage communications and electronic navigational equipment. Although lightning has been suspected of igniting fuel vapors and causing an explosion, serious accidents due to lightning strikes are rare. Nearby lightning can blind the pilot, rendering him or her momentarily unable to navigate either by instrument or by visual reference. Nearby lightning can also induce permanent errors in the magnetic compass. Lightning discharges, even distant ones, can disrupt radio communications on low and medium frequencies. Though lightning intensity and frequency have no simple relationship to other storm parameters, severe storms, as a rule, have a high frequency of lightning.

Engine Water Ingestion

Turbine engines have a limit on the amount of water they can ingest. Updrafts are present in many thunderstorms, particularly those in the developing stages. If the updraft velocity in the thunderstorm approaches or exceeds the terminal velocity of the falling raindrops, very high concentrations of water may occur. It is possible that these concentrations can be in excess of the quantity of water turbine engines are designed to ingest. Therefore, severe thunderstorms may contain areas of high water concentration which could result in flameout and/or structural failure of one or more engines.

Chapter Summary

Knowledge of the atmosphere and the forces acting within it to create weather is essential to understand how weather affects a flight. By understanding basic weather theories, a pilot can make sound decisions during flight planning after receiving weather briefings. For additional information on the topics discussed in this chapter, see AC 00-6, Aviation Weather For Pilots and Flight Operations Personnel; AC 00-24, Thunderstorms; AC 00-45, Aviation Weather Services; AC 91-74, Pilot Guide Flight in Icing Conditions; and chapter 7, section 2 of the Aeronautical Information Manual (AIM).

Chapter 12
Aviation Weather Services

Introduction

In aviation, weather service is a combined effort of the National Weather Service (NWS), Federal Aviation Administration (FAA), Department of Defense (DOD), other aviation groups, and individuals. Because of the increasing need for worldwide weather services, foreign weather organizations also provide vital input.

While weather forecasts are not 100 percent accurate, meteorologists, through careful scientific study and computer modeling, have the ability to predict weather patterns, trends, and characteristics with increasing accuracy. Through a complex system of weather services, government agencies, and independent weather observers, pilots and other aviation professionals receive the benefit of this vast knowledge base in the form of up-to-date weather reports and forecasts. These reports and forecasts enable pilots to make informed decisions regarding weather and flight safety before and during a flight.

Observations

The data gathered from surface and upper altitude observations form the basis of all weather forecasts, advisories, and briefings. There are four types of weather observations: surface, upper air, radar, and satellite.

Surface Aviation Weather Observations

Surface aviation weather observations (METARs) are a compilation of elements of the current weather at individual ground stations across the United States. The network is made up of government and privately contracted facilities that provide continuous up-to-date weather information. Automated weather sources, such as the Automated Weather Observing Systems (AWOS), Automated Surface Observing Systems (ASOS), Air Route Traffic Control Center (ARTCC) facilities, as well as other automated facilities, also play a major role in the gathering of surface observations.

Surface observations provide local weather conditions and other relevant information for a radius of five miles of a specific airport. This information includes the type of report, station identifier, date and time, modifier (as required), wind, visibility, runway visual range (RVR), weather phenomena, sky condition, temperature/dew point, altimeter reading, and applicable remarks. The information gathered for the surface observation may be from a person, an automated station, or an automated station that is updated or enhanced by a weather observer. In any form, the surface observation provides valuable information about individual airports around the country. Although the reports cover only a small radius, the pilot can generate a good picture of the weather over a wide area when many reporting stations are looked at together.

Air Route Traffic Control Center (ARTCC)

The ARTCC facilities are responsible for maintaining separation between flights conducted under instrument flight rules (IFR) in the en route structure. Center radars (Air Route Surveillance Radar (ARSR)) acquire and track transponder returns using the same basic technology as terminal radars. Earlier center radars displayed weather as an area of slashes (light precipitation) and Hs (moderate rainfall). Because the controller could not detect higher levels of precipitation, pilots had to be wary of areas showing moderate rainfall. Newer radar displays show weather as three shades of blue. Controllers can select the level of weather to be displayed. Weather displays of higher levels of intensity make it difficult for controllers to see aircraft data blocks, so pilots should not expect air traffic control (ATC) to keep weather displayed continuously.

Upper Air Observations

Observations of upper air weather are more challenging than surface observations. There are only two methods by which upper air weather phenomena can be observed: radiosonde observations and pilot weather reports (PIREPs). A radiosonde is a small cubic instrumentation package which is suspended below a six foot hydrogen or helium filled balloon. Once released, the balloon rises at a rate of approximately 1,000 feet per minute (fpm). As it ascends, the instrumentation gathers various pieces of data such as air temperature and pressure, as well as wind speed and direction. Once the information is gathered, it is relayed to ground stations via a 300 milliwatt radio transmitter.

The balloon flight can last as long as 2 hours or more and can ascend to altitudes as high as 115,000 feet and drift as far as 125 miles. The temperatures and pressures experienced during the flight can be as low as -130 °F and pressures as low as a few thousandths of what is experienced at sea level.

Since the pressure decreases as the balloon rises in the atmosphere, the balloon expands until it reaches the limits of its elasticity. This point is reached when the diameter has increased to over 20 feet. At this point, the balloon pops and the radiosonde falls back to Earth. The descent is slowed by means of a parachute. The parachute aids in protecting people and objects on the ground. Each year over 75,000 balloons are launched. Of that number, 20 percent are recovered and returned for reconditioning. Return instructions are printed on the side of each radiosonde.

Pilots also provide vital information regarding upper air weather observations and remain the only real-time source of information regarding turbulence, icing, and cloud heights. This information is gathered and filed by pilots in flight. Together, PIREPs and radiosonde observations provide information on upper air conditions important for flight planning. Many domestic and international airlines have equipped their aircraft with instrumentation that automatically transmits inflight weather observations through the DataLink system to the airline dispatcher who disseminates the data to appropriate weather forecasting authorities.

Radar Observations

Weather observers use four types of radar to provide information about precipitation, wind, and weather systems.

1. The WSR-88D NEXRAD radar, commonly called Doppler radar, provides in-depth observations that inform surrounding communities of impending weather. Doppler radar has two operational modes: clear air and precipitation. In clear air mode, the radar is in its most sensitive operational mode because a slow antenna rotation allows the radar to sample the atmosphere longer. Images are updated about every 10 minutes in this mode.

Precipitation targets provide stronger return signals therefore the radar is operated in the Precipitation mode when precipitation is present. A faster antenna rotation in this mode allows images to update at a faster rate, approximately every 4 to 6 minutes. Intensity values in both modes are measured in dBZ (decibels of Z) and depicted in color on the radar image. *[Figure 12-1]* Intensities are correlated to intensity terminology (phraseology) for air traffic control purposes. *[Figure 12-2 and 12-3]*

Figure 12-1. *Example of a weather radar scope.*

Reflectivity (dBZ) Ranges	Weather Radar Echo Intensity
<30 dBZ	Light
30–40 dBZ	Moderate
>40–50	Heavy
50+ dBZ	Extreme

Figure 12-3. *WSR-88D Weather Radar Precipitation Intensity Terminology.*

3. The third type of radar commonly used in the detection of precipitation is the FAA airport surveillance radar. This radar is used primarily to detect aircraft, but it also detects the location and intensity of precipitation which is used to route aircraft traffic around severe weather in an airport environment.

4. Airborne radar is equipment carried by aircraft to locate weather disturbances. The airborne radars generally operate in the C or X bands (around 6 GHz or around 10 GHz, respectively) permitting both penetration of heavy precipitation, required for determining the extent of thunderstorms, and sufficient reflection from less intense precipitation.

Satellite

Advancement in satellite technologies has recently allowed for commercial use to include weather uplinks. Through the use of satellite subscription services, individuals are now able to receive satellite transmitted signals that provide near real-time weather information for the North American continent.

Satellite Weather

Recently private enterprise and satellite technology have expanded the realm of weather services. Pilots now have the capability of receiving continuously updated weather across the entire country at any altitude. No longer are pilots restricted by radio range or geographic isolations such as mountains or valleys.

In addition, pilots no longer have to request specific information from weather briefing personnel directly. When the weather becomes questionable, radio congestion often increases, delaying the timely exchange of valuable inflight weather updates for a pilot's specific route of flight. Flight Service Station (FSS) personnel can communicate with only one pilot at a time, which leaves other pilots waiting and flying in uncertain weather conditions. Satellite weather provides the pilot with a powerful resource for enhanced situational awareness at any time. Due to continuous satellite broadcasts, pilots can obtain a weather briefing by looking at a display screen. Pilots have a choice between FAA-certified devices or portable receivers as a source of weather data.

Clean Air Mode	Precipitation Mode
DBZ	DBZ
+28	75
+24	70
+20	65
+16	60
+12	55
+8	50
+4	45
0	40
-4	35
-8	30
-12	25
-16	20
-20	15
-24	10
-28	5
ND	ND

Figure 12-2. *WSR-88D Weather Radar Echo Intensity Legend.*

2. FAA terminal doppler weather radar (TDWR), installed at some major airports around the country, also aids in providing severe weather alerts and warnings to ATC. Terminal radar ensures pilots are aware of wind shear, gust fronts, and heavy precipitation, all of which are dangerous to arriving and departing aircraft.

Satellite Weather Products

Significant Meteorological Information (SIGMET)

SIGMETs are weather advisories issued concerning weather significant to the safety of all aircraft. SIGMET advisories can cover an area of at least 3,000 square miles and provide data regarding severe and extreme turbulence, severe icing, and widespread dust or sandstorms that reduce visibility to less than three miles. *[Figure 12-4]*

Figure 12-4. *Satellite SIGMET.*

Airmen's Meteorological Information (AIRMET)

AIRMETs are weather advisories issued only to amend the area forecast concerning weather phenomena which are of operational interest to all aircraft and potentially hazardous to aircraft having limited capability because of lack of equipment, instrumentation, or pilot qualifications. AIRMETs concern weather of less severity than that covered by SIGMETs or convective SIGMETs. AIRMETs cover moderate icing, moderate turbulence, sustained winds of 30 knots or more at the surface, widespread areas of ceilings less than 1,000 feet and/or visibility less than three miles, and extensive mountain obscurement. *[Figure 12-5]*

Figure 12-5. *Satellite AIRMET.*

Service Outlets

Service outlets are government or private facilities that provide aviation weather services. Several different government agencies, including the FAA, National Oceanic and Atmospheric Administration (NOAA), and the NWS work in conjunction with private aviation companies to provide different means of accessing weather information.

Automated Flight Service Station (AFSS)

The AFSS is the primary source for preflight weather information. A preflight weather briefing from an AFSS can be obtained 24 hours a day by calling 1-800-WX BRIEF from almost anywhere in the United States. In areas not served by an AFSS, NWS facilities may provide pilot weather briefings. Telephone numbers for NWS facilities and additional numbers for AFSS can be found in the Airport/Facility Directory (A/FD) or in the United States Government section of the telephone book.

The AFSS also provides inflight weather briefing services, as well as scheduled and unscheduled weather broadcasts. An AFSS may also furnish weather advisories to flights within the AFSS region of authority.

Transcribed Information Briefing Service (TIBS)

The Transcribed Information Briefing Service (TIBS) is a service prepared and disseminated by selected AFSS. It provides continuous telephone recordings of meteorological and aeronautical information. Specifically, TIBS provides area and route briefings, airspace procedures, and special announcements. It is designed to be a preliminary briefing tool and is not intended to replace a standard briefing from a FSS specialist. The TIBS service is available 24 hours a day and is updated when conditions change, but it can only be accessed by a touchtone phone. The phone numbers for the TIBS service are listed in the A/FD.

Direct User Access Terminal Service (DUATS)

The Direct User Access Terminal Service (DUATS), which is funded by the FAA, allows any pilot with a current medical certificate to access weather information and file a flight plan via computer. Two methods of access are available to connect with DUATS. The first is via the Internet at http://www.duats.com. The second method requires a modem and a communications program supplied by a DUATS provider. To access the weather information and file a flight plan by this method, pilots use a toll free telephone number to connect the user's computer directly to the DUATS computer. The current vendors of DUATS service and the associated phone numbers are listed in Chapter 7, Safety of Flight, of the Aeronautical Information Manual (AIM).

En Route Flight Advisory Service (EFAS)

A service specifically designed to provide timely en route weather information upon pilot request is known as the en route flight advisory service (EFAS), or Flight Watch. EFAS provides a pilot with weather advisories tailored to the type of flight, route, and cruising altitude. EFAS can be one of the best sources for current weather information along the route of flight.

A pilot can usually contact an EFAS specialist from 6 a.m. to 10 p.m. anywhere in the conterminous United States and Puerto Rico. The common EFAS frequency, 122.0 MHz, is established for pilots of aircraft flying between 5,000 feet above ground level (AGL) and 17,500 feet mean sea level (MSL).

Hazardous Inflight Weather Advisory (HIWAS)

Hazardous Inflight Weather Advisory (HIWAS) is a national program for broadcasting hazardous weather information continuously over selected navigation aids (NAVAIDs). The broadcasts include advisories such as AIRMETS, SIGMETS, convective SIGMETS, and urgent PIREPs. These broadcasts are only a summary of the information, and pilots should contact a FSS or EFAS for detailed information. NAVAIDs that have HIWAS capability are depicted on sectional charts with an "H" in the upper right corner of the identification box. *[Figure 12-6]*

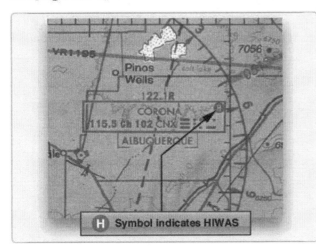

Figure 12-6. *HIWAS availability is shown on sectional chart.*

Transcribed Weather Broadcast (TWEB) (Alaska Only)

Equipment is provided in Alaska by which meteorological and aeronautical data are recorded on tapes and broadcast continuously over selected low or medium frequency (L/MF) and very high frequency (VHF) omnidirectional radio range navigation system (VOR) facilities. Broadcasts are made from a series of individual tape recordings, and changes, as they occur, are transcribed onto the tapes. The information provided varies depending on the type equipment available.

Generally, the broadcast contains a summary of adverse conditions, surface weather observations, PIREPS, and a density altitude statement (if applicable). At the discretion of the broadcast facility, recordings may also include a synopsis, winds aloft forecast, en route and terminal forecast data, and radar reports. At selected locations, telephone access to the TWEB has been provided (TEL-TWEB). Telephone numbers for this service are found in the Supplement Alaska A/FD. These broadcasts are made available primarily for preflight and inflight planning, and as such, should not be considered as a substitute for specialist-provided preflight briefings.

Weather Briefings

Prior to every flight, pilots should gather all information vital to the nature of the flight. This includes an appropriate weather briefing obtained from a specialist at a FSS, AFSS, or NWS.

For weather specialists to provide an appropriate weather briefing, they need to know which of the three types of briefings is needed—standard, abbreviated, or outlook. Other helpful information is whether the flight is visual flight rules (VFR) or IFR, aircraft identification and type, departure point, estimated time of departure (ETD), flight altitude, route of flight, destination, and estimated time en route (ETE).

This information is recorded in the flight plan system and a note is made regarding the type of weather briefing provided. If necessary, it can be referenced later to file or amend a flight plan. It is also used when an aircraft is overdue or is reported missing.

Standard Briefing

A standard briefing is the most complete report and provides the overall weather picture. This type of briefing should be obtained prior to the departure of any flight and should be used during flight planning. A standard briefing provides the following information in sequential order if it is applicable to the route of flight.

1. Adverse conditions—this includes information about adverse conditions that may influence a decision to cancel or alter the route of flight. Adverse conditions include significant weather, such as thunderstorms or aircraft icing, or other important items such as airport closings.

2. VFR flight not recommended—if the weather for the route of flight is below VFR minimums, or if it is doubtful the flight could be made under VFR conditions due to the forecast weather, the briefer may state that VFR is not recommended. It is the pilot's decision whether or not to continue the flight under VFR, but this advisory should be weighed carefully.

3. Synopsis—an overview of the larger weather picture. Fronts and major weather systems that affect the general area are provided.

4. Current conditions—this portion of the briefing contains the current ceilings, visibility, winds, and temperatures. If the departure time is more than 2 hours away, current conditions are not included in the briefing.

5. En route forecast—a summary of the weather forecast for the proposed route of flight.

6. Destination forecast—a summary of the expected weather for the destination airport at the estimated time of arrival (ETA).

7. Winds and temperatures aloft—a report of the winds at specific altitudes for the route of flight. The temperature information is provided only on request.

8. Notices to Airmen (NOTAM)—information pertinent to the route of flight which has not been published in the NOTAM publication. Published NOTAM information is provided during the briefing only when requested.

9. ATC delays—an advisory of any known ATC delays that may affect the flight.

10. Other information—at the end of the standard briefing, the FSS specialist provides the radio frequencies needed to open a flight plan and to contact EFAS. Any additional information requested is also provided at this time.

Abbreviated Briefing

An abbreviated briefing is a shortened version of the standard briefing. It should be requested when a departure has been delayed or when weather information is needed to update the previous briefing. When this is the case, the weather specialist needs to know the time and source of the previous briefing so the necessary weather information will not be omitted inadvertently. It is always a good idea to update weather whenever a pilot has additional time.

Outlook Briefing

An outlook briefing should be requested when a planned departure is 6 hours or more away. It provides initial forecast information that is limited in scope due to the timeframe of the planned flight. This type of briefing is a good source of flight planning information that can influence decisions regarding route of flight, altitude, and ultimately the go/no-go decision. A prudent pilot requests a follow-up briefing prior to departure since an outlook briefing generally only contains information based on weather trends and existing weather in geographical areas at or near the departure airport. A standard briefing near the time of departure ensures that the pilot has the latest information available prior to their flight.

Aviation Weather Reports

Aviation weather reports are designed to give accurate depictions of current weather conditions. Each report provides current information that is updated at different times. Some typical reports are METAR, PIREPs, and radar weather reports (SDs).

Aviation Routine Weather Report (METAR)

A METAR is an observation of current surface weather reported in a standard international format. While the METAR code has been adopted worldwide, each country is allowed to make modifications to the code. Normally, these differences are minor but necessary to accommodate local procedures or particular units of measure. This discussion of METAR will cover elements used in the United States.

Metars are issued hourly unless significant weather changes have occurred. A special METAR (SPECI) can be issued at any interval between routine METAR reports.

Example:
METAR KGGG 161753Z AUTO 14021G26 3/4SM +TSRA BR BKN008 OVC012CB 18/17 A2970 RMK PRESFR

A typical METAR report contains the following information in sequential order:

1. Type of report—there are two types of METAR reports. The first is the routine METAR report that is transmitted every hour. The second is the aviation selected SPECI. This is a special report that can be given at any time to update the METAR for rapidly changing weather conditions, aircraft mishaps, or other critical information.

2. Station identifier—a four-letter code as established by the International Civil Aviation Organization (ICAO). In the 48 contiguous states, a unique three-letter identifier is preceded by the letter "K." For example, Gregg County Airport in Longview, Texas, is identified by the letters "KGGG," K being the country designation and GGG being the airport identifier. In other regions of the world, including Alaska and Hawaii, the first two letters of the four-letter ICAO identifier indicate the region, country, or state. Alaska identifiers always begin with the letters "PA" and Hawaii identifiers always begin with the letters "PH." A list of station identifiers can be found at an FSS or NWS office.

3. Date and time of report—depicted in a six-digit group (161753Z). The first two digits are the date. The last four digits are the time of the METAR, which is always given in coordinated universal time (UTC). A "Z" is appended to the end of the time to denote the time is given in Zulu time (UTC) as opposed to local time.

4. Modifier—denotes that the METAR came from an automated source or that the report was corrected. If the notation "AUTO" is listed in the METAR, the report came from an automated source. It also lists "AO1" or "AO2" in the remarks section to indicate the type of precipitation sensors employed at the automated station.

   When the modifier "COR" is used, it identifies a corrected report sent out to replace an earlier report that contained an error (for example: METAR KGGG 161753Z COR).

5. Wind—reported with five digits (14021) unless the speed is greater than 99 knots, in which case the wind is reported with six digits. The first three digits indicate the direction the true wind is blowing in tens of degrees. If the wind is variable, it is reported as "VRB." The last two digits indicate the speed of the wind in knots unless the wind is greater than 99 knots, in which case it is indicated by three digits. If the winds are gusting, the letter "G" follows the wind speed (G26). After the letter "G," the peak gust recorded is provided. If the wind varies more than 60° and the wind speed is greater than six knots, a separate group of numbers, separated by a "V," will indicate the extremes of the wind directions. *Figure 12-7* shows how the TDWR/Weather System Processor (WSP) determines the true wind, as well as gust front/wind shear location.

Figure 12-7. *Example of what the controller sees on the ribbon display in the tower cab.*

6. Visibility—the prevailing visibility (¾ SM) is reported in statute miles as denoted by the letters "SM." It is reported in both miles and fractions of miles. At times, runway visual range (RVR) is reported following the

prevailing visibility. RVR is the distance a pilot can see down the runway in a moving aircraft. When RVR is reported, it is shown with an R, then the runway number followed by a slant, then the visual range in feet. For example, when the RVR is reported as R17L/1400FT, it translates to a visual range of 1,400 feet on runway 17 left.

7. Weather—can be broken down into two different categories: qualifiers and weather phenomenon (+TSRA BR). First, the qualifiers of intensity, proximity, and the descriptor of the weather will be given. The intensity may be light (-), moderate ( ), or heavy (+). Proximity only depicts weather phenomena that are in the airport vicinity. The notation "VC" indicates a specific weather phenomenon is in the vicinity of five to ten miles from the airport. Descriptors are used to describe certain types of precipitation and obscurations. Weather phenomena may be reported as being precipitation, obscurations, and other phenomena such as squalls or funnel clouds. Descriptions of weather phenomena as they begin or end, and hailstone size are also listed in the remarks sections of the report. *[Figure 12-8]*

8. Sky condition—always reported in the sequence of amount, height, and type or indefinite ceiling/ height (vertical visibility) (BKN008 OVC012CB). The heights of the cloud bases are reported with a three-digit number in hundreds of feet AGL. Clouds above 12,000 feet are not detected or reported by an automated station. The types of clouds, specifically towering cumulus (TCU) or cumulonimbus (CB) clouds, are reported with their height. Contractions are used to describe the amount of cloud coverage and obscuring phenomena. The amount of sky coverage is reported in eighths of the sky from horizon to horizon. *[Figure 12-9]*

9. Temperature and dew point—the air temperature and dew point are always given in degrees Celsius (C) or (°C 18/17). Temperatures below 0 °C are preceded by the letter "M" to indicate minus.

10. Altimeter setting—reported as inches of mercury ("Hg) in a four-digit number group (A2970). It is always preceded by the letter "A." Rising or falling pressure may also be denoted in the remarks sections as "PRESRR" or "PRESFR" respectively.

11. Zulu time—a term used in aviation for UTC which places the entire world on one time standard.

Qualifier		Weather Phenomena		
Intensity or Proximity 1	Descriptor 2	Precipitation 3	Obscuration 4	Other 5
− Light	**MI** Shallow	**DZ** Drizzle	**BR** Mist	**PO** Dust/sand whirls
Moderate (no qualifier)	**BC** Patches	**RA** Rain	**FG** Fog	**SQ** Squalls
+ Heavy	**DR** Low drifting	**SN** Snow	**FU** Smoke	**FC** Funnel cloud
VC in the vicinity	**BL** Blowing	**SG** Snow grains	**DU** Dust	**+FC** Tornado or waterspout
	SH Showers	**IC** Ice crystals (diamond dust)	**SA** Sand	**SS** Sandstorm
	TS Thunderstorms	**PL** Ice pellets	**HZ** Haze	**DS** Dust storm
	FZ Freezing	**GR** Hail	**PY** Spray	
	PR Partial	**GS** Small hail or snow pellets	**VA** Volcanic ash	
		UP *Unknown precipitation		

The weather groups are constructed by considering columns 1–5 in this table in sequence: intensity, followed by descriptor, followed by weather phenomena (e.g., heavy rain showers(s) is coded as +SHRA).
* Automated stations only

Figure 12-8. *Descriptors and weather phenomena used in a typical METAR.*

Sky Cover	Contraction
Less than ⅛ (Clear)	SKC, CLR, FEW
⅛-⅜ (Few)	FEW
⅜-½ (Scattered)	SCT
⅝-⅞ (Broken)	BKN
⅞ or (Overcast)	OVC

Figure 12-9. *Reportable contractions for sky condition.*

12. Remarks—the remarks section always begins with the letters "RMK." Comments may or may not appear in this section of the METAR. The information contained in this section may include wind data, variable visibility, beginning and ending times of particular phenomenon, pressure information, and various other information deemed necessary. An example of a remark regarding weather phenomenon that does not fit in any other category would be: OCNL LTGICCG. This translates as occasional lightning in the clouds and from cloud to ground. Automated stations also use the remarks section to indicate the equipment needs maintenance.

Example:
METAR KGGG 161753Z AUTO 14021G26 3/4SM +TSRA BR BKN008 OVC012CB 18/17 A2970 RMK PRESFR

Explanation:
Routine METAR for Gregg County Airport for the 16th day of the month at 1753Z automated source. Winds are 140 at 21 knots gusting to 26. Visibility is ¾ statute mile. Thunderstorms with heavy rain and mist. Ceiling is broken at 800 feet, overcast at 1,200 feet with cumulonimbus clouds. Temperature 18 °C and dew point 17 °C. Barometric pressure is 29.70 "Hg and falling rapidly.

Pilot Weather Reports (PIREPs)

PIREPs provide valuable information regarding the conditions as they actually exist in the air, which cannot be gathered from any other source. Pilots can confirm the height of bases and tops of clouds, locations of wind shear and turbulence, and the location of inflight icing. If the ceiling is below 5,000 feet, or visibility is at or below five miles, ATC facilities are required to solicit PIREPs from pilots in the area. When unexpected weather conditions are encountered, pilots are encouraged to make a report to a FSS or ATC. When a pilot weather report is filed, the ATC facility or FSS will add it to the distribution system to brief other pilots and provide inflight advisories.

PIREPs are easy to file and a standard reporting form outlines the manner in which they should be filed. *Figure 12-10* shows the elements of a PIREP form. Item numbers 1 through 5 are required information when making a report, as well as at least one weather phenomenon encountered. A PIREP is normally transmitted as an individual report, but may be appended to a surface report. Pilot reports are easily decoded and most contractions used in the reports are self-explanatory.

Encoding Pilot Weather Reports (PIREPS)

1	XXX	3-letter station identifier	Nearest weather reporting location to the reported phenomenon
2	UA	Routine PIREP, UUA-Urgent PIREP.	
3	/OV	Location	Use 3-letter NAVAID idents only. a. Fix: /OV ABC, /OV ABC 090025. b. Fix: /OV ABC 045020-DEF, /OV ABC-DEF-GHI
4	/TM	Time	4 digits in UTC: /TM 0915.
5	/FL	Altitude/Flight level	3 digits for hundreds of feet. If not known, use UNKN: /FL095, /FL310, /FLUNKN.
6	/TP	Type Aircraft	4 digits maximum. If not known, use UNKN: /TP L329, /TP B727, /TP UNKN.
7	/SK	Sky cover/Cloud layers	Describe as follows: a. Height of cloud base in hundreds of feet. If unknown, use UNKN. b. Cloud cover symbol. c. Height of cloud tops in hundreds of feet.
8	/WX	Weather	Flight visibility reported first: Use standard weather symbols; intensity is not reported: /WX FV02 R H, /WX FV01 TRW.
9	/TA	Air temperature in Celsius (C)	If below zero, prefix with a hyphen: /TA 15, /TA -06.
10	/WV	Wind	Direction in degrees magnetic north and speed in six digits: /WV 270045, WV 280110.
11	/TB	Turbulence	Use standard contractions for intensity and type (use CAT or CHOP when appropriate). Include altitude only if different from /FL, /TB EXTREME, /TB LGT-MDT BLO 090.
12	/IC	Icing	Describe using standard intensity and type contractions. Include altitude only if different than /FL: /IC LGT-MDT RIME, /IC SVR CLR 028-045.
13	/RM	Remarks	Use free from to clarify the report and type hazardous elements first: /RM LLWS -15KT SFC-030 DURC RNWY 22 JFK.

Figure 12-10. *PIREP encoding and decoding.*

Example:
UA/OV GGG 090025/TM 1450/FL 060/TP C182/SK 080 OVC/WX FV 04R/TA 05/WV 270030/TB LGT/RM HVY RAIN

Explanation:
Type: ....Routine pilot report
Location: ....25 NM out on the 090° radial, Gregg County VOR
Time: ....1450 Zulu
Altitude or Flight Level: 6,000 feet
Aircraft Type: ....Cessna 182
Sky Cover: ....8,000 overcast
Visibility/Weather: ....4 miles in rain
Temperature: ....5 °Celsius
Wind: ....270° at 30 knots
Turbulence: ....Light
Icing: .... None reported
Remarks: .... Rain is heavy

Radar Weather Reports (RAREP)

Areas of precipitation and thunderstorms are observed by radar on a routine basis. Radar weather reports (RAREPs) or storm detections (SDs) are issued by radar stations at 35 minutes past the hour, with special reports issued as needed.

RAREPs provide information on the type, intensity, and location of the echo top of the precipitation. *[Figure 12-11]* These reports may also include direction and speed of the area of precipitation, as well as the height and base of the precipitation in hundreds of feet MSL. RAREPs are especially valuable for preflight planning to help avoid areas of severe weather. However, radar only detects objects

Symbol	Meaning
R	Rain
RW	Rain Shower
S	Snow
SW	Snow Shower
T	Thunderstorm

Symbol	Intensity
-	Light
(none)	Moderate
+	Heavy
++	Very Heavy
x	Intense
xx	Extreme

Contraction	Operational Status
PPINE	Radar is operating normally but there are no echoes being detected.
PPINA	Radar observation is not available.
PPIOM	Radar is inoperative or out of service.
AUTO	Automated radar report from WSR-88D.

Figure 12-11. *Radar weather report codes.*

in the atmosphere that are large enough to be considered precipitation. Cloud bases and tops, ceilings, and visibility are not detected by radar.

A typical RAREP will include:

- Location identifier and time of radar observation

- Echo pattern

  1. Line (LN)—a line of precipitation echoes at least 30 miles long, at least four times as long as it is wide, and at least 25 percent coverage within the line.

  2. Area (AREA)—a group of echoes of similar type and not classified as a line.

  3. Single cell (CELL)—a single isolated convective echo such as a rain shower.

- Area coverage in tenths

- Type and intensity of weather

- Azimuth, referenced to true north and range, in nautical miles from the radar site of points defining the echo pattern. For lines and areas, there will be two azimuth and range sets that define the pattern. For cells, there will be only one azimuth and range set.

- Dimension of echo pattern—given when the azimuth and range define only the center line of the pattern.

- Cell movement—movement is coded only for cells; it will not be coded for lines or areas.

- Maximum top of precipitation and location— maximum tops may be coded with the symbols "MT" or "MTS." If it is coded with "MTS," it means that satellite data, as well as radar information was used to measure the top of the precipitation.

- If the contraction "AUTO" appears in the report, it means the report is automated from WSR-88D weather radar data.

- The last section is primarily used to prepare radar summary charts, but can be used during preflight to determine the maximum precipitation intensity within a specific grid box. The higher the number, the greater the intensity. Two or more numbers appearing after a grid box reference, such as PM34, indicates precipitation in consecutive grid boxes.

Example:
TLX 1935 LN 8 TRW++ 86/40 199/115
20W C2425 MTS 570 AT 159/65 AUTO
^MO1 NO2 ON3 PM34 QM3 RL2=

Explanation:
The radar report gives the following information: The report is automated from Oklahoma City and was made at 1935 UTC. The echo pattern for this radar report indicates a line of echos covering 8/10 of the area. Thunderstorms and very heavy rain showers are indicated. The next set of numbers indicates the azimuth that defines the echo (86° at 40 NM and 199° at 115 NM). The dimension of this echo is given as 20 NM wide (10 NM on either side of the line defined by the azimuth and range). The cells within the line are moving from 240° at 25 knots. The maximum top of the precipitation, as determined by radar and satellite, is 57,000 feet and it is located on the 159° radial, 65 NM out. The last line indicates the intensity of the precipitation, for example in grid QM the intensity is 3, or heavy precipitation. (1 is light and 6 is extreme.)

Aviation Forecasts

Observed weather condition reports are often used in the creation of forecasts for the same area. A variety of different forecast products are produced and designed to be used in the preflight planning stage. The printed forecasts that pilots need to be familiar with are the terminal aerodrome forecast (TAF), aviation area forecast (FA), inflight weather advisories (SIGMET, AIRMET), and the winds and temperatures aloft forecast (FD).

Terminal Aerodrome Forecasts (TAF)

A TAF is a report established for the five statute mile radius around an airport. TAF reports are usually given for larger airports. Each TAF is valid for a 30-hour time period, and is updated four times a day at 0000Z, 0600Z, 1200Z, and 1800Z. The TAF utilizes the same descriptors and abbreviations as used in the METAR report. The TAF includes the following information in sequential order:

1. Type of report—a TAF can be either a routine forecast (TAF) or an amended forecast (TAF AMD).

2. ICAO station identifier—the station identifier is the same as that used in a METAR.

3. Date and time of origin—time and date of TAF origination is given in the six-number code with the first two being the date, the last four being the time. Time is always given in UTC as denoted by the Z following the number group.

4. Valid period date and time—the valid forecast time period is given by a six-digit number group. The first two numbers indicate the date, followed by the two-digit beginning time for the valid period, and the last two digits are the ending time.

5. Forecast wind—the wind direction and speed forecast are given in a five-digit number group. The first three indicate the direction of the wind in reference to true north. The last two digits state the windspeed in knots as denoted by the letters "KT." Like the METAR, winds greater than 99 knots are given in three digits.

6. Forecast visibility—given in statute miles and may be in whole numbers or fractions. If the forecast is greater than six miles, it will be coded as "P6SM."

7. Forecast significant weather—weather phenomena are coded in the TAF reports in the same format as the METAR. If no significant weather is expected during the forecast time period, the denotation "NSW" is included in the "becoming" or "temporary" weather groups.

8. Forecast sky condition—given in the same manner as the METAR. Only cumulonimbus (CB) clouds are forecast in this portion of the TAF report as opposed to CBs and towering cumulus in the METAR.

9. Forecast change group—for any significant weather change forecast to occur during the TAF time period, the expected conditions and time period are included in this group. This information may be shown as from (FM), becoming (BECMG), and temporary (TEMPO). "FM" is used when a rapid and significant change, usually within an hour, is expected. "BECMG" is used when a gradual change in the weather is expected over a period of no more than 2 hours. "TEMPO" is used for temporary fluctuations of weather, expected to last less than one hour.

10. Probability forecast—a given percentage that describes the probability of thunderstorms and precipitation occurring in the coming hours. This forecast is not used for the first 6 hours of the 24-hour forecast.

Example:
TAF
KPIR 111130Z 111212 15012KT P6SM BKN090
TEMPO 1214 5SM BR
FM1500 16015G25KT P6SM SCT040 BKN250
FM0000 14012KT P6SM BKN080 OVC150 PROB40 0004
3SM TSRA BKN030CB
FM0400 1408KT P6SM SCT040 OVC080
TEMPO 0408 3SM TSRA OVC030CB
BECMG 0810 32007KT=

Explanation:
Routine TAF for Pierre, South Dakota…on the 11th day of the month, at 1130Z…valid for 24 hours from 1200Z on the 11th to 1200Z on the 12th…wind from 150° at 12 knots…visibility greater than 6 sm…broken clouds at 9,000 feet…temporarily, between 1200Z and 1400Z, visibility 5 sm in mist…from 1500Z winds from 160° at 15 knots, gusting to 25 knots visibility greater than 6 sm…clouds scattered at 4,000 feet and broken at 25,000 feet…from 0000Z wind from 140° at 12 knots…visibility greater than 6 sm…clouds broken at 8,000 feet, overcast at 15,000 feet…between 0000Z and 0400Z, there is 40 percent probability of visibility 3 sm…thunderstorm with moderate rain showers…clouds broken at 3,000 feet with cumulonimbus clouds…from 0400Z…winds from 140° at 8 knots…visibility greater than 6 miles…clouds at 4,000 scattered and overcast at 8,000…temporarily between 0400Z and 0800Z…visibility 3 miles…thunderstorms with moderate rain showers…clouds overcast at 3,000 feet with cumulonimbus clouds…becoming between 0800Z and 1000Z…wind from 320° at 7 knots…end of report (=).

Area Forecasts (FA)

The FA gives a picture of clouds, general weather conditions, and visual meteorological conditions (VMC) expected over a large area encompassing several states. There are six areas for which area forecasts are published in the contiguous 48 states. Area forecasts are issued three times a day and are valid for 18 hours. This type of forecast gives information vital to en route operations, as well as forecast information for smaller airports that do not have terminal forecasts.

Area forecasts are typically disseminated in four sections and include the following information:

1. Header—gives the location identifier of the source of the FA, the date and time of issuance, the valid forecast time, and the area of coverage.

Example:
DFWC FA 120945
SYNOPSIS AND VFR CLDS/WX
SYNOPSIS VALID UNTIL 130400
CLDS/WX VALID UNTIL 122200…OTLK VALID
122200-130400
OK TX AR LA MS AL AND CSTL WTRS

Explanation:
The area forecast shows information given by Dallas Fort Worth, for the region of Oklahoma, Texas, Arkansas, Louisiana, Mississippi, and Alabama, as well as a portion of the Gulf coastal waters. It was issued on the 12th day of the month at 0945. The synopsis is valid from the time of issuance until 0400 hours on the 13th. VFR clouds and weather information on this area forecast are valid until 2200 hours on the 12th and the outlook is valid until 0400 hours on the 13th.

2. Precautionary statements—IFR conditions, mountain obscurations, and thunderstorm hazards are described in this section. Statements made here regarding height are given in MSL, and if given otherwise, AGL or ceiling (CIG) will be noted.

Example:

SEE AIRMET SIERRA FOR IFR CONDS AND MTN OBSCN.

TS IMPLY SEV OR GTR TURB SEV ICE LLWS AND IFR CONDS.

NON MSL HGTS DENOTED BY AGL OR CIG.

Explanation:

The area forecast covers VFR clouds and weather, so the precautionary statement warns that AIRMET Sierra should be referenced for IFR conditions and mountain obscuration. The code TS indicates the possibility of thunderstorms and implies there may be occurrences of severe or greater turbulence, severe icing, low-level wind shear, and IFR conditions. The final line of the precautionary statement alerts the user that heights, for the most part, are MSL. Those that are not MSL will be AGL or CIG.

3. Synopsis—gives a brief summary identifying the location and movement of pressure systems, fronts, and circulation patterns.

Example:

SYNOPSIS...LOW PRES TROF 10Z OK/TX PNHDL AREA FCST MOV EWD INTO CNTRL-SWRN OK BY 04Z. WRMFNT 10Z CNTRL OK-SRN AR-NRN MS FCST LIFT NWD INTO NERN OK-NRN AR EXTRM NRN MS BY 04Z.

Explanation:

As of 1000Z, there is a low pressure trough over the Oklahoma and Texas panhandle area, which is forecast to move eastward into central southwestern Oklahoma by 0400Z. A warm front located over central Oklahoma, southern Arkansas, and northern Mississippi at 1000Z is forecast to lift northwestward into northeastern Oklahoma, northern Arkansas, and extreme northern Mississippi by 0400Z.

4. VFR Clouds and Weather—This section lists expected sky conditions, visibility, and weather for the next 12 hours and an outlook for the following 6 hours.

Example:

S CNTRL AND SERN TX
AGL SCT-BKN010. TOPS 030. VIS 3-5SM BR. 14-16Z BECMG AGL SCT030. 19Z AGL SCT050.
OTLK...VFR

OK
PNDLAND NW...AGL SCT030 SCT-BKN100.
TOPS FL200.
15Z AGL SCT040 SCT100. AFT 20Z SCT TSRA DVLPG..
FEW POSS SEV. CB TOPS FL450.
OTLK...VFR

Explanation:

In south central and southeastern Texas, there is a scattered to broken layer of clouds from 1,000 feet AGL with tops at 3,000 feet, visibility is 3 to 5 sm in mist. Between 1400Z and 1600Z, the cloud bases are expected to increase to 3,000 feet AGL. After 1900Z, the cloud bases are expected to continue to increase to 5,000 feet AGL and the outlook is VFR.

In northwestern Oklahoma and panhandle, the clouds are scattered at 3,000 feet with another scattered to broken layer at 10,000 feet AGL, with the tops at 20,000 feet. At 1500 Z, the lowest cloud base is expected to increase to 4,000 feet AGL with a scattered layer at 10,000 feet AGL. After 2000Z, the forecast calls for scattered thunderstorms with rain developing and a few becoming severe; the CB clouds will have tops at flight level 450 or 45,000 feet MSL.

It should be noted that when information is given in the area forecast, locations may be given by states, regions, or specific geological features such as mountain ranges. *Figure 12-12* shows an area forecast chart with six regions of forecast, states, regional areas, and common geographical features.

Inflight Weather Advisories

Inflight weather advisories, which are provided to en route aircraft, are forecasts that detail potentially hazardous weather. These advisories are also available to pilots prior to departure for flight planning purposes. An inflight weather advisory is issued in the form of either an AIRMET, SIGMET, or convective SIGMET.

AIRMET

AIRMETs (WAs) are examples of inflight weather advisories that are issued every 6 hours with intermediate updates issued as needed for a particular area forecast region. The information contained in an AIRMET is of operational interest to all aircraft, but the weather section concerns phenomena considered potentially hazardous to light aircraft and aircraft with limited operational capabilities.

An AIRMET includes forecast of moderate icing, moderate turbulence, sustained surface winds of 30 knots or greater, widespread areas of ceilings less than 1,000 feet and/or visibilities less than three miles, and extensive mountain obscurement.

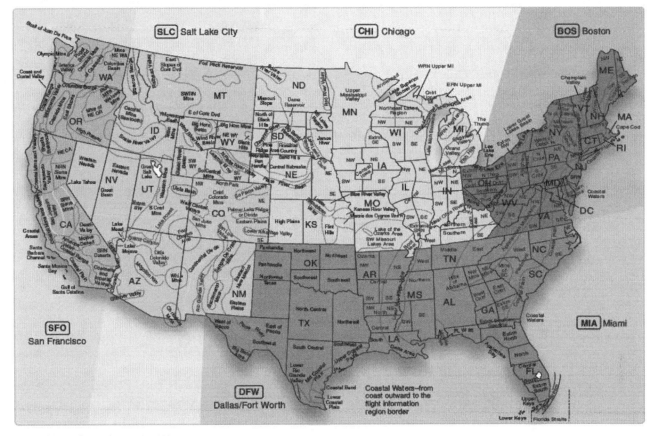

Figure 12-12. *Area forecast region map.*

Each AIRMET bulletin has a fixed alphanumeric designator, numbered sequentially for easy identification, beginning with the first issuance of the day. Sierra is the AIRMET code used to denote IFR and mountain obscuration; Tango is used to denote turbulence, strong surface winds, and low-level wind shear; and Zulu is used to denote icing and freezing levels.

Example:
DFWTWA 241650
AIRMET TANGO UPDT 3 FOR TURBC... STG
SFC WINDS AND LLWS VALID UNTIL 242000
AIRMET TURBC... OK TX...UPDT
FROM OKC TO DFW TO SAT TO MAF TO CDS
TO OKC OCNL MDT TURBC BLO 60 DUE TO
STG AND GUSTY LOW LVL WINDS. CONDS
CONTG BYD 2000Z

Explanation:
This AIRMET was issued by Dallas–Fort Worth on the 24th day of the month, at 1650Z time. On this third update, the AIRMET Tango is issued for turbulence, strong surface winds, and low-level wind shear until 2000Z on the same day. The turbulence section of the AIRMET is an update for Oklahoma and Texas. It defines an area from Oklahoma City to Dallas, Texas, to San Antonio, to Midland, Texas, to Childress, Texas, to Oklahoma City that will experience occasional moderate turbulence below 6,000 feet due to strong and gusty low-level winds. It also notes that these conditions are forecast to continue beyond 2000Z.

SIGMET

SIGMETs (WSs) are inflight advisories concerning nonconvective weather that is potentially hazardous to all aircraft. They report weather forecasts that include severe icing not associated with thunderstorms, severe or extreme turbulence or clear air turbulence (CAT) not associated with thunderstorms, dust storms or sandstorms that lower surface or inflight visibilities to below three miles, and volcanic ash. SIGMETs are unscheduled forecasts that are valid for 4 hours, but if the SIGMET relates to hurricanes, it is valid for 6 hours.

A SIGMET is issued under an alphabetic identifier, from November through Yankee, excluding Sierra and Tango. The first issuance of a SIGMET is designated as an Urgent Weather SIGMET (UWS). Reissued SIGMETs for the same weather phenomenon are sequentially numbered until the weather phenomenon ends.

Example:
SFOR WS 100130
SIGMET ROME02 VALID UNTIL 100530
OR WA
FROM SEA TO PDT TO EUG TO SEA
OCNL MOGR CAT BTN 280 AND 350 EXPCD
DUE TO JTSTR.
CONDS BGNG AFT 0200Z CONTG BYD 0530Z .

Explanation:
This is SIGMET Romeo 2, the second issuance for this weather phenomenon. It is valid until the 10th day of the month at 0530Z time. This SIGMET is for Oregon and Washington, for a defined area from Seattle to Portland to Eugene to Seattle. It calls for occasional moderate or greater clear air turbulence between 28,000 and 35,000 feet due to the location of the jet stream. These conditions will be beginning after 0200Z and will continue beyond the forecast scope of this SIGMET of 0530Z.

Convective Significant Meteorological Information (WST)

A convective SIGMET (WST) is an inflight weather advisory issued for hazardous convective weather that affects the safety of every flight. Convective SIGMETs are issued for severe thunderstorms with surface winds greater than 50 knots, hail at the surface greater than or equal to ¾ inch in diameter, or tornadoes. They are also issued to advise pilots of embedded thunderstorms, lines of thunderstorms, or thunderstorms with heavy or greater precipitation that affect 40 percent or more of a 3,000 square foot or greater region.

Convective SIGMETs are issued for each area of the contiguous 48 states but not Alaska or Hawaii. Convective SIGMETs are issued for the eastern (E), western (W), and central (C) United States. Each report is issued at 55 minutes past the hour, but special reports can be issued during the interim for any reason. Each forecast is valid for 2 hours. They are numbered sequentially each day from 1–99, beginning at 00Z time. If no hazardous weather exists, the convective SIGMET is still issued; however, it states "CONVECTIVE SIGMET…NONE."

Example:
MKCC WST 221855
CONVECTIVE SIGMET 21C
VALID UNTIL 2055
KS OK TX
VCNTY GLD-CDS LINE
NO SGFNT TSTMS RPRTD
LINE TSTMS DVLPG BY 1955Z WILL MOV EWD
30-35 KT THRU 2055Z
HAIL TO 2 IN PSBL

Explanation:
The WST indicates this report is a convective SIGMET. The current date is the 22nd of the month and it was issued at 1855Z. It is convective SIGMET number 21C, indicating that it is the 21st consecutive report issued for the central United States. This report is valid for 2 hours until 2055Z time. The convective SIGMET is for an area from Kansas to Oklahoma to Texas, in the vicinity of a line from Goodland, Kansas, to Childress, Texas. No significant thunderstorms are being reported, but a line of thunderstorms will develop by 1955 Zulu time and will move eastward at a rate of 30–35 knots through 2055Z. Hail up to 2 inches in size is possible with the developing thunderstorms.

Winds and Temperature Aloft Forecast (FD)

Winds and temperatures aloft forecasts (FD) provide wind and temperature forecasts for specific locations in the contiguous United States, including network locations in Hawaii and Alaska. The forecasts are made twice a day based on the radiosonde upper air observations taken at 0000Z and 1200Z.

Through 12,000 feet are true altitudes and above 18,000 feet are pressure altitudes. Wind direction is always in reference to true north and wind speed is given in knots. The temperature is given in degrees Celsius. No winds are forecast when a given level is within 1,500 feet of the station elevation. Similarly, temperatures are not forecast for any station within 2,500 feet of the station elevation.

If the wind speed is forecast to be greater than 100 knots but less than 199 knots, the computer adds 50 to the direction and subtracts 100 from the speed. To decode this type of data group, the reverse must be accomplished. For example, when the data appears as "731960," subtract 50 from the 73 and add 100 to the 19, and the wind would be 230° at 119 knots with a temperature of –60 °C. If the wind speed is forecast to be 200 knots or greater, the wind group is coded as 99 knots. For example, when the data appears as "7799," subtract 50 from 77 and add 100 to 99, and the wind is 270° at 199 knots or greater. When the forecast wind speed is calm or less than 5 knots, the data group is coded "9900," which means light and variable. [Figure 12-13]

FD KWBC 151640
BASED ON 151200Z DATA
VALID 151800Z FOR USE 1700-2100Z
TEMPS NEGATIVE ABV 24000

FD	3000	6000	9000	12000	18000	24000	30000
AMA		2714	2725+00	2625 04	2531 15	2542 27	265842
DEN				2321 04	2532 08	2434 19	2441 31	235347

Figure 12-13. *Winds and temperature aloft report.*

Explanation of *Figure 12-13:*
The heading indicates that this FD was transmitted on the 15th of the month at 1640Z and is based on the 1200Z radiosonde. The valid time is 1800Z on the same day and should be used for the period between 1700Z and 2100Z. The heading also indicates that the temperatures above 24,000 feet MSL are negative. Since the temperatures above 24,000 feet are negative, the minus sign is omitted.

A four-digit data group shows the wind direction in reference to true north and the wind speed in knots. The elevation at Amarillo, Texas (AMA) is 3,605 feet, so the lowest reportable altitude is 6,000 feet for the forecast winds. In this case, "2714" means the wind is forecast to be from 270° at a speed of 14 knots.

A six-digit group includes the forecast temperature aloft. The elevation at Denver (DEN) is 5,431 feet, so the lowest reportable altitude is 9,000 feet for the winds and temperature forecast. In this case, "2321-04" indicates the wind is forecast to be from 230° at a speed of 21 knots with a temperature of –4 °C.

Weather Charts

Weather charts are graphic charts that depict current or forecast weather. They provide an overall picture of the United States and should be used in the beginning stages of flight planning. Typically, weather charts show the movement of major weather systems and fronts. Surface analysis, weather depiction, and radar summary charts are sources of current weather information. Significant weather prognostic charts provide an overall forecast weather picture.

Surface Analysis Chart

The surface analysis chart depicts an analysis of the current surface weather. *[Figure 12-14]* This chart is a computer prepared report that is transmitted every 3 hours and covers the contiguous 48 states and adjacent areas. A surface analysis chart shows the areas of high and low pressure, fronts, temperatures, dew points, wind directions and speeds, local weather, and visual obstructions.

Surface weather observations for reporting points across the United States are also depicted on this chart. Each of these reporting points is illustrated by a station model. *[Figure 12-15]* A station model includes:

- Type of observation—a round model indicates an official weather observer made the observation. A square model indicates the observation is from an automated station. Stations located offshore give data from ships, buoys, or offshore platforms.

- Sky cover—the station model depicts total sky cover and is shown as clear, scattered, broken, overcast, or obscured/partially obscured.

- Clouds—represented by specific symbols. Low cloud symbols are placed beneath the station model, while middle and high cloud symbols are placed directly above the station model. Typically, only one type of cloud will be depicted with the station model.

Figure 12-14. *Surface analysis chart.*

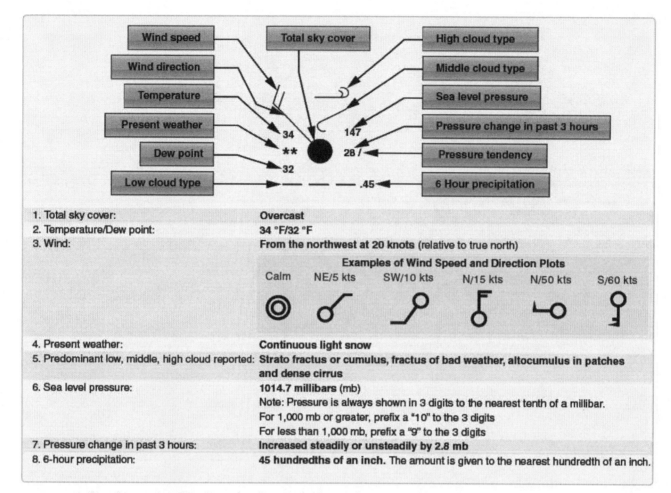

1. Total sky cover:	**Overcast**
2. Temperature/Dew point:	**34 °F/32 °F**
3. Wind:	**From the northwest at 20 knots** (relative to true north)

Examples of Wind Speed and Direction Plots

Calm	NE/5 kts	SW/10 kts	N/15 kts	N/50 kts	S/60 kts

4. Present weather:	**Continuous light snow**
5. Predominant low, middle, high cloud reported:	**Strato fractus or cumulus, fractus of bad weather, altocumulus in patches and dense cirrus**
6. Sea level pressure:	**1014.7 millibars (mb)** Note: Pressure is always shown in 3 digits to the nearest tenth of a millibar. For 1,000 mb or greater, prefix a "10" to the 3 digits For less than 1,000 mb, prefix a "9" to the 3 digits
7. Pressure change in past 3 hours:	**Increased steadily or unsteadily by 2.8 mb**
8. 6-hour precipitation:	**45 hundredths of an inch.** The amount is given to the nearest hundredth of an inch.

Figure 12-15. *Sample station model and weather chart symbols.*

- Sea level pressure—given in three digits to the nearest tenth of a millibar (mb). For 1,000 mbs or greater, prefix a 10 to the three digits. For less than 1,000 mbs, prefix a 9 to the three digits.

- Pressure change/tendency—pressure change in tenths of mb over the past 3 hours. This is depicted directly below the sea level pressure.

- Precipitation—a record of the precipitation that has fallen over the last 6 hours to the nearest hundredth of an inch.

- Dew point—given in degrees Fahrenheit.

- Present weather—over 100 different weather symbols are used to describe the current weather.

- Temperature—given in degrees Fahrenheit.

- Wind—true direction of wind is given by the wind pointer line, indicating the direction from which the wind is coming. A short barb is equal to 5 knots of wind, a long barb is equal to 10 knots of wind, and a pennant is equal to 50 knots.

Weather Depiction Chart

A weather depiction chart details surface conditions as derived from METAR and other surface observations. The weather depiction chart is prepared and transmitted by computer every 3 hours beginning at 0100Z time, and is valid at the time of the plotted data. It is designed to be used for flight planning by giving an overall picture of the weather across the United States. *[Figure 12-16]*

This type of chart typically displays major fronts or areas of high and low pressure. The weather depiction chart also provides a graphic display of IFR, VFR, and MVFR (marginal VFR) weather. Areas of IFR conditions (ceilings less than 1,000 feet and visibility less than three miles) are shown by a hatched area outlined by a smooth line. MVFR regions (ceilings 1,000 to 3,000 feet, visibility 3 to 5 miles) are shown by a nonhatched area outlined by a smooth line. Areas of VFR (no ceiling or ceiling greater than 3,000 feet and visibility greater than five miles) are not outlined.

Figure 12-16. *Weather depiction chart.*

Weather depiction charts show a modified station model that provides sky conditions in the form of total sky cover, cloud height or ceiling, weather, and obstructions to visibility, but does not include winds or pressure readings like the surface analysis chart. A bracket ( ]) symbol to the right of the station indicates the observation was made by an automated station. A detailed explanation of a station model is depicted in the previous discussion of surface analysis charts.

Radar Summary Chart

A radar summary chart is a graphically depicted collection of radar weather reports (SDs). *[Figure 12-17]* The chart is published hourly at 35 minutes past the hour. It displays areas of precipitation, as well as information regarding the characteristics of the precipitation. *[Figure 12-18]* A radar summary chart includes:

- No information—if information is not reported, the chart will say "NA." If no echoes are detected, the chart will say "NE."

- Precipitation intensity contours—intensity can be described as one of six levels and is shown on the chart by three contour intervals.

- Height of tops—the heights of the echo tops are given in hundreds of feet MSL.

Movement of cells—individual cell movement is indicated by an arrow pointing in the direction of movement. The speed of movement in knots is the number at the top of the arrow head. "LM" indicates little movement.

- Type of precipitation—the type of precipitation is marked on the chart using specific symbols. These symbols are not the same as used on the METAR charts.

- Echo configuration—echoes are shown as being areas, cells, or lines.

- Weather watches—severe weather watch areas for tornadoes and severe thunderstorms are depicted by boxes outlined with heavy dashed lines.

The radar summary chart is a valuable tool for preflight planning. It does, however, contain several limitations for the usage of the chart. This chart depicts only areas of precipitation. It will not show areas of clouds and fog with no appreciable precipitation, or the height of the tops and bases of the clouds. Radar summary charts are a depiction of current precipitation and should be used in conjunction with current METAR and weather forecasts.

Figure 12-17. *Radar summary chart.*

Figure 12-18. *Intensity levels, contours, and precipitation type symbols.*

Symbol	Meaning
R	Rain
RW	Rain shower
S	Snow
SW	Snow shower
T	Thunderstorm
NA	Not available
NE	No echoes
OM	Out for maintenance
⬈ 35	Cell movement to the northeast at 35 knots
LM	Little movement
WS999	Severe thunderstorm watch number 999
WT210	Tornado watch number 210
SLD	8/10 or greater coverage in a line
／	Line of echoes

Significant Weather Prognostic Charts

Significant weather prognostic charts are available for low-level significant weather from the surface to FL 240 (24,000 feet), also referred to as the 400 mb level, and high-level significant weather from FL 250 to FL 600 (25,000 to 60,000 feet). The primary concern of this discussion is the low-level significant weather prognostic chart.

The low-level chart comes in two forms: the 12– and 24–hour forecast chart, and the 36- and 48-hour surface forecast chart. The first chart is a four-panel chart that includes 12– and 24–hour forecasts for significant weather and surface weather. Charts are issued four times a day at 0000Z, 0600Z, 1200Z, and 1800Z. The valid time for the chart is printed on the lower left corner of each panel.

The upper two panels show forecast significant weather, which may include nonconvective turbulence, freezing levels, and IFR or MVFR weather. Areas of moderate or greater turbulence are enclosed in dashed lines. Numbers within these areas give the height of the turbulence in hundreds of feet MSL. Figures below the line show the anticipated base, while figures above the line show the top of the zone of turbulence. Also shown on this panel are areas of VFR, IFR, and MVFR. IFR areas are enclosed by solid lines, MVFR areas are enclosed by scalloped lines, and the remaining, unenclosed area is designated VFR. Zigzag lines and the letters "SFC" indicate freezing levels in that area are at the surface. Freezing level height contours for the highest freezing level are drawn at 4,000-foot intervals with dashed lines.

The lower two panels show the forecast surface weather and depicts the forecast locations and characteristics of pressure systems, fronts, and precipitation. Standard symbols are used to show fronts and pressure centers. Direction of movement of the pressure center is depicted by an arrow. The speed in knots is shown next to the arrow. In addition, areas of forecast precipitation and thunderstorms are outlined. Areas of precipitation that are shaded indicate at least one-half of the area is being affected by the precipitation. Unique symbols indicate the type of precipitation and the manner in which it occurs.

Figure 12-19 depicts a typical significant weather prognostic chart as well as the symbols typically used to depict precipitation. Prognostic charts are an excellent source of information for preflight planning; however, this chart should be viewed in light of current conditions and specific local area forecasts.

The 36- and 48-hour significant weather prognostic chart is an extension of the 12- and 24-hour forecast. It provides information regarding surface weather forecasts and includes a discussion of the forecast. This chart is issued twice a day. It typically contains forecast positions and characteristics of pressure patterns, fronts, and precipitation. An example of a 36- and 48-hour surface prognostic chart is shown in *Figure 12-20*.

ATC Radar Weather Displays

Although ATC systems cannot always detect the presence or absence of clouds, they can often determine the intensity of a precipitation area, but the specific character of that area (snow, rain, hail, VIRGA, etc.) cannot be determined. For this reason, ATC refers to all weather areas displayed on ATC radar scopes as "precipitation."

ARTCC facilities normally use a Weather and Radar Processor (WARP) to display a mosaic of data obtained from multiple NEXRAD sites. There is a time delay between actual conditions and those displayed to the controller. The precipitation data on the ARTCC controller's display could be up to 6 minutes old. The WARP processor is only used in ARTCC facilities. All ATC facilities using radar weather processors with the ability to determine precipitation intensity, describe the intensity to pilots as:

- Light,
- Moderate,
- Heavy, or
- Extreme.

Figure 12-19. *Significant weather prognostic chart and legend (inset).*

Figure 12-20. *36- (top) and 48-hour (bottom) surface prognostic chart.*

When the WARP is not available, a second system, the narrowband Air Route Surveillance Radar (ARSR) can display two distinct levels of precipitation intensity that will be described to pilots as "MODERATE and "HEAVY TO EXTREME."

ATC facilities that cannot display the intensity levels of precipitation due to equipment limitations will describe the location of the precipitation area by geographic position, or position relative to the aircraft. Since the intensity level is not available, the controller will state "INTENSITY UNKNOWN."

ATC radar is not able to detect turbulence. Generally, turbulence can be expected to occur as the rate of rainfall or intensity of precipitation increases. Turbulence associated with greater rates of rainfall/precipitation will normally be more severe than any associated with lesser rates of rainfall/precipitation. Turbulence should be expected to occur near convective activity, even in clear air. Thunderstorms are a form of convective activity that imply severe or greater turbulence. Operation within 20 miles of thunderstorms should be approached with great caution, as the severity of turbulence can be much greater than the precipitation intensity might indicate.

Weather Avoidance Assistance

To the extent possible, controllers will issue pertinent information on weather and assist pilots in avoiding such areas when requested. Pilots should respond to a weather advisory by either acknowledging the advisory or by acknowledging the advisory and requesting an alternative course of action as follows:

- Request to deviate off course by stating the number of miles and the direction of the requested deviation.

- Request a new route to avoid the affected area.

- Request a change of altitude.

- Request radar vectors around the affected areas.

It should be remembered that the controller's primary function is to provide safe separation between aircraft. Any additional service, such as weather avoidance assistance, can only be provided to the extent that it does not detract from the primary function. It's also worth noting that the separation workload is generally greater than normal when weather disrupts the usual flow of traffic. ATC radar limitations and frequency congestion may also be a factor in limiting the controller's capability to provide additional service.

Electronic Flight Displays (EFD) /Multi-Function Display (MFD) Weather

Many aircraft manufacturers now include satellite weather services with new electronic flight display (EFD) systems. EFDs give a pilot access to many of the satellite weather services available.

Products available to a pilot on the display pictured in *Figure 12-21* are listed as follows. The letters in parentheses indicate the soft key to press in order to access the data.

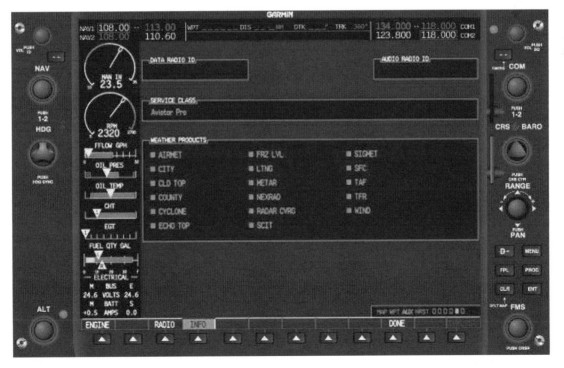

Figure 12-21. *Information page.*

- Graphical NEXRAD data (NEXRAD)
- Graphical METAR data (METAR)
- Textual METAR data
- Textual terminal aerodrome forecasts (TAF)
- City forecast data
- Graphical wind data (WIND)
- Graphical echo tops (ECHO TOPS)
- Graphical cloud tops (CLD TOPS)
- Graphical lightning strikes (LTNG)
- Graphical storm cell movement (CELL MOV)
- NEXRAD radar coverage (information displayed with the NEXRAD data)
- SIGMETs/AIRMETs (SIG/AIR)
- Surface analysis to include city forecasts (SFC)
- County warnings (COUNTY)
- Freezing levels (FRZ LVL)
- Hurricane track (CYCLONE)
- Temporary flight restrictions (TFR)

Pilots must be familiar with any EFD or MFD used and the satellite weather products available on the display.

Weather Products Age and Expiration

The information displayed using a satellite weather link is near real time but should not be thought of as instantaneous up-to-date information. Each type of weather display is stamped with the age information on the MFD. The time is referenced from Zulu when the information was assembled at the ground station. The age should not be assumed to be the time when the FIS received the information from the satellite.

Two types of weather are displayed on the screen: "current" weather and forecast data. Current information is displayed by an age while the forecast data has a data stamp in the form of "__/__ __ : __". [Figure 12-22]

The Next Generation Weather Radar System (NEXRAD)

The NEXRAD system is comprised of a series of 159 Weather Surveillance Radar–1988 Doppler (WSR-88D) sites situated throughout the United States as well as selected oversees sites. The NEXRAD system is a joint venture between the United States Department of Commerce (DOC), the United States Department of Defense, (DOD) as well as the United States Department of Transportation (DOT). The individual agencies that have control over the system are the NWS, Air Force Weather Agency (AFWA) and the FAA. [Figure 12-23]

Figure 12-22. *List of weather products and the expiration times of each.*

NEXRAD radar produces two levels of products: level II and level III.

Level II Data Products

All NEXRAD level-II data products are available through the National Climatic Data Center (NCDC). Level II data consists of the three meteorological base data quantities: reflectivity, mean radial velocity, and spectrum width.

Level III Data Products

There are 41 products routinely available through the NCDC. Level III graphic products are available as digital images, color hard copy, gray scale hard copy, or acetate overlay copies. This information is then encoded and disseminated through the satellite weather system as well as other sources.

NEXRAD level III data for up to a 2,000 mile range can be displayed. It is important to realize that the radar image is not real time and can be up to 5 minutes old. At no time should the images be used as storm penetrating radar nor to navigate through a line of storms. The images display should only be used as a reference.

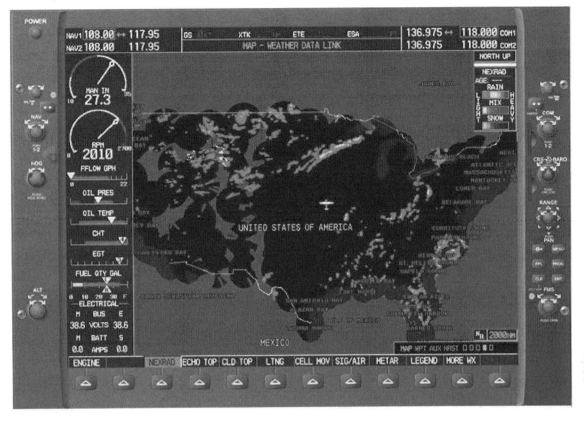

Figure 12-23. *NEXRAD radar display.*

NEXRAD radar is mutually exclusive of Topographic (TOPO), TERRAIN and STORMSCOPE. When NEXRAD is turned on, TOPO, TERRAIN, and STORMSCOPE are turned off because the colors used to display intensities are very similar.

Lightning information is available to assist when NEXRAD is enabled. This presents a more vivid picture of the weather in the surrounding area.

In addition to utilizing the soft keys to activate the NEXRAD display, the pilot also has the option of setting the desired range. It is possible to zoom in on a specific area of the display in order to gain a more detailed picture of the radar display. *[Figure 12-24]*

NEXRAD Abnormalities

Although NEXRAD is a compilation of stations across the country, there can be abnormalities associated with the system. Some of the abnormalities are listed below.

- Ground clutter

- Strobes and spurious radar data

- Sun strobes, when the radar antenna points directly at the sun

- Interference from buildings or mountains, which may cause shadows

- Military aircraft which deploy metallic dust and may reflect the radar signature

NEXRAD Limitations

In addition to the abnormalities listed, the NEXRAD system does have some specific limitations.

Base Reflectivity

The NEXRAD base reflectivity does not provide adequate information from which to determine cloud layers or type of precipitation with respect to hail versus rain. Therefore, a pilot may mistake rain for hail.

In addition, the base reflectivity is sampled at the minimum antenna elevation angle. With this minimum angle, an individual site cannot depict high altitude storms directly over the station. This will leave an area of null coverage if an adjacent site does not also cover the affected area.

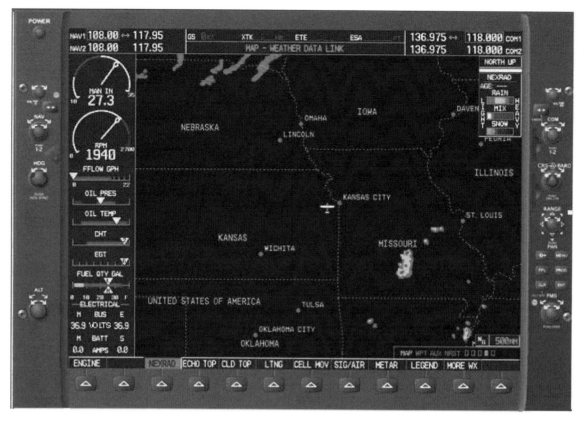

Figure 12-24. *NEXRAD radar display (500 mile range). The individual color gradients can be easily discerned and interpreted via the legend in the upper right corner of the screen. Additional information can be gained by pressing the LEGEND soft key, which displays the legend page.*

Resolution Display

The resolution of the displayed data will pose additional concerns when the range is decreased. The minimum resolution for NEXRAD returns is two kilometers. This means that when the display range is zoomed in to approximately ten miles, the individual square return boxes will be more prevalent. Each square will indicate the strongest display return within that two kilometer square area.

AIRMET/SIGMET Display

AIRMET/SIGMET information is available for the displayed viewing range on the MFD. Some displays are capable of displaying weather information for a 2,000 mile range. AIRMETS/SIGMETS are displayed by dashed lines on the map. *[Figure 12-25]*

The legend box denotes the various colors used to depict the AIRMETs such as icing, turbulence, IFR weather, mountain obscuration as well as surface winds. *[Figure 12-26]* The great advantage of the graphically displayed AIRMET/SIGMET boundary box is the pilot can see the extent of the area that the report covers. The pilot does not need to manually plot the points to determine the full extent of the coverage area.

Graphical METARs

METARs can be displayed on the multi-function display. Each reporting station that has a METAR/TAF available is depicted by a flag from the center of the airport symbol. Each flag is color coded to depict the type of weather that is currently reported at that station. A legend is available to assist users in determining what each flag color represents. *[Figure 12-27]*

The graphical METAR display shows all available reporting stations within the set viewing range. By setting the range knob up to a 2,000 mile range, pilots can pan around the display map to check the current conditions of various airports along the route of flight.

By understanding what each colored flag indicates, a pilot can quickly determine where weather patterns display marginal weather, IFR, or areas of VFR. These flags make it easy to determine weather at a specific airport should the need arise to divert from the intended airport of landing.

Figure 12-25. *The AIRMET information box instructs the pilot to press the enter button to gain additional information on the selected area of weather. Once the enter soft key (ENT) is depressed, the specific textual information is displayed on the right side of the screen.*

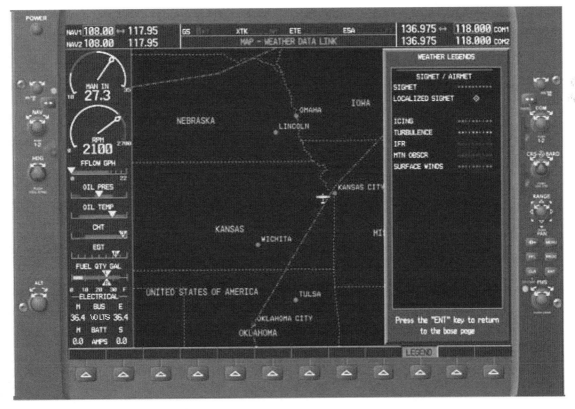

Figure 12-26. *SIGMET/AIRMET legend display.*

Figure 12-27. *Graphical METAR legend display.*

Chapter Summary

While no weather forecast is guaranteed to be 100 percent accurate, pilots have access to a myriad of weather information on which to base flight decisions. Weather products available for preflight planning to en route information received over the radio or via satellite link provide the pilot with the most accurate and up-to-date information available. Each report provides a piece of the weather puzzle. Pilots must use several reports to get an overall picture and gain an understanding of the weather that will affect the safe completion of a flight.

Chapter 13

Airport Operations

Introduction

Each time a pilot operates an aircraft, the flight normally begins and ends at an airport. An airport may be a small sod field or a large complex utilized by air carriers. This chapter examines airport operations, identifies features of an airport complex, and provides information on operating on or in the vicinity of an airport.

Types of Airports

There are two types of airports—towered and nontowered. These types can be further subdivided to:

- Civil Airports—airports that are open to the general public.

- Military/Federal Government airports—airports operated by the military, National Aeronautics and Space Administration (NASA), or other agencies of the Federal Government.

- Private airports—airports designated for private or restricted use only, not open to the general public.

Towered Airport

A towered airport has an operating control tower. Air traffic control (ATC) is responsible for providing the safe, orderly, and expeditious flow of air traffic at airports where the type of operations and/or volume of traffic requires such a service. Pilots operating from a towered airport are required to maintain two-way radio communication with air traffic controllers, and to acknowledge and comply with their instructions. Pilots must advise ATC if they cannot comply with the instructions issued and request amended instructions. A pilot may deviate from an air traffic instruction in an emergency, but must advise ATC of the deviation as soon as possible.

Nontowered Airport

An nontowered airport does not have an operating control tower. Two-way radio communications are not required, although it is a good operating practice for pilots to transmit their intentions on the specified frequency for the benefit of other traffic in the area. The key to communicating at an airport without an operating control tower is selection of the correct common frequency. The acronym CTAF, which stands for Common Traffic Advisory Frequency, is synonymous with this program. A CTAF is a frequency designated for the purpose of carrying out airport advisory practices while operating to or from an airport without an operating control tower. The CTAF may be a Universal Integrated Community (UNICOM), MULTICOM, Flight Service Station (FSS), or tower frequency and is identified in appropriate aeronautical publications. UNICOM is a nongovernment air/ground radio communication station which may provide airport information at public use airports where there is no tower or FSS. On pilot request, UNICOM stations may provide pilots with weather information, wind direction, the recommended runway, or other necessary information. If the UNICOM frequency is designated as the CTAF, it will be identified in appropriate aeronautical publications. *Figure 13-1* lists recommended communication procedures. More information on radio communications is discussed later in this chapter.

Sources for Airport Data

When a pilot flies into a different airport, it is important to review the current data for that airport. This data provides the pilot with information, such as communication frequencies, services available, closed runways, or airport construction. Three common sources of information are:

- Aeronautical Charts
- Airport/Facility Directory (A/FD)
- Notices to Airmen (NOTAMs)

Facility at Airport	Frequency Use	Cummunication/Broadcast Procedures		
		Outbound	Inbound	Practice Instrument Approach
UNICOM (no tower or FSS)	Communicate with UNICOM station on published CTAF frequency (122.7, 122.8, 122.725, 122.975, or 123.0). If unable to contact UNICOM station, use self-announce procedures on CTAF.	Before taxiing and before taxiing on the runway for departure.	10 miles out. Entering downwind, base, and final. Leaving the runway.	
No tower, FSS, or UNICOM	Self-announce on MULTICOM frequency 122.9.	Before taxiing and before taxiing on the runway for departure.	10 miles out. Entering downwind, base, and final. Leaving the runway.	Departing final approach fix (name) or on final approach segment inbound.
No tower in operation, FSS open	Communicate with FSS on CTAF frequency.	Before taxiing and before taxiing on the runway for departure.	10 miles out. Entering downwind, base, and final. Leaving the runway.	Approach completed/terminated.
FSS closed (no tower)	Self-announce on CTAF.	Before taxiing and before taxiing on the runway for departure.	10 miles out. Entering downwind, base, and final. Leaving the runway.	
Tower or FSS not in operation	Self-announce on CTAF.	Before taxiing and before taxiing on the runway for departure.	10 miles out. Entering downwind, base, and final. Leaving the runway.	

Figure 13-1. *Recommended communication procedures.*

Aeronautical Charts

Aeronautical charts provide specific information on airports. Chapter 15, Navigation, contains an excerpt from an aeronautical chart and an aeronautical chart legend, which provides guidance on interpreting the information on the chart.

Airport/Facility Directory (A/FD)

The A/FD provides the most comprehensive information on a given airport. It contains information on airports, heliports, and seaplane bases that are open to the public. The A/FD is published in seven books, which are organized by regions and are revised every 56 days. The A/FD is also available digitally at www.naco.faa.gov. *Figure 13-2* contains an excerpt from a directory. For a complete listing of information provided in an A/FD and how the information may be decoded, refer to the "Directory Legend Sample" located in the front of each A/FD.

In addition to airport information, each A/FD contains information such as special notices, Federal Aviation Administration (FAA) and National Weather Service (NWS) telephone numbers, preferred instrument flight rules (IFR) routing, visual flight rules (VFR) waypoints, a listing of very high frequency (VHF) omnidirectional range (VOR) receiver checkpoints, aeronautical chart bulletins, land and hold short operations (LAHSO) for selected airports, airport diagrams for selected towered airports, en route flight advisory service (EFAS) outlets, parachute jumping areas, and facility telephone numbers. It would be helpful to review an A/FD to become familiar with the information it contains.

Notices to Airmen (NOTAMs)

NOTAMs provide the most current information available. They provide time-critical information on airports and changes that affect the national airspace system (NAS) and are of concern to IFR operations. NOTAM information is classified into three categories. These are NOTAM-D or distant, NOTAM-L or local, and flight data center (FDC) NOTAMs. NOTAM-Ds are attached to hourly weather reports and are available at automated flight service stations (AFSS) or FSS.

FDC NOTAMs are issued by the National Flight Data Center and contain regulatory information, such as temporary flight restrictions or an amendment to instrument approach

Figure 13-2. *Airport/Facility Directory excerpt.*

procedures. The NOTAM-Ds and FDC NOTAMs are contained in the NOTAM publication, which is issued every 28 days. Prior to any flight, pilots should check for any NOTAMs that could affect their intended flight.

NOTAM-D information includes such data as taxiway closures, personnel and equipment near or crossing runways, and airport lighting aids that do not affect instrument approach criteria, such as visual approach slope indicator (VASI). NOTAM-D information is distributed locally only and is not attached to the hourly weather reports. A separate file of local NOTAMs is maintained at each FSS for facilities in their area only. NOTAM-D information for other FSS areas must be specifically requested directly from the FSS that has responsibility for the airport concerned.

Airport Markings and Signs

There are markings and signs used at airports, which provide directions and assist pilots in airport operations. Some of the most common markings and signs are discussed. Additional information may be found in Chapter 2, Aeronautical Lighting and Other Airport Visual Aids, in the Aeronautical Information Manual (AIM).

Runway Markings

Runway markings vary depending on the type of operations conducted at the airport. *Figure 13-3* shows a runway that is approved as a precision instrument approach runway and some other common runway markings. A basic VFR runway may only have centerline markings and runway numbers.

Figure 13-3. *Selected airport markings and surface lighting.*

Since aircraft are affected by the wind during takeoffs and landings, runways are laid out according to the local prevailing winds. Runway numbers are in reference to magnetic north. Certain airports have two or even three runways laid out in the same direction. These are referred to as parallel runways and are distinguished by a letter added to the runway number (e.g., runway 36L (left), 36C (center), and 36R (right)).

Another feature of some runways is a displaced threshold. A threshold may be displaced because of an obstruction near the end of the runway. Although this portion of the runway is not to be used for landing, it may be available for taxiing, takeoff, or landing rollout. Some airports may have a blast pad/stopway area. The blast pad is an area where a propeller or jet blast can dissipate without creating a hazard. The stopway area is paved in order to provide space for an aircraft to decelerate and stop in the event of an aborted takeoff. These areas cannot be used for takeoff or landing.

Taxiway Markings

Aircraft use taxiways to transition from parking areas to the runway. Taxiways are identified by a continuous yellow centerline stripe and may include edge markings to define the edge of the taxiway. This is usually done when the taxiway edge does not correspond with the edge of the pavement. If an edge marking is a continuous line, the paved shoulder is not intended to be used by an aircraft. If it is a dashed marking, an aircraft may use that portion of the pavement. Where a taxiway approaches a runway, there may be a holding position marker. These consist of four yellow lines (two solid and two dashed). The solid lines are where the aircraft is to hold. At some towered airports, holding position markings may be found on a runway. They are used when there are intersecting runways, and ATC issues instructions such as "cleared to land—hold short of runway 30."

Other Markings

Some other markings found on the airport include vehicle roadway markings, VOR receiver checkpoint markings, and non-movement area boundary markings.

Vehicle roadway markings are used when necessary to define a pathway for vehicle crossing areas that are also intended for aircraft. These markings usually consist of a solid white line to delineate each edge of the roadway and a dashed line to separate lanes within the edges of the roadway. In lieu of the solid lines, zipper markings may be used to delineate the edges of the vehicle roadway. [Figure 13-4]

A VOR receiver checkpoint marking consists of a painted circle with an arrow in the middle. The arrow is aligned in the direction of the checkpoint azimuth. This allows pilots to check aircraft instruments with navigational aid signals.

Figure 13-4. *Vehicle roadway markings.*

A non-movement area boundary marking delineates a movement area under ATC. These markings are yellow and located on the boundary between the movement and non-movement area. They normally consist of two yellow lines (one solid and one dashed).

Airport Signs

There are six types of signs that may be found at airports. The more complex the layout of an airport, the more important the signs become to pilots. *Figure 13-5* shows examples of signs, their purpose, and appropriate pilot action. The six types of signs are:

- Mandatory instruction signs—red background with white inscription. These signs denote an entrance to a runway, critical area, or prohibited area.

- Location signs—black with yellow inscription and a yellow border, no arrows. They are used to identify a taxiway or runway location, to identify the boundary of the runway, or identify an instrument landing system (ILS) critical area.

- Direction signs—yellow background with black inscription. The inscription identifies the designation of the intersecting taxiway(s) leading out of an intersection.

- Destination signs—yellow background with black inscription and also contain arrows. These signs provide information on locating things, such as runways, terminals, cargo areas, and civil aviation areas.

- Information signs—yellow background with black inscription. These signs are used to provide the pilot with information on such things as areas that cannot be seen from the control tower, applicable radio frequencies, and noise abatement procedures. The airport operator determines the need, size, and location of these signs.

- Runway distance remaining signs—black background with white numbers. The numbers indicate the distance of the remaining runway in thousands of feet.

Airport Lighting

The majority of airports have some type of lighting for night operations. The variety and type of lighting systems depends on the volume and complexity of operations at a given airport. Airport lighting is standardized so that airports use the same light colors for runways and taxiways.

Airport Beacon

Airport beacons help a pilot identify an airport at night. The beacons are operated from dusk till dawn. Sometimes they are turned on if the ceiling is less than 1,000 feet and/or the ground visibility is less than 3 statute miles (VFR minimums). However, there is no requirement for this, so a pilot has the responsibility of determining if the weather meets VFR requirements. The beacon has a vertical light

Type of Sign	Action or Purpose	Type of Sign	Action or Purpose
4-22	**Taxiway/Runway Hold Position:** Hold short of runway on taxiway	▬ ▬ ▬	**Runway Safety Area/Obstacle Free Zone Boundary:** Exit boundary of runway protected areas
26-8	**Runway/Runway Hold Position:** Hold short of intersecting runway	ꚃꚃꚃ	**ILS Critical Area Boundary:** Exit boundary of ILS critical area
8-APCH	**Runway Approach Hold Position:** Hold short of aircraft on approach	J→	**Taxiway Direction:** Defines direction & designation of intersecting taxiway(s)
ILS	**ILS Critical Area Hold Position:** Hold short of ILS approach critical area	↙L	**Runway Exit:** Defines direction & designation of exit taxiway from runway
⊖	**No Entry:** Identifies paved areas where aircraft entry is prohibited	22↑	**Outbound Destination:** Defines directions to takeoff runways
B	**Taxiway Location:** Identifies taxiway on which aircraft is located	↖MIL	**Inbound Destination:** Defines directions for arriving aircraft
22	**Runway Location:** Identifies runway on which aircraft is located	▨▨▨	**Taxiway Ending Marker:** Indicates taxiway does not continue
4	**Runway Distance Remaining:** Provides remaining runway length in 1,000 feet increments	↙A G L→	**Direction Sign Array:** Identifies location in conjunction with multiple intersecting taxiways

Figure 13-5. *Airport signs.*

distribution to make it most effective from 1–10° above the horizon, although it can be seen well above or below this spread. The beacon may be an omnidirectional capacitor-discharge device, or it may rotate at a constant speed, which produces the visual effect of flashes at regular intervals. The combination of light colors from an airport beacon indicates the type of airport. *[Figure 13-6]* Some of the most common beacons are:

- Flashing white and green for civilian land airports;

- Flashing white and yellow for a water airport;

- Flashing white, yellow, and green for a heliport; and

- Two quick white flashes alternating with a green flash identifying a military airport.

Figure 13-6. *Airport rotating beacons.*

Approach Light Systems

Approach light systems are primarily intended to provide a means to transition from instrument flight to visual flight for landing. The system configuration depends on whether the runway is a precision or nonprecision instrument runway. Some systems include sequenced flashing lights, which appear to the pilot as a ball of light traveling toward the runway at high speed. Approach lights can also aid pilots operating under VFR at night.

Visual Glideslope Indicators

Visual glideslope indicators provide the pilot with glidepath information that can be used for day or night approaches. By maintaining the proper glidepath as provided by the system, a pilot should have adequate obstacle clearance and should touch down within a specified portion of the runway.

Visual Approach Slope Indicator (VASI)

VASI installations are the most common visual glidepath systems in use. The VASI provides obstruction clearance within 10° of the runway extended runway centerline, and to four nautical miles (NM) from the runway threshold.

The VASI consists of light units arranged in bars. There are 2-bar and 3-bar VASIs. The 2-bar VASI has near and far light bars and the 3-bar VASI has near, middle, and far light bars. Two-bar VASI installations provide one visual glidepath which is normally set at 3°. The 3-bar system provides two glidepaths, the lower glidepath normally set at 3° and the upper glidepath ¼ degree above the lower glidepath.

The basic principle of the VASI is that of color differentiation between red and white. Each light unit projects a beam of light, a white segment in the upper part of the beam and a red segment in the lower part of the beam. The lights are arranged so the pilot sees the combination of lights shown in *Figure 13-7* to indicate below, on, or above the glidepath.

Figure 13-7. *Two-bar VASI system.*

Other Glidepath Systems

A precision approach path indicator (PAPI) uses lights similar to the VASI system except they are installed in a single row, normally on the left side of the runway. *[Figure 13-8]*

A tri-color system consists of a single light unit projecting a three-color visual approach path. Below the glidepath is indicated by red, on the glidepath is indicated by green, and above the glidepath is indicated by amber. When descending below the glidepath, there is a small area of dark amber. Pilots should not mistake this area for an "above the glidepath" indication. *[Figure 13-9]*

Pulsating visual approach slope indicators normally consist of a single light unit projecting a two-color visual approach path into the final approach area of the runway upon which the indicator is installed. The on glidepath indication is a steady white light. The slightly below glidepath indication is a steady red light. If the aircraft descends further below the glidepath, the red light starts to pulsate. The above glidepath indication is a pulsating white light. The pulsating rate increases as the aircraft gets further above or below the desired glideslope.

Figure 13-8. *Precision approach path indicator.*

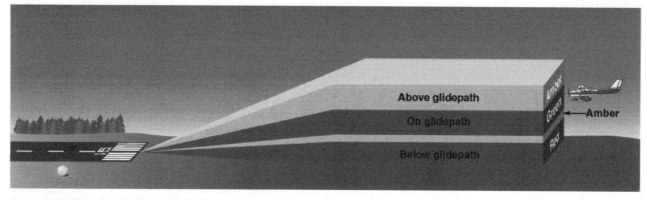

Figure 13-9. *Tri-color visual approach slope indicator.*

The useful range of the system is about four miles during the day and up to ten miles at night. *[Figure 13-10]*

Runway Lighting

There are various lights that identify parts of the runway complex. These assist a pilot in safely making a takeoff or landing during night operations.

Runway End Identifier Lights (REIL)

Runway end identifier lights (REIL) are installed at many airfields to provide rapid and positive identification of the approach end of a particular runway. The system consists of a pair of synchronized flashing lights located laterally on each side of the runway threshold. REILs may be either omnidirectional or unidirectional facing the approach area.

Runway Edge Lights

Runway edge lights are used to outline the edges of runways at night or during low visibility conditions. These lights are classified according to the intensity they are capable of producing: high intensity runway lights (HIRL), medium intensity runway lights (MIRL), and low intensity runway lights (LIRL). The HIRL and MIRL have variable intensity settings. These lights are white, except on instrument runways

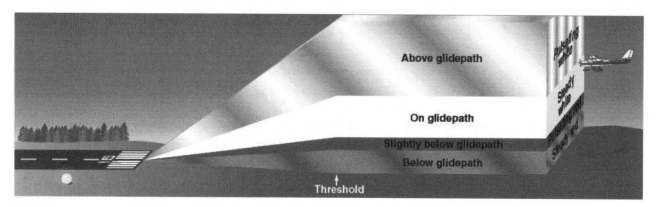

Figure 13-10. *Pulsating visual approach slope indicator.*

where amber lights are used on the last 2,000 feet or half the length of the runway, whichever is less. The lights marking the end of the runway are red.

In-Runway Lighting

Runway centerline lighting system (RCLS)—installed on some precision approach runways to facilitate landing under adverse visibility conditions. They are located along the runway centerline and are spaced at 50-foot intervals. When viewed from the landing threshold, the runway centerline lights are white until the last 3,000 feet of the runway. The white lights begin to alternate with red for the next 2,000 feet. For the remaining 1,000 feet of the runway, all centerline lights are red.

Touchdown zone lights (TDZL)—installed on some precision approach runways to indicate the touchdown zone when landing under adverse visibility conditions. They consist of two rows of transverse light bars disposed symmetrically about the runway centerline. The system consists of steady-burning white lights which start 100 feet beyond the landing threshold and extend to 3,000 feet beyond the landing threshold or to the midpoint of the runway, whichever is less.

Taxiway centerline lead-off lights—provide visual guidance to persons exiting the runway. They are color-coded to warn pilots and vehicle drivers that they are within the runway environment or ILS/MLS critical area, whichever is more restrictive. Alternate green and yellow lights are installed, beginning with green, from the runway centerline to one centerline light position beyond the runway holding position or ILS/MLS critical area holding position.

Taxiway centerline lead-on lights—provide visual guidance to persons entering the runway. These "lead-on" lights are also color-coded with the same color pattern as lead-off lights to warn pilots and vehicle drivers that they are within the runway environment or instrument landing system/microwave landing system (ILS/MLS) critical area, whichever is more conservative. The fixtures used for lead-on lights are bidirectional (i.e., one side emits light for the lead-on function while the other side emits light for the lead-off function). Any fixture that emits yellow light for the lead-off function also emits yellow light for the lead-on function.

Land and hold short lights—used to indicate the hold short point on certain runways which are approved for LAHSO. Land and hold short lights consist of a row of pulsing white lights installed across the runway at the hold short point. Where installed, the lights are on anytime LAHSO is in effect. These lights are off when LAHSO is not in effect.

Control of Airport Lighting

Airport lighting is controlled by air traffic controllers at towered airports. At nontowered airports, the lights may be on a timer, or where an FSS is located at an airport, the FSS personnel may control the lighting. A pilot may request various light systems be turned on or off and also request a specified intensity, if available, from ATC or FSS personnel. At selected nontowered airports, the pilot may control the lighting by using the radio. This is done by selecting a specified frequency and clicking the radio microphone. For information on pilot controlled lighting at various airports, refer to the A/FD. [Figure 13-11]

Key Mike	Function
7 times within 5 seconds	Highest intensity available
5 times within 5 seconds	Medium or lower intensity (Lower REIL or REIL off)
3 times within 5 seconds	Lowest intensity available (Lower REIL or REIL off)

Figure 13-11. Radio controlled runway lighting.

Taxiway Lights

Omnidirectional taxiway lights outline the edges of the taxiway and are blue in color. At many airports, these edge lights may have variable intensity settings that may be adjusted by an air traffic controller when deemed necessary or when requested by the pilot. Some airports also have taxiway centerline lights that are green in color.

Obstruction Lights

Obstructions are marked or lighted to warn pilots of their presence during daytime and nighttime conditions. Obstruction lighting can be found both on and off an airport to identify obstructions. They may be marked or lighted in any of the following conditions.

- Red obstruction lights—flash or emit a steady red color during nighttime operations, and the obstructions are painted orange and white for daytime operations.

- High intensity white obstruction lights—flash high intensity white lights during the daytime with the intensity reduced for nighttime.

- Dual lighting—a combination of flashing red beacons and steady red lights for nighttime operation, and high intensity white lights for daytime operations.

Wind Direction Indicators

It is important for a pilot to know the direction of the wind. At facilities with an operating control tower, this information is provided by ATC. Information may also be provided by FSS personnel located at a particular airport or by requesting information on a CTAF at airports that have the capacity to receive and broadcast on this frequency.

When none of these services is available, it is possible to determine wind direction and runway in use by visual wind indicators. A pilot should check these wind indicators even when information is provided on the CTAF at a given airport because there is no assurance that the information provided is accurate.

The wind direction indicator can be a wind cone, wind sock, tetrahedron, or wind tee. These are usually located in a central location near the runway and may be placed in the center of a segmented circle, which identifies the traffic pattern direction, if it is other than the standard left-hand pattern. *[Figures 13-12 and 13-13]*

The wind sock is a good source of information since it not only indicates wind direction, but allows the pilot to estimate the wind velocity and gusts or factor. The wind sock extends out straighter in strong winds and tends to move back and forth when the wind is gusty. Wind tees and tetrahedrons can swing freely, and align themselves with the wind direction. The wind tee and tetrahedron can also be manually set to align with the runway in use; therefore, a pilot should also look at the wind sock, if available.

Traffic Patterns

At those airports without an operating control tower, a segmented circle visual indicator system *[Figure 13-13]*, if installed, is designed to provide traffic pattern information. Usually located in a position affording maximum visibility to pilots in the air and on the ground and providing a centralized location for other elements of the system, the segmented circle consists of the following components: wind direction indicators, landing direction indicators, landing strip indicators, and traffic pattern indicators.

A tetrahedron is installed to indicate the direction of landings and takeoffs when conditions at the airport warrant its use. It may be located at the center of a segmented circle and may be lighted for night operations. The small end of the tetrahedron points in the direction of landing. Pilots are cautioned against using a tetrahedron for any purpose other than as an indicator of landing direction. At airports with control towers, the tetrahedron should only be referenced when the control tower is not in operation. Tower instructions supersede tetrahedron indications.

Landing strip indicators are installed in pairs as shown in *Figure 13-13* and are used to show the alignment of landing strips. Traffic pattern indicators are arranged in pairs in conjunction with landing strip indicators and used to indicate the direction of turns when there is a variation from the normal left traffic pattern. (If there is no segmented circle installed at the airport, traffic pattern indicators may be installed on or near the end of the runway.)

Figure 13-12. *Wind direction indicators.*

Figure 13-13. *Segmented circle.*

At most airports and military air bases, traffic pattern altitudes for propeller-driven aircraft generally extend from 600 feet to as high as 1,500 feet above ground level (AGL). Pilots can obtain the traffic pattern altitude for an airport from the A/FD. Also, traffic pattern altitudes for military turbojet aircraft sometimes extend up to 2,500 feet AGL. Therefore, pilots of en route aircraft should be constantly on the alert for other aircraft in traffic patterns and avoid these areas whenever possible. When operating at an airport, traffic pattern altitudes should be maintained unless otherwise required by the applicable distance from cloud criteria in Title 14 of the Code of Federal Regulations (14 CFR) section 91.155. Additional information on airport traffic pattern operations can be found in Chapter 4, Air Traffic Control, of the AIM. Pilots can find traffic pattern information and restrictions such as noise abatement in the A/FD.

Example: Key to Traffic Pattern Operations— Single Runway

1. Enter pattern in level flight, abeam the midpoint of the runway, at pattern altitude. (1,000' AGL) is recommended pattern altitude unless established otherwise.)

2. Maintain pattern altitude until abeam approach end of the landing runway on downwind leg.

3. Complete turn to final at least ¼ mile from the runway.

4. Continue straight ahead until beyond departure end of runway.

5. If remaining in the traffic pattern, commence turn to crosswind leg beyond the departure end of the runway within 300 feet of pattern altitude.

6. If departing the traffic pattern, continue straight out, or exit with a 45° turn (to the left when in a left-hand traffic pattern; to the right when in a right-hand traffic pattern) beyond the departure end of the runway, after reaching pattern altitude. *[Figure 13-14]*

Example: Key to Traffic Pattern Operations— Parallel Runways

1. Enter pattern in level flight, abeam the midpoint of the runway, at pattern altitude. (1,000' AGL is recommended pattern altitude unless established otherwise.)

2. Maintain pattern altitude until abeam approach end of the landing runway on downwind leg.

3. Complete turn to final at least ¼ mile from the runway.

4. Continue straight ahead until beyond departure end of runway.

5. If remaining in the traffic pattern, commence turn to crosswind leg beyond the departure end of the runway within 300 feet of pattern altitude.

6. If departing the traffic pattern, continue straight out, or exit with a 45° turn (to the left when in a left-hand traffic pattern; to the right when in a right-hand traffic pattern) beyond the departure end of the runway, after reaching pattern altitude.

7. Do not overshoot final or continue on a track which penetrates the final approach of the parallel runway.

8. Do not continue on a track which penetrates the departure path of the parallel runway. *[Figure 13-15]*

Radio Communications

Operating in and out of a towered airport, as well as in a good portion of the airspace system, requires that an aircraft have two-way radio communication capability. For this reason, a pilot should be knowledgeable of radio station license requirements and radio communications equipment and procedures.

Radio License

There is no license requirement for a pilot operating in the United States; however, a pilot who operates internationally is required to hold a restricted radiotelephone permit issued by the Federal Communications Commission (FCC). There

Figure 13-14. *Traffic pattern operations—single runway.*

is also no station license requirement for most general aviation aircraft operating in the United States. A station license is required however for an aircraft which is operating internationally, which uses other than a VHF radio, and which meets other criteria.

Radio Equipment

In general aviation, the most common types of radios are VHF. A VHF radio operates on frequencies between 118.0 and 136.975 and is classified as 720 or 760 depending on the number of channels it can accommodate. The 720 and 760 use .025 spacing (118.025, 118.050) with the 720 having a frequency range up to 135.975 and the 760 going up to 136.975. VHF radios are limited to line of sight transmissions; therefore, aircraft at higher altitudes are able to transmit and receive at greater distances.

In March of 1997, the International Civil Aviation Organization (ICAO) amended its International Standards and Recommended Practices to incorporate a channel plan specifying 8.33 kHz channel spacings in the Aeronautical Mobile Service. The 8.33 kHz channel plan was adopted to alleviate the shortage of VHF ATC channels experienced in western Europe and in the United Kingdom. Seven western European countries and the United Kingdom implemented the 8.33 kHz channel plan on January 1, 1999. Accordingly, aircraft operating in the airspace of these countries must have

the capability of transmitting and receiving on the 8.33 kHz spaced channels.

Using proper radio phraseology and procedures contribute to a pilot's ability to operate safely and efficiently in the airspace system. A review of the Pilot/Controller Glossary contained in the AIM assists a pilot in the use and understanding of standard terminology. The AIM also contains many examples of radio communications.

ICAO has adopted a phonetic alphabet, which should be used in radio communications. When communicating with ATC, pilots should use this alphabet to identify their aircraft. *[Figure 13-16]*

Lost Communication Procedures

It is possible that a pilot might experience a malfunction of the radio. This might cause the transmitter, receiver, or both to become inoperative. If a receiver becomes inoperative and a pilot needs to land at a towered airport, it is advisable to remain outside or above Class D airspace until the direction and flow of traffic is determined. A pilot should then advise the tower of the aircraft type, position, altitude, and intention to land. The pilot should continue, enter the pattern, report a position as appropriate, and watch for light signals from the tower. Light signal colors and their meanings are contained in *Figure 13-17*.

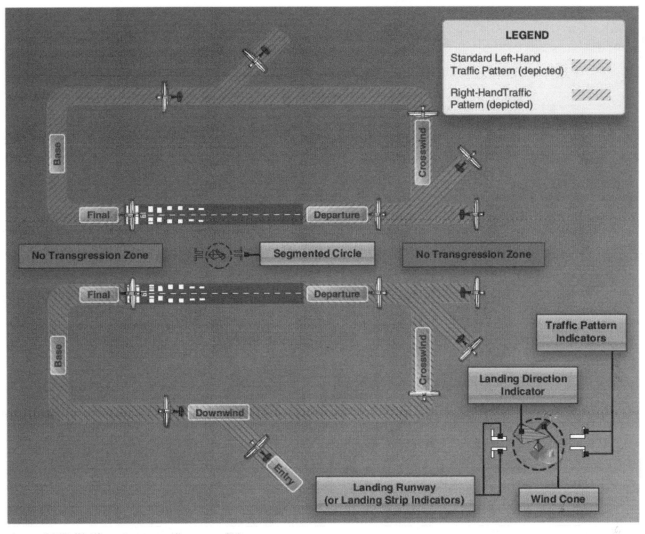

Figure 13-15. *Traffic pattern operation—parallel runways.*

If the transmitter becomes inoperative, a pilot should follow the previously stated procedures and also monitor the appropriate ATC frequency. During daylight hours ATC transmissions may be acknowledged by rocking the wings, and at night by blinking the landing light.

When both receiver and transmitter are inoperative, the pilot should remain outside of Class D airspace until the flow of traffic has been determined and then enter the pattern and watch for light signals.

If a radio malfunctions prior to departure, it is advisable to have it repaired, if possible. If this is not possible, a call should be made to ATC and the pilot should request authorization to depart without two-way radio communications. If authorization is given to depart, the pilot is advised to monitor the appropriate frequency and/or watch for light signals as appropriate.

Air Traffic Control (ATC) Services

Besides the services provided by an FSS as discussed in Chapter 12, Aviation Weather Services, numerous other services are provided by ATC. In many instances a pilot is required to have contact with ATC, but even when not required, a pilot finds it helpful to request their services.

Primary Radar

Radar is a device which provides information on range, azimuth, and/or elevation of objects in the path of the transmitted pulses. It measures the time interval between transmission and reception of radio pulses and correlates the angular orientation of the radiated antenna beam or beams in azimuth and/or elevation. Range is determined by measuring the time it takes for the radio wave to go out to the object and then return to the receiving antenna. The direction of a detected object from a radar site is determined by the position

Character	Morse Code	Telephony	Phonic Pronunciation
A	•—	Alfa	(AL-FAH)
B	—•••	Bravo	(BRAH-VOH)
C	—•—•	Charlie	(CHAR-LEE) or (SHAR-LEE)
D	—••	Delta	(DELL-TAH)
E	•	Echo	(ECK-OH)
F	••—•	Foxtrot	(FOKS-TROT)
G	——•	Golf	(GOLF)
H	••••	Hotel	(HOH-TEL)
I	••	India	(IN-DEE-AH)
J	•———	Juliett	(JEW-LEE-ETT)
K	—•—	Kilo	(KEY-LOH)
L	•—••	Lima	(LEE-MAH)
M	——	Mike	(MIKE)
N	—•	November	(NO-VEM-BER)
O	———	Oscar	(OSS-CAH)
P	•——•	Papa	(PAH-PAH)
Q	——•—	Quebec	(KEH-BECK)
R	•—•	Romeo	(ROW-ME-OH)
S	•••	Sierra	(SEE-AIR-RAH)
T	—	Tango	(TANG-GO)
U	••—	Uniform	(YOU-NEE-FORM) or (OO-NEE-FORM)
V	•••—	Victor	(VIK-TAH)
W	•——	Whiskey	(WISS-KEY)
X	—••—	Xray	(ECKS-RAY)
Y	—•——	Yankee	(YANG-KEY)
Z	——••	Zulu	(ZOO-LOO)
1	•————	One	(WUN)
2	••———	Two	(TOO)
3	•••——	Three	(TREE)
4	••••—	Four	(FOW-ER)
5	•••••	Five	(FIFE)
6	—••••	Six	(SIX)
7	——•••	Seven	(SEV-EN)
8	———••	Eight	(AIT)
9	————•	Nine	(NIN-ER)
0	—————	Zero	(ZEE-RO)

Figure 13-16. *Phonetic alphabet.*

of the rotating antenna when the reflected portion of the radio wave is received.

Modern radar is very reliable and there are seldom outages. This is due to reliable maintenance and improved equipment. There are, however, some limitations which may affect ATC services and prevent a controller from issuing advisories concerning aircraft which are not under his or her control and cannot be seen on radar.

The characteristics of radio waves are such that they normally travel in a continuous straight line unless they are "bent" by atmospheric phenomena such as temperature inversions, reflected or attenuated by dense objects such as heavy clouds and precipitation, or screened by high terrain features.

ATC Radar Beacon System (ATCRBS)

The ATC radar beacon system (ATCRBS) is often referred to as "secondary surveillance radar." This system consists of three components and helps in alleviating some of the limitations associated with primary radar. The three components are an interrogator, transponder, and radarscope. The advantages of ATCRBS are the reinforcement of radar targets, rapid target identification, and a unique display of selected codes.

Transponder

The transponder is the airborne portion of the secondary surveillance radar system and a system with which a pilot should be familiar. The ATCRBS cannot display the secondary information unless an aircraft is equipped with a transponder. A transponder is also required to operate in certain controlled airspace as discussed in Chapter 14, Airspace.

A transponder code consists of four numbers from 0 to 7 (4,096 possible codes). There are some standard codes, or ATC may issue a four-digit code to an aircraft. When a controller requests a code or function on the transponder, the word "squawk" may be used. *Figure 13-18* lists some standard transponder phraseology. Additional information concerning transponder operation can be found in the AIM, chapter 4.

Radar Traffic Advisories

Radar equipped ATC facilities provide radar assistance to aircraft on instrument flight plans and VFR aircraft provided the aircraft can communicate with the facility and are within radar coverage. This basic service includes safety alerts, traffic advisories, limited vectoring when requested, and sequencing at locations where this procedure has been established. ATC issues traffic advisories based on observed radar targets. The traffic is referenced by azimuth from the aircraft in terms of the 12-hour clock. Also, distance in nautical miles, direction in which the target is moving, and type and altitude of the aircraft, if known, are given. An example would be: "Traffic 10 o'clock 5 miles east bound, Cessna 152, 3,000 feet." The pilot should note that traffic position is based on the aircraft track, and that wind correction can affect the clock position

Color and Type of Signal	Movement of Vehicles, Equipment and Personnel	Aircraft on the Ground	Aircraft in Flight
Steady green	Cleared to cross, proceed or go	Cleared for takeoff	Cleared to land
Flashing green	Not applicable	Cleared for taxi	Return for landing (to be followed by steady green at the proper time)
Steady red	Stop	Stop	Give way to other aircraft and continue circling
Flashing red	Clear the taxiway/runway	Taxi clear of the runway in use	Airport unsafe, do not land
Flashing white	Return to starting point on airport	Return to starting point on airport	Not applicable
Alternating red and green	Exercise extreme caution!!!!	Exercise extreme caution!!!!	Exercise extreme caution!!!!

Figure 13-17. *Light gun signals.*

at which a pilot locates traffic. This service is not intended to relieve the pilot of the responsibility to see and avoid other aircraft. *[Figure 13-19]*

In addition to basic radar service, terminal radar service area (TRSA) has been implemented at certain terminal locations. TRSAs are depicted on sectional aeronautical charts and listed in the A/FD. The purpose of this service is to provide separation between all participating VFR aircraft and all IFR aircraft operating within the TRSA. Class C service provides approved separation between IFR and VFR aircraft, and

sequencing of VFR aircraft to the primary airport. Class B service provides approved separation of aircraft based on IFR, VFR, and/or weight, and sequencing of VFR arrivals to the primary airport(s).

Wake Turbulence

All aircraft generate wake turbulence while in flight. This disturbance is caused by a pair of counter-rotating vortices trailing from the wingtips. The vortices from larger aircraft pose problems to encountering aircraft. The wake of these aircraft can impose rolling moments exceeding the roll-

Radar Beacon Phraseology	
SQUAWK (number)	Operate radar beacon transponder on designated code in MODE A/3.
IDENT	Engage the "IDENT" feature (military I/P) of the transponder.
SQUAWK (number) and IDENT	Operate transponder on specified code in MODE A/3 and engage the "IDENT" (military I/P) feature.
SQUAWK Standby	Switch transponder to standby position.
SQUAWK Low/Normal	Operate transponder on low or normal sensitivity as specified. Transponder is operated in "NORMAL" position unless ATC specifies "LOW" ("ON" is used instead of "NORMAL" as a master control label on some types of transponders).
SQUAWK Altitude	Activate MODE C with automatic altitude reporting.
STOP Altitude SQUAWK	Turn off altitude reporting switch and continue transmitting MODE C framing pulses. If your equipment does not have this capability, turn off MODE C.
STOP SQUAWK (mode in use)	Switch off specified mode. (Used for military aircraft when the controller is unaware of military service requirements for the aircraft to continue operation on another MODE.)
STOP SQUAWK	Switch off transponder.
SQUAWK Mayday	Operate transponder in the emergency position (MODE A Code 7700 for civil transponder, MODE 3 Code 7700 and emergency feature for military transponder).
SQUAWK VFR	Operate radar beacon transponder on Code 1200 in MODE A/3, or other appropriate VFR code.

Figure 13-18. *Transponder phraseology.*

Traffic information would be issued to the pilot of aircraft "A" as 12 o'clock. The actual position of the traffic as seen by the pilot of aircraft "A" would be 1 o'clock. Traffic information issued to aircraft "B" would also be given as 12 o'clock, but in this case the pilot of "B" would see traffic at 10 o'clock.

Figure 13-19. *Traffic advisories.*

control authority of the encountering aircraft. Also, the turbulence generated within the vortices can damage aircraft components and equipment if encountered at close range. For this reason, a pilot must envision the location of the vortex wake and adjust the flightpath accordingly.

During ground operations and during takeoff, jet engine blast (thrust stream turbulence) can cause damage and upset smaller aircraft at close range. For this reason, pilots of small aircraft should consider the effects of jet-engine blast and maintain adequate separation. Also, pilots of larger aircraft should consider the effects of their aircraft's jet-engine blast on other aircraft and equipment on the ground.

Vortex Generation

Lift is generated by the creation of a pressure differential over the wing surface. The lowest pressure occurs over the upper wing surface, and the highest pressure under the wing. This pressure differential triggers the rollup of the airflow aft of the wing resulting in swirling air masses trailing downstream of the wingtips. After the rollup is completed, the wake consists of two counter rotating cylindrical vortices. Most of the energy is within a few feet of the center of each vortex, but pilots should avoid a region within about 100 feet of the vortex core. *[Figure 13-20]*

Vortex Strength

The strength of the vortex is governed by the weight, speed, and shape of the wing of the generating aircraft. The vortex characteristics of any given aircraft can also be changed by the extension of flaps or other wing configuration devices as well as by a change in speed. The greatest vortex strength occurs when the generating aircraft is heavy, clean, and slow.

Vortex Behavior

Trailing vortices have certain behavioral characteristics that can help a pilot visualize the wake location and take avoidance precautions.

Vortices are generated from the moment an aircraft leaves the ground (until it touches down), since trailing vortices are the byproduct of wing lift. *[Figure 13-21]* The vortex circulation is outward, upward, and around the wingtips when viewed from either ahead or behind the aircraft. Tests have shown that vortices remain spaced a bit less than a wingspan apart, drifting with the wind, at altitudes greater than a wingspan from the ground. Tests have also shown that the vortices sink at a rate of several hundred feet per minute, slowing their descent and diminishing in strength with time and distance behind the generating aircraft.

Figure 13-20. *Vortex generation.*

Figure 13-21. *Vortex behavior.*

When the vortices of larger aircraft sink close to the ground (within 100 to 200 feet), they tend to move laterally over the ground at a speed of 2–3 knots. A crosswind decreases the lateral movement of the upwind vortex and increases the movement of the downwind vortex. A tailwind condition can move the vortices of the preceding aircraft forward into the touchdown zone.

Vortex Avoidance Procedures

- Landing behind a larger aircraft on the same runway—stay at or above the larger aircraft's approach flightpath and land beyond its touchdown point.

- Landing behind a larger aircraft on a parallel runway closer than 2,500 feet—consider the possibility of drift and stay at or above the larger aircraft's final approach flightpath and note its touch down point.

- Landing behind a larger aircraft on crossing runway—cross above the larger aircraft's flightpath.

- Landing behind a departing aircraft on the same runway—land prior to the departing aircraft's rotating point.

- Landing behind a larger aircraft on a crossing runway—note the aircraft's rotation point and, if that point is past the intersection, continue and land prior to the intersection. If the larger aircraft rotates prior to the intersection, avoid flight below its flightpath. Abandon the approach unless a landing is ensured well before reaching the intersection.

- Departing behind a large aircraft—rotate prior to the large aircraft's rotation point and climb above its climb path until turning clear of the wake.

- For intersection takeoffs on the same runway—be alert to adjacent larger aircraft operations, particularly upwind of the runway of intended use. If an intersection takeoff clearance is received, avoid headings that cross below the larger aircraft's path.

- If departing or landing after a large aircraft executing a low approach, missed approach, or touch and go landing (since vortices settle and move laterally near the ground, the vortex hazard may exist along the runway and in the flightpath, particularly in a quartering tailwind), it is prudent to wait at least 2 minutes prior to a takeoff or landing.

- En route it is advisable to avoid a path below and behind a large aircraft, and if a large aircraft is observed above on the same track, change the aircraft position laterally and preferably upwind.

Collision Avoidance

14 CFR part 91 has established right-of-way rules, minimum safe altitudes, and VFR cruising altitudes to enhance flight safety. The pilot can contribute to collision avoidance by being alert and scanning for other aircraft. This is particularly important in the vicinity of an airport.

Effective scanning is accomplished with a series of short, regularly spaced eye movements that bring successive areas of the sky into the central visual field. Each movement should not exceed 10°, and each should be observed for at least 1 second to enable detection. Although back and forth eye movements seem preferred by most pilots, each pilot should develop a scanning pattern that is most comfortable and then adhere to it to assure optimum scanning. Even if entitled to the right-of-way, a pilot should yield if another aircraft seems too close.

Clearing Procedures

The following procedures and considerations should assist a pilot in collision avoidance under various situations.

- Before takeoff—prior to taxiing onto a runway or landing area in preparation for takeoff, pilots should scan the approach area for possible landing traffic, executing appropriate maneuvers to provide a clear view of the approach areas.

- Climbs and descents—during climbs and descents in flight conditions which permit visual detection of other traffic, pilots should execute gentle banks left and right at a frequency which permits continuous visual scanning of the airspace.

- Straight and level—during sustained periods of straight-and-level flight, a pilot should execute appropriate clearing procedures at periodic intervals.

- Traffic patterns—entries into traffic patterns while descending should be avoided.

- Traffic at VOR sites—due to converging traffic, sustained vigilance should be maintained in the vicinity of VORs and intersections.

- Training operations—vigilance should be maintained and clearing turns should be made prior to a practice maneuver. During instruction, the pilot should be asked to verbalize the clearing procedures (call out "clear left, right, above, and below").

High-wing and low-wing aircraft have their respective blind spots. The pilot of a high-wing aircraft should momentarily raise the wing in the direction of the intended turn and look for traffic prior to commencing the turn. The pilot of a low-wing aircraft should momentarily lower the wing and look for traffic prior to commencing the turn.

Runway Incursion Avoidance

A runway incursion is "any occurrence in the airport runway environment involving an aircraft, vehicle, person, or object on the ground that creates a collision hazard or results in a loss of required separation with an aircraft taking off, intending to take off, landing, or intending to land." It is important to give the same attention to operating on the surface as in other phases of flights. Proper planning can prevent runway incursions and the possibility of a ground collision. A pilot should be aware of the aircraft's position on the surface at all times and be aware of other aircraft and vehicle operations on the airport. At times towered airports can be busy and taxi instructions complex. In this situation it may be advisable to write down taxi instructions. The following are some practices to help prevent a runway incursion:

- Read back all runway crossing and/or hold instructions.

- Review airport layouts as part of preflight planning, before descending to land and while taxiing, as needed.

- Know airport signage.

- Review NOTAM for information on runway/taxiway closures and construction areas.

- Request progressive taxi instructions from ATC when unsure of the taxi route.

- Check for traffic before crossing any runway hold line and before entering a taxiway.

- Turn on aircraft lights and the rotating beacon or strobe lights while taxing.

- When landing, clear the active runway as soon as possible, then wait for taxi instructions before further movement.

- Study and use proper phraseology in order to understand and respond to ground control instructions.

- Write down complex taxi instructions at unfamiliar airports.

For more detailed information, contact the FAA's Office of Runway Safety and Operational Services web site at http://www.faa.gov/runwaysafety/ or visit http://www.aopa.org/asf/accident_data/incursions.html to access a learning tool developed by the FAA and the Aircraft Owners and Pilots Association (AOPA) to help pilots and maintenance technicians avoid runway incursions involving taxiing aircraft. Additional information can also be found in Advisory Circular (AC) 91-73, Part 91, Pilot and Flightcrew Procedures During Taxi Operations, and Part 135, Single-Pilot Procedures During Taxi Operations.

Chapter Summary

This chapter focused on airport operations both in the air and on the surface. For specific information about an unfamiliar airport, consult the A/FD and NOTAMS before flying. For further information regarding procedures discussed in this chapter, refer to 14 CFR part 91 and the AIM. By adhering to established procedures, both airport operations and safety are enhanced.

Chapter 14

Airspace

The two categories of airspace are: regulatory and nonregulatory. Within these two categories there are four types: controlled, uncontrolled, special use, and other airspace. *Figure 14-1* presents a profile view of the dimensions of various classes of airspace. Also, there are excerpts from sectional charts which are discussed in Chapter 15, Navigation, that are used to illustrate how airspace is depicted.

Figure 14-1. *Airspace profile.*

Controlled Airspace

Controlled airspace is a generic term that covers the different classifications of airspace and defined dimensions within which air traffic control (ATC) service is provided in accordance with the airspace classification. Controlled airspace consists of:

- Class A
- Class B
- Class C
- Class D
- Class E

Class A Airspace

Class A airspace is generally the airspace from 18,000 feet mean sea level (MSL) up to and including flight level (FL) 600, including the airspace overlying the waters within 12 nautical miles (NM) of the coast of the 48 contiguous states and Alaska. Unless otherwise authorized, all operation in Class A airspace is conducted under instrument flight rules (IFR).

Class B Airspace

Class B airspace is generally airspace from the surface to 10,000 feet MSL surrounding the nation's busiest airports in terms of airport operations or passenger enplanements. The configuration of each Class B airspace area is individually tailored, consists of a surface area and two or more layers (some Class B airspace areas resemble upside-down wedding cakes), and is designed to contain all published instrument procedures once an aircraft enters the airspace. An ATC clearance is required for all aircraft to operate in the area, and all aircraft that are so cleared receive separation services within the airspace.

Class C Airspace

Class C airspace is generally airspace from the surface to 4,000 feet above the airport elevation (charted in MSL) surrounding those airports that have an operational control tower, are serviced by a radar approach control, and have a certain number of IFR operations or passenger enplanements. Although the configuration of each Class C area is individually tailored, the airspace usually consists of a surface area with a five NM radius, an outer circle with a ten NM radius that extends from 1,200 feet to 4,000 feet above the airport elevation, and an outer area. Each aircraft must establish two-way radio communications with the ATC facility providing air traffic services prior to entering the airspace and thereafter maintain those communications while within the airspace.

Class D Airspace

Class D airspace is generally airspace from the surface to 2,500 feet above the airport elevation (charted in MSL) surrounding those airports that have an operational control tower. The configuration of each Class D airspace area is individually tailored and when instrument procedures are published, the airspace is normally designed to contain the procedures. Arrival extensions for instrument approach procedures (IAPs) may be Class D or Class E airspace. Unless otherwise authorized, each aircraft must establish two-way radio communications with the ATC facility providing air traffic services prior to entering the airspace and thereafter maintain those communications while in the airspace.

Class E Airspace

If the airspace is not Class A, B, C, or D, and is controlled airspace, then it is Class E airspace. Class E airspace extends upward from either the surface or a designated altitude to the overlying or adjacent controlled airspace. When designated as a surface area, the airspace is configured to contain all instrument procedures. Also in this class are federal airways, airspace beginning at either 700 or 1,200 feet above ground level (AGL) used to transition to and from the terminal or en route environment, and en route domestic and offshore airspace areas designated below 18,000 feet MSL. Unless designated at a lower altitude, Class E airspace begins at 14,500 MSL over the United States, including that airspace overlying the waters within 12 NM of the coast of the 48 contiguous states and Alaska, up to but not including 18,000 feet MSL, and the airspace above FL 600.

Uncontrolled Airspace

Class G Airspace

Uncontrolled airspace or Class G airspace is the portion of the airspace that has not been designated as Class A, B, C, D, or E. It is therefore designated uncontrolled airspace. Class G airspace extends from the surface to the base of the overlying Class E airspace. Although ATC has no authority or responsibility to control air traffic, pilots should remember there are visual flight rules (VFR) minimums which apply to Class G airspace.

Special Use Airspace

Special use airspace or special area of operation (SAO) is the designation for airspace in which certain activities must be confined, or where limitations may be imposed on aircraft operations that are not part of those activities. Certain special use airspace areas can create limitations on the mixed use of airspace. The special use airspace depicted on instrument charts includes the area name or number, effective altitude, time and weather conditions of operation, the controlling agency, and the chart panel location. On National Aeronautical Charting Group (NACG) en route charts, this information is available on one of the end panels. Special use airspace usually consists of:

- Prohibited areas
- Restricted areas
- Warning areas
- Military operation areas (MOAs)
- Alert areas
- Controlled firing areas (CFAs)

Prohibited Areas

Prohibited areas contain airspace of defined dimensions within which the flight of aircraft is prohibited. Such areas are established for security or other reasons associated with the national welfare. These areas are published in the Federal Register and are depicted on aeronautical charts. The area is charted as a "P" followed by a number (e.g., P-49). Examples of prohibited areas include Camp David and the National Mall in Washington, D.C., where the White House and the Congressional buildings are located. *[Figure 14-2]*

Figure 14-2. *An example of a prohibited area is Crawford, Texas.*

Restricted Areas

Restricted areas are areas where operations are hazardous to nonparticipating aircraft and contain airspace within which the flight of aircraft, while not wholly prohibited, is subject to restrictions. Activities within these areas must be confined because of their nature, or limitations may be imposed upon aircraft operations that are not a part of those activities, or both. Restricted areas denote the existence of unusual, often invisible, hazards to aircraft (e.g., artillery firing, aerial gunnery, or guided missiles). IFR flights may be authorized to transit the airspace and are routed accordingly. Penetration of restricted areas without authorization from the using or controlling agency may be extremely hazardous to the aircraft and its occupants. ATC facilities apply the following procedures when aircraft are operating on an IFR clearance (including those cleared by ATC to maintain VFR on top) via a route which lies within joint-use restricted airspace:

1. If the restricted area is not active and has been released to the Federal Aviation Administration (FAA), the ATC facility allows the aircraft to operate in the restricted airspace without issuing specific clearance for it to do so.

2. If the restricted area is active and has not been released to the FAA, the ATC facility issues a clearance which ensures the aircraft avoids the restricted airspace.

Restricted areas are charted with an "R" followed by a number (e.g., R-4401) and are depicted on the en route chart appropriate for use at the altitude or FL being flown. *[Figure 14-3]* Restricted area information can be obtained on the back of the chart.

Figure 14-3. *Restricted areas on a sectional chart.*

Warning Areas

Warning areas are similar in nature to restricted areas; however, the United States government does not have sole jurisdiction over the airspace. A warning area is airspace of defined dimensions, extending from 12 NM outward from the coast of the United States, containing activity that may be hazardous to nonparticipating aircraft. The purpose of such areas is to warn nonparticipating pilots of the potential danger. A warning area may be located over domestic or international waters or both. The airspace is designated with a "W" followed by a number (e.g., W-237). *[Figure 14-4]*

Military Operation Areas (MOAs)

MOAs consist of airspace with defined vertical and lateral limits established for the purpose of separating certain

Figure 14-4. *Requirements for airspace operations.*

military training activities from IFR traffic. Whenever an MOA is being used, nonparticipating IFR traffic may be cleared through an MOA if IFR separation can be provided by ATC. Otherwise, ATC reroutes or restricts nonparticipating IFR traffic. MOAs are depicted on sectional, VFR terminal area, and en route low altitude charts and are not numbered (e.g., "Camden Ridge MOA"). *[Figure 14-5]* However, the MOA is also further defined on the back of the sectional charts with times of operation, altitudes affected, and the controlling agency.

Alert Areas

Alert areas are depicted on aeronautical charts with an "A" followed by a number (e.g., A-211) to inform nonparticipating pilots of areas that may contain a high volume of pilot training or an unusual type of aerial activity. Pilots should exercise caution in alert areas. All activity within an alert area shall be conducted in accordance with regulations, without waiver, and pilots of participating aircraft, as well as pilots transiting the area, shall be equally responsible for collision avoidance. *[Figure 14-6]*

Controlled Firing Areas (CFAs)

CFAs contain activities, which, if not conducted in a controlled environment, could be hazardous to nonparticipating aircraft. The difference between CFAs and other special use airspace is that activities must be suspended when a spotter aircraft, radar, or ground lookout position indicates an aircraft might be approaching the area. There is no need to chart CFAs since they do not cause a nonparticipating aircraft to change its flightpath.

Other Airspace Areas

"Other airspace areas" is a general term referring to the majority of the remaining airspace. It includes:

- Local airport advisory
- Military training route (MTR)
- Temporary flight restriction (TFR)
- Parachute jump aircraft operations
- Published VFR routes
- Terminal radar service area (TRSA)
- National security area (NSA)

Local Airport Advisory (LAA)

A service provided by facilities, which are located on the landing airport, have a discrete ground-to-air communication frequency or the tower frequency when the tower is closed, automated weather reporting with voice broadcasting, and a continuous ASOS/AWOS data display, other continuous direct reading instruments, or manual observations available to the specialist.

Figure 14-5. *Camden Ridge MOA is an example of a military operations area.*

Figure 14-6. *Alert area (A-211).*

Military Training Routes (MTRs)

MTRs are routes used by military aircraft to maintain proficiency in tactical flying. These routes are usually established below 10,000 feet MSL for operations at speeds in excess of 250 knots. Some route segments may be defined at higher altitudes for purposes of route continuity. Routes are identified as IFR (IR), and VFR (VR), followed by a number. *[Figure 14-7]* MTRs with no segment above 1,500 feet AGL are identified by four number characters (e.g., IR1206, VR1207). MTRs that include one or more segments above 1,500 feet AGL are identified by three number characters (e.g., IR206, VR207). IFR low altitude en route charts depict all IR routes and all VR routes that accommodate operations above 1,500 feet AGL. IR routes are conducted in accordance with IFR regardless of weather conditions. VFR sectional charts depict military training activities such as IR, VR, MOA, restricted area, warning area, and alert area information.

Figure 14-7. *Military training route (MTR) chart symbols.*

Temporary Flight Restrictions (TFR)

A flight data center (FDC) Notice to Airmen (NOTAM) is issued to designate a TFR. The NOTAM begins with the phrase "FLIGHT RESTRICTIONS" followed by the location of the temporary restriction, effective time period, area defined in statute miles, and altitudes affected. The NOTAM also contains the FAA coordination facility and telephone number, the reason for the restriction, and any other information deemed appropriate. The pilot should check the NOTAMs as part of flight planning.

Some of the purposes for establishing a TFR are:

- Protect persons and property in the air or on the surface from an existing or imminent hazard.

- Provide a safe environment for the operation of disaster relief aircraft.

- Prevent an unsafe congestion of sightseeing aircraft above an incident or event, which may generate a high degree of public interest.

- Protect declared national disasters for humanitarian reasons in the State of Hawaii.

- Protect the President, Vice President, or other public figures.

- Provide a safe environment for space agency operations.

Since the events of September 11, 2001, the use of TFRs has become much more common. There have been a number of incidents of aircraft incursions into TFRs, which have resulted in pilots undergoing security investigations and certificate suspensions. It is a pilot's responsibility to be aware of TFRs in their proposed area of flight. One way to check is to visit the FAA website, www.tfr.faa.gov, and verify that there is not a TFR in the area.

Parachute Jump Aircraft Operations

Parachute jump aircraft operations are published in the Airport/Facility Directory (A/FD). Sites that are used frequently are depicted on sectional charts.

Published VFR Routes

Published VFR routes are for transitioning around, under, or through some complex airspace. Terms such as VFR flyway, VFR corridor, Class B airspace VFR transition route, and terminal area VFR route have been applied to such routes. These routes are generally found on VFR terminal area planning charts.

Terminal Radar Service Areas (TRSAs)

TRSAs are areas where participating pilots can receive additional radar services. The purpose of the service is to provide separation between all IFR operations and participating VFR aircraft.

The primary airport(s) within the TRSA become(s) Class D airspace. The remaining portion of the TRSA overlies other controlled airspace, which is normally Class E airspace beginning at 700 or 1,200 feet and established to transition to/from the en route/terminal environment. TRSAs are depicted on VFR sectional charts and terminal area charts with a solid black line and altitudes for each segment. The Class D portion is charted with a blue segmented line. Participation in TRSA services is voluntary; however, pilots operating under VFR are encouraged to contact the radar approach control and take advantage of TRSA service.

National Security Areas (NSAs)

NSAs consist of airspace of defined vertical and lateral dimensions established at locations where there is a requirement for increased security and safety of ground facilities. Flight in NSAs may be temporarily prohibited by regulation under the provisions of Title 14 of the Code of Federal Regulations (14 CFR) part 99, and prohibitions are disseminated via NOTAM. Pilots are requested to voluntarily avoid flying through these depicted areas.

Air Traffic Control and the National Airspace System

The primary purpose of the ATC system is to prevent a collision between aircraft operating in the system and to organize and expedite the flow of traffic. In addition to its primary function, the ATC system has the capability to provide (with certain limitations) additional services. The ability to provide additional services is limited by many factors, such as the volume of traffic, frequency congestion, quality of radar, controller workload, higher priority duties, and the pure physical inability to scan and detect those situations that fall in this category. It is recognized that these services cannot be provided in cases in which the provision of services is precluded by the above factors.

Consistent with the aforementioned conditions, controllers shall provide additional service procedures to the extent permitted by higher priority duties and other circumstances. The provision of additional services is not optional on the part of the controller, but rather is required when the work situation permits. Provide ATC service in accordance with the procedures and minima in this order except when:

1. A deviation is necessary to conform with ICAO Documents, National Rules of the Air, or special agreements where the United States provides ATC service in airspace outside the country and its possessions or:

2. Other procedures/minima are prescribed in a letter of agreement, FAA directive, or a military document, or:

3. A deviation is necessary to assist an aircraft when an emergency has been declared.

Coordinating the Use of Airspace

ATC is responsible for ensuring that the necessary coordination has been accomplished before allowing an aircraft under their control to enter another controller's area of jurisdiction.

Before issuing control instructions directly or relaying through another source to an aircraft which is within another controller's area of jurisdiction that will change that aircraft's heading, route, speed, or altitude, ATC ensures that coordination has been accomplished with each of the controllers listed below whose area of jurisdiction is affected by those instructions unless otherwise specified by a letter of agreement or a facility directive:

1. The controller within whose area of jurisdiction the control instructions are issued.

2. The controller receiving the transfer of control.

3. Any intervening controller(s) through whose area of jurisdiction the aircraft will pass.

If ATC issues control instructions to an aircraft through a source other than another controller (e.g., Aeronautical Radio, Incorporated (ARINC), Automated Flight Service Station/ Flight Service Station (AFSS/FSS), another pilot) they ensure that the necessary coordination has been accomplished with any controllers listed above, whose area of jurisdiction is affected by those instructions unless otherwise specified by a letter of agreement or a facility directive.

Operating in the Various Types of Airspace

It is important that pilots be familiar with the operational requirements for each of the various types or classes of airspace. Subsequent sections cover each class in sufficient detail to facilitate understanding with regard to weather, type of pilot certificate held, as well as equipment required.

Basic VFR Weather Minimums

No pilot may operate an aircraft under basic VFR when the flight visibility is less, or at a distance from clouds that is less, than that prescribed for the corresponding altitude and class of airspace. *[Figure 14-9]* Except as provided in 14 CFR Section 91.157, Special VFR Weather Minimums, no person may operate an aircraft beneath the ceiling under VFR within the lateral boundaries of controlled airspace designated to the surface for an airport when the ceiling is less than 1,000 feet. Additional information can be found in 14 CFR section 91.155(c).

Operating Rules and Pilot/Equipment Requirements

The safety of flight is a top priority of all pilots and the responsibilities associated with operating an aircraft should always be taken seriously. The air traffic system maintains a high degree of safety and efficiency with strict regulatory oversight of the FAA. Pilots fly in accordance with regulations that have served the United States well, as evidenced by the fact that the country has the safest aviation system in the world.

All aircraft operating in today's National Airspace System (NAS) has complied with the CFR governing its certification and maintenance; all pilots operating today have completed rigorous pilot certification training and testing. Of equal importance is the proper execution of preflight planning, aeronautical decision-making (ADM) and risk management. ADM involves a systematic approach to risk assessment and stress management in aviation, illustrates how personal attitudes can influence decision-making, and how those attitudes can be modified to enhance safety in the flight deck. More detailed information regarding ADM and risk mitigation can be found in Chapter 17, Aeronautical Decision-Making.

Pilots also comply with very strict FAA general operating and flight rules as outlined in the CFR, including the FAA's important "see and avoid" mandate. These regulations provide the historical foundation of the FAA regulations governing the aviation system and the individual classes of airspace. *Figure 14-10* lists the operational and equipment requirements for these various classes of airspace. It will be helpful to refer to this figure as the specific classes are discussed in greater detail.

Class A

Pilots operating an aircraft in Class A airspace must conduct that operation under IFR and only under an ATC clearance received prior to entering the airspace. Unless otherwise authorized by ATC, each aircraft operating in Class A airspace must be equipped with a two-way radio capable of communicating with ATC on a frequency assigned by ATC. Unless otherwise authorized by ATC, all aircraft within Class A airspace must be equipped with the appropriate transponder equipment meeting all applicable specifications found in 14 CFR section 91.215.

Class B

All pilots operating an aircraft within a Class B airspace area must receive an ATC clearance from the ATC facility having jurisdiction for that area. The pilot in command (PIC) may not take off or land an aircraft at an airport within a Class B airspace unless he or she has met one of the following requirements:

1. A private pilot certificate.

2. A recreational pilot certificate and all requirements contained within 14 CFR section 61.101(d), or the

Airspace			Flight Visibility	Distance from Clouds
Class A			Not applicable	Not applicable
Class B			3 statute miles	Clear of clouds
Class C			3 statute miles	1,000 feet above 500 feet below 2,000 feet horizontal
Class D			3 statute miles	1,000 feet above 500 feet below 2,000 feet horizontal
Class E	At or above 10,000 feet MSL		5 statute miles	1,000 feet above 1,000 feet below 1 statute mile horizontal
	Less than 10,000 feet MSL		3 statute miles	1,000 feet above 500 feet below 2,000 feet horizontal
Class G	1,200 feet or less above the surface (regardless of MSL altitude).	Day, except as provided in section 91.155(b)	1 statute mile	Clear of clouds
		Night, except as provided in section 91.155(b)	3 statute miles	1,000 feet above 500 feet below 2,000 feet horizontal
	More than 1,200 feet above the surface but less than 10,000 feet MSL.	Day	1 statute mile	1,000 feet above 500 feet below 2,000 feet horizontal
		Night	3 statute miles	1,000 feet above 500 feet below 2,000 feet horizontal
	More than 1,200 feet above the surface and at or above 10,000 feet MSL.		5 statute miles	1,000 feet above 1,000 feet below 1 statute mile horizontal

Figure 14-9. *Visual flight rule weather minimums.*

requirements for a student pilot seeking a recreational pilot certificate in 14 CFR section 61.94.

3. A sport pilot certificate and all requirements contained within 14 CFR section 61.325, or the requirements for a student pilot seeking a recreational pilot certificate in 14 CFR section 61.94, or the aircraft is operated by a student pilot who has met the requirements of 14 CFR sections 61.94 and 61.95, as applicable.

Unless otherwise authorized by ATC, all aircraft within Class B airspace must be equipped with the applicable operating transponder and automatic altitude reporting equipment specified in 14 CFR section 91.215(a) and an operable two-way radio capable of communications with ATC on appropriate frequencies for that Class B airspace area.

Class C

For the purpose of this section, the primary airport is the airport for which the Class C airspace area is designated. A satellite airport is any other airport within the Class C airspace area. No pilot may take off or land an aircraft at a satellite airport within a Class C airspace area except in compliance with FAA arrival and departure traffic patterns.

Two-way radio communications must be established and maintained with the ATC facility providing air traffic services prior to entering the airspace and thereafter maintained while within the airspace.

A pilot departing from the primary airport or satellite airport with an operating control tower must establish and maintain two-way radio communications with the control tower, and thereafter as instructed by ATC while operating in the Class C airspace area. If departing from a satellite airport without an operating control tower, the pilot must establish and maintain two-way radio communications with the ATC facility having jurisdiction over the Class C airspace area as soon as practicable after departing.

Unless otherwise authorized by the ATC having jurisdiction over the Class C airspace area, all aircraft within Class C airspace must be equipped with the appropriate transponder equipment meeting all applicable specifications found in 14 CFR section 91.215.

Class D

No pilot may take off or land an aircraft at a satellite airport within a Class D airspace area except in compliance with FAA arrival and departure traffic patterns. A pilot departing from the primary airport or satellite airport with an operating control tower must establish and maintain two-way radio communications with the control tower, and thereafter as instructed by ATC while operating in the Class D airspace area. If departing from a satellite airport without an operating control tower, the pilot must establish and maintain two-way radio communications with the ATC facility having jurisdiction over the Class D airspace area as soon as practicable after departing.

Two-way radio communications must be established and maintained with the ATC facility providing air traffic services prior to entering the airspace and thereafter maintained while within the airspace.

If the aircraft radio fails in flight under IFR, the pilot should continue the flight by the route assigned in the last ATC clearance received; or, if being radar vectored, by the direct route from the point of radio failure to the fix, route, or airway specified in the vector clearance. In the absence of an assigned route, the pilot should continue by the route

Class Airspace	Entry Requirements	Equipment	Minimum Pilot Certificate
A	ATC clearance	IFR equipped	Instrument rating
B	ATC clearance	Two-way radio, transponder with altitude reporting capability	Private—(However, a student or recreational pilot may operate at other than the primary airport if seeking private pilot certification and if regulatory requirements are met.)
C	Two-way radio communications prior to entry	Two-way radio, transponder with altitude reporting capability	No specific requirement
D	Two-way radio communications prior to entry	Two-way radio	No specific requirement
E	None for VFR	No specific requirement	No specific requirement
G	None	No specific requirement	No specific requirement

Figure 14-10. *Requirements for airspace operations.*

that ATC advised may be expected in a further clearance; or, if a route had not been advised, by the route filed in the flight plan.

If the aircraft radio fails in flight under VFR, the PIC may operate that aircraft and land if weather conditions are at or above basic VFR weather minimums, visual contact with the tower is maintained, and a clearance to land is received.

Class E

Unless otherwise required by 14 CFR part 93 or unless otherwise authorized or required by the ATC facility having jurisdiction over the Class E airspace area, each pilot operating an aircraft on or in the vicinity of an airport in a Class E airspace area must comply with the requirements of Class G airspace. Each pilot must also comply with any traffic patterns established for that airport in 14 CFR part 93.

Unless otherwise authorized or required by ATC, no person may operate an aircraft to, from, through, or on an airport having an operational control tower unless two-way radio communications are maintained between that aircraft and the control tower. Communications must be established prior to four nautical miles from the airport, up to and including 2,500 feet AGL. However, if the aircraft radio fails in flight, the PIC may operate that aircraft and land if weather conditions are at or above basic VFR weather minimums, visual contact with the tower is maintained, and a clearance to land is received.

If the aircraft radio fails in flight under IFR, the pilot should continue the flight by the route assigned in the last ATC clearance received; or, if being radar vectored, by the direct route from the point of radio failure to the fix, route, or airway specified in the vector clearance. In the absence of an assigned route, the pilot should continue by the route that ATC advised may be expected in a further clearance; or, if a route had not been advised, by the route filed in the flight plan.

Class G

When approaching to land at an airport without an operating control tower in Class G airspace:

1. Each pilot of an airplane must make all turns of that airplane to the left unless the airport displays approved light signals or visual markings indicating that turns should be made to the right, in which case the pilot must make all turns to the right.

2. Each pilot of a helicopter or a powered parachute must avoid the flow of fixed-wing aircraft.

Unless otherwise authorized or required by ATC, no person may operate an aircraft to, from, through, or on an airport having an operational control tower unless two-way radio communications are maintained between that aircraft and the control tower. Communications must be established prior to four nautical miles from the airport, up to and including 2,500 feet AGL. However, if the aircraft radio fails in flight, the pilot in command may operate that aircraft and land if weather conditions are at or above basic VFR weather minimums, visual contact with the tower is maintained, and a clearance to land is received.

If the aircraft radio fails in flight under IFR, the pilot should continue the flight by the route assigned in the last ATC clearance received; or, if being radar vectored, by the direct route from the point of radio failure to the fix, route, or airway specified in the vector clearance. In the absence of an assigned route, the pilot should continue by the route that ATC advised may be expected in a further clearance; or, if a route had not been advised, by the route filed in the flight plan.

Ultralight Vehicles

No person may operate an ultralight vehicle within Class A, Class B, Class C, or Class D airspace or within the lateral boundaries of the surface area of Class E airspace designated for an airport unless that person has prior authorization from the ATC facility having jurisdiction over that airspace. (See 14 CFR part 103.)

Unmanned Free Balloons

Unless otherwise authorized by ATC, no person may operate an unmanned free balloon below 2,000 feet above the surface within the lateral boundaries of Class B, Class C, Class D, or Class E airspace designated for an airport. (See 14 CFR part 101.)

Parachute Jumps

No person may make a parachute jump, and no PIC may allow a parachute jump to be made from that aircraft, in or into Class A, Class B, Class C, or Class D airspace without, or in violation of, the terms of an ATC authorization issued by the ATC facility having jurisdiction over the airspace. (See 14 CFR part 105.)

Chapter Summary

This chapter introduces the various classifications of airspace and provides information on the requirements to operate in such airspace. For further information, consult the AIM and 14 CFR parts 71, 73, and 91.

Chapter 15

Navigation

Introduction

This chapter provides an introduction to cross-country flying under visual flight rules (VFR). It contains practical information for planning and executing cross-country flights for the beginning pilot.

Air navigation is the process of piloting an aircraft from one geographic position to another while monitoring one's position as the flight progresses. It introduces the need for planning, which includes plotting the course on an aeronautical chart, selecting checkpoints, measuring distances, obtaining pertinent weather information, and computing flight time, headings, and fuel requirements. The methods used in this chapter include pilotage—navigating by reference to visible landmarks, dead reckoning—computations of direction and distance from a known position, and radio navigation—by use of radio aids.

Aeronautical Charts

An aeronautical chart is the road map for a pilot flying under VFR. The chart provides information which allows pilots to track their position and provides available information which enhances safety. The three aeronautical charts used by VFR pilots are:

- Sectional
- VFR Terminal Area
- World Aeronautical

A free catalog listing aeronautical charts and related publications including prices and instructions for ordering is available at the National Aeronautical Charting Group (NACG) web site: www.naco.faa.gov.

Sectional Charts

Sectional charts are the most common charts used by pilots today. The charts have a scale of 1:500,000 (1 inch = 6.86 nautical miles (NM) or approximately 8 statute miles (SM)) which allows for more detailed information to be included on the chart.

The charts provide an abundance of information, including airport data, navigational aids, airspace, and topography. *Figure 15-1* is an excerpt from the legend of a sectional chart. By referring to the chart legend, a pilot can interpret most of the information on the chart. A pilot should also check the chart for other legend information, which includes air traffic control (ATC) frequencies and information on airspace. These charts are revised semiannually except for some areas outside the conterminous United States where they are revised annually.

VFR Terminal Area Charts

VFR terminal area charts are helpful when flying in or near Class B airspace. They have a scale of 1:250,000 (1 inch = 3.43 NM or approximately 4 SM). These charts provide a more detailed display of topographical information and are revised semiannually, except for several Alaskan and Caribbean charts. *[Figure 15-2]*

World Aeronautical Charts

World aeronautical charts are designed to provide a standard series of aeronautical charts, covering land areas of the

Figure 15-1. *Sectional chart and legend.*

Figure 15-2. *VFR terminal area chart and legend.*

world, at a size and scale convenient for navigation by moderate speed aircraft. They are produced at a scale of 1:1,000,000 (1 inch = 13.7 NM or approximately 16 SM). These charts are similar to sectional charts and the symbols are the same except there is less detail due to the smaller scale. *[Figure 15-3]*

These charts are revised annually except several Alaskan charts and the Mexican/Caribbean charts which are revised every 2 years.

Lattitude and Longitude (Meridians and Parallels)

The equator is an imaginary circle equidistant from the poles of the Earth. Circles parallel to the equator (lines running east and west) are parallels of latitude. They are used to measure degrees of latitude north (N) or south (S) of the equator. The angular distance from the equator to the pole is one-fourth of a circle or 90°. The 48 conterminous states of the United States are located between 25° and 49° N latitude. The arrows in *Figure 15-4* labeled "Latitude" point to lines of latitude.

Meridians of longitude are drawn from the North Pole to the South Pole and are at right angles to the Equator. The "Prime Meridian" which passes through Greenwich, England, is used as the zero line from which measurements are made in degrees east (E) and west (W) to 180°. The 48 conterminous states of the United States are between 67° and 125° W longitude. The arrows in *Figure 15-4* labeled "Longitude" point to lines of longitude.

Any specific geographical point can be located by reference to its longitude and latitude. Washington, D.C., for example, is approximately 39° N latitude, 77° W longitude. Chicago is approximately 42° N latitude, 88° W longitude.

Time Zones

The meridians are also useful for designating time zones. A day is defined as the time required for the Earth to make one complete rotation of 360°. Since the day is divided into 24 hours, the Earth revolves at the rate of 15° an hour. Noon is the time when the sun is directly above a meridian; to the west of that meridian is morning, to the east is afternoon.

Figure 15-3. *World aeronautical chart.*

Figure 15-4. *Meridians and parallels—the basis of measuring time, distance, and direction.*

The standard practice is to establish a time zone for each 15° of longitude. This makes a difference of exactly 1 hour between each zone. In the United States, there are four time zones. The time zones are Eastern (75°), Central (90°), Mountain (105°), and Pacific (120°). The dividing lines are somewhat irregular because communities near the boundaries often find it more convenient to use time designations of neighboring communities or trade centers.

Figure 15-5 shows the time zones in the United States. When the sun is directly above the 90th meridian, it is noon Central Standard Time. At the same time, it is 1 p.m. Eastern Standard Time, 11 a.m. Mountain Standard Time, and 10 a.m. Pacific Standard Time. When Daylight Saving Time is in effect, generally between the second Sunday in March and the first Sunday in November, the sun is directly above the 75th meridian at noon, Central Daylight Time.

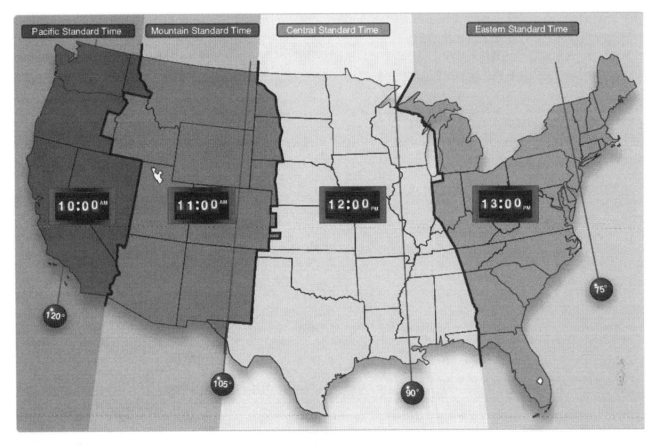

Figure 15-5. *Time zones.*

These time zone differences must be taken into account during long flights eastward—especially if the flight must be completed before dark. Remember, an hour is lost when flying eastward from one time zone to another, or perhaps even when flying from the western edge to the eastern edge of the same time zone. Determine the time of sunset at the destination by consulting the flight service stations (AFSS/FSS) or National Weather Service (NWS) and take this into account when planning an eastbound flight.

In most aviation operations, time is expressed in terms of the 24-hour clock. ATC instructions, weather reports and broadcasts, and estimated times of arrival are all based on this system. For example: 9 a.m. is expressed as 0900, 1 p.m. is 1300, and 10 p.m. is 2200.

Because a pilot may cross several time zones during a flight, a standard time system has been adopted. It is called Universal Coordinated Time (UTC) and is often referred to as Zulu time. UTC is the time at the 0° line of longitude which passes through Greenwich, England. All of the time zones around

the world are based on this reference. To convert to this time, a pilot should do the following:

Eastern Standard Time..........Add 5 hours

Central Standard Time..........Add 6 hours

Mountain Standard Time...... Add 7 hours

Pacific Standard Time.......... Add 8 hours

For Daylight Saving Time, 1 hour should be subtracted from the calculated times.

Measurement of Direction

By using the meridians, direction from one point to another can be measured in degrees, in a clockwise direction from true north. To indicate a course to be followed in flight, draw a line on the chart from the point of departure to the destination and measure the angle which this line forms with a meridian. Direction is expressed in degrees, as shown by the compass rose in *Figure 15-6.*

Figure 15-6. *Compass rose.*

Because meridians converge toward the poles, course measurement should be taken at a meridian near the midpoint of the course rather than at the point of departure. The course measured on the chart is known as the true course (TC). This is the direction measured by reference to a meridian or true north. It is the direction of intended flight as measured in degrees clockwise from true north.

As shown in *Figure 15-7*, the direction from A to B would be a true course of 065°, whereas the return trip (called the reciprocal) would be a true course of 245°.

Figure 15-7. *Courses are determined by reference to meridians on aeronautical charts.*

The true heading (TH) is the direction in which the nose of the aircraft points during a flight when measured in degrees clockwise from true north. Usually, it is necessary to head the aircraft in a direction slightly different from the true course to offset the effect of wind. Consequently, numerical value of the true heading may not correspond with that of

the true course. This is discussed more fully in subsequent sections in this chapter. For the purpose of this discussion, assume a no-wind condition exists under which heading and course would coincide. Thus, for a true course of 065°, the true heading would be 065°. To use the compass accurately, however, corrections must be made for magnetic variation and compass deviation.

Variation

Variation is the angle between true north and magnetic north. It is expressed as east variation or west variation depending upon whether magnetic north (MN) is to the east or west of true north (TN).

The north magnetic pole is located close to 71° N latitude, 96° W longitude and is about 1,300 miles from the geographic or true north pole, as indicated in *Figure 15-8*. If the Earth were uniformly magnetized, the compass needle would point toward the magnetic pole, in which case the variation between true north (as shown by the geographical meridians) and magnetic north (as shown by the magnetic meridians) could be measured at any intersection of the meridians.

Figure 15-8. *Magnetic meridians are in red while the lines of longitude and latitude are in blue. From these lines of variation (magnetic meridians), one can determine the effect of local magnetic variations on a magnetic compass.*

Actually, the Earth is not uniformly magnetized. In the United States, the needle usually points in the general direction of the magnetic pole, but it may vary in certain geographical localities by many degrees. Consequently, the exact amount of variation at thousands of selected locations in the United States has been carefully determined. The amount and the direction of variation, which change slightly from time to time, are shown on most aeronautical charts as broken magenta lines, called isogonic lines, which connect points of equal magnetic variation. (The line connecting points at which there is no variation between true north and magnetic north is the agonic line.) An isogonic chart is shown in *Figure 15-9*. Minor bends and turns in the isogonic and agonic lines are caused by unusual geological conditions affecting magnetic forces in these areas.

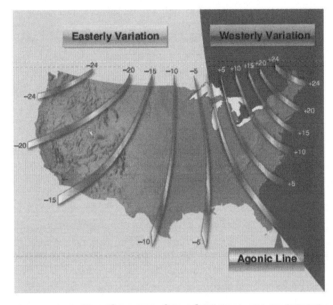

Figure 15-9. *Note the agonic line where magnetic variation is zero.*

On the west coast of the United States, the compass needle points to the east of true north; on the east coast, the compass needle points to the west of true north.

Zero degree variation exists on the agonic line, where magnetic north and true north coincide. This line runs roughly west of the Great Lakes, south through Wisconsin, Illinois, western Tennessee, and along the border of Mississippi and Alabama. *[Compare Figures 15-9 and 15-10.]*

Because courses are measured in reference to geographical meridians which point toward true north, and these courses are maintained by reference to the compass which points along a magnetic meridian in the general direction of magnetic north, the true direction must be converted into magnetic direction for the purpose of flight. This conversion is made by adding or subtracting the variation which is indicated by the nearest isogonic line on the chart.

For example, a line drawn between two points on a chart is called a true course as it is measured from true north. However, flying this course off the magnetic compass would not provide an accurate course between the two points due to three elements that must be considered. The first is magnetic variation, the second is compass deviation, and the third is wind correction. All three must be considered for accurate navigation.

Magnetic Variation

As mentioned in the paragraph discussing variation, the appropriate variation for the geographical location of the flight must be considered and added or subtracted as appropriate. If flying across an area where the variation changes, then the values must be applied along the route of flight appropriately. Once applied, this new course is called the magnetic course.

Magnetic Deviation

Because each aircraft has its own internal effect upon the onboard compass systems from its own localized magnetic influencers, the pilot must add or subtract these influencers based upon the direction he or she is flying. The application of

Figure 15-10. *Effect of variation on the compass.*

deviation (taken from a compass deviation card) compensates the magnetic course unique to that aircraft's compass system (as affected by localized magnetic influencers) and it now becomes the compass course. Therefore, the compass course when followed (in a no wind condition) takes the aircraft from point A to point B even though the aircraft heading may not match the original course line drawn on the chart.

If the variation is shown as "9° E," this means that magnetic north is 9° east of true north. If a true course of 360° is to be flown, 9° must be subtracted from 360°, which results in a magnetic heading of 351°. To fly east, a magnetic course of 081° (090° − 9°) would be flown. To fly south, the magnetic course would be 171° (180° − 9°). To fly west, it would be 261° (270° − 9°). To fly a true heading of 060°, a magnetic course of 051° (060° − 9°) would be flown.

Remember, if variation is west, add; if east, subtract. One method for remembering whether to add or subtract variation is the phrase "east is least (subtract) and west is best (add)."

Deviation

Determining the magnetic heading is an intermediate step necessary to obtain the correct compass heading for the flight. To determine compass heading, a correction for deviation must be made. Because of magnetic influences within an aircraft such as electrical circuits, radio, lights, tools, engine, and magnetized metal parts, the compass needle is frequently deflected from its normal reading. This deflection is deviation. The deviation is different for each aircraft, and it also may vary for different headings in the same aircraft. For instance, if magnetism in the engine attracts the north end of the compass, there would be no effect when the plane is on a heading of magnetic north. On easterly or westerly headings, however, the compass indications would be in error, as shown in *Figure 15-11*. Magnetic attraction can come from many other parts of the aircraft; the assumption of attraction in the engine is merely used for the purpose of illustration.

Some adjustment of the compass, referred to as compensation, can be made to reduce this error, but the remaining correction must be applied by the pilot.

Proper compensation of the compass is best performed by a competent technician. Since the magnetic forces within the aircraft change, because of landing shocks, vibration, mechanical work, or changes in equipment, the pilot should occasionally have the deviation of the compass checked. The procedure used to check the deviation (called "swinging the compass") is briefly outlined.

The aircraft is placed on a magnetic compass rose, the engine started, and electrical devices normally used (such as radio)

Figure 15-11. *Magnetized portions of the airplane cause the compass to deviate from its normal indications.*

are turned on. Tailwheel-type aircraft should be jacked up into flying position. The aircraft is aligned with magnetic north indicated on the compass rose and the reading shown on the compass is recorded on a deviation card. The aircraft is then aligned at 30° intervals and each reading is recorded. If the aircraft is to be flown at night, the lights are turned on and any significant changes in the readings are noted. If so, additional entries are made for use at night.

The accuracy of the compass can also be checked by comparing the compass reading with the known runway headings.

A deviation card, similar to *Figure 15-12*, is mounted near the compass, showing the addition or subtraction required to correct for deviation on various headings, usually at intervals of 30°. For intermediate readings, the pilot should be able to interpolate mentally with sufficient accuracy. For example, if the pilot needed the correction for 195° and noted the correction for 180° to be 0° and for 210° to be +2°, it could be assumed that the correction for 195° would be +1°. The magnetic heading, when corrected for deviation, is known as compass heading.

For (Magnetic)	N	30	60	E	120	150
Steer (Compass)	0	28	57	86	117	148

For (Magnetic	S	210	240	W	300	330
Steer (Compass)	180	212	243	274	303	332

Figure 15-12. *Compass deviation card.*

Effect of Wind

The preceding discussion explained how to measure a true course on the aeronautical chart and how to make corrections for variation and deviation, but one important factor has not been considered—wind. As discussed in the study of the atmosphere, wind is a mass of air moving over the surface of the Earth in a definite direction. When the wind is blowing from the north at 25 knots, it simply means that air is moving southward over the Earth's surface at the rate of 25 NM in 1 hour.

Under these conditions, any inert object free from contact with the Earth is carried 25 NM southward in 1 hour. This effect becomes apparent when such things as clouds, dust, and toy balloons are observed being blown along by the wind. Obviously, an aircraft flying within the moving mass of air is similarly affected. Even though the aircraft does not float freely with the wind, it moves through the air at the same time the air is moving over the ground, thus is affected by wind. Consequently, at the end of 1 hour of flight, the aircraft is in a position which results from a combination of the following two motions:

- Movement of the air mass in reference to the ground

- Forward movement of the aircraft through the air mass

Actually, these two motions are independent. It makes no difference whether the mass of air through which the aircraft is flying is moving or is stationary. A pilot flying in a 70-knot gale would be totally unaware of any wind (except for possible turbulence) unless the ground were observed. In reference to the ground, however, the aircraft would appear to fly faster with a tailwind or slower with a headwind, or to drift right or left with a crosswind.

As shown in *Figure 15-13*, an aircraft flying eastward at an airspeed of 120 knots in still air has a groundspeed (GS) exactly the same—120 knots. If the mass of air is moving eastward at 20 knots, the airspeed of the aircraft is not affected, but the progress of the aircraft over the ground is 120 plus 20, or a GS of 140 knots. On the other hand, if the mass of air is moving westward at 20 knots, the airspeed of the aircraft remains the same, but GS becomes 120 minus 20, or 100 knots.

Assuming no correction is made for wind effect, if an aircraft is heading eastward at 120 knots, and the air mass moving southward at 20 knots, the aircraft at the end of 1 hour is almost 120 miles east of its point of departure because of its progress through the air. It is 20 miles south because of the motion of the air. Under these circumstances, the airspeed remains 120 knots, but the GS is determined by combining

Figure 15-13. *Motion of the air affects the speed with which aircraft move over the Earth's surface. Airspeed, the rate at which an aircraft moves through the air, is not affected by air motion.*

the movement of the aircraft with that of the air mass. GS can be measured as the distance from the point of departure to the position of the aircraft at the end of 1 hour. The GS can be computed by the time required to fly between two points a known distance apart. It also can be determined before flight by constructing a wind triangle, which is explained later in this chapter. *[Figure 15-14]*

The direction in which the aircraft is pointing as it flies is heading. Its actual path over the ground, which is a combination of the motion of the aircraft and the motion of the air, is its track. The angle between the heading and the track is drift angle. If the aircraft heading coincides with the true course and the wind is blowing from the left, the track does not coincide with the true course. The wind causes the aircraft to drift to the right, so the track falls to the right of the desired course or true course. *[Figure 15-15]*

Figure 15-14. *Aircraft flightpath resulting from its airspeed and direction, and the wind speed and direction.*

Figure 15-15. *Effects of wind drift on maintaining desired course.*

The following method is used by many pilots to determine compass heading: after the TC is measured, and wind correction applied resulting in a TH, the sequence TH ± variation (V) = magnetic heading (MH) ± deviation (D) = compass heading (CH) is followed to arrive at compass heading. *[Figure 15-16]*

By determining the amount of drift, the pilot can counteract the effect of the wind and make the track of the aircraft coincide with the desired course. If the mass of air is moving across the course from the left, the aircraft drifts to the right, and a correction must be made by heading the aircraft sufficiently to the left to offset this drift. To state in another way, if the wind is from the left, the correction is made by pointing the aircraft to the left a certain number of degrees, therefore correcting for wind drift. This is the wind correction angle (WCA) and is expressed in terms of degrees right or left of the true course. *[Figure 15-17]*

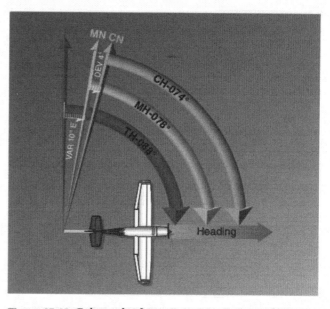

Figure 15-16. *Relationship between true, magnetic, and compass headings for a particular instance.*

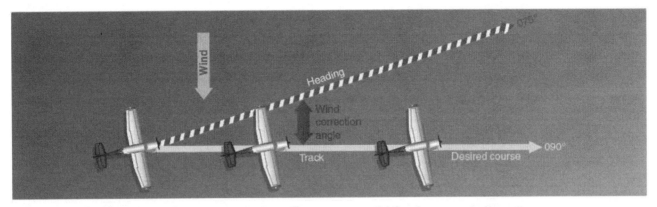

Figure 15-17. *Establishing a wind correction angle that will counteract wind drift and maintain the desired course.*

To summarize:

- Course—intended path of an aircraft over the ground or the direction of a line drawn on a chart representing the intended aircraft path, expressed as the angle measured from a specific reference datum clockwise from 0° through 360° to the line.

- Heading—direction in which the nose of the aircraft points during flight.

- Track—actual path made over the ground in flight. (If proper correction has been made for the wind, track and course are identical.)

- Drift angle—angle between heading and track.

- WCA—correction applied to the course to establish a heading so that track coincides with course.

- Airspeed—rate of the aircraft's progress through the air.

- GS—rate of the aircraft's inflight progress over the ground.

Basic Calculations

Before a cross-country flight, a pilot should make common calculations for time, speed, and distance, and the amount of fuel required.

Converting Minutes to Equivalent Hours

Frequently, it is necessary to convert minutes into equivalent hours when solving speed, time, and distance problems. To convert minutes to hours, divide by 60 (60 minutes = 1 hour). Thus, 30 minutes is 30/60 = 0.5 hour. To convert hours to minutes, multiply by 60. Thus, 0.75 hour equals 0.75 × 60 = 45 minutes.

Time T = D/GS

To find the time (T) in flight, divide the distance (D) by the GS. The time to fly 210 NM at a GS of 140 knots is 210 ÷ 140, or 1.5 hours. (The 0.5 hour multiplied by 60 minutes equals 30 minutes.) Answer: 1:30.

Distance D = GS X T

To find the distance flown in a given time, multiply GS by time. The distance flown in 1 hour 45 minutes at a GS of 120 knots is 120 x 1.75, or 210 NM.

GS GS = D/T

To find the GS, divide the distance flown by the time required. If an aircraft flies 270 NM in 3 hours, the GS is 270 ÷ 3 = 90 knots.

Converting Knots to Miles Per Hour

Another conversion is that of changing knots to miles per hour (mph). The aviation industry is using knots more frequently than mph, but it might be well to discuss the conversion for those that use mph when working with speed problems. The NWS reports both surface winds and winds aloft in knots. However, airspeed indicators in some aircraft are calibrated in mph (although many are now calibrated in both miles per hour and knots). Pilots, therefore, should learn to convert wind speeds that are reported in knots to mph.

A knot is 1 nautical mile per hour (NMPH). Because there are 6,076.1 feet in 1 NM and 5,280 feet in 1 SM, the conversion factor is 1.15. To convert knots to miles per hour, multiply speed in knots by 1.15. For example: a wind speed of 20 knots is equivalent to 23 mph.

Most flight computers or electronic calculators have a means of making this conversion. Another quick method of conversion is to use the scales of NM and SM at the bottom of aeronautical charts.

Fuel Consumption

Aircraft fuel consumption is computed in gallons per hour. Consequently, to determine the fuel required for a given flight, the time required for the flight must be known. Time in flight multiplied by rate of consumption gives the quantity of fuel required. For example, a flight of 400 NM at a GS of 100 knots requires 4 hours. If an aircraft consumes 5 gallons an hour, the total consumption is 4 x 5, or 20 gallons.

The rate of fuel consumption depends on many factors: condition of the engine, propeller/rotor pitch, propeller/rotor revolutions per minute (rpm), richness of the mixture, and particularly the percentage of horsepower used for flight at cruising speed. The pilot should know the approximate consumption rate from cruise performance charts, or from experience. In addition to the amount of fuel required for the flight, there should be sufficient fuel for reserve.

Flight Computers

Up to this point, only mathematical formulas have been used to determine such items as time, distance, speed, and fuel consumption. In reality, most pilots use a mechanical or electronic flight computer. These devices can compute numerous problems associated with flight planning and navigation. The mechanical or electronic computer has an instruction book that probably includes sample problems so the pilot can become familiar with its functions and operation. [Figure 15-18]

Plotter

Another aid in flight planning is a plotter, which is a protractor and ruler. The pilot can use this when determining true course and measuring distance. Most plotters have a ruler which measures in both NM and SM and has a scale for a sectional chart on one side and a world aeronautical chart on the other. [Figure 15-18]

Pilotage

Pilotage is navigation by reference to landmarks or checkpoints. It is a method of navigation that can be used on any course that has adequate checkpoints, but it is more commonly used in conjunction with dead reckoning and VFR radio navigation.

The checkpoints selected should be prominent features common to the area of the flight. Choose checkpoints that can be readily identified by other features such as roads, rivers, railroad tracks, lakes, and power lines. If possible, select features that make useful boundaries or brackets on each side of the course, such as highways, rivers, railroads, and mountains. A pilot can keep from drifting too far off course by referring to and not crossing the selected brackets. Never place complete reliance on any single checkpoint. Choose

ample checkpoints. If one is missed, look for the next one while maintaining the heading. When determining position from checkpoints, remember that the scale of a sectional chart is 1 inch = 8 SM or 6.86 NM. For example, if a checkpoint selected was approximately one-half inch from the course line on the chart, it is 4 SM or 3.43 NM from the course on the ground. In the more congested areas, some of the smaller features are not included on the chart. If confused, hold the heading. If a turn is made away from the heading, it is easy to become lost.

Roads shown on the chart are primarily the well-traveled roads or those most apparent when viewed from the air. New roads and structures are constantly being built, and may not be shown on the chart until the next chart is issued. Some structures, such as antennas may be difficult to see. Sometimes TV antennas are grouped together in an area near a town. They are supported by almost invisible guy wires. Never approach an area of antennas less than 500 feet above the tallest one. Most of the taller structures are marked with strobe lights to make them more visible to a pilot. However, some weather conditions or background lighting may make them difficult to see. Aeronautical charts display the best information available at the time of printing, but a pilot should be cautious for new structures or changes that have occurred since the chart was printed.

Dead Reckoning

Dead reckoning is navigation solely by means of computations based on time, airspeed, distance, and direction. The products derived from these variables, when adjusted by wind speed and velocity, are heading and GS. The predicted heading takes the aircraft along the intended path and the GS establishes the time to arrive at each checkpoint and the destination. Except for flights over water, dead reckoning is usually used with pilotage for cross-country flying. The heading and GS as calculated is constantly monitored and corrected by pilotage as observed from checkpoints.

The Wind Triangle or Vector Analysis

If there is no wind, the aircraft's ground track is the same as the heading and the GS is the same as the true airspeed. This condition rarely exists. A wind triangle, the pilot's version of vector analysis, is the basis of dead reckoning.

The wind triangle is a graphic explanation of the effect of wind upon flight. GS, heading, and time for any flight can be determined by using the wind triangle. It can be applied to the simplest kind of cross-country flight as well as the most complicated instrument flight. The experienced pilot becomes so familiar with the fundamental principles that estimates can be made which are adequate for visual flight without actually drawing the diagrams. The beginning student, however, needs

Figure 15-18. *A plotter (A), the computational and wind side of a mechanical flight computer (B), and an electronic flight computer (C).*

to develop skill in constructing these diagrams as an aid to the complete understanding of wind effect. Either consciously or unconsciously, every good pilot thinks of the flight in terms of wind triangle.

If flight is to be made on a course to the east, with a wind blowing from the northeast, the aircraft must be headed somewhat to the north of east to counteract drift. This can be represented by a diagram as shown in *Figure 15-19*. Each line represents direction and speed. The long blue and white hashed line shows the direction the aircraft is heading, and its length represents the distance the airspeed for 1 hour. The short blue arrow at the right shows the wind direction, and its length represents the wind velocity for 1 hour. The solid

yellow line shows the direction of the track or the path of the aircraft as measured over the earth, and its length represents the distance traveled in 1 hour, or the GS.

In actual practice, the triangle illustrated in *Figure 15-19* is not drawn; instead, construct a similar triangle as shown by the blue, yellow, and black lines in *Figure 15-20*, which is explained in the following example.

Suppose a flight is to be flown from E to P. Draw a line on the aeronautical chart connecting these two points; measure its direction with a protractor, or plotter, in reference to a meridian. This is the true course, which in this example is assumed to be 090° (east). From the NWS, it is learned that

Figure 15-19. *Principle of the wind triangle.*

Figure 15-20. *The wind triangle as is drawn in navigation practice.*

the wind at the altitude of the intended flight is 40 knots from the northeast (045°). Since the NWS reports the wind speed in knots, if the true airspeed of the aircraft is 120 knots, there is no need to convert speeds from knots to mph or vice versa.

Now, on a plain sheet of paper draw a vertical line representing north to south. (The various steps are shown in *Figure 15-21.*)

Step 1

Place the protractor with the base resting on the vertical line and the curved edge facing east. At the center point of the base, make a dot labeled "E" (point of departure), and at the curved edge, make a dot at 90° (indicating the direction of the true course) and another at 45° (indicating wind direction).

Step 2

With the ruler, draw the true course line from E, extending it somewhat beyond the dot by 90°, and labeling it "TC 090°."

Step 3

Next, align the ruler with E and the dot at 45°, and draw the wind arrow from E, not toward 045°, but downwind in the direction the wind is blowing, making it 40 units long, to correspond with the wind velocity of 40 knots. Identify this line as the wind line by placing the letter "W" at the end to show the wind direction.

Step 4

Finally, measure 120 units on the ruler to represent the airspeed, making a dot on the ruler at this point. The units used may be of any convenient scale or value (such as ¼ inch = 10 knots), but once selected, the same scale must be used for each of the linear movements involved. Then place the ruler so that the end is on the arrowhead (W) and the 120-knot dot intercepts the true course line. Draw the line and label it "AS 120." The point "P" placed at the intersection represents the position of the aircraft at the end of 1 hour. The diagram is now complete.

Figure 15-21. *Steps in drawing the wind triangle.*

The distance flown in 1 hour (GS) is measured as the numbers of units on the true course line (88 NMPH, or 88 knots). The true heading necessary to offset drift is indicated by the direction of the airspeed line, which can be determined in one of two ways:

- By placing the straight side of the protractor along the north-south line, with its center point at the intersection of the airspeed line and north-south line, read the true heading directly in degrees (076°). *[Figure 15-22]*

- By placing the straight side of the protractor along the true course line, with its center at P, read the angle between the true course and the airspeed line. This is the WCA, which must be applied to the true course to obtain the true heading. If the wind blows from the right of true course, the angle is added; if from the left, it is subtracted. In the example given, the WCA is 14° and the wind is from the left; therefore, subtract 14° from true course of 090°, making the true heading 076°. *[Figure 15-23]*

Figure 15-22. *Finding true heading by the wind correction angle.*

Figure 15-23. *Finding true heading by direct measurement.*

After obtaining the true heading, apply the correction for magnetic variation to obtain magnetic heading, and the correction for compass deviation to obtain a compass heading. The compass heading can be used to fly to the destination by dead reckoning.

To determine the time and fuel required for the flight, first find the distance to destination by measuring the length of the course line drawn on the aeronautical chart (using the appropriate scale at the bottom of the chart). If the distance measures 220 NM, divide by the GS of 88 knots, which gives 2.5 hours, or 2:30, as the time required. If fuel consumption is 8 gallons an hour, 8 × 2.5 or about 20 gallons is used. Briefly summarized, the steps in obtaining flight information are as follows:

- TC—direction of the line connecting two desired points, drawn on the chart and measured clockwise in degrees from true north on the mid-meridian.

- WCA—determined from the wind triangle. (Added to TC if the wind is from the right; subtracted if wind is from the left).

- TH—direction measured in degrees clockwise from true north, in which the nose of the plane should point to make good the desired course.

- Variation—obtained from the isogonic line on the chart (added to TH if west; subtracted if east).

- MH—an intermediate step in the conversion (obtained by applying variation to true heading).

- Deviation—obtained from the deviation card on the aircraft (added to MH or subtracted from, as indicated).

- Compass heading—reading on the compass (found by applying deviation to MH) which is followed to make good the desired course.

- Total distance—obtained by measuring the length of the TC line on the chart (using the scale at the bottom of the chart).

- GS—obtained by measuring the length of the TC line on the wind triangle (using the scale employed for drawing the diagram).

- Estimated time en route (ETE)—total distance divided by GS.

- Fuel rate—predetermined gallons per hour used at cruising speed.

NOTE: Additional fuel for adequate reserve should be added as a safety measure.

Flight Planning

Title 14 of the Code of Federal Regulations (14 CFR) part 91 states, in part, that before beginning a flight, the pilot in command (PIC) of an aircraft shall become familiar with all available information concerning that flight. For flights not in the vicinity of an airport, this must include information on available current weather reports and forecasts, fuel requirements, alternatives available if the planned flight cannot be completed, and any known traffic delays of which the pilot in command has been advised by ATC.

Assembling Necessary Material

The pilot should collect the necessary material well before the flight. An appropriate current sectional chart and charts for areas adjoining the flight route should be among this material if the route of flight is near the border of a chart.

Additional equipment should include a flight computer or electronic calculator, plotter, and any other item appropriate to the particular flight. For example, if a night flight is to be undertaken, carry a flashlight; if a flight is over desert country, carry a supply of water and other necessities.

Weather Check

It is wise to check the weather before continuing with other aspects of flight planning to see, first of all, if the flight is feasible and, if it is, which route is best. Chapter 12, Aviation Weather Services, discusses obtaining a weather briefing.

Use of Airport/Facility Directory (A/FD)

Study available information about each airport at which a landing is intended. This should include a study of the Notices to Airmen (NOTAMs) and the A/FD. *[Figure 15-24]* This includes location, elevation, runway and lighting facilities, available services, availability of aeronautical advisory station frequency (UNICOM), types of fuel available (use to decide on refueling stops), AFSS/FSS located on the airport, control tower and ground control frequencies, traffic information, remarks, and other pertinent information. The NOTAMs, issued every 28 days, should be checked for additional information on hazardous conditions or changes that have been made since issuance of the A/FD.

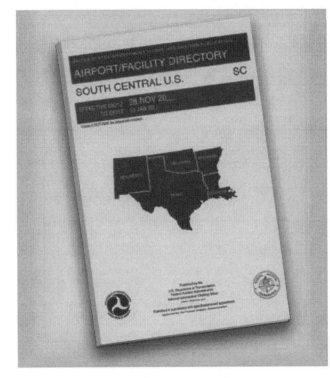

Figure 15-24. *Airport/Facility Directory.*

The sectional chart bulletin subsection should be checked for major changes that have occurred since the last publication date of each sectional chart being used. Remember, the chart may be up to 6 months old. The effective date of the chart appears at the top of the front of the chart. The A/FD generally has the latest information pertaining to such matters and should be used in preference to the information on the back of the chart, if there are differences.

Airplane Flight Manual or Pilot's Operating Handbook (AFM/POH)

The Aircraft Flight Manual or Pilot's Operating Handbook (AFM/POH) should be checked to determine the proper loading of the aircraft (weight and balance data). The weight of the usable fuel and drainable oil aboard must be known. Also, check the weight of the passengers, the weight of all baggage to be carried, and the empty weight of the aircraft to be sure that the total weight does not exceed the maximum allowable. The distribution of the load must be known to tell if the resulting center of gravity (CG) is within limits. Be sure to use the latest weight and balance information in the FAA-approved AFM or other permanent aircraft records, as appropriate, to obtain empty weight and empty weight CG information.

Determine the takeoff and landing distances from the appropriate charts, based on the calculated load, elevation of the airport, and temperature; then compare these distances with the amount of runway available. Remember, the heavier the load and the higher the elevation, temperature, or humidity, the longer the takeoff roll and landing roll and the lower the rate of climb.

Check the fuel consumption charts to determine the rate of fuel consumption at the estimated flight altitude and power settings. Calculate the rate of fuel consumption, and then compare it with the estimated time for the flight so that refueling points along the route can be included in the plan.

Charting the Course

Once the weather has been checked and some preliminary planning done, it is time to chart the course and determine the data needed to accomplish the flight. The following sections provide a logical sequence to follow in charting the course, filling out a flight log, and filing a flight plan. In the following example, a trip is planned based on the following data and the sectional chart excerpt in *Figure 15-25.*

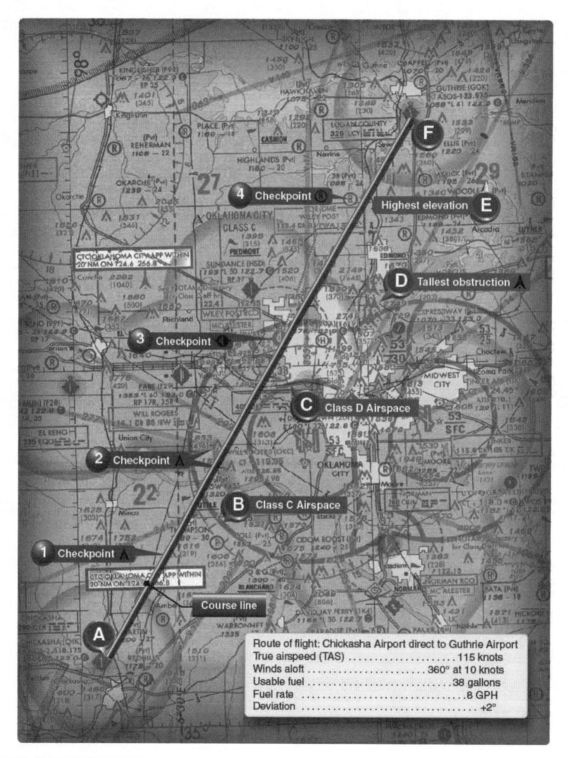

Figure 15-25. *Sectional chart excerpt.*

Route of flight: Chickasha Airport direct to Guthrie Airport

True airspeed (TAS)..115 knots

Winds aloft...360° at 10 knots

Usable fuel..38 gallons

Fuel rate...8 GPH

Deviation...+2°

Steps in Charting the Course

The following is a suggested sequence for arriving at the pertinent information for the trip. As information is determined, it may be noted as illustrated in the example of a flight log in *Figure 15-26*. Where calculations are required, the pilot may use a mathematical formula or a manual or electronic flight computer. If unfamiliar with the use of a manual or electronic computer, it would be advantageous to read the operation manual and work several practice problems at this point.

First draw a line from Chickasha Airport (point A) directly to Guthrie Airport (point F). The course line should begin at the center of the airport of departure and end at the center of the destination airport. If the route is direct, the course line consists of a single straight line. If the route is not direct, it consists of two or more straight line segments. For example, a VOR station which is off the direct route, but which makes navigating easier, may be chosen (radio navigation is discussed later in this chapter).

Appropriate checkpoints should be selected along the route and noted in some way. These should be easy-to-locate points such as large towns, large lakes and rivers, or combinations of recognizable points such as towns with an airport, towns with a network of highways, and railroads entering and departing. Normally, choose only towns indicated by splashes of yellow on the chart. Do not choose towns represented by a small circle—these may turn out to be only a half-dozen houses. (In isolated areas, however, towns represented by a small circle can be prominent checkpoints.) For this trip, four checkpoints have been selected. Checkpoint 1 consists of a tower located east of the course and can be further identified by the highway and railroad track, which almost parallels the course at this point. Checkpoint 2 is the obstruction just to the west of the course and can be further identified by Will Rogers World

PILOT'S PLANNING SHEET

PLANE IDENTIFICATION N123DB   DATE

COURSE	TC	Wind Knots	Wind From	WCA R+ L-	TH	WCA R+ L-	MH	DEV	CH	TOTAL MILES	GS	TOTAL TIME	FUEL RATE	TOTAL FUEL
From Chickasha	031°	10	360°	3° L	28	7° E	21°	+2°	23	53	106 kts	35 min	8 GPH	38 gal
To Guthrie														
From														
To														

VISUAL FLIGHT LOG

TIME OF DEPARTURE	NAVIGATION AIDS	COURSE		DISTANCE		ELAPSED TIME		GS	CH	REMARKS
POINT OF DEPARTURE Chickasha Airport	NAVAID IDENT. FREQ.	TO	FROM	POINT TO POINT	CUMULATIVE	ESTIMATED	ACTUAL	ESTIMATED ACTUAL	ESTIMATED ACTUAL	WEATHER AIRSPACE ETC.
CHECKPOINT #1				11 NM		6 min +5		106 kts	023°	
CHECKPOINT #2				10 NM	21 NM	6 min		106 kts	023°	
CHECKPOINT #3				10.5 NM	31.5 NM	6 min		106 kts	023°	
CHECKPOINT #4				13 NM	44.5 NM	7 min		106 kts	023°	
DESTINATION Guthrie Airport				8.5 NM	53 NM	5 min				

Figure 15-26. *Pilot's planning sheet and visual flight log.*

Airport which is directly to the east. Checkpoint 3 is Wiley Post Airport, which the aircraft should fly directly over. Checkpoint 4 is a private, non-surfaced airport to the west of the course and can be further identified by the railroad track and highway to the east of the course.

The course and areas on either side of the planned route should be checked to determine if there is any type of airspace with which the pilot should be concerned or which has special operational requirements. For this trip, it should be noted that the course passes through a segment of the Class C airspace surrounding Will Rogers World Airport where the floor of the airspace is 2,500 feet mean sea level (MSL) and the ceiling is 5,300 feet MSL (point B). Also, there is Class D airspace from the surface to 3,800 feet MSL surrounding Wiley Post Airport (point C) during the time the control tower is in operation.

Study the terrain and obstructions along the route. This is necessary to determine the highest and lowest elevations as well as the highest obstruction to be encountered so that an appropriate altitude which conforms to 14 CFR part 91 regulations can be selected. If the flight is to be flown at an altitude more than 3,000 feet above the terrain, conformance to the cruising altitude appropriate to the direction of flight is required. Check the route for particularly rugged terrain so it can be avoided. Areas where a takeoff or landing is made should be carefully checked for tall obstructions. Television transmitting towers may extend to altitudes over 1,500 feet above the surrounding terrain. It is essential that pilots be aware of their presence and location. For this trip, it should be noted that the tallest obstruction is part of a series of antennas with a height of 2,749 feet MSL (point D). The highest elevation should be located in the northeast quadrant and is 2,900 feet MSL (point E).

Since the wind is no factor and it is desirable and within the aircraft's capability to fly above the Class C and D airspace to be encountered, an altitude of 5,500 feet MSL is chosen. This altitude also gives adequate clearance of all obstructions as well as conforms to the 14 CFR part 91 requirement to fly at an altitude of odd thousand plus 500 feet when on a magnetic course between 0 and 179°.

Next, the pilot should measure the total distance of the course as well as the distance between checkpoints. The total distance is 53 NM and the distance between checkpoints is as noted on the flight log in *Figure 15-26*.

After determining the distance, the true course should be measured. If using a plotter, follow the directions on the plotter. The true course is 031°. Once the true heading is established, the pilot can determine the compass heading.

This is done by following the formula given earlier in this chapter. The formula is:

$$TC \pm WCA = TH \pm V = MH \pm D = CH$$

The WCA can be determined by using a manual or electronic flight computer. Using a wind of 360° at 10 knots, it is determined the WCA is 3° left. This is subtracted from the TC making the TH 28°. Next, the pilot should locate the isogonic line closest to the route of the flight to determine variation. *Figure 15-25* shows the variation to be 6.30° E (rounded to 7° E), which means it should be subtracted from the TH, giving an MH of 21°. Next, add 2° to the MH for the deviation correction. This gives the pilot the compass heading which is 23°.

Now, the GS can be determined. This is done using a manual or electronic calculator. The GS is determined to be 106 knots. Based on this information, the total trip time, as well as time between checkpoints, and the fuel burned can be determined. These calculations can be done mathematically or by using a manual or electronic calculator.

For this trip, the GS is 106 knots and the total time is 35 minutes (30 minutes plus 5 minutes for climb) with a fuel burn of 4.7 gallons. Refer to the flight log in *Figure 15-26* for the time between checkpoints.

As the trip progresses, the pilot can note headings and time and make adjustments in heading, GS, and time.

Filing a VFR Flight Plan

Filing a flight plan is not required by regulations; however, it is a good operating practice, since the information contained in the flight plan can be used in search and rescue in the event of an emergency.

Flight plans can be filed in the air by radio, but it is best to file a flight plan by phone just before departing. After takeoff, contact the AFSS by radio and give them the takeoff time so the flight plan can be activated.

When a VFR flight plan is filed, it is held by the AFSS until 1 hour after the proposed departure time and then canceled unless: the actual departure time is received; a revised proposed departure time is received; or at the time of filing, the AFSS is informed that the proposed departure time is met, but actual time cannot be given because of inadequate communication. The FSS specialist who accepts the flight plan does not inform the pilot of this procedure, however.

Figure 15-27 shows the flight plan form a pilot files with the AFSS. When filing a flight plan by telephone or radio, give the information in the order of the numbered spaces. This enables the AFSS specialist to copy the information more efficiently. Most of the fields are either self-explanatory or non-applicable to the VFR flight plan (such as item 13). However, some fields may need explanation.

- Item 3 is the aircraft type and special equipment. An example would be C-150/X, which means the aircraft has no transponder. A listing of special equipment codes is found in the Aeronautical Information Manual (AIM).

- Item 6 is the proposed departure time in UTC (indicated by the "Z").

- Item 7 is the cruising altitude. Normally, "VFR" can be entered in this block, since the pilot chooses a cruising altitude to conform to FAA regulations.

- Item 8 is the route of flight. If the flight is to be direct, enter the word "direct;" if not, enter the actual route to be followed such as via certain towns or navigation aids.

- Item 10 is the estimated time en route. In the sample flight plan, 5 minutes was added to the total time to allow for the climb.

- Item 12 is the fuel on board in hours and minutes. This is determined by dividing the total usable fuel aboard in gallons by the estimated rate of fuel consumption in gallons.

Remember, there is every advantage in filing a flight plan; but do not forget to close the flight plan on arrival. Do this by telephone to avoid radio congestion.

Radio Navigation

Advances in navigational radio receivers installed in aircraft, the development of aeronautical charts which show the exact location of ground transmitting stations and their frequencies, along with refined flight deck instrumentation make it possible for pilots to navigate with precision to almost any point desired. Although precision in navigation is obtainable through the proper use of this equipment, beginning pilots should use this equipment to supplement navigation by visual reference to the ground (pilotage). This method provides the

Figure 15-27. *Flight plan form.*

pilot with an effective safeguard against disorientation in the event of radio malfunction.

There are four radio navigation systems available for use for VFR navigation. These are:

- VHF Omnidirectional Range (VOR)
- Nondirectional Radio Beacon (NDB)
- Long Range Navigation (LORAN-C)
- Global Positioning System (GPS)

Very High Frequency (VHF) Omnidirectional Range (VOR)

The VOR system is present in three slightly different navigation aids (NAVAIDs): VOR, VOR/DME, and VORTAC. By itself it is known as a VOR, and it provides magnetic bearing information to and from the station. When DME is also installed with a VOR, the NAVAID is referred to as a VOR/DME. When military tactical air navigation (TACAN) equipment is installed with a VOR, the NAVAID is known as a VORTAC. DME is always an integral part of a VORTAC. Regardless of the type of NAVAID utilized (VOR, VOR/DME or VORTAC), the VOR indicator behaves the same. Unless otherwise noted, in this section, VOR, VOR/DME and VORTAC NAVAIDs are all referred to hereafter as VORs.

The prefix "omni-" means all, and an omnidirectional range is a VHF radio transmitting ground station that projects straight line courses (radials) from the station in all directions. From a top view, it can be visualized as being similar to the spokes from the hub of a wheel. The distance VOR radials are projected depends upon the power output of the transmitter.

The course or radials projected from the station are referenced to magnetic north. Therefore, a radial is defined as a line of magnetic bearing extending outward from the VOR station. Radials are identified by numbers beginning with 001, which is 1° east of magnetic north, and progress in sequence through all the degrees of a circle until reaching 360. To aid in orientation, a compass rose reference to magnetic north is superimposed on aeronautical charts at the station location.

VOR ground stations transmit within a VHF frequency band of 108.0–117.95 MHz. Because the equipment is VHF, the signals transmitted are subject to line-of-sight restrictions. Therefore, its range varies in direct proportion to the altitude of receiving equipment. Generally, the reception range of the signals at an altitude of 1,000 feet above ground level (AGL) is about 40 to 45 miles. This distance increases with altitude. [Figure 15-28]

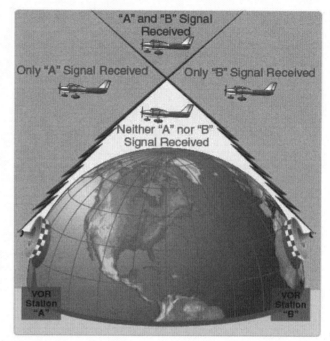

Figure 15-28. *VHF transmissions follow a line-of-sight course.*

VORs and VORTACs are classed according to operational use. There are three classes:

- T (Terminal)
- L (Low altitude)
- H (High altitude)

The normal useful range for the various classes is shown in the following table:

VOR/VORTAC NAVAIDS
Normal Usable Altitudes and Radius Distances

Class	Altitudes	Distance (Miles)
T	12,000' and below	25
L	Below 18,000'	40
H	Below 14,500'	40
H	Within the conterminous 48 states only, between 14,500 and 17,999'	100
H	18,000'—FL 450	130
H	60,000'—FL 450	100

The useful range of certain facilities may be less than 50 miles. For further information concerning these restrictions, refer to the Communication/NAVAID Remarks in the A/FD.

The accuracy of course alignment of VOR radials is considered to be excellent. It is generally within plus or minus 1°. However, certain parts of the VOR receiver equipment deteriorate, and this affects its accuracy. This is particularly true at great distances from the VOR station. The best assurance of maintaining an accurate VOR receiver is periodic checks and calibrations. VOR accuracy checks are not a regulatory requirement for VFR flight. However, to assure accuracy of the equipment, these checks should be accomplished quite frequently and a complete calibration each year. The following means are provided for pilots to check VOR accuracy:

- FAA VOR test facility (VOT)
- Certified airborne checkpoints
- Certified ground checkpoints located on airport surfaces

If an aircraft has two VOR receivers installed, a dual VOR receiver check can be made. To accomplish the dual receiver check, a pilot tunes both VOR receivers to the same VOR ground facility. The maximum permissible variation between the two indicated bearings is 4 degrees. A list of the airborne and ground checkpoints is published in the A/FD.

Basically, these checks consist of verifying that the VOR radials the aircraft equipment receives are aligned with the radials the station transmits. There are not specific tolerances in VOR checks required for VFR flight. But as a guide to assure acceptable accuracy, the required IFR tolerances can be used—±4° for ground checks and ±6° for airborne checks. These checks can be performed by the pilot.

The VOR transmitting station can be positively identified by its Morse code identification or by a recorded voice identification which states the name of the station followed by "VOR." Many FSS transmit voice messages on the same frequency that the VOR operates. Voice transmissions should not be relied upon to identify stations, because many FSS remotely transmit over several omniranges, which have names different from that of the transmitting FSS. If the VOR is out of service for maintenance, the coded identification is removed and not transmitted. This serves to alert pilots that this station should not be used for navigation. VOR receivers are designed with an alarm flag to indicate when signal strength is inadequate to operate the navigational equipment. This happens if the aircraft is too far from the VOR or the aircraft is too low and, therefore, is out of the line of sight of the transmitting signals.

Using the VOR

In review, for VOR radio navigation, there are two components required: ground transmitter and aircraft

receiving equipment. The ground transmitter is located at a specific position on the ground and transmits on an assigned frequency. The aircraft equipment includes a receiver with a tuning device and a VOR or omninavigation instrument. The navigation instrument could be a course deviation indicator (CDI), horizontal situation indicator (HSI), or a radio magnetic indicator (RMI). Each of these instruments indicates the course to the tuned VOR.

Course Deviation Indicator (CDI)

The CDI is found in most training aircraft. It consists of (1) omnibearing selector (OBS) sometimes referred to as the course selector, (2) a CDI needle (Left-Right Needle), and (3) a TO/FROM indicator.

The course selector is an azimuth dial that can be rotated to select a desired radial or to determine the radial over which the aircraft is flying. In addition, the magnetic course "TO" or "FROM" the station can be determined.

When the course selector is rotated, it moves the CDI or needle to indicate the position of the radial relative to the aircraft. If the course selector is rotated until the deviation needle is centered, the radial (magnetic course "FROM" the station) or its reciprocal (magnetic course "TO" the station) can be determined. The course deviation needle also moves to the right or left if the aircraft is flown or drifting away from the radial which is set in the course selector.

By centering the needle, the course selector indicates either the course "FROM" the station or the course "TO" the station. If the flag displays a "TO," the course shown on the course selector must be flown to the station. *[Figure 15-29]* If

Figure 15-29. *VOR indicator.*

"FROM" is displayed and the course shown is followed, the aircraft is flown away from the station.

Horizontal Situation Indicator

The HSI is a direction indicator that uses the output from a flux valve to drive the compass card. The HSI *[Figure 15-30]* combines the magnetic compass with navigation signals and a glideslope. The HSI gives the pilot an indication of the location of the aircraft with relationship to the chosen course or radial.

In *Figure 15-30,* the aircraft magnetic heading displayed on the compass card under the lubber line is 184°. The course select pointer shown is set to 295°; the tail of the pointer indicates the reciprocal, 115°. The course deviation bar operates with a VOR/Localizer (VOR/LOC) or GPS navigation receiver to indicate left or right deviations from the course selected with the course select pointer; operating

in the same manner, the angular movement of a conventional VOR/LOC needle indicates deviation from course.

The desired course is selected by rotating the course select pointer, in relation to the compass card, by means of the course select knob. The HSI has a fixed aircraft symbol and the course deviation bar displays the aircraft's position relative to the selected course. The TO/FROM indicator is a triangular pointer. When the indicator points to the head of the course select pointer, the arrow shows the course selected. If properly intercepted and flown, the course will take the aircraft to the chosen facility. When the indicator points to the tail of the course, the arrow shows that the course selected, if properly intercepted and flown, will take the aircraft directly away from the chosen facility.

When the NAV warning flag appears it indicates no reliable signal is being received. The appearance of the HDG flag indicates the compass card is not functioning properly.

The glideslope pointer indicates the relation of the aircraft to the glideslope. When the pointer is below the center position, the aircraft is above the glideslope and an increased rate of descent is required. In some installations, the azimuth card is a remote indicating compass; however, in others the heading must be checked occasionally against the magnetic compass and reset.

Radio Magnetic Indicator (RMI)

The RMI *[Figure 15-31]* is a navigational aid providing aircraft magnetic or directional gyro heading and very high frequency omnidirectional range (VOR), GPS, and automatic direction finder (ADF) bearing information. Remote indicating

Figure 15-30. *Horizontal situation indicator.*

Figure 15-31. *Radio magnetic indicator.*

compasses were developed to compensate for errors in and limitations of older types of heading indicators.

The remote compass transmitter is a separate unit usually mounted in a wingtip to eliminate the possibility of magnetic interference. The RMI consists of a compass card, a heading index, two bearing pointers, and pointer function switches. The two pointers are driven by any two combinations of a GPS, an ADF, and/or a VOR. The pilot has the ability to select the navigation aid to be indicated. The pointer indicates course to selected NAVAID or waypoint. In *Figure 15-31* the green pointer is indicating the station tuned on the ADF. The yellow pointer is indicating the course to a VOR of GPS waypoint. Note that there is no requirement for a pilot to select course with the RMI, but only the NAVAID is to be indicated.

Tracking With VOR

The following describes a step-by-step procedure to use when tracking to and from a VOR station using a CDI. *Figure 15-32* illustrates the procedure.

First, tune the VOR receiver to the frequency of the selected VOR station. For example, 115.0 to receive Bravo VOR. Next, check the identifiers to verify that the desired VOR is being received. As soon as the VOR is properly tuned, the course deviation needle deflects either left or right. Then, rotate the azimuth dial to the course selector until the course deviation needle centers and the TO-FROM indicator indicates "TO." If the needle centers with a "FROM" indication, the azimuth should be rotated 180° because, in this case, it is desired to fly "TO" the station. Now, turn the aircraft to the heading indicated on the VOR azimuth dial or course selector, 350° in this example.

If a heading of 350° is maintained with a wind from the right as shown, the aircraft drifts to the left of the intended track. As the aircraft drifts off course, the VOR course deviation needle gradually moves to the right of center or indicates the direction of the desired radial or track.

To return to the desired radial, the aircraft heading must be altered to the right. As the aircraft returns to the desired track, the deviation needle slowly returns to center. When centered, the aircraft is on the desired radial and a left turn must be made toward, but not to the original heading of 350° because a wind drift correction must be established. The amount of correction depends upon the strength of the wind. If the wind velocity is unknown, a trial-and-error method can be used to find the correct heading. Assume, for this example, a 10° correction for a heading of 360° is maintained.

Figure 15-32. *Tracking a radial in a crosswind.*

While maintaining a heading of 360°, assume that the course deviation begins to move to the left. This means that the wind correction of 10° is too great and the aircraft is flying to the right of course. A slight turn to the left should be made to permit the aircraft to return to the desired radial.

When the deviation needle centers, a small wind drift correction of 5° or a heading correction of 355° should be flown. If this correction is adequate, the aircraft remains on the radial. If not, small variations in heading should be made to keep the needle centered, and consequently keep the aircraft on the radial.

As the VOR station is passed, the course deviation needle fluctuates, then settles down, and the "TO" indication changes to "FROM." If the aircraft passes to one side of the station, the needle deflects in the direction of the station as the indicator changes to "FROM."

Generally, the same techniques apply when tracking outbound as those used for tracking inbound. If the intent is to fly over the station and track outbound on the reciprocal of the inbound radial, the course selector should not be changed. Corrections are made in the same manner to keep the needle centered. The only difference is that the omnidirectional range indicator indicates "FROM."

If tracking outbound on a course other than the reciprocal of the inbound radial, this new course or radial must be set in the course selector and a turn made to intercept this course. After this course is reached, tracking procedures are the same as previously discussed.

Tips on Using the VOR

- Positively identify the station by its code or voice identification.

- Keep in mind that VOR signals are "line-of-sight." A weak signal or no signal at all is received if the aircraft is too low or too far from the station.

- When navigating to a station, determine the inbound radial and use this radial. Fly a heading that will maintain the course. If the aircraft drifts, fly a heading to re-intercept the course then apply a correction to compensate for wind drift.

- If minor needle fluctuations occur, avoid changing headings immediately. Wait momentarily to see if the needle recenters; if it does not, then correct.

- When flying "TO" a station, always fly the selected course with a "TO" indication. When flying "FROM" a station, always fly the selected course with a "FROM" indication. If this is not done, the action of the course

deviation needle is reversed. To further explain this reverse action, if the aircraft is flown toward a station with a "FROM" indication or away from a station with a "TO" indication, the course deviation needle indicates in an direction opposite to that which it should indicate. For example, if the aircraft drifts to the right of a radial being flown, the needle moves to the right or points away from the radial. If the aircraft drifts to the left of the radial being flown, the needle moves left or in the direction opposite to the radial.

- When navigating using the VOR it is important to fly headings that maintain or re-intercept the course. Just turning toward the needle will cause overshooting the radial and flying an S turn to the left and right of course.

Time and Distance Check From a Station

To compute time and distance from a station, first turn the aircraft to place the bearing pointer on the nearest 90° index. Note time and maintain heading. When the bearing pointer has moved 10°, note the elapsed time in seconds and apply the formulas in the following example to determine time and distance. [Figure 15-33]

Figure 15-33. *Time-distance check example.*

The time from station may also be calculated by using a short method based on the above formula, if a 10° bearing change is flown. If the elapsed time for the bearing change is noted in seconds and a 10° bearing change is made, the time from the station in minutes is determined by counting off one decimal point. Thus, if 75 seconds are required to fly a 10° bearing change, the aircraft is 7.5 minutes from the station. When the bearing pointer is moving rapidly or when several corrections are required to place the pointer on the wingtip position, the aircraft is at station passage.

The distance from the station is computed by multiplying TAS or GS (in miles per minute) by the previously determined time in minutes. For example, if the aircraft is 7.5 minutes from station, flying at a TAS of 120 knots or 2 NM per minute, the distance from station is 15 NM (7.5 x 2 = 15).

The preceding are methods of computing approximate time and distance. The accuracy of time and distance checks is governed by existing wind, degree of bearing change, and accuracy of timing. The number of variables involved causes the result to be only an approximation. However, by flying an accurate heading and checking the time and bearing closely, the pilot can make a reasonable estimate of time and distance from the station.

Course Intercept

Course interceptions are performed in most phases of instrument navigation. The equipment used varies, but an intercept heading must be flown that results in an angle or rate of intercept sufficient to solve a particular problem.

Rate of Intercept

Rate of intercept, seen by the aviator as bearing pointer or HSI movement, is a result of the following factors:

- The angle at which the aircraft is flown toward a desired course (angle of intercept)

- True airspeed and wind (GS)

- Distance from the station

Angle of Intercept

The angle of intercept is the angle between the heading of the aircraft (intercept heading) and desired course. Controlling this angle by selection/adjustment of the intercept heading is the easiest and most effective way to control course interceptions. Angle of intercept must be greater than the degrees from course, but should not exceed 90°. Within this limit, adjust to achieve the most desirable rate of intercept.

When selecting an intercept heading, the key factor is the relationship between distance from the station and degrees from the course. Each degree, or radial, is 1 NM wide at a distance of 60 NM from the station. Width increases or decreases in proportion to the 60 NM distance. For example, 1 degree is 2 NM wide at 120 NM—and ½ NM wide at 30 NM. For a given GS and angle of intercept, the resultant rate of intercept varies according to the distance from the station. When selecting an intercept heading to form an angle of intercept, consider the following factors:

- Degrees from course

- Distance from the station

- True airspeed and wind (GS)

Distance Measuring Equipment (DME)

Distance measuring equipment (DME) consists of an ultra high frequency (UHF) navigational aid with VOR/DMEs and VORTACs. It measures, in NM, the slant range distance of an aircraft from a VOR/DME or VORTAC (both hereafter

referred to as a VORTAC). Although DME equipment is very popular, not all aircraft are DME equipped.

To utilize DME, the pilot should select, tune, and identify a VORTAC, as previously described. The DME receiver, utilizing what is called a "paired frequency" concept, automatically selects and tunes the UHF DME frequency associated with the VHF VORTAC frequency selected by the pilot. This process is entirely transparent to the pilot. After a brief pause, the DME display shows the slant range distance to or from the VORTAC. Slant range distance is the direct distance between the aircraft and the VORTAC, and is therefore affected by aircraft altitude. (Station passage directly over a VORTAC from an altitude of 6,076 feet above ground level (AGL) would show approximately 1.0 NM on the DME.) DME is a very useful adjunct to VOR navigation. A VOR radial alone merely gives line of position information. With DME, a pilot may precisely locate the aircraft on that line (radial).

Most DME receivers also provide GS and time-to-station modes of operation. The GS is displayed in knots (NMPH). The time-to-station mode displays the minutes remaining to VORTAC station passage, predicated upon the present GS. GS and time-to-station information is only accurate when tracking directly to or from a VORTAC. DME receivers typically need a minute or two of stabilized flight directly to or from a VORTAC before displaying accurate GS or time-to-station information.

Some DME installations have a hold feature that permits a DME signal to be retained from one VORTAC while the course indicator displays course deviation information from an ILS or another VORTAC.

VOR/DME RNAV

Area navigation (RNAV) permits electronic course guidance on any direct route between points established by the pilot. While RNAV is a generic term that applies to a variety of navigational aids, such as LORAN-C, GPS, and others, this section deals with VOR/DME-based RNAV. VOR/DME RNAV is not a separate ground-based NAVAID, but a method of navigation using VOR/DME and VORTAC signals specially processed by the aircraft's RNAV computer. [Figure 15-34]

NOTE: In this section, the term "VORTAC" also includes VOR/DME NAVAIDs.

In its simplest form, VOR/DME RNAV allows the pilot to electronically move VORTACs around to more convenient locations. Once electronically relocated, they are referred to as waypoints. These waypoints are described as a

Figure 15-34. *Flying an RNAV course.*

combination of a selected radial and distance within the service volume of the VORTAC to be used. These waypoints allow a straight course to be flown between almost any origin and destination, without regard to the orientation of VORTACs or the existence of airways.

While the capabilities and methods of operation of VOR/DME RNAV units differ, there are basic principles of operation that are common to all. Pilots are urged to study the manufacturer's operating guide and receive instruction prior to the use of VOR/DME RNAV or any unfamiliar navigational system. Operational information and limitations should also be sought from placards and the supplement section of the AFM/POH.

VOR/DME-based RNAV units operate in at least three modes: VOR, en route, and approach. A fourth mode, VOR Parallel, may also be found on some models. The units need both VOR and DME signals to operate in any RNAV mode. If the NAVAID selected is a VOR without DME, RNAV mode will not function.

In the VOR (or non-RNAV) mode, the unit simply functions as a VOR receiver with DME capability. *[Figure 15-35]* The unit's display on the VOR indicator is conventional in all respects. For operation on established airways or any other ordinary VOR navigation, the VOR mode is used.

Figure 15-35. *RNAV controls.*

To utilize the unit's RNAV capability, the pilot selects and establishes a waypoint or a series of waypoints to define

a course. To operate in any RNAV mode, the unit needs both radial and distance signals; therefore, a VORTAC (or VOR/DME) needs to be selected as a NAVAID. To establish a waypoint, a point somewhere within the service range of a VORTAC is defined on the basis of radial and distance. Once the waypoint is entered into the unit and the RNAV en route mode is selected, the CDI displays course guidance to the waypoint, not the original VORTAC. DME also displays distance to the waypoint. Many units have the capability to store several waypoints, allowing them to be programmed prior to flight, if desired, and called up in flight.

RNAV waypoints are entered into the unit in magnetic bearings (radials) of degrees and tenths (i.e., 275.5°) and distances in NM and tenths (i.e., 25.2 NM). When plotting RNAV waypoints on an aeronautical chart, pilots find it difficult to measure to that level of accuracy, and in practical application, it is rarely necessary. A number of flight planning publications publish airport coordinates and waypoints with this precision and the unit accepts those figures. There is a subtle, but important difference in CDI operation and display in the RNAV modes.

In the RNAV modes, course deviation is displayed in terms of linear deviation. In the RNAV en route mode, maximum deflection of the CDI typically represents 5 NM on either side of the selected course, without regard to distance from the waypoint. In the RNAV approach mode, maximum deflection of the CDI typically represents 1¼ NM on either side of the selected course. There is no increase in CDI sensitivity as the aircraft approaches a waypoint in RNAV mode.

The RNAV approach mode is used for instrument approaches. Its narrow scale width (¼ of the en route mode) permits very precise tracking to or from the selected waypoint. In visual flight rules (VFR) cross-country navigation, tracking a course in the approach mode is not desirable because it requires a great deal of attention and soon becomes tedious.

A fourth, lesser-used mode on some units is the VOR Parallel mode. This permits the CDI to display linear (not angular) deviation as the aircraft tracks to and from VORTACs. It derives its name from permitting the pilot to offset (or parallel) a selected course or airway at a fixed distance of the pilot's choosing, if desired. The VOR parallel mode has the same effect as placing a waypoint directly over an existing VORTAC. Some pilots select the VOR parallel mode when utilizing the navigation (NAV) tracking function of their autopilot for smoother course following near the VORTAC.

Confusion is possible when navigating an aircraft with VOR/DME-based RNAV, and it is essential that the pilot become familiar with the equipment installed. It is not unknown for pilots to operate inadvertently in one of the RNAV modes when the operation was not intended by overlooking switch positions or annunciators. The reverse has also occurred with a pilot neglecting to place the unit into one of the RNAV modes by overlooking switch positions or annunciators. As always, the prudent pilot is not only familiar with the equipment used, but never places complete reliance in just one method of navigation when others are available for cross-check.

Automatic Direction Finder (ADF)

Many general aviation-type aircraft are equipped with ADF radio receiving equipment. To navigate using the ADF, the pilot tunes the receiving equipment to a ground station known as a nondirectional radio beacon (NDB). The NDB stations normally operate in a low or medium frequency band of 200 to 415 kHz. The frequencies are readily available on aeronautical charts or in the A/FD.

All radio beacons except compass locators transmit a continuous three-letter identification in code except during voice transmissions. A compass locator, which is associated with an instrument landing system, transmits a two-letter identification.

Standard broadcast stations can also be used in conjunction with ADF. Positive identification of all radio stations is extremely important and this is particularly true when using standard broadcast stations for navigation.

NDBs have one advantage over the VOR. This advantage is that low or medium frequencies are not affected by line-of-sight. The signals follow the curvature of the Earth; therefore, if the aircraft is within the range of the station, the signals can be received regardless of altitude.

The following table gives the class of NDB stations, their power, and usable range:

NONDIRECTIONAL RADIOBEACON (NDB)
(Usable Radius Distances for All Altitudes)

Class	Power (Watts)	Distance (Miles)
Compass Locator	Under 25	15
MH	Under 50	25
H	50–1999	*50
HH	2000 or more	75

*Service range of individual facilities may be less than 50 miles.

One of the disadvantages that should be considered when using low frequency (LF) for navigation is that low frequency signals are very susceptible to electrical disturbances, such as lightning. These disturbances create excessive static, needle deviations, and signal fades. There may be interference from distant stations. Pilots should know the conditions under which these disturbances can occur so they can be more alert to possible interference when using the ADF.

Basically, the ADF aircraft equipment consists of a tuner, which is used to set the desired station frequency, and the navigational display.

The navigational display consists of a dial upon which the azimuth is printed, and a needle which rotates around the dial and points to the station to which the receiver is tuned.

Some of the ADF dials can be rotated to align the azimuth with the aircraft heading; others are fixed with 0° representing the nose of the aircraft, and 180° representing the tail. Only the fixed azimuth dial is discussed in this handbook. [Figure 15-36]

Figure 15-36. *ADF with fixed azimuth and magnetic compass.*

Figure 15-37 illustrates terms that are used with the ADF and should be understood by the pilot.

To determine the magnetic bearing "FROM" the station, 180° is added to or subtracted from the magnetic bearing to the station. This is the reciprocal bearing and is used when plotting position fixes.

Figure 15-37. *ADF terms.*

Keep in mind that the needle of fixed azimuth points to the station in relation to the nose of the aircraft. If the needle is deflected 30° to the left for a relative bearing of 330°, this means that the station is located 30° left. If the aircraft is turned left 30°, the needle moves to the right 30° and indicates a relative bearing of 0°, or the aircraft is pointing toward the station. If the pilot continues flight toward the station keeping the needle on 0°, the procedure is called homing to the station. If a crosswind exists, the ADF needle continues to drift away from zero. To keep the needle on zero, the aircraft must be turned slightly resulting in a curved flightpath to the station. Homing to the station is a common procedure, but results in drifting downwind, thus lengthening the distance to the station.

Tracking to the station requires correcting for wind drift and results in maintaining flight along a straight track or bearing to the station. When the wind drift correction is established, the ADF needle indicates the amount of correction to the right or left. For instance, if the magnetic bearing to the station is 340°, a correction for a left crosswind would result in a magnetic heading of 330°, and the ADF needle would indicate 10° to the right or a relative bearing of 010°. *[Figure 15-38]*

When tracking away from the station, wind corrections are made similar to tracking to the station, but the ADF needle points toward the tail of the aircraft or the 180° position on the azimuth dial. Attempting to keep the ADF needle on the 180° position during winds results in the aircraft flying a curved flight leading further and further from the desired track. To correct for wind when tracking outbound, correction should be made in the direction opposite of that in which the needle is pointing.

Figure 15-38. *ADF tracking.*

Although the ADF is not as popular as the VOR for radio navigation, with proper precautions and intelligent use, the ADF can be a valuable aid to navigation.

Loran-C Navigation

Long range navigation, version C (LORAN-C) is another form of RNAV, but one that operates from chains of transmitters broadcasting signals in the LF spectrum. World Aeronautical Chart (WAC), sectional charts, and VFR terminal area charts do not show the presence of LORAN-C transmitters. Selection of a transmitter chain is either made automatically by the unit, or manually by the pilot using guidance information provided by the manufacturer. LORAN-C is a highly accurate, supplemental form of navigation typically installed as an adjunct to VOR and ADF equipment. Databases of airports, NAVAIDs, and ATC facilities are frequently features of LORAN-C receivers.

LORAN-C is an outgrowth of the original LORAN-A developed for navigation during World War II. The LORAN-C system is used extensively in maritime applications. It experienced a dramatic growth in popularity with pilots with the advent of the small, panel-mounted LORAN-C receivers available at relatively low cost. These units are frequently very sophisticated and capable, with a wide variety of navigational functions.

With high levels of LORAN-C sophistication and capability, a certain complexity in operation is an unfortunate necessity. Pilots are urged to read the operating handbooks and to consult the supplements section of the AFM/POH prior to utilizing LORAN-C for navigation. Many units offer so many features that the manufacturers often publish two different sets of instructions: (1) a brief operating guide and (2) in-depth operating manual.

While coverage is not global, LORAN-C signals are suitable for navigation in all of the conterminous United States, and parts of Canada and Alaska. Several foreign countries also operate their own LORAN-C systems. In the United States, the U.S. Coast Guard operates the LORAN-C system. LORAN-C system status is available from: USCG Navigation Center, Alexandria, Virginia at (703) 313-5900.

LORAN-C absolute accuracy is excellent—position errors are typically less than .25 NM. Repeatable accuracy, or the ability to return to a waypoint previously visited, is even better. While LORAN-C is a form of RNAV, it differs significantly from VOR/DME-based RNAV. It operates in a 90–110 kHz frequency range and is based upon measurement of the difference in arrival times of pulses of radio frequency (RF) energy emitted by a chain of transmitters hundreds of miles apart.

Within any given chain of transmitters, there is a master station, and from three to five secondary stations. LORAN-C units must be able to receive at least a master and two secondary stations to provide navigational information. Unlike VOR/DME-based RNAV, where the pilot must select the appropriate VOR/DME or VORTAC frequency, there is not a frequency selection in LORAN-C. The most advanced units automatically select the optimum chain for navigation. Other units rely upon the pilot to select the appropriate chain with a manual entry.

After the LORAN-C receiver has been turned on, the unit must be initialized before it can be used for navigation. While this can be accomplished in flight, it is preferable to perform this task, which can take several minutes, on the ground. The methods for initialization are as varied as the number of different models of receivers. Some require pilot input during the process, such as verification or acknowledgment of the information displayed.

Most units contain databases of navigational information. Frequently, such databases contain not only airport and NAVAID locations, but also extensive airport, airspace, and ATC information. While the unit can operate with an expired database, the information should be current or verified to be correct prior to use. The pilot can update some databases, while others require removal from the aircraft and the services of an avionics technician.

VFR navigation with LORAN-C can be as simple as telling the unit where the pilot wishes to go. The course guidance provided is a great circle (shortest distance) route to the destination. Older units may need a destination entered in terms of latitude and longitude, but recent designs need only the identifier of the airport or NAVAID. The unit also permits database storage and retrieval of pilot defined waypoints. LORAN-C signals follow the curvature of the Earth and are generally usable hundreds of miles from their transmitters.

The LORAN-C signal is subject to degradation from a variety of atmospheric disturbances. It is also susceptible to interference from static electricity buildup on the airframe and electrically "noisy" airframe equipment. Flight in precipitation or even dust clouds can cause occasional interference with navigational guidance from LORAN-C signals. To minimize these effects, static wicks and bonding straps should be installed and properly maintained.

LORAN-C navigation information is presented to the pilot in a variety of ways. All units have self-contained displays, and some elaborate units feature built-in moving map displays. Some installations can also drive an external moving map display, a conventional VOR indicator, or a horizontal situation indicator (HSI). Course deviation information is presented as a linear deviation from course—there is no increase in tracking sensitivity as the aircraft approaches the waypoint or destination. Pilots must carefully observe placards, selector switch positions, and annunciator indications when utilizing LORAN-C because aircraft installations can vary widely. The pilot's familiarity with unit operation through AFM/POH supplements and operating guides cannot be overemphasized.

LORAN-C Notices to Airmen (NOTAMs) should be reviewed prior to relying on LORAN-C for navigation. LORAN-C NOTAMs are issued to announce outages for specific chains and transmitters. Pilots may obtain LORAN-C NOTAMs from FSS briefers only upon request.

The prudent pilot never relies solely on one means of navigation when others are available for backup and cross-check. Pilots should never become so dependent upon the extensive capabilities of LORAN-C that other methods of navigation are neglected.

Global Positioning System

The GPS is a satellite-based radio navigation system. Its RNAV guidance is worldwide in scope. There are no symbols for GPS on aeronautical charts as it is a space-based system with global coverage. Development of the system is underway so that GPS is capable of providing the primary means of electronic navigation. Portable and yoke mounted units are proving to be very popular in addition to those permanently installed in the aircraft. Extensive navigation databases are common features in aircraft GPS receivers.

The GPS is a satellite radio navigation and time dissemination system developed and operated by the U.S. Department of Defense (DOD). Civilian interface and GPS system status is available from the U.S. Coast Guard.

It is not necessary to understand the technical aspects of GPS operation to use it in VFR/instrument flight rules (IFR) navigation. It does differ significantly from conventional, ground-based electronic navigation, and awareness of those differences is important. Awareness of equipment approvals and limitations is critical to the safety of flight.

The GPS navigation system broadcasts a signal that is used by receivers to determine precise position anywhere in the world. The receiver tracks multiple satellites and determines a pseudorange measurement to determine the user location. A minimum of four satellites is necessary to establish an accurate three-dimensional position. The Department of Defense (DOD) is responsible for operating the GPS satellite constellation and monitors the GPS satellites to ensure proper operation.

The status of a GPS satellite is broadcast as part of the data message transmitted by the satellite. GPS status information is also available by means of the U.S. Coast Guard navigation information service at (703) 313-5907 or online at http://www.navcen.uscg.gov/. Additionally, satellite status is available through the Notice to Airmen (NOTAM) system.

The GPS receiver verifies the integrity (usability) of the signals received from the GPS constellation through receiver autonomous integrity monitoring (RAIM) to determine if a satellite is providing corrupted information. At least one satellite, in addition to those required for navigation, must be in view for the receiver to perform the RAIM function; thus, RAIM needs a minimum of five satellites in view, or four

satellites and a barometric altimeter (baro-aiding) to detect an integrity anomaly. For receivers capable of doing so, RAIM needs six satellites in view (or five satellites with baro-aiding) to isolate the corrupt satellite signal and remove it from the navigation solution. Baro-aiding is a method of augmenting the GPS integrity solution by using a nonsatellite input source. GPS derived altitude should not be relied upon to determine aircraft altitude since the vertical error can be quite large and no integrity is provided. To ensure that baro-aiding is available, the current altimeter setting must be entered into the receiver as described in the operating manual.

RAIM messages vary somewhat between receivers; however, generally there are two types. One type indicates that there are not enough satellites available to provide RAIM integrity monitoring and another type indicates that the RAIM integrity monitor has detected a potential error that exceeds the limit for the current phase of flight. Without RAIM capability, the pilot has no assurance of the accuracy of the GPS position.

Selective Availability

Selective Availability (SA) is a method by which the accuracy of GPS is intentionally degraded. This feature is designed to deny hostile use of precise GPS positioning data. SA was discontinued on May 1, 2000, but many GPS receivers are designed to assume that SA is still active.

The GPS constellation of 24 satellites is designed so that a minimum of five satellites are always observable by a user anywhere on earth. The receiver uses data from a minimum of four satellites above the mask angle (the lowest angle above the horizon at which a receiver can use a satellite).

VFR Use of GPS

GPS navigation has become a great asset to VFR pilots, providing increased navigation capability and enhanced situational awareness, while reducing operating costs due to greater ease in flying direct routes. While GPS has many benefits to the VFR pilot, care must be exercised to ensure that system capabilities are not exceeded.

Types of receivers used for GPS navigation under VFR are varied, from a full IFR installation being used to support a VFR flight, to a VFR only installation (in either a VFR or IFR capable aircraft) to a hand-held receiver. The limitations of each type of receiver installation or use must be understood by the pilot to avoid misusing navigation information. In all cases, VFR pilots should never rely solely on one system of navigation. GPS navigation must be integrated with other forms of electronic navigation as well as pilotage and dead reckoning. Only through the integration of these techniques can the VFR pilot ensure accuracy in navigation.

Some critical concerns in VFR use of GPS include RAIM capability, database currency and antenna location.

RAIM Capability

Many VFR GPS receivers and all hand-held units have no RAIM alerting capability. Loss of the required number of satellites in view, or the detection of a position error, cannot be displayed to the pilot by such receivers. In receivers with no RAIM capability, no alert would be provided to the pilot that the navigation solution had deteriorated, and an undetected navigation error could occur. A systematic cross-check with other navigation techniques would identify this failure, and prevent a serious deviation.

In many receivers, an up-datable database is used for navigation fixes, airports, and instrument procedures. These databases must be maintained to the current update for IFR operation, but no such requirement exists for VFR use. However, in many cases, the database drives a moving map display which indicates Special Use Airspace and the various classes of airspace, in addition to other operational information. Without a current database the moving map display may be outdated and offer erroneous information to VFR pilots wishing to fly around critical airspace areas, such as a Restricted Area or a Class B airspace segment. Numerous pilots have ventured into airspace they were trying to avoid by using an outdated database. If there is not a current data base in the receiver, disregard the moving map display when making critical navigation decisions.

In addition, waypoints are added, removed, relocated, or re-named as required to meet operational needs. When using GPS to navigate relative to a named fix, a current database must be used to properly locate a named waypoint. Without the update, it is the pilot's responsibility to verify the waypoint location referencing to an official current source, such as the A/FD, sectional chart, or en route chart.

In many VFR installations of GPS receivers, antenna location is more a matter of convenience than performance. In IFR installations, care is exercised to ensure that an adequate clear view is provided for the antenna to see satellites. If an alternate location is used, some portion of the aircraft may block the view of the antenna, causing a greater opportunity to lose navigation signal.

This is especially true in the case of hand-helds. The use of hand-held receivers for VFR operations is a growing trend, especially among rental pilots. Typically, suction cups are used to place the GPS antennas on the inside of aircraft windows. While this method has great utility, the antenna location is limited by aircraft structure for optimal reception of available satellites. Consequently, signal losses may occur in certain situations of aircraft-satellite geometry, causing a loss of navigation signal. These losses, coupled with a lack of RAIM capability, could present erroneous position and navigation information with no warning to the pilot.

While the use of a hand-held GPS for VFR operations is not limited by regulation, modification of the aircraft, such as installing a panel- or yoke-mounted holder, is governed by 14 CFR part 43. Pilots should consult with a mechanic to ensure compliance with the regulation and a safe installation.

Tips for Using GPS for VFR Operations

Always check to see if the unit has RAIM capability. If no RAIM capability exists, be suspicious of a GPS displayed position when any disagreement exists with the position derived from other radio navigation systems, pilotage, or dead reckoning.

Check the currency of the database, if any. If expired, update the database using the current revision. If an update of an expired database is not possible, disregard any moving map display of airspace for critical navigation decisions. Be aware that named waypoints may no longer exist or may have been relocated since the database expired. At a minimum, the waypoints planned to be used should be checked against a current official source, such as the A/FD, or a Sectional Aeronautical Chart.

While a hand-held GPS receiver can provide excellent navigation capability to VFR pilots, be prepared for intermittent loss of navigation signal, possibly with no RAIM warning to the pilot. If mounting the receiver in the aircraft, be sure to comply with 14 CFR part 43.

Plan flights carefully before taking off. If navigating to user-defined waypoints, enter them before flight, not on the fly. Verify the planned flight against a current source, such as a current sectional chart. There have been cases in which one pilot used waypoints created by another pilot that were not where the pilot flying was expecting. This generally resulted in a navigation error. Minimize head-down time in the aircraft and keep a sharp lookout for traffic, terrain, and obstacles. Just a few minutes of preparation and planning on the ground makes a great difference in the air.

Another way to minimize head-down time is to become very familiar with the receiver's operation. Most receivers are not intuitive. The pilot must take the time to learn the various keystrokes, knob functions, and displays that are used in the operation of the receiver. Some manufacturers provide computer-based tutorials or simulations of their receivers. Take the time to learn about the particular unit before using it in flight.

In summary, be careful not to rely on GPS to solve all VFR navigational problems. Unless an IFR receiver is installed in accordance with IFR requirements, no standard of accuracy or integrity has been assured. While the practicality of GPS is compelling, the fact remains that only the pilot can navigate the aircraft, and GPS is just one of the pilot's tools to do the job.

VFR Waypoints

VFR waypoints provide VFR pilots with a supplementary tool to assist with position awareness while navigating visually in aircraft equipped with area navigation receivers. VFR waypoints should be used as a tool to supplement current navigation procedures. The uses of VFR waypoints include providing navigational aids for pilots unfamiliar with an area, waypoint definition of existing reporting points, enhanced navigation in and around Class B and Class C airspace, and enhanced navigation around Special Use Airspace. VFR pilots should rely on appropriate and current aeronautical charts published specifically for visual navigation. If operating in a terminal area, pilots should take advantage of the Terminal Area Chart available for that area, if published. The use of VFR waypoints does not relieve the pilot of any responsibility to comply with the operational requirements of 14 CFR part 91.

VFR waypoint names (for computer entry and flight plans) consist of five letters beginning with the letters "VP" and are retrievable from navigation databases. The VFR waypoint names are not intended to be pronounceable, and they are not for use in ATC communications. On VFR charts, a stand-alone VFR waypoint is portrayed using the same four-point star symbol used for IFR waypoints. VFR waypoint collocated with a visual checkpoint on the chart is identified by a small magenta flag symbol. A VFR waypoint collocated with a visual checkpoint is pronounceable based on the name of the visual checkpoint and may be used for ATC communications. Each VFR waypoint name appears in parentheses adjacent to the geographic location on the chart. Latitude/longitude data for all established VFR waypoints may be found in the appropriate regional A/FD.

When filing VFR flight plans, use the five-letter identifier as a waypoint in the route of flight section if there is an intended course change at that point or if used to describe the planned route of flight. This VFR filing would be similar to VOR use in a route of flight. Pilots must use the VFR waypoints only when operating under VFR conditions.

Any VFR waypoints intended for use during a flight should be loaded into the receiver while on the ground and prior to departure. Once airborne, pilots should avoid programming routes or VFR waypoint chains into their receivers.

Pilots should be especially vigilant for other traffic while operating near VFR waypoints. The same effort to see and avoid other aircraft near VFR waypoints is necessary, as is the case when operating near VORs and NDBs. In fact, the increased accuracy of navigation through the use of GPS demands even greater vigilance, as off-course deviations among different pilots and receivers is less. When operating near a VFR waypoint, use whatever ATC services are available, even if outside a class of airspace where communications are required. Regardless of the class of airspace, monitor the available ATC frequency closely for information on other aircraft operating in the vicinity. It is also a good idea to turn on landing light(s) when operating near a VFR waypoint to make the aircraft more conspicuous to other pilots, especially when visibility is reduced.

Lost Procedures

Getting lost in an aircraft is a potentially dangerous situation especially when low on fuel. If a pilot becomes lost, there are some good common sense procedures to follow. If a town or city cannot be seen, the first thing to do is climb, being mindful of traffic and weather conditions. An increase in altitude increases radio and navigation reception range, and also increases radar coverage. If flying near a town or city, it might be possible to read the name of the town on a water tower.

If the aircraft has a navigational radio, such as a VOR or ADF receiver, it can be possible to determine position by plotting an azimuth from two or more navigational facilities. If GPS is installed, or a pilot has a portable aviation GPS on board, it can be used to determine the position and the location of the nearest airport.

Communicate with any available facility using frequencies shown on the sectional chart. If contact is made with a controller, radar vectors may be offered. Other facilities may offer direction finding (DF) assistance. To use this procedure, the controller requests the pilot to hold down the transmit button for a few seconds and then release it. The controller may ask the pilot to change directions a few times and repeat the transmit procedure. This gives the controller enough information to plot the aircraft position and then give vectors to a suitable landing site. If the situation becomes threatening, transmit the situation on the emergency frequency 121.5 MHz and set the transponder to 7700. Most facilities, and even airliners, monitor the emergency frequency.

Flight Diversion

There probably comes a time when a pilot is not able to make it to the planned destination. This can be the result of unpredicted weather conditions, a system malfunction, or poor preflight planning. In any case, the pilot needs to be able to safely and efficiently divert to an alternate destination. Before any cross-country flight, check the charts for airports or suitable landing areas along or near the route of flight. Also, check for navigational aids that can be used during a diversion.

Computing course, time, speed, and distance information in flight requires the same computations used during preflight planning. However, because of the limited flight deck space, and because attention must be divided between flying the aircraft, making calculations, and scanning for other aircraft, take advantage of all possible shortcuts and rule-of-thumb computations.

When in flight, it is rarely practical to actually plot a course on a sectional chart and mark checkpoints and distances. Furthermore, because an alternate airport is usually not very far from your original course, actual plotting is seldom necessary.

A course to an alternate can be measured accurately with a protractor or plotter, but can also be measured with reasonable accuracy using a straightedge and the compass rose depicted around VOR stations. This approximation can be made on the basis of a radial from a nearby VOR or an airway that closely parallels the course to your alternate. However, remember that the magnetic heading associated with a VOR radial or printed airway is outbound from the station. To find the course TO the station, it may be necessary to determine the reciprocal of that heading. It is typically easier to navigate to an alternate airport that has a VOR or NDB facility on the field.

After selecting the most appropriate alternate, approximate the magnetic course to the alternate using a compass rose or airway on the sectional chart. If time permits, try to start the diversion over a prominent ground feature. However, in an emergency, divert promptly toward your alternate. Attempting to complete all plotting, measuring, and computations involved before diverting to the alternate may only aggravate an actual emergency.

Once established on course, note the time, and then use the winds aloft nearest to your diversion point to calculate a heading and GS. Once a GS has been calculated, determine a new arrival time and fuel consumption. Give priority to flying the aircraft while dividing attention between navigation and planning. When determining an altitude to use while diverting, consider cloud heights, winds, terrain, and radio reception.

Chapter Summary

This chapter has discussed the fundamentals of VFR navigation. Beginning with an introduction to the charts that can be used for navigation to the more technically advanced concept of GPS, there is one aspect of navigation that remains the same. The pilot is responsible for proper planning and the execution of that planning to ensure a safe flight.

Chapter 16

Aeromedical Factors

Introduction

It is important for a pilot to be aware of the mental and physical standards required for the type of flying done. This chapter provides information on medical certification and on a variety of aeromedical factors related to flight activities.

Rods and Cones

Rod Concentration

Lens

Iris

Optic Nerve

Retina

PUPIL
The pupil (aperture) is the opening at the center of the **iris**. The size of the pupil is adjusted to control the amount of light entering the eye.

CORNEA
Light passes through the **cornea** (the transparent window on the front of the eye) and then through the **lens** to focus on the retina.

YAW

ROLL

ROLL

PITCH

YAW

The semicircular tubes are arranged at approximately right angles to each other, in the roll, pitch, and yaw axes.

Ampulla of Semicirc

Semicircul

Otoli

Endolymph Fluid

Vestibular Nerve

Cupo

Hair Cells

Obtaining a Medical Certificate

Most pilots must have a valid medical certificate to exercise the privileges of their airman certificates. Glider and free balloon pilots are not required to hold a medical certificate. Sport pilots may hold either a medical certificate or a valid state driver's license.

Acquisition of a medical certificate requires an examination by an aviation medical examiner (AME), a physician with training in aviation medicine designated by the Civil Aerospace Medical Institute (CAMI). There are three classes of medical certificates. The class of certificate needed depends on the type of flying the pilot plans to do.

A third-class medical certificate is required for a private or recreational pilot certificate. It is valid for 3 years for those individuals who have not reached the age of 40; otherwise it is valid for 2 years. A commercial pilot certificate requires at least a second-class medical certificate, which is valid for 1 year. First-class medical certificates are required for airline transport pilots, and are valid for 6 months.

The standards are more rigorous for the higher classes of certificates. A pilot with a higher class medical certificate has met the requirements for the lower classes as well. Since the required medical class applies only when exercising the privileges of the pilot certificate for which it is required, a first-class medical certificate would be valid for 1 year if exercising the privileges of a commercial certificate, and 2 or 3 years, as appropriate, for exercising the privileges of a private or recreational certificate. The same applies for a second-class medical certificate. The standards for medical certification are contained in Title 14 of the Code of Federal Regulations (14 CFR) part 67 and the requirements for obtaining medical certificates can be found in 14 CFR part 61.

Students who have physical limitations, such as impaired vision, loss of a limb, or hearing impairment may be issued a medical certificate valid for "student pilot privileges only" while learning to fly. Pilots with disabilities may require special equipment installed in the aircraft, such as hand controls for pilots with paraplegia. Some disabilities necessitate a limitation on the individual's certificate; for example, impaired hearing would require the limitation "not valid for flight requiring the use of radio." When all the knowledge, experience, and proficiency requirements have been met and a student can demonstrate the ability to operate the aircraft with the normal level of safety, a "statement of demonstrated ability" (SODA) can be issued. This waiver, or SODA, is valid as long as the physical impairment does not worsen. Contact the local Flight Standards District Office (FSDO) for more information on this subject.

Health and Physiological Factors Affecting Pilot Performance

A number of health factors and physiological effects can be linked to flying. Some are minor, while others are important enough to require special attention to ensure safety of flight. In some cases, physiological factors can lead to inflight emergencies. Some important medical factors that a pilot should be aware of include hypoxia, hyperventilation, middle ear and sinus problems, spatial disorientation, motion sickness, carbon monoxide (CO) poisoning, stress and fatigue, dehydration, and heatstroke. Other subjects include the effects of alcohol and drugs, anxiety, and excess nitrogen in the blood after scuba diving.

Hypoxia

Hypoxia means "reduced oxygen" or "not enough oxygen." Although any tissue will die if deprived of oxygen long enough, usually the most concern is with getting enough oxygen to the brain, since it is particularly vulnerable to oxygen deprivation. Any reduction in mental function while flying can result in life-threatening errors. Hypoxia can be caused by several factors, including an insufficient supply of oxygen, inadequate transportation of oxygen, or the inability of the body tissues to use oxygen. The forms of hypoxia are based on their causes: hypoxic hypoxia, hypemic hypoxia, stagnant hypoxia, and histotoxic hypoxia.

Hypoxic Hypoxia

Hypoxic hypoxia is a result of insufficient oxygen available to the body as a whole. A blocked airway and drowning are obvious examples of how the lungs can be deprived of oxygen, but the reduction in partial pressure of oxygen at high altitude is an appropriate example for pilots. Although the percentage of oxygen in the atmosphere is constant, its partial pressure decreases proportionately as atmospheric pressure decreases. As the airplane ascends during flight, the percentage of each gas in the atmosphere remains the same, but there are fewer molecules available at the pressure required for them to pass between the membranes in the respiratory system. This decrease in number of oxygen molecules at sufficient pressure can lead to hypoxic hypoxia.

Hypemic Hypoxia

Hypemic hypoxia occurs when the blood is not able to take up and transport a sufficient amount of oxygen to the cells in the body. Hypemic means "not enough blood." This type of hypoxia is a result of oxygen deficiency in the blood, rather than a lack of inhaled oxygen, and can be caused by a variety of factors. It may be due to reduced blood volume (due to severe bleeding), or it may result from certain blood diseases, such as anemia. More often hypemic hypoxia occurs because hemoglobin, the actual blood molecule that transports oxygen, is chemically unable to bind oxygen molecules. The most common form of hypemic hypoxia is CO poisoning. This is explained in greater detail on page 16-11. Hypemic hypoxia can also be caused by the loss of blood due to blood donation. Blood can require several weeks to return to normal following a donation. Although the effects of the blood loss are slight at ground level, there are risks when flying during this time.

Stagnant Hypoxia

Stagnant means "not flowing," and stagnant hypoxia, or ischemia, results when the oxygen-rich blood in the lungs is not moving, for one reason or another, to the tissues that need it. An arm or leg "going to sleep" because the blood flow has accidentally been shut off is one form of stagnant hypoxia. This kind of hypoxia can also result from shock, the heart failing to pump blood effectively, or a constricted artery. During flight, stagnant hypoxia can occur with excessive acceleration of gravity (Gs). Cold temperatures also can reduce circulation and decrease the blood supplied to extremities.

Histotoxic Hypoxia

The inability of the cells to effectively use oxygen is defined as histotoxic hypoxia. "Histo" refers to tissues or cells, and "toxic" means poisonous. In this case, enough oxygen is being transported to the cells that need it, but they are unable to make use of it. This impairment of cellular respiration can be caused by alcohol and other drugs, such as narcotics and poisons. Research has shown that drinking one ounce of alcohol can equate to about an additional 2,000 feet of physiological altitude.

Symptoms of Hypoxia

High-altitude flying can place a pilot in danger of becoming hypoxic. Oxygen starvation causes the brain and other vital organs to become impaired. One noteworthy attribute of the onset of hypoxia is that the first symptoms are euphoria and a carefree feeling. With increased oxygen starvation, the extremities become less responsive and flying becomes less coordinated. The symptoms of hypoxia vary with the individual, but common symptoms include:

- Cyanosis (blue fingernails and lips)
- Headache
- Decreased reaction time
- Impaired judgment
- Euphoria
- Visual impairment
- Drowsiness

- Lightheaded or dizzy sensation
- Tingling in fingers and toes
- Numbness

As hypoxia worsens, the field of vision begins to narrow, and instrument interpretation can become difficult. Even with all these symptoms, the effects of hypoxia can cause a pilot to have a false sense of security and be deceived into believing everything is normal. The treatment for hypoxia includes flying at lower altitudes and/or using supplemental oxygen.

All pilots are susceptible to the effects of oxygen starvation, regardless of physical endurance or acclimatization. When flying at high altitudes, it is paramount that oxygen be used to avoid the effects of hypoxia. The term "time of useful consciousness" describes the maximum time the pilot has to make rational, life-saving decisions and carry them out at a given altitude without supplemental oxygen. As altitude increases above 10,000 feet, the symptoms of hypoxia increase in severity, and the time of useful consciousness rapidly decreases. [Figure 16-1]

Altitude	Time of Useful Consciousness
45,000 feet MSL	9 to 15 seconds
40,000 feet MSL	15 to 20 seconds
35,000 feet MSL	30 to 60 seconds
30,000 feet MSL	1 to 2 minutes
28,000 feet MSL	2½ to 3 minutes
25,000 feet MSL	3 to 5 minutes
22,000 feet MSL	5 to 10 minutes
20,000 feet MSL	30 minutes or more

Figure 16-1. Time of useful consciousness.

Since symptoms of hypoxia can be different for each individual, the ability to recognize hypoxia can be greatly improved by experiencing and witnessing the effects of it during an altitude chamber "flight." The Federal Aviation Administration (FAA) provides this opportunity through aviation physiology training, which is conducted at the FAA CAMI and at many military facilities across the United States. For information about the FAA's one-day physiological training course with altitude chamber and vertigo demonstrations, visit the FAA web site: www.faa.gov/pilots/training/airman_education/aerospace_physiology/index.cfm.

Hyperventilation

Hyperventilation is the excessive rate and depth of respiration leading to abnormal loss of carbon dioxide from the blood. This condition occurs more often among pilots than is generally recognized. It seldom incapacitates completely, but it causes disturbing symptoms that can alarm the uninformed pilot. In such cases, increased breathing rate and anxiety further aggravate the problem. Hyperventilation can lead to unconsciousness due to the respiratory system's overriding mechanism to regain control of breathing.

Pilots encountering an unexpected stressful situation may subconsciously increase their breathing rate. If flying at higher altitudes, either with or without oxygen, a pilot may have a tendency to breathe more rapidly than normal, which often leads to hyperventilation.

Since many of the symptoms of hyperventilation are similar to those of hypoxia, it is important to correctly diagnose and treat the proper condition. If using supplemental oxygen, check the equipment and flow rate to ensure the symptoms are not hypoxia related. Common symptoms of hyperventilation include:

- Visual impairment
- Unconsciousness
- Lightheaded or dizzy sensation
- Tingling sensations
- Hot and cold sensations
- Muscle spasms

The treatment for hyperventilation involves restoring the proper carbon dioxide level in the body. Breathing normally is both the best prevention and the best cure for hyperventilation. In addition to slowing the breathing rate, breathing into a paper bag or talking aloud helps to overcome hyperventilation. Recovery is usually rapid once the breathing rate is returned to normal.

Middle Ear and Sinus Problems

During climbs and descents, the free gas formerly present in various body cavities expands due to a difference between the pressure of the air outside the body and that of the air inside the body. If the escape of the expanded gas is impeded, pressure builds up within the cavity and pain is experienced. Trapped gas expansion accounts for ear pain and sinus pain, as well as a temporary reduction in the ability to hear.

The middle ear is a small cavity located in the bone of the skull. It is closed off from the external ear canal by the eardrum. Normally, pressure differences between the middle ear and the outside world are equalized by a tube leading from inside each ear to the back of the throat on each side, called the Eustachian tube. These tubes are usually closed, but open during chewing, yawning, or swallowing to equalize pressure. Even a slight difference between external pressure and middle ear pressure can cause discomfort. *[Figure 16-2]*

Figure 16-2. *The Eustachian tube allows air pressure to equalize in the middle ear.*

During a climb, middle ear air pressure may exceed the pressure of the air in the external ear canal, causing the eardrum to bulge outward. Pilots become aware of this pressure change when they experience alternate sensations of "fullness" and "clearing." During descent, the reverse happens. While the pressure of the air in the external ear canal increases, the middle ear cavity, which equalized with the lower pressure at altitude, is at lower pressure than the external ear canal. This results in the higher outside pressure, causing the eardrum to bulge inward.

This condition can be more difficult to relieve due to the fact that the partial vacuum tends to constrict the walls of the Eustachian tube. To remedy this often painful condition, which also causes a temporary reduction in hearing sensitivity, pinch the nostrils shut, close the mouth and lips, and blow slowly and gently in the mouth and nose.

This procedure forces air through the Eustachian tube into the middle ear. It may not be possible to equalize the pressure in the ears if a pilot has a cold, an ear infection, or sore throat. A flight in this condition can be extremely painful, as well as damaging to the eardrums. If experiencing minor congestion, nose drops or nasal sprays may reduce the risk of a painful ear blockage. Before using any medication, check with an AME to ensure that it will not affect the ability to fly.

In a similar way, air pressure in the sinuses equalizes with the pressure in the flight deck through small openings that connect the sinuses to the nasal passages. An upper respiratory infection, such as a cold or sinusitis, or a nasal allergic condition can produce enough congestion around an opening to slow equalization. As the difference in pressure between the sinuses and the flight deck increases, congestion may plug the opening. This "sinus block" occurs most frequently during descent. Slow descent rates can reduce the associated pain. A sinus block can occur in the frontal sinuses, located above each eyebrow, or in the maxillary sinuses, located in each upper cheek. It will usually produce excruciating pain over the sinus area. A maxillary sinus block can also make the upper teeth ache. Bloody mucus may discharge from the nasal passages.

Sinus block can be avoided by not flying with an upper respiratory infection or nasal allergic condition. Adequate protection is usually not provided by decongestant sprays or drops to reduce congestion around the sinus openings. Oral decongestants have side effects that can impair pilot performance. If a sinus block does not clear shortly after landing, a physician should be consulted.

Spatial Disorientation and Illusions

Spatial disorientation specifically refers to the lack of orientation with regard to the position, attitude, or movement of the airplane in space. The body uses three integrated systems working together to ascertain orientation and movement in space.

- Vestibular system—organs found in the inner ear that sense position by the way we are balanced.

- Somatosensory system—nerves in the skin, muscles, and joints, which, along with hearing, sense position based on gravity, feeling, and sound.

- Visual system—eyes, which sense position based on what is seen.

All this information comes together in the brain and, most of the time, the three streams of information agree, giving a clear idea of where and how the body is moving. Flying can sometimes cause these systems to supply conflicting information to the brain, which can lead to disorientation. During flight in visual meteorological conditions (VMC), the eyes are the major orientation source and usually prevail over false sensations from other sensory systems. When these visual cues are removed, as they are in instrument meteorological conditions (IMC), false sensations can cause a pilot to quickly become disoriented.

The vestibular system in the inner ear allows the pilot to sense movement and determine orientation in the surrounding environment. In both the left and right inner ear, three semicircular canals are positioned at approximate right angles to each other. *[Figure 16-3]* Each canal is filled with fluid and has a section full of fine hairs. Acceleration of the inner ear in any direction causes the tiny hairs to deflect, which in turn stimulates nerve impulses, sending messages to the brain. The vestibular nerve transmits the impulses from the utricle, saccule, and semicircular canals to the brain to interpret motion.

The somatosensory system sends signals from the skin, joints, and muscles to the brain that are interpreted in relation to the Earth's gravitational pull. These signals determine posture. Inputs from each movement update the body's position to the brain on a constant basis. "Seat of the pants" flying is largely dependent upon these signals. Used in conjunction with visual and vestibular clues, these sensations can be fairly reliable. However, the body cannot distinguish between acceleration forces due to gravity and those resulting from maneuvering the aircraft, which can lead to sensory illusions and false impressions of an aircraft's orientation and movement.

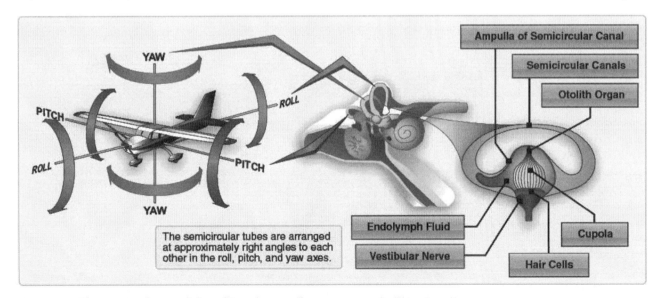

Figure 16-3. *The semicircular canals lie in three planes and sense motions of roll, pitch, and yaw.*

No turning
No sensation.

Start of turn
Sensation of turning
as moving fluid deflects
hairs.

Constant rate turn
No sensation after fluid
accelerates to same
speed as tube wall.

Turn stopped
Sensation of turning in
opposite direction as moving
fluid deflects hairs in opposite
direction.

Figure 16-4. *Human sensation of angular acceleration.*

Under normal flight conditions, when there is a visual reference to the horizon and ground, the sensory system in the inner ear helps to identify the pitch, roll, and yaw movements of the aircraft. When visual contact with the horizon is lost, the vestibular system becomes unreliable. Without visual references outside the aircraft, there are many situations in which combinations of normal motions and forces create convincing illusions that are difficult to overcome.

Prevention is usually the best remedy for spatial disorientation. Unless a pilot has many hours of training in instrument flight, flight should be avoided in reduced visibility or at night when the horizon is not visible. A pilot can reduce susceptibility to disorienting illusions through training and awareness, and learning to rely totally on flight instruments.

Vestibular Illusions

The Leans

A condition called the leans can result when a banked attitude, to the left for example, may be entered too slowly to set in motion the fluid in the "roll" semicircular tubes. *[Figure 16-4]* An abrupt correction of this attitude sets the fluid in motion, creating the illusion of a banked attitude to the right. The disoriented pilot may make the error of rolling the aircraft into the original left banked attitude, or if level flight is maintained, will feel compelled to lean in the perceived vertical plane until this illusion subsides.

Coriolis Illusion

The coriolis illusion occurs when a pilot has been in a turn long enough for the fluid in the ear canal to move at the same speed as the canal. A movement of the head in a different plane, such as looking at something in a different part of the flight deck, may set the fluid moving and create the illusion of turning or accelerating on an entirely different axis. This action causes the pilot to think the aircraft is doing a maneuver that it is not. The disoriented pilot may maneuver the aircraft into a dangerous attitude in an attempt to correct the aircraft's perceived attitude.

For this reason, it is important that pilots develop an instrument cross-check or scan that involves minimal head movement. Take care when retrieving charts and other objects in the flight deck—if something is dropped, retrieve it with minimal head movement and be alert for the coriolis illusion.

Graveyard Spiral

As in other illusions, a pilot in a prolonged coordinated, constant-rate turn, will have the illusion of not turning. During the recovery to level flight, the pilot will experience the sensation of turning in the opposite direction. The disoriented pilot may return the aircraft to its original turn. Because an aircraft tends to lose altitude in turns unless the pilot compensates for the loss in lift, the pilot may notice a loss of altitude. The absence of any sensation of turning creates the illusion of being in a level descent. The pilot may pull back on the controls in an attempt to climb or stop the descent. This action tightens the spiral and increases the loss of altitude; this illusion is referred to as a graveyard spiral. *[Figure 16-5]* At some point, this could lead to a loss of aircraft control.

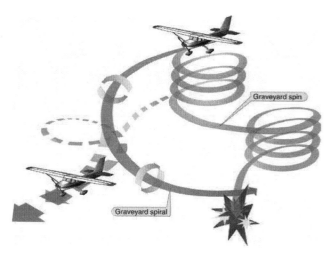

Figure 16-5. *Graveyard spiral.*

Somatogravic Illusion

A rapid acceleration, such as experienced during takeoff, stimulates the otolith organs in the same way as tilting the head backwards. This action creates the somatogravic illusion of being in a nose-up attitude, especially in situations without good visual references. The disoriented pilot may push the aircraft into a nose-low or dive attitude. A rapid deceleration by quick reduction of the throttle(s) can have the opposite effect, with the disoriented pilot pulling the aircraft into a nose-up or stall attitude.

Inversion Illusion

An abrupt change from climb to straight-and-level flight can stimulate the otolith organs enough to create the illusion of tumbling backwards, or inversion illusion. The disoriented pilot may push the aircraft abruptly into a nose-low attitude, possibly intensifying this illusion.

Elevator Illusion

An abrupt upward vertical acceleration, as can occur in an updraft, can stimulate the otolith organs to create the illusion of being in a climb. This is called elevator illusion. The disoriented pilot may push the aircraft into a nose-low attitude. An abrupt downward vertical acceleration, usually in a downdraft, has the opposite effect, with the disoriented pilot pulling the aircraft into a nose-up attitude.

Visual Illusions

Visual illusions are especially hazardous because pilots rely on their eyes for correct information. Two illusions that lead to spatial disorientation, false horizon and autokinesis, are concerned with only the visual system.

False Horizon

A sloping cloud formation, an obscured horizon, an aurora borealis, a dark scene spread with ground lights and stars, and certain geometric patterns of ground lights can provide inaccurate visual information, or false horizon, for aligning the aircraft correctly with the actual horizon. The disoriented pilot may place the aircraft in a dangerous attitude.

Autokinesis

In the dark, a stationary light will appear to move about when stared at for many seconds. The disoriented pilot could lose control of the aircraft in attempting to align it with the false movements of this light, called autokinesis.

Postural Considerations

The postural system sends signals from the skin, joints, and muscles to the brain that are interpreted in relation to the Earth's gravitational pull. These signals determine posture. Inputs from each movement update the body's position to the brain on a constant basis. "Seat of the pants" flying is largely dependent upon these signals. Used in conjunction with visual and vestibular clues, these sensations can be fairly reliable. However, because of the forces acting upon the body in certain flight situations, many false sensations can occur due to acceleration forces overpowering gravity. *[Figure 16-6]* These situations include uncoordinated turns, climbing turns, and turbulence.

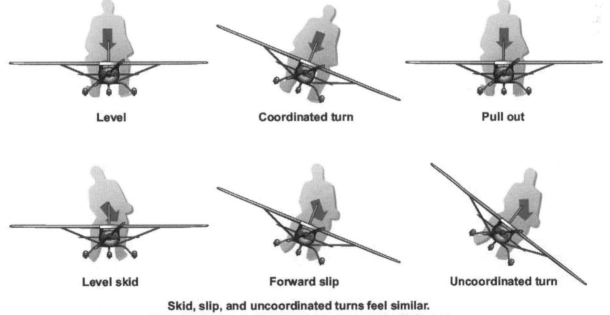

Level   **Coordinated turn**   **Pull out**

Level skid   **Forward slip**   **Uncoordinated turn**

**Skid, slip, and uncoordinated turns feel similar.
Pilots feel they are being forced sideways in their seat.**

Figure 16-6. *Sensations from centrifugal force.*

Demonstration of Spatial Disorientation

There are a number of controlled aircraft maneuvers a pilot can perform to experiment with spatial disorientation. While each maneuver will normally create a specific illusion, any false sensation is an effective demonstration of disorientation. Thus, even if there is no sensation during any of these maneuvers, the absence of sensation is still an effective demonstration because it illustrates the inability to detect bank or roll. There are several objectives in demonstrating these various maneuvers.

1. They teach pilots to understand the susceptibility of the human system to spatial disorientation.

2. They demonstrate that judgments of aircraft attitude based on bodily sensations are frequently false.

3. They help decrease the occurrence and degree of disorientation through a better understanding of the relationship between aircraft motion, head movements, and resulting disorientation.

4. They help instill a greater confidence in relying on flight instruments for assessing true aircraft attitude.

A pilot should not attempt any of these maneuvers at low altitudes, or in the absence of an instructor pilot or an appropriate safety pilot.

Climbing While Accelerating

With the pilot's eyes closed, the instructor pilot maintains approach airspeed in a straight-and-level attitude for several seconds, then accelerates while maintaining straight-and-level attitude. The usual illusion during this maneuver, without visual references, is that the aircraft is climbing.

Climbing While Turning

With the pilot's eyes still closed and the aircraft in a straight-and-level attitude, the instructor pilot now executes, with a relatively slow entry, a well coordinated turn of about 1.5 positive G (approximately 50° bank) for 90°. While in the turn, without outside visual references and under the effect of the slight positive G, the usual illusion produced is that of a climb. Upon sensing the climb, the pilot should immediately open the eyes to see that a slowly established, coordinated turn produces the same sensation as a climb.

Diving While Turning

Repeating the previous procedure, except the pilot's eyes should be kept closed until recovery from the turn is approximately one-half completed, can create the illusion of diving while turning.

Tilting to Right or Left

While in a straight-and-level attitude, with the pilot's eyes closed, the instructor pilot executes a moderate or slight skid to the left with wings level. This creates the illusion of the body being tilted to the right.

Reversal of Motion

This illusion can be demonstrated in any of the three planes of motion. While straight and level, with the pilot's eyes closed, the instructor pilot smoothly and positively rolls the aircraft to approximately 45° bank attitude while maintaining heading and pitch attitude. This creates the illusion of a strong sense of rotation in the opposite direction. After this illusion is noted, the pilot should open his or her eyes and observe that the aircraft is in a banked attitude.

Diving or Rolling Beyond the Vertical Plane

This maneuver may produce extreme disorientation. While in straight-and-level flight, the pilot should sit normally, either with eyes closed or gaze lowered to the floor. The instructor pilot starts a positive, coordinated roll toward a 30° or 40° angle of bank. As this is in progress, the pilot tilts his or her head forward, looks to the right or left, then immediately returns his or her head to an upright position. The instructor pilot should time the maneuver so the roll is stopped as the pilot returns his or her head upright. An intense disorientation is usually produced by this maneuver, and the pilot experiences the sensation of falling downward into the direction of the roll.

In the descriptions of these maneuvers, the instructor pilot is doing the flying, but having the pilot do the flying can also be a very effective demonstration. The pilot should close his or her eyes and tilt the head to one side. The instructor pilot tells the pilot what control inputs to perform. The pilot then attempts to establish the correct attitude or control input with eyes closed and head tilted. While it is clear the pilot has no idea of the actual attitude, he or she will react to what the senses are saying. After a short time, the pilot will become disoriented and the instructor pilot then tells the pilot to look up and recover. The benefit of this exercise is that the pilot experiences the disorientation while flying the aircraft.

Coping with Spatial Disorientation

To prevent illusions and their potentially disastrous consequences, pilots can:

1. Understand the causes of these illusions and remain constantly alert for them. Take the opportunity to experience spatial disorientation illusions in a device such as a Barany chair, a Vertigon, or a Virtual Reality Spatial Disorientation Demonstrator.

2. Always obtain and understand preflight weather briefings.

3. Before flying in marginal visibility (less than 3 miles) or where a visible horizon is not evident, such as flight over open water during the night, obtain training and maintain proficiency in airplane control by reference to instruments.

4. Do not continue flight into adverse weather conditions or into dusk or darkness unless proficient in the use of flight instruments. If intending to fly at night, maintain night-flight currency and proficiency. Include cross-country and local operations at various airfields.

5. Ensure that when outside visual references are used, they are reliable, fixed points on the Earth's surface.

6. Avoid sudden head movement, particularly during takeoffs, turns, and approaches to landing.

7. Be physically tuned for flight into reduced visibility. That is, ensure proper rest, adequate diet, and, if flying at night, allow for night adaptation Remember that illness, medication, alcohol, fatigue, sleep loss, and mild hypoxia are likely to increase susceptibility to spatial disorientation.

8. Most importantly, become proficient in the use of flight instruments and rely upon them. Trust the instruments and disregard your sensory perceptions.

The sensations that lead to illusions during instrument flight conditions are normal perceptions experienced by pilots. These undesirable sensations cannot be completely prevented, but through training and awareness, pilots can ignore or suppress them by developing absolute reliance on the flight instruments. As pilots gain proficiency in instrument flying, they become less susceptible to these illusions and their effects.

Optical Illusions

Of the senses, vision is the most important for safe flight. However, various terrain features and atmospheric conditions can create optical illusions. These illusions are primarily associated with landing. Since pilots must transition from reliance on instruments to visual cues outside the flight deck for landing at the end of an instrument approach, it is imperative they be aware of the potential problems associated with these illusions, and take appropriate corrective action. The major illusions leading to landing errors are described below.

Runway Width Illusion

A narrower-than-usual runway can create an illusion the aircraft is at a higher altitude than it actually is, especially when runway length-to-width relationships are comparable. *[Figure 16-7]* The pilot who does not recognize this illusion

will fly a lower approach, with the risk of striking objects along the approach path or landing short. A wider-than-usual runway can have the opposite effect, with the risk of the pilot leveling out the aircraft high and landing hard, or overshooting the runway.

Runway and Terrain Slopes Illusion

An upsloping runway, upsloping terrain, or both, can create an illusion that the aircraft is at a higher altitude than it actually is. *[Figure 16-7]* The pilot who does not recognize this illusion will fly a lower approach. Downsloping runways and downsloping approach terrain can have the opposite effect.

Featureless Terrain Illusion

An absence of surrounding ground features, as in an overwater approach, over darkened areas, or terrain made featureless by snow, can create an illusion the aircraft is at a higher altitude than it actually is. This illusion, sometimes referred to as the "black hole approach," causes pilots to fly a lower approach than is desired.

Water Refraction

Rain on the windscreen can create an illusion of being at a higher altitude due to the horizon appearing lower than it is. This can result in the pilot flying a lower approach.

Haze

Atmospheric haze can create an illusion of being at a greater distance and height from the runway. As a result, the pilot will have a tendency to be low on the approach. Conversely, extremely clear air (clear bright conditions of a high attitude airport) can give the pilot the illusion of being closer than he or she actually is, resulting in a high approach, which may result in an overshoot or go around. The diffusion of light due to water particles on the windshield can adversely affect depth perception. The lights and terrain features normally used to gauge height during landing become less effective for the pilot.

Fog

Flying into fog can create an illusion of pitching up. Pilots who do not recognize this illusion will often steepen the approach quite abruptly.

Ground Lighting Illusions

Lights along a straight path, such as a road or lights on moving trains, can be mistaken for runway and approach lights. Bright runway and approach lighting systems, especially where few lights illuminate the surrounding terrain, may create the illusion of less distance to the runway. The pilot who does not recognize this illusion will often fly a higher approach.

Runway width illusion

- A narrower-than-usual runway can create an illusion that the aircraft is higher than it actually is, leading to a lower approach.

- A wider-than-usual runway can create an illusion that the aircraft is lower than it actually is, leading to a higher approach.

Runway slope illusion

- A downsloping runway can create the illusion that the aircraft is lower than it actually is, leading to a higher approach.

- An upsloping runway can create the illusion that the aircraft is higher than it actually is, leading to a lower approach.

···· Normal approach
◄ Approach due to illusion

Figure 16-7. *Runway illusions.*

How To Prevent Landing Errors Due to Optical Illusions

To prevent these illusions and their potentially hazardous consequences, pilots can:

1. Anticipate the possibility of visual illusions during approaches to unfamiliar airports, particularly at night or in adverse weather conditions. Consult airport diagrams and the Airport/Facility Directory (A/FD) for information on runway slope, terrain, and lighting.

2. Make frequent reference to the altimeter, especially during all approaches, day and night.

3. If possible, conduct aerial visual inspection of unfamiliar airports before landing.

4. Use Visual Approach Slope Indicator (VASI) or Precision Approach Path Indicator (PAPI) systems for a visual reference, or an electronic glideslope, whenever they are available.

5. Utilize the visual descent point (VDP) found on many nonprecision instrument approach procedure charts.

6. Recognize that the chances of being involved in an approach accident increase when some emergency or other activity distracts from usual procedures.

7. Maintain optimum proficiency in landing procedures.

In addition to the sensory illusions due to misleading inputs to the vestibular system, a pilot may also encounter various visual illusions during flight. Illusions rank among the most common factors cited as contributing to fatal aviation accidents.

Sloping cloud formations, an obscured horizon, a dark scene spread with ground lights and stars, and certain geometric patterns of ground light can create illusions of not being aligned correctly with the actual horizon. Various surface features and atmospheric conditions encountered in landing can create illusions of being on the wrong approach path. Landing errors due to these illusions can be prevented by anticipating them during approaches, inspecting unfamiliar airports before landing, using electronic glideslope or VASI systems when available, and maintaining proficiency in landing procedures.

Motion Sickness

Motion sickness, or airsickness, is caused by the brain receiving conflicting messages about the state of the body. A pilot may experience motion sickness during initial flights, but it generally goes away within the first few lessons. Anxiety and stress, which may be experienced at the beginning of flight training, can contribute to motion sickness. Symptoms of motion sickness include general discomfort, nausea, dizziness, paleness, sweating, and vomiting.

It is important to remember that experiencing airsickness is no reflection on one's ability as a pilot. If prone to motion sickness, let the flight instructor know, there are techniques that can be used to overcome this problem. For example, avoid lessons in turbulent conditions until becoming more comfortable in the aircraft, or start with shorter flights and graduate to longer instruction periods. If symptoms of motion sickness are experienced during a lesson, opening fresh air vents, focusing on objects outside the airplane, and avoiding unnecessary head movements may help alleviate some of the discomfort. Although medications like Dramamine can prevent airsickness in passengers, they are not recommended while flying since they can cause drowsiness and other problems.

Carbon Monoxide (CO) Poisoning

CO is a colorless and odorless gas produced by all internal combustion engines. Attaching itself to the hemoglobin in the blood about 200 times more easily than oxygen, CO prevents the hemoglobin from carrying oxygen to the cells, resulting in hypemic hypoxia. The body requires up to 48 hours to dispose of CO. If severe enough, the CO poisoning can result in death. Aircraft heater vents and defrost vents may provide CO a passageway into the cabin, particularly if the engine exhaust system has a leak or is damaged. If a strong odor of exhaust gases is detected, assume that CO is present. However, CO may be present in dangerous amounts even if no exhaust odor is detected. Disposable, inexpensive CO detectors are widely available. In the presence of CO, these detectors change color to alert the pilot of the presence of CO. Some effects of CO poisoning are headache, blurred vision, dizziness, drowsiness, and/or loss of muscle power. Any time a pilot smells exhaust odor, or any time that these symptoms are experienced, immediate corrective actions should be taken. These include turning off the heater, opening fresh air vents and windows, and using supplemental oxygen, if available.

Tobacco smoke also causes CO poisoning. Smoking at sea level can raise the CO concentration in the blood and result in physiological effects similar to flying at 8,000 feet. Besides hypoxia, tobacco causes diseases and physiological debilitation that are medically disqualifying for pilots.

Stress

Stress is the body's response to physical and psychological demands placed upon it. The body's reaction to stress includes releasing chemical hormones (such as adrenaline) into the blood, and increasing metabolism to provide more energy to the muscles. Blood sugar, heart rate, respiration, blood pressure, and perspiration all increase. The term "stressor" is used to describe an element that causes an individual to experience stress. Examples of stressors include physical stress (noise or vibration), physiological stress (fatigue), and psychological stress (difficult work or personal situations).

Stress falls into two broad categories, acute (short term) and chronic (long term). Acute stress involves an immediate threat that is perceived as danger. This is the type of stress that triggers a "fight or flight" response in an individual, whether the threat is real or imagined. Normally, a healthy person can cope with acute stress and prevent stress overload. However, ongoing acute stress can develop into chronic stress.

Chronic stress can be defined as a level of stress that presents an intolerable burden, exceeds the ability of an individual to cope, and causes individual performance to fall sharply. Unrelenting psychological pressures, such as loneliness, financial worries, and relationship or work problems can produce a cumulative level of stress that exceeds a person's ability to cope with the situation. When stress reaches these levels, performance falls off rapidly. Pilots experiencing this level of stress are not safe and should not exercise their airman privileges. Pilots who suspect they are suffering from chronic stress should consult a physician.

Fatigue

Fatigue is frequently associated with pilot error. Some of the effects of fatigue include degradation of attention and concentration, impaired coordination, and decreased ability to communicate. These factors seriously influence the ability to make effective decisions. Physical fatigue results from sleep loss, exercise, or physical work. Factors such as stress and prolonged performance of cognitive work result in mental fatigue.

Like stress, fatigue falls into two broad categories: acute and chronic. Acute fatigue is short term and is a normal occurrence in everyday living. It is the kind of tiredness people feel after a period of strenuous effort, excitement, or lack of sleep. Rest after exertion and 8 hours of sound sleep ordinarily cures this condition.

A special type of acute fatigue is skill fatigue. This type of fatigue has two main effects on performance:

- Timing disruption—Appearing to perform a task as usual, but the timing of each component is slightly off. This makes the pattern of the operation less smooth, because the pilot performs each component as though it were separate, instead of part of an integrated activity.

- Disruption of the perceptual field—Concentrating attention upon movements or objects in the center of vision and neglecting those in the periphery. This is accompanied by loss of accuracy and smoothness in control movements.

Acute fatigue has many causes, but the following are among the most important for the pilot:

- Mild hypoxia (oxygen deficiency)
- Physical stress
- Psychological stress and
- Depletion of physical energy resulting from psychological stress
- Sustained psychological stress

Sustained psychological stress accelerates the glandular secretions that prepare the body for quick reactions during an emergency. These secretions make the circulatory and respiratory systems work harder, and the liver releases energy to provide the extra fuel needed for brain and muscle work. When this reserve energy supply is depleted, the body lapses into generalized and severe fatigue.

Acute fatigue can be prevented by proper diet and adequate rest and sleep. A well-balanced diet prevents the body from needing to consume its own tissues as an energy source. Adequate rest maintains the body's store of vital energy.

Chronic fatigue, extending over a long period of time, usually has psychological roots, although an underlying disease is sometimes responsible. Continuous high stress levels produce chronic fatigue. Chronic fatigue is not relieved by proper diet and adequate rest and sleep, and usually requires treatment by a physician. An individual may experience this condition in the form of weakness, tiredness, palpitations of the heart, breathlessness, headaches, or irritability. Sometimes chronic fatigue even creates stomach or intestinal problems and generalized aches and pains throughout the body. When the condition becomes serious enough, it leads to emotional illness.

If suffering from acute fatigue, stay on the ground. If fatigue occurs in the flight deck, no amount of training or experience can overcome the detrimental effects. Getting adequate rest is the only way to prevent fatigue from occurring. Avoid flying without a full night's rest, after working excessive hours, or after an especially exhausting or stressful day. Pilots who suspect they are suffering from chronic fatigue should consult a physician.

Dehydration and Heatstroke

Dehydration is the term given to a critical loss of water from the body. Causes of dehydration are hot flight decks and flight lines, wind, humidity, and diuretic drinks—coffee, tea, alcohol, and caffeinated soft drinks. Some common signs of dehydration are headache, fatigue, cramps, sleepiness, and dizziness.

The first noticeable effect of dehydration is fatigue, which in turn makes top physical and mental performance difficult, if not impossible. Flying for long periods in hot summer temperatures or at high altitudes increases the susceptibility to dehydration because these conditions tend to increase the rate of water loss from the body.

To help prevent dehydration, drink two to four quarts of water every 24 hours. Since each person is physiologically different, this is only a guide. Most people are aware of the eight-glasses-a-day guide: If each glass of water is eight ounces, this equates to 64 ounces, which is two quarts. If this fluid is not replaced, fatigue progresses to dizziness, weakness, nausea, tingling of hands and feet, abdominal cramps, and extreme thirst.

The key for pilots is to be continually aware of their condition. Most people become thirsty with a 1.5 quart deficit, or a loss of 2 percent of total body weight. This level of dehydration triggers the "thirst mechanism." The problem is that the thirst mechanism arrives too late and is turned off too easily. A small amount of fluid in the mouth will turn this mechanism off and the replacement of needed body fluid is delayed.

Other steps to prevent dehydration include:

- Carrying a container in order to measure daily water intake.

- Staying ahead—not relying on the thirst sensation as an alarm. If plain water is offensive, add some sport drink flavoring to make it more acceptable.

- Limiting daily intake of caffeine and alcohol (both are diuretics and stimulate increased production of urine).

Heatstroke is a condition caused by any inability of the body to control its temperature. Onset of this condition may be recognized by the symptoms of dehydration, but also has been known to be recognized only by complete collapse.

To prevent these symptoms, it is recommended that an ample supply of water be carried and used at frequent intervals on any long flight, whether thirsty or not. The body normally absorbs water at the rate of 1.2 to 1.5 quarts per hour. Individuals should drink one quart per hour for severe heat stress conditions or one pint per hour for moderate stress conditions. If the aircraft has a canopy or roof window, wearing light-colored, porous clothing and a hat will help provide protection from the sun. Keeping the flight deck well ventilated aids in dissipating excess heat.

Alcohol

Alcohol impairs the efficiency of the human body. [Figure 16-8] Studies have proved that drinking and performance deterioration are closely linked. Pilots must make hundreds of decisions, some of them time-critical, during the course of a flight. The safe outcome of any flight depends on the ability to make the correct decisions and take the appropriate actions during routine occurrences, as well as abnormal situations. The influence of alcohol drastically reduces the chances of completing a flight without incident. Even in small amounts, alcohol can impair judgment, decrease sense of responsibility, affect coordination, constrict visual field, diminish memory, reduce reasoning power, and lower attention span. As little as one ounce of alcohol can decrease the speed and strength of muscular reflexes, lessen

Type Beverage	Typical Serving (oz)	Pure Alcohol Content (oz)
Table Wine	4.0	.48
Light Beer	12.0	.48
Aperitif Liquor	1.5	.38
Champagne	4.0	.48
Vodka	1.0	.50
Whiskey	1.25	.50
0.01–0.05 (10–50 mg%)	average individual appears normal	
0.03–0.12* (30–120 mg%)	mild euphoria, talkativeness, decreased inhibitions, decreased attention, impaired judgment, increased reaction time	
0.09–0.25 (90–250 mg%)	emotional instability, loss of critical judgment, impairment of memory and comprehension, decreased sensory response, mild muscular incoordination	
0.18–0.30 (180–300 mg%)	confusion, dizziness, exaggerated emotions (anger, fear, grief) impaired visual perception, decreased pain sensation, impaired balance, staggering gait, slurred speech, moderate muscular incoordination	
0.27–0.40 (270–400 mg%)	apathy, impaired consciousness, stupor, significantly decreased response to stimulation, severe muscular incoordination, inability to stand or walk, vomiting, incontinence of urine and feces	
0.35–0.50 (350–500 mg%)	unconsciousness, depressed or abolished reflexes, abnormal body temperature, coma; possible death from respiratory paralysis (450 mg% or above)	

* Legal limit for motor vehicle operation in most states is 0.08 or 0.10% (80–100 mg of alcohol per dL of blood).

Figure 16-8. *Impairement scale with alcohol use.*

the efficiency of eye movements while reading, and increase the frequency at which errors are committed. Impairments in vision and hearing occur at alcohol blood levels due to as little as one drink.

The alcohol consumed in beer and mixed drinks is ethyl alcohol, a central nervous system depressant. From a medical point of view, it acts on the body much like a general anesthetic. The "dose" is generally much lower and more slowly consumed in the case of alcohol, but the basic effects on the human body are similar. Alcohol is easily and quickly absorbed by the digestive tract. The bloodstream absorbs about 80 to 90 percent of the alcohol in a drink within 30 minutes when ingested on an empty stomach. The body requires about 3 hours to rid itself of all the alcohol contained in one mixed drink or one beer.

While experiencing a hangover, a pilot is still under the influence of alcohol. Although a pilot may think he or she is functioning normally, motor and mental response impairment is still present. Considerable amounts of alcohol can remain in the body for over 16 hours, so pilots should be cautious about flying too soon after drinking.

Altitude multiplies the effects of alcohol on the brain. When combined with altitude, the alcohol from two drinks may have the same effect as three or four drinks. Alcohol interferes with the brain's ability to utilize oxygen, producing a form of histotoxic hypoxia. The effects are rapid because alcohol passes quickly into the bloodstream. In addition, the brain is a highly vascular organ that is immediately sensitive to changes in the blood's composition. For a pilot, the lower oxygen availability at altitude and the lower capability of the brain to use what oxygen is there, add up to a deadly combination.

Intoxication is determined by the amount of alcohol in the bloodstream. This is usually measured as a percentage by weight in the blood. 14 CFR part 91 requires that blood alcohol level be less than .04 percent and that 8 hours pass between drinking alcohol and piloting an airplane. A pilot with a blood alcohol level of .04 percent or greater after 8 hours cannot fly until the blood alcohol falls below that amount. Even though blood alcohol may be well below .04 percent, a pilot cannot fly sooner than 8 hours after drinking alcohol. Although the regulations are quite specific, it is a good idea to be more conservative than the regulations.

Drugs

Pilot performance can be seriously degraded by both prescription and over-the-counter medications, as well as by the medical conditions for which they are taken. Many medications, such as tranquilizers, sedatives, strong pain relievers, and cough suppressants have primary effects that may impair judgment, memory, alertness, coordination, vision, and the ability to make calculations. [Figure 16-9] Others, such as antihistamines, blood pressure drugs, muscle relaxants, and agents to control diarrhea and motion sickness have side effects that may impair the same critical functions. Any medication that depresses the nervous system, such as a sedative, tranquilizer, or antihistamine, can make a pilot more susceptible to hypoxia.

Painkillers are grouped into two broad categories: analgesics and anesthetics. Analgesics are drugs that reduce pain, while anesthetics are drugs that deaden pain or cause loss of consciousness.

Over-the-counter analgesics, such as acetylsalicylic acid (aspirin), acetaminophen (Tylenol), and ibuprofen (Advil) have few side effects when taken in the correct dosage. Although some people are allergic to certain analgesics or may suffer from stomach irritation, flying usually is not restricted when taking these drugs. However, flying is almost always precluded while using prescription analgesics, such as drugs containing propoxyphene (e.g., Darvon), oxycodone (e.g., Percodan), meperidine (e.g., Demerol), and codeine since these drugs are known to cause side effects such as mental confusion, dizziness, headaches, nausea, and vision problems.

Anesthetic drugs are commonly used for dental and surgical procedures. Most local anesthetics used for minor dental and outpatient procedures wear off within a relatively short period of time. The anesthetic itself may not limit flying as much as the actual procedure and subsequent pain.

Stimulants are drugs that excite the central nervous system and produce an increase in alertness and activity. Amphetamines, caffeine, and nicotine are all forms of stimulants. Common uses of these drugs include appetite suppression, fatigue reduction, and mood elevation. Some of these drugs may cause a stimulant reaction, even though this reaction is not their primary function. In some cases, stimulants can produce anxiety and mood swings, both of which are dangerous when flying.

Depressants are drugs that reduce the body's functioning in many areas. These drugs lower blood pressure, reduce mental processing, and slow motor and reaction responses. There are several types of drugs that can cause a depressing effect on the body, including tranquilizers, motion sickness medication, some types of stomach medication, decongestants, and antihistamines. The most common depressant is alcohol.

Some drugs that are classified as neither stimulants nor depressants have adverse effects on flying. For example, some antibiotics can produce dangerous side effects, such as balance disorders, hearing loss, nausea, and vomiting. While many antibiotics are safe for use while flying, the infection requiring the antibiotic may prohibit flying. In addition, unless specifically prescribed by a physician, do not take more than one drug at a time, and never mix drugs with alcohol, because the effects are often unpredictable.

The dangers of illegal drugs also are well documented. Certain illegal drugs can have hallucinatory effects that occur days or weeks after the drug is taken. Obviously, these drugs have no place in the aviation community.

14 CFR prohibits pilots from performing crewmember duties while using any medication that affects the body in any way contrary to safety. The safest rule is not to fly as a crewmember while taking any medication, unless approved to do so by the FAA. If there is any doubt regarding the effects of any medication, consult an AME before flying.

Psychoactive Drugs	Range of Effects		Development of Tolerance	Prolonged Use of Large Amounts	Withdrawal Symptoms After Prolonged Use
	From	To			
Alcohol Beer Wine Hard Liquor	Relaxation, lowered inhibitions, reduced intensity of physical sensations, digestive upsets, body heat loss, reduced muscular coordination.	Loss of body control, passing out (also causing physical injuries), susceptibility to pneumonia, cessation of breathing	Moderate	Liver damage, ulcers, chronic diarrhea, amnesia, vomiting, brain damage, internal bleeding, debilitation	Convulsions, shakes, hallucinations, loss of memory, uncontrolled muscular spasms, psychosis
Sedative Hypnotics *Barbiturates:* - Nembutal - Phenobarbital - Seconal *Tranquilizers:* - Valium - Librium - Quaaludes	Relaxation, lowered inhibitions, reduced intensity of physical sensations, digestive upsets, body heat loss, reduced muscular coordination	Passing out, loss of body control, stupor, severe depression of respiration, possible death (Effects are exaggerated when used in combination with alcohol—synergistic effect.)	Moderate	Amnesia, confusion, drowsiness, personality changes	
Opiates Opium Morphine Heroin Codeine Dilaudid Percodan Darvon Methadone	Suppression of pain, lowered blood pressure and respiratory rate, constipation, disruption of menstrual cycle, hallucinations, sleep	Clammy skin, convulsions, coma, respiratory depression, possible death	High	Depressed sexual drive, lethargy, general physical debilitation, infections, hepatitis	Watery eyes, runny nose, severe back pains, stomach cramps, sleeplessness, nausea, diarrhea, sweating, muscle spasms
Stimulants Dexedrine Methamphetamine Diet Pills Ritalin Cocaine Caffeine	Increased blood pressure and pulse rate, appetite loss, increased alertness, dilated and dried out bronchi, restlessness, insomnia	Paranoid reaction, temporary psychosis, irritability, convulsions, palpitations (not generally true for caffeine)	High	Psychosis, insomnia, paranoia, nervous system damage (not generally true for caffeine)	Severe depression, both physical and mental (not true for caffeine)
Psychedelics LSD Mescaline Psilocybin PCP	Distorted perceptions, hallucinations, confusion, vomiting	Psychosis, hallucinations, vomiting, anxiety, panic, stupor. With PCP: Aggressive behavior, catatonia, convulsions, coma, high blood pressure	High	Psychosis, continued hallucinations, mental disruption	Occasional flashback phenomena, depression
THC Marijuana Hashish	Sedation, euphoria, increased appetite, altered mental processes	Distorted perception, anxiety, panic	Moderate	Amotivation (loss of drive)	No true withdrawal symptoms except possible depression

Figure 16-9. *Adverse affects of various drugs.*

16-15

Altitude-Induced Decompression Sickness (DCS)

Decompression sickness (DCS) describes a condition characterized by a variety of symptoms resulting from exposure to low barometric pressures that cause inert gases (mainly nitrogen), normally dissolved in body fluids and tissues, to come out of physical solution and form bubbles. Nitrogen is an inert gas normally stored throughout the human body (tissues and fluids) in physical solution. When the body is exposed to decreased barometric pressures (as in flying an unpressurized aircraft to altitude, or during a rapid decompression), the nitrogen dissolved in the body comes out of solution. If the nitrogen is forced to leave the solution too rapidly, bubbles form in different areas of the body, causing a variety of signs and symptoms. The most common symptom is joint pain, which is known as "the bends." *[Figure 16-10]*

What to do when altitude-induced DCS occurs:

- Put on oxygen mask immediately and switch the regulator to 100 percent oxygen.

- Begin an emergency descent and land as soon as possible. Even if the symptoms disappear during descent, land and seek medical evaluation while continuing to breathe oxygen.

- If one of the symptoms is joint pain, keep the affected area still; do not try to work pain out by moving the joint around.

- Upon landing seek medical assistance from an FAA medical officer, AME, military flight surgeon, or a hyperbaric medicine specialist. Be aware that a physician not specialized in aviation or hypobaric medicine may not be familiar with this type of medical problem.

- Definitive medical treatment may involve the use of a hyperbaric chamber operated by specially trained personnel.

- Delayed signs and symptoms of altitude-induced DCS can occur after return to ground level regardless of presence during flight.

DCS After Scuba Diving

Scuba diving subjects the body to increased pressure, which allows more nitrogen to dissolve in body tissues and fluids. *[Figure 16-11]* The reduction of atmospheric pressure that accompanies flying can produce physical problems for scuba divers. A pilot or passenger who intends to fly after scuba

DCS Type	Bubble Location	Signs & Symptoms (Clinical Manifestations)
BENDS	Mostly large joints of the body (elbows, shoulders, hip, wrists, knees, ankles)	• Localized deep pain, ranging from mild (a "niggle") to excruciating—sometimes a dull ache, but rarely a sharp pain • Active and passive motion of the joint aggravating the pain • Pain occurring at altitude, during the descent, or many hours later
NEUROLOGIC Manifestations	Brain	• Confusion or memory loss • Headache • Spots in visual field (scotoma), tunnel vision, double vision (diplopia), or blurry vision • Unexplained extreme fatigue or behavior changes • Seizures, dizziness, vertigo, nausea, vomiting, and unconsciousness
	Spinal Cord	• Abnormal sensations such as burning, stinging, and tingling around the lower chest and back • Symptoms spreading from the feet up and possibly accompanied by ascending weakness or paralysis • Girdling abdominal or chest pain
	Peripheral Nerves	• Urinary and rectal incontinence • Abnormal sensations, such as numbness, burning, stinging and tingling (paresthesia) • Muscle weakness or twitching
CHOKES	Lungs	• Burning deep chest pain (under the sternum) • Pain aggravated by breathing • Shortness of breath (dyspnea) • Dry constant cough
SKIN BENDS	Skin	• Itching usually around the ears, face, neck, arms, and upper torso • Sensation of tiny insects crawling over the skin • Mottled or marbled skin usually around the shoulders, upper chest, and abdomen, accompanied by itching • Swelling of the skin, accompanied by tiny scar-like skin depressions (pitting edema)

Figure 16-10. *Signs and symptoms of altitude decompression sickness.*

Figure 16-11. *To avoid the bends, scuba divers must not fly for specific time periods following dives.*

diving should allow the body sufficient time to rid itself of excess nitrogen absorbed during diving. If not, DCS due to evolved gas can occur during exposure to low altitude and create a serious inflight emergency.

The recommended waiting time before going to flight altitudes of up to 8,000 feet is at least 12 hours after diving that does not require controlled ascent (nondecompression stop diving), and at least 24 hours after diving that does require controlled ascent (decompression stop diving). The waiting time before going to flight altitudes above 8,000 feet should be at least 24 hours after any scuba dive. These recommended altitudes are actual flight altitudes above mean sea level (AMSL) and not pressurized cabin altitudes. This takes into consideration the risk of decompression of the aircraft during flight.

Vision in Flight

Of all the senses, vision is the most important for safe flight. Most of the things perceived while flying are visual or heavily supplemented by vision. As remarkable and vital as it is, vision is subject to limitations, such as illusions and blind spots. The more a pilot understands about the eyes and how they function, the easier it is to use vision effectively and compensate for potential problems.

The eye functions much like a camera. Its structure includes an aperture, a lens, a mechanism for focusing, and a surface for registering images. Light enters through the cornea at the front of the eyeball, travels through the lens, and falls on the retina. The retina contains light sensitive cells that convert light energy into electrical impulses that travel through nerves to the brain. The brain interprets the electrical signals to form images. There are two kinds of light-sensitive cells in the eyes: rods and cones. *[Figure 16-12]*

The cones are responsible for all color vision, from appreciating a glorious sunset to discerning the subtle shades in a fine painting. Cones are present throughout the retina, but

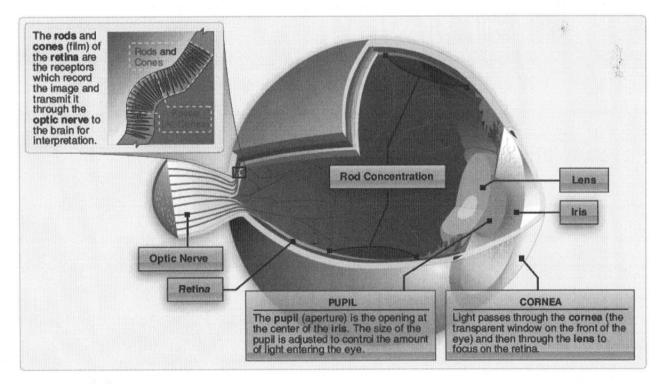

The **rods** and **cones** (film) of the **retina** are the receptors which record the image and transmit it through the **optic nerve** to the brain for interpretation.

Rods and Cones

Rod Concentration

Lens

Iris

Optic Nerve

Retina

PUPIL
The pupil (aperture) is the opening at the center of the iris. The size of the pupil is adjusted to control the amount of light entering the eye.

CORNEA
Light passes through the **cornea** (the transparent window on the front of the eye) and then through the **lens** to focus on the retina.

Figure 16-12. *The human eye.*

are concentrated toward the center of the field of vision at the back of the retina. There is a small pit called the fovea where almost all the light sensing cells are cones. This is the area where most "looking" occurs (the center of the visual field where detail, color sensitivity, and resolution are highest).

While the cones and their associated nerves are well suited to detecting fine detail and color in high light levels, the rods are better able to detect movement and provide vision in dim light. The rods are unable to discern color but are very sensitive at low light levels. The trouble with rods is that a large amount of light overwhelms them, and they take a long time to "reset" and adapt to the dark again. There are so many cones in the fovea that the very center of the visual field hardly has virtually no rods at all. So in low light, the middle of the visual field is not very sensitive, but farther from the fovea, the rods are more numerous and provide the major portion of night vision.

The area where the optic nerve enters the eyeball has no rods or cones, leaving a blind spot in the field of vision. Normally, each eye compensates for the other's blind spot. *Figure 16-13* provides a dramatic example of the eye's blind spot. Cover the right eye and hold this page at arm's length. Focus the left eye on the X on the right side of the windshield and notice what happens to the airplane while slowly bringing the page closer to the eye.

Empty-Field Myopia

Empty-field myopia is a condition that usually occurs when flying above the clouds or in a haze layer that provides nothing specific to focus on outside the aircraft. This causes the eyes to relax and seek a comfortable focal distance which may range from 10 to 30 feet. For the pilot, this means looking without seeing, which is dangerous. Searching out

and focusing on distant light sources, no matter how dim, helps prevent the onset of empty-field myopia.

Night Vision

It is estimated that once fully adapted to darkness, the rods are 10,000 times more sensitive to light than the cones, making them the primary receptors for night vision. Since the cones are concentrated near the fovea, the rods are also responsible for much of the peripheral vision. The concentration of cones in the fovea can make a night blind spot in the center of the field of vision. To see an object clearly at night, the pilot must expose the rods to the image. This can be done by looking 5° to 10° off center of the object to be seen. This can be tried in a dim light in a darkened room. When looking directly at the light, it dims or disappears altogether. When looking slightly off center, it becomes clearer and brighter.

Refer to *Figure 16-14*. When looking directly at an object, the image is focused mainly on the fovea, where detail is best seen. At night, the ability to see an object in the center of the visual field is reduced as the cones lose much of their sensitivity and the rods become more sensitive. Looking off center can help compensate for this night blind spot. Along with the loss of sharpness (acuity) and color at night, depth perception and judgment of size may be lost.

While the cones adapt rapidly to changes in light intensities, the rods take much longer. Walking from bright sunlight into a dark movie theater is an example of this dark adaptation period experience. The rods can take approximately 30 minutes to fully adapt to darkness. A bright light, however, can completely destroy night adaptation, leaving night vision severely compromised while the adaptation process is repeated.

Figure 16-13. *The eye's blind spot.*

Figure 16-14. *Night blind spot.*

Hypoxia also affects vision. Sharp clear vision, (with the best being equal to 20-20 vision) requires significant oxygen especially at night. As altitude increases, the available oxygen decreases, degrading night vision. Compounding the problem is fatigue, which minimizes physiological well being. Adding fatigue to high altitude exposure is a recipe for disaster. In fact, if flying at night at an altitude of 12,000 feet, the pilot may actually see elements of his or her normal vision missing or not in focus. Missing visual elements resemble the missing pixels in a digital image while unfocused vision is dim and washed out.

For the pilot suffering the effects of hypoxic hypoxia, a simple descent to a lower altitude may not be sufficient to reestablish vision. For example, a climb from 8,000 feet to 12,000 feet for 30 minutes does not mean a descent to 8,000 feet will rectify the problem. Visual acuity may not be regained for over an hour. Thus, it is important to remember, altitude and fatigue have a profound effect on a pilot's ability to see.

Several things can be done to keep the eyes adapted to darkness. The first is obvious: avoid bright lights before and during flight. For 30 minutes before a night flight, avoid any bright light sources, such as headlights, landing lights, strobe lights, or flashlights. If a bright light is encountered, close one eye to keep it light sensitive. This allows the use of that eye to see again when the light is gone.

Red flight deck lighting also helps preserve night vision, but red light severely distorts some colors and completely washes out the color red. This makes reading an aeronautical chart difficult. A dim white light or a carefully directed flashlight can enhance night reading ability. While flying at night, keep the instrument panel and interior lights turned up no higher than necessary. This helps to see outside references more easily. If the eyes become blurry, blinking more frequently often helps.

Diet and general physical health have an impact on how well a pilot can see in the dark. Deficiencies in vitamins A and C have been shown to reduce night acuity. Other factors, such as CO poisoning, smoking, alcohol, certain drugs, and a lack of oxygen also can greatly decrease night vision.

Night Vision Illusions

There are many different types of visual illusions that commonly occur at night. Anticipating and staying aware of them is usually the best way to avoid them.

Autokinesis

Autokinesis is caused by staring at a single point of light against a dark background for more than a few seconds. After a few moments, the light appears to move on its own. To prevent this illusion, focus the eyes on objects at varying distances and avoid fixating on one target. Be sure to maintain a normal scan pattern.

False Horizon

A false horizon can occur when the natural horizon is obscured or not readily apparent. It can be generated by confusing bright stars and city lights. It can also occur while flying toward the shore of an ocean or a large lake. Because of the relative darkness of the water, the lights along the shoreline can be mistaken for stars in the sky. *[Figure 16-15]*

Night Landing Illusions

Landing illusions occur in many forms. Above featureless terrain at night, there is a natural tendency to fly a lower-than-normal approach. Elements that cause any type of visual obscurities, such as rain, haze, or a dark runway environment can also cause low approaches. Bright lights, steep surrounding terrain, and a wide runway can produce the illusion of being too low, with a tendency to fly a higher-than-normal approach. A set of regularly spaced lights along a road or highway can appear to be runway lights. Pilots have even mistaken the lights on moving trains as runway or approach lights. Bright runway or approach lighting systems can create the illusion that the airplane is closer to the runway, especially where few lights illuminate the surrounding terrain.

Figure 16-15. *At night, the horizon may be hard to discern due to dark terrain and misleading light patterns on the ground.*

Pilots who are flying at night should strongly consider oxygen supplementation at altitudes and times not required by the FAA, especially at night, when critical judgement and hand-eye coordination is necessary (e.g., IFR), or if a smoker or not perfectly healthy.

Chapter Summary

This chapter provides an introduction to aeromedical factors relating to flight activities. More detailed information on the subjects discussed in this chapter is available in the Aeronautical Information Manual (AIM) and online at www. faa.gov/pilots/safety/pilotsafetybrochures.

Chapter 17

Aeronautical Decision-Making

Introduction

Aeronautical decision-making (ADM) is decision-making in a unique environment—aviation. It is a systematic approach to the mental process used by pilots to consistently determine the best course of action in response to a given set of circumstances. It is what a pilot intends to do based on the latest information he or she has.

The importance of learning and understanding effective ADM skills cannot be overemphasized. While progress is continually being made in the advancement of pilot training methods, aircraft equipment and systems, and services for pilots, accidents still occur. Despite all the changes in technology to improve flight safety, one factor remains the same: the human factor which leads to errors. It is estimated that approximately 80 percent of all aviation accidents are related to human factors and the vast majority of these accidents occur during landing (24.1 percent) and takeoff (23.4 percent). *[Figure 17-1]*

ADM is a systematic approach to risk assessment and stress management. To understand ADM is to also understand how personal attitudes can influence decision-making and how those attitudes can be modified to enhance safety in the flight deck. It is important to understand the factors that cause humans to make decisions and how the decision-making process not only works, but can be improved.

This chapter focuses on helping the pilot improve his or her ADM skills with the goal of mitigating the risk factors associated with flight. Advisory Circular (AC) 60-22, Aeronautical Decision-Making, provides background references, definitions, and other pertinent information about ADM training in the general aviation (GA) environment. *[Figure 17-2]*

History of ADM

For over 25 years, the importance of good pilot judgment, or aeronautical decision-making (ADM), has been recognized as critical to the safe operation of aircraft, as well as accident avoidance. The airline industry, motivated by the need to reduce accidents caused by human factors, developed the first training programs based on improving ADM. Crew resource management (CRM) training for flight crews is focused on the effective use of all available resources: human resources, hardware, and information supporting ADM to facilitate crew cooperation and improve decision-making. The goal of all flight crews is good ADM and the use of CRM is one way to make good decisions.

Research in this area prompted the Federal Aviation Administration (FAA) to produce training directed at improving the decision-making of pilots and led to current FAA regulations that require that decision-making be taught as part of the pilot training curriculum. ADM research, development, and testing culminated in 1987 with the publication of six manuals oriented to the decision-making needs of variously rated pilots. These manuals provided multifaceted materials designed to reduce the number of decision related accidents. The effectiveness of these materials was validated in independent studies where student pilots received such training in conjunction with the standard flying curriculum. When tested, the pilots who had received ADM training made fewer inflight errors than those who had

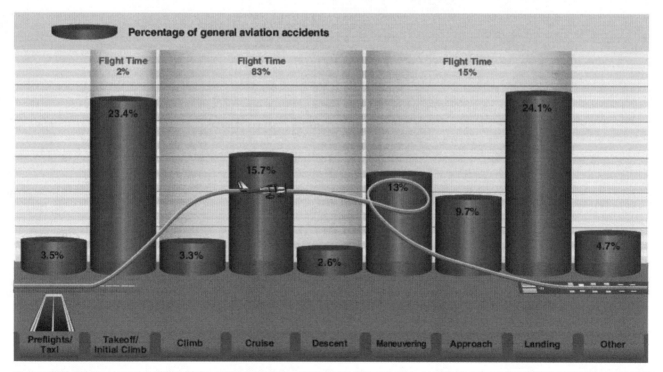

Figure 17-1. *The percentage of aviation accidents as they relate to the different phases of flight. Note that the greatest percentage of accidents take place during a minor percentage of the total flight.*

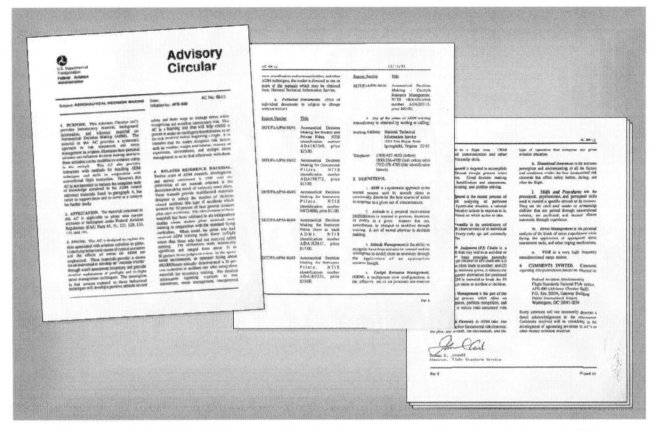

Figure 17 2. *Advisory Circular (AC) 60-22, Aeronautical Decision Making, carries a wealth of information for the pilot to learn.*

Crew Resource Management (CRM) and Single-Pilot Resource Management

While CRM focuses on pilots operating in crew environments, many of the concepts apply to single-pilot operations. Many CRM principles have been successfully applied to single-pilot aircraft, and led to the development of Single-Pilot Resource Management (SRM). SRM is defined as the art and science of managing all the resources (both on-board the aircraft and from outside sources) available to a single pilot (prior and during flight) to ensure that the successful outcome of the flight. SRM includes the concepts of ADM, Risk Management (RM), Task Management (TM), Automation Management (AM), Controlled Flight Into Terrain (CFIT) Awareness, and Situational Awareness (SA). SRM training helps the pilot maintain situational awareness by managing the automation and associated aircraft control and navigation tasks. This enables the pilot to accurately assess and manage risk and make accurate and timely decisions.

SRM is all about helping pilots learn how to gather information, analyze it, and make decisions. Although the flight is coordinated by a single person and not an onboard flight crew, the use of available resources such as air traffic control (ATC) and flight service station (FSS) replicates the principles of CRM.

Hazard and Risk

Two defining elements of ADM are hazard and risk. Hazard is a real or perceived condition, event, or circumstance that a pilot encounters. When faced with a hazard, the pilot makes an assessment of that hazard based upon various factors. The pilot assigns a value to the potential impact of the hazard, which qualifies the pilot's assessment of the hazard—risk.

Therefore, risk is an assessment of the single or cumulative hazard facing a pilot; however, different pilots see hazards differently. For example, the pilot arrives to preflight and discovers a small, blunt type nick in the leading edge at the middle of the aircraft's prop. Since the aircraft is parked on the tarmac, the nick was probably caused by another aircraft's prop wash blowing some type of debris into the propeller. The nick is the hazard (a present condition). The risk is prop fracture if the engine is operated with damage to a prop blade.

The seasoned pilot may see the nick as a low risk. He realizes this type of nick diffuses stress over a large area, is located in the strongest portion of the propeller, and based on experience, he doesn't expect it to propagate a crack which can lead to high risk problems. He does not cancel his flight. The inexperienced pilot may see the nick as a high risk factor because he is unsure of the affect the nick will have on the

prop's operation and he has been told that damage to a prop could cause a catastrophic failure. This assessment leads him to cancel his flight.

Therefore, elements or factors affecting individuals are different and profoundly impact decision-making. These are called human factors and can transcend education, experience, health, physiological aspects, etc.

Another example of risk assessment was the flight of a Beechcraft King Air equipped with deicing and anti-icing. The pilot deliberately flew into moderate to severe icing conditions while ducking under cloud cover. A prudent pilot would assess the risk as high and beyond the capabilities of the aircraft, yet this pilot did the opposite. Why did the pilot take this action?

Past experience prompted the action. The pilot had successfully flown into these conditions repeatedly although the icing conditions were previously forecast 2,000 feet above the surface. This time, the conditions were forecast from the surface. Since the pilot was in a hurry and failed to factor in the difference between the forecast altitudes, he assigned a low risk to the hazard and took a chance. He and the passengers died from a poor risk assessment of the situation.

Hazardous Attitudes and Antidotes

Being fit to fly depends on more than just a pilot's physical condition and recent experience. For example, attitude will affect the quality of decisions. Attitude is a motivational predisposition to respond to people, situations, or events in a given manner. Studies have identified five hazardous attitudes that can interfere with the ability to make sound decisions and exercise authority properly: anti-authority, impulsivity, invulnerability, macho, and resignation. *[Figure 17-3]*

Hazardous attitudes contribute to poor pilot judgment but can be effectively counteracted by redirecting the hazardous attitude so that correct action can be taken. Recognition of hazardous thoughts is the first step toward neutralizing them. After recognizing a thought as hazardous, the pilot should label it as hazardous, then state the corresponding antidote. Antidotes should be memorized for each of the hazardous attitudes so they automatically come to mind when needed.

Risk

During each flight, the single pilot makes many decisions under hazardous conditions. To fly safely, the pilot needs to assess the degree of risk and determine the best course of action to mitigate risk.

The Five Hazardous Attitudes

Anti-Authority: "Don't tell me."
This attitude is found in people who do not like anyone telling them what to do. In a sense, they are saying, "No one can tell me what to do." They may be resentful of having someone tell them what to do, or may regard rules, regulations, and procedures as silly or unnecessary. However, it is always your prerogative to question authority if you feel it is in error.

Impulsivity: "Do it quickly."
This is the attitude of people who frequently feel the need to do something, anything, immediately. They do not stop to think about what they are about to do; they do not select the best alternative, and they do the first thing that comes to mind.

Invulnerability: "It won't happen to me."
Many people falsely believe that accidents happen to others, but never to them. They know accidents can happen, and they know that anyone can be affected. However, they never really feel or believe that they will be personally involved. Pilots who think this way are more likely to take chances and increase risk.

Macho: "I can do it."
Pilots who are always trying to prove that they are better than anyone else think, "I can do it—I'll show them." Pilots with this type of attitude will try to prove themselves by taking risks in order to impress others. While this pattern is thought to be a male characteristic, women are equally susceptible.

Resignation: "What's the use?"
Pilots who think, "What's the use?" do not see themselves as being able to make a great deal of difference in what happens to them. When things go well, the pilot is apt to think that it is good luck. When things go badly, the pilot may feel that someone is out to get me, or attribute it to bad luck. The pilot will leave the action to others, for better or worse. Sometimes, such pilots will even go along with unreasonable requests just to be a "nice guy."

Figure 17-3. *The five hazardous attitudes identified through past and contemporary study.*

Assessing Risk

For the single pilot, assessing risk is not as simple as it sounds. For example, the pilot acts as his or her own quality control in making decisions. If a fatigued pilot who has flown 16 hours is asked if he or she is too tired to continue flying, the answer may be no. Most pilots are goal oriented and when asked to accept a flight, there is a tendency to deny personal limitations while adding weight to issues not germane to the mission. For example, pilots of helicopter emergency services (EMS) have been known (more than other groups) to make flight decisions that add significant weight to the patient's welfare. These pilots add weight to intangible factors (the patient in this case) and fail to appropriately quantify actual hazards such as fatigue or weather when making flight decisions. The single pilot who has no other crew member for consultation must wrestle with the intangible factors that draw one into a hazardous position. Therefore, he or she has a greater vulnerability than a full crew.

Examining National Transportation Safety Board (NTSB) reports and other accident research can help a pilot learn to assess risk more effectively. For example, the accident rate during night VFR decreases by nearly 50 percent once a pilot obtains 100 hours, and continues to decrease until the 1,000 hour level. The data suggest that for the first 500 hours, pilots flying VFR at night might want to establish higher personal limitations than are required by the regulations and, if applicable, apply instrument flying skills in this environment.

Several risk assessment models are available to assist in the process of assessing risk. The models, all taking slightly different approaches, seek a common goal of assessing risk in an objective manner. Two are illustrated below.

The most basic tool is the risk matrix. *[Figure 17-4]* It assesses two items: the likelihood of an event occurring and the consequence of that event.

Figure 17-4. *This risk matrix can be used for almost any operation by assigning likelihood and consequence. In the case presented, the pilot assigned a likelihood of occassional and the severity as catastrophic. As one can see, this falls in the high risk area.*

17-5

Likelihood of an Event

Likelihood is nothing more than taking a situation and determining the probability of its occurrence. It is rated as probable, occasional, remote, or improbable. For example, a pilot is flying from point A to point B (50 miles) in marginal visual flight rules (MVFR) conditions. The likelihood of encountering potential instrument meteorological conditions (IMC) is the first question the pilot needs to answer. The experiences of other pilots coupled with the forecast, might cause the pilot to assign "occasional" to determine the probability of encountering IMC.

The following are guidelines for making assignments.

- Probable—an event will occur several times.
- Occasional—an event will probably occur sometime.
- Remote—an event is unlikely to occur, but is possible.
- Improbable—an event is highly unlikely to occur.

Severity of an Event

The next element is the severity or consequence of a pilot's action(s). It can relate to injury and/or damage. If the individual in the example above is not an instrument flight rules (IFR) pilot, what are the consequences of him or her encountering inadvertent IMC conditions? In this case, because the pilot is not IFR rated, the consequences are catastrophic. The following are guidelines for this assignment.

- Catastrophic—results in fatalities, total loss
- Critical—severe injury, major damage
- Marginal—minor injury, minor damage
- Negligible—less than minor injury, less than minor system damage

Simply connecting the two factors as shown in *Figure 17-4* indicates the risk is high and the pilot must either not fly, or fly only after finding ways to mitigate, eliminate, or control the risk.

Although the matrix in *Figure 17-4* provides a general viewpoint of a generic situation, a more comprehensive program can be made that is tailored to a pilot's flying. *[Figure 17-5]* This program includes a wide array of aviation related activities specific to the pilot and assesses health, fatigue, weather, capabilities, etc. The scores are added and the overall score falls into various ranges, with the range representative of actions that a pilot imposes upon himself or herself.

Mitigating Risk

Risk assessment is only part of the equation. After determining the level of risk, the pilot needs to mitigate the risk. For example, the pilot flying from point A to point B (50 miles) in MVFR conditions has several ways to reduce risk:

- Wait for the weather to improve to good visual flight rules (VFR) conditions.
- Take a pilot who is certified as an IFR pilot.
- Delay the flight.
- Cancel the flight.
- Drive.

One of the best ways to single pilots can mitigate risk is to use the IMSAFE checklist to determine physical and mental readiness for flying:

1. Illness—Am I sick? Illness is an obvious pilot risk.

2. Medication—Am I taking any medicines that might affect my judgment or make me drowsy?

3. Stress—Am I under psychological pressure from the job? Do I have money, health, or family problems? Stress causes concentration and performance problems. While the regulations list medical conditions that require grounding, stress is not among them. The pilot should consider the effects of stress on performance.

4. Alcohol—Have I been drinking within 8 hours? Within 24 hours? As little as one ounce of liquor, one bottle of beer, or four ounces of wine can impair flying skills. Alcohol also renders a pilot more susceptible to disorientation and hypoxia.

5. Fatigue—Am I tired and not adequately rested? Fatigue continues to be one of the most insidious hazards to flight safety, as it may not be apparent to a pilot until serious errors are made.

6. Eating—Have I eaten enough of the proper foods to keep adequately nourished during the entire flight?

The PAVE Checklist

Another way to mitigate risk is to perceive hazards. By incorporating the PAVE checklist into preflight planning, the pilot divides the risks of flight into four categories: **P**ilot-in-command (PIC), **A**ircraft, en**V**ironment, and **E**xternal pressures (PAVE) which form part of a pilot's decision-making process.

RISK ASSESSMENT

Pilot's Name

Flight From   To

SLEEP
1. Did not sleep well or less than 8 hours   2
2. Slept well   0

HOW DO YOU FEEL?
1. Have a cold or ill   4
2. Feel great   0
3. Feel a bit off   2

WEATHER AT TERMINATION
1. Greater than 5 miles visibility and 3,000 feet ceilings   1
2. At least 3 miles visibility and 1,000 feet ceilings, but less than 3,000 feet ceilings and 5 miles visibility   3
3. IMC conditions   4

Column total

HOW IS THE DAY GOING?
1. Seems like one thing after another (late, making errors, out of step)   3
2. Great day   0

IS THE FLIGHT
1. Day?   1
2. Night?   3

PLANNING
1. Rush to get off ground   3
2. No hurry   1
3. Used charts and computer to assist   0
4. Used computer program for all planning   Yes 3
                                             No   0
5. Did you verify weight and balance?   Yes 0
                                         No   3
6. Did you evaluate performance?   Yes 0
                                    No   3
7. Do you brief your passangers on the ground and in flight?   Yes 0
                                                                No   2

Column total

TOTAL SCORE

Low Risk | Endangerment

0 Not Complex Flight 10 Exercise Caution 20 Area of Concern 30

Figure 17-5. *Example of a more comprehensive risk assessment program.*

With the PAVE checklist, pilots have a simple way to remember each category to examine for risk prior to each flight. Once a pilot identifies the risks of a flight, he or she needs to decide whether the risk or combination of risks can be managed safely and successfully. If not, make the decision to cancel the flight. If the pilot decides to continue with the flight, he or she should develop strategies to mitigate the risks. One way a pilot can control the risks is to set personal minimums for items in each risk category. These are limits unique to that individual pilot's current level of experience and proficiency.

For example, the aircraft may have a maximum crosswind component of 15 knots listed in the aircraft flight manual (AFM), and the pilot has experience with 10 knots of direct crosswind. It could be unsafe to exceed a 10 knots crosswind component without additional training. Therefore, the 10 kts crosswind experience level is that pilot's personal limitation until additional training with a certificated flight instructor (CFI) provides the pilot with additional experience for flying in crosswinds that exceed 10 knots.

One of the most important concepts that safe pilots understand is the difference between what is "legal" in terms of the regulations, and what is "smart" or "safe" in terms of pilot experience and proficiency.

P = Pilot in Command (PIC)

The pilot is one of the risk factors in a flight. The pilot must ask, "Am I ready for this trip?" in terms of experience, recency, currency, physical and emotional condition. The IMSAFE checklist provides the answers.

A = Aircraft

What limitations will the aircraft impose upon the trip? Ask the following questions:

- Is this the right aircraft for the flight?

- Am I familiar with and current in this aircraft? Aircraft performance figures and the AFM are based on a brand new aircraft flown by a professional test pilot. Keep that in mind while assessing personal and aircraft performance.

- Is this aircraft equipped for the flight? Instruments? Lights? Navigation and communication equipment adequate?

- Can this aircraft use the runways available for the trip with an adequate margin of safety under the conditions to be flown?

- Can this aircraft carry the planned load?

- Can this aircraft operate at the altitudes needed for the trip?

- Does this aircraft have sufficient fuel capacity, with reserves, for trip legs planned?

- Does the fuel quantity delivered match the fuel quantity ordered?

V = EnVironment

Weather

Weather is an major environmental consideration. Earlier it was suggested pilots set their own personal minimums, especially when it comes to weather. As pilots evaluate the weather for a particular flight, they should consider the following:

- What are the current ceiling and visibility? In mountainous terrain, consider having higher minimums for ceiling and visibility, particularly if the terrain is unfamiliar.

- Consider the possibility that the weather may be different than forecast. Have alternative plans and be ready and willing to divert, should an unexpected change occur.

- Consider the winds at the airports being used and the strength of the crosswind component.

- If flying in mountainous terrain, consider whether there are strong winds aloft. Strong winds in mountainous terrain can cause severe turbulence and downdrafts and be very hazardous for aircraft even when there is no other significant weather.

- Are there any thunderstorms present or forecast?

- If there are clouds, is there any icing, current or forecast? What is the temperature/dew point spread and the current temperature at altitude? Can descent be made safely all along the route?

- If icing conditions are encountered, is the pilot experienced at operating the aircraft's deicing or anti-icing equipment? Is this equipment in good condition and functional? For what icing conditions is the aircraft rated, if any?

Terrain

Evaluation of terrain is another important component of analyzing the flight environment.

- To avoid terrain and obstacles, especially at night or in low visibility, determine safe altitudes in advance by using the altitudes shown on VFR and IFR charts during preflight planning.

- Use maximum elevation figures (MEFs) and other easily obtainable data to minimize chances of an inflight collision with terrain or obstacles.

Airport

- What lights are available at the destination and alternate airports? VASI/PAPI or ILS glideslope guidance? Is the terminal airport equipped with them? Are they working? Will the pilot need to use the radio to activate the airport lights?

- Check the Notices to Airmen (NOTAMS) for closed runways or airports. Look for runway or beacon lights out, nearby towers, etc.

- Choose the flight route wisely. An engine failure gives the nearby airports supreme importance.

- Are there shorter or obstructed fields at the destination amd/or alternate airports?

Airspace

- If the trip is over remote areas, are appropriate clothing, water, and survival gear onboard in the event of a forced landing?

- If the trip includes flying over water or unpopulated areas with the chance of losing visual reference to the horizon, the pilot must be prepared to fly IFR.

- Check the airspace and any temporary flight restriction (TFRs) along the route of flight.

Nighttime

Night flying requires special consideration.

- If the trip includes flying at night over water or unpopulated areas with the chance of losing visual reference to the horizon, the pilot must be prepared to fly IFR.

- Will the flight conditions allow a safe emergency landing at night?

- Preflight all aircraft lights, interior and exterior, for a night flight. Carry at least two flashlights—one for exterior preflight and a smaller one that can be dimmed and kept nearby.

E = External Pressures

External pressures are influences external to the flight that create a sense of pressure to complete a flight—often at the expense of safety. Factors that can be external pressures include the following:

- Someone waiting at the airport for the flight's arrival.

- A passenger the pilot does not want to disappoint.

- The desire to demonstrate pilot qualifications.

- The desire to impress someone. (Probably the two most dangerous words in aviation are "Watch this!")

- The desire to satisfy a specific personal goal ("get-home-itis," "get-there-itis," and "let's-go-itis").

- The pilot's general goal-completion orientation.

- Emotional pressure associated with acknowledging that skill and experience levels may be lower than a pilot would like them to be. Pride can be a powerful external factor!

Managing External Pressures

Management of external pressure is the single most important key to risk management because it is the one risk factor category that can cause a pilot to ignore all the other risk factors. External pressures put time-related pressure on the pilot and figure into a majority of accidents.

The use of personal standard operating procedures (SOPs) is one way to manage external pressures. The goal is to supply a release for the external pressures of a flight. These procedures include but are not limited to:

- Allow time on a trip for an extra fuel stop or to make an unexpected landing because of weather.

- Have alternate plans for a late arrival or make backup airline reservations for must-be-there trips.

- For really important trips, plan to leave early enough so that there would still be time to drive to the destination.

- Advise those who are waiting at the destination that the arrival may be delayed. Know how to notify them when delays are encountered.

- Manage passengers' expectations. Make sure passengers know that they might not arrive on a firm schedule, and if they must arrive by a certain time, they should make alternative plans.

- Eliminate pressure to return home, even on a casual day flight, by carrying a small overnight kit containing prescriptions, contact lens solutions, toiletries, or other necessities on every flight.

The key to managing external pressure is to be ready for and accept delays. Remember that people get delayed when traveling on airlines, driving a car, or taking a bus. The pilot's goal is to manage risk, not create hazards. *[Figure 17-6]*

Figure 17-6. *The PAVE checklist.*

Human Behavior

Studies of human behavior have tried to determine an individual's predisposition to taking risks and the level of an individual's involvement in accidents. In 1951, a study regarding injury-prone children was published by Elizabeth Mechem Fuller and Helen B. Baune, of the University of Minnesota. The study was comprised of two separate groups of second grade students. Fifty-five students were considered accident repeaters and 48 students had no accidents. Both groups were from the same school of 600 and their family demographics were similar.

The accident-free group showed a superior knowledge of safety, were considered industrious and cooperative with others, but were not considered physically inclined. The accident-repeater group had better gymnastic skills, were considered aggressive and impulsive, demonstrated rebellious behavior when under stress, were poor losers, and liked to be the center of attention. One interpretation of this data—an adult predisposition to injury stems from childhood behavior and environment—leads to the conclusion that any pilot group should be comprised only of pilots who are safety-conscious, industrious, and cooperative.

Clearly, this is not only an inaccurate inference, it is impossible. Pilots are drawn from the general population and exhibit all types of personality traits. Thus, it is important that good decision-making skills be taught to all pilots.

Historically, the term "pilot error" has been used to describe an accident in which an action or decision made by the pilot was the cause or a contributing factor that led to the accident. This definition also includes the pilot's failure to make a correct decision or take proper action. From a broader perspective, the phrase "human factors related" more aptly describes these accidents. A single decision or event does not lead to an accident, but a series of events and the resultant decisions together form a chain of events leading to an outcome.

In his article "Accident-Prone Pilots," Dr. Patrick R. Veillette uses the history of "Captain Everyman" to demonstrate how aircraft accidents are caused more by a chain of poor choices rather than one single poor choice. In the case of Captain Everyman, after a gear-up landing accident, he became involved in another accident while taxiing a Beech 58P Baron out of the ramp. Interrupted by a radio call from the dispatcher, Everyman neglected to complete the fuel cross-feed check before taking off. Everyman, who was flying solo, left the right-fuel selector in the cross-feed position. Once aloft and cruising, he noticed a right roll tendency and corrected with aileron trim. He did not realize that both engines were feeding off the left wing's tank, making the wing lighter.

After two hours of flight, the right engine quit when Everyman was flying along a deep canyon gorge. While he was trying to troubleshoot the cause of the right engine's failure, the left engine quit. Everyman landed the aircraft on a river sand bar but it sank into ten feet of water.

Several years later Everyman flew a de Havilland Twin Otter to deliver supplies to a remote location. When he returned to home base and landed, the aircraft veered sharply to the left, departed the runway, and ran into a marsh 375 feet from the runway. The airframe and engines sustained considerable damage. Upon inspecting the wreck, accident investigators found the nose wheel steering tiller in the fully deflected position. Both the after takeoff and before landing checklists required the tiller to be placed in the neutral position. Everyman had overlooked this item.

Now, is Everyman accident prone or just unlucky? Skipping details on a checklist appears to be a common theme in the preceding accidents. While most pilots have made similar mistakes, these errors were probably caught prior to a mishap due to extra margin, good warning systems, a sharp copilot, or just good luck. What makes a pilot less prone to accidents?

The successful pilot possesses the ability to concentrate, manage workloads, monitor and perform several simultaneous tasks. Some of the latest psychological screenings used in aviation test applicants for their ability to multitask, measuring both accuracy, as well as the individual's ability to focus attention on several subjects simultaneously. The FAA oversaw an extensive research study on the similarities and dissimilarities of accident-free pilots and those who were not. The project surveyed over 4,000 pilots, half of whom had "clean" records while the other half had been involved in an accident.

Five traits were discovered in pilots prone to having accidents. These pilots:

- Have disdain toward rules.
- Have very high correlation between accidents on their flying records and safety violations on their driving records.
- Frequently fall into the "thrill and adventure seeking" personality category.

- Are impulsive rather than methodical and disciplined, both in their information gathering and in the speed and selection of actions to be taken.
- A disregard for or under utilization of outside sources of information, including copilots, flight attendants, flight service personnel, flight instructors, and air traffic controllers.

The Decision-Making Process

An understanding of the decision-making process provides the pilot with a foundation for developing ADM and SRM skills. While some situations, such as engine failure, require an immediate pilot response using established procedures, there is usually time during a flight to analyze any changes that occur, gather information, and assess risk before reaching a decision.

Risk management and risk intervention is much more than the simple definitions of the terms might suggest. Risk management and risk intervention are decision-making processes designed to systematically identify hazards, assess the degree of risk, and determine the best course of action. These processes involve the identification of hazards, followed by assessments of the risks, analysis of the controls, making control decisions, using the controls, and monitoring the results.

The steps leading to this decision constitute a decision-making process. Three models of a structured framework for problem-solving and decision-making are the 5-P, the 3P, the 3 with CARE and TEAM, the OODA, and the DECIDE models. They provide assistance in organizing the decision process. All these models have been identified as helpful to the single pilot in organizing critical decisions.

SRM and the 5P Check

SRM is about how to gather information, analyze it, and make decisions. Learning how to identify problems, analyze the information, and make informed and timely decisions is not as straightforward as the training involved in learning specific maneuvers. Learning how to judge a situation and "how to think" in the endless variety of situations encountered while flying out in the "real world" is more difficult.

There is no one right answer in ADM, rather each pilot is expected to analyze each situation in light of experience level, personal minimums, and current physical and mental readiness level, and make his or her own decision.

SRM sounds good on paper, but it requires a way for pilots to understand and use it in their daily flights. One practical application is called the "Five Ps (5 Ps)" *[Figure 17-7]* The

The SRM Five "P" Check
▢ The Plan
▢ The Plane
▢ The Pilot
▢ The Passengers
▢ The Programming

Figure 17-7. *The Five P checklist.*

check reminds the pilot that the day's flight plan is real life and subject to change at any time.

Obviously weather is a huge part of any plan. The addition of datalink weather information give the advanced avionics pilot a real advantage in inclement weather, but only if the pilot is trained to retrieve, and evaluate the weather in real time without sacrificing situational awareness. And of course, weather information should drive a decision, even if that decision is to continue on the current plan. Pilots of aircraft without datalink weather should get updated weather in flight through a Flight Service Station (FSS) and/or Flight Watch.

The Plane

Both the "plan" and the "plane" are fairly familiar to most pilots. The "plane" consists of the usual array of mechanical and cosmetic issues that every aircraft pilot, owner, or operator can identify. With the advent of advanced avionics, the "plane" has expanded to include database currency, automation status, and emergency backup systems that were unknown a few years ago. Much has been written about single pilot IFR flight both with and without an autopilot. While this is a personal decision, it is just that—a decision. Low IFR in a non-autopilot equipped aircraft may depend on several of the other Ps to be discussed. Pilot proficiency, currency, and fatigue are among them.

The Pilot

Flying, especially when used for business transportation, can expose the pilot to high altitude flying, long distance and endurance, and more challenging weather. An advanced avionics aircraft, simply due to their advanced capabilities can expose a pilot to even more of these stresses. The traditional "IMSAFE" checklist (see page 17-6) is a good start.

The combination of late night, pilot fatigue, and the effects of sustained flight above 5,000 feet may cause pilots to become less discerning, less critical of information, less decisive and more compliant and accepting. Just as the most critical portion of the flight approaches (for instance a night instrument approach, in the weather, after a 4-hour flight) the pilot's guard is down the most. The 5P process helps a pilot recognize the physiological situation at the end of the flight before takeoff, and continues to update personal conditions as the flight progresses. Once risks are identified, the pilot is in an infinitely better place to make alternate plans that lessen the effect of these factors and provide a safer solution.

The Passengers

One of the key differences between CRM and SRM is the way passengers interact with the pilot. The pilot of a highly capable single-engine aircraft has entered into a very personal relationship with the passengers. In fact, the pilot and passengers sit within an arm's reach all of the time.

The desire of the passengers to make airline connections or important business meetings easily enters into this pilot's decision-making loop. Done in a healthy and open way, this can be a positive factor. Consider a flight to Dulles Airport and the passengers, both close friends and business partners, need to get to Washington, D.C., for an important meeting. The weather is VFR all the way to southern Virginia then turns to low IFR as the pilot approaches Dulles. A pilot employing the 5P approach might consider reserving a rental car at an airport in northern North Carolina or southern Virginia to coincide with a refueling stop. Thus, the passengers have a way to get to Washington, and the pilot has an out to avoid being pressured into continuing the flight if the conditions do not improve.

Passengers can also be pilots. If no one is designated as pilot in command (PIC) and unplanned circumstances arise, the decision-making styles of several self-confident pilots may come into conflict.

Pilots also need to understand that non-pilots may not understand the level of risk involved in the flight. There is an element of risk in every flight. That is why SRM calls it risk management, not risk elimination. While a pilot may feel comfortable with the risk present in a night IFR flight, the passengers may not. A pilot employing SRM should ensure the passengers are involved in the decision-making and given tasks and duties to keep them busy and involved. If, upon a factual description of the risks present, the passengers decide to buy an airline ticket or rent a car, then a good decision has generally been made. This discussion also allows the pilot to move past what he or she thinks the passengers want to do and find out what they actually want to do. This removes self-induced pressure from the pilot.

The Programming

The advanced avionics aircraft adds an entirely new dimension to the way GA aircraft are flown. The electronic instrument displays, GPS, and autopilot reduce pilot workload and increase pilot situational awareness. While programming and operation of these devices are fairly simple and straightforward, unlike the analog instruments they replace, they tend to capture the pilot's attention and hold it for long periods of time. To avoid this phenomenon, the pilot should plan in advance when and where the programming for approaches, route changes, and airport information gathering should be accomplished as well as times it should not. Pilot familiarity with the equipment, the route, the local air traffic control environment, and personal capabilities vis-à-vis the automation should drive when, where, and how the automation is programmed and used.

The pilot should also consider what his or her capabilities are in response to last minute changes of the approach (and the reprogramming required) and ability to make large-scale changes (a reroute for instance) while hand flying the aircraft. Since formats are not standardized, simply moving from one manufacturer's equipment to another should give the pilot pause and require more conservative planning and decisions.

The SRM process is simple. At least five times before and during the flight, the pilot should review and consider the "Plan, the Plane, the Pilot, the Passengers, and the Programming" and make the appropriate decision required by the current situation. It is often said that failure to make a decision is a decision. Under SRM and the 5 Ps, even the decision to make no changes to the current plan, is made through a careful consideration of all the risk factors present.

Perceive, Process, Perform (3P)

The Perceive, Process, Perform (3P) model for ADM offers a simple, practical, and systematic approach that can be used during all phases of flight. To use it, the pilot will:

- Perceive the given set of circumstances for a flight.

- Process by evaluating their impact on flight safety.

- Perform by implementing the best course of action.

In the first step, the goal is to develop situational awareness by perceiving hazards, which are present events, objects, or circumstances that could contribute to an undesired future event. In this step, the pilot will systematically identify and list hazards associated with all aspects of the flight: pilot, aircraft, environment, and external pressures. It is important to consider how individual hazards might combine. Consider, for example, the hazard that arises when a new instrument pilot with no experience in actual instrument conditions wants to make a cross-country flight to an airport with low ceilings in order to attend an important business meeting.

In the second step, the goal is to process this information to determine whether the identified hazards constitute risk, which is defined as the future impact of a hazard that is not controlled or eliminated. The degree of risk posed by a given hazard can be measured in terms of exposure (number of people or resources affected), severity (extent of possible loss), and probability (the likelihood that a hazard will cause a loss). If the hazard is low ceilings, for example, the level of risk depends on a number of other factors, such as pilot training and experience, aircraft equipment and fuel capacity, and others.

In the third step, the goal is to perform by taking action to eliminate hazards or mitigate risk, and then continuously evaluate the outcome of this action. With the example of low ceilings at destination, for instance, the pilot can perform good ADM by selecting a suitable alternate, knowing where to find good weather, and carrying sufficient fuel to reach it. This course of action would mitigate the risk. The pilot also has the option to eliminate it entirely by waiting for better weather.

Once the pilot has completed the 3P decision process and selected a course of action, the process begins anew because now the set of circumstances brought about by the course of action requires analysis. The decision-making process is a continuous loop of perceiving, processing and performing.

With practice and consistent use, running through the 3P cycle can become a habit that is as smooth, continuous, and automatic as a well-honed instrument scan. This basic set of practical risk management tools can be used to improve risk management. The 3P model has been expanded to include the CARE and TEAM models which offers pilots another way to assess and reduce risks associated with flying.

Perceive, Process, Perform with CARE and TEAM

Most flight training activities take place in the "time-critical" timeframe for risk management. *Figures 17-8* and *17-9* combine the six steps of risk management into an easy-to-remember 3P model for practical risk management: Perceive, Process, Perform with the CARE and TEAM models. Pilots can help perceive hazards by using the PAVE checklist of: Pilot, Aircraft, enVironment, and External pressures. They can process hazards by using the CARE checklist of: Consequences, Alternatives, Reality, External factors. Finally, pilots can perform risk management by using the TEAM choice list of: Transfer, Eliminate, Accept, or Mitigate. These concepts are relatively new in the GA training world, but have been shown to be extraordinarily useful in lowering accident rates in the world of air carriers.

Pilots can perceive hazards by using the PAVE checklist:

Pilot

Gayle is a healthy and well-rested private pilot with approximately 300 hours total flight time. Hazards include her lack of overall and cross-country experience and the fact that she has not flown at all in two months.

Aircraft

Although it does not have a panel-mount GPS or weather avoidance gear, the aircraft—a C182 Skylane with long-range fuel tanks—is in good mechanical condition with no inoperative equipment. The instrument panel is a standard "six-pack."

EnVironment

Departure and destination airports have long runways. Weather is the main hazard. Although it is VFR, it is a typical summer day in the Mid-Atlantic region: hot (near 90 °F) hazy (visibility 7 miles), and humid with a density altitude of 2,500 feet. Weather at the destination airport (located in the mountains) is still IMC, but forecast to improve to visual meteorological conditions (VMC) prior to her arrival. En route weather is VMC, but there is an AIRMET Sierra for pockets of IMC over mountain ridges along the proposed route of flight.

External Pressures

Gayle is making the trip to spend a weekend with relatives she does not see very often. Her family is very excited and has made a number of plans for the visit.

Pilots can perform risk management by using the TEAM choice list:

Pilot

To manage the risk associated with her inexperience and lack of recent flight time, Gayle can:
- Transfer the risk entirely by having another pilot act as PIC.
- Eliminate the risk by canceling the trip.
- Accept the risk and fly anyway.
- Mitigate the risk by flying with another pilot.

Gayle chooses to mitigate the major risk by hiring a CFI to accompany her and provide dual cross-country instruction. An added benefit is the opportunity to broaden her flying experience.

Aircraft

To manage risk associated with any doubts about the aircraft's mechanical condition, Gayle can:
- Transfer the risk by using a different airplane.
- Eliminate the risk by canceling the trip.
- Accept the risk.
- Mitigate the remaining (residual) risk through review of aircraft performance and careful preflight inspection.

Since she finds no problems with the aircraft's mechanical condition, Gayle chooses to mitigate any remaining risk through careful preflight inspection of the aircraft.

Environment

To manage the risk associated with hazy conditions and mountainous terrain, Gayle can:
- Transfer the risk of VFR in these conditions by asking an instrument-rated pilot to fly the trip under IFR.
- Eliminate the risk by canceling the trip.
- Accept the risk.
- Mitigate the risk by careful preflight planning, filing a VFR flight plan, requesting VFR flight following, and using resources such as Flight Watch.

Detailed preflight planning must be a vital part of Gayle's weather risk mitigation strategy. The most direct route would put her over mountains for most of the trip. Because of the thick haze and pockets of IMC over mountains, Gayle might mitigate the risk by modifying the route to fly over valleys. This change will add 30 minutes to her estimated time of arrival (ETA), but the extra time is a small price to pay for avoiding possible IMC over mountains. Because her destination airport is IMC at the time of departure, Gayle needs to establish that VFR conditions exist at other airports within easy driving distance of her original destination. In addition, Gayle should review basic information (e.g., traffic pattern altitude, runway layout, frequencies) for these alternate airports. To further mitigate risk and practice good cockpit resource management, Gayle should file a VFR flight plan, use VFR flight following, and call Flight Watch to get weather updates en route. Finally, basic functions on her handheld GPS should also be practiced.

External Pressures

To mitigate the risk of emotional pressure from family expectations that can drive a "get-there" mentality, Gayle can:
- Transfer the risk by having her co-pilot act as PIC and make the continue/divert decision.
- Eliminate the risk by canceling the trip.
- Accept the risk.
- Mitigate the risk by managing family expectations and making alternative arrangements in the event of diversion to another airport.

Gayle and her co-pilot choose to address this risk by agreeing that each pilot has a veto on continuing the flight, and that they will divert if either becomes uncomfortable with flight conditions. Because the destination airport is still IMC at the time of departure, Gayle establishes a specific point in the trip—an en route VORTAC located between the destination airport and the two alternates—as the logical place for her "final" continue/divert decision. Rather than give her family a specific ETA that might make Gayle feel pressured to meet the schedule, she manages her family's expectations by advising them that she will call when she arrives.

Figure 17-8. *A real-world example of how the 3P model guides decisions on a cross-country trip.*

Pilots can perceive hazards by using the CARE checklist:

Pilot

- Consequences: Gayle's inexperience and lack of recent flight time create some risk of an accident, primarily because she plans to travel over mountains on a hazy day and land at an unfamiliar mountain airport that is still in IMC conditions.
- Alternatives: Gayle might mitigate the pilot-related risk by hiring a CFI to accompany her and provide dual cross-country instruction. An added benefit is the opportunity to broaden her flying experience in safe conditions.
- Reality: Accepting the reality that limited experience can create additional risk is a key part of sound risk management and mitigation.
- External Factors: Like many pilots, Gayle must contend with the emotional pressure associated with acknowledging that her skill and experience levels may be lower than she would like them to be. Pride can be a powerful external factor!

Environment

- Consequences: For a pilot whose experience consists mostly of local flights in good VMC, launching a long cross-country flight over mountainous terrain in hazy conditions could lead to pilot disorientation and increase the risk of an accident.
- Alternatives: Options include postponing the trip until the visibility improves, or modifying the route to avoid extended periods of time over the mountains.
- Reality: Hazy conditions and mountainous terrain clearly create risk for an inexperienced VFR-only pilot.
- External Factors: Few pilots are immune to the pressure of "get-there-itis," which can sometimes induce a decision to launch or continue in less than ideal weather conditions.

Aircraft

- Consequences: This area presents low risk because the aircraft is in excellent mechanical condition and Gayle is familiar with its avionics.
- Alternatives: Had there been a problem with her aircraft, Gayle might have considered renting another plane from her flight school. Bear in mind, however, that alternatives sometimes create new hazards. In this instance, there may be hazards associated with flying an unfamiliar aircraft with different avionics.
- Reality: It is important to recognize the reality of an aircraft's mechanical condition. If you find a maintenance discrepancy and then find yourself saying that it is "probably" okay to fly with it anyway, you need to revisit the consequences part of this checklist.
- External Factors: Pilot decision-making can sometimes be influenced by the external pressure of needing to return the airplane to the FBO by a certain date and time. Because Gayle owns the airplane, there was no such pressure in this case.

External Pressures

- Consequences: Any number of factors can create risk of emotional pressure from a "get-there" mentality. In Gayle's case, the consequences of her strong desire to visit family, her family's expectations, and personal pride could induce her to accept unnecessary risk.
- Alternatives: Gayle clearly needs to develop a mitigating strategy for each of the external factors associated with this trip.
- Reality: Pilots sometimes tend to discount or ignore the potential impact of these external factors. Gayle's open acknowledgement of these factors (e.g., "I might be pressured into pressing on so my mother won't have to worry about our late arrival.") is a critical element of effective risk management.
- External Factors: (see above)

Figure 17-9. *Additional real-world examples of how the 3P model guides decisions on a cross-country trip.*

Forming Good Safety Habits

While the 3P model is similar to other methods, there are two good reasons to use the 3P model. First, the 3P model gives pilots a structured, efficient, and systematic way to identify hazards, assess risk, and implement effective risk controls. Second, practicing risk management needs to be as automatic in GA flying as basic aircraft control. As is true for other flying skills, risk management thinking habits are best developed through repetition and consistent adherence to specific procedures.

The OODA Loop

Colonel John Boyd, United States Air Forces (Retired), coined the term and developed the concept of the "OODA Loop" (Observation, Orientation, Decision, Action). The ideas, words, and phrases contained in Boyd's briefings have penetrated not only the United States military services, but the business community and worldwide academia. The OODA Loop is now used as a standard description of decision-making cycles.

The Loop is an interlaced decision model which provides immediate feedback throughout the decision-making process. For SRM purposes, an abbreviated version of the concept *[Figure 17-10]* provides an easily understood tool for the pilot.

The first node of the Loop, Observe, reflects the need for situational awareness. A pilot must be aware of those things around him or her that may impact the flight. Continuous monitoring of aircraft controls, weather, etc., provides a constant reference point by which the pilot knows his or her starting point on the loop which permits the ability to immediately move to the next step.

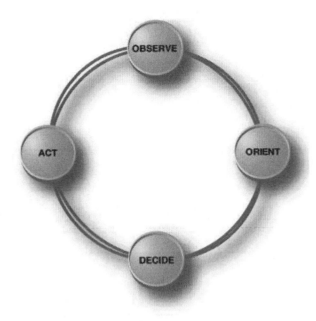

Figure 17-10. *The OODA Loop.*

Orient, the second node of the Loop, focuses the pilot's attention on one or more discrepancies in the flight. For example, there is a low oil pressure reading. The pilot is aware of this deviation and considers available options in view of potential hazards to continued flight.

The pilot then moves to the third node, Decide, in which he or she makes a positive determination about a specific effect. That decision is made based on experience and knowledge of potential results, and to take that particular action will produce the desired result. The pilot then Acts on that decision, making a physical input to cause the aircraft to react in the desired fashion.

Once the loop has been completed, the pilot is once again in the Observe position. The assessment of the resulting action is added to the previously perceived aspects of the flight to further define the flight's progress. The advantage of the OODA Loop model is that it may be cumulative, as well as having the potential of allowing for multiple progressions to occur at any given point in the flight.

The DECIDE Model

Using the acronym "DECIDE," the six-step process DECIDE Model is another continuous loop process that provides the pilot with a logical way of making decisions. *[Figure 17-11]* DECIDE means to Detect, Estimate, Choose a course of action, Identify solutions, Do the necessary actions, and Evaluate the effects of the actions.

First, consider a recent accident involving a Piper Apache (PA-23). The aircraft was substantially damaged during impact with terrain at a local airport in Alabama. The certificated airline transport pilot (ATP) received minor injuries and the certificated private pilot was not injured. The private pilot was receiving a checkride from the ATP (who was also a designated examiner) for a commercial pilot certificate with a multi-engine rating. After performing airwork at altitude, they returned to the airport and the private pilot performed a single-engine approach to a full stop landing. He then taxied back for takeoff, performed a short field takeoff, and then joined the traffic pattern to return for another landing. During the approach for the second landing, the ATP simulated a right engine failure by reducing power on the right engine to zero thrust. This caused the aircraft to yaw right.

The procedure to identify the failed engine is a two-step process. First, bring power to maximum controllable on both engines. Because the left engine is the only engine delivering thrust, the yaw increases to the right, which necessitates application of additional left rudder application. The failed engine is the side that requires no rudder pressure, in this case the right engine. Second, having identified the failed right engine, the procedure is to feather the right engine and adjust power to maintain descent angle to a landing.

However, in this case the pilot feathered the left engine because he assumed the engine failure was a left engine failure. During twin-engine training, the left engine out is emphasized more than the right engine because the left engine on most light twins is the critical engine. This is due to multiengine airplanes being subject to P-factor, as are single-engine airplanes. The descending propeller blade of each engine will produce greater thrust than the ascending blade when the airplane is operated under power and at positive angles of attack. The descending propeller blade of the right engine is also a greater distance from the center of gravity, and therefore has a longer moment arm than the descending propeller blade of the left engine. As a result, failure of the left engine will result in the most asymmetrical thrust (adverse yaw) because the right engine will be providing the remaining thrust. Many twins are designed with a counter-rotating right engine. With this design, the degree of asymmetrical thrust is the same with either engine inoperative. Neither engine is more critical than the other.

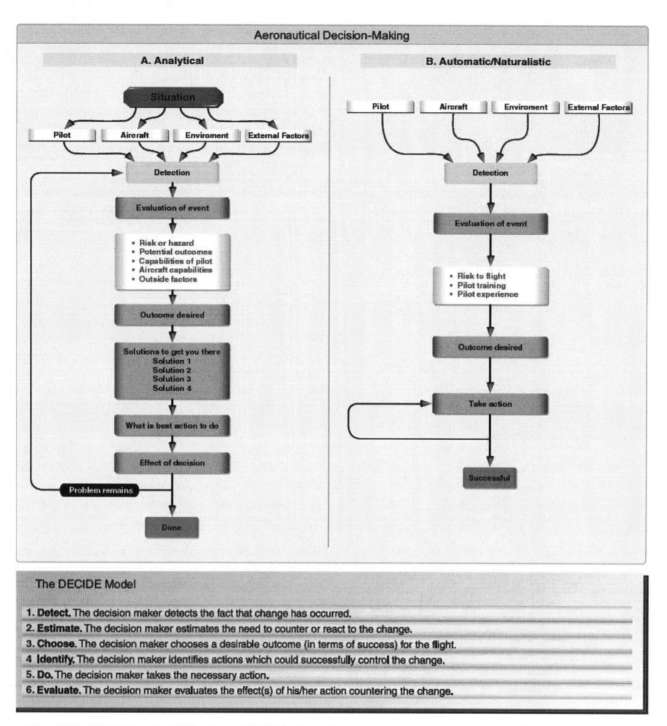

Aeronautical Decision-Making

A. Analytical

Situation
→ Pilot · Aircraft · Enviroment · External Factors
→ Detection
→ Evaluation of event
→ • Risk or hazard
  • Potential outcomes
  • Capabilities of pilot
  • Aircraft capabilities
  • Outside factors
→ Outcome desired
→ Solutions to get you there
  Solution 1
  Solution 2
  Solution 3
  Solution 4
→ What is best action to do
→ Effect of decision
→ Problem remains
→ Done

B. Automatic/Naturalistic

Pilot · Aircraft · Enviroment · External Factors
→ Detection
→ Evaluation of event
→ • Risk to flight
  • Pilot training
  • Pilot experience
→ Outcome desired
→ Take action
→ Successful

The DECIDE Model

1. **Detect.** The decision maker detects the fact that change has occurred.
2. **Estimate.** The decision maker estimates the need to counter or react to the change.
3. **Choose.** The decision maker chooses a desirable outcome (in terms of success) for the flight.
4. **Identify.** The decision maker identifies actions which could successfully control the change.
5. **Do.** The decision maker takes the necessary action.
6. **Evaluate.** The decision maker evaluates the effect(s) of his/her action countering the change.

Figure 17-11. *The DECIDE model has been recognized worldwide. Its application is illustrated in A while automatic/naturalistic decision-making is shown in B.*

Since the pilot never executed the first step of identifying which engine failed, he feathered the left engine and set the right engine at zero thrust. This essentially restricted the aircraft to a controlled glide. Upon realizing that he was not going to make the runway, the pilot increased power to both engines causing an enormous yaw to the left (the left propeller was feathered) whereupon the aircraft started to turn left. In desperation, the instructor closed both throttles and the aircraft hit the ground and was substantially damaged.

This case is interesting because it highlights two particular issues. First, taking action without forethought can be just as dangerous as taking no action at all. In this case, the pilot's actions were incorrect; yet, there was sufficient time to take the necessary steps to analyze the simulated emergency. The second and more subtle issue is that decisions made under pressure are sometimes executed based upon limited experience and the actions taken may be incorrect, incomplete, or insufficient to handle the situation.

Detect (the Problem)

Problem detection is the first step in the decision-making process. It begins with recognizing a change occurred or an expected change did not occur. A problem is perceived first by the senses and then it is distinguished through insight and experience. These same abilities, as well as an objective analysis of all available information, are used to determine the nature and severity of the problem. One critical error made during the decision-making process is incorrectly detecting the problem. In the example above, the change that occurred was a yaw.

Estimate (the Need To React)

In the engine-out example, the aircraft yawed right, the pilot was on final approach, and the problem warranted a prompt solution. In many cases, overreaction and fixation excludes a safe outcome. For example, what if the cabin door of a Mooney suddenly opened in flight while the aircraft climbed through 1,500 feet on a clear sunny day? The sudden opening would be alarming, but the perceived hazard the open door presents is quickly and effectively assessed as minor. In fact, the door's opening would not impact safe flight and can almost be disregarded. Most likely, a pilot would return to the airport to secure the door after landing.

The pilot flying on a clear day faced with this minor problem may rank the open cabin door as a low risk. What about the pilot on an IFR climb out in IMC conditions with light intermittent turbulence in rain who is receiving an amended clearance from air traffic control (ATC)? The open cabin door now becomes a higher risk factor. The problem has not changed, but the perception of risk a pilot assigns it changes because of the multitude of ongoing tasks and the environment. Experience, discipline, awareness, and knowledge will influence how a pilot ranks a problem.

Choose (a Course of Action)

After the problem has been identified and its impact estimated, the pilot must determine the desirable outcome and choose a course of action. In the case of the multiengine pilot given the simulated failed engine, the desired objective is to safely land the airplane.

Identify (Solutions)

The pilot formulates a plan that will take him or her to the objective. Sometimes, there may be only one course of action available. In the case of the engine failure, already at 500 feet or below, the pilot solves the problem by identifying one or more solutions that lead to a successful outcome. It is important for the pilot not to become fixated on the process to the exclusion of making a decision.

Do (the Necessary Actions)

Once pathways to resolution are identified, the pilot selects the most suitable one for the situation. The multiengine pilot given the simulated failed engine must now safely land the aircraft.

Evaluate (the Effect of the Action)

Finally, after implementing a solution, evaluate the decision to see if it was correct. If the action taken does not provide the desired results, the process may have to be repeated.

Decision-Making in a Dynamic Environment

The common approach to decision-making has been through the use of analytical models such as 5P, 3P, OODA, and DECIDE. Good decisions result when pilots gather all available information, review it, analyze the options, rate the options, select a course of action, and evaluate that course of action for correctness.

In some situations, there isn't always time to make decisions based on analytical decision-making skills. A good example is a quarterback whose actions are based upon a highly fluid and changing situation. He intends to execute a plan, but new circumstances dictate decision-making on the fly. This type of decision-making is called automatic decision-making or naturalized decision-making. *[Figure 17-11B]*

Automatic Decision-Making

In an emergency situation, a pilot might not survive if he or she rigorously applied analytical models to every decision made; there is not enough time to go through all the options. But under these circumstances does he or she find the best possible solution to every problem?

For the past several decades, research into how people actually make decisions has revealed that when pressed for time, experts faced with a task loaded with uncertainty, first assess whether the situation strikes them as familiar. Rather than comparing the pros and cons of different approaches, they quickly imagine how one or a few possible courses of action in such situations will play out. Experts take the first workable option they can find. While it may not be the best of all possible choices, it often yields remarkably good results.

The terms naturalistic and automatic decision-making have been coined to describe this type of decision-making. The ability to make automatic decisions holds true for a range of experts from fire fighters to chess players. It appears the expert's ability hinges on the recognition of patterns and consistencies that clarify options in complex situations. Experts appear to make provisional sense of a situation, without actually reaching a decision, by launching experience-based actions that in turn trigger creative revisions.

This is a reflexive type of decision-making anchored in training and experience and is most often used in times of emergencies when there is no time to practice analytical decision-making. Naturalistic or automatic decision-making improves with training and experience, and a pilot will find himself or herself using a combination of decision-making tools that correlate with individual experience and training.

Operational Pitfalls

Although more experienced pilots are likely to make more automatic decisions, there are tendencies or operational pitfalls that come with the development of pilot experience. These are classic behavioral traps into which pilots have been known to fall. More experienced pilots (as a rule) try to complete a flight as planned, please passengers, and meet schedules. The desire to meet these goals can have an adverse effect on safety and contribute to an unrealistic assessment of piloting skills. All experienced pilots have fallen prey to, or have been tempted by, one or more of these tendencies in their flying careers. These dangerous tendencies or behavior patterns, which must be identified and eliminated, include the operational pitfalls shown in *Figure 17-12*.

Stress Management

Everyone is stressed to some degree almost all of the time. A certain amount of stress is good since it keeps a person alert and prevents complacency. Effects of stress are cumulative and, if the pilot does not cope with them in an appropriate way, they can eventually add up to an intolerable burden. Performance generally increases with the onset of stress, peaks, and then begins to fall off rapidly as stress levels exceed a person's ability to cope. The ability to make effective decisions during flight can be impaired by stress. There are two categories of stress—acute and chronic. These are both explained in Chapter 16, Aeromedical Factors.

Factors referred to as stressors can increase a pilot's risk of error in the flight deck. *[Figure 17-13]* Remember the cabin door that suddenly opened in flight on the Mooney climbing through 1,500 feet on a clear sunny day? It may startle the pilot, but the stress would wane when it became apparent the situation was not a serious hazard. Yet, if the cabin door opened in IMC conditions, the stress level makes significant impact on the pilot's ability to cope with simple tasks. The key to stress management is to stop, think, and analyze before jumping to a conclusion. There is usually time to think before drawing unnecessary conclusions.

There are several techniques to help manage the accumulation of life stresses and prevent stress overload. For example, to help reduce stress levels, set aside time for relaxation each day or maintain a program of physical fitness. To prevent stress overload, learn to manage time more effectively to avoid pressures imposed by getting behind schedule and not meeting deadlines.

Use of Resources

To make informed decisions during flight operations, a pilot must also become aware of the resources found inside and outside the flight deck. Since useful tools and sources of information may not always be readily apparent, learning to recognize these resources is an essential part of ADM training. Resources must not only be identified, but a pilot must also develop the skills to evaluate whether there is time to use a particular resource and the impact its use will have upon the safety of flight. For example, the assistance of ATC may be very useful if a pilot becomes lost, but in an emergency situation, there may be no time available to contact ATC.

Internal Resources

One of the most underutilized resources may be the person in the right seat, even if the passenger has no flying experience. When appropriate, the PIC can ask passengers to assist with certain tasks, such as watching for traffic or reading checklist items. Some other ways a passenger can assist:

- Provide information in an irregular situation, especially if familiar with flying. A strange smell or sound may alert a passenger to a potential problem.

Operational Pitfalls

Peer Pressure
Poor decision-making may be based upon an emotional response to peers, rather than evaluating a situation objectively.

Mind Set
A pilot displays mind set through an inability to recognize and cope with changes in a given situation.

Get-there-itis
This disposition impairs pilot judgment through a fixation on the original goal or destination, combined with a disregard for any alternative course of action.

Duck-Under Syndrome
A pilot may be tempted to make it into an airport by descending below minimums during an approach. There may be a belief that there is a built-in margin of error in every approach procedure, or a pilot may want to admit that the landing cannot be completed and a missed approach must be initiated.

Scud Running
This occurs when a pilot tries to maintain visual contact with the terrain at low altitudes while instrument conditions exist.

Continuing Visual Flight Rules (VFR) into Instrument Conditions
Spatial disorientation or collision with ground/obstacles may occur when a pilot continues VFR into instrument conditions. This can be even more dangerous if the pilot is not instrument rated or current.

Getting Behind the Aircraft
This pitfall can be caused by allowing events or the situation to control pilot actions. A constant state of surprise at what happens next may be exhibited when the pilot is getting behind the aircraft.

Loss of Positional or Situational Awareness
In extreme cases, when a pilot gets behind the aircraft, a loss of positional or situational awareness may result. The pilot may not know the aircraft's geographical location, or may be unable to recognize deteriorating circumstances.

Operating Without Adequate Fuel Reserves
Ignoring minimum fuel reserve requirements is generally the result of overconfidence, lack of flight planning, or disregarding applicable regulations.

Descent Below the Minimum En Route Altitude
The duck-under syndrome, as mentioned above, can also occur during the en route portion of an IFR flight.

Flying Outside the Envelope
The assumed high performance capability of a particular aircraft may cause a mistaken belief that it can meet the demands imposed by a pilot's overestimated flying skills.

Neglect of Flight Planning, Preflight Inspections, and Checklists
A pilot may rely on short- and long-term memory, regular flying skills, and familiar routes instead of established procedures and published checklists. This can be particularly true of experienced pilots.

Figure 17-12. *Typical operational pitfalls requiring pilot awareness.*

Stressors

Environmental
Conditions associated with the environment, such as temperature and humidity extremes, noise, vibration, and lack of oxygen.

Physiological Stress
Physical conditions, such as fatigue, lack of physical fitness, sleep loss, missed meals (leading to low blood sugar levels), and illness.

Psychological Stress
Social or emotional factors, such as a death in the family, a divorce, a sick child, or a demotion at work. This type of stress may also be related to mental workload, such as analyzing a problem, navigating an aircraft, or making decisions.

Figure 17-13. *System stressors. Environmental, physiological, and psychological stress are factors which affect decision-making skills. These stressors have a profound impact especially during periods of high workload.*

- Confirm after the pilot that the landing gear is down.

- Learn to look at the altimeter for a given altitude in a descent.

- Listen to logic or lack of logic.

Also, the process of a verbal briefing (which can happen whether or not passengers are aboard) can help the PIC in the decision-making process. For example, assume a pilot provides a lone passenger a briefing of the forecast landing weather before departure. When the Automatic Terminal Information Service (ATIS) is picked up, the weather has significantly changed. The discussion of this forecast change can lead the pilot to reexamine his or her activities and decision-making. *[Figure 17-14]* Other valuable internal resources include ingenuity, aviation knowledge, and flying skill. Pilots can increase flight deck resources by improving these characteristics.

When flying alone, another internal resource is verbal communication. It has been established that verbal communication reinforces an activity; touching an object while communicating further enhances the probability an activity has been accomplished. For this reason, many solo pilots read the checklist out loud; when they reach critical items, they touch the switch or control. For example, to ascertain the landing gear is down, the pilot can read the checklist. But, if he or she touches the gear handle during the process, a safe extension of the landing gear is confirmed.

It is necessary for a pilot to have a thorough understanding of all the equipment and systems in the aircraft being flown. Lack of knowledge, such as knowing if the oil pressure gauge is direct reading or uses a sensor, is the difference between making a wise decision or poor one that leads to a tragic error.

Checklists are essential flight deck internal resources. They are used to verify the aircraft instruments and systems are checked, set, and operating properly, as well as ensuring the proper procedures are performed if there is a system malfunction or inflight emergency. Students reluctant to use checklists can be reminded that pilots at all levels of experience refer to checklists, and that the more advanced the aircraft is, the more crucial checklists become. In addition, the pilot's operating handbook (POH) is required to be carried on board the aircraft and is essential for accurate flight planning and resolving inflight equipment malfunctions. However, the most valuable resource a pilot has is the ability to manage workload whether alone or with others.

External Resources

Air traffic controllers and flight service specialists are the best external resources during flight. In order to promote the safe, orderly flow of air traffic around airports and, along flight routes, the ATC provides pilots with traffic advisories, radar vectors, and assistance in emergency situations. Although it is the PIC's responsibility to make the flight as safe as possible, a pilot with a problem can request assistance from ATC. *[Figure 17-15]* For example, if a pilot needs to level off, be given a vector, or decrease speed, ATC assists and

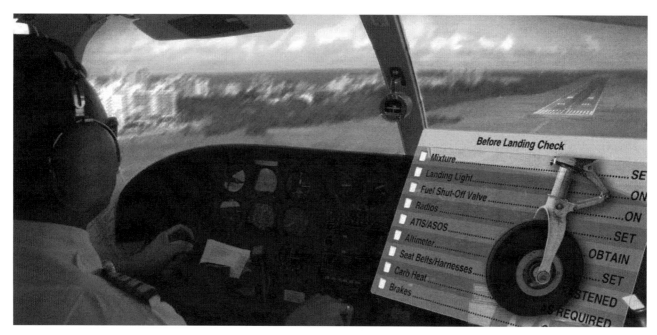

Figure 17-14. *When possible, have a passenger reconfirm that critical tasks are completed.*

Figure 17-15. *Controllers work to make flights as safe as possible.*

becomes integrated as part of the crew. The services provided by ATC can not only decrease pilot workload, but also help pilots make informed inflight decisions.

The FSS are air traffic facilities that provide pilot briefing, en route communications, VFR search and rescue services, assist lost aircraft and aircraft in emergency situations, relay ATC clearances, originate Notices to Airmen (NOTAM), broadcast aviation weather and National Airspace System (NAS) information, receive and process IFR flight plans, and monitor navigational aids (NAVAIDs). In addition, at selected locations, FSSs provide En Route Flight Advisory Service (Flight Watch), issue airport advisories, and advise Customs and Immigration of transborder flights. Selected FSSs in Alaska also provide TWEB recordings and take weather observations.

Another external resource available to pilots is the VHF Direction Finder (VHF/DF). This is one of the common systems that helps pilots without their being aware of its operation. FAA facilities that provide VHF/DF service are identified in the A/FD. DF equipment has long been used to locate lost aircraft and to guide aircraft to areas of good weather or to airports. DF instrument approaches may be given to aircraft in a distress or urgency condition.

Experience has shown that most emergencies requiring DF assistance involve pilots with little flight experience. With this in mind, DF approach procedures provide maximum flight stability in the approach by using small turns, and wings-level descents. The DF specialist will give the pilot headings to fly and tell the pilot when to begin descent. If followed, the headings will lead the aircraft to a predetermined point such as the DF station or an airport. To become familiar with the procedures and other benefits of DF, pilots are urged to request practice DF guidance and approaches in VFR weather conditions.

Situational Awareness

Situational awareness is the accurate perception and understanding of all the factors and conditions within the five fundamental risk elements (flight, pilot, aircraft, environment, and type of operation that comprise any given aviation situation) that affect safety before, during, and after the flight. Monitoring radio communications for traffic, weather discussion, and ATC communication can enhance situational awareness by helping the pilot develop a mental picture of what is happening.

Maintaining situational awareness requires an understanding of the relative significance of all flight related factors and their future impact on the flight. When a pilot understands what is going on and has an overview of the total operation, he or she is not fixated on one perceived significant factor. Not only is it important for a pilot to know the aircraft's geographical location, it is also important he or she understand what is happening. For instance, while flying above Richmond, Virginia, toward Dulles Airport or Leesburg, the pilot should know why he or she is being vectored and be able to anticipate spatial location. A pilot who is simply making turns without understanding why has added an additional burden to his or her management in the event of an emergency. To maintain situational awareness, all of the skills involved in ADM are used.

Obstacles to Maintaining Situational Awareness

Fatigue, stress, and work overload can cause a pilot to fixate on a single perceived important item and reduce an overall situational awareness of the flight. A contributing factor in many accidents is a distraction that diverts the pilot's attention from monitoring the instruments or scanning outside the aircraft. Many flight deck distractions begin as a minor problem, such as a gauge that is not reading correctly, but result in accidents as the pilot diverts attention to the perceived problem and neglects to properly control the aircraft.

Workload Management

Effective workload management ensures essential operations are accomplished by planning, prioritizing, and sequencing tasks to avoid work overload. *[Figure 17-16]* As experience is gained, a pilot learns to recognize future workload requirements and can prepare for high workload periods during times of low workload. Reviewing the appropriate chart and setting radio frequencies well in advance of when they are needed helps reduce workload as the flight nears the airport. In addition, a pilot should listen to ATIS, Automated Surface Observing System (ASOS), or Automated Weather

Recognizing a work overload situation is also an important component of managing workload. The first effect of high workload is that the pilot may be working harder but accomplishing less. As workload increases, attention cannot be devoted to several tasks at one time, and the pilot may begin to focus on one item. When a pilot becomes task saturated, there is no awareness of input from various sources, so decisions may be made on incomplete information and the possibility of error increases. *[Figure 17-17]*

When a work overload situation exists, a pilot needs to stop, think, slow down, and prioritize. It is important to understand how to decrease workload. For example, in the case of the cabin door that opened in VFR flight, the impact on workload should be insignificant. If the cabin door opens under IFR different conditions, its impact on workload will change. Therefore, placing a situation in the proper perspective, remaining calm, and thinking rationally are key elements in reducing stress and increasing the capacity to fly safely. This ability depends upon experience, discipline, and training.

Figure 17-16. *Balancing workloads can be a difficult task.*

Observing System (AWOS), if available, and then monitor the tower frequency or Common Traffic Advisory Frequency (CTAF) to get a good idea of what traffic conditions to expect. Checklists should be performed well in advance so there is time to focus on traffic and ATC instructions. These procedures are especially important prior to entering a high-density traffic area, such as Class B airspace.

Managing Risks

The ability to manage risk begins with preparation. Here are some things a pilot can do to manage overall risk:

- Assess the flight's risk based upon experience. Use some form of risk assessment. For example, if the weather is marginal and the pilot has low IMC training, it is probably a good idea to cancel the flight.

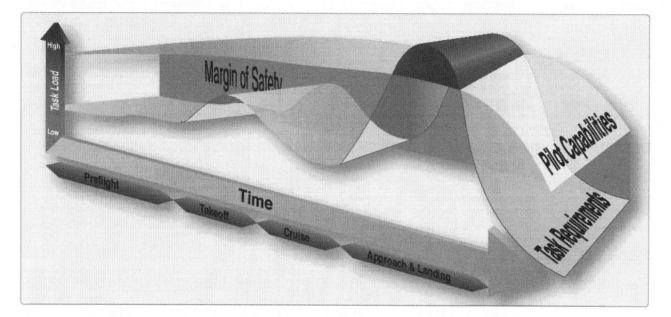

Figure 17-17. *The pilot has a certain capacity of doing work and handling tasks. However, there is a point where the tasking exceeds the pilot's capability. When this happens, tasks are either not done properly or some are not done at all.*

- Brief passengers using the SAFETY list:

  S Seat belts fastened for taxi, takeoff, landing

     Shoulder harness fastened for takeoff, landing

     Seat position adjusted and locked in place

  A Air vents (location and operation)

     All environmental controls (discussed)

     Action in case of any passenger discomfort

  F Fire extinguisher (location and operation)

  E Exit doors (how to secure; how to open)

     Emergency evacuation plan

     Emergency/survival kit (location and contents)

  T Traffic (scanning, spotting, notifying pilot)

     Talking, ("sterile flight deck" expectations)

  Y Your questions? (Speak up!)

- In addition to the SAFETY list, discuss with passengers whether or not smoking is permitted, flight route altitudes, time en route, destination, weather during flight, expected weather at the destination, controls and what they do, and the general capabilities and limitations of the aircraft.

- Use a sterile flight deck (one that is completely silent with no pilot communication with passengers or by passengers) from the time of departure to the first intermediate altitude and clearance from the local airspace.

- Use a sterile flight deck during arrival from the first radar vector for approach or descent for the approach.

- Keep the passengers informed during times when the workload is low.

- Consider using the passenger in the right seat for simple tasks such as holding the chart. This relieves the pilot of a task.

Automation

In the GA community, an automated aircraft is generally comprised of an integrated advanced avionics system consisting of a primary flight display (PFD), a multifunction flight display (MFD) including an instrument-certified Global Positioning System (GPS) with traffic and terrain graphics, and a fully integrated autopilot. This type of aircraft is commonly known as an advanced avionics aircraft. In an advanced avionics aircraft, there are typically two display (computer) screens, PFD (left display screen) and the MFD.

Automation is the single most important advance in aviation technologies. Electronic flight displays (EFDs) have made vast improvements in how information is displayed and what information is available to the pilot. Pilots can access electronic databases that contain all of the information traditionally contained in multiple handbooks, reducing clutter in the flight deck. *[Figure 17-18]*

Multifunction displays (MFDs) are capable of displaying moving maps that mirror sectional charts. These detailed displays depict all airspace, including Temporary Flight Restrictions (TFRs). MFDs are so descriptive that many pilots fall into the trap of relying solely on the moving maps for navigation. Pilots also draw upon the database to familiarize themselves with departure and destination airport information.

More pilots now rely on electronic databases for flight planning and use automated flight planning tools rather than planning the flight by the traditional methods of laying out charts, drawing the course, identifying navigation points (assuming a VFR flight), and using the POH to figure out the weight and balance and performance charts. Whichever method a pilot chooses to plan a flight, it is important to remember to check and confirm calculations

Although automation has made flying safer, automated systems can make some errors more evident, and sometimes hide other errors or make them less evident. There are concerns about the effect of automation on pilots. In a study published in 1995, the British Airline Pilots Association officially voiced its concern that "Airline pilots increasingly lack 'basic flying skills' as a result of reliance on automation."

This reliance on automation translates into a lack of basic flying skills that may affect the pilot's ability to cope with an inflight emergency, such as sudden mechanical failure. The worry that pilots are becoming too reliant on automated systems and are not being encouraged or trained to fly manually has grown with the increase in the number of MFD flight decks.

As automated flight decks began entering everyday line operations, instructors and check airmen grew concerned about some of the unanticipated side effects. Despite the promise of reducing human mistakes, the flight managers reported the automation actually created much larger errors at times. In the terminal environment, the workload in an automated flight deck actually seemed higher than in the older analog flight decks. At other times, the automation seemed to lull the flight crews into complacency. Over time, concern surfaced that the manual flying skills of the automated flight

Figure 17-18. *Electronic flight instrumentation comes in many systems and provides a myriad of information to the pilot.*

crews deteriorated due to over-reliance on computers. The flight crew managers said they worried that pilots would have less "stick-and-rudder" proficiency when those skills were needed to manually resume direct control of the aircraft.

A major study was conducted to evaluate the performance of two groups of pilots. The control group was composed of pilots who flew an older version of a common twin-jet airliner equipped with analog instrumentation and the experimental group was composed of pilots who flew the same aircraft, but newer models equipped with an electronic flight instrument system (EFIS) and a flight management system (FMS). The pilots were evaluated in maintaining aircraft parameters such as heading, altitude, airspeed, glideslope, and localizer deviations, as well as pilot control inputs. These were recorded during a variety of normal, abnormal, and emergency maneuvers during 4 hours of simulator sessions.

Results of the Study

When pilots who had flown EFIS for several years were required to fly various maneuvers manually, the aircraft parameters and flight control inputs clearly showed some erosion of flying skills. During normal maneuvers such as turns to headings without a flight director, the EFIS group exhibited somewhat greater deviations than the analog group. Most of the time, the deviations were within the practical test standards (PTS), but the pilots definitely did not keep on the localizer and glideslope as smoothly as the analog group.

The differences in hand-flying skills between the two groups became more significant during abnormal maneuvers such as slam-dunks. When given close crossing restrictions, the analog crews were more adept at the mental math and usually maneuvered the aircraft in a smoother manner to make the restriction. On the other hand, the EFIS crews tended to go "heads down" and tried to solve the crossing restriction on the FMS. *[Figure 17-19]*

Another situation used in the simulator experiment reflected real world changes in approach that are common and can be assigned on short notice. Once again, the analog crews transitioned more easily to the parallel runway's localizer, whereas the EFIS crews had a much more difficult time, with the pilot going head down for a significant amount of time trying to program the new approach into the FMS.

While a pilot's lack of familiarity with the EFIS is often an issue, the approach would have been made easier by disengaging the automated system and manually flying the approach. At the time of this study, the general guidelines in the industry were to let the automated system do as much of the flying as possible. That view has since changed and it is recommended that pilots use their best judgment when choosing which level of automation will most efficiently do the task considering the workload and situational awareness.

Emergency maneuvers clearly broadened the difference in manual flying skills between the two groups. In general, the analog pilots tended to fly raw data, so when they were given an emergency such as an engine failure and were instructed to fly the maneuver without a flight director, they performed it expertly. By contrast, SOP for EFIS operations at the time was to use the flight director. When EFIS crews had their flight directors disabled, their eye scan again began a more erratic searching pattern and their manual flying subsequently suffered.

Those who reviewed the data saw that the EFIS pilots who better managed the automation also had better flying skills. While the data did not reveal whether those skills preceded or followed automation, it did indicate that automation management needed to be improved. Recommended "best practices" and procedures have remedied some of the earlier problems with automation.

Pilots need to maintain their flight skills and ability to maneuver aircraft manually within the standards set forth in the PTS. It is recommended that pilots of automated aircraft occasionally disengage the automation and manually fly the aircraft to maintain stick-and-rudder proficiency. It is imperative pilots understand that the EFD adds to the overall quality of the flight experience, but it can also lead to catastrophe if not utilized properly. At no time is the moving map meant to substitute for a VFR sectional or low altitude en route chart.

Equipment Use

Autopilot Systems

In a single-pilot environment, an autopilot system can greatly reduce workload. *[Figure 17-20]* As a result, the pilot is free to focus his or her attention on other flight deck duties. This can improve situational awareness and reduce the possibility of a CFIT accident. While the addition of an autopilot may certainly be considered a risk control measure, the real challenge comes in determining the impact of an inoperative unit. If the autopilot is known to be inoperative prior to departure, this may factor into the evaluation other risks.

Figure 17-20. *An example of an autopilot system.*

For example, the pilot may be planning for a VHF omnidirectional range (VOR) approach down to minimums on a dark night into an unfamiliar airport. In such a case, the pilot may have been relying heavily on a functioning autopilot capable of flying a coupled approach. This would free the pilot to monitor aircraft performance. A malfunctioning autopilot could be the single factor that takes this from a medium to a serious risk. At this point, an alternative needs to be considered. On the other hand, if the autopilot were to fail at a critical (high workload) portion of this same flight, the pilot must be prepared to take action. Instead of simply being an inconvenience, this could quickly turn into an emergency if not properly handled. The best way to ensure a pilot is prepared for such an event is to carefully study the issue prior to departure and determine well in advance how an autopilot failure is to be handled.

Familiarity

As previously discussed, pilot familiarity with all equipment is critical in optimizing both safety and efficiency. If a pilot is unfamiliar with any aircraft systems, this will add to workload and may contribute to a loss of situational awareness. This level of proficiency is critical and should be looked upon as a requirement, not unlike carrying an adequate supply of fuel. As a result, pilots should not look upon unfamiliarity with the aircraft and its systems as a risk control measure, but instead as a hazard with high risk potential. Discipline is key to success.

Respect for Onboard Systems

Automation can assist the pilot in many ways, but a thorough understanding of the system(s) in use is essential to gaining the benefits it can offer. Understanding leads to respect which is achieved through discipline and the mastery of the onboard systems. It is important to fly the airplane using minimal information from the primary flight display (PFD). This includes turns, climbs, descents, and being able to fly approaches.

Reinforcement of Onboard Suites

The use of an electronic flight display may not seem intuitive, but competency becomes better with understanding and practice. Computer-based software and incremental training help the pilot become comfortable with the onboard suites. Then the pilot needs to practice what was learned in order to gain experience. Reinforcement not only yields dividends in the use of automation, it also reduces workload significantly.

Getting Beyond Rote Workmanship

The key to working effectively with automation is getting beyond the sequential process of executing an action. If a pilot has to analyze what key to push next, or always uses the same sequence of keystrokes when others are available, he or she may be trapped in a rote process. This mechanical process indicates a shallow understanding of the system. Again, the desire is to become competent and know what to do without having to think about, "what keystroke is next." Operating the system with competency and comprehension benefits a pilot when situations become more diverse and tasks increase.

Understand the Platform

Contrary to popular belief, flight in aircraft equipped with different electronic management suites requires the same attention as aircraft equipped with analog instrumentation and a conventional suite of avionics. The pilot should review and understand the different ways in which EFD are used in a particular aircraft. *[Figure 17-21]*

Two simple rules for use of an EFD:

- Be able to fly the aircraft to the standards in the PTS. Although this may seem insignificant, knowing how to fly the aircraft to a standard makes a pilot's airmanship smoother and allows him or her more time to attend to the system instead of managing multiple tasks.

- Read and understand the installed electronic flight systems manuals to include the use of the autopilot and the other onboard electronic management tools.

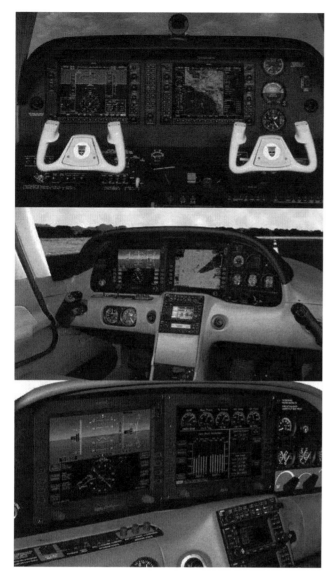

Figure 17-21. *Examples of different platforms. Top to bottom are the Beechcraft Baron G58, Cirrus SR22, and Cirrus Entega.*

Managing Aircraft Automation

Before any pilot can master aircraft automation, he or she must first know how to fly the aircraft. Maneuvers training remains an important component of flight training because almost 40 percent of all GA accidents take place in the landing phase, one realm of flight that still does not involve programming a computer to execute. Another 15 percent of all GA accidents occurs during takeoff and initial climb.

An advanced avionics safety issue identified by the FAA concerns pilots who apparently develop an unwarranted over-reliance in their avionics and the aircraft, believing that the equipment will compensate for pilot shortcomings. Related to the over-reliance is the role of ADM, which is probably the most significant factor in the GA accident record of high performance aircraft used for cross country flight. The FAA

advanced avionics aircraft Safety Study found that poor decision-making seems to afflict new advanced avionics pilots at a rate higher than that of GA as a whole. The review of advanced avionics accidents cited in this study shows the majority are not caused by something directly related to the aircraft, but by the pilot's lack of experience and a chain of poor decisions. One consistent theme in many of the fatal accidents is continued VFR flight into IMC.

Thus, pilot skills for normal and emergency operations hinge not only on mechanical manipulation of the stick and rudder, but also include the mental mastery of the EFD. Three key flight management skills are needed to fly the advanced avionics safely: information, automation, and risk.

Information Management

For the newly transitioning pilot, the PFD, MFD, and GPS/VHF navigator screens seem to offer too much information presented in colorful menus and submenus. In fact, the pilot may be drowning in information but unable to find a specific piece of information. It might be helpful to remember these systems are similar to computers which store some folders on a desktop and some within a hierarchy.

The first critical information management skill for flying with advanced avionics is to understand the system at a conceptual level. Remembering how the system is organized helps the pilot manage the available information. It is important to understanding that learning knob-and-dial procedures is not enough. Learning more about how advanced avionics systems work leads to better memory for procedures and allows pilots to solve problems they have not seen before.

There are also limits to understanding. It is generally impossible to understand all of the behaviors of a complex avionics system. Knowing to expect surprises, and to continually learn new things is more effective than attempting to memorize mechanical manipulation of the knobs. Simulation software and books on the specific system used are of great value.

The second critical information management skill is stop, look, and read. Pilots new to advanced avionics often become fixated on the knobs and try to memorize each and every sequence of button pushes, pulls, and turns. A far better strategy for accessing and managing the information available in advanced avionics computers is to stop, look, and read. Reading before pushing, pulling, or twisting can often save a pilot some trouble.

Once behind the display screens on an advanced avionics aircraft, the pilot's goal is to meter, manage, and prioritize the information flow to accomplish specific tasks. Certificated flight instructors (CFIs) as well as pilots transitioning to advanced avionics will find it helpful to corral the information flow. This is possible through such tactics as configuring the aspects of the PFD and MFD screens according to personal preferences. For example, most systems offer map orientation options that include "north up," "track up," "DTK" (desired track up), and "heading up." Another tactic is to decide, when possible, how much (or how little) information to display. Pilots can also tailor the information displayed to suit the needs of a specific flight.

Information flow can also be managed for a specific operation. The pilot has the ability to prioritize information for a timely display of exactly the information needed for any given flight operation. Examples of managing information display for a specific operation include:

- Program map scale settings for en route versus terminal area operation.

- Utilize the terrain awareness page on the MFD for a night or IMC flight in or near the mountains.

- Use the nearest airports inset on the PFD at night or over inhospitable terrain.

- Program the weather datalink set to show echoes and METAR status flags.

Enhanced Situational Awareness

An advanced avionics aircraft offers increased safety with enhanced situational awareness. Although aircraft flight manuals (AFM) explicitly prohibit using the moving map, topography, terrain awareness, traffic, and weather datalink displays as the primary data source, these tools nonetheless give the pilot unprecedented information for enhanced situational awareness. Without a well-planned information management strategy, these tools also make it easy for an unwary pilot to slide into the complacent role of passenger in command.

Consider the pilot whose navigational information management strategy consists solely of following the magenta line on the moving map. He or she can easily fly into geographic or regulatory disaster, if the straight-line GPS course goes through high terrain or prohibited airspace, or if the moving map display fails.

A good strategy for maintaining situational awareness information management should include practices that help ensure that awareness is enhanced by the use of automation, not diminished. Two basic procedures are to always double-check the system and verbal callouts. At a minimum, ensure the presentation makes sense. Was the correct destination fed into the navigation system? Callouts—even for single-pilot operations—are an excellent way to maintain situational awareness as well as manage information.

Other ways to maintain situational awareness include:

- Perform verification check of all programming. Before departure, check all information programmed while on the ground.

- Check the flight routing. Before departure, ensure all routing matches the planned flight route. Enter the planned route and legs, to include headings and leg length, on a paper log. Use this log to evaluate what has been programmed. If the two do not match, do not assume the computer data is correct, double check the computer entry.

- Verify waypoints.

- Make use of all onboard navigation equipment. For example, use VOR to back up GPS and vice versa.

- Match the use of the automated system with pilot proficiency. Stay within personal limitations.

- Plan a realistic flight route to maintain situational awareness. For example, although the onboard equipment allows a direct flight from Denver, Colorado, to Destin, Florida, the likelihood of rerouting around Eglin Air Force Base's airspace is high.

- Be ready to verify computer data entries. For example, incorrect keystrokes could lead to loss of situational awareness because the pilot may not recognize errors made during a high workload period.

Automation Management

Advanced avionics offer multiple levels of automation, from strictly manual flight to highly automated flight. No one level of automation is appropriate for all flight situations, but in order to avoid potentially dangerous distractions when flying with advanced avionics, the pilot must know how to manage the course deviation indicator (CDI), the navigation source, and the autopilot. It is important for a pilot to know the peculiarities of the particular automated system being used. This ensures the pilot knows what to expect, how to monitor for proper operation, and promptly take appropriate action if the system does not perform as expected.

For example, at the most basic level, managing the autopilot means knowing at all times which modes are engaged and which modes are armed to engage. The pilot needs to verify that armed functions (e.g., navigation tracking or altitude capture) engage at the appropriate time. Automation management is another good place to practice the callout technique, especially after arming the system to make a change in course or altitude.

In advanced avionics aircraft, proper automation management also requires a thorough understanding of how the autopilot interacts with the other systems. For example, with some autopilots, changing the navigation source on the e-HSI from GPS to LOC or VOR while the autopilot is engaged in NAV (course tracking mode) will cause the autopilot's NAV mode to disengage. The autopilot's lateral control will default to ROL (wing level) until the pilot takes action to reengage the NAV mode to track the desired navigation source.

Risk Management

Risk management is the last of the three flight management skills needed for mastery of the glass flight deck aircraft. The enhanced situational awareness and automation capabilities offered by a glass flight deck airplane vastly expand its safety and utility, especially for personal transportation use. At the same time, there is some risk that lighter workloads could lead to complacency.

Humans are characteristically poor monitors of automated systems. When asked to passively monitor an automated system for faults, abnormalities, or other infrequent events, humans perform poorly. The more reliable the system, the poorer the human performance. For example, the pilot only monitors a backup alert system, rather than the situation that the alert system is designed to safeguard. It is a paradox of automation that technically advanced avionics can both increase and decrease pilot awareness.

It is important to remember that electronic flight displays do not replace basic flight knowledge and skills. They are a tool for improving flight safety. Risk increases when the pilot believes the gadgets will compensate for lack of skill and knowledge. It is especially important to recognize there are limits to what the electronic systems in any light GA aircraft can do. Being PIC requires sound ADM which sometimes means saying "no" to a flight.

Risk is also increased when the pilot fails to monitor the systems. By failing to monitor the systems and failing to check the results of the processes, the pilot becomes detached from the aircraft operation and slides into the complacent role of passenger in command. Complacency led to tragedy in a 1999 aircraft accident.

In Colombia, a multi-engine aircraft crewed with two pilots struck the face of the Andes Mountains. Examination of their FMS revealed they entered a waypoint into the FMS incorrectly by one degree resulting in a flightpath taking them to a point 60 NM off their intended course. The pilots were equipped with the proper charts, their route was posted on the charts, and they had a paper navigation log indicating the direction of each leg. They had all the tools to manage and monitor their flight, but instead allowed the automation to fly and manage itself. The system did exactly what it was programmed to do; it flew on a programmed course into a mountain resulting in multiple deaths. The pilots simply failed to manage the system and inherently created their own hazard. Although this hazard was self-induced, what is notable is the risk the pilots created through their own inattention. By failing to evaluate each turn made at the direction of automation, the pilots maximized risk instead of minimizing it. In this case, a totally avoidable accident become a tragedy through simple pilot error and complacency.

For the GA pilot transitioning to automated systems, it is helpful to note that all human activity involving technical devices entails some element of risk. Knowledge, experience, and mission requirements tilt the odds in favor of safe and successful flights. The advanced avionics aircraft offers many new capabilities and simplifies the basic flying tasks, but only if the pilot is properly trained and all the equipment is working as advertised.

Chapter Summary

This chapter focused on helping the pilot improve his or her ADM skills with the goal of mitigating the risk factors associated with flight in both classic and automated aircraft. In the end, the discussion is not so much about aircraft, but about the people who fly them.

Appendix

Short Field Takeoff Distance at 2,450 Pounds for a Cessna Model 172R

CONDITIONS:

Flaps 10°
Full Throttle Prior to Brake Release
Paved, level, dry runway
Zero Wind
Lift Off: 51 KIAS
Speed at 50 Ft: 57 KIAS

Press Alt In Feet	0°C		10°C		20°C		30°C		40°C	
	Grnd Roll Ft	Total Ft To Clear 50 Ft Obst	Grnd Roll Ft	Total Ft To Clear 50 Ft Obst	Grnd Roll Ft	Total Ft To Clear 50 Ft Obst	Grnd Roll Ft	Total Ft To Clear 50 Ft Obst	Grnd Roll Ft	Total Ft To Clear 50 Ft Obst
S. L.	845	1510	910	1625	980	1745	1055	1875	1135	2015
1000	925	1660	1000	1790	1075	1925	1160	2070	1245	2220
2000	1015	1830	1095	1970	1185	2125	1275	2290	1365	2455
3000	1115	2020	1205	2185	1305	2360	1400	2540	1505	2730
4000	1230	2245	1330	2430	1435	2630	1545	2830	1655	3045
5000	1355	2500	1470	2715	1585	2945	1705	3175	1830	3430
6000	1500	2805	1625	3060	1750	3315	1880	3590	2020	3895
7000	1660	3170	1795	3470	1935	3770	2085	4105	2240	4485
8000	1840	3620	1995	3975	2150	4345	2315	4775	---	---

NOTES:

1. Short field technique as specified in Section 4.
2. Prior to takeoff from fields above 3000 feet elevation, the mixture should be leaned to give maximum RPM in a full throttle, static runup.
3. Decrease distances 10% for each 9 knots headwind. For operation with tail winds up to 10 knots, increase distances by 10% for each 2 knots.
4. For operation on dry, grass runway, increase distances by 15% of the "ground roll" figure.
5. Where distance value has been deleted, climb performance is minimal.

Time, Fuel, and Distance to Climb at 2,450 Pounds for a Cessna Model 172R

CONDITIONS:

Flaps Up
Full Throttle
Standard Temperature

PRESS ALT FT	TEMP °C	CLIMB SPEED KIAS	RATE OF CLIMB FPM	FROM SEA LEVEL		
				TIME IN MIN	FUEL USED GAL	DIST NM
S.L.	15	79	720	0	0.0	0
1000	13	78	670	1	0.4	2
2000	11	77	625	3	0.7	4
3000	9	76	575	5	1.2	6
4000	7	76	560	6	1.5	8
5000	5	75	515	8	1.8	11
6000	3	74	465	10	2.1	14
7000	1	73	415	13	2.5	17
8000	-1	72	365	15	3.0	21
9000	-3	72	315	18	3.4	25
10,000	-5	71	270	22	4.0	29
11,000	-7	70	220	26	4.6	35
12,000	-9	69	170	31	5.4	43

NOTES:

1. Add 1.1 gallons of fuel for engine start, taxi and takeoff allowance.
2. Mixture leaned above 3000 feet for maximum RPM.
3. Increase time, fuel and distance by 10% for each 10°C above standard temperature.
4. Distances shown are based on zero wind.

Cruise Performance for a Cessna Model 172R

CONDITIONS:
2450 Pounds
Recommended Lean Mixture At All Altitudes (Refer to Section 4, Cruise)

PRESS ALT FT	RPM	20°C BELOW STANDARD TEMP			STANDARD TEMPERATURE			20°C ABOVE STANDARD TEMP		
		% BHP	KTAS	GPH	% BHP	KTAS	GPH	% BHP	KTAS	GPH
2000	2250	---	---	---	79	115	9.0	74	114	8.5
	2200	79	112	9.1	74	112	8.5	70	111	8.0
	2100	69	107	7.9	65	106	7.5	62	105	7.1
	2000	61	101	7.0	58	99	6.6	55	97	6.4
	1900	54	94	6.2	51	91	5.9	50	89	5.8
4000	2300	--	---	---	79	117	9.1	75	117	8.6
	2250	80	115	9.2	75	114	8.6	70	114	8.1
	2200	75	112	8.6	70	111	8.1	66	110	7.6
	2100	66	106	7.6	62	105	7.1	59	103	6.8
	2000	58	100	6.7	55	98	6.4	53	95	6.2
	1900	52	92	6.0	50	90	5.8	49	87	5.6
6000	2350	--	---	---	80	120	9.2	75	119	8.6
	2300	80	117	9.2	75	117	8.6	71	116	8.1
	2250	76	115	8.7	71	114	8.1	67	113	7.7
	2200	71	112	8.1	67	111	7.7	64	109	7.3
	2100	63	105	7.2	60	104	6.9	57	101	6.6
	2000	56	98	6.4	53	96	6.2	52	93	6.0

NOTE:

1. Cruise speeds are shown for an airplane equipped with speed fairings. Without speed fairings, decrease speeds shown by 2 knots.

Short Field Landing Distance at 2,450 Pounds for a Cessna Model 172R

CONDITIONS:

Flaps 30°
Power Off
Maximum Braking
Paved, level, dry runway
Zero Wind
Speed at 50 Ft: 62 KIAS

Press Alt In Feet	0°C		10°C		20°C		30°C		40°C	
	Grnd Roll Ft	Total Ft To Clear 50 Ft Obst	Grnd Roll Ft	Total Ft To Clear 50 Ft Obst	Grnd Roll Ft	Total Ft To Clear 50 Ft Obst	Grnd Roll Ft	Total Ft To Clear 50 Ft Obst	Grnd Roll Ft	Total Ft To Clear 50 Ft Obst
S. L.	525	1250	540	1280	560	1310	580	1340	600	1370
1000	545	1280	560	1310	580	1345	600	1375	620	1405
2000	565	1310	585	1345	605	1375	625	1410	645	1440
3000	585	1345	605	1380	625	1415	650	1445	670	1480
4000	605	1380	630	1415	650	1450	670	1485	695	1520
5000	630	1415	650	1455	675	1490	700	1525	720	1560
6000	655	1455	675	1490	700	1530	725	1565	750	1605
7000	680	1495	705	1535	730	1570	755	1610	775	1650
8000	705	1535	730	1575	755	1615	780	1655	810	1695

NOTES:

1. Short field technique as specified in Section 4.
2. Decrease distances 10% for each 9 knots headwind. For operation with tail winds up to 10 knots, increase distances by 10% for each 2 knots.
3. For operation on dry, grass runway, increase distances by 45% of the "ground roll" figure.
4. If landing with flaps up, increase the approach speed by 7 KIAS and allow for 35% longer distances.

Challenger 605 Range/Payload Profile

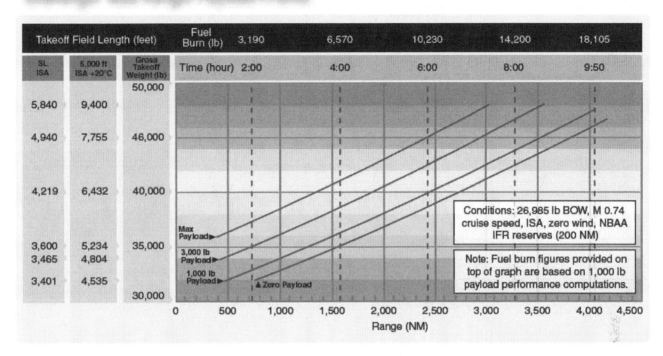

Takeoff Field Length (feet)		Fuel Burn (lb)	3,190	6,570	10,230	14,200	18,105
SL ISA	5,000 ft ISA +20°C	Gross Takeoff Weight (lb)	Time (hour) 2:00	4:00	6:00	8:00	9:50
		50,000					
5,840	9,400						
4,940	7,755	46,000					
4,219	6,432	40,000					
3,600	5,234	35,000					
3,465	4,804						
3,401	4,535						
		30,000					

Max Payload▶

3,000 lb Payload▶

1,000 lb Payload▶

▲ Zero Payload

Conditions: 26,985 lb BOW, M 0.74 cruise speed, ISA, zero wind, NBAA IFR reserves (200 NM)

Note: Fuel burn figures provided on top of graph are based on 1,000 lb payload performance computations.

Range (NM): 0   500   1,000   1,500   2,000   2,500   3,000   3,500   4,000   4,500

Challenger 605 Time and Fuel Versus Distance

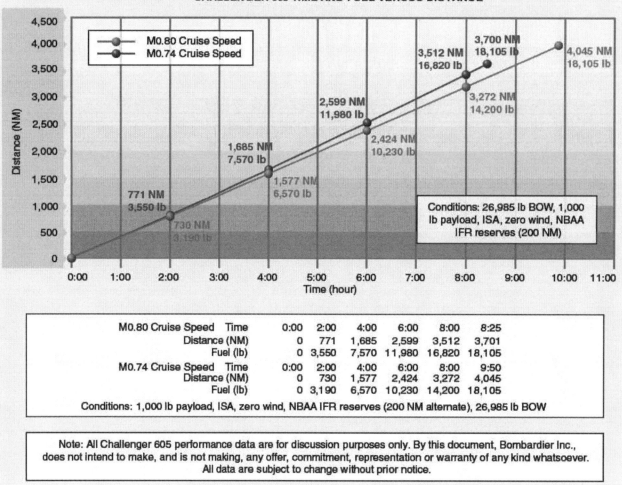

CHALLENGER 605 TIME AND FUEL VERSUS DISTANCE

M0.80 Cruise Speed	Time	0:00	2:00	4:00	6:00	8:00	8:25
	Distance (NM)	0	771	1,685	2,599	3,512	3,701
	Fuel (lb)	0	3,550	7,570	11,980	16,820	18,105
M0.74 Cruise Speed	Time	0:00	2:00	4:00	6:00	8:00	9:50
	Distance (NM)	0	730	1,577	2,424	3,272	4,045
	Fuel (lb)	0	3,190	6,570	10,230	14,200	18,105

Conditions: 1,000 lb payload, ISA, zero wind, NBAA IFR reserves (200 NM alternate), 26,985 lb BOW

Note: All Challenger 605 performance data are for discussion purposes only. By this document, Bombardier Inc., does not intend to make, and is not making, any offer, commitment, representation or warranty of any kind whatsoever. All data are subject to change without prior notice.

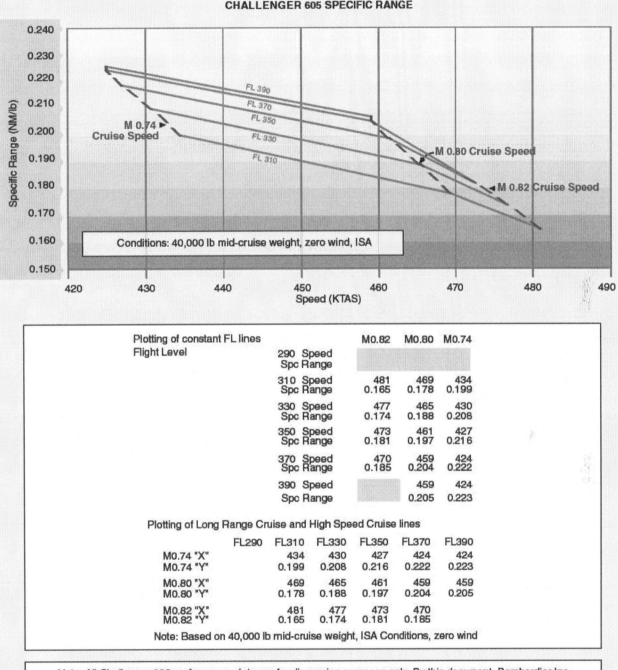

CHALLENGER 605 SPECIFIC RANGE

Conditions: 40,000 lb mid-cruise weight, zero wind, ISA

Plotting of constant FL lines

Flight Level			M0.82	M0.80	M0.74
290	Speed				
	Spc Range				
310	Speed		481	469	434
	Spc Range		0.165	0.178	0.199
330	Speed		477	465	430
	Spc Range		0.174	0.188	0.208
350	Speed		473	461	427
	Spc Range		0.181	0.197	0.216
370	Speed		470	459	424
	Spc Range		0.185	0.204	0.222
390	Speed			459	424
	Spc Range			0.205	0.223

Plotting of Long Range Cruise and High Speed Cruise lines

	FL290	FL310	FL330	FL350	FL370	FL390
M0.74 "X"		434	430	427	424	424
M0.74 "Y"		0.199	0.208	0.216	0.222	0.223
M0.80 "X"		469	465	461	459	459
M0.80 "Y"		0.178	0.188	0.197	0.204	0.205
M0.82 "X"		481	477	473	470	
M0.82 "Y"		0.165	0.174	0.181	0.185	

Note: Based on 40,000 lb mid-cruise weight, ISA Conditions, zero wind

Note: All Challenger 605 performance data are for discussion purposes only. By this document, Bombardier Inc., does not intend to make, and is not making, any offer, commitment, representation or warranty of any kind whatsoever. All data are subject to change without prior notice.

Glossary

14 CFR. See Title 14 of the Code of Federal Regulations.

100-hour inspection. An inspection identical in scope to an annual inspection. Conducted every 100 hours of flight on aircraft of under 12,500 pounds that are used to carry passengers for hire.

Absolute accuracy. The ability to determine present position in space independently, and is most often used by pilots.

Absolute altitude. The actual distance between an aircraft and the terrain over which it is flying.

Absolute pressure. Pressure measured from the reference of zero pressure, or a vacuum.

A.C. Alternating current.

Acceleration. Force involved in overcoming inertia, and which may be defined as a change in velocity per unit of time.

Acceleration error. A magnetic compass error apparent when the aircraft accelerates while flying on an easterly or westerly heading, causing the compass card to rotate toward North.

Accelerate-go distance. The distance required to accelerate to V_1 with all engines at takeoff power, experience an engine failure at V_1, and continue the takeoff on the remaining engine(s). The runway required includes the distance required to climb to 35 feet by which time V_2 speed must be attained.

Accelerate-stop distance. The distance required to accelerate to V_1 with all engines at takeoff power, experience an engine failure at V_1, and abort the takeoff and bring the airplane to a stop using braking action only (use of thrust reversing is not considered).

Accelerometer. A part of an inertial navigation system (INS) that accurately measures the force of acceleration in one direction.

ADC. See air data computer.

ADF. See automatic direction finder.

ADI. See attitude director indicator.

Adiabatic cooling. A process of cooling the air through expansion. For example, as air moves up slope it expands with the reduction of atmospheric pressure and cools as it expands.

Adiabatic heating. A process of heating dry air through compression. For example, as air moves down a slope it is compressed, which results in an increase in temperature.

Adjustable-pitch propeller. A propeller with blades whose pitch can be adjusted on the ground with the engine not running, but which cannot be adjusted in flight. Also referred to as a ground adjustable propeller. Sometimes also used to refer to constant-speed propellers that are adjustable in flight.

Adjustable stabilizer. A stabilizer that can be adjusted in flight to trim the airplane, thereby allowing the airplane to fly hands-off at any given airspeed.

ADM. See aeronautical decision-making.

ADS-B. See automatic dependent surveillance-broadcast.

Advection fog. Fog resulting from the movement of warm, humid air over a cold surface.

Adverse yaw. A condition of flight in which the nose of an airplane tends to yaw toward the outside of the turn. This is caused by the higher induced drag on the outside wing, which is also producing more lift. Induced drag is a by-product of the lift associated with the outside wing.

Aerodynamics. The science of the action of air on an object, and with the motion of air on other gases. Aerodynamics deals with the production of lift by the aircraft, the relative wind, and the atmosphere.

Aeronautical chart. A map used in air navigation containing all or part of the following: topographic features, hazards and obstructions, navigation aids, navigation routes, designated airspace, and airports.

Aeronautical decision-making (ADM). A systematic approach to the mental process used by pilots to consistently determine the best course of action in response to a given set of circumstances.

A/FD. See Airport/Facility Directory.

Agonic line. An irregular imaginary line across the surface of the Earth along which the magnetic and geographic poles are in alignment, and along which there is no magnetic variation.

Ailerons. Primary flight control surfaces mounted on the trailing edge of an airplane wing, near the tip. Ailerons control roll about the longitudinal axis.

Aircraft. A device that is used, or intended to be used, for flight.

Aircraft altitude. The actual height above sea level at which the aircraft is flying.

Aircraft approach category. A performance grouping of aircraft based on a speed of 1.3 times the stall speed in the landing configuration at maximum gross landing weight.

Air data computer (ADC). An aircraft computer that receives and processes pitot pressure, static pressure, and temperature to calculate very precise altitude, indicated airspeed, true airspeed, and air temperature.

Airfoil. Any surface, such as a wing, propeller, rudder, or even a trim tab, which provides aerodynamic force when it interacts with a moving stream of air.

Air mass. An extensive body of air having fairly uniform properties of temperature and moisture.

AIRMET. Inflight weather advisory issued as an amendment to the area forecast, concerning weather phenomena of operational interest to all aircraft and that is potentially hazardous to aircraft with limited capability due to lack of equipment, instrumentation, or pilot qualifications.

Airplane. An engine-driven, fixed-wing aircraft heavier than air that is supported in flight by the dynamic reaction of air against its wings.

Airplane Flight Manual (AFM). A document developed by the airplane manufacturer and approved by the Federal Aviation Administration (FAA). It is specific to a particular make and model airplane by serial number and it contains operating procedures and limitations.

Airplane Owner/Information Manual. A document developed by the airplane manufacturer containing general information about the make and model of an airplane. The airplane owner's manual is not FAA approved and is not specific to a particular serial numbered airplane. This manual is not kept current, and therefore cannot be substituted for the AFM/POH.

Airport diagram. The section of an instrument approach procedure chart that shows a detailed diagram of the airport. This diagram includes surface features and airport configuration information.

Airport/Facility Directory (A/FD). An FAA publication containing information on all airports, communications, and NAVAIDs.

Airport surface detection equipment (ASDE). Radar equipment specifically designed to detect all principal features and traffic on the surface of an airport, presenting the entire image on the control tower console; used to augment visual observation by tower personnel of aircraft and/or vehicular movements on runways and taxiways.

Airport surveillance radar (ASR). Approach control radar used to detect and display an aircraft's position in the terminal area.

Airport surveillance radar approach. An instrument approach in which ATC issues instructions for pilot compliance based on aircraft position in relation to the final approach course and the distance from the end of the runway as displayed on the controller's radar scope.

Air route surveillance radar (ARSR). Air route traffic control center (ARTCC) radar used primarily to detect and display an aircraft's position while en route between terminal areas.

Air route traffic control center (ARTCC). Provides ATC service to aircraft operating on IFR flight plans within controlled airspace and principally during the en route phase of flight.

Airspeed. Rate of the aircraft's progress through the air.

Airspeed indicator. A differential pressure gauge that measures the dynamic pressure of the air through which the aircraft is flying. Displays the craft's airspeed, typically in knots, to the pilot.

Air traffic control radar beacon system (ATCRBS). Sometimes called secondary surveillance radar (SSR), which utilizes a transponder in the aircraft. The ground equipment is an interrogating unit, in which the beacon antenna is mounted so it rotates with the surveillance antenna. The interrogating unit transmits a coded pulse sequence that actuates the aircraft transponder. The transponder answers the coded sequence by transmitting a preselected coded sequence back to the ground equipment, providing a strong return signal and positive aircraft identification, as well as other special data.

Airway. An airway is based on a centerline that extends from one navigation aid or intersection to another navigation aid (or through several navigation aids or intersections); used to establish a known route for en route procedures between terminal areas.

Airworthiness Certificate. A certificate issued by the FAA to all aircraft that have been proven to meet the minimum standards set down by the Code of Federal Regulations.

Airworthiness Directive. A regulatory notice sent out by the FAA to the registered owner of an aircraft informing the owner of a condition that prevents the aircraft from continuing to meet its conditions for airworthiness. Airworthiness Directives (AD notes) are to be complied with within the required time limit, and the fact of compliance, the date of compliance, and the method of compliance are recorded in the aircraft's maintenance records.

Alert area. An area in which there is a high volume of pilot training or an unusual type of aeronautical activity.

Almanac data. Information the global positioning system (GPS) receiver can obtain from one satellite which describes the approximate orbital positioning of all satellites in the constellation. This information is necessary for the GPS receiver to know what satellites to look for in the sky at a given time.

ALS. See approach lighting system.

Alternate airport. An airport designated in an IFR flight plan, providing a suitable destination if a landing at the intended airport becomes inadvisable.

Alternate static source valve. A valve in the instrument static air system that supplies reference air pressure to the altimeter, airspeed indicator, and vertical speed indicator if the normal static pickup should become clogged or iced over.

Altimeter. A flight instrument that indicates altitude by sensing pressure changes.

Altimeter setting. Station pressure (the barometric pressure at the location the reading is taken) which has been corrected for the height of the station above sea level.

Altitude engine. A reciprocating aircraft engine having a rated takeoff power that is producible from sea level to an established higher altitude.

Ambient pressure. The pressure in the area immediately surrounding the aircraft.

Ambient temperature. The temperature in the area immediately surrounding the aircraft.

AME. See aviation medical examiner.

Amendment status. The circulation date and revision number of an instrument approach procedure, printed above the procedure identification.

Ammeter. An instrument installed in series with an electrical load used to measure the amount of current flowing through the load.

Aneroid. The sensitive component in an altimeter or barometer that measures the absolute pressure of the air. It is a sealed, flat capsule made of thin disks of corrugated metal soldered together and evacuated by pumping all of the air out of it.

Aneroid barometer. An instrument that measures the absolute pressure of the atmosphere by balancing the weight of the air above it against the spring action of the aneroid.

Angle of attack. The acute angle formed between the chord line of an airfoil and the direction of the air striking the airfoil.

Angle of incidence. The angle formed by the chord line of the wing and a line parallel to the longitudinal axis of the airplane.

Anhedral. A downward slant from root to tip of an aircraft's wing or horizontal tail surface.

Annual inspection. A complete inspection of an aircraft and engine, required by the Code of Federal Regulations, to be accomplished every 12 calendar months on all certificated aircraft. Only an A&P technician holding an Inspection Authorization can conduct an annual inspection.

Anti-ice. Preventing the accumulation of ice on an aircraft structure via a system designed for that purpose.

Antiservo tab. An adjustable tab attached to the trailing edge of a stabilator that moves in the same direction as the primary control. It is used to make the stabilator less sensitive.

Approach lighting system (ALS). Provides lights that will penetrate the atmosphere far enough from touchdown to give directional, distance, and glidepath information for safe transition from instrument to visual flight.

Area chart. Part of the low-altitude en route chart series, this chart furnishes terminal data at a larger scale for congested areas.

Area forecast (FA). A report that gives a picture of clouds, general weather conditions, and visual meteorological conditions (VMC) expected over a large area encompassing several states.

Area navigation (RNAV). Allows a pilot to fly a selected course to a predetermined point without the need to overfly ground-based navigation facilities, by using waypoints.

Arm. See moment arm.

ARSR. See air route surveillance radar.

ARTCC. See air route traffic control center.

ASDE. See airport surface detection equipment.

ASOS. See Automated Surface Observing System.

Aspect ratio. Span of a wing divided by its average chord.

ASR. See airport surveillance radar.

Asymmetric thrust. Also known as P-factor. A tendency for an aircraft to yaw to the left due to the descending propeller blade on the right producing more thrust than the ascending blade on the left. This occurs when the aircraft's longitudinal axis is in a climbing attitude in relation to the relative wind.

The P-factor would be to the right if the aircraft had a counterclockwise rotating propeller.

ATC. Air Traffic Control.

ATCRBS. See air traffic control radar beacon system.

ATIS. See automatic terminal information service.

Atmospheric propagation delay. A bending of the electromagnetic (EM) wave from the satellite that creates an error in the GPS system.

Attitude. A personal motivational predisposition to respond to persons, situations, or events in a given manner that can, nevertheless, be changed or modified through training as sort of a mental shortcut to decision-making.

Attitude and heading reference system (AHRS). A system composed of three-axis sensors that provide heading, attitude, and yaw information for aircraft. AHRS are designed to replace traditional mechanical gyroscopic flight instruments and provide superior reliability and accuracy.

Attitude director indicator (ADI). An aircraft attitude indicator that incorporates flight command bars to provide pitch and roll commands.

Attitude indicator. The foundation for all instrument flight, this instrument reflects the airplane's attitude in relation to the horizon.

Attitude instrument flying. Controlling the aircraft by reference to the instruments rather than by outside visual cues.

Attitude management. The ability to recognize hazardous attitudes in oneself and the willingness to modify them as necessary through the application of an appropriate antidote thought.

Autokinesis. Nighttime visual illusion that a stationary light is moving, which becomes apparent after several seconds of staring at the light.

Automated Surface Observing System (ASOS). Weather reporting system which provides surface observations every minute via digitized voice broadcasts and printed reports.

Automated Weather Observing System (AWOS). Automated weather reporting system consisting of various sensors, a processor, a computer-generated voice subsystem, and a transmitter to broadcast weather data.

Automatic dependent surveillance—broadcast (ADS-B). A device used in aircraft that repeatedly broadcasts a message that includes position (such as latitude, longitude, and altitude), velocity, and possibly other information.

Automatic direction finder (ADF). Electronic navigation equipment that operates in the low- and medium-frequency bands. Used in conjunction with the ground-based nondirectional beacon (NDB), the instrument displays the number of degrees clockwise from the nose of the aircraft to the station being received.

Automatic terminal information service (ATIS). The continuous broadcast of recorded non-control information in selected terminal areas. Its purpose is to improve controller effectiveness and relieve frequency congestion by automating repetitive transmission of essential but routine information.

Autopilot. An automatic flight control system which keeps an aircraft in level flight or on a set course. Automatic pilots can be directed by the pilot, or they may be coupled to a radio navigation signal.

Aviation medical examiner (AME). A physician with training in aviation medicine designated by the Civil Aerospace Medical Institute (CAMI).

Aviation Routine Weather Report (METAR). Observation of current surface weather reported in a standard international format.

AWOS. See Automated Weather Observing System.

Axes of an aircraft. Three imaginary lines that pass through an aircraft's center of gravity. The axes can be considered as imaginary axles around which the aircraft rotates. The three axes pass through the center of gravity at 90° angles to each other. The axis from nose to tail is the longitudinal axis (pitch), the axis that passes from wingtip to wingtip is the lateral axis (roll), and the axis that passes vertically through the center of gravity is the vertical axis (yaw).

Axial flow compressor. A type of compressor used in a turbine engine in which the airflow through the compressor is essentially linear. An axial-flow compressor is made up of several stages of alternate rotors and stators. The compressor ratio is determined by the decrease in area of the succeeding stages.

Azimuth card. A card that may be set, gyroscopically controlled, or driven by a remote compass.

Back course (BC). The reciprocal of the localizer course for an ILS. When flying a back-course approach, an aircraft approaches the instrument runway from the end at which the localizer antennas are installed.

Balance tab. An auxiliary control mounted on a primary control surface, which automatically moves in the direction opposite the primary control to provide an aerodynamic assist in the movement of the control. Sometimes referred to as a servo tab.

Baro-aiding. A method of augmenting the GPS integrity solution by using a nonsatellite input source. To ensure that baro-aiding is available, the current altimeter setting must be entered as described in the operating manual.

Barometric scale. A scale on the dial of an altimeter to which the pilot sets the barometric pressure level from which the altitude shown by the pointers is measured.

Basic empty weight (GAMA). Basic empty weight includes the standard empty weight plus optional and special equipment that has been installed.

BC. See back course.

Bernoulli's Principle. A principle that explains how the pressure of a moving fluid varies with its speed of motion. An increase in the speed of movement causes a decrease in the fluid's pressure.

Biplanes. Airplanes with two sets of wings.

Block altitude. A block of altitudes assigned by ATC to allow altitude deviations; for example, "Maintain block altitude 9 to 11 thousand."

Bypass ratio. The ratio of the mass airflow in pounds per second through the fan section of a turbofan engine to the mass airflow that passes through the gas generator portion of the engine.

Cabin altitude. Cabin pressure in terms of equivalent altitude above sea level.

Cage. The black markings on the ball instrument indicating its neutral position.

Calibrated. The instrument indication compared with a standard value to determine the accuracy of the instrument.

Calibrated orifice. A hole of specific diameter used to delay the pressure change in the case of a vertical speed indicator.

Calibrated airspeed. The speed at which the aircraft is moving through the air, found by correcting IAS for instrument and position errors.

Camber. The camber of an airfoil is the characteristic curve of its upper and lower surfaces. The upper camber is more pronounced, while the lower camber is comparatively flat. This causes the velocity of the airflow immediately above the wing to be much higher than that below the wing.

Canard. A horizontal surface mounted ahead of the main wing to provide longitudinal stability and control. It may be a fixed, movable, or variable geometry surface, with or without control surfaces.

Canard configuration. A configuration in which the span of the forward wings is substantially less than that of the main wing.

Cantilever. A wing designed to carry loads without external struts.

CAS. Calibrated airspeed.

CDI. Course deviation indicator.

Ceiling. The height above the earth's surface of the lowest layer of clouds, which is reported as broken or overcast, or the vertical visibility into an obscuration.

Center of gravity (CG). The point at which an airplane would balance if it were possible to suspend it at that point. It is the mass center of the airplane, or the theoretical point at which the entire weight of the airplane is assumed to be concentrated. It may be expressed in inches from the reference datum, or in percentage of mean aerodynamic chord (MAC). The location depends on the distribution of weight in the airplane.

Center of gravity limits. The specified forward and aft points within which the CG must be located during flight. These limits are indicated on pertinent airplane specifications.

Center of gravity range. The distance between the forward and aft CG limits indicated on pertinent airplane specifications.

Center of pressure. A point along the wing chord line where lift is considered to be concentrated. For this reason, the center of pressure is commonly referred to as the center of lift.

Centrifugal flow compressor. An impeller-shaped device that receives air at its center and slings the air outward at high velocity into a diffuser for increased pressure. Also referred to as a radial outflow compressor.

Centrifugal force. An outward force, that opposes centripetal force, resulting from the effect of inertia during a turn.

Centripetal force. A center-seeking force directed inward toward the center of rotation created by the horizontal component of lift in turning flight.

CG. See center of gravity.

Changeover point (COP). A point along the route or airway segment between two adjacent navigation facilities or waypoints where changeover in navigation guidance should occur.

Checklist. A tool that is used as a human factors aid in aviation safety. It is a systematic and sequential list of all operations that must be performed to properly accomplish a task.

Chord line. An imaginary straight line drawn through an airfoil from the leading edge to the trailing edge.

Circling approach. A maneuver initiated by the pilot to align the aircraft with a runway for landing when a straight-in landing from an instrument approach is not possible or is not desirable.

Class A airspace. Airspace from 18,000 feet MSL up to and including FL 600, including the airspace overlying the waters within 12 NM of the coast of the 48 contiguous states and Alaska; and designated international airspace beyond 12 NM of the coast of the 48 contiguous states and Alaska within areas of domestic radio navigational signal or ATC radar coverage, and within which domestic procedures are applied.

Class B airspace. Airspace from the surface to 10,000 feet MSL surrounding the nation's busiest airports in terms of IFR operations or passenger numbers. The configuration of each Class B airspace is individually tailored and consists of a surface area and two or more layers, and is designed to contain all published instrument procedures once an aircraft enters the airspace. For all aircraft, an ATC clearance is required to operate in the area, and aircraft so cleared receive separation services within the airspace.

Class C airspace. Airspace from the surface to 4,000 feet above the airport elevation (charted in MSL) surrounding those airports having an operational control tower, serviced by radar approach control, and having a certain number of IFR operations or passenger numbers. Although the configuration of each Class C airspace area is individually tailored, the airspace usually consists of a 5 NM radius core surface area that extends from the surface up to 4,000 feet above the airport elevation, and a 10 NM radius shelf area that extends from 1,200 feet to 4,000 feet above the airport elevation.

Class D airspace. Airspace from the surface to 2,500 feet above the airport elevation (charted in MSL) surrounding those airports that have an operational control tower. The configuration of each Class D airspace area is individually tailored, and when instrument procedures are published, the airspace is normally designed to contain the procedures.

Class E airspace. Airspace that is not Class A, Class B, Class C, or Class D, and is controlled airspace.

Class G airspace. Airspace that is uncontrolled, except when associated with a temporary control tower, and has not been designated as Class A, Class B, Class C, Class D, or Class E airspace.

Clean configuration. A configuration in which all flight control surfaces have been placed to create minimum drag. In most aircraft this means flaps and gear retracted.

Clearance. ATC permission for an aircraft to proceed under specified traffic conditions within controlled airspace, for the purpose of providing separation between known aircraft.

Clearance delivery. Control tower position responsible for transmitting departure clearances to IFR flights.

Clearance limit. The fix, point, or location to which an aircraft is cleared when issued an air traffic clearance.

Clearance on request. An IFR clearance not yet received after filing a flight plan.

Clearance void time. Used by ATC, the time at which the departure clearance is automatically canceled if takeoff has not been made. The pilot must obtain a new clearance or cancel the IFR flight plan if not off by the specified time.

Clear ice. Glossy, clear, or translucent ice formed by the relatively slow freezing of large, supercooled water droplets.

Coefficient of lift. The ratio between lift pressure and dynamic pressure.

Cold front. The boundary between two air masses where cold air is replacing warm air.

Compass course. A true course corrected for variation and deviation errors.

Compass locator. A low-power, low- or medium-frequency (L/MF) radio beacon installed at the site of the outer or middle marker of an ILS.

Compass rose. A small circle graduated in 360° increments, to show direction expressed in degrees.

Complex aircraft. An aircraft with retractable landing gear, flaps, and a controllable pitch propeller.

Compressor pressure ratio. The ratio of compressor discharge pressure to compressor inlet pressure.

Compressor stall. In gas turbine engines, a condition in an axial-flow compressor in which one or more stages of rotor blades fail to pass air smoothly to the succeeding stages. A stall condition is caused by a pressure ratio that is incompatible with the engine rpm. Compressor stall will be indicated by a rise in exhaust temperature or rpm fluctuation, and if allowed to continue, may result in flameout and physical damage to the engine.

Computer navigation fix. A point used to define a navigation track for an airborne computer system such as GPS or FMS.

Concentric rings. Dashed-line circles depicted in the plan view of IAP charts, outside of the reference circle, that show en route and feeder facilities.

Condensation. A change of state of water from a gas (water vapor) to a liquid.

Condensation nuclei. Small particles of solid matter in the air on which water vapor condenses.

Cone of confusion. A cone-shaped volume of airspace directly above a VOR station where no signal is received, causing the CDI to fluctuate.

Configuration. This is a general term, which normally refers to the position of the landing gear and flaps.

Constant-speed propeller. A controllable-pitch propeller whose pitch is automatically varied in flight by a governor to maintain a constant rpm in spite of varying air loads.

Continuous flow oxygen system. System that supplies a constant supply of pure oxygen to a rebreather bag that dilutes the pure oxygen with exhaled gases and thus supplies a healthy mix of oxygen and ambient air to the mask. Primarily used in passenger cabins of commercial airliners.

Control and performance. A method of attitude instrument flying in which one instrument is used for making attitude changes, and the other instruments are used to monitor the progress of the change.

Control display unit. A display interfaced with the master computer, providing the pilot with a single control point for all navigations systems, thereby reducing the number of required flight deck panels.

Controllability. A measure of the response of an aircraft relative to the pilot's flight control inputs.

Controlled airspace. An airspace of defined dimensions within which ATC service is provided to IFR and VFR flights in accordance with the airspace classification. It includes Class A, Class B, Class C, Class D, and Class E airspace.

Control pressures. The amount of physical exertion on the control column necessary to achieve the desired attitude.

Convective weather. Unstable, rising air found in cumiliform clouds.

Convective SIGMET. Weather advisory concerning convective weather significant to the safety of all aircraft, including thunderstorms, hail, and tornadoes.

Conventional landing gear. Landing gear employing a third rear-mounted wheel. These airplanes are also sometimes referred to as tailwheel airplanes.

Coordinated flight. Flight with a minimum disturbance of the forces maintaining equilibrium, established via effective control use.

COP. See changeover point.

Coriolis illusion. The illusion of rotation or movement in an entirely different axis, caused by an abrupt head movement, while in a prolonged constant-rate turn that has ceased to stimulate the brain's motion sensing system.

Coupled ailerons and rudder. Rudder and ailerons are connected with interconnected springs in order to counteract adverse yaw. Can be overridden if it becomes necessary to slip the aircraft.

Course. The intended direction of flight in the horizontal plane measured in degrees from north.

Cowl flaps. Shutter-like devices arranged around certain air-cooled engine cowlings, which may be opened or closed to regulate the flow of air around the engine.

Crew resource management (CRM). The application of team management concepts in the flight deck environment. It was initially known as cockpit resource management, but as CRM programs evolved to include cabin crews, maintenance personnel, and others, the phrase "crew resource management" was adopted. This includes single pilots, as in most general aviation aircraft. Pilots of small aircraft, as well as crews of larger aircraft, must make effective use of all available resources; human resources, hardware, and information. A current definition includes all groups routinely working with the flight crew who are involved in decisions required to operate a flight safely. These groups include, but are not limited to pilots, dispatchers, cabin crewmembers, maintenance personnel, and air traffic controllers. CRM is one way of addressing the challenge of optimizing the human/machine interface and accompanying interpersonal activities.

Critical altitude. The maximum altitude under standard atmospheric conditions at which a turbocharged engine can produce its rated horsepower.

Critical angle of attack. The angle of attack at which a wing stalls regardless of airspeed, flight attitude, or weight.

Critical areas. Areas where disturbances to the ILS localizer and glideslope courses may occur when surface vehicles or aircraft operate near the localizer or glideslope antennas.

CRM. See crew resource management.

Cross-check. The first fundamental skill of instrument flight, also known as "scan," the continuous and logical observation of instruments for attitude and performance information.

Cruise clearance. An ATC clearance issued to allow a pilot to conduct flight at any altitude from the minimum IFR altitude up to and including the altitude specified in the clearance. Also authorizes a pilot to proceed to and make an approach at the destination airport.

Current induction. An electrical current being induced into, or generated in, any conductor that is crossed by lines of flux from any magnet.

DA. See decision altitude.

Datum (Reference Datum). An imaginary vertical plane or line from which all measurements of arm are taken. The datum is established by the manufacturer. Once the datum has been selected, all moment arms and the location of CG range are measured from this point.

D.C. Direct current.

Dark adaptation. Physical and chemical adjustments of the eye that make vision possible in relative darkness.

Dead reckoning. Navigation of an airplane solely by means of computations based on airspeed, course, heading, wind direction and speed, groundspeed, and elapsed time.

Deceleration error. A magnetic compass error that occurs when the aircraft decelerates while flying on an easterly or westerly heading, causing the compass card to rotate toward South.

Decision altitude (DA). A specified altitude in the precision approach, charted in feet MSL, at which a missed approach must be initiated if the required visual reference to continue the approach has not been established.

Decision height (DH). A specified altitude in the precision approach, charted in height above threshold elevation, at which a decision must be made either to continue the approach or to execute a missed approach.

Deice. The act of removing ice accumulation from an aircraft structure.

Delta. A Greek letter expressed by the symbol Δ to indicate a change of values. As an example, ΔCG indicates a change (or movement) of the CG.

Density altitude. Pressure altitude corrected for nonstandard temperature. Density altitude is used in computing the performance of an aircraft and its engines.

Departure procedure (DP). Preplanned IFR ATC departure, published for pilot use, in textual and graphic format.

Deposition. The direct transformation of a gas to a solid state, in which the liquid state is bypassed. Some sources use sublimation to describe this process instead of deposition.

Detonation. The sudden release of heat energy from fuel in an aircraft engine caused by the fuel-air mixture reaching its critical pressure and temperature. Detonation occurs as a violent explosion rather than a smooth burning process.

Deviation. A magnetic compass error caused by local magnetic fields within the aircraft. Deviation error is different on each heading.

Dew. Moisture that has condensed from water vapor. Usually found on cooler objects near the ground, such as grass, as the near-surface layer of air cools faster than the layers of air above it.

Dewpoint. The temperature at which air reaches a state where it can hold no more water.

DGPS. Differential global positioning system.

DH. See decision height.

Differential ailerons. Control surface rigged such that the aileron moving up moves a greater distance than the aileron moving down. The up aileron produces extra parasite drag to compensate for the additional induced drag caused by the down aileron. This balancing of the drag forces helps minimize adverse yaw.

Differential Global Positioning System (DGPS). A system that improves the accuracy of Global Navigation Satellite Systems (GNSS) by measuring changes in variables to provide satellite positioning corrections.

Differential pressure. A difference between two pressures. The measurement of airspeed is an example of the use of differential pressure.

Dihedral. The positive acute angle between the lateral axis of an airplane and a line through the center of a wing or horizontal stabilizer. Dihedral contributes to the lateral stability of an airplane.

Diluter-demand oxygen system. An oxygen system that delivers oxygen mixed or diluted with air in order to maintain a constant oxygen partial pressure as the altitude changes.

Direct indication. The true and instantaneous reflection of aircraft pitch-and-bank attitude by the miniature aircraft, relative to the horizon bar of the attitude indicator.

Direct User Access Terminal System (DUATS). A system that provides current FAA weather and flight plan filing services to certified civil pilots, via personal computer, modem, or telephone access to the system. Pilots can request specific types of weather briefings and other pertinent data for planned flights.

Directional stability. Stability about the vertical axis of an aircraft, whereby an aircraft tends to return, on its own, to flight aligned with the relative wind when disturbed from that equilibrium state. The vertical tail is the primary contributor to directional stability, causing an airplane in flight to align with the relative wind.

Distance circle. See reference circle.

Distance measuring equipment (DME). A pulse-type electronic navigation system that shows the pilot, by an instrument-panel indication, the number of nautical miles between the aircraft and a ground station or waypoint.

DME. See distance measuring equipment.

DME arc. A flight track that is a constant distance from the station or waypoint.

DOD. Department of Defense.

Doghouse. A turn-and-slip indicator dial mark in the shape of a doghouse.

Domestic Reduced Vertical Separation Minimum (DRVSM). Additional flight levels between FL 290 and FL 410 to provide operational, traffic, and airspace efficiency.

Double gimbal. A type of mount used for the gyro in an attitude instrument. The axes of the two gimbals are at right angles to the spin axis of the gyro, allowing free motion in two planes around the gyro.

DP. See departure procedure.

Drag. The net aerodynamic force parallel to the relative wind, usually the sum of two components: induced drag and parasite drag.

Drag curve. The curve created when plotting induced drag and parasite drag.

Drift angle. Angle between heading and track.

DRVSM. See Domestic Reduced Vertical Separation Minimum.

DUATS. See direct user access terminal system.

Duplex. Transmitting on one frequency and receiving on a separate frequency.

Dutch roll. A combination of rolling and yawing oscillations that normally occurs when the dihedral effects of an aircraft are more powerful than the directional stability. Usually dynamically stable but objectionable in an airplane because of the oscillatory nature.

Dynamic hydroplaning. A condition that exists when landing on a surface with standing water deeper than the tread depth of the tires. When the brakes are applied, there is a possibility that the brake will lock up and the tire will ride on the surface of the water, much like a water ski. When the tires are hydroplaning, directional control and braking action are virtually impossible. An effective anti-skid system can minimize the effects of hydroplaning.

Dynamic stability. The property of an aircraft that causes it, when disturbed from straight-and-level flight, to develop forces or moments that restore the original condition of straight and level.

Eddy currents. Current induced in a metal cup or disc when it is crossed by lines of flux from a moving magnet.

Eddy current damping. The decreased amplitude of oscillations by the interaction of magnetic fields. In the case of a vertical card magnetic compass, flux from the oscillating permanent magnet produces eddy currents in a damping disk or cup. The magnetic flux produced by the eddy currents opposes the flux from the permanent magnet and decreases the oscillations.

EFAS. See En Route Flight Advisory Service.

EFC. See expect-further-clearance.

EFD. See electronic flight display.

EGT. See exhaust gas temperature.

Electronic flight display (EFD). For the purpose of standardization, any flight instrument display that uses LCD or other image-producing system (cathode ray tube (CRT), etc.)

Elevator. The horizontal, movable primary control surface in the tail section, or empennage, of an airplane. The elevator is hinged to the trailing edge of the fixed horizontal stabilizer.

Elevator illusion. The sensation of being in a climb or descent, caused by the kind of abrupt vertical accelerations that result from up- or downdrafts.

Emergency. A distress or urgent condition.

Empennage. The section of the airplane that consists of the vertical stabilizer, the horizontal stabilizer, and the associated control surfaces.

Emphasis error. The result of giving too much attention to a particular instrument during the cross-check, instead of relying on a combination of instruments necessary for attitude and performance information.

Empty-field myopia. Induced nearsightedness that is associated with flying at night, in instrument meteorological conditions and/or reduced visibility. With nothing to focus on, the eyes automatically focus on a point just slightly ahead of the airplane.

EM wave. Electromagnetic wave.

Encoding altimeter. A special type of pressure altimeter used to send a signal to the air traffic controller on the ground, showing the pressure altitude the aircraft is flying.

Engine pressure ratio (EPR). The ratio of turbine discharge pressure divided by compressor inlet pressure, which is used as an indication of the amount of thrust being developed by a turbine engine.

En route facilities ring. Depicted in the plan view of IAP charts, a circle which designates NAVAIDs, fixes, and intersections that are part of the en route low altitude airway structure.

En Route Flight Advisory Service (EFAS). An en route weather-only AFSS service.

En route high-altitude charts. Aeronautical charts for en route instrument navigation at or above 18,000 feet MSL.

En route low-altitude charts. Aeronautical charts for en route IFR navigation below 18,000 feet MSL.

EPR. See engine pressure ratio.

Equilibrium. A condition that exists within a body when the sum of the moments of all of the forces acting on the body is equal to zero. In aerodynamics, equilibrium is when all opposing forces acting on an aircraft are balanced (steady, unaccelerated flight conditions).

Equivalent airspeed. Airspeed equivalent to CAS in standard atmosphere at sea level. As the airspeed and pressure altitude increase, the CAS becomes higher than it should be, and a correction for compression must be subtracted from the CAS.

Evaporation. The transformation of a liquid to a gaseous state, such as the change of water to water vapor.

Exhaust gas temperature (EGT). The temperature of the exhaust gases as they leave the cylinders of a reciprocating engine or the turbine section of a turbine engine.

Expect-further-clearance (EFC). The time a pilot can expect to receive clearance beyond a clearance limit.

Explosive decompression. A change in cabin pressure faster than the lungs can decompress. Lung damage is possible.

FA. See area forecast.

FAA. Federal Aviation Administration.

FAF. See final approach fix.

False horizon. Inaccurate visual information for aligning the aircraft, caused by various natural and geometric formations that disorient the pilot from the actual horizon.

FDI. See flight director indicator.

Federal airways. Class E airspace areas that extend upward from 1,200 feet to, but not including, 18,000 feet MSL, unless otherwise specified.

Feeder facilities. Used by ATC to direct aircraft to intervening fixes between the en route structure and the initial approach fix.

Final approach. Part of an instrument approach procedure in which alignment and descent for landing are accomplished.

Final approach fix (FAF). The fix from which the IFR final approach to an airport is executed, and which identifies the beginning of the final approach segment. An FAF is designated on government charts by a Maltese cross symbol for nonprecision approaches, and a lightning bolt symbol for precision approaches.

Fixating. Staring at a single instrument, thereby interrupting the cross-check process.

Fixed-pitch propellers. Propellers with fixed blade angles. Fixed-pitch propellers are designed as climb propellers, cruise propellers, or standard propellers.

Fixed slot. A fixed, nozzle shaped opening near the leading edge of a wing that ducts air onto the top surface of the wing. Its purpose is to increase lift at higher angles of attack.

FL. See flight level.

Flameout. A condition in the operation of a gas turbine engine in which the fire in the engine goes out due to either too much or too little fuel sprayed into the combustors.

Flaps. Hinged portion of the trailing edge between the ailerons and fuselage. In some aircraft ailerons and flaps are interconnected to produce full-span "flaperons." In either case, flaps change the lift and drag on the wing.

Floor load limit. The maximum weight the floor can sustain per square inch/foot as provided by the manufacturer.

Flight configurations. Adjusting the aircraft control surfaces (including flaps and landing gear) in a manner that will achieve a specified attitude.

Flight director indicator (FDI). One of the major components of a flight director system, it provides steering commands that the pilot (or the autopilot, if coupled) follows.

Flight level (FL). A measure of altitude (in hundreds of feet) used by aircraft flying above 18,000 feet with the altimeter set at 29.92 "Hg.

Flight management system (FMS). Provides pilot and crew with highly accurate and automatic long-range navigation capability, blending available inputs from long- and short-range sensors.

Flight path. The line, course, or track along which an aircraft is flying or is intended to be flown.

Flight patterns. Basic maneuvers, flown by reference to the instruments rather than outside visual cues, for the purpose of practicing basic attitude flying. The patterns simulate maneuvers encountered on instrument flights such as holding patterns, procedure turns, and approaches.

Flight strips. Paper strips containing instrument flight information, used by ATC when processing flight plans.

FMS. See flight management system.

FOD. See foreign object damage.

Fog. Cloud consisting of numerous minute water droplets and based at the surface; droplets are small enough to be suspended in the earth's atmosphere indefinitely. (Unlike drizzle, it does not fall to the surface. Fog differs from a cloud only in that a cloud is not based at the surface, and is distinguished from haze by its wetness and gray color.)

Force (F). The energy applied to an object that attempts to cause the object to change its direction, speed, or motion. In aerodynamics, it is expressed as F, T (thrust), L (lift), W (weight), or D (drag), usually in pounds.

Foreign object damage (FOD). Damage to a gas turbine engine caused by some object being sucked into the engine while it is running. Debris from runways or taxiways can cause foreign object damage during ground operations, and the ingestion of ice and birds can cause FOD in flight.

Form drag. The drag created because of the shape of a component or the aircraft.

Frise-type aileron. Aileron having the nose portion projecting ahead of the hinge line. When the trailing edge of the aileron moves up, the nose projects below the wing's lower surface and produces some parasite drag, decreasing the amount of adverse yaw.

Front. The boundary between two different air masses.

Frost. Ice crystal deposits formed by sublimation when temperature and dewpoint are below freezing.

Fuel load. The expendable part of the load of the airplane. It includes only usable fuel, not fuel required to fill the lines or that which remains trapped in the tank sumps.

Fundamental skills. Pilot skills of instrument cross-check, instrument interpretation, and aircraft control.

Fuselage. The section of the airplane that consists of the cabin and/or cockpit, containing seats for the occupants and the controls for the airplane.

GAMA. General Aviation Manufacturers Association.

Gimbal ring. A type of support that allows an object, such as a gyroscope, to remain in an upright condition when its base is tilted.

Glideslope (GS). Part of the ILS that projects a radio beam upward at an angle of approximately 3° from the approach end of an instrument runway. The glideslope provides vertical guidance to aircraft on the final approach course for the aircraft to follow when making an ILS approach along the localizer path.

Glideslope intercept altitude. The minimum altitude of an intermediate approach segment prescribed for a precision approach that ensures obstacle clearance.

Global landing system (GLS). An instrument approach with lateral and vertical guidance with integrity limits (similar to barometric vertical navigation (BARO VNAV).

Global navigation satellite system (GNSS). Satellite navigation system that provides autonomous geospatial positioning with global coverage. It allows small electronic receivers to determine their location (longitude, latitude, and altitude) to within a few meters using time signals transmitted along a line of sight by radio from satellites.

Global positioning system (GPS). Navigation system that uses satellite rather than ground-based transmitters for location information.

GLS. See global landing system.

GNSS. See global navigation satellite system.

Goniometer. As used in radio frequency (RF) antenna systems, a direction-sensing device consisting of two fixed loops of wire oriented 90° from each other, which separately sense received signal strength and send those signals to two rotors (also oriented 90°) in the sealed direction-indicating instrument. The rotors are attached to the direction-indicating needle of the instrument and rotated by a small motor until minimum magnetic field is sensed near the rotors.

GPS. See global positioning system.

GPS Approach Overlay Program. An authorization for pilots to use GPS avionics under IFR for flying designated existing nonprecision instrument approach procedures, with the exception of LOC, LDA, and SDF procedures.

GPWS. See ground proximity warning system.

Graveyard spiral. The illusion of the cessation of a turn while still in a prolonged, coordinated, constant rate turn, which can lead a disoriented pilot to a loss of control of the aircraft.

Great circle route. The shortest distance across the surface of a sphere (the Earth) between two points on the surface.

Ground adjustable trim tab. Non-movable metal trim tab on a control surface. Bent in one direction or another while on the ground to apply trim forces to the control surface.

Ground effect. The condition of slightly increased air pressure below an airplane wing or helicopter rotor system that increases the amount of lift produced. It exists within approximately one wing span or one rotor diameter from the ground. It results from a reduction in upwash, downwash, and wingtip vortices, and provides a corresponding decrease in induced drag.

Ground proximity warning system (GPWS). A system designed to determine an aircraft's clearance above the Earth and provides limited predictability about aircraft position relative to rising terrain.

Groundspeed. Speed over the ground, either closing speed to the station or waypoint, or speed over the ground in whatever direction the aircraft is going at the moment, depending upon the navigation system used.

GS. See glideslope.

GWPS. See ground proximity warning system.

Gyroscopic precession. An inherent quality of rotating bodies, which causes an applied force to be manifested 90° in the direction of rotation from the point where the force is applied.

HAA. See height above airport.

HAL. See height above landing.

HAT. See height above touchdown elevation.

Hazardous attitudes. Five aeronautical decision-making attitudes that may contribute to poor pilot judgment: anti-authority, impulsivity, invulnerability, machismo, and resignation.

Hazardous Inflight Weather Advisory Service (HIWAS). Service providing recorded weather forecasts broadcast to airborne pilots over selected VORs.

Head-up display (HUD). A special type of flight viewing screen that allows the pilot to watch the flight instruments and other data while looking through the windshield of the aircraft for other traffic, the approach lights, or the runway.

Heading. The direction in which the nose of the aircraft is pointing during flight.

Heading indicator. An instrument which senses airplane movement and displays heading based on a 360° azimuth, with the final zero omitted. The heading indicator, also called a directional gyro (DG), is fundamentally a mechanical instrument designed to facilitate the use of the magnetic compass. The heading indicator is not affected by the forces that make the magnetic compass difficult to interpret.

Headwork. Required to accomplish a conscious, rational thought process when making decisions. Good decision-making involves risk identification and assessment, information processing, and problem solving.

Height above airport (HAA). The height of the MDA above the published airport elevation.

Height above landing (HAL). The height above a designated helicopter landing area used for helicopter instrument approach procedures.

Height above touchdown elevation (HAT). The DA/DH or MDA above the highest runway elevation in the touchdown zone (first 3,000 feet of the runway).

HF. High frequency.

Hg. Abbreviation for mercury, from the Latin hydrargyrum.

High performance aircraft. An aircraft with an engine of more than 200 horsepower.

Histotoxic hypoxia. The inability of cells to effectively use oxygen. Plenty of oxygen is being transported to the cells that need it, but they are unable to use it.

HIWAS. See Hazardous Inflight Weather Advisory Service.

Holding. A predetermined maneuver that keeps aircraft within a specified airspace while awaiting further clearance from ATC.

Holding pattern. A racetrack pattern, involving two turns and two legs, used to keep an aircraft within a prescribed airspace with respect to a geographic fix. A standard pattern uses right turns; nonstandard patterns use left turns.

Homing. Flying the aircraft on any heading required to keep the needle pointing to the 0° relative bearing position.

Horizontal situation indicator (HSI). A flight navigation instrument that combines the heading indicator with a CDI, in order to provide the pilot with better situational awareness of location with respect to the courseline.

Horsepower. The term, originated by inventor James Watt, means the amount of work a horse could do in one second. One horsepower equals 550 foot-pounds per second, or 33,000 foot-pounds per minute.

Hot start. In gas turbine engines, a start which occurs with normal engine rotation, but exhaust temperature exceeds prescribed limits. This is usually caused by an excessively rich mixture in the combustor. The fuel to the engine must be terminated immediately to prevent engine damage.

HSI. See horizontal situation indicator.

HUD. See head-up display.

Human factors. A multidisciplinary field encompassing the behavioral and social sciences, engineering, and physiology, to consider the variables that influence individual and crew performance for the purpose of optimizing human performance and reducing errors.

Hung start. In gas turbine engines, a condition of normal light off but with rpm remaining at some low value rather than increasing to the normal idle rpm. This is often the result of insufficient power to the engine from the starter. In the event of a hung start, the engine should be shut down.

Hydroplaning. A condition that exists when landing on a surface with standing water deeper than the tread depth of the tires. When the brakes are applied, there is a possibility that the brake will lock up and the tire will ride on the surface of the water, much like a water ski. When the tires are hydroplaning, directional control and braking action are virtually impossible. An effective anti-skid system can minimize the effects of hydroplaning.

Hypemic hypoxia. A type of hypoxia that is a result of oxygen deficiency in the blood, rather than a lack of inhaled oxygen. It can be caused by a variety of factors. Hypemic means "not enough blood."

Hyperventilation. Occurs when an individual is experiencing emotional stress, fright, or pain, and the breathing rate and depth increase, although the carbon dioxide level in the blood is already at a reduced level. The result is an excessive loss of carbon dioxide from the body, which can lead to unconsciousness due to the respiratory system's overriding mechanism to regain control of breathing.

Hypoxia. A state of oxygen deficiency in the body sufficient to impair functions of the brain and other organs.

Hypoxic hypoxia. This type of hypoxia is a result of insufficient oxygen available to the lungs. A decrease of oxygen molecules at sufficient pressure can lead to hypoxic hypoxia.

IAF. See initial approach fix.

IAP. See instrument approach procedures.

IAS. See indicated airspeed.

ICAO. See International Civil Aviation Organization.

Ident. Air Traffic Control request for a pilot to push the button on the transponder to identify return on the controller's scope.

IFR. See instrument flight rules.

ILS. See instrument landing system.

ILS categories. Categories of instrument approach procedures allowed at airports equipped with the following types of instrument landing systems:

> **ILS Category I:** Provides for approach to a height above touchdown of not less than 200 feet, and with runway visual range of not less than 1,800 feet.

> **ILS Category II:** Provides for approach to a height above touchdown of not less than 100 feet and with runway visual range of not less than 1,200 feet.

> **ILS Category IIIA:** Provides for approach without a decision height minimum and with runway visual range of not less than 700 feet.

> **ILS Category IIIB:** Provides for approach without a decision height minimum and with runway visual range of not less than 150 feet.

> **ILS Category IIIC:** Provides for approach without a decision height minimum and without runway visual range minimum.

IMC. See instrument meteorological conditions.

Inclinometer. An instrument consisting of a curved glass tube, housing a glass ball, and damped with a fluid similar to kerosene. It may be used to indicate inclination, as a level, or, as used in the turn indicators, to show the relationship between gravity and centrifugal force in a turn.

Indicated airspeed (IAS). Shown on the dial of the instrument airspeed indicator on an aircraft. Indicated airspeed (IAS) is the airspeed indicator reading uncorrected for instrument, position, and other errors. Indicated airspeed means the speed of an aircraft as shown on its pitot static airspeed indicator calibrated to reflect standard atmosphere adiabatic compressible flow at sea level uncorrected for airspeed system errors. Calibrated airspeed (CAS) is IAS corrected for instrument errors, position error (due to incorrect pressure at the static port) and installation errors.

Indicated altitude. The altitude read directly from the altimeter (uncorrected) when it is set to the current altimeter setting.

Indirect indication. A reflection of aircraft pitch-and-bank attitude by instruments other than the attitude indicator.

Induced drag. Drag caused by the same factors that produce lift; its amount varies inversely with airspeed. As airspeed decreases, the angle of attack must increase, in turn increasing induced drag.

Induction icing. A type of ice in the induction system that reduces the amount of air available for combustion. The most commonly found induction icing is carburetor icing.

Inertial navigation system (INS). A computer-based navigation system that tracks the movement of an aircraft via signals produced by onboard accelerometers. The initial location of the aircraft is entered into the computer, and all subsequent movement of the aircraft is sensed and used to keep the position updated. An INS does not require any inputs from outside signals.

Initial approach fix (IAF). The fix depicted on IAP charts where the instrument approach procedure (IAP) begins unless otherwise authorized by ATC.

Inoperative components. Higher minimums are prescribed when the specified visual aids are not functioning; this information is listed in the Inoperative Components Table found in the United States Terminal Procedures Publications.

INS. See inertial navigation system.

Instantaneous vertical speed indicator (IVSI). Assists in interpretation by instantaneously indicating the rate of climb or descent at a given moment with little or no lag as displayed in a vertical speed indicator (VSI).

Instrument approach procedures (IAP). A series of predetermined maneuvers for the orderly transfer of an aircraft under IFR from the beginning of the initial approach to a landing or to a point from which a landing may be made visually.

Instrument flight rules (IFR). Rules and regulations established by the Federal Aviation Administration to govern flight under conditions in which flight by outside visual reference is not safe. IFR flight depends upon flying by reference to instruments in the flight deck, and navigation is accomplished by reference to electronic signals.

Instrument landing system (ILS). An electronic system that provides both horizontal and vertical guidance to a specific runway, used to execute a precision instrument approach procedure.

Instrument meteorological conditions (IMC). Meteorological conditions expressed in terms of visibility, distance from clouds, and ceiling less than the minimums specified for visual meteorological conditions, requiring operations to be conducted under IFR.

Instrument takeoff. Using the instruments rather than outside visual cues to maintain runway heading and execute a safe takeoff.

Intercooler. A device used to reduce the temperatures of the compressed air before it enters the fuel metering device. The resulting cooler air has a higher density, which permits the engine to be operated with a higher power setting.

Interference drag. Drag generated by the collision of airstreams creating eddy currents, turbulence, or restrictions to smooth flow.

International Civil Aviation Organization (ICAO). The United Nations agency for developing the principles and techniques of international air navigation, and fostering planning and development of international civil air transport.

International standard atmosphere (IAS). A model of standard variation of pressure and temperature.

Interpolation. The estimation of an intermediate value of a quantity that falls between marked values in a series. Example: In a measurement of length, with a rule that is marked in eighths of an inch, the value falls between 3/8 inch and 1/2 inch. The estimated (interpolated) value might then be said to be 7/16 inch.

Inversion. An increase in temperature with altitude.

Inversion illusion. The feeling that the aircraft is tumbling backwards, caused by an abrupt change from climb to straight-and-level flight while in situations lacking visual reference.

Inverter. A solid-state electronic device that converts D.C. into A.C. current of the proper voltage and frequency to operate A.C. gyro instruments.

Isobars. Lines which connect points of equal barometric pressure.

Isogonic lines. Lines drawn across aeronautical charts to connect points having the same magnetic variation.

IVSI. See instantaneous vertical speed indicator.

Jet route. A route designated to serve flight operations from 18,000 feet MSL up to and including FL 450.

Jet stream. A high-velocity narrow stream of winds, usually found near the upper limit of the troposphere, which flows generally from west to east.

Judgment. The mental process of recognizing and analyzing all pertinent information in a particular situation, a rational evaluation of alternative actions in response to it, and a timely decision on which action to take.

KIAS. Knots indicated airspeed.

Kollsman window. A barometric scale window of a sensitive altimeter used to adjust the altitude for the altimeter setting.

LAAS. See local area augmentation system.

Lag. The delay that occurs before an instrument needle attains a stable indication.

Land breeze. A coastal breeze flowing from land to sea caused by temperature differences when the sea surface is warmer than the adjacent land. The land breeze usually occurs at night and alternates with the sea breeze that blows in the opposite direction by day.

Land as soon as possible. Land without delay at the nearest suitable area, such as an open field, at which a safe approach and landing is assured.

Land as soon as practical. The landing site and duration of flight are at the discretion of the pilot. Extended flight beyond the nearest approved landing area is not recommended.

Land immediately. The urgency of the landing is paramount. The primary consideration is to ensure the survival of the occupants. Landing in trees, water, or other unsafe areas should be considered only as a last resort.

Lateral axis. An imaginary line passing through the center of gravity of an airplane and extending across the airplane from wingtip to wingtip.

Lateral stability (rolling). The stability about the longitudinal axis of an aircraft. Rolling stability or the ability of an airplane to return to level flight due to a disturbance that causes one of the wings to drop.

Latitude. Measurement north or south of the equator in degrees, minutes, and seconds. Lines of latitude are also referred to as parallels.

LDA. See localizer-type directional aid.

Lead radial. The radial at which the turn from the DME arc to the inbound course is started.

Leading edge. The part of an airfoil that meets the airflow first.

Leading edge devices. High lift devices which are found on the leading edge of the airfoil. The most common types are fixed slots, movable slats, and leading edge flaps.

Leading-edge flap. A portion of the leading edge of an airplane wing that folds downward to increase the camber, lift, and drag of the wing. The leading-edge flaps are extended for takeoffs and landings to increase the amount of aerodynamic lift that is produced at any given airspeed.

Leans, the. A physical sensation caused by an abrupt correction of a banked attitude entered too slowly to stimulate the motion sensing system in the inner ear. The abrupt correction can create the illusion of banking in the opposite direction.

Licensed empty weight. The empty weight that consists of the airframe, engine(s), unusable fuel, and undrainable oil plus standard and optional equipment as specified in the equipment list. Some manufacturers used this term prior to GAMA standardization.

Lift. A component of the total aerodynamic force on an airfoil and acts perpendicular to the relative wind.

Limit load factor. Amount of stress, or load factor, that an aircraft can withstand before structural damage or failure occurs.

Lines of flux. Invisible lines of magnetic force passing between the poles of a magnet.

L/MF. See low or medium frequency.

LMM. See locator middle marker.

Load factor. The ratio of a specified load to the total weight of the aircraft. The specified load is expressed in terms of any of the following: aerodynamic forces, inertial forces, or ground or water reactions.

Loadmeter. A type of ammeter installed between the generator output and the main bus in an aircraft electrical system.

LOC. See localizer.

Local area augmentation system (LAAS). A differential global positioning system (DGPS) that improves the accuracy of the system by determining position error from the GPS satellites, then transmitting the error, or corrective factors, to the airborne GPS receiver.

Localizer (LOC). The portion of an ILS that gives left/right guidance information down the centerline of the instrument runway for final approach.

Localizer-type directional aid (LDA). A NAVAID used for nonprecision instrument approaches with utility and accuracy comparable to a localizer but which is not a part of a complete ILS and is not aligned with the runway. Some LDAs are equipped with a glideslope.

Locator middle marker (LMM). Nondirectional radio beacon (NDB) compass locator, collocated with a middle marker (MM).

Locator outer marker (LOM). NDB compass locator, collocated with an outer marker (OM).

LOM. See locator outer marker.

Longitude. Measurement east or west of the Prime Meridian in degrees, minutes, and seconds. The Prime Meridian is 0° longitude and runs through Greenwich, England. Lines of longitude are also referred to as meridians.

Longitudinal axis. An imaginary line through an aircraft from nose to tail, passing through its center of gravity. The longitudinal axis is also called the roll axis of the aircraft. Movement of the ailerons rotates an airplane about its longitudinal axis.

Longitudinal stability (pitching). Stability about the lateral axis. A desirable characteristic of an airplane whereby it tends to return to its trimmed angle of attack after displacement.

Long range navigation (LORAN). An electronic navigational system by which hyperbolic lines of position are determined by measuring the difference in the time of reception of synchronized pulse signals from two fixed transmitters. LORAN-A operates in the 1750–1950 kHz frequency band. LORAN-C and -D operate in the 100–110 kHz frequency band.

LORAN. See long range navigation.

LORAN-C. A radio navigation system that utilizes master and slave stations transmitting timed pulses. The time difference in reception of pulses from several stations establishes a hyperbolic line of position, which can be identified on a LORAN chart. A fix in position is obtained by utilizing signals from two or more stations.

Low or medium frequency. A frequency range between 190 and 535 kHz with the medium frequency above 300 kHz. Generally associated with nondirectional beacons transmitting a continuous carrier with either a 400 or 1,020 Hz modulation.

Lubber line. The reference line used in a magnetic compass or heading indicator.

MAA. See maximum authorized altitude.

MAC. See mean aerodynamic chord.

Mach number. The ratio of the true airspeed of the aircraft to the speed of sound in the same atmospheric conditions, named in honor of Ernst Mach, late 19th century physicist.

Mach meter. The instrument that displays the ratio of the speed of sound to the true airspeed an aircraft is flying.

Magnetic bearing (MB). The direction to or from a radio transmitting station measured relative to magnetic north.

Magnetic compass. A device for determining direction measured from magnetic north.

Magnetic dip. A vertical attraction between a compass needle and the magnetic poles. The closer the aircraft is to a pole, the more severe the effect.

Magnetic heading (MH). The direction an aircraft is pointed with respect to magnetic north.

Magneto. A self-contained, engine-driven unit that supplies electrical current to the spark plugs; completely independent of the airplane's electrical system. Normally there are two magnetos per engine.

Magnus effect. Lifting force produced when a rotating cylinder produces a pressure differential. This is the same effect that makes a baseball curve or a golf ball slice.

Mandatory altitude. An altitude depicted on an instrument approach chart with the altitude value both underscored and overscored. Aircraft are required to maintain altitude at the depicted value.

Mandatory block altitude. An altitude depicted on an instrument approach chart with two underscored and overscored altitude values between which aircraft are required to maintain altitude.

Maneuverability. Ability of an aircraft to change directions along a flightpath and withstand the stresses imposed upon it.

Maneuvering speed (V_A). The maximum speed at which full, abrupt control movement can be used without overstressing the airframe.

Manifold absolute pressure. The absolute pressure of the fuel/air mixture within the intake manifold, usually indicated in inches of mercury.

MAP. See missed approach point.

Margin identification. The top and bottom areas on an instrument approach chart that depict information about the procedure, including airport location and procedure identification.

Marker beacon. A low-powered transmitter that directs its signal upward in a small, fan-shaped pattern. Used along the flight path when approaching an airport for landing, marker beacons indicate both aurally and visually when the aircraft is directly over the facility.

Mass. The amount of matter in a body.

Maximum altitude. An altitude depicted on an instrument approach chart with overscored altitude value at which or below aircraft are required to maintain altitude.

Maximum authorized altitude (MAA). A published altitude representing the maximum usable altitude or flight level for an airspace structure or route segment.

Maximum landing weight. The greatest weight that an airplane normally is allowed to have at landing.

Maximum ramp weight. The total weight of a loaded aircraft, including all fuel. It is greater than the takeoff weight due to the fuel that will be burned during the taxi and runup operations. Ramp weight may also be referred to as taxi weight.

Maximum takeoff weight. The maximum allowable weight for takeoff.

Maximum weight. The maximum authorized weight of the aircraft and all of its equipment as specified in the Type Certificate Data Sheets (TCDS) for the aircraft.

Maximum zero fuel weight (GAMA). The maximum weight, exclusive of usable fuel.

MB. See magnetic bearing.

MCA. See minimum crossing altitude.

MDA. See minimum descent altitude.

MEA. See minimum en route altitude.

Mean aerodynamic chord (MAC). The average distance from the leading edge to the trailing edge of the wing.

Mean sea level. The average height of the surface of the sea at a particular location for all stages of the tide over a 19-year period.

MEL. See minimum equipment list.

Meridians. Lines of longitude.

Mesosphere. A layer of the atmosphere directly above the stratosphere.

METAR. See Aviation Routine Weather Report.

MFD. See multi-function display.

MH. See magnetic heading.

MHz. Megahertz.

Microbursts. A strong downdraft which normally occurs over horizontal distances of 1 NM or less and vertical distances of less than 1,000 feet. In spite of its small horizontal scale, an intense microburst could induce windspeeds greater than 100 knots and downdrafts as strong as 6,000 feet per minute.

Microwave landing system (MLS). A precision instrument approach system operating in the microwave spectrum which normally consists of an azimuth station, elevation station, and precision distance measuring equipment.

Mileage breakdown. A fix indicating a course change that appears on the chart as an "x" at a break between two segments of a federal airway.

Military operations area (MOA). Airspace established for the purpose of separating certain military training activities from IFR traffic.

Military training route (MTR). Airspace of defined vertical and lateral dimensions established for the conduct of military training at airspeeds in excess of 250 knots indicated airspeed (KIAS).

Minimum altitude. An altitude depicted on an instrument approach chart with the altitude value underscored. Aircraft are required to maintain altitude at or above the depicted value.

Minimum crossing altitude (MCA). The lowest allowed altitude at certain fixes an aircraft must cross when proceeding in the direction of a higher minimum en route altitude (MEA).

Minimum descent altitude (MDA). The lowest altitude (in feet MSL) to which descent is authorized on final approach, or during circle-to-land maneuvering in execution of a nonprecision approach.

Minimum drag. The point on the total drag curve where the lift-to-drag ratio is the greatest. At this speed, total drag is minimized.

Minimum en route altitude (MEA). The lowest published altitude between radio fixes that ensures acceptable navigational signal coverage and meets obstacle clearance requirements between those fixes.

Minimum equipment list (MEL). A list developed for larger aircraft that outlines equipment that can be inoperative for various types of flight including IFR and icing conditions. This list is based on the master minimum equipment list (MMEL) developed by the FAA and must be approved by the FAA for use. It is specific to an individual aircraft make and model.

Minimum obstruction clearance altitude (MOCA). The lowest published altitude in effect between radio fixes on VOR airways, off-airway routes, or route segments, which meets obstacle clearance requirements for the entire route segment and which ensures acceptable navigational signal coverage only within 25 statute (22 nautical) miles of a VOR.

Minimum reception altitude (MRA). The lowest altitude at which an airway intersection can be determined.

Minimum safe altitude (MSA). The minimum altitude depicted on approach charts which provides at least 1,000 feet of obstacle clearance for emergency use within a specified distance from the listed navigation facility.

Minimum vectoring altitude (MVA). An IFR altitude lower than the minimum en route altitude (MEA) that provides terrain and obstacle clearance.

Minimums section. The area on an IAP chart that displays the lowest altitude and visibility requirements for the approach.

Missed approach. A maneuver conducted by a pilot when an instrument approach cannot be completed to a landing.

Missed approach point (MAP). A point prescribed in each instrument approach at which a missed approach procedure shall be executed if the required visual reference has not been established.

Mixed ice. A mixture of clear ice and rime ice.

MLS. See microwave landing system.

MM. Middle marker.

MOA. See military operations area.

MOCA. See minimum obstruction clearance altitude.

Mode C. Altitude reporting transponder mode.

Moment. The product of the weight of an item multiplied by its arm. Moments are expressed in pound-inches (lb-in). Total moment is the weight of the airplane multiplied by the distance between the datum and the CG.

Moment arm. The distance from a datum to the applied force.

Moment index (or index). A moment divided by a constant such as 100, 1,000, or 10,000. The purpose of using a moment index is to simplify weight and balance computations of airplanes where heavy items and long arms result in large, unmanageable numbers.

Monocoque. A shell-like fuselage design in which the stressed outer skin is used to support the majority of imposed stresses. Monocoque fuselage design may include bulkheads but not stringers.

Monoplanes. Airplanes with a single set of wings.

Movable slat. A movable auxiliary airfoil on the leading edge of a wing. It is closed in normal flight but extends at high angles of attack. This allows air to continue flowing over the top of the wing and delays airflow separation.

MRA. See minimum reception altitude.

MSA. See minimum safe altitude.

MSL. See mean sea level.

MTR. See military training route.

Multi-function display (MFD). Small screen (CRT or LCD) in an aircraft that can be used to display information to the pilot in numerous configurable ways. Often an MFD will be used in concert with a primary flight display.

MVA. See minimum vectoring altitude.

N_1. Rotational speed of the low pressure compressor in a turbine engine.

N₂. Rotational speed of the high pressure compressor in a turbine engine.

Nacelle. A streamlined enclosure on an aircraft in which an engine is mounted. On multiengine propeller-driven airplanes, the nacelle is normally mounted on the leading edge of the wing.

NACG. See National Aeronautical Charting Group.

NAS. See National Airspace System.

National Airspace System (NAS). The common network of United States airspace—air navigation facilities, equipment and services, airports or landing areas; aeronautical charts, information and services; rules, regulations and procedures, technical information; and manpower and material.

National Aeronautical Charting Group (NACG). A Federal agency operating under the FAA, responsible for publishing charts such as the terminal procedures and en route charts.

National Route Program (NRP). A set of rules and procedures designed to increase the flexibility of user flight planning within published guidelines.

National Security Area (NSA). Areas consisting of airspace of defined vertical and lateral dimensions established at locations where there is a requirement for increased security and safety of ground facilities. Pilots are requested to voluntarily avoid flying through the depicted NSA. When it is necessary to provide a greater level of security and safety, flight in NSAs may be temporarily prohibited. Regulatory prohibitions are disseminated via NOTAMs.

National Transportation Safety Board (NTSB). A United States Government independent organization responsible for investigations of accidents involving aviation, highways, waterways, pipelines, and railroads in the United States. NTSB is charged by congress to investigate every civil aviation accident in the United States.

NAVAID. Naviagtional aid.

NAV/COM. Navigation and communication radio.

NDB. See nondirectional radio beacon.

Negative static stability. The initial tendency of an aircraft to continue away from the original state of equilibrium after being disturbed.

Neutral static stability. The initial tendency of an aircraft to remain in a new condition after its equilibrium has been disturbed.

NM. Nautical mile.

NOAA. National Oceanic and Atmospheric Administration.

No-gyro approach. A radar approach that may be used in case of a malfunctioning gyro-compass or directional gyro. Instead of providing the pilot with headings to be flown, the controller observes the radar track and issues control instructions "turn right/left" or "stop turn," as appropriate.

Nondirectional radio beacon (NDB). A ground-based radio transmitter that transmits radio energy in all directions.

Nonprecision approach. A standard instrument approach procedure in which only horizontal guidance is provided.

No procedure turn (NoPT). Term used with the appropriate course and altitude to denote that the procedure turn is not required.

NoPT. See no procedure turn.

NOTAM. See Notice to Airmen.

Notice to Airmen (NOTAM). A notice filed with an aviation authority to alert aircraft pilots of any hazards en route or at a specific location. The authority in turn provides means of disseminating relevant NOTAMs to pilots.

NRP. See National Route Program.

NSA. See National Security Area.

NTSB. See National Transportation Safety Board.

NWS. National Weather Service.

Obstacle departure procedures (ODP). A preplanned instrument flight rule (IFR) departure procedure printed for pilot use in textual or graphic form to provide obstruction clearance via the least onerous route from the terminal area to the appropriate en route structure. ODPs are recommended for obstruction clearance and may be flown without ATC clearance unless an alternate departure procedure (SID or radar vector) has been specifically assigned by ATC.

Obstruction lights. Lights that can be found both on and off an airport to identify obstructions.

Occluded front. A frontal occlusion occurs when a fast-moving cold front catches up with a slow moving warm front. The difference in temperature within each frontal system is a major factor in determining whether a cold or warm front occlusion occurs.

ODP. See obstacle departure procedures.

OM. Outer marker.

Omission error. The failure to anticipate significant instrument indications following attitude changes; for example, concentrating on pitch control while forgetting about heading or roll information, resulting in erratic control of heading and bank.

Optical illusion. A misleading visual image. For the purpose of this handbook, the term refers to the brain's misinterpretation of features on the ground associated with landing, which causes a pilot to misread the spatial relationships between the aircraft and the runway.

Orientation. Awareness of the position of the aircraft and of oneself in relation to a specific reference point.

Otolith organ. An inner ear organ that detects linear acceleration and gravity orientation.

Outer marker. A marker beacon at or near the glideslope intercept altitude of an ILS approach. It is normally located four to seven miles from the runway threshold on the extended centerline of the runway.

Outside air temperature (OAT). The measured or indicated air temperature (IAT) corrected for compression and friction heating. Also referred to as true air temperature.

Overcontrolling. Using more movement in the control column than is necessary to achieve the desired pitch-and-bank condition.

Overboost. A condition in which a reciprocating engine has exceeded the maximum manifold pressure allowed by the manufacturer. Can cause damage to engine components.

Overpower. To use more power than required for the purpose of achieving a faster rate of airspeed change.

P-static. See precipitation static.

PAPI. See precision approach path indicator.

PAR. See precision approach radar.

Parallels. Lines of latitude.

Parasite drag. Drag caused by the friction of air moving over the aircraft structure; its amount varies directly with the airspeed.

Payload (GAMA). The weight of occupants, cargo, and baggage.

Personality. The embodiment of personal traits and characteristics of an individual that are set at a very early age and extremely resistant to change.

P-factor. A tendency for an aircraft to yaw to the left due to the descending propeller blade on the right producing more thrust than the ascending blade on the left. This occurs when the aircraft's longitudinal axis is in a climbing attitude in relation to the relative wind. The P-factor would be to the right if the aircraft had a counterclockwise rotating propeller.

PFD. See primary flight display.

Phugoid oscillations. Long-period oscillations of an aircraft around its lateral axis. It is a slow change in pitch accompanied by equally slow changes in airspeed. Angle of attack remains constant, and the pilot often corrects for phugoid oscillations without even being aware of them.

PIC. See pilot in command.

Pilotage. Navigation by visual reference to landmarks.

Pilot in command (PIC). The pilot responsible for the operation and safety of an aircraft.

Pilot report (PIREP). Report of meteorological phenomena encountered by aircraft.

Pilot's Operating Handbook/Airplane Flight Manual (POH/AFM). FAA-approved documents published by the airframe manufacturer that list the operating conditions for a particular model of aircraft.

PIREP. See pilot report.

Pitot pressure. Ram air pressure used to measure airspeed.

Pitot-static head. A combination pickup used to sample pitot pressure and static air pressure.

Plan view. The overhead view of an approach procedure on an instrument approach chart. The plan view depicts the routes that guide the pilot from the en route segments to the IAF.

Planform. The shape or form of a wing as viewed from above. It may be long and tapered, short and rectangular, or various other shapes.

Pneumatic. Operation by the use of compressed air.

POH/AFM. See Pilot's Operating Handbook/Airplane Flight Manual.

Point-in-space approach. A type of helicopter instrument approach procedure to a missed approach point more than 2,600 feet from an associated helicopter landing area.

Poor judgment chain. A series of mistakes that may lead to an accident or incident. Two basic principles generally associated with the creation of a poor judgment chain are: (1) one bad decision often leads to another; and (2) as a string of bad decisions grows, it reduces the number of subsequent alternatives for continued safe flight. ADM is intended to break the poor judgment chain before it can cause an accident or incident.

Position error. Error in the indication of the altimeter, ASI, and VSI caused by the air at the static system entrance not being absolutely still.

Position report. A report over a known location as transmitted by an aircraft to ATC.

Positive static stability. The initial tendency to return to a state of equilibrium when disturbed from that state.

Power. Implies work rate or units of work per unit of time, and as such, it is a function of the speed at which the force is developed. The term "power required" is generally associated with reciprocating engines.

Powerplant. A complete engine and propeller combination with accessories.

Precession. The characteristic of a gyroscope that causes an applied force to be felt, not at the point of application, but 90° from that point in the direction of rotation.

Precipitation. Any or all forms of water particles (rain, sleet, hail, or snow) that fall from the atmosphere and reach the surface.

Precipitation static (P-static). A form of radio interference caused by rain, snow, or dust particles hitting the antenna and inducing a small radio-frequency voltage into it.

Precision approach. A standard instrument approach procedure in which both vertical and horizontal guidance is provided.

Precision approach path indicator (PAPI). A system of lights similar to the VASI, but consisting of one row of lights in two- or four-light systems. A pilot on the correct glideslope will see two white lights and two red lights. See VASI.

Precision approach radar (PAR). A type of radar used at an airport to guide an aircraft through the final stages of landing, providing horizontal and vertical guidance. The radar operator directs the pilot to change heading or adjust the descent rate to keep the aircraft on a path that allows it to touch down at the correct spot on the runway.

Precision runway monitor (PRM). System allows simultaneous, independent instrument flight rules (IFR) approaches at airports with closely spaced parallel runways.

Preferred IFR routes. Routes established in the major terminal and en route environments to increase system efficiency and capacity. IFR clearances are issued based on these routes, listed in the A/FD except when severe weather avoidance procedures or other factors dictate otherwise.

Preignition. Ignition occurring in the cylinder before the time of normal ignition. Preignition is often caused by a local hot spot in the combustion chamber igniting the fuel-air mixture.

Pressure altitude. Altitude above the standard 29.92 "Hg plane.

Pressure demand oxygen system. A demand oxygen system that supplies 100 percent oxygen at sufficient pressure above the altitude where normal breathing is adequate. Also referred to as a pressure breathing system.

Prevailing visibility. The greatest horizontal visibility equaled or exceeded throughout at least half the horizon circle (which is not necessarily continuous).

Preventive maintenance. Simple or minor preservative operations and the replacement of small standard parts not involving complex assembly operation as listed in 14 CFR part 43, appendix A. Certificated pilots may perform preventive maintenance on any aircraft that is owned or operated by them provided that the aircraft is not used in air carrier service.

Primary and supporting. A method of attitude instrument flying using the instrument that provides the most direct indication of attitude and performance.

Primary flight display (PFD). A display that provides increased situational awareness to the pilot by replacing the traditional six instruments used for instrument flight with an easy-to-scan display that provides the horizon, airspeed, altitude, vertical speed, trend, trim, and rate of turn among other key relevant indications.

PRM. See precision runway monitor.

Procedure turn. A maneuver prescribed when it is necessary to reverse direction to establish an aircraft on the intermediate approach segment or final approach course.

Profile view. Side view of an IAP chart illustrating the vertical approach path altitudes, headings, distances, and fixes.

Prohibited area. Designated airspace within which flight of aircraft is prohibited.

Propeller. A device for propelling an aircraft that, when rotated, produces by its action on the air, a thrust approximately perpendicular to its plane of rotation. It includes the control components normally supplied by its manufacturer.

Propeller/rotor modulation error. Certain propeller rpm settings or helicopter rotor speeds can cause the VOR course deviation indicator (CDI) to fluctuate as much as ±6°. Slight changes to the rpm setting will normally smooth out this roughness.

Rabbit, the. High-intensity flasher system installed at many large airports. The flashers consist of a series of brilliant blue-white bursts of light flashing in sequence along the approach lights, giving the effect of a ball of light traveling toward the runway.

Radar. A system that uses electromagnetic waves to identify the range, altitude, direction, or speed of both moving and fixed objects such as aircraft, weather formations, and terrain. The term RADAR was coined in 1941 as an acronym for Radio Detection and Ranging. The term has since entered the English language as a standard word, radar, losing the capitalization in the process.

Radar approach. The controller provides vectors while monitoring the progress of the flight with radar, guiding the pilot through the descent to the airport/heliport or to a specific runway.

Radar services. Radar is a method whereby radio waves are transmitted into the air and are then received when they have been reflected by an object in the path of the beam. Range is determined by measuring the time it takes (at the speed of light) for the radio wave to go out to the object and then return to the receiving antenna. The direction of a detected object from a radar site is determined by the position of the rotating antenna when the reflected portion of the radio wave is received.

Radar summary chart. A weather product derived from the national radar network that graphically displays a summary of radar weather reports.

Radar weather report (SD). A report issued by radar stations at 35 minutes after the hour, and special reports as needed. Provides information on the type, intensity, and location of the echo tops of the precipitation.

Radials. The courses oriented from a station.

Radio or radar altimeter. An electronic altimeter that determines the height of an aircraft above the terrain by measuring the time needed for a pulse of radio-frequency energy to travel from the aircraft to the ground and return.

Radio frequency (RF). A term that refers to alternating current (AC) having characteristics such that, if the current is input to antenna, an electromagnetic (EM) field is generated suitable for wireless broadcasting and/or communications.

Radio magnetic indicator (RMI). An electronic navigation instrument that combines a magnetic compass with an ADF or VOR. The card of the RMI acts as a gyro-stabilized magnetic compass, and shows the magnetic heading the aircraft is flying.

Radiosonde. A weather instrument that observes and reports meteorological conditions from the upper atmosphere. This instrument is typically carried into the atmosphere by some form of weather balloon.

Radio wave. An electromagnetic (EM) wave with frequency characteristics useful for radio transmission.

RAIM. See receiver autonomous integrity monitoring.

RAM recovery. The increase in thrust as a result of ram air pressures and density on the front of the engine caused by air velocity.

Random RNAV routes. Direct routes, based on area navigation capability, between waypoints defined in terms of latitude/longitude coordinates, degree-distance fixes, or offsets from established routes/airways at a specified distance and direction.

Ranging signals. Transmitted from the GPS satellite, signals allowing the aircraft's receiver to determine range (distance) from each satellite.

Rapid decompression. The almost instantaneous loss of cabin pressure in aircraft with a pressurized cockpit or cabin.

RB. See relative bearing.

RBI. See relative bearing indicator.

RCO. See remote communications outlet.

Receiver autonomous integrity monitoring (RAIM). A system used to verify the usability of the received GPS signals and warns the pilot of any malfunction in the navigation system. This system is required for IFR-certified GPS units.

Recommended altitude. An altitude depicted on an instrument approach chart with the altitude value neither underscored nor overscored. The depicted value is an advisory value.

Receiver-transmitter (RT). A system that receives and transmits a signal and an indicator.

Reduced vertical separation minimum (RVSM). Reduces the vertical separation between flight levels (FL) 290 and 410 from 2,000 feet to 1,000 feet, and makes six additional FLs available for operation. Also see DRVSM.

Reference circle (also, distance circle). The circle depicted in the plan view of an IAP chart that typically has a 10 NM radius, within which chart the elements are drawn to scale.

Regions of command. The "regions of normal and reversed command" refers to the relationship between speed and the power required to maintain or change that speed in flight.

Region of reverse command. Flight regime in which flight at a higher airspeed requires a lower power setting and a lower airspeed requires a higher power setting in order to maintain altitude.

REIL. See runway end identifier lights.

Relative bearing (RB). The angular difference between the aircraft heading and the direction to the station, measured clockwise from the nose of the aircraft.

Relative bearing indicator (RBI). Also known as the fixed-card ADF, zero is always indicated at the top of the instrument and the needle indicates the relative bearing to the station.

Relative humidity. The ratio of the existing amount of water vapor in the air at a given temperature to the maximum amount that could exist at that temperature; usually expressed in percent.

Relative wind. Direction of the airflow produced by an object moving through the air. The relative wind for an airplane in flight flows in a direction parallel with and opposite to the direction of flight; therefore, the actual flight path of the airplane determines the direction of the relative wind.

Remote communications outlet (RCO). An unmanned communications facility that is remotely controlled by air traffic personnel.

Required navigation performance (RNP). A specified level of accuracy defined by a lateral area of confined airspace in which an RNP-certified aircraft operates.

Restricted area. Airspace designated under 14 CFR part 73 within which the flight of aircraft, while not wholly prohibited, is subject to restriction.

Reverse sensing. The VOR needle appearing to indicate the reverse of normal operation.

RF. Radio frequency.

Rhodopsin. The photosensitive pigments that initiate the visual response in the rods of the eye.

Rigging. The final adjustment and alignment of an aircraft and its flight control system that provides the proper aerodynamic characteristics.

Rigidity. The characteristic of a gyroscope that prevents its axis of rotation tilting as the Earth rotates.

Rigidity in space. The principle that a wheel with a heavily weighted rim spinning rapidly will remain in a fixed position in the plane in which it is spinning.

Rime ice. Rough, milky, opaque ice formed by the instantaneous freezing of small supercooled water droplets.

Risk. The future impact of a hazard that is not eliminated or controlled.

Risk elements. There are four fundamental risk elements in aviation: the pilot, the aircraft, the environment, and the type of operation that comprise any given aviation situation.

Risk management. The part of the decision-making process which relies on situational awareness, problem recognition, and good judgment to reduce risks associated with each flight.

RMI. See radio magnetic indicator.

RNAV. See area navigation.

RNP. See required navigation performance.

RT. See receiver-transmitter.

Rudder. The movable primary control surface mounted on the trailing edge of the vertical fin of an airplane. Movement of the rudder rotates the airplane about its vertical axis.

Ruddervator. A pair of control surfaces on the tail of an aircraft arranged in the form of a V. These surfaces, when moved together by the control wheel, serve as elevators, and when moved differentially by the rudder pedals, serve as a rudder.

Runway centerline lights. Runway lighting which consists of flush centerline lights spaced at 50-foot intervals beginning 75 feet from the landing threshold.

Runway edge lights. A component of the runway lighting system that is used to outline the edges of runways at night or during low visibility conditions. These lights are classified according to the intensity they are capable of producing.

Runway end identifier lights (REIL). A pair of synchronized flashing lights, located laterally on each side of the runway threshold, providing rapid and positive identification of the approach end of a runway.

Runway visibility value (RVV). The visibility determined for a particular runway by a transmissometer.

Runway visual range (RVR). The instrumentally derived horizontal distance a pilot should be able to see down the runway from the approach end, based on either the sighting of high-intensity runway lights, or the visual contrast of other objects.

RVR. See runway visual range.

RVV. See runway visibility value.

SA. See selective availability.

St. Elmo's Fire. A corona discharge which lights up the aircraft surface areas where maximum static discharge occurs.

Satellite ephemeris data. Data broadcast by the GPS satellite containing very accurate orbital data for that satellite, atmospheric propagation data, and satellite clock error data.

Sea breeze. A coastal breeze blowing from sea to land caused by the temperature difference when the land surface is warmer than the sea surface. The sea breeze usually occurs during the day and alternates with the land breeze that blows in the opposite direction at night.

Sea level engine. A reciprocating aircraft engine having a rated takeoff power that is producible only at sea level.

Scan. The first fundamental skill of instrument flight, also known as "cross-check;" the continuous and logical observation of instruments for attitude and performance information.

Sectional aeronautical charts. Designed for visual navigation of slow- or medium-speed aircraft. Topographic information on these charts features the portrayal of relief, and a judicious selection of visual check points for VFR flight. Aeronautical information includes visual and radio aids to navigation, airports, controlled airspace, restricted areas, obstructions and related data.

SDF. See simplified directional facility.

Selective availability (SA). A satellite technology permitting the Department of Defense (DOD) to create, in the interest of national security, a significant clock and ephemeris error in the satellites, resulting in a navigation error.

Semicircular canal. An inner ear organ that detects angular acceleration of the body.

Semimonocoque. A fuselage design that includes a substructure of bulkheads and/or formers, along with stringers, to support flight loads and stresses imposed on the fuselage.

Sensitive altimeter. A form of multipointer pneumatic altimeter with an adjustable barometric scale that allows the reference pressure to be set to any desired level.

Service ceiling. The maximum density altitude where the best rate-of-climb airspeed will produce a 100-feet-per-minute climb at maximum weight while in a clean configuration with maximum continuous power.

Servo. A motor or other form of actuator which receives a small signal from the control device and exerts a large force to accomplish the desired work.

Servo tab. An auxiliary control mounted on a primary control surface, which automatically moves in the direction opposite the primary control to provide an aerodynamic assist in the movement of the control.

SIDS. See standard instrument departure procedures.

SIGMET. The acronym for Significant Meteorological information. A weather advisory issued concerning weather significant to the safety of all aircraft.

Signal-to-noise ratio. An indication of signal strength received compared to background noise, which is a measure of the adequacy of the received signal.

Significant weather prognostic. Presents four panels showing forecast significant weather.

Simplex. Transmission and reception on the same frequency.

Simplified directional facility (SDF). A NAVAID used for nonprecision instrument approaches. The final approach course is similar to that of an ILS localizer; however, the SDF course may be offset from the runway, generally not more than 3°, and the course may be wider than the localizer, resulting in a lower degree of accuracy.

Single-pilot resource management (SRM). The ability for a pilot to manage all resources effectively to ensure the outcome of the flight is successful.

Situational awareness. Pilot knowledge of where the aircraft is in regard to location, air traffic control, weather, regulations, aircraft status, and other factors that may affect flight.

Skidding turn. An uncoordinated turn in which the rate of turn is too great for the angle of bank, pulling the aircraft to the outside of the turn.

Skills and procedures. The procedural, psychomotor, and perceptual skills used to control a specific aircraft or its systems. They are the airmanship abilities that are gained through conventional training, are perfected, and become almost automatic through experience.

Skin friction drag. Drag generated between air molecules and the solid surface of the aircraft.

Slant range. The horizontal distance from the aircraft antenna to the ground station, due to line-of-sight transmission of the DME signal.

Slaved compass. A system whereby the heading gyro is "slaved to," or continuously corrected to bring its direction readings into agreement with a remotely located magnetic direction sensing device (usually a flux valve or flux gate compass).

Slipping turn. An uncoordinated turn in which the aircraft is banked too much for the rate of turn, so the horizontal lift component is greater than the centrifugal force, pulling the aircraft toward the inside of the turn.

Small airplane. An airplane of 12,500 pounds or less maximum certificated takeoff weight.

Somatogravic illusion. The misperception of being in a nose-up or nose-down attitude, caused by a rapid acceleration or deceleration while in flight situations that lack visual reference.

Spatial disorientation. The state of confusion due to misleading information being sent to the brain from various sensory organs, resulting in a lack of awareness of the aircraft position in relation to a specific reference point.

Special flight permit. A flight permit issued to an aircraft that does not meet airworthiness requirements but is capable of safe flight. A special flight permit can be issued to move an aircraft for the purposes of maintenance or repair, buyer delivery, manufacturer flight tests, evacuation from danger, or customer demonstration. Also referred to as a ferry permit.

Special use airspace. Airspace in which flight activities are subject to restrictions that can create limitations on the mixed use of airspace. Consists of prohibited, restricted, warning, military operations, and alert areas.

Special fuel consumption. The amount of fuel in pounds per hour consumed or required by an engine per brake horsepower or per pound of thrust.

Speed. The distance traveled in a given time.

Spin. An aggravated stall that results in an airplane descending in a helical, or corkscrew path.

Spiral instability. A condition that exists when the static directional stability of the airplane is very strong as compared to the effect of its dihedral in maintaining lateral equilibrium.

Spiraling slipstream. The slipstream of a propeller-driven airplane rotates around the airplane. This slipstream strikes the left side of the vertical fin, causing the aircraft to yaw slightly. Rudder offset is sometimes used by aircraft designers to counteract this tendency.

Spoilers. High-drag devices that can be raised into the air flowing over an airfoil, reducing lift and increasing drag. Spoilers are used for roll control on some aircraft. Deploying spoilers on both wings at the same time allows the aircraft to descend without gainingspeed. Spoilers are also used to shorten the ground roll after landing.

SRM. See single-pilot resource management.

SSR. See secondary surveillance radar.

SSV. See standard service volume.

Stabilator. A single-piece horizontal tail surface on an airplane that pivots around a central hinge point. A stabilator serves the purposes of both the horizontal stabilizer and the elevators.

Stability. The inherent quality of an airplane to correct for conditions that may disturb its equilibrium, and to return or to continue on the original flightpath. It is primarily an airplane design characteristic.

Stagnant hypoxia. A type of hypoxia that results when the oxygen-rich blood in the lungs is not moving to the tissues that need it.

Stall. A rapid decrease in lift caused by the separation of airflow from the wing's surface, brought on by exceeding the critical angle of attack. A stall can occur at any pitch attitude or airspeed.

Standard atmosphere. At sea level, the standard atmosphere consists of a barometric pressure of 29.92 inches of mercury ("Hg) or 1013.2 millibars, and a temperature of 15 °C (59 °F). Pressure and temperature normally decrease as altitude increases. The standard lapse rate in the lower atmosphere for each 1,000 feet of altitude is approximately 1 "Hg and 2 °C (3.5 °F). For example, the standard pressure and temperature at 3,000 feet mean sea level (MSL) are 26.92 "Hg (29.92 "Hg − 3 "Hg) and 9 °C (15 °C − 6 °C).

Standard empty weight (GAMA). This weight consists of the airframe, engines, and all items of operating equipment that have fixed locations and are permanently installed in the airplane including fixed ballast, hydraulic fluid, unusable fuel, and full engine oil.

Standard holding pattern. A holding pattern in which all turns are made to the right.

Standard instrument departure procedures (SIDS). Published procedures to expedite clearance delivery and to facilitate transition between takeoff and en route operations.

Standard rate turn. A turn in which an aircraft changes its direction at a rate of 3° per second (360° in 2 minutes) for low- or medium-speed aircraft. For high-speed aircraft, the standard rate turn is 1½° per second (360° in 4 minutes).

Standard service volume (SSV). Defines the limits of the volume of airspace which the VOR serves.

Standard terminal arrival route (STAR). A preplanned IFR ATC arrival procedure published for pilot use in graphic and/or textual form.

Standard weights. Weights established for numerous items involved in weight and balance computations. These weights should not be used if actual weights are available.

STAR. See standard terminal arrival route.

Static longitudinal stability. The aerodynamic pitching moments required to return the aircraft to the equilibrium angle of attack.

Static pressure. Pressure of air that is still or not moving, measured perpendicular to the surface of the aircraft.

Static stability. The initial tendency an aircraft displays when disturbed from a state of equilibrium.

Station. A location in the airplane that is identified by a number designating its distance in inches from the datum. The datum is, therefore, identified as station zero. An item located at station +50 would have an arm of 50 inches.

Stationary front. A front that is moving at a speed of less than 5 knots.

Steep turns. In instrument flight, any turn greater than standard rate; in visual flight, anything greater than a 45° bank.

Stepdown fix. The point after which additional descent is permitted within a segment of an IAP.

Strapdown system. An INS in which the accelerometers and gyros are permanently "strapped down" or aligned with the three axes of the aircraft.

Stratoshere. A layer of the atmosphere above the tropopause extending to a height of approximately 160,000 feet.

Stress. The body's response to demands placed upon it.

Stress management. The personal analysis of the kinds of stress experienced while flying, the application of appropriate stress assessment tools, and other coping mechanisms.

Structural icing. The accumulation of ice on the exterior of the aircraft.

Sublimation. Process by which a solid is changed to a gas without going through the liquid state.

Suction relief valve. A relief valve in an instrument vacuum system required to maintain the correct low pressure inside the instrument case for the proper operation of the gyros.

Supercharger. An engine- or exhaust-driven air compressor used to provide additional pressure to the induction air so the engine can produce additional power.

Supercooled water droplets. Water droplets that have been cooled below the freezing point, but are still in a liquid state.

Surface analysis chart. A report that depicts an analysis of the current surface weather. Shows the areas of high and low pressure, fronts, temperatures, dewpoints, wind directions and speeds, local weather, and visual obstructions.

Synchro. A device used to transmit indications of angular movement or position from one location to another.

Synthetic vision. A realistic display depiction of the aircraft in relation to terrain and flight path.

TAA. See terminal arrival area.

TACAN. See tactical air navigation.

Tactical air navigation (TACAN). An electronic navigation system used by military aircraft, providing both distance and direction information.

Takeoff decision speed (V_1). Per 14 CFR section 23.51: "the calibrated airspeed on the ground at which, as a result of engine failure or other reasons, the pilot assumed to have made a decision to continue or discontinue the takeoff."

Takeoff distance. The distance required to complete an all-engines operative takeoff to the 35-foot height. It must be at least 15 percent less than the distance required for a one-engine inoperative engine takeoff. This distance is not normally a limiting factor as it is usually less than the one-engine inoperative takeoff distance.

Takeoff safety speed (V_2). Per 14 CFR part 1: "A referenced airspeed obtained after lift-off at which the required one-engine-inoperative climb performance can be achieved."

TAWS. See terrain awareness and warning system.

Taxiway lights. Omnidirectional lights that outline the edges of the taxiway and are blue in color.

Taxiway turnoff lights. Lights that are flush with the runway which emit a steady green color.

TCAS. See traffic alert collision avoidance system.

TCH. See threshold crossing height.

TDZE. See touchdown zone elevation.

TEC. See Tower En Route Control.

Technique. The manner in which procedures are executed.

Telephone information briefing service (TIBS). Telephone recording of area and/or route meteorological briefings, airspace procedures, and special aviation-oriented announcements.

Temporary flight restriction (TFR). Restriction to flight imposed in order to:

1. Protect persons and property in the air or on the surface from an existing or imminent flight associated hazard;

2. Provide a safe environment for the operation of disaster relief aircraft;

3. Prevent an unsafe congestion of sightseeing aircraft above an incident;

4. Protect the President, Vice President, or other public figures; and,

5. Provide a safe environment for space agency operations.

Pilots are expected to check appropriate NOTAMs during flight planning when conducting flight in an area where a temporary flight restriction is in effect.

Tension. Maintaining an excessively strong grip on the control column, usually resulting in an overcontrolled situation.

Terminal aerodrome forecast (TAF). A report established for the 5 statute mile radius around an airport. Utilizes the same descriptors and abbreviations as the METAR report.

Terminal arrival area (TAA). A procedure to provide a new transition method for arriving aircraft equipped with FMS and/or GPS navigational equipment. The TAA contains a "T" structure that normally provides a NoPT for aircraft using the approach.

Terminal instrument approach procedure (TERP). Prescribes standardized methods for use in designing instrument flight procedures.

TERP. See terminal instrument approach procedure.

Terminal radar service areas (TRSA). Areas where participating pilots can receive additional radar services. The purpose of the service is to provide separation between all IFR operations and participating VFR aircraft.

Terrain awareness and warning system (TAWS). A timed-based system that provides information concerning potential hazards with fixed objects by using GPS positioning and a database of terrain and obstructions to provide true predictability of the upcoming terrain and obstacles.

TFR. See temporary flight restriction.

Thermosphere. The last layer of the atmosphere that begins above the mesosphere and gradually fades away into space.

Threshold crossing height (TCH). The theoretical height above the runway threshold at which the aircraft's glideslope antenna would be if the aircraft maintained the trajectory established by the mean ILS glideslope or MLS glidepath.

Thrust. The force which imparts a change in the velocity of a mass. This force is measured in pounds but has no element of time or rate. The term "thrust required" is generally associated with jet engines. A forward force which propels the airplane through the air.

Thrust (aerodynamic force). The forward aerodynamic force produced by a propeller, fan, or turbojet engine as it forces a mass of air to the rear, behind the aircraft.

Thrust line. An imaginary line passing through the center of the propeller hub, perpendicular to the plane of the propeller rotation.

Time and speed table. A table depicted on an instrument approach procedure chart that identifies the distance from the FAF to the MAP, and provides the time required to transit that distance based on various groundspeeds.

Timed turn. A turn in which the clock and the turn coordinator are used to change heading a definite number of degrees in a given time.

TIS. See traffic information service.

Title 14 of the Code of Federal Regulations (14 CFR). Includes the federal aviation regulations governing the operation of aircraft, airways, and airmen.

Torque. (1) A resistance to turning or twisting. (2) Forces that produce a twisting or rotating motion. (3) In an airplane, the tendency of the aircraft to turn (roll) in the opposite direction of rotation of the engine and propeller. (4) In helicopters with a single, main rotor system, the tendency of the helicopter to turn in the opposite direction of the main rotor rotation.

Torquemeter. An instrument used with some of the larger reciprocating engines and turboprop or turboshaft engines to measure the reaction between the propeller reduction gears and the engine case.

Total drag. The sum of the parasite drag and induced drag.

Touchdown zone elevation (TDZE). The highest elevation in the first 3,000 feet of the landing surface, TDZE is indicated on the instrument approach procedure chart when straight-in landing minimums are authorized.

Touchdown zone lights. Two rows of transverse light bars disposed symmetrically about the runway centerline in the runway touchdown zone.

Tower En Route Control (TEC). The control of IFR en route traffic within delegated airspace between two or more adjacent approach control facilities, designed to expedite traffic and reduce control and pilot communication requirements.

TPP. See United States Terminal Procedures Publication.

Track. The actual path made over the ground in flight.

Tracking. Flying a heading that will maintain the desired track to or from the station regardless of crosswind conditions.

Traffic Alert Collision Avoidance System (TCAS). An airborne system developed by the FAA that operates independently from the ground-based Air Traffic Control system. Designed to increase flight deck awareness of proximate aircraft and to serve as a "last line of defense" for the prevention of midair collisions.

Traffic information service (TIS). A ground-based service providing information to the flight deck via data link using the S-mode transponder and altitude encoder to improve the safety and efficiency of "see and avoid" flight through an automatic display that informs the pilot of nearby traffic.

Trailing edge. The portion of the airfoil where the airflow over the upper surface rejoins the lower surface airflow.

Transcribed Weather Broadcast (TWEB). Meteorological and aeronautical data recorded on tapes and broadcast over selected NAVAIDs. Generally, the broadcast contains route-oriented data with specially prepared NWS forecasts, inflight advisories, and winds aloft. It also includes selected current information such as weather reports (METAR/SPECI), NOTAMs, and special notices.

Transponder. The airborne portion of the ATC radar beacon system.

Transponder code. One of 4,096 four-digit discrete codes ATC assigns to distinguish between aircraft.

Trend. Immediate indication of the direction of aircraft movement, as shown on instruments.

Tricycle gear. Landing gear employing a third wheel located on the nose of the aircraft.

Trim. To adjust the aerodynamic forces on the control surfaces so that the aircraft maintains the set attitude without any control input.

Trim tab. A small auxiliary hinged portion of a movable control surface that can be adjusted during flight to a position resulting in a balance of control forces.

Tropopause. The boundary layer between the troposphere and the mesosphere which acts as a lid to confine most of the water vapor, and the associated weather, to the troposphere.

Troposphere. The layer of the atmosphere extending from the surface to a height of 20,000 to 60,000 feet, depending on latitude.

True airspeed. Actual airspeed, determined by applying a correction for pressure altitude and temperature to the CAS.

True altitude. The vertical distance of the airplane above sea level—the actual altitude. It is often expressed as feet above mean sea level (MSL). Airport, terrain, and obstacle elevations on aeronautical charts are true altitudes.

Truss. A fuselage design made up of supporting structural members that resist deformation by applied loads. The truss-type fuselage is constructed of steel or aluminum tubing. Strength and rigidity is achieved by welding the tubing together into a series of triangular shapes, called trusses.

T-tail. An aircraft with the horizontal stabilizer mounted on the top of the vertical stabilizer, forming a T.

Turbine discharge pressure. The total pressure at the discharge of the low-pressure turbine in a dual-turbine axial-flow engine.

Turbine engine. An aircraft engine which consists of an air compressor, a combustion section, and a turbine. Thrust is produced by increasing the velocity of the air flowing through the engine.

Turbocharger. An air compressor driven by exhaust gases, which increases the pressure of the air going into the engine through the carburetor or fuel injection system.

Turbofan engine. A fanlike turbojet engine designed to create additional thrust by diverting a secondary airflow around the combustion chamber.

Turbojet engine. A turbine engine which produces its thrust entirely by accelerating the air through the engine.

Turboprop engine. A turbine engine which drives a propeller through a reduction gearing arrangement. Most of the energy in the exhaust gases is converted into torque, rather than using its acceleration to drive the aircraft.

Turboshaft engine. A gas turbine engine that delivers power through a shaft to operate something other than a propeller.

Turn-and-slip indicator. A flight instrument consisting of a rate gyro to indicate the rate of yaw and a curved glass inclinometer to indicate the relationship between gravity and centrifugal force. The turn-and-slip indicator indicates the relationship between angle of bank and rate of yaw. Also called a turn-and-bank indicator.

Turn coordinator. A rate gyro that senses both roll and yaw due to the gimbal being canted. Has largely replaced the turn-and-slip indicator in modern aircraft.

TWEB. See Transcribed Weather Broadcast.

UHF. See ultra-high frequency.

Ultra-high frequency (UHF). The range of electromagnetic frequencies between 962 MHz and 1213 MHz.

Ulitmate load factor. In stress analysis, the load that causes physical breakdown in an aircraft or aircraft component during a strength test, or the load that according to computations, should cause such a breakdown.

Uncaging. Unlocking the gimbals of a gyroscopic instrument, making it susceptible to damage by abrupt flight maneuvers or rough handling.

Uncontrolled airspace. Class G airspace that has not been designated as Class A, B, C, D, or E. It is airspace in which air traffic control has no authority or responsibility to control air traffic; however, pilots should remember there are VFR minimums which apply to this airspace.

Underpower. Using less power than required for the purpose of achieving a faster rate of airspeed change.

United States Terminal Procedures Publication (TPP). Booklets published in regional format by the NACO that include DPs, STARs, IAPs, and other information pertinent to IFR flight.

Unusual attitude. An unintentional, unanticipated, or extreme aircraft attitude.

Useful load. The weight of the pilot, copilot, passengers, baggage, usable fuel, and drainable oil. It is the basic empty weight subtracted from the maximum allowable gross weight. This term applies to general aviation aircraft only.

User-defined waypoints. Waypoint location and other data which may be input by the user, this is the only GPS database information that may be altered (edited) by the user.

V_1. See takeoff decision speed.

V_2. See takeoff safety speed.

V_A. The design maneuvering speed. The maximum speed at which full, abrupt control movement can be used without overstressing the airframe.

Vapor lock. A problem that mostly affects gasoline-fuelled internal combustion engines. It occurs when the liquid fuel changes state from liquid to gas while still in the fuel delivery system. This disrupts the operation of the fuel pump, causing loss of feed pressure to the carburetor or fuel injection system, resulting in transient loss of power or complete stalling. Restarting the engine from this state may be difficult. The fuel can vaporise due to being heated by the engine, by the local climate or due to a lower boiling point at high altitude.

Variation. Compass error caused by the difference in the physical locations of the magnetic north pole and the geographic north pole.

VASI. See visual approach slope indicator.

VDP. See visual descent point.

Vector. A force vector is a graphic representation of a force and shows both the magnitude and direction of the force.

Vectoring. Navigational guidance by assigning headings.

Velocity. The speed or rate of movement in a certain direction.

Venturi tube. A specially shaped tube attached to the outside of an aircraft to produce suction to allow proper operation of gyro instruments.

Vertical axis. An imaginary line passing vertically through the center of gravity of an aircraft. The vertical axis is called the z-axis or the yaw axis.

Vertical card compass. A magnetic compass that consists of an azimuth on a vertical card, resembling a heading indicator with a fixed miniature airplane to accurately present the heading of the aircraft. The design uses eddy current damping to minimize lead and lag during turns.

Vertical speed indicator (VSI). A rate-of-pressure change instrument that gives an indication of any deviation from a constant pressure level.

Vertical stability. Stability about an aircraft's vertical axis. Also called yawing or directional stability.

Very-high frequency (VHF). A band of radio frequencies falling between 30 and 300 MHz.

Very-high frequency omnidirectional range (VOR). Electronic navigation equipment in which the flight deck instrument identifies the radial or line from the VOR station, measured in degrees clockwise from magnetic north, along which the aircraft is located.

Vestibule. The central cavity of the bony labyrinth of the ear, or the parts of the membranous labyrinth that it contains.

V$_{FE}$. The maximum speed with the flaps extended. The upper limit of the white arc.

VFR. See visual flight rules.

VFR on top. ATC authorization for an IFR aircraft to operate in VFR conditions at any appropriate VFR altitude.

VFR over the top. A VFR operation in which an aircraft operates in VFR conditions on top of an undercast.

VFR terminal area chart. At a scale of 1:250,000, a chart that depicts Class B airspace, which provides for the control or segregation of all the aircraft within the Class B airspace. The chart depicts topographic information and aeronautical information including visual and radio aids to navigation, airports, controlled airspace, restricted areas, obstructions, and related data.

V-G diagram. A chart that relates velocity to load factor. It is valid only for a specific weight, configuration and altitude and shows the maximum amount of positive or negative lift the airplane is capable of generating at a given speed. Also shows the safe load factor limits and the load factor that the aircraft can sustain at various speeds.

Victor airways. Airways based on a centerline that extends from one VOR or VORTAC navigation aid or intersection, to another navigation aid (or through several navigation aids or intersections); used to establish a known route for en route procedures between terminal areas.

Visual approach slope indicator (VASI). A visual aid of lights arranged to provide descent guidance information during the approach to the runway. A pilot on the correct glideslope will see red lights over white lights.

Visual descent point (VDP). A defined point on the final approach course of a nonprecision straight-in approach procedure from which normal descent from the MDA to the runway touchdown point may be commenced, provided the runway environment is clearly visible to the pilot.

Visual flight rules (VFR). Flight rules adopted by the FAA governing aircraft flight using visual references. VFR operations specify the amount of ceiling and the visibility the pilot must have in order to operate according to these rules. When the weather conditions are such that the pilot can not operate according to VFR, he or she must use instrument flight rules (IFR).

Visual meteorological conditions (VMC). Meteorological conditions expressed in terms of visibility, distance from cloud, and ceiling meeting or exceeding the minimums specified for VFR.

V$_{LE}$. Landing gear extended speed. The maximum speed at which an airplane can be safely flown with the landing gear extended.

V$_{LO}$. Landing gear operating speed. The maximum speed for extending or retracting the landing gear if using an airplane equipped with retractable landing gear.

V$_{MC}$. Minimum control airspeed. This is the minimum flight speed at which a light, twin-engine airplane can be satisfactorily controlled when an engine suddenly becomes inoperative and the remaining engine is at takeoff power.

VMC. See visual meteorological conditions.

V$_{NE}$. The never-exceed speed. Operating above this speed is prohibited since it may result in damage or structural failure. The red line on the airspeed indicator.

V$_{NO}$. The maximum structural cruising speed. Do not exceed this speed except in smooth air. The upper limit of the green arc.

VOR. See very-high frequency omnidirectional range.

VORTAC. A facility consisting of two components, VOR and TACAN, which provides three individual services: VOR azimuth, TACAN azimuth, and TACAN distance (DME) at one site.

VOR test facility (VOT). A ground facility which emits a test signal to check VOR receiver accuracy. Some VOTs are available to the user while airborne, while others are limited to ground use only.

VOT. See VOR test facility.

VSI. See vertical speed indicator.

V$_{S0}$. The stalling speed or the minimum steady flight speed in the landing configuration. In small airplanes, this is the power-off stall speed at the maximum landing weight in the landing configuration (gear and flaps down). The lower limit of the white arc.

V$_{S1}$. The stalling speed or the minimum steady flight speed obtained in a specified configuration. For most airplanes, this is the power-off stall speed at the maximum takeoff weight in the clean configuration (gear up, if retractable, and flaps up). The lower limit of the green arc.

V-tail. A design which utilizes two slanted tail surfaces to perform the same functions as the surfaces of a conventional elevator and rudder configuration. The fixed surfaces act as both horizontal and vertical stabilizers.

V$_X$. Best angle-of-climb speed. The airspeed at which an airplane gains the greatest amount of altitude in a given distance. It is used during a short-field takeoff to clear an obstacle.

V$_Y$. Best rate-of-climb speed. This airspeed provides the most altitude gain in a given period of time.

V$_{YSE}$. Best rate-of-climb speed with one engine inoperative. This airspeed provides the most altitude gain in a given period of time in a light, twin-engine airplane following an engine failure.

WAAS. See wide area augmentation system.

Wake turbulence. Wingtip vortices that are created when an airplane generates lift. When an airplane generates lift, air spills over the wingtips from the high pressure areas below the wings to the low pressure areas above them. This flow causes rapidly rotating whirlpools of air called wingtip vortices or wake turbulence.

Warm front. The boundary area formed when a warm air mass contacts and flows over a colder air mass. Warm fronts cause low ceilings and rain.

Warning area. An area containing hazards to any aircraft not participating in the activities being conducted in the area. Warning areas may contain intensive military training, gunnery exercises, or special weapons testing.

WARP. See weather and radar processing.

Waste gate. A controllable valve in the tailpipe of an aircraft reciprocating engine equipped with a turbocharger. The valve is controlled to vary the amount of exhaust gases forced through the turbocharger turbine.

Waypoint. A designated geographical location used for route definition or progress-reporting purposes and is defined in terms of latitude/longitude coordinates.

WCA. See wind correction angle.

Weather and radar processor (WARP). A device that provides real-time, accurate, predictive, and strategic weather information presented in an integrated manner in the National Airspace System (NAS).

Weather depiction chart. Details surface conditions as derived from METAR and other surface observations.

Weight. The force exerted by an aircraft from the pull of gravity.

Wide area augmentation system (WAAS). A differential global positioning system (DGPS) that improves the accuracy of the system by determining position error from the GPS satellites, then transmitting the error, or corrective factors, to the airborne GPS receiver.

Wind correction angle (WCA). The angle between the desired track and the heading of the aircraft necessary to keep the aircraft tracking over the desired track.

Wind direction indicators. Indicators that include a wind sock, wind tee, or tetrahedron. Visual reference will determine wind direction and runway in use.

Wind shear. A sudden, drastic shift in windspeed, direction, or both that may occur in the horizontal or vertical plane.

Winds and temperature aloft forecast (FD). A twice daily forecast that provides wind and temperature forecasts for specific locations in the contiguous United States.

Wing area. The total surface of the wing (in square feet), which includes control surfaces and may include wing area covered by the fuselage (main body of the airplane), and engine nacelles.

Wings. Airfoils attached to each side of the fuselage and are the main lifting surfaces that support the airplane in flight.

Wing span. The maximum distance from wingtip to wingtip.

Wingtip vortices. The rapidly rotating air that spills over an airplane's wings during flight. The intensity of the turbulence depends on the airplane's weight, speed, and configuration. Also referred to as wake turbulence. Vortices from heavy aircraft may be extremely hazardous to small aircraft.

Wing twist. A design feature incorporated into some wings to improve aileron control effectiveness at high angles of attack during an approach to a stall.

Work. A measurement of force used to produce movement.

World Aeronautical Charts (WAC). A standard series of aeronautical charts covering land areas of the world at a size and scale convenient for navigation (1:1,000,000) by moderate speed aircraft. Topographic information includes cities and towns, principal roads, railroads, distinctive landmarks, drainage, and relief. Aeronautical information includes visual and radio aids to navigation, airports, airways, restricted areas, obstructions and other pertinent data.

Zone of confusion. Volume of space above the station where a lack of adequate navigation signal directly above the VOR station causes the needle to deviate.

Zulu time. A term used in aviation for coordinated universal time (UTC) which places the entire world on one time standard.

Index

100-hour inspection 8-9

A

Abbreviated briefing 12-5
Absolute altitude 7-6
Accelerate-go distance 10-28
Accelerate-stop distance 10-28
Adjustable-pitch propeller 6-6
Adjustable stabilizer 5-11
Advection fog 11-15
Adverse balance 9-3
Adverse conditions 12-5
Adverse yaw 5-3
Advisory circular (AC) 1-10
Aeromedical factors 16-1
Aeronautical charts 13-3
Aeronautical decision-making 17-1
Aeronautical information manual (AIM) 1-9
Ailerons 5-3
Airborne radar 12-3
Aircraft documents 8-6
Aircraft engine 6-1
Aircraft inspections 8-8
Aircraft maintenance 8-8
Aircraft owner/operator responsibilities 8-13
Aircraft Owners and Pilots Association (AOPA) 2-16
Aircraft types and categories 1-12
Airfoil 3-7, 3-8
Airframe 2-7
Airframe systems 6-25
Airline Deregulation Act of 1978 1-7
Airline transport pilot 1-14
Airmen's Meteorological Information (AIRMET)
.... 12-3, 12-12
Airplane Flight Manuals (AFM) 8-1
Airport/facility directory (A/FD) 13-3
Airport beacon 13-6
Airport lighting 13-6, 13-9
Airport markings and signs 13-4
Airport signs 13-6
Airport surveillance radar 12-3
Airspace 14-1

Airspeed 8-2
Airspeed indicator (ASI) 7-1, 7-8, 10-2
Airspeed tape 7-12
Airworthiness certificate 8-7
Airworthiness directives (ADs) 8-12
Air Commerce Act 1-4
Air data computer (ADC) 7-14
Air masses 11-18
Air route surveillance radar (ARSR) 12-2
Air route traffic control center (ARTCC) 12-2
Air traffic control (ATC) 1-6, 13-13, 14-7
Alcohol 16-13
Alert areas 14-4
Alternator 6-28
Altimeter 7-1, 7-3, 7-5, 7-12
Altimeter setting 12-7
Altimeter system inspection 8-9
Altitude 11-6
Altitude-induced decompression sickness (DCS) 16-16
Alto 11-17
Ammeter 6-30
Aneroid barometer 11-5
Angle of attack (AOA) 5-4
Annual inspection 8-8
Anti-ice 6-37
Antiservo tab 2-6, 5-11
Approach light systems 13-7
Area forecasts (FA) 12-11
Arm 9-5
Assessing risk 17-5
Asymmetric loading 4-27
ATC delays 12-5
ATC radar beacon system (ATCRBS) 13-14
Atmosphere 3-1, 10-2, 11-2
Atmospheric circulation 11-3
Atmospheric pressure 3-2, 10-2, 11-3
Atmospheric stability 11-12
Attitude and heading reference system (AHRS) 7-12, 7-20
Attitude indicator 7-12, 7-18
Autokinesis 16-7, 16-19
Automated Surface Observing System (ASOS) 12-2
Automated Weather Observing System (AWOS) 12-2

Automatic decision-making 17-20
Automatic terminal information service (ATIS)............7-5
Automation 17-25
Automation management 17-31
Autopilot 5-12
Autopilot systems 17-27
Aviation forecasts 12-10
Aviation gasoline (AVGAS)......................................6-26
Aviation medical examiner (AME) 16-2
Aviation routine weather report (METAR) 11-18, 12-6
Aviation safety inspector (ASI) 1-9
Aviation weather reports..12-6
Axes of an aircraft...4-11
Axes of rotation...5-3

B

Balance..9-2
Balanced field length...10-28
Balance tabs 5-11
Barbs 11-12
Basic aerodynamics 2-2
Basic empty weight..9-5
Before takeoff 13-18
Benoist, Tom..1-3
Bernoulli, Daniel...3-7
Bernoulli's Principle of Differential Pressure.............3-7
Best angle-of-climb speed (V_X)................................7-9
Best rate-of-climb speed (V_Y).................................7-9
Blade angle...4-24
Blocked pitot system...7-10
Blocked static system...7-11
Boundary layer.. 4-4, 4-39
Brakes 2-7, 6-32
Brake horsepower (BHP)................................... 6-6, 6-24
Bus bar 6-29

C

Cabin pressure control system 6-33
Cabin pressurization system 6-32
Calibrated airspeed (CAS).............................. 7-8, 10-17
Canard..5-7
Cannula 6-35
Carbon monoxide (CO) poisoning...........................16-11
Carburetor air temperature gauge 6-10
Carburetor heat..6-9
Carburetor icing 6-8
Carburetor systems..6-7
Castellanus 11-17
Catastrophic 17-6
Cayley, Sir George...1-2
Ceiling...11-17

Center of gravity 9-2, 9-5
Certificated flight instructor (CFI) 1-16, 1-20
Certificate of aircraft registration..............................8-6
CG limits...9-5
CG range 9-5
Chandelles...4-33
Change in lift-off technique 10-27
Charles, Professor Jacques...1-2
Cirrus...11-17
Civil Aeronautics Act 1-5
Civil Aeronautics Authority (CAA)...........................1-5
Civil Aeronautics Board (CAB)................................1-5
Civil airports 13-1
Class A Airspace 14-2
Class B Airspace 14-2
Class C Airspace 14-2
Class D Airspace 14-2
Class E Airspace 14-2
Class G Airspace 14-3
Climbs and descents..13-18
Climb performance 10-6
Climb performance expressed as percent gradient
of Climb 10-27
Climb requirements..10-29
Clouds 11-15, 12-16
Cloud classification 11-17
Code of Federal Regulations (CFR) 1-7
Cold front..11-20
Collision avoidance...13-17
Combustion 6-18
Commercial pilot 1-14
Compass systems 7-22
Composites...2-9
Compressor stalls 6-23
Continuous-flow oxygen system................................6-36
Control 9-3
Controllability 4-13, 4-36
Controlled airspace 13-2, 14-2
Controlled firing areas (CFAs)..................................14-4
Control instruments...2-12
Convective currents 11-7
Convective significant meteorological information
(WST) 12-13
Cooling..6-1
Coriolis force 11-3
Coriolis illusion...16-6
Corkscrew effect..4-26
Coupled ailerons 5-4
Crew resource management (CRM) 17-4
Critical...17-6
Crosswind and headwind component chart 10-24

Cumulus 11-17
Current conditions 12-5

D

Datum 9-5
DECIDE Model 17-17
Decision-making in a dynamic environment 17-19
Decision-making process 17-11
Dehydration 16-12
Deice system 6-37
Delta 9-5
Density altitude 3-3, 7-6, 10-3, 11-5
Density altitude charts 10-19
Department of Homeland Security (DHS) 1-6
Department of Transportation (DOT) 1-6
Deposition 11-15
Designated pilot examiner 1-20
Design maneuvering speed (VA) 7-9
Destination forecast 12-5
Destination signs 13-6
Determining loaded weight and CG 9-7
Deviation 7-24
Dew point 11-13, 12-16
Differential ailerons 5-4
Dihedral 4-16
Diluter-demand oxygen systems 6-36
Dip errors 7-24
Direction signs 13-6
Direct User Access Terminal Service (DUATS) 12-4
Doppler radar 12-2
Drag 2-2, 4-2, 4-3
Drugs 16-14
Dual lighting 13-9
Dutch roll 4-18
Dynamic hydroplaning 10-12
Dynamic stability 4-13

E

Eddy current damping 7-26
Electrical 6-1
Electrical pulse-demand oxygen system 6-36
Electrical system 2-7, 6-28
Electronic flight displays (EFD) 2-12, 7-12, 12-18
Elevator 2-5, 5-5
Elevator illusion 16-7
Emergency locator transmitter (ELT) 8-9
Empennage 2-3, 2-5
Empty-field myopia 16-18
Engine 6-1
Engine cooling systems 6-16
Engine pressure ratio (EPR) 6-22

Engine temperature limitations 6-22
Engine water ingestion 11-25
Enhanced Situational Awareness 17-31
Environmental control systems 6-1
En Route Flight Advisory Service (EFAS) 12-4
En route forecast 12-5
Equipment Use 17-27
Equivalent airspeed (EAS) 10-17
Equivalent shaft horsepower (ESHP) 6-24
Exhaust gas temperature (EGT) gauge 6-8, 6-22
Exhaust systems 6-17
Explosive decompression 6-33
External resources 17-22

F

FAA Safety Team (FAASTeam) 1-9
Fairings 4-4
False horizon 16-7, 16-19
Familiarity 17-29
Fansler, P. E. 1-3
Fast-moving cold front 11-21
Fatigue 16-12
Featureless terrain illusion 16-9
Federal Aviation Act of 1958 1-6
Federal Aviation Administration (FAA) 1-6
Federal Aviation Agency (FAA) 1-6
Federal Certification of Pilots and Mechanics 1-4
Federal Communications Commission (FCC) . 8-14, 13-11
Field offices 1-8
First airmail flight 1-4
First license 1-4
Fixed-pitch propeller 6-5
Flameout 6-23
Flaperons 5-5
Flaps 5-8
Flight controls 2-7, 5-2
Flight control systems 5-1
Flight instruments 7-1
Flight limits 8-4
Flight maneuvers 4-32
Flight publications 1-11
Flight school 1-15
Flight service station 12-4
Flight Standards District Office (FSDO) 1-8
Flight Standards Service (AFS) 1-8
Float-type carburetor 6-7
Floor load limit 9-5
Flux gate compass system 7-20
Fog 11-15, 16-9
Forces in climbs 4-21
Forces in descents 4-22

Forces in turns..4-19
Forecast change group 12-10
Forecast significant weather........................12-10
Forecast sky condition 12-10
Forecast visibility...12-10
Forecast wind...12-10
Foreign object damage (FOD) 6-23
Forming good safety habits............................17-16
Four-stroke engines...6-3
Fowler flaps..5-9
Fracto 11-17
Free-stream velocity..4-4
Free directional oscillations 4-18
Friction...3-5
Frise-type ailerons...5-4
Fronts 11-18
Fuel 6-1
Fuel-pump system 6-25
Fuel contamination..6-27
Fuel gauges...6-25
Fuel grades...6-26
Fuel injection system 6-10
Fuel load...9-5
Fuel primer...6-25
Fuel selectors 6-26
Fuel strainers..6-26
Fuel systems...6-25
Fuel tanks 6-25
Full authority digital engine control (FADEC)...........6-19
Full temperature accountability 10-27
Fuselage 2-3

G

General Aviation Manufacturers Association (GAMA) 8-2
Generator...6-28
Getting beyond rote workmanship...........17-29
Global positioning system (GPS) 2-16
Graphical METARs 12-23
Graveyard spiral..16-6
Gravity-feed system 6-25
Ground adjustable tabs...................................5-11
Ground effect 4-9
Ground lighting illusions 16-9
Ground power unit (GPU) 6-28
Gyroscopic action 4-27
Gyroscopic action 4-27
Gyroscopic attitude indicators 5-12
Gyroscopic flight instruments........................7-14
Gyroscopic principles 7-15

H

Hail...11-24
Handbooks 1-10
Hazard...17-4
Hazardous attitudes...17-4
Hazardous Inflight Weather Advisory (HIWAS) 12-4
Haze 16-9
Heading indicator.............................. 7-13, 7-20
Heatstroke 16-12
Henson, William Samuel 1-3
High intensity white obstruction lights 13-9
High speed flight..4-38
High speed flight controls 4-43
High speed stalls 4-32
History of ADM..17-2
History of flight...1-2
History of the Federal Aviation Administration (FAA) 1-3
Histotoxic hypoxia...16-3
Horizontally opposed engine 6-2
Horizontal situation indicator (HSI) 7-13
Human behavior...17-10
Humidity 11-13
Humidity 3-3
Hydraulic systems..6-30
Hydromechanical 5-2
Hypemic hypoxia...16-2
Hypersonic...4-38
Hyperventilation 16-3
Hypoxia..16-2
Hypoxic hypoxia..16-2

I

ICAO station identifier.................................12-10
Ice..4-23
Ice fog 11-15
Icing 11-24
Ignition..6-1
Ignition system...6-14
Illusions..16-5
Impact pressure chamber 7-2
Improbable 17-6
Inflight Weather Advisories.........................12-12
In-line engines..6-2
In-runway lighting 13-9
Inches of mercury 11-4
Inclinometer...7-18
Indicated airspeed (IAS) 4-39, 7-8, 10-17
Indicated altitude..7-6

Induced drag.. 4-3, 4-5
Induction 6-1
Induction system 6-7
Information management 17-30
Information signs 13-6
Instantaneous vertical speed indicator (IVSI)..............7-7
Instrument check..7-7
Instrument landing system (ILS) 2-12
Intelligent flight control systems (IFCS).......................5-2
Interference drag 4-4
Internal resources 17-20
International Civil Aviation Organization (ICAO)
.... 3-2, 13-12
International Standard Atmosphere (ISA) .. 3-2, 10-2, 11-5
Interpolation...10-19
Inversion 11-13
Inversion illusion 16-7
Isobars 11-12

J

Jet-fueled piston engine 6-4

K

Keel effect..4-17
Knowledge examination 1-17
Kollsman window 7-4

L

Lags..7-26
Landing 10-27
Landing charts...10-25
Landing gear 2-3, 2-6, 6-1, 6-31
Landing gear extended speed (V_{LE})...........................7-9
Landing gear operating speed (V_{LO})..........................7-9
Landing performance 10-15, 10-33
Landing strip indicators 13-10
Land and hold short lights.......................................13-9
Lateral stability 4-16
Lazy eights..4-33
leading edge 3-8
    cuffs...5-10
    device 5-9
    flaps 5-9
Leads 7-26
Leans, the 16-6
Lenticularus...11-17
Licensed empty weight 9-5
Lift..2-2, 4-2
Lift/drag ratio 4-6
Lightning..11-25
Lightning strike protection......................................2-11

Light sport aircraft (LSA) 1-12, 8-7
Likelihood of an event 17-6
Lilienthal, Otto...1-3
loadmeter...6-30
Load distribution..4-36
Local airport advisory 14-4
Location signs 13-6
Longitudinal stability 4-14
Low-level wind shear..11-11
Low-Level Wind Shear Alert System (LLWAS) 11-11
Lubrication...6-1

M

MacCracken, William P., Jr.,...1-4
Mach buffet...4-42
Mach number 4-39
Magnetic compass.. 5-12, 7-22
Magnus, Heinrich Gustav 3-4
Magnus effect...3-4
Maintenance entries 8-11
Managing aircraft automation 17-29
Managing risks..17-24
Mandatory instruction signs...................................13-6
Maneuverability 4-13
Manifold absolute pressure (MAP).............................6-6
Marginal..17-6
Maximum landing weight..9-5
Maximum ramp weight..9-5
Maximum takeoff weight...9-5
Maximum weight 9-5
Maximum zero fuel weight.......................................9-5
Mean aerodynamic chord (MAC)....................... 4-12, 9-5
Medical certificate...16-2
Medical certification requirements 1-16
Mesosphere 11-3
Meteorologists..12-1
Microjets 6-20
Middle ear 16-4
Military/Federal government airports 13-1
Military operation areas (MOAs)...............................14-4
Military training routes (MTRs) 14-6
Minimum control speed (VMC) 7-10
Minimum equipment lists (MEL) 8-9
Mitigating risk..17-6
Mixture control 6-8
Modifier...12-6
Moisture 11-13
Moment 4-12, 9-5
Moment arm 4-12, 9-5
Moment index 9-5
Monocoque 2-3, 2-8

Montgolfier, Joseph and Etienne.....................................1-2
Motion sickness 16-11
Multi-function display (MFD) 2-12, 7-13, 12-18

N

N_1 indicator 6-22
N_2 indicator 6-22
National Aeronautics and Space Administration (NASA) .
....2-16, 5-2
National Airspace System..14-7
National Oceanic and Atmospheric Administration
(NOAA) 3-4
National Security Areas (NSAs).................................14-6
National Transportation Safety Board (NTSB) 1-6
National Weather Service (NWS)................................12-1
Navigation instruments 2-12
Negative arm..9-10
Negative dynamic stability 4-13
Negative static stability..4-13
Negligible...17-6
Net thrust...6-24
Neutral dynamic stability..4-13
Neutral static stability 4-13
Newton's basic laws of motion.....................................3-4
Newton's First Law of Motion 3-4, 4-19
Newton's Second Law of Motion.................................3-4
Newton's Third Law of Motion.......................3-4, 4-26
Next Generation Weather Radar System (NEXRAD)12-21
Night vision...16-18
Nimbus...11-17
Non-movement area boundary marking 13-6
Nondirectional beacon (NDB) 2-12
Notices to Airmen (NOTAM)..................1-11, 12-5, 13-3

O

Obstacles to maintaining situational awareness.........17-23
Obstructions on wind 11-8
Obstruction lights...13-9
Occasional..17-6
Occluded front 11-22
Oil systems..6-15
OODA loop 17-16
Operational pitfalls...17-20
Optical illusions 16-9
Original equipment manufacturer (OEM) 6-4
Oscillation error 7-26
Other information...12-5
Other markings...13-5
Outlook briefing 12-5
Outside air temperature (OAT) gauge 6-10, 7-26

Oxygen masks...6-35
Oxygen systems 6-34

P

Parachute jumps..14-10
Parachute jump aircraft operations 14-6
Parasite drag..4-3
PAVE Checklist...17-6
Payload..9-5
Pennants 11-12
Perceive, Process, Perform (3P)...............................17-14
Perceive, Process, Perform with CARE and TEAM..17-14
Performance 10-5
Performance charts...10-18
Performance data 10-1
Performance instruments 2-12
Performance requirements 10-27
Performance speeds 10-17
Pheil, A. C..1-3
Pilot in command (PIC) 1-14
Pilot's operating handbook (POH)..............................8-1
Pilot certifications 1-13
Pilot weather reports (PIREPs) 12-8
Pitch 4-11
Pitching 4-14
Pitot-static flight instruments 7-1
Placards 8-4
Plain flap 5-8
Plan, the..17-12
Positive dynamic stability 4-13
Positive static stability 4-13
Postural considerations 16-7
Powerplant 2-3, 2-7, 6-1, 8-3
Practical examination..1-18
Precession 7-15
Precipitation 11-18, 12-16
Precision approach path indicator (PAPI)....................13-7
Preflight inspections...8-9
Present weather 12-16
Pressure-demand oxygen systems...............................6-36
Pressure-type carburetor 6-8
Pressure altitude 3-2, 7-6, 10-3
Pressure change/tendency 12-16
Pressurized aircraft...6-32
Preventive maintenance 8-11
Primary flight controls 5-2
Primary flight display...2-12
Primary locations of the FAA 1-8
Primary radar 13-13
Private airports 13-1

Private pilot 1-14
Probability forecast 12-10
Probable 17-6
Professional Air Traffic Controllers Organization
(PATCO) Strike 1-7
Prohibited areas 14-3
Propeller 2-7, 6-1, 6-4
Propeller anti-ice 6-38
Propeller blade 4-24
Propeller principles 4-24
Published VFR routes 14-6
Pulsating visual approach slope 13-7
Pulse oximeters 6-37
P-factor 4-26, 4-27

Q

Quesada, General Elwood Richard "Pete" 1-6

R

Radar observations 12-2
Radar summary chart 12-17
Radar traffic advisories 13-14
Radar Weather Reports (RAREP) 12-9
Radial engines 6-2
Radiation fog 11-15
Radiosonde 12-2
Radio communications 13-11
Radio equipment 13-12
Range performance 10-8
Rapid decompression 6-34
Rate of turn 4-30
Reciprocating engines 6-2
Red obstruction lights 13-9
Reference datum 9-5
Refueling procedures 6-27
Region of reversed command 10-10
Reinforcement of onboard suites 17-29
Relative humidity 11-13
Remarks 12-8
Remote 17-6
Remote indicating compass 7-21
Repairs and alterations 8-12
Respect for onboard systems 17-29
Restricted areas 14-3
Retractable landing gear 6-31
Rigidity in space 7-15
Risk 17-4
Risk management 17-32
Roll 4-11
Rolling 4-16
Rough air 4-33

Rudder 5-4, 5-7
Rudder 2-6
Ruddervators 5-8
Runway and terrain slopes illusion 16-9
Runway centerline lighting system (RCLS) 13-9
Runway distance remaining signs 13-6
Runway edge lights 13-8
Runway end identifier lights (REIL) 13-8
Runway incursion avoidance 13-18
Runway lighting 13-8
Runway markings 13-4
Runway surface and gradient 10-11
Runway width illusion 16-9

S

Safety Program Airmen Notification System (SPANS)
.... 1-12
Satellite 12-3
Satellite weather 12-3
Sea level pressure 12-16
Sea smoke 11-15
Segmented circle visual indicator system 13-10
Semimonocoque 2-3, 2-8
Servicing of oxygen systems 6-37
Severity of an event 17-6
Shock wave 4-40
Shock waves 4-40
Significant Meteorological Information (SIGMET)
.... 12-3, 12-13
Significant weather prognostic charts 12-18
Single-engine best rate of climb (V_{YSE}) 7-10
Single-pilot resource management 17-4
Sinus problems 16-4
Situational awareness 17-23
Skidding turn 4-21
Skin friction drag 4-4
Sky condition 12-7
Slipping turn 4-20
Slotted flap 5-8
Somatogravic illusion 16-7
Sources of power 7-16
Spatial disorientation 16-5
Special airworthiness certificate 8-8
Special flight permits 8-12
Special use airspace 14-3
Spins 4-32
Spiral instability 4-18
Split flap 5-8
Spoilers 5-10
Sport pilot 1-14
Sport pilot certificate 1-12

Squall line 11-23
SRM and the 5P Check 17-11
Stabilator 5-6
Stability 4-13, 4-36, 9-2, 9-3
Stagnant hypoxia 16-3
Stalls 4-22, 4-32
Stall speed performance charts 10-26
Standard airworthiness certificate 8-7
Standard briefing 12-5
Standard datum plane (SDP) 10-3
Standard empty weight 9-5
Standard temperature lapse rate 10-2
Standard weights 9-5
Starting system 6-18
Static pressure chamber 7-2
Static stability 4-13
Station 9-5
Stationary front 11-22
Station identifier 12-6
Steam fog 11-15
Straight-and-level flight 10-5, 13-18
Stratosphere 11-3
Stratus 11-17
Stress 16-11
Stress management 17-20
Student pilot 1-16
Student pilot solo requirements 1-16
Subcomponents of an airplane 2-7
Sublimation 11-15
Subsonic 4-38
Sumps 6-26
Superchargers 6-11, 6-12
Supersonic 4-38
Supersonic flow 4-38
Supplemental type certificate (STC) 6-26
Surface analysis chart 12-14
Surface aviation weather observations (METARs) 12-2
Sweepback 4-17, 4-41
Synopsis 12-5

T

T-tail configuration 5-6
Tachometer 7-13
Tailwheel landing gear airplanes 6-31
Takeoff 10-27
Takeoff charts 10-19
Takeoff distance 10-28
Takeoff performance 10-13
Taxiway centerline lead-off lights 13-9
Taxiway centerline lead-on lights 13-9
Taxiway lights 13-9

Taxiway markings 13-5
Temperature 11-13, 12-16
Temperature and dew point 12-7
Temporary flight restrictions (TFR) 14-6
Terminal aerodrome forecasts (TAF) 12-10
Terminal doppler weather radar (TDWR) 12-3
Terminal radar service area (TRSA) 13-15, 14-6
Tetrahedron 13-10
Thermosphere 11-3
Thielert, Frank 6-4
Three-color visual approach path 13-7
Thrust 2-2
Thrust horsepower (THP) 6-6, 6-24
Thunderstorms 11-22
Tornadoes 11-23
Torque 4-26
Torquemeter 6-22
Touchdown zone lights (TDZL) 13-9
Traffic patterns 13-18
Trailing edge 3-8
Training operations 13-18
Transcontinental mail route 1-4
Transcribed information briefing service (TIBS) 12-4
Transcribed Weather Broadcast (TWEB) 12-4
Transonic 4-38
Transponder 13-14
Transponder inspection 8-9
Transport category airplane performance 10-27
Trend vectors 7-14
Tricycle landing gear airplanes 6-31
Trim systems 5-10
Trim tabs 2-5, 5-10
Tropopause 11-3
Troposphere 11-2
True airspeed (TAS) 4-39, 7-8, 10-17
True altitude 7-6
Truss structure 2-8
Turbine engines 6-20
Turbofan 6-20
Turbojet 6-20
Turboprop 6-20
Turboshaft 6-20
Turbosuperchargers 6-11, 6-12
Turbulence 11-24
Turn-and-slip indicator 7-17
Turn coordinator 7-17
Turn indicator 7-13, 7-16
Two-stroke engine 6-3
Types of airports 13-1
Type certificate data sheet (TCDS) 9-3

Type of report 12-6, 12-10

U

Ultralight 1-12, 14-10
Uncontrolled airport.....................................13-2
Uncontrolled airspace 14-3
Understand the platform 17-29
Unmanned free balloons 14-10
Upper air observations 12-2
Upslope fog...11-15
Useful load...9-5
Use of resources..17-20

V

V-tail 5-8
V_1 10-28
V_2 10-28
V_A...10-18
Variable inlet guide vane (VIGV).................6-23
Vehicle roadway markings 13-5
Vertical card magnetic compass 7-26
Vertical speed indicator (VSI) 7-1, 7-7, 7-13
Vertical stability...4-17
Very high frequency (VHF) omnidirectional radio
range (VOR)...2-12
Very light jets (VLJs).....................................6-20
Vestibular illusions 16-6
Vestibular system...16-5
V_{FE} 10-18
V_{FS} 10-28
Vg diagram...4-33
Vinci, Leonardo da...1-2
Visibility 11-18, 12-7
Vision...16-17
Visual approach slope indicator (VASI).........13-7
Visual glide slope indicators..........................13-7
Visual illusions 16-7
V_{LE} 10-17
V_{LO} 10-18
V_{LOF} 10-28
V_{MCA} 10-28
V_{MCG} 10-28
V_{NE} 10-18
V_{NO} 10-18
Vortex 4-8
Vortex generation..13-16
VOR receiver checkpoint marking 13-5
V_R...10-28
V_S...10-27
V_{S0}..10-17
V_{S1}..10-17

V_X...10-17
V_Y...10-17

W

Wake turbulence 4-8, 13-15
Warm front.. 11-19
Warning areas 14-4
Water refraction 16-9
Weather... 11-1, 12-7
Weather briefings...12-5
Weather charts 12-14
Weather depiction chart 12-16
Weight.. 2-2, 4-2, 4-7, 4-35, 9-1
Weight and balance...................................... 4-35
  computations 9-6
  restrictions 9-7
Weight and loading distribution.....................8-3
Weight control 9-1
White arc...7-9
Wind.. 12-6, 12-16
Windscreen anti-ice 6-38
Winds and temperatures aloft 12-5
Winds and temperature aloft forecast (FD) ...12-14
Wind direction indicators..............................13-10
Wind patterns 11-7
Wind shear 11-11
Wind shifts 11-22
Wind sock 13-10
Winglets...3-10
Wings 2-3, 2-4
Wingtip vortices..4-8
Workload management 17-23
Wright, Wilbur and Orville.............................1-3
WSR-88D NEXRAD radar...............................12-2

Y

Yaw...4-11
Yawing..4-17
Yaw string...7-18

Z

Zero fuel weight..9-10
Zulu time...12-8

15840626R00264